Sports Business Management

Sports Business Management will equip students with a comprehensive understanding of the sports industry. Covering management, strategy, marketing, and finance, the decision making approach of the book emphasizes key concepts while translating them into practice.

Foster, O'Reilly, and Dávila present a set of modular chapters supported by plenty of examples, mini-cases, and exercises to help students apply a decision making approach to real-world situations. Covering an international array of sports and organizations – including the Olympic Games, FIFA World Cup, US Major League Baseball, and more – the book also covers unique topics such as diversity in sports, the impact of technology, and social media. Rounding this out, the book provides about 50 Harvard/Stanford cases, along with case notes for instructors.

This is an ideal textbook for upper-level undergraduate and graduate students of sports business and management, fully supported by a companion website featuring PowerPoint slides, test questions, teaching notes, and other tools for instructors.

George Foster is the Konosuke Matsushita Professor of Management at Stanford University, USA. His research and teaching includes entrepreneurship, financial analysis, and sports business management. He holds two honorary doctorates. George Foster interacts extensively with executives of many key stakeholders in the sports business ecosystem.

Norm O'Reilly is the Richard P. and Joan S. Fox Professor of Management, and Chair of the Department of Sports Administration at Ohio University, USA. He teaches courses in sport management, sport finance, and sport marketing, and is a lifetime Research Fellow of the North American Society for Sport Management. Norm O'Reilly consults regularly across the industry.

Antonio Dávila is Professor of Entrepreneurship and Accounting and Control at IESE, University of Navarra, Spain, where he also teaches MBA and PhD courses on sports management. He has authored several books and journal articles on management and received recognition for his writing from the Strategic Management Society.

Sports Business Management

Decision Making Around the Globe

George Foster, Norm O'Reilly, and Antonio Dávila

Assisted by
Carlos Shimizu and Kevin Hurd

Routledge
Taylor & Francis Group

NEW YORK AND LONDON

First published 2016
by Routledge
711 Third Avenue, New York, NY 10017

and by Routledge
2 Park Square, Milton Park, Abingdon, Oxon OX14 4RN

Routledge is an imprint of the Taylor & Francis Group, an informa business

Library of Congress Cataloging in Publication Data
A catalog record for this book has been requested.

ISBN: 978-1-138-91953-2 (hbk)
ISBN: 978-1-138-91954-9 (pbk)
ISBN: 978-1-315-68782-7 (ebk)

Typeset in Times New Roman
by Out of House Publishing

Table of Contents

Preface

Sport as a business continues to grow and thrive. We, as a group of authors, have been fortunate to have spent many years studying the field very closely: attending events, working for and with many diverse sporting organizations, and researching and teaching on the topic. When we embarked on this project, we felt that a book was needed that provides deep and informed insight into the decisions that sport managers are faced with in this ever-expanding and ever-more sophisticated industry. So, decision making was the first core element. Second, we knew a stakeholder approach to these decisions was necessary. As sports business management becomes more complex, more competitive, more digital, increasingly data-centric, and highly scrutinized, the sport manager needs to make decisions with a keen knowledge of the impact of these decisions on all of the other stakeholders in the industry. Third, given the global nature of the sports industry, it was important that our analysis and examples cover sports, leagues, clubs, and athletes from many countries and the rich business ecosystem that underlies their on-field games and events.

The book is organized into three sections. Part I provides background on two of the three fundamental elements of the book: decision making (Chapter 1) and stakeholders (Chapter 2). Part II comprises seven chapters (Chapters 3 through 9) that deeply review the important sport industry stakeholders. Part III of the book showcases business management applications of the concepts and structures presented in Parts I and II: marketing (Chapter 10), sponsorship and athlete endorsements (Chapters 11 and 12), ticketing and venue-building management (Chapters 13 and 17), sports engagement (Chapter 14), sport broadcasting (Chapters 15 and 16), and the valuation of clubs (Chapter 18). The final fundamental element of this book – perspectives from different parts of the globe – is threaded through each of the 18 chapters.

We hope you enjoy the book and its content. We hope it informs your learning and provides an edge on your career journey.

George Foster
Norm O'Reilly
Antonio Dávila

Acknowledgments

The authors wish to acknowledge the support of a large number of people. First, we would like to thank our universities, our colleagues, and our students, who make coming to work each day such a rewarding experience. We are very blessed to work in such stimulating environments. Second, we feel very fortunate to be able to work in a business field – sport – where there is so much passion and that has such an exciting future. Third, we would like to acknowledge all of those industry leaders and experts who have provided resources, content, advice, direction, and learning that has much enhanced what is presented in this book. Fourth, two of our colleagues, Carlos Shimizu (Stanford University) and Kevin Hurd (Ohio University) were very instrumental in supporting the development and writing of this book. Over an extended period, each was devoted to continually improving the final product. Fifth, thanks to John Kissick for his belief and commitment to Stanford University in general, and specifically for his encouragement and support to our desire to change the way sports business management is analyzed and taught. George Foster would like to acknowledge his deep appreciation for the friendship and the many insights he gained from his years of stimulating co-teaching with Bill Walsh. Finally and most importantly, we'd like to thank our families who put up with the late nights, lengthy discussions, and our long devotion to producing a book such as this.

We would also like to acknowledge a few individuals who supported the writing of particular chapters or who aided in the overall book production process. Chapter contributors include Gashaw Abeza, Elisa Beselt, Jared Dudas, Matt Dewire, Nolan Dewire, Mark Dottori, Kevin Hurd, Chris Glynn, Joey Vagnier, Melissa Wells and Daisy Rojas provided much valued assistance at multiple stages. At Routledge and Taylor & Francis, we are thankful for the vision, patience, and high-quality support of Sharon Golan and Erin Arata.

There are many with whom we have worked over the years in the industry, most of whom have taught us and provided business and sport-based experiences included in the content presented in the pages of this book. These people are too many to name, but we are sincerely grateful to have their insights embedded in what we have presented.

PART I INTRODUCTION TO SPORTS BUSINESS MANAGEMENT

1

DECISION MAKING
A STRUCTURED APPROACH

Decisions made by multiple stakeholders at all levels drive the changing landscape of the sporting industry. This book analyzes many of these decisions and provides a structure to help stakeholders make more informed decisions. This chapter provides an overview of the key concepts underlying informed decision making, with illustrations from ten decision contexts faced by the San Francisco Giants of Major League Baseball (MLB). These decision contexts have greatly shaped the path that the Giants have travelled over multiple decades. These concepts include objectives, timeframe/horizon period, alternatives, constraints, and uncertainty. Other aspects of decision making we highlight include differences between the quality of decision making and the desirability of a given outcome, and the differences across stakeholders' objectives. After decisions have been made, execution becomes central to increasing the likelihood that good outcomes will be achieved. In many cases, the decision making analysis will include the steps to be taken to implement the decision, the resources required, and milestones along the way that track progress being made.

Decision making in the sporting world often happens in a fishbowl, with many from the outside making public judgments, often with very limited information, and with hidden or not-so-hidden agendas. Ever-present in the sporting world is the very public backdrop of second-guessing decision makers, questioning their motives, and criticizing them with the benefit of hindsight. This is an industry that is simultaneously exciting to work in, difficult to keep the incentives of key stakeholders well aligned, and receives the highest levels of publicity and commentary. In this environment, the better the quality of the decision making processes used by stakeholders, the more likely that the sporting industry will continue to grow in a positive way and deliver many benefits to the large numbers of people who "eat, breathe, and live" multiple aspects of the sporting landscape.

1.1 SOME KEY CONCEPTS FOR INFORMED GOOD DECISIONS

Informed good decisions often have a common underpinning in their structure:

1.1.1 Objectives that are Well Articulated and Defined

Decision makers benefit greatly from making explicit and understanding the objective(s) they are pursuing. These objectives can have a mixture of financial/non-financial and quantitative and qualitative aspects. We will illustrate these aspects later in this chapter with respect to decisions by several groups to buy an MLB sporting club franchise. Where a decision is being made by a group of individuals, it is important at the outset (or at least by the time the decision is made) to have a shared understanding of the main objective(s). Oftentimes decisions that result in outcomes that are viewed by some as negative arise because there was a lack of agreement from the outset as to the key objective being pursued.

1.1.2 Timeframe / Horizon Period of Decision that is Realistic

Decisions vary greatly in the timeframe being considered. A coach on a given game day typically has an objective to win the game with whatever resources he brings to the field of play that day. Once the game begins, the timeframe can further shorten, often dramatically. In a game such as basketball, where the coach has great ability to change who is in the game, the timeframe can be simply the very next play. In contrast, consider the general manager of a basketball club who is in charge of building a squad of players that can compete over several years at the highest championship level. Here there is a much longer time-frame and the general manager's decisions will be less affected by the ups and downs of individual games.

A key aspect of an informed decision is an understanding of what is a realistic timeframe. By having a realistic long timeframe, it is more likely that the objective will be achieved. Too often in sports, individuals are given unrealistically short time horizons and can be fired before they have a chance to achieve their targeted objective. A club-owner building a club that aims to consistently challenge for the championship each year, and yet has hired and fired five coaches in an eight-year period is very likely operating with very unrealistic timeframes. Of course, coaches, when hired by such an owner, likely have sizable information about the low likelihood of being the coach at that club for the next five years. One informed coach, who accepted the position in these circumstances, demanded and received a five-year guaranteed contract at several million dollars each year. The point here is that a potential coach could still agree to terms with the owner with a "hire and then fire" reputation by making his own informed decision. This could include building in extra protection should the likely outcome of an early coach tenure exit eventuate.[1]

1.1.3 Alternatives Aggressively Pursued and Examined

Having a reasonable number of available options increases the likelihood that a good decision is made and a good outcome is more likely to occur. Consider a baseball team looking to build a new stadium and having to negotiate with the city where the stadium will be built. These negotiations could include rental agreements if the city owns the land, sharing of parking revenues with the city, and provision of security on game days by the local police. The Atlanta Braves of MLB had this situation after it was decided that its existing stadium was "well past its use-by date."[2] Many observers and City of Atlanta officials expected the team to stay in downtown Atlanta and negotiate with the city to either build a new stadium or make a very major upgrade of the existing standard. The Braves' existing stadium was built in 1996 for the Olympic Games, was located downtown, and had limited parking. The trend of most recent new baseball parks has been to build on downtown sites. During the planning process in 2012/13, however, the Braves expanded the alternatives to include local county sites as well as down-town sites. The Braves eventually settled on a Cobb County location 20 miles from downtown Atlanta that had multiple benefits to the Braves over the downtown sites considered.

Some clubs considering new stadiums will add alternative cities/counties to their options in the belief that cities will compete against each other and further offer extra enhancements they would not have had if only one site was considered from the outset. These enhancements could be many, including offering the club lower rental, a higher share of parking revenue, additional security at no extra cost, and/or rezoning land that the club could use for its own real estate development project. Bargaining power in a negotiation is often enhanced by having more than one viable alternative option. Aggressively seeking to expand the available alternatives is often a hallmark of a successful decision maker.

1.1.4 Constraints Understood

Most decision makers have constraints within which they have to operate. Informed decision makers understand the nature of these constraints and how binding they actually are. Some potential investors in sporting clubs have a "operating profit or at a minimum breakeven" constraint and exclude from their analysis clubs that are for sale that have high ongoing operating losses. Some potential investors interested in buying the Phoenix Coyotes of the National Hockey League (NHL) lost interest when they were shown the very large magnitude of the operating losses of the club.[3]

Each sport has its own regulations, operating rules, and institutional structures. For instance, world soccer is regulated by FIFA, the world soccer federation. Among the multiple aspects of the sport, FIFA regulates the transfer of players from professional players all the way to kids that are offered a contract. FIFA has set two transfer windows, one around New Year and the main one in the July–August timeframe. During these windows, teams can hire free agents as well as buy the contracts of existing players from other teams. The New Year window is often the last chance for soccer clubs struggling with relegation to reinforce their squads; creativity and negotiation ability is crucial here because the selling clubs know of the desperate needs of these relegation-threatened clubs.[4]

1.1.5 Uncertainty Explicitly Recognized

Uncertainty is a central aspect of decision making. Consider negotiations between the general manager and a potential player that is a "free agent," available to join the club for the coming season. Other clubs are known to be interested, although there is uncertainty over how many and the likely financial package offered. The general manager in question is well known for making decisions in a very structured way and is comfortable assessing how different amounts offered to the player affect the likelihood of different outcomes. Given other financial constraints at the club, the maximum that can be offered is $20 million for the season. Two important areas of uncertainty for the general manager are:

1   The likelihood of the player accepting packages of different amounts (such as a $20 million offer that has a 90 percent likelihood of acceptance; $15 million, a 55 percent likelihood; and $10 million, a 5 percent likelihood).
2   The likelihood the player will stay fit and perform to expectation during the number of contracted seasons if he or she does accept the offer.

General managers face both areas of uncertainty on an ongoing basis. Not all decisions result in outcomes that were the most desirable at the time of the original decision.

1.2 DECISION MAKING EXAMPLES FROM THE SAN FRANCISCO GIANTS OF MLB[5]

In November 2014, the San Francisco Giants celebrated their third World Series win in five years, having previously won in 2010 and 2012. The term "dynasty" was used by some to describe this high level of championship-winning achievement. Behind this celebration lay many decisions made by a syndicate starting in 1992 and an earlier syndicate that enabled the Giants to be in the position to achieve this success on the field. During this period there was also a sizable increase in the valuation and financial success of the Giants. An overview of some key decisions by the Giants highlights the decision making concepts introduced earlier in this chapter. This sequence of decisions also illustrates the roller-coaster journey that decision makers in the world of sports find themselves on.

Exhibits 1.1–1.3 highlight some of the timelines and key events associated with the ten decisions now discussed. Exhibit 1.1 has the timeline; Exhibit 1.2 has the on-field performance tableau. The yearly estimated revenues, payroll, and attendance are presented in Exhibit 1.3.

Decision #1: Bob Lurie decides in late 1992 to sell the Giants

The Giants moved from New York in 1958 to become the San Francisco Giants. The then-owner Horace Stoneham retained ownership until 1976, when San Francisco-born Bob Lurie led a syndicate to purchase the club for a reported $8 million. Lurie was a successful real estate investor, who further built on San Francisco real estate properties bought or built by his father. One prompt to Lurie's 1976 decision to buy the Giants was to pre-empt the purchase of the club by a Canadian syndicate who planned to move the club to Toronto.

The Giants moved to playing at Candlestick Park in 1960 and then later shared that stadium with the San Francisco 49ers of the NFL. In 1989, the Giants made the World Series, which they lost to their cross-town rival, Oakland Athletics. Minutes before Game 3 of the 1989 World Series, the Loma Prieta earthquake occurred. Candlestick Park by the late 1980s (or indeed earlier) had become a below-standard ballpark. The Giants were suffering operating losses each and every year in the 1980/92 period. Average per game attendance in the 1980/92 period was only 17,871; this average was frequently in the bottom half of MLB clubs. The frequent cold swirling winds at Candlestick made for difficult playing conditions and difficult viewing conditions. Lurie made multiple efforts to build an alternative baseball stadium. Four attempts by the Giants – in 1987, 1989, 1990, and 1992 – to seek public financing for a new stadium failed to receive voter approval. In 1992, Lurie stated:

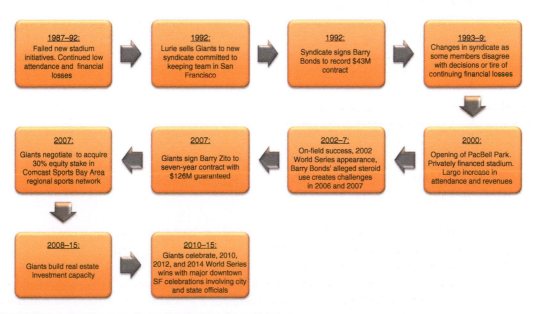

EXHIBIT 1.1 San Francisco Giants Ten Decision Points Timeline

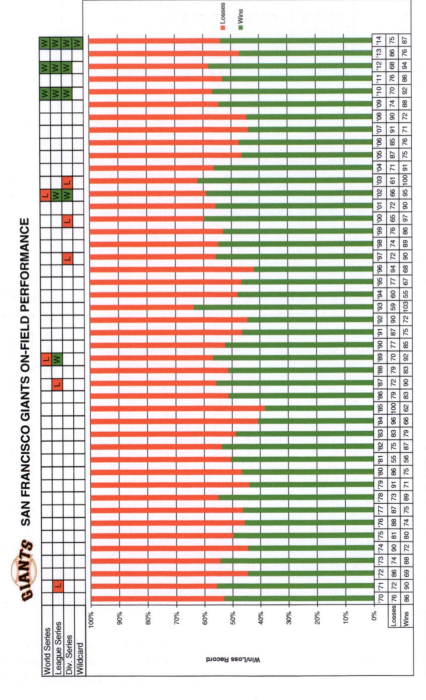

EXHIBIT 1.2 San Francisco Giants On-Field Performance

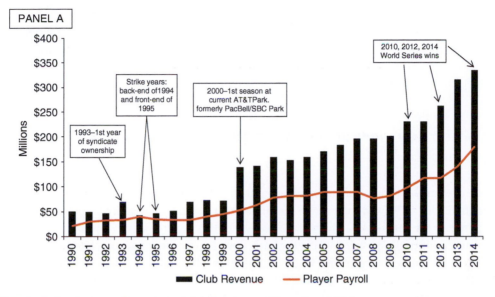

EXHIBIT 1.3A San Francisco Giants Annual Club Revenue and Player Payroll ($M)

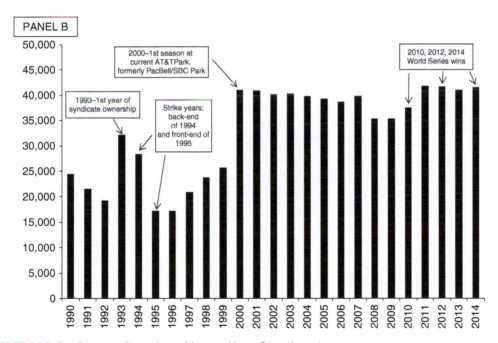

EXHIBIT 1.3B San Francisco Giants Annual Average Home Game Attendance

When I bought the Giants 17 years ago, certainly one of the main things in my mind was to make sure they did not leave San Francisco or the Bay Area. But in a few years it became apparent to me that Candlestick Park was no longer an adequate facility for the Giants or our wonderful fans.[6]

The 1992 rejection by the voters was the final prompt to Lurie deciding to put the club up for sale. He viewed that he had kept the club in San Francisco for 17 years, despite the year-by-year losses, and had experienced the pain of four failed efforts to gain public funding support for a new stadium. He received in 1992 an offer from a syndicate wishing to relocate the club to St. Petersburg, Florida. The offer was reported to be $115 million, but did not receive immediate approval by MLB, which strongly preferred to keep the club in San Francisco. Attempts in late 1992 were made by the mayor and other officials in San Francisco to seek investor groups to purchase the Giants from Lurie.

Decision #2: New syndicate decides in 1992 to buy the Giants and keep them in San Francisco

Multiple investors looked at purchasing the Giants in 1992. The likely minimum purchase price was $100 million. Not all viewed the purchase as an attractive one. One wealthy potential investor opted not to purchase the Giants. A key financial objective for this investor was to buy a club that, at a minimum, had zero (ideally positive) operating cash flow. For this investor, purchasing the Giants was not an attractive alternative, given his financial objectives.[7] The Giants were likely to sustain operating losses each year they remained at Candlestick Park.

Another group of investors, however, decided in late 1992 to form an investment syndicate to purchase the Giants for a reported $100 million. The syndicate was well-aware that operating losses would occur going forward in 1993 and beyond while the Giants played at Candlestick Park. The investment syndicate included many wealthy San Francisco citizens and individuals who had connections with that city. They included Peter Magowan, Walter Shorenstein, Donald Fisher, and Charles Schwab. The individual syndicate members had differing mixes of objectives. Some investors had financial objectives underlying their decision to join the syndicate and believed that both on-field player/coach decisions and off-field business decisions should have a strong focus on building the financial value of their investment. Other investors were motivated by the objective to see the Giants stay in San Francisco. Once that objective appeared to be achieved, they decided to sell or reduce their interest in the syndicate. One such investor was sufficiently tired of writing checks each year to cover his share of the operating losses that he reportedly sold his share to another investor for a nominal amount. The annual operating losses of the Giants in 1994 were deepened by a MLB strike that led to post-strike attendance declines at Candlestick. This higher level of operating losses likely accelerated the decision by several individuals to exit the syndicate.

Decision #3: New syndicate signs Barry Bonds in 1992 to a then-record $43 million contract

The new syndicate believed that it was important to "jump-start the franchise" in the eyes of multiple stakeholders. Decisions related to hiring new players were considered. The alternatives included signing a leading hitter or a leading pitcher. The new syndicate opted to make a record setting offer to Barry Bonds, who was the pre-eminent free agent at that time. The contract was for six years with a total guarantee of $43.75 million at an average of $7.3 million per year. This contract broke Cal Ripken's total guarantee record contract by $11 million. There were many qualitative and non-financial aspects to the 1992 signing of Bonds. Bonds was the son of the former star Giants player Bobby Bonds. He was the godson of Willie Mays, the Hall of Fame Giants player. Larry Baer described the 1992 decision context as follows:

We needed to jump-start the franchise. We felt we had to establish operating credibility. Some people were calling our investor group the billionaire boys club … We had to show we cared about baseball and operating the team and it wasn't just an ego-driven instrument. So we were able to go out and preemptively bring Barry Bonds home – he grew up in the clubhouse of Candlestick Park as a three- or four-year-old at the feet of his father. In addition to helping the team, people saw two other things. First, it was a great baseball name in San Francisco coming home. Second, there was the huge symbolism that the new owners of the Giants cared about making the team good and they wanted to do it quickly.[8]

One aspect of the sporting industry is the public domain in which many decisions are made. The Bonds hiring decision in 1992 is illustrative. The contract was signed at the winter meetings of MLB before ownership of the Giants was transferred from the Lurie syndicate to the new syndicate. A December 1992 article in *The Baltimore Sun* reported:

The new ownership group of the San Francisco Giants finally got outfielder Barry Bonds under contract yesterday, completing the six-year deal that current club owner Bob Lurie had refused to guarantee. The Giants seemed prepared to open the winter meetings with a major splash Saturday night, but the cryptic announcement was scuttled when current Giants owner Bob Lurie angrily asserted that he had not approved the deal. "You have to have control of the team to sign a ball-player," Lurie said, "and they don't have a team. We do not want Barry Bonds to be a San Francisco Giant at that price."[9]

The new ownership group contracted with Lurie to "guarantee" the contract with Barry Bonds if the sale of the Giants by Lurie did not occur. In many industries, such a side-contract would remain private between the contracting parties. But such a thing is rarely the case in the sporting industry!

Decision #4: Team payroll decisions result in conflicts among the syndicate that are then aired in the press

Peter Magowan was appointed CEO of the Giants in 1992. Magowan was a key person in building the new investor syndicate. After the signing of Barry Bonds, the Giants in the mid-1990s did not contract additional all-star players at the level of Bonds to its team roster. Walter Shorenstein, one of the wealthiest members of the syndicate, strongly disagreed with this policy. He feuded with Magowan, arguing a much higher player payroll was required for both on-field and off-field success. In 1994, Shorenstein exited the syndicate; however, he continued to voice his disagreements. A 1998 *San Francisco Chronicle* article included multiple quotations from Shorenstein, including:

If I had stayed in the franchise, it would be infinitely better … We would have built a winner by signing more ballplayers like Barry Bonds and filled Candlestick. San Francisco will only support a winner.[10]

The 1998 article noted that while Giants executives "declined to comment on Shorenstein's statements … several investors in the team privately said the San Francisco business icon [Shorenstein] was not interested in a downtown stadium, 'If he had his way' said one investor, 'the team would be on the block. We could not survive long term in Candlestick – regardless of our payroll.'" Larry Baer, current CEO of the Giants (COO in 1998), was quoted in the same article as saying no amount of payroll guarantees success:

> You have to be beyond a certain threshold, say $35 million, to be competitive ... Beyond that, nothing is a lock. The Baltimore Orioles spent $72 million on their payroll, and they will not make the playoffs. Yet Houston and San Diego are around $40 million and they're in.

Decisions about the level of club payrolls are central to the management of sporting clubs. Chapters 4 (Clubs, Owners, and Management), 5 (Professional Athletes and Players' Associations/Unions), and 6 (Club Player-Side Decision Making) of this book discuss this area, including factors that affect the payroll levels chosen by a club at a particular point in time.

The San Francisco Giants has long operated with a club total player payroll that is below that of several other MLB clubs. For example, information related to the 2010 to 2014 period that includes their three World Series wins is:

Year	Giants Payroll	MLB Rank	MLB Highest	MLB Lowest
2010	$98 million	10th	$206 million (New York Yankees)	$35 million (Pittsburgh Pirates)
2011	$118 million	7th	$202 million (New York Yankees)	$36 million (Kansas City Royals)
2012	$118 million	7th	$200 million (New York Yankees)	$53 million (Oakland Athletics)
2013	$136 million	7th	$228 million (New York Yankees)	$26 million (Houston Astros)
2014	$149 million	7th	$229 million (Los Angeles Dodgers)	$46 million (Miami Marlins)

As further highlighted in Decision #6 and #7 below, the Giants face payroll decisions on an ongoing basis. Some decisions have a relatively long time horizon, such as offering a record salary for an extended period as with the 1992 Barry Bonds contract. Other decisions have a much shorter time horizon, such as offering a half-year contract mid-season to a veteran to overcome a higher-than-expected number of injuries in a key position.

Decision #5: New ballpark decisions result in the Giants 2000 season opening in new privately financed baseball park in downtown San Francisco

Right from the outset of assuming ownership in late 1992, the syndicate knew that moving to a new ballpark would enable the Giants to better achieve the objectives of its members. A new stadium could potentially increase annual revenues by at least $40 million per year according to some conservative estimates in the late 1990s. This sizable increase in revenues could potentially be used to eliminate operating losses (related to the profitability objective of some syndicate members) or to add some more high-impact players to the club (related to the Giants being a consistently on-the-field, championship-challenging club objective).

There were many sites for the new stadium available in the Bay Area, including both downtown sites and sites in other parts of the Bay Area. The Giants decided on a downtown location on the waterfront that had the potential to become one of the most scenically located ballparks in North America. Given that four previous attempts to have public financing for a new stadium had failed, the Giants opted for a privately financed ballpark. Realistically, this was the only option available. Moreover, the existing syndicate took the risk of using debt financing rather than raise more equity capital that would have diluted their equity interests.

April 11, 2000 saw the Giants on opening day in their new Pacific Bell Park. It had an estimated construction cost of $360 million. In the 1997/2000 period, the Giants made many decisions that were part of building a waterfront stadium without access to public financing. Approximately $180 million of debt was part of the financing. The remaining $180 million was raised by the sale of (a) seat licenses, (b) naming rights (Pacific Bell[11]), and (c) sponsorship, advertising, and concessionaire contracts with some front-end cash payments. One constraint added by the $180 million debt was that the Giants had a 20-year cash outflow for interest and debt repayment that many other clubs with city-financed stadiums did not have to pay.

Decision #6: Giants have on-field success, a 2002 World Series appearance, and a dramatic increase in revenues with new stadium (however, steroid-use allegations regarding Barry Bonds creates difficult decisions for Giants management in 2006 and 2007)

The 2000/4 period saw the Giants make great strides in both the on-field and off-field areas. The Giants made the playoffs three times between 2000 and 2004 and had the third best winning percentage in the National League in that period. In 2002, they went to the World Series, losing to the Los Angeles Angels in a seven-game series. Barry Bonds was a key part of this success: in 2001, he broke the single season home run record by hitting 73 home runs. Regarding attendance, in the 1993/9 period, the Giants at Candlestick Park averaged 23,625 per game; this rose to an average of 40,409 for the five years from 2000 to 2004. This 71 percent increase was further enhanced by the higher average ticket prices and suite revenue at the new stadium and better sponsorship deals. *Forbes* estimated that Giants revenues increased 93 percent from $72 million in 1999 to $139 million in 2000. This quantum increase was above that initially budgeted in the Giants' early projections.

Barry Bonds' outstanding hitting from 2000 onwards led some to call AT&T Park, the "house that Barry built." However, in the mid-2000s, allegations surfaced that Bonds was taking illegal performance-enhancing drugs. A 2006 book alleged that Bonds used steroids from at least 1998 to 2002. Media reports in 2005 and 2006 made frequent references linking steroids with Barry Bonds. Bonds denied the allegations. The extensive media attention put the San Francisco Giants in a difficult position. Bonds' five-year contract ended in 2006; he was then the highest paid Giants player. He also had a reputation for being a very difficult person off the field, as echoed by a number of media columnists:

- "He's a prima donna, they say, and a whiner, a hot dog, a phony, a cancer on the team" (Scott Ostler in the *San Francisco Chronicle*, 1992)
- "The Giants often are perceived as 24 guys and Barry. He has his own corner of the clubhouse. Three locker cubicles are kept empty between him and the rest of the team ... the other players are content to let 'Barry be Barry' because he's so darn talented" (Mark Emmons in the *San Francisco Chronicle*, 2003).

At the end of the 2006 season, the Giants faced the decision of whether to offer Bonds an attractive contract for the 2007 season and possibly beyond. The 2007 year was pivotal to Bonds as he was highly likely to break Hank Aaron's record for career home runs of 755. This record is one of the landmark achievements in baseball history for a hitter. If the Giants did not sign Bonds for 2007, what would be the reaction of the Giants fans seeing him break the record in a different uniform? Bonds continued to deny the steroid allegations and no definitive evidence had appeared to contradict his denials. However, many viewed the circumstantial evidence of steroid use by Bonds as damming.

In January 2007, the Giants signed Bonds to a one-year, $15.8 million extension for the 2007 season. As expected, Bonds did break Aaron's record in 2007 in a Giants uniform and much to the thrill of Giants fans it was at AT&T Park. MLB commissioner Bud Selig issued a statement saying: "While the issues which have swirled around this record will continue to work themselves toward resolution, today is a day for congratulations on a truly remarkable achievement."[12] While many Giants fans roared with excitement when Bonds hit his 756th home run, others in the baseball world and beyond viewed the achievement as tainted.

Larry Baer, current CEO of the Giants, commented on the 2007 decision to offer Bonds a one-year contract as follows:

> It was a highly complex, highly difficult, highly emotional decision – a real potpourri of mixture of qualitative, quantitative, perception, image considerations. At the end of the day, what we had to determine in 2006 was first could he help the team win. A lot of people didn't think that was a consideration. They thought it was to sell tickets or thought it was to see him set the home run record in a Giants uniform. While there were elements of that, especially the latter, a key factor was "could he help the team win?"

Baer also noted that prior to the 2007 decision, the Giants had already made deliberate efforts to separate the Giants brand from the Bonds brand:

> Though Bonds was very much part of the Giants franchise and connected to us in many ways, we also had to try to create some separation. As we got further along into the steroid allegations, the separation had to be made more clear, between the Giants and Bonds. So some of the marketing of the team had to split off from Bonds. And certainly there was trepidation about making him the centerpiece of everything.

After the 2007 season, the Giants decided not to offer Bonds a contract for the 2008 season and beyond. To the surprise of some, no other MLB club made a 2008 contract offer that Bonds viewed as acceptable. Bonds' 2007 season with the Giants was to be his last in MLB.

Decision #7: Giants sign Barry Zito to a seven-year contract starting in 2007 for $126 million of guaranteed money

Decisions to contract players for coming seasons have uncertainty on multiple dimensions, including future performance, health, and attitude. In late 2006, the Giants signed Barry Zito to a $126 million, seven-year contract. This was their then-largest contract for a pitcher.[13] At the time, it made Zito the highest paid pitcher in the MLB. The contract was questioned by many, in large part due to the Giants offering a 29-year-old pitcher a seven-year contract at an average of $18 million per year. Most pitchers suffer a sizable decline in performance in their 30s. The Giants press release on December 29, 2006 included the following comments:[14]

When you have an opportunity to acquire a pitcher of Barry's caliber, you have to exhaust every effort to get him on your club.

> Brian Sabean, senior vice-president and general manager of the Giants

Barry's signing is as big a moment in recent Giants history as when we signed Barry Bonds for the first time back in 1992. Barry is at the same point in his career now as Bonds was back then – an established major leaguer with a rigorous work ethic entering the prime of his career … In terms of the contract, after examining Barry's track record of durability, his age, and work ethic, we are excited that he'll be a Giant for at least the next seven years.

> Peter Magowan, president of the Giants

Zito's subsequent record at the Giants was not the performance outcome that the Giants had bet on. In his seven years with the Athletics, Zito (aged 22 to 28 years) won 102 and lost 63 regular season games for a win percentage of 61.8 percent. In his seven years with the Giants, Zito (aged 29 to 35 years) won 63 games and lost 80 for a win percentage of 44.1 percent. The Giants chose not to use him in their 2010 post-season, but did use him in their 2012 post-season when he pitched 13 innings across the three post-season series. Not surprisingly, the Zito contract came under continued criticism. In March 2012, one commentator listed the Zito contract with the Giants as "the worst free agent contract ever."[15]

Decision #8: Giants decide to acquire a 30 percent equity stake in a regional sports network

Many MLB clubs have contracts with a regional sports network (RSN) to show many of their games live on cable television. Prior to the 2000s, almost all MLB clubs signed a long-term contract in return for a guaranteed annual payment. In the 1999/2001 period, the New York Yankees led negotiations that resulted in the creation of the YES Network in which it had a major equity interest. The YES Network was a cable RSN that would show live the majority of Yankees games. This positioned the New York Yankees to share in any asset creation (and dividends) associated with the YES Network as well as the annual payment for the right to show Yankees games live.

In late 2007, the Giants negotiated with the two co-owners of their RSN (then FSN Bay Area) to acquire an equity share. The prior equity share was 60 percent Comcast and 40 percent Fox Sports. The revised equity share was Comcast 45 percent, San Francisco Giants 30 percent, and Fox Sports 25 percent. As part of the agreement, the Giants signed a 25-year contract to provide 135 games exclusively to the RSN.[16] Larry Baer stated at the time: "We are excited to deepen our relationship with FSN Bay Area, one of the signature regional sports networks in the country."[17]

Decision #9: Giants decide to expand their asset base through real estate and events

The San Francisco Giants have long sought multiple avenues to expand their asset base beyond their management of the baseball club and its players/coaches. The first major asset-build project after acquiring the club in 1992 was the privately funded new stadium that opened in 2000. This project transformed the asset value of the Giants. Ongoing asset-building activities associated with the ballpark beyond baseball have included hosting multiple events on non-baseball playing days. Examples are hosting college bowl games, the annual Giant race (half-marathon, 10km, 5km), international soccer games, and concerts. The second major asset transformative project was acquiring a 30 percent equity in their RSN as described in Decision #8. The third major transformative project is a real estate project known as Mission Rock.

The Mission Rock project is a $1.6 billion plan to redevelop 28 acres that currently has aging pier warehouses and surface parking on land adjacent to AT&T Park. The proposal is to build corporate offices, retail, and housing, as well as park areas on land not owned by the Giants. A key element in this project is obtaining approval from city and state bodies for various aspects of the project. The project started in 2008 as a partnership with several real estate development groups. The Port of San Francisco asked for bids and then selected the Giants-led group to undertake and manage the redevelopment. As with many downtown redevelopment projects, many approvals are part of the process. However, the Giants are investing sizable resources on this project, which has a very large upside to the value of the assets owned or managed by the San Francisco Giants syndicate. One aspect here is that the timelines can be very long and the skillsets of real estate executives very different from other areas of the San Francisco Giants organization. In general, as sporting clubs seek to diversify their assets, personnel expansion into different competencies will be an ongoing challenge. Fran Weld, director of real estate for the San Francisco Giants, commented:

> One of the primary reasons that we are leading the Mission Rock project is because we care about the future of our community. We have at least another 50 years left to play at AT&T Park, and we consider the immediate neighborhood around the ballpark to be our front door. We want to create the best waterfront experience for fans, neighbors who live and work nearby, and visitors to San Francisco. In addition, controlling our only dedicated parking resource is a critical goal for protecting the operational functionality of our urban site. While we have one of the highest modal splits of MLB, with over 50 percent of our fans walking, biking, or taking public transit, we still have to take care of those fans who chose to drive to games. Finally, as a multi-faceted business operation, we are strategically pursuing the asset diversification that real estate brings to our portfolio, which will provide future financial stability to our organization.[18]

Development and management of the association of real estate assets with sporting stadiums and arenas is an increasingly important part of asset creation in sports.

Decision #10: Giants decide to celebrate 2010, 2012, and 2014 World Series wins with major downtown celebrations involving city and state officials

There are many stakeholders that have an interest in seeing the San Francisco Giants succeed as a MLB franchise on the field as well as be financially secure as a business. On at least two occasions, San Franciscan groups have worked with city officials to pre-empt attempts to relocate the Giants to other cities. Decisions #1 and #2 reference successful efforts to pre-empt attempts to move the Giants to Toronto in 1976 and to St. Petersburg in 1992.

After each of the recent World Series wins in 2010, 2012, and 2014, the Giants led broad community celebrations that recognized the contributions of the many groups that played roles in their successes on and off the field. The Giants recognized the contributions of past owners (such as Bob Lurie), former players (such as Willie Mays and Barry Bonds), early investors and former management (such as Peter Magowan and Bill Neukom), and the many city officials and city bodies such as the police and fire departments, as well the many fans of the Giants. These celebrations attracted huge crowds for a ticker tape parade as well as at City Hall. Celebrations such as these showcase the important role that sporting clubs play in building the fabric of a city and creating important bonds across many diverse groups in that city and beyond. The link to the city is reinforced in the club's 2015 marketing campaign with the slogan "We are SF, we are Giant."

Decisions to make the celebrations a showcase for the many stakeholders highlights the importance the Giants syndicate and its management place on continuing to reinforce and strengthen their relationships with these stakeholders.

1.3 SOME GENERAL COMMENTS ON DECISION MAKING

The ten decision areas overviewed for the San Francisco Giants illustrate some general points that occur frequently in subsequent chapters and that provide a guide and rich example for the rest of the book.

1.3.1 Good Decisions Do Not Guarantee Desired Outcomes

It is essential to distinguish between the quality of a decision as opposed to the desirability of the outcome. A good decision is one where there is consistency between the pre-set objectives and the actual objectives used to make a choice and where all available information and data was used in a consistent way to make the final choice. However, in an uncertain world with many uncontrollable factors, there is no guarantee that a "good" decision process will lead to the desired outcome. Assume a general manager (GM) of a professional basketball club negotiates very successfully with a 26-year-old superstar seven-foot forward who is a five-time all-star. The GM negotiates a five-year contract that adds the superstar player to the club at a reasonable salary. In the first year of the contract, the club experiences major on-court success and goes deep in the playoffs with the new hire making outstanding contributions. However, during the first game of their second season, the player suffers a devastating, career-ending knee injury. This is clearly a "bad outcome" for both the club and the player. However, it does not mean that the decision made one year earlier to offer the five-year contract was a "bad decision." Injuries are part of sport at all levels. The best protection against bad outcomes is using a good decision making process and then following the decision with effective execution.

1.3.2 Differences Across Stakeholders and Often Within Stakeholder Groups Are To Be Expected

Decision making involving different stakeholders needs to balance differences between parties. Consider the interests of a syndicate group owning a club moving to a new stadium and the interests of fans. The norm in these settings is that the new stadium has higher ticket prices and higher food and beverage charges. There may even be the requirement that season ticket holders purchase seat licenses, which have the right to then buy tickets at the higher prices. These seat licenses in some stadiums have ranged from as low as $1,000 to as high as $80,000. Not surprisingly, some existing ticket holders at the old stadium resent the new charges and a subset may not be able to afford to make the transition to the new stadium. As a second example, clubs may prefer to offer players shorter contracts at lower amounts with lower guarantees. In contrast, players likely will prefer longer contracts at higher amounts with higher guarantees. Contracting in these settings typically involves negotiations that require compromises by one or both parties in order for an agreement to be made. The San Francisco Giants decision analysis also highlights how differences can exist among individual members of a stakeholder group. The 1992 syndicate that purchased the Giants quickly had several exits by individuals who had differences in their objectives from those remaining in the syndicate.

A consequence of these frequently encountered differences across stakeholders is that successful negotiation skills have high value in the sporting world. Executives who are experienced in negotiations can add great value to the investments made or assets held by stakeholders whose interests they are advancing.

1.3.3 Decision Making and Actions in a Fish Bowl

There is a very high level of public interest in many decisions made in the sporting industry. The highest rated programs on television are frequently sports-related. Cable stations such as ESPN attract high ratings and command very high carriage fees for distributors. Newspapers for many years have had separate sports sections, and in some cases sporting stories can even occupy the front pages. Online sporting news websites attract many hits. In short, there is a very high demand for sports content. In many cases, what some see as relatively trivial information content or even gossip, to others is seen something that it is well worth spending time consuming. Part of this high interest in sports content results in differences of opinions and positions by key participants in the sports industry being showcased in public. This showcasing can be deliberate in some cases, while in others it is accidental or unintentional.

The advent of social media and mobile technology has further increased the interest in stories about the sports industry. An extreme example here is how decisions made by players in their off-field activities are very much in the public domain now on a continual 24/7 basis. This creates greater onus on players to be more measured in their activities and to make day-by-day decisions that protect their brand rather than diminish their brand (as well as the brands of their club, league, sponsors, etc.).

1.3.4 Second-Guessing Decisions and Reinventing History

Another consequence of the high interest in many aspects of the sporting industry is that many decisions are "second-guessed" or, at a later stage, heavily criticized on the basis of information not available at the time the initial decision was made. Sporting columnists often seek to attract attention to their thoughts and writings by making "shock value" comments or taking extreme positions that do not necessarily represent their own opinions. The result is that many individuals making key decisions in the sporting industry will see their decisions heavily criticized by some, and their character may be mischaracterized or even lampooned. For example, every GM of long standing with a club will have made player acquisition decisions that after the fact underperform relative to their informed expectations at the time the hire decision was made. They likely will also have made decisions to cut players that subsequently outperform while playing for a competing club, relative to what they expected at the time the decision to fire/not renew was made.

Executives who are uncomfortable with public criticism of themselves or their decisions need to learn to accept this criticism in a less personal way or not seek high-profile positions in the sporting industry. Similarly, players whose quality of performance is likely affected by public criticism have to quickly develop coping mechanisms so that they can perform to the best of their abilities.

1.4 SUMMARY

Every chapter in this book highlights multiple decisions by one or more stakeholders in the sporting industry in different contexts and from different perspectives. Informed decision making increases the likelihood that good outcomes will result from these decisions. However, uncertainty at the time of a decision or its poor execution can result in the actual outcomes diverging from the preferred outcomes at the time of the decision. In many cases, however, there will be a sequence of decisions such that those individuals who possess good judgment will be identified as effective decision makers who attract the respect of others inside and outside the sporting industry.

BOX 1.1 MANAGING THE SAN FRANCISCO GIANTS AS A MULTI-BUSINESS ORGANIZATION[19]

The dominant focus of sporting clubs historically was achieving success on the field. Individuals with limited business backgrounds often managed the clubs. The current management and investor syndicate of the San Francisco Giants illustrates the change that has occurred in how many leading sporting clubs are managed. Larry Baer graduated from the University of California at Berkeley and joined the Giants as marketing director. After four years, he attended the Harvard Business School, graduating with a MBA. Post-Harvard, he spent four years at Westinghouse Broadcasting in San Francisco and New York. A major division of Westinghouse was CBS, then one of the three major broadcast networks. Baer was special assistant to the chairman of CBS. In 1992, Baer returned to the Giants as executive vice-president. He played a key role with Peter Magowan (the first Giants CEO) in building the syndicate that purchased the Giants from the Bob Lurie group. He was named chief operating officer (COO) in May 1996, president in 2008, and CEO in 2012.

Baer views the CEO role at the Giants as managing a multi-business organization: "We are definitely in the business of winning MLB baseball games and competing at the highest levels for playoff and championship success. However, we are also in the customer service and entertainment businesses, in the promotion and delivery of non-baseball events, in the media business with our partnerships and equity in broadcast media and radio, in the technology business, and also in the community service activity area. Add to that our important investments in real estate. Our aim is to be a high performance organization across all our many businesses."

Baer is on the board of directors of multiple key partner organizations of the Giants, including Comcast Sports Net Bay Area and KQED. He is president and CEO of Giants Development Services, the company developing the real estate project near AT&T Park.

Part of Baer's management style is to create a culture of inclusiveness. He says that the organization's aim is to have "employees pulling on the same rope. When we are in the World Series we take all our employees on the road to the games, and not just those focused on the baseball team. That involved chartering 747s. And each time we won, Bruce Bochy [manager], Brian Sabean [general manager], and myself presented a World Series ring to every employee."

An important role of a sporting club CEO is representing the organization to the broader community. Baer has embraced this aspect of his role as a Bay Area community leader. He and his wife have been actively involved in multiple Bay Area organizations, including San Francisco General Hospital and the Boys and Girls Clubs of America.

BOX 1.2 GIANTS LEVERAGE TECHNOLOGY TO ADOPT DYNAMIC PRICING WITH INCREASES IN GAME DAY REVENUES

For many decades, most MLB clubs had a policy of having different price zones for tickets in a stadium but not having price differences for the same seat at different games. Yet it has always been apparent that market demand for the same seat is not uniform since "not all games are created equal." Rather, factors such as the quality and brand of the opponent, the starting pitchers, the month of the year, the day of the week, and on whether the game is at day or night can make a big difference. Chapter 13 discusses how leagues and clubs are rethinking their ticket pricing structures to reflect these demand factors. The San Francisco Giants has been an early aggressive user of technology in the ticketing arena. Two key areas are: (a) using dynamic pricing to set the prices of tickets sold on a single game basis; and (b) allowing season ticket holders to sell their tickets on in a secondary market in which the Giants participate on a revenue-sharing basis. Russ Stanley, managing vice-president of ticket sales and services, credited both as important to the many sellout games at AT&T Park. He noted they have "42,000 seats and 29,000 full season ticket holders, so we have 13,000 single-game tickets to sell."[20]

Dynamic pricing is where market factors on a game-by-game basis are used to set market clearing prices. Historically, it has been used in the airline industry and the lodging industry for many years. Typically those involved in setting the dynamic pricing architecture at a sporting club will be the head of information technology, the head of ticketing, and a third-party advisory company that has expertise in analyzing large databases in the setting of dynamic prices. The Giants chose Qcue as the third-party advisor. The Giants trialed dynamic pricing in 2009 to sell outfield and upper-deck seats that were sold on a game-by-game basis. In 2010, dynamic pricing was expanded to all tickets sold on a game-by-game basis. Initially, Jerry Drobny (vice-president of strategic revenue services), Devin Lutes (director of ticket services), and Stanley reviewed the Qcue-recommended prices and made adjustments. One factor considered was not setting prices so low that season ticket holders felt that the price they were paying for their own seats was a bad investment. However, many tickets were still priced lower than the previous year's face value of the ticket. Bill Schlough, head of information technology, noted that "dynamic pricing enables us to capture a larger share of consumer surplus."[21]

Stanley estimated "about an $8,000,000 increase in revenue year-over-year in 2010 from 2009" from their adoption of dynamic pricing. He noted that "we had a great year in 2010 that came down to the wire and we won the World Series. Had we not been able to be nimble and react to market value shifts, we would have left that money on the table."

Many season ticket holders buy packages of 81 regular season games. By creating an authenticated secondary market in which season ticket holders could sell on some of their tickets, the Giants were able to reduce the number of "black market" tickets sold. Fans who were willing to pay premium prices could go onto the Giants affiliated secondary market and know that the tickets they purchased were "authentic." The Giants benefited here in two direct ways – an increase in the number of people buying tickets (and spending at the park) due to the higher "trust factor," and sharing in the prices paid by those purchasing on the secondary market. A third benefit was the likely increase in season ticket renewals as season ticket holders were less likely to have "unused tickets." Season-ticket holders with many "unused tickets" they have paid for are less likely to renew their packages for the next season.

NOTES

1 A similar situation exists when a league has no guaranteed contracts for its players. Players in the NFL can be cut mid-stream in their contract periods and the club not have to pay the remaining payments outlined in the contract. One result is that agents and players not contract for larger amounts of a total "nominal " contract to be paid up front, reducing the risks to a player being cut mid-stream in a nominally long-term contract.

2 See T. Tucker, "Braves plan to build new stadium in Cobb," *The Atlanta Journal-Constitution*, November 12, 2013. *The Atlanta Journal-Constitution* is a good source that tracks the timeline and key aspects of the Braves' efforts to find the "best" location for their new stadium.

3 See, for example, M. Sunnucks, "Phoenix Coyotes buyers may be running into financial challenges," *Phoenix Business Journal*, July 31, 2013.

4 Chapter 3 outlines the relegation structure found in many major soccer leagues.

5 Much of the information and quotations in this section are taken from a Stanford GSB case "San Francisco Giants: opportunities and challenges in different eras" (2015).

6 "San Jose rejects Giants," *The New York Times*, June 4, 1992.

7 This investor was Irv Grousbeck, who subsequently was a lead investor in the syndicate that purchased the Boston Celtics in 2002 for a reported $360 million. The Celtics passed Grousbeck's business model criteria and has been a very successful investment for the syndicate.

8 Quotes from Larry Baer are taken from interviews with Baer for a Stanford GSB case or comments made by Baer during Stanford GSB classes in which Baer was a guest speaker.

9 P. Schmuck, "Bonds signs deal with Giants-to-be: Lurie protected in $43 million pact," *The Baltimore Sun*, December 9, 1992.

10 J. Swartz, "Giants' pricey new park may lower team quality/debt could hamper keeping top players," *San Francisco Chronicle*, September 11, 1998.

11 Pacific Bell was a telecommunications company strong in the Pacific Coast region. Subsequently, Pacific Bell was acquired by SBC. SBC was subsequently acquired by AT&T in 2005 and assumed the AT&T name The San Francisco ballpark had name changes that mirrored these corporate changes. It has been called AT&T Park since 2006.

12 MLB press release. Quoted in "Barry Bonds breaks home run record!!!," *MediaTakeOut.com*, August 8, 2007.

13 H. Schulman and S. Slusser, "Giants finally make a big splash, sign Zito to largest pitcher contract ever," *San Francisco Chronicle*, December 28, 2006.

14 "Giants sign Cy Young winner Barry Zito to seven-year deal," San Francisco Giants press release, December 29, 2006.

15 J. Heyman, "Here's the answer to whether Zito's is the worst free agent contract ever," *Baseball Insider*, March 25, 2012.

16 "SF Giants take stake in FSN," *Variety*, December 10, 2007.

17 "San Francisco Giants, FSN Bay Area announce long-term rights extension," San Francisco Giants press release, December 10, 2007.

18 See J.K. Dineen, "SF Giants real estate director talks beer and building and Mission Rock," *Bay Area /Biz Talk*, April 12, 2013. Official plans are found in City and County of San Francisco, Port of San Francisco, "Seawall lot 337 (SWL 337) & Pier 48," March 12, 2013.

19 Box 1.1 draws on comments made by Larry Baer at multiple Stanford GSB classes plus several media interviews including: "KNBR conversation, Larry Baer, Giants president," *SFGATE*, October 26, 2013, and B. Costa, "Baseball champions' CEO on creating a culture of success," *The Wall Street Journal*, February 22, 2015.

20 J. McCarthy, "Selling out with Russ Stanley," *Selling Out*, November 20, 2013.

21 S. Overby, "For San Francisco Giants, dynamic pricing software hits a home run," *CIO* June 29, 2011.

2

THE WORLD OF SPORTS AND ITS BUSINESS ECOSYSTEM

S port plays many roles in societies around the globe. At the most visible level from a media perspective are events where elite athletes are paid to perform at the highest levels with highly paid coaching staff, and where audiences can pay sizable amounts to witness the spectacle. Here, athleticism, entertainment, and community are key dimensions to the sporting experience. At the other end of the spectrum, there are many events and games, such as weekend children's sporting competitions with parents and friends watching from the sidelines or training sessions with voluntary coaches. These two extremes illustrate the very diverse roles for sport in society, including physical and mental health-building and personal development, as well as entertainment and community-building. This book examines the global business ecosystem for the diverse sports platforms that underlie and ideally promote the many benefits that the world of sports brings to society. We also highlight areas where tensions exist between the goals or actions of key stakeholders in the sports world and other parts of society. Box 2.1 describes the sport of diving in China, where it is one of the most popular sports; however, in the rest of the world, the sport is typically only followed by the general population around the time of the Olympic Games.

BOX 2.1 PASSIONATE FANS EXAMPLE: CHINA AND DIVING

We can learn a great deal about the importance of fan passion to the business of sport by looking at any sport and its core followers in its main countries of play. Each country (or regions in many cases) has its own passion for certain sports: think cycling in France, football in the United States, ice hockey in Canada, rugby in New Zealand, cricket in India, hurling in Ireland, Australian rules football in Australia, and so on. In each case, the country or region has a deep passion – or at least a good chunk of its population does – for the sport. Its players are often national heroes. In sports where there are multiple countries playing the sport at an elite level, the outcomes of games in which the national team competes can be cause for celebration and pride (in the case of victory) or disappointment (in the case of failure).

At the 2008 Olympic Games in Beijing, the Chinese national passion for the sport of diving was showcased. Relatively minor in many other countries, diving is one of the very top sports in China. Heading into the 2008 Games, China's top competing divers were national celebrities – on par with Yao Ming (NBA star) and Liu Xiang (star hurdler). Tickets to diving events were among the hardest to get for the Games. The Beijing aquatic facility built for the Games ("the Cube") was world-class and for once in aquatic sport, it was diving (and not swimming) that drove the venue project. China's stars in 2008 – Guo Jingjing, Zhou Lüxin, He Chong, Qin Kai, Chen Ruolin, and Wang Xin – were and remain household names in China. At the 2008 Games, they were expected to capture gold in each and every event. Fortunately for national pride, the Chinese divers came close to a sweep, winning gold in seven of the eight diving events and silver in the other event (due to an upset victory by Australian Matthew Mitcham in the ten-meter platform). China's legendary diver Gao Min – gold medal winner in the 1988 and 1992 games – carried the Olympic Torch in the stadium at the Beijing Opening Ceremony.

2.1 THE SPORTS BUSINESS ECOSYSTEM

Exhibit 2.1 provides an overview of some key stakeholders in the sports business ecosystem. Many, if not all of these stakeholders can be found in both professional and amateur sports. Professional sports

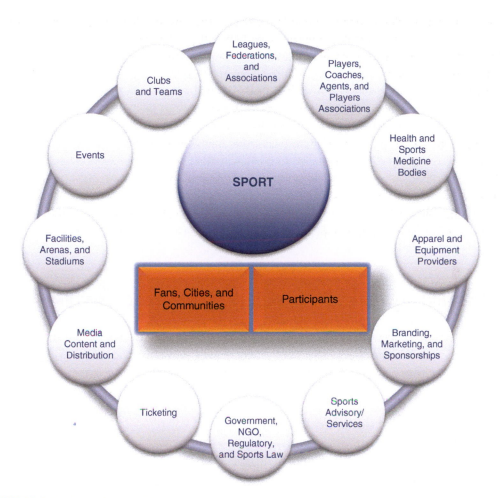

EXHIBIT 2.1 The Sports Business Ecosystem

contests are distinguished by monetary payments being made to individual athletes engaged in the sporting competition. Amateur sport refers to contexts where individual participants do not receive financial compensation. With amateur sports there often is a contest, although that is not always the case. An amateur swimmer or runner may be a lone participant with the focus on personal health rather than any attempt to win over one or more other participants. Professional athletes typically form a small minority of the total participants in most sports. For example, professional golfers and runners comprise less than 1 percent of the total participants in these sports.

Professional sports and amateur sports are best viewed as ends of a spectrum. Rankings of the highest paid athletes highlight examples of professional sporting contexts. These rankings typically include athletes from both team-based sports (such as soccer, football, basketball, cricket, and baseball) and individual athlete sports (such as boxing, MMA, golf, and tennis). Amateur participants in these same sports include many youths in high schools and weekend sports as well as adults playing for enjoyment and health. Between these two extremes are some sporting contests where many key parties are paid but those on the "sporting field" itself are not financially compensated. For example, while several US college sports have many aspects of professional sporting contests (such as football with highly paid coaches, large stadiums, and large media contracts), at present the governing sports body mandates that college players are amateur athletes. Over time, the trend has been that sports that have key aspects of professional sports but with amateur athletes will switch to having their athletes become professional athletes. An example is rugby union, where prior to 1995 the sport's governing body (then the International Rugby Board, now called World Rugby) imposed bans on players who had accepted financial payments to play. Since 1995, rugby union has embraced financial payments to its players. There is growing pressure in the United States for some financial compensation (beyond tuition scholarships) to be paid to some college student athletes.

An important aspect on the amateur extreme is the noted uncertainty around when an athlete is professional and when they are amateur. As a result, alternative terminology has emerged in defining sport that is not professional. This includes the use of terms such as 'Olympic sport' (including any sport activity related to a sport that is part of the program of the Olympic Summer Games or Olympic Winter Games) and 'grassroots sport' (referring to any sport-related activity at the community level, where play is largely for enjoyment and not about high performance). These terms have varying degrees of accuracy in any specific context.[1]

2.2 KEY STAKEHOLDERS IN THE SPORTS BUSINESS ECOSYSTEM

There are twelve major stakeholders in the sports business ecosystem outlined in Exhibit 2.1 in addition to the fans, cities, and communities. The role of these major stakeholders can often differ depending on whether the context relates to a professional sports context or an amateur sport participant context.

2.2.1 Leagues, Federations, and Associations

Most sports at either the professional or amateur level have one or more bodies that govern major aspects of the game. Examples occur at many levels. These include the global level (such as FIBA for basketball, which has more than 200 country members), the country level (such as EPL for English soccer with 20 member clubs and the NHL for North American ice hockey with 30 clubs), the college level (such as the NCAA in the US with more than 1,200 colleges who comprise member conferences such as the SEC and Pac-12), and at the junior sport level (such as Pop Warner Little Scholars for junior football in the US, with more than 400,000 juniors between the ages of five and 16). Decisions by these bodies can be far-reaching. They can relate to such diverse areas as the number of participants playing on a team at any one time, the allowed equipment, length of a game, and game integrity protocols (such as procedures to detect performance-enhancing drugs and potential game-fixing). The enforcement of these decisions is pivotal to professional sporting contexts but much less so in some amateur settings (Chapters 3 and 7 discuss the key decisions and issues for this group of stakeholders).

2.2.2 Clubs and Teams

Many sports have a club/team as well as an individual participant aspect. The engine of fan engagement for many sporting leagues are the individual teams in those leagues. Examples from professional leagues include soccer (Manchester United and FC Barcelona), football (Dallas Cowboys), basketball (Los Angeles Lakers), baseball (New York Yankees), ice hockey (Toronto Maple Leafs), and Australian rules football (West Coast Eagles). Professional motorsport often has teams that consist of multiple drivers (such as the Ferrari team in Formula 1 and the Hendrick Motorsports team in NASCAR). Several chapters in this book cover issues arising with these teams, including strategy and execution (Chapter 4), marketing and sponsorship (Chapters 10 and 11), and valuation (Chapter 18). Teams in amateur sports are often the first exposure that many children have to the sporting participant experience.

2.2.3 Players, Coaches, Agents, and Player Associations

At the professional sports level, much of the media attention focuses on key players and coaches. Decisions here have multiple aspects, depending on the perspective. Clubs making hiring and contracting decisions are very interested in elements such as player and coach contributions to winning and club branding as well as player compensation. Players/coaches and their agents are very interested in the club's ability to win championships as well as compensation. The growing role of analytics in many player-related areas has created a vibrant industry in data collection and data analysis using increasingly sophisticated tools. Many new startup companies showcase with innovative data presentations on the field action by professional and amateur athletes. Associations representing players or coaches in collective bargaining exist for professional athletes in many sports. Chapter 5 includes detailed discussions of this stakeholder area.

2.2.4 Events

Many sporting activities are associated with organized events, including some global mega sport events that can attract television audiences of more than half the world's population. At the high-performance team (or country) sports level, examples include mega global events such as the Summer and Winter Olympic Games, the World Cups (e.g., soccer, rugby, and cricket), major world championships (e.g., IAAF World Championships in Athletics), global team events for individual sports (such as the Ryder Cup in golf and the Davis Cup in tennis), and major national championship games that are globally broadcast (such as the NFL's Super Bowl). Examples at the individual professional athlete level include globally recognized tournaments in tennis (such as Wimbledon), motorsports (such as the Formula 1 Grand Prix) and golf (such as the Masters). Many participant sports have seen increasingly sophisticated events being created and executed, beyond the more traditional offerings of marathons, triathlons, cycling events, walks, and regattas. Examples of this new wave of events include the Tough Mudder, Titan Desert, and Spartan Warrior obstacle/adventure events as well as many charity- and theme-related golf, cycling, running, and walking events. Chapter 9 discusses key decisions in the creation and execution of the many diverse types of sporting events.

2.2.5 Facilities, Arenas, and Stadiums

Sporting events at the professional level can attract mega-crowds "housed" in facilities such as courses, centers, stadiums, and arenas. Examples include: (a) the Indianapolis Motor Speedway, which has attracted crowds of more than 200,000; (b) the Sydney Olympic Stadium with more than 110,000 seats built for the 2000 Summer Olympic Games; and (c) multiple US college football stadiums with space for more than 100,000 spectators (such as the stadiums at the University of Michigan and Ohio State). In recent years, facilities have become technology showcases with construction costs of over $1 billion, including the Levi Stadium for the San Francisco 49ers and AT&T Stadium for the Dallas Cowboys. Golf courses have increasingly become developed as integral parts of larger real estate investments. At the community level, governments build sporting facilities ranging from soccer fields to ice arenas to swimming pools, where amateurs at all levels can develop or engage in their sporting passions. Key financing, construction, and operating challenges with such facilities are discussed in Chapter 17.

2.2.6 Health and Sport Medicine Bodies

A key role of sports in society is promoting physical and mental health. Sport medicine organizations and practitioners are an important element of the sport ecosystem. The first stage of sports involvement for many can start at a very young age and often via parental influence. Early school years often involve mandatory sports programs and many individuals continue for years with sports activities as part of a balanced approach to living without any attempt (or ability) to be an elite athlete. Running, cycling, and swimming are examples of sporting activities with such a participation base. At the elite athlete end of sports, ongoing health and medical initiatives are aimed at both (a) enhancing ability to play ("a pivotal ability of a professional athlete is availability"), and (b) being able to play at a maximum level of ability when they do play. There is increasing sophistication in both "legitimate" and "illegitimate" initiatives by athletes related to either (a) or (b). Chapter 6 examines the many initiatives and challenges in this area and the topics are referenced throughout the book.

2.2.7 Apparel and Equipment Providers

Sports differ greatly in the apparel and equipment required to be a participant. At one extreme are sports with minimal requirements, such as soccer or basketball, which in part explains their growing popularity in many parts of the globe where there is limited funding available for sports and where you can play with not much more than a ball. The other extreme would be Formula 1 motor sports where the annual budget of some teams exceeds $200 million. A major growth area of the sports eco-system in recent decades has been major apparel companies such as Nike and Under Armour and major equipment providers such as Callaway Golf and Wilson. Professional athletes are often paid large endorsement fees to showcase apparel and equipment to their often large amateur participant and/or fan markets. Chapter 12 discusses the diversity of challenges and opportunities in this area.

2.2.8 Media Content and Distribution

A major financial pillar of many sporting leagues and clubs is payments received from broadcast, cable, and digital media companies. For example, in 2015 the National Football League (NFL) received in excess of $6 billion from its various media partners in return for the rights to broadcast its games. The sports experience for all stakeholders has been greatly enhanced by the growing diversity of media platforms and the ever-increasing sophistication of media technology. These enhancements have occurred for recording the amateur level of sports as well as the professional level. New innovations, such as the GoPro camera, continue to add further dimensions to the sports experience for active participants as well as those interested in observing that experience. For example, the attractiveness of attending sport events has increased for certain individuals who like to share their experience of "being at the game" with others via social media. Chapters 14, 15 and 16 cover the rich contributions to many areas of sports that come from the ever-increasing number of media-related content or distribution companies.

2.2.9 Branding, Marketing, and Sponsorship

Branding occurs at multiple areas of the sports ecosystem. In fact, brand is an important aspect for every stakeholder in sport. Leagues, clubs, and players in the professional arena can benefit from developing brands that create a positive image to key stakeholders such as fans, corporate sponsors, and media companies. Tactically, marketing initiatives can play an important role in this brand-building, as well as providing value in other management roles such as promoting attendance at games, purchasing merchandise, and building sporting club memberships. Corporate sponsors of leagues, federations, clubs, or players often see sporting platforms as an effective way to promote their own brands or to enhance the sales of their own products and/or services. NASCAR, for example, has a fan base that is renowned for its high level of brand loyalty to its major sponsors and for the major sponsors of the individual teams and their drivers. Chapters 10 and 11 discuss the many dimensions of this pivotal area of the business of sports.

2.2.10 Ticketing

Ticketing companies play multiple roles in the sports ecosystem. Many sporting clubs and events contract with ticketing companies to provide the ticket exchange platform by which they transact with buyers of their tickets. To many fans, a major part of their commercial interaction with a sporting event starts with a ticketing company such as Ticketmaster, AXS, or Tickets.com. Ticketing companies have been an important stimulus to innovation in the marketing arena. New initiatives such as dynamic pricing and paperless tickets have been either stimulated by or refined by ticketing companies. These companies also attract much criticism due to allegations of excessive ticket service charges and having dominant market positions. The advent of organized and legal secondary markets has the potential to greatly change the ticketing landscape. Chapter 13 outlines key issues in the ticketing area. Ticketing companies are collecting vast amounts of private information about buyers and sellers that have great commercial value.

2.2.11 Sports Advisory/Service Companies

Sporting leagues, clubs, event-holders, and other stakeholders often use the services of many third-party companies who have sizable expertise in areas of importance to much decision making in the sporting industry. Companies such as AEG, GMR, IMG, Octagon, WMG, and CAA have broad expertise in many areas such as venue management, athlete representation, marketing, and sponsorship. Moreover, much of their expertise has a broader base in many non-sports areas of the entertainment industry. Information technology companies such as Cisco, IBM, Oracle, and SAP are playing leading roles in the ways that technology is being used to improve the fan and in-stadium experience. Also included here are banks and law firms that are essential to many important transactions being conducted in an efficient and effective way.

2.2.12 Government, NGOs, Regulatory, and Sports Law

Government has a vital interest in many areas of sports. In fact, in some countries, government is the primary funder of sport. Activities that have the ability to increase the general level of health (both physical and mental) of individuals are highly attractive to governments at all levels. Based on sport's role in this regard, many levels of government make sporting-related investments to promote the health of its different age groups and citizens. Many governments have sport ministries, departments, or branches. Sports can also play an important role in building national and regional community pride and engagement. Government initiatives in this regard can include policies/laws to guide sport, assistance/support in attracting global sporting events (e.g., Olympic Games, world cups and world championships) via hosting programs, the building of sporting facilities, and providing safe environments for fans to enjoy sporting events. Regulatory bodies can provide incentives and penalties that affect the behavior of leagues, clubs, and/or players. For example, the combat sports of boxing and mixed martial arts in the US are governed state by state through regulations relating to permissible areas of hitting/striking during combat, as well as the use of steroids and other performance-enhancing drugs by participants. Non-government organizations (NGOs) can also be important stakeholders in the business of sports. NGOs are often supported by government funding as well as via funding from sporting bodies. For example, the World Anti-Doping Agency (WADA) is a global NGO that is funded by the governments of multiple countries as well as individual sporting associations. WADA regularly provides a list of prohibited substances that athletes are not allowed to take in sanctioned sporting contests, which is recognized widely by most sporting organizations. Topics related to this stakeholder group are discussed in detail in Chapter 7.

This book examines the decisions, the opportunities, and the challenges facing each of these stakeholders. Business concepts, managerial approaches, examples, and case studies are provided to illustrate. Importantly, we take a global perspective on the world of sports, providing concepts and frameworks that are applicable across countries and contexts. Specifically, key aspects are illustrated using examples from different countries and regions and different sports. Overall, we highlight how, despite differences in the game of sport(s) played in different countries or regions, there are many similarities in the decisions and challenges faced by key stakeholders in their own ecosystems.

2.3 FANS, CITIES, AND COMMUNITIES

Exhibit 2.1 includes fans and communities as a central part of the sports ecosystem. Exhibit 2.2 showcases how fans are far from homogeneous. They vary significantly in their composition, ranging from diehard, loyal fans to those who get interested for social or business reasons.

Located within these levels of fan are subcategories. For instance, the diehards, who regularly consume sports and support their teams both financially and emotionally, can be divided into three distinct categories that all share the characteristic that their schedules revolve around sports. There are: (a) overall sport diehards (i.e., those who love sport), (b) local sport diehards (i.e., those who live and die for the home team), and (c) single sport diehards (i.e., those who have a deep love for one particular sport).

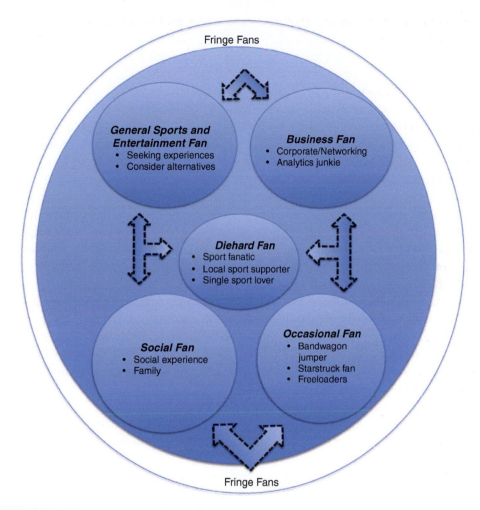

EXHIBIT 2.2 The Rich Heterogeneity of Sports Fans

The overall sport diehards follow all sports and attempt to know as much as possible about everything going on in the sports world. They consume sport in person, as well as via multiple media formats. They are involved with fantasy sport, they gamble on sport, they purchase sport merchandise, and they support sponsors of sport. They buy tickets and would have a hard time turning down an invitation to a sport event. The local diehards follow everything going on in their "home" market. They go often to home games and are likely to buy or share season ticket packages for their team. They go crazy when the team wins and are depressed when they lose. The single sport diehard fan has an interest that runs very deep in their favorite sport. They follow it religiously. They know about multiple players in the league/sport, they know the statistics of their team and players intimately, they will travel to championships or high-value games, and they'll purchase extra television or online packages about the sport, league, or club.

The largest category of fan is the general sport and entertainment fan. These are individuals who seek experiences (sport and non-sport) for their entertainment value. When they are deciding what to watch, attend, or follow, they consider a number of options (again both sport and non-sport) before making their decision. They may be a sport fan or just a general entertainment fan, but in either case they will consider sport products in their options. The general sports fan enjoys sports for what they are, they may attend a couple of games a year, but their lives don't revolve around them as is the case for a diehard fan. Similarly, the general entertainment fan does not take a major interest in sports, but they love the enormity of the events, particularly when they attract interest in a large proportion of the population (e.g., the local team qualifies for the championship round, or their national team plays for a gold medal in a high-profile Olympic sport).

A category of fan that is increasingly important in the sport business and corporate partnerships is the business fan. This category of fan can fall into two distinct subcategories: (a) the corporate/networking fan, and (b) the analytics fan. The corporate/networking fan consumes sports and purchases suites for the purpose of entertaining clients and building partnerships. The analytics fan is drawn to sport for the mathematical "measurables" that can be taken from sport. Leagues and clubs are increasing the amount of information collected and make it available to third parties such as analytics fans.

Another category that must be taken into consideration is the social fan. This fan enjoys the unique social environment that sports bring, and thus they consume sport for the social dynamic it provides. This may be a family coming to the game for entertainment and time together, or a young group of single professionals looking for a good time or different experience. The purpose is social in nature. Note that this category (like many of the categories) may overlap with others in certain cases. For example, a social fan going to the game with their family may also be a diehard single sport fan.

The last two categories displayed in Exhibit 2.2, occasional fans and fringe fans, may be the target of many sports marketers. With a rather large base, the occasional fan is one that does not regularly consume sports or even care that much about them, however, on occasion, they will consume sport. This category is divided into three subcategories: (a) the bandwagon fan, (b) the star-struck fan, and (c) the freeloaders. The bandwagon fans have no measurable loyalty and are only interested in sport when certain teams are successful. However, they do invest in tickets, merchandise, and sponsor product/service when the bandwagon is full. The star-struck fan is interested in sport, because they are drawn to certain athletes. For example, David Beckham and Roger Federer have brought thousands of new fans to their sports simply due to the fans' affinity for each of these stars and their celebrity status. Some fans in this category have been attracted by the growth of reality shows, where the fan has built their affinity to a given star via that show. The freeloader is a fan that sport marketers are advised to ignore, although some do not. They will go to games but only if they get a free ticket from a friend or work contact, but they will never pay for a ticket or purchase merchandise or watch sport on television at home. The last category, the fringe fan, is a fan that can take or leave sports as something they might do on occasion but with no regularity or interest beyond that. They may get interested at times, but for the most part sports are not an important part of their lives.

As noted, fans from all categories can switch from any category at any time, or even be in more than one category at a time. One of the main goals of professionals in the sports business is to drive fans into higher levels of fandom or "up the ladder" as some often describe the process. The more passionate the fan, the more likely they are to consume in the various economic outlets of sport.

In seeking to attract new or more fans, sport can have a defining advantage over many other products, in that its consumers are often also fans, sometimes even fanatics for the product. Few other industries experience this phenomenon. First, the passion (or potential passion) that exists allows sport organizations to develop programs to turn fans or spectators into loyal fans. These loyal fans then support their sponsors, buy their merchandise, watch their games on television or via the internet, purchase bulk tickets (season tickets, ticket packages, single-day tickets), use sport for a business event, and convince friends and acquaintances to watch or attend a game, and so on. Although a process similar to other businesses (from awareness to allegiance) must be followed, the ability to create and keep loyal fans is special in sport, whether the affinity is for a professional club, a star athlete, a national team, or a league. Second, this passion allows for the ability to build secondary or satellite fan bases where fans of the organization may live far from where it plays and may never attend a game in person. Examples include the fan clubs of all of the top professional clubs around the globe, such as Manchester United (EPL), the Montreal Canadians (NHL), the New York Yankees (MLB), and the Dallas Cowboys (NFL).

2.4 PROFESSIONAL VERSUS AMATEUR SPORT

As noted in Section 2.1, there are two "sides" to the sport industry, the professional sport side and the non-professional side – often termed "amateur sport," but also known as or to include amateur sport, grassroots sport, and Olympic sport. This could also include leisure, sport participation, and recreation efforts related to sport. In distinguishing between the two, "professional sports" are defined as sports built around players making enough money to play their sport as their job, while "amateur sports" refer to sporting activities that players practice for fulfillment. Importantly, although amateur sport is home to many professionals such as coaches, trainers, or administrators, the players (or participants) are not professional.

From a management perspective, professional and amateur sports are managed differently and have different rules, yet they are intimately related. The mixing of the two is relatively new, however, as up until the 1988 Olympic Games, the International Olympic Committee banned professional athletes from competing in the Games. The emergence of professional sports is still creating tensions on the operation of amateur sport federations, since many of these organizations were created to manage and support amateur sports because of their values and social relevance, often funded by governments around the world. Chapter 7 covers federations, the organizations responsible for much of the amateur sport aspect of the industry.

Some professional sport organizations have recently organized themselves like federations. For example, the Association of Tennis Professionals (ATP, for men) and the Women's Tennis Association (WTA, for women) manage professional tennis while the International Tennis Federation (ITF) is responsible for the amateur elements of the sport and the feeder system from amateur to professional tennis. Similarly, Euroleague Basketball is a breakaway from FIBA Europe to manage the top European competition with the interests of professional basketball as a key objective. Similar situations have occurred in European football/soccer and professional cycling.

2.5 PLAYERS AS A PIVOTAL STAKEHOLDER IN PROFESSIONAL SPORTS

The single largest cost category for many professional team sports organizations is player salaries. Exhibit 2.3 reports the average percentage of estimated revenues allocated to player salaries for the four major North American sport leagues (Panel A) and the five major European soccer leagues (Panel B). The percentages range both across the nine leagues in Exhibit 2.3 and over time for each of the nine leagues. However, most of the observations are in the range of 40 percent to 60 percent. No other single cost category in these nine leagues is of this magnitude. Exhibit 2.3 highlights the pivotal importance of relationships between leagues, clubs, and their players. These relationships can, at times, be very confrontational. As discussed in Chapter 5, lockouts and strikes are part of the professional sporting landscape for many leagues. Lockouts are where the owners prevent the players from working. Conversely, a strike is where the players refuse to play under the current work conditions. The financial health of leagues is enhanced by key stakeholders structuring relationships where the emphasis is first and foremost on growing the pie, and then negotiating shares of the pie that both sides are "uncomfortably comfortable" with.

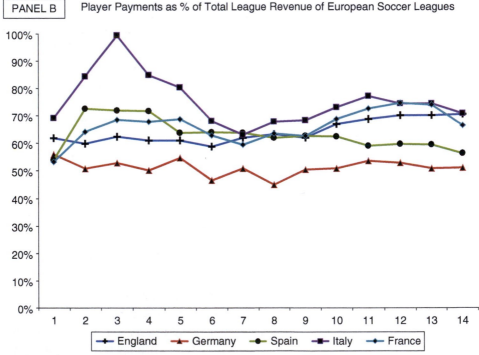

EXHIBIT 2.3 Players as a Pivotal Stakeholder

Panel A: North America Professional Sports Leagues.

Note: The NHL time series is discontinuous at 2005 due to a season lockout and 2013 due to lockout/partial season.

Source: *Forbes/USA* Today/Spotrac Estimates of Club Player Payroll to Revenue Ratios.

Panel B: European Major Soccer Leagues: Deloitte's Report of Club Player Payroll to Revenue Ratios.

Source: Deloitte

Exhibit 2.3 presents data at the aggregate league level. For any individual club, the percentages vary substantially. Chapter 6 examines decision making in the pivotal player-side of sports clubs.

2.6 MANAGEMENT IN THE SPORTS INDUSTRY VERSUS MANAGEMENT IN OTHER INDUSTRIES

Exhibit 2.4 lists ten areas of commonality that sport shares with most other industries and ten areas of differentiation where sport is typically different from other industries.

2.6.1 Areas of Commonality

The ten areas of commonality are briefly described here:

1　In any industry, strong leadership and a clear (and often evolving) strategy increase the likelihood of business success. For example, sports commissioners in the US, such as Pete Rozelle in the NFL (1960 to 1989) and David Stern in the NBA (1984 to 2014), are widely recognized as leading major business transformations of their respective sports and leagues.

2　Value creation is a major focus in the sport business. The success here is most evident in the ten-fold increase in the valuations of many professional sport clubs in Europe and North America over the past two decades. Associated with value creation is much debate over value-sharing among the key contributors to that creation. For example, a key factor in collective bargaining negotiations between the National Hockey League (NHL) and the NHL Players' Association (NHLPA) is the percentage of total NHL revenues "captured" by players. In the 2013 Collective Bargaining Agreement this is approximately 50 percent as compared to 57 percent in the prior agreement (signed in 2005).

3　Business executives in most industries continually pursue opportunities to grow revenues and drive profitability. Growth brings with it many benefits, an important part of which is providing more promotion opportunities for high performers.

Areas of Commonality	Areas of Differentiation
1. Leadership and Strategy Matters	1. Winning on the Field is Central
2. Value Creation and Value Sharing	2. Diverse Owner Objectives
3. Search for Revenue Growth	3. Managing in the Fishbowl
4. Broadening of Product Activity	4. Supporting the Weakest
5. New Product Innovation	5. Handicapping the Strongest
6. Astute and Creative Contracting Rules	6. Revenue Pools and Allocation
7. Quality of the Product Matters	7. Athletes as Business Assets
8. Branding Matters	8. Managing with the "Badly Behaved"
9. Fans and Customers as a Business Pillar	9. Limited Financial Disclosures
10. Globalization	10. Sports and Entertainment Cocktail

EXHIBIT 2.4 Managing in the Sports Industry Vis-à-vis Managing in Other Industries

4   Executives seek to expand into areas where value-increments to their business arise. Ownership investments by many MLB clubs in their regional sports networks are illustrative of such activities. For example, in 2000, the New York Yankees negotiated for equity in the YES Network. Just over a decade later, in 2013, increased value was evident when 21st Century Fox acquired a controlling interest in YES Network at a valuation of over $3 billion.

5   Competitors in any industry seek innovative new products to enhance the customer experience and drive new revenue sources. An example is sport broadcasters adding new online channels/distribution outlets that provide additional content for fans. There is an increasing number of viewers using "second screens" when viewing sports on television, with the resultant growth in startups that provide content for the "second screen."

6   Creative contracting rules provide key individuals with focused incentives in areas viewed as adding high value to an organization. In sports, an example is European soccer (football) coaches being paid incentives related to their team advancing to high-reward elite competitions, such as the Champions League. This is a European competition that only the top teams from the country-based leagues, such as the English Premier League and the German Bundesliga, qualify. In 2014, Spanish Premier League club Real Madrid received more than €62 million for winning this competition.

7   Quality matters! This is true of any business in any domain, where a quality product is a necessary requirement for return customers. The major broadcast success of the NFL is illustrative of this concept, where the stop–start nature of the NFL game allows broadcasters multiple playbacks showcasing the complexity of each play using superb camerawork and media technology. It is a game made for and enhanced by quality broadcasting.

8   Branding – or the perceptions that consumers have of your organization and/or products – is a major strategic concern for organizations of all sizes. The brand of tennis player Roger Federer, for instance, has many attractive attributes (such as style and class, as well as elite performance) and a large following that have enabled his total sponsorship payments to be in the top three of all athletes each year for many years.

9   The sport industry has customers like any industry, however they take the form of fans (such as spectators at PGA golf events) or participants (participation sport, such as the Berlin Marathon).

10 Business is global and companies compete for resources, customers, and revenues across many borders. As a result, many sports have growing global dimensions. Section 2.7 gives examples of how globalization is affecting many of the key stakeholders outlined in Exhibit 2.1.

2.6.2 Areas of Differentiation

Notwithstanding the many similarities discussed above, Exhibit 2.4 also highlights how the business of sports has multiple differentiated, highly differentiated, or even unique aspects.

1   Winning (on the field) is very public and has direct impacts on fan behavior and management decisions. In most sporting contexts, there is only one winner whereas in most other industries there can be several companies viewed as having winning strategies. Coaches in many sports are the source of "memorable" quotes in this area. Examples include "Show me a good loser, and I'll show you a loser" (Vince Lombardi, NFL coach)[2] and "Win any way as long as you can get away with it. Nice guys finish last" (Leo Durocher).[3]

2   Owners of sporting assets are a varied lot (e.g., single owners, syndicate owners, corporate owners, etc.) and can have very different objectives, including performance, profit, and profile. Chapter 4 discusses eight motives for owning sporting clubs.

3   Media attention on major sport is very high and media attacks on owners, players, clubs, and management are common. Many business executives who sell their original business and then acquire ownership of a sporting club note that their public profile becomes far more magnified even though the revenues and assets of their sporting club may be only a small percentage of the revenues and assets of their prior business interests.

4   Many leagues have policies in place to support the weaker clubs and promote competitive balance. Chapter 3 discusses different approaches adopted to enable the "weaker" clubs to better compete on the playing field and have a realistic chance of competing for end-of-season trophies – for example, drafting rules that give higher draft choices to clubs with below average on-the-field performance.

5   Often related to "supporting the weakest" is "handicapping the strongest." The MLB's revenue-sharing rules mandate that high revenue clubs, such as the Boston Red Sox, transfer ("share") part of their revenues to the low-revenue clubs such as the Kansas City Royals. Salary caps and salary taxes in many leagues constrain the payrolls of clubs who, absent of these caps or taxes, would have player payrolls many times that of some other clubs in the same league.

6   Unlike almost any other industry, many sporting leagues pool major portions of the league revenues and share them equally or according to a predetermined formula. More than 50 percent of the NFL league-wide aggregate revenues are classified as "central revenues" that are shared equally among the 32 NFL clubs. The English Premier League (EPL) pools their broadcast revenues and shares 50 percent of them on an equal basis with the individual EPL clubs.

7   Many individual athletes are well known to their fans in a way that even key employees in other businesses are not. The growth of fantasy sports has accentuated the amount of time that fans invest in building their player-by-player knowledge.

8   Related to the previous point, athletes that attract negative attention by their behavior are subject to intense and continued publicity and criticism. "Athlete behaving badly" is a goldmine story for many in the media. There are no shortage of stories associated with partner abuse, drugs, steroids, and alcohol abuse, to name some regularly occurring in the media. For example, the multiple Alex Rodriguez steroid stories had negative effects not only on his own brand, but also the brands of Major League Baseball (league), the New York Yankees (club), and associated companies (such as sponsor's).

9   Many sport organizations, leagues, and clubs are private organizations and are not required to make the same level of financial disclosure as publicly traded companies in most industries. The lack of publicly audited financials for many NBA and NHL clubs has led to skepticism by players and player associations/unions when claims are made by leagues that many clubs are "financially strapped"/unprofitable and not viable if player salaries are substantially increased. Transparency of club financials in many regions is the exception rather than the norm.

10 Sport and entertainment have a special mix, where each is intertwined into the other, with halftime shows, cheerleaders, music, etc. that are now hallmarks of live sports. Executives who have live event expertise from concerts and other non-sports areas are increasingly being seen as a source of valuable insights for the sports world.

2.7 THE GROWING GLOBAL DIMENSIONS OF THE BUSINESS OF SPORTS

The sports world has long had several sports played in many different countries. Soccer is the standout example from a global business of sports perspective. The FIFA World Cups for men and women are played every four years with countries from all continents seeking to appear in the tournament. Similar world cups for younger age groups (U23, U19, etc.) are also held for men and women. Multiple individual countries have their own soccer leagues that are the dominant professional league in that country. On many criteria, from a business of sports viewpoint, soccer is the posterchild of a global sport. Notwithstanding this position, all sports – even the world of soccer – are being shaped by strong globalization forces that are affecting the business side of the sports world across the key stakeholders in the sports ecosystem (Exhibit 2.1). Examples are described briefly here.

2.7.1 Leagues, Federations, and Associations

Both men's (ATP) and women's (WTA) professional tennis now hold "end of season tournaments" for their leading eight players to grow their global following. The men's tournament is held in London and the women's tournament is played in Singapore. The NFL historically has had more than 95 percent of its revenues from within the US so higher priority is now being given to building a presence in other countries. An example is the increase in the number of regular season games being played in London, England.

2.7.2 Clubs/Teams

Multiple soccer clubs are attempting to build their global brands, one purpose of which is to enable those clubs to have pre-season friendlies in other countries. On August 2, 2014, Manchester United played Real Madrid in a pre-season "friendly" at the University of Michigan football stadium in front of a US record crowd for soccer of 100,000 spectators. It was reported that all 100,000 tickets sold out in the first day of sales. There is a growing number of sporting clubs with ownership outside their host country. Box 2.2 discusses how Manchester City of the EPL, with Abu Dhabi ownership, has invested in soccer clubs in the US, Japan, and Australia. Manchester City is one of multiple English clubs with non-English ownership. Other EPL examples include Manchester United and Arsenal (both with US majority owners), and Chelsea (Russian owner). Paris Saint-Germain in the French Ligue 1 (Qatar investor) and the Brooklyn Nets in the NBA (Russian investor) are other examples of clubs being owned by non-domestic investors.

BOX 2.2 ABU DHABI USES SPORT AS PART OF A GLOBAL BRANDING STRATEGY

Abu Dhabi, one of the two major emirates in the United Arab Emirates (UAE) along with Dubai, has invested heavily in global branding. One key leg of this branding has been starting and building a global airline carrier. Abu Dhabi started Etihad Airways in 2003 and now has flights to all six continents. In its early years, Etihad placed the largest ever single order for airlines at the Paris Air Show. Sports have also been a major aspect of Abu Dhabi's branding strategies. Two major areas of branding have been sponsorship associated with sporting properties (such as clubs and events) and sporting club ownership.

Etihad's sports sponsorships include the English cricket team, the Mumbai Indian Cricket Team in the Indian Premier League, and the Gaelic Athletic Association Hurling Senior Championship in Ireland. It is also the major sponsor of elite sporting events that have been brought to Abu Dhabi, including the Formula 1 Etihad Airways Abu Dhabi Grand Prix and the Abu Dhabi Golf Championships.

In 2008, a member of the Abu Dhabi royal family led an investment group to buy Manchester City FC, a mid-range club in the English Premier League. Manchester City for many years had been the second team to Manchester United in the city of Manchester. The player payroll for Manchester City has been greatly increased by the Abu Dhabi investment group. The year prior to the ownership change (2007/8), Manchester City's payroll of £54 million was eighth highest in the EPL, with Chelsea the highest at £172 million, more than triple Manchester City's level of investment. By 2012/13, City's payroll of £233 million was the highest in the EPL by more than a £50 million margin. In that year (2012/13), Manchester United had the second highest payroll with £183 million. Etihad Airlines became the main sponsor of Manchester City in 2009, including the front shirt sponsor. In 2011, Manchester City signed what was reported to be a £400 million sponsorship deal with Etihad "making it the largest deal of its kind in sport and reinforcing City's position as a football club with unprecedented financial power."[4] The Abu Dhabi investment has brought success on the field. Manchester City won the FA Cup in 2011 and the Premier League title in 2012 and 2014.

Manchester City has become the platform (with its City Football Group) for further global investment in soccer. In 2013, the City Football Group joined the New York Yankees in a $100 million investment in New York City FC, a new franchise in Major League Soccer, the elite North American league. Etihad is the front shirt sponsor for the New York club. In 2014, the City Football Group purchased a controlling interest in Melbourne Heart, a club in Australia's elite soccer league (the A-League) for a reported $11.5 million – the name of the club was then changed to Melbourne City. Etihad became the front shirt sponsor for Melbourne City FC starting in 2014. Also in 2014, the City Football Group bought an equity stake in the Japanese J-League club Yokohama F-Marinos FC. Ferran Soriano, Manchester City's CEO, stated when announcing the Melbourne club acquisition: "We want all our teams to take benefit from our global organization. We have experience in football performance, medicine, sports science, and of course tactics and technical development. We also know about player recruitment and have large scouting networks all over the world to look for players for the Melbourne team as well as the others."[5]

One indicator of the magnitude of the Abu Dhabi investment in Manchester City after their acquisition of the club in 2008 can be seen in their audited financials – see Exhibit 2.5. The accumulated pre-tax losses from 2008/9 to 2013/14 are more than £580 million. The "Message from the chairman" (Khaldoon Al Mubarak) in the 2013/14 Annual Report stated: "In the 2013/14 season, Manchester City won its second Barclay Premier League title in three years and also the Capital One Cup. This means the Club has now won every major domestic competition at least once in the last four seasons … We have moved beyond the period of heavy investment that was required to make the Club competitive again … The commercial growth we are seeing today will underpin and support our operations in the future. Importantly, Manchester City is entering the next phase of its development with zero financial debt." The City Football Group also invested a reported $300 million in a new City Football Academy near Manchester, which also includes its global headquarters.[6]

Year	Revenues	Wages	Pre-Tax Profits (Losses)
2004–5	60.864	37.677	(15.624)
2005–6	61.802	34.341	10.062
2006–7	56.925	36.381	(11.035)
2007–8	82.295	54.222	(32.648)
2008–9	87.033	82.633	(92.562)
2009–10	125.050	133.306	(121.300)
2010–11	153.186	173.977	(197.491)
2011–12	231.140	201.789	(98.705)
2012–13	271.775	233.106	(51.621)
2013–14	346.512	xx	(22.929)

EXHIBIT 2.5 Manchester City FC Financials (£ millions)
Source: Deloitte Annual Review of Football Finance (successive years)

Box 11.1, later in the book, discusses the use of sponsorships by Emirates, which is the flagship carrier of Dubai, the other of the two major emirates in the UAE. Dubai, like Abu Dhabi, has used sports sponsorship as part of a global branding platform.

2.7.3 Players, Coaches, Agents, and Player Associations

European soccer leagues have long been the "target home" of promising South American youth players. More recently, the soccer leagues in many countries have players from all over the world with the emergence of an active global player transfer market. Similarly, the growing number of non-North American players in the NBA, MLB, NHL, and MLS illustrates the global forces occurring at the elite player level. The NBA, the leading professional basketball league with regards to player salaries, not surprisingly attracts elite athletes from around the globe. A NBA October 2014 press release noted that "A record 101 international players from 37 countries and territories are on opening night rosters for the 2014/15 season, up from last year's record of 92 international players. It has more than doubled since 2000/01 (45 international players) and nearly quintupled since 1990/91 (21 international players)."[7] Box 2.3 shows the broad country representation of male tennis players on the ATP ranking of the Top 100 players.

BOX 2.3 THE GLOBAL DIVERSITY OF MEN'S PROFESSIONAL TENNIS TOP 100 PLAYERS OF ASSOCIATION OF TENNIS PROFESSIONALS (ATP)

Player associations for individual athlete sports, such as golf and tennis, have a rich country catchment area for their members that showcases the very global nature of their sports. The Association of Tennis Professionals (ATP) was formed in 1972 by three well-known US tennis identities – Donald Dell, Cliff Drysdale, and Jack Kramer – to better represent the interests of male tennis players. Its global headquarters is in London. Starting in 1990, the ATP has also organized the men's global tennis circuit after the shutdown of World Championship Tennis.

A comparison of the 1995/2004 and 2005/14 periods showcases the continued breadth of countries from which the top 100 ranked players have their heritage. For each of these two ten-year periods with 100 players ranked each year, there are 1,000 player/year ranks. For the 1995/2004 period, the top seven countries in representation constituted 55.6 percent of all year ranks. The seven countries were Spain (13.5 percent), USA (10.3 percent), France (7.8 percent), Sweden (6.7 percent), Germany (6.2 percent), Australia (5.6 percent), and Argentina (5.5 percent). For the 2005/14 period, the top seven countries constituted a very similar 56.6 percent of all year ranks– Spain (12.7 percent), France (11.5 percent), Argentina (7.9 percent), Germany (7.8 percent), USA (7.3 percent), Russia (4.9 percent), and Italy (4.5 percent). Exhibit 2.6 plots the year-by-year variations in the percentages for these top seven countries over the 2005/14 period. Between these two ten-year periods, there were shifts within the percentages of players from individual countries. For example, in the 2005/14 period there were sizable decreases in the percentage of athletes from Sweden, the US, Australia, and the Netherlands vis-à-vis the 1995/2004 period. The major increases came from France, Italy, Serbia, Croatia, and Argentina.

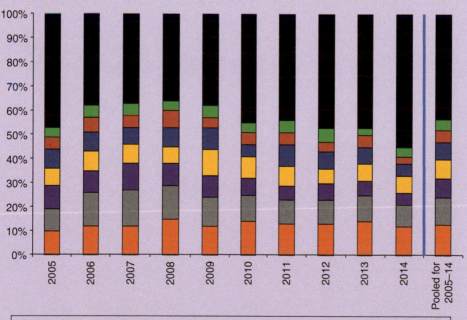

EXHIBIT 2.6 ATP Top 100 Players Country Representation 2005/14

Within the ATP, there is a marked tiering of money earned by a small number of players. For example, four leading players in the 2005/14 period dominated the major tournaments – Roger Federer of Switzerland, Rafael Nadal of Spain, Novak Djokovic of Serbia, and Andy Murray of Great Britain. These four leading players have dominated both tournament earnings and sponsorship earnings. Many other players on the ATP circuits struggle to do more than cover basic costs and have a minimum surplus. Yet, having a broad number of athletes playing in tournaments at different levels is essential to the ATP global game in which the next generation of players can develop and a small number of superstars emerge.

Box 2.4 illustrates how the majority of Australian's Top 50 paid sports stars in 2014 played in leagues and competitions outside of Australia.

BOX 2.4 AUSTRALIAN ATHLETES SEEK RICHES PLAYING ABROAD: TOP 50 EARNING AUSTRALIAN SPORTS STARS

Elite athletes in global sports often have to play in competitions beyond their domestic base to maximize their earnings. Australia illustrates this phenomenon. Each year *BRW* (an Australian business magazine) publishes a list of the "50 highest paid sports stars" with Australian heritage. Of the top 25 paid athletes in the 2014 ranking,[8] 17 played in leagues or competitions outside of Australia. The sports of these 17 athletes were as follows:

- Basketball (four in NBA: Andrew Bogut, Patrick Mills, Dante Exum, and Aron Baynes)
- Golf (four in PGA: Adam Scott, Jason Day, John Senden, and Marc Leishman)
- Soccer (four in non-Australian leagues: Tim Cahill, Mile Jedinak, Brett Holman, and Ryan McGowan)
- Motor sports (two: Marcos Ambrose in NASCAR, and Daniel Ricciardo in Formula 1)
- Baseball (one in MLB: Grant Balfour)
- Surfing (one in ASP: Mick Fanning)
- Cycling (one from global circuit: Cadel Evans)

The other athletes in the top 25 were all cricketers who played on the Australian team and also in other leagues around the globe such as the Indian Premier League. All of the top 25 highest paid athletes were male.

The next 25 highest paid athletes (#26 to #50) followed a similar pattern, but with more representation from Australian domestic competitions. Sports with athletes based outside of Australia in those next 25 highest paid were golf (five), surfing (five), motor sports (two), soccer (one), boxing (one), and horse racing (one). Cricket had five athletes in this #26 to #50 list. The remaining athletes were from Australian domestic competitions: motor racing (three), Australian rules (one) and rugby (one). There were two female athletes in the #25 to #50 ranking: Stephanie Gilmore on the ASP surfing tour, and Karrie Webb on the LPGA tour.

2.7.4 Events

At both the professional and the amateur levels, leagues and event organizers are seeking to hold events in multiple countries. An example is Tough Mudder, the company that runs events for participants who pay to enter challenging long-distance, obstacle-based running events. Starting in 2010, the first Tough Mudder race was run in the US. Subsequently, it has expanded to Canada, the United Kingdom, Australia, and Germany. Formula 1, in its early years, was dominated by races on European racing tracks. Recently, new countries hosting F1 races include Bahrain (starting in 2004), China (2004), Singapore (2008), Abu Dhabi (2009), India (2011), and Russia (2014).

2.7.5 Facilities, Arenas, and Stadiums

The construction of new stadiums, arenas, pools, tennis centers, and other sporting facilities is an ongoing activity in many parts of the world. Leading architecture, design and construction companies increasingly look beyond their own country base when seeking new projects. The demanding digital and technology aspects of new stadiums and arenas mean that companies investing in building strong skillsets in these areas are likely to be leading candidates for projects in many parts of the world (as opposed to being from the host country).

2.7.6 Health, Sports, and Medicine Bodies

Advances in medical knowledge about preventative medicine and injury rehabilitation come from many countries. Clubs and players will seek the best advice irrespective of whether it is from their own country or from other countries. Concerns about performance-enhancing drugs/supplements is of global importance to sports administrators. The International Olympic Committee (IOC), the World Anti-Doping Agency (WADA), the National Anti-Doping Agencies (NADAs), and governments have invested heavily in being able to monitor athlete intake of prohibited substances at global events.

2.7.7 Apparel and Equipment Providers

Companies such as Nike and Adidas have increased their global footprints over many years. For example, up to the mid-1980s, Nike (based in Oregon, US) had non-US revenues of less than 20 percent. By 2014, however, Nike had increased this ratio to be more than 55 percent of its revenues being from outside of North America. More recent entrants into this market, such as Under Armour (based in Maryland, US), are following a similar path of early years with a high percentage of revenues from the US and then seeing their global business grow as an opportunity that is an increasingly important pillar of continued high growth.

2.7.8 Media, Content, and Distribution

Fans of different sports are increasingly being able to access content from many countries. The English Premier League has been very aggressive at expanding the global distribution of its live games to broadcast networks in different countries. The NBA has expanded its footprint well beyond North America over the past two decades. Part of this expansion has been to increase the number of countries where live NBA games are broadcast. One NBA game in 2007 featured the Houston Rockets (with Yao Ming from Shanghai) versus the Milwaukee Bucks (with Yi Jianlian from Guangdong). Promoted as "Yao versus Yi," it was reported to draw more than 200 million viewers in China.[9] Online content platforms, such as YouTube, are enabling live games of sports (such as cricket) to be seen by fans in all parts of the globe.

2.7.9 Branding, Marketing, and Sponsorship

Surveys of global brands highlight that many companies have used sports as an important platform in their brand build. The International Olympic Committee (IOC) has 11 "TOP" (The Olympic Programme) sponsors, which each pay the IOC an average of $87 million for the four years of this partnership. The 11 sponsors for the 2009/12 cycle were Acer, Atos Origin, Coca-Cola, Dow Chemical, General Electric, McDonald's, Omega, Panasonic, Procter & Gamble, Samsung, and Visa. The majority of these TOP partners are regularly ranked on global brand lists. Many different media outlets have helped a small set of elite athletes become global brands in their own right, even in countries where their sport is not the dominant one and with people who are not fans of their sport. Examples include Michael Jordan, David Beckham, Cristiano Ronaldo, Lionel Messi, Roger Federer, Rafael Nadal, Serena Williams, and Maria Sharapova.

2.7.10 Government/NGO/Regulatory/Sport Law

Key challenges facing the sports industry increasingly require coordination across governments and regulatory bodies in multiple countries. The detection and hopefully minimization of game-fixing by betting/gambling syndicates is central to maintaining the integrity of sporting outcomes. Match-fixing in soccer is likewise a major concern in many leagues and international tournaments, leading FIFA to seek the cooperation of Interpol to identify potential or actual examples. *The New York Times* reported results of an investigation of possible match-fixing in the 2010 FIFA World Cup held in South Africa. It referred to an internal FIFA report that was not made public. The *Times* stated that the FIFA report included the following comment: "Were the listed matches fixed … On the balance of probabilities, yes!"[10] The global nature of soccer and the many geographies in which gambling syndicates operate require global coordination across many organizations (such as police and banks as well as leagues) to better detect attempts by gamblers to fix games.

2.8 SUMMARY

Decision makers in the sporting industry operate in a broad ecosystem that creates opportunities for leveraging the impact of their decisions. Most decisions by any one stakeholder will impact one or more other stakeholders. In some cases, conflicts between the interests of individual stakeholders can create tension and restrictions on planned strategies and their execution. A better understanding of this broad ecosystem of the sports industry will enable more informed decision making by the many stakeholders.

NOTES

1 For example, an increasing number of sports in the Olympics have professional players participating. Examples are basketball, tennis, and golf. Other sports have a strong amateur focus – such as boxing.
2 www.brainyquote.com/quotes/authors/v/vince_lombardi.html.
3 http://rightwingnews.com/quotes/great-quotes-from-great-coaches-2.
4 D. Taylor, "Manchester City bank record £400m sponsorship deal with Etihad Airways," *The Guardian*, July 8, 2011.
5 M. Lynch, "Manchester City buy A-League club Melbourne Heart," *Sydney Morning Herald*, January 23, 2014.
6 J. Price-Wright, "New York City FC: an inside look at the beginning of the Big Apple's MLS team," prosoccer-talk.nbcsports.com, February 20, 2015.
7 "Record 101 international players on opening day rosters," NBA press release, October 29, 2014.
8 "Australia's highest paid sports stars," Yahoo! 7 Sport, February 17, 2015.
9 "Yao Ming's Rockets beat Yi Jianlian's Bucks 104–88," *ESPN*, November 9, 2007.
10 D. Hill and J. Longman, "Fixed soccer matches cast shadow over World Cup," *The New York Times*, May 31, 2014.

PART II STAKEHOLDERS

3 LEAGUES

The league is the main organizing body of professional sport. A league has at its apex a governing body that manages and regulates (a) a competition comprising multiple clubs where the winner will be a club team, or (b) a competition comprising athletes where the winner will be an individual athlete. Classic examples of sports with team-based leagues include soccer, football, basketball, baseball, softball, rugby, and cricket. For individual athlete-focused leagues, typical examples are tennis, golf, motor racing, boxing, skiing, and surfing.[1] Often there are global and continental bodies or federations that coordinate and manage country-based competitions and other aspects of these sports that "sit above" the country-based leagues. Examples include FIFA (soccer), FIBA (basketball), ICC (cricket), and World Rugby (rugby). Global bodies and federations will be discussed in detail in Chapter 7. Several of the high-profile individual athlete-based leagues operate with tournaments that are held in many parts of the globe. Examples include the ATP and WTA in tennis and the ASP World Tour for surfing professionals.

Two words of caution here. First, not all sports have a well-defined hierarchy of a single governing body that manages and regulates that sport. Boxing is an example of a sport where there are multiple "leagues" that have some but not all "overarching authority" (see Box 3.1). In such cases, there can be extra challenges over and above those described in much of this chapter as regards management decision making. Second, the personalities and negotiating skills of key individuals can shape the way a sport evolves and those key individuals may or may not have "official" positions in that league's organization structure.

BOX 3.1 THE WORLD OF PROFESSIONAL BOXING: MULTIPLE LEAGUES, MANY TITLES, AND BOXERS OFTEN "COLLATERAL DAMAGE"

Many sports have a well-defined organization structure where there is an observable governing body and agreement as to what are the "rules of the game" on and off the field. The world of boxing illustrates the downside of the absence of such a well-defined infrastructure. Key aspects of the boxing world include:

1. Multiple sanctioning bodies leading to lack of agreement as to who is the World Champion. There are four major bodies that award titles to professional boxers:

   ■ World Boxing Association (WBA) – headquartered in Panama City, Panama. Has experienced allegations of corruption and bribes to officials.
   ■ World Boxing Organization (WBO) – headquartered in San Juan, Puerto Rico. Breakaway from the WBA, in part over disputes as regards rules.
   ■ World Boxing Council (WBC) – headquartered in Mexico City, Mexico. Allegations that it has made decisions counter to its own regulations due to pressure of key promoters.
   ■ International Boxing Federation (IBF) – headquartered in Springfield, New Jersey, USA. Allegations made that a long-term president was involved in racketeering.

   Each of the four leagues has multiple weight classes. Boxers in a given weight class can be ranked high in one league, lower in another league, or not even ranked by yet another league. Many fans find this lack of agreement confusing.

2. Powerful promoters of fights, such as Don King and Bob Arum, have historically appeared to have operated by their own rules in deciding which boxers get into the ring for some title

fights. Fights between highly ranked boxers have sometimes not occurred due to disputes between promoters. Moreover, multiple promoters are alleged to have underpaid boxers. Shifting coalitions between promoters and their key advisors can create much uncertainty for boxers as to what fights might occur and the financial arrangements for those fights.

3. States within the US and in multiple countries differ in their regulations –such as testing for "banned substances" and what are permissible in-ring fighting rules. These differences can enable promoters to shop around/search for the lowest regulatory rules to the detriment of boxers and other stakeholders.

4. Multiple boxers having limited education. Stories of young boxers being exploited by promoters occur with seemingly never-ending frequency.

5. Subjective nature of judging boxing events. Allegations of fixed matches are fueled when individual judges score the same fight differently or when a result is announced that seems at variance with third-party perspectives on who "clearly won."

6. Large amounts of betting on events that can be "fixed" in multiple ways – such as one boxer deliberately underperforming, a referee favoring one boxer over another, judges deliberately scoring one or more rounds wrong, and so on.

Within this relatively chaotic structure, many boxers are not well protected as regards their own health, welfare, and financial interests. The consequence can be many boxers who after a short time period become "collateral damage" in a structure that can lack a strong level of high integrity. Moreover, there is the very real possibility that potentially elite athletes are not able to fulfill their promise to become a "World Champion" due to that not being in the vested interests of pivotal promoters, league officials, or other players in the boxing world.

3.1 DIFFERING ARCHITECTURES OF SPORTS LEAGUES

To illustrate some of the aspects of the architecture of leagues, several examples are provided.

3.1.1 Team-Based Sporting Leagues

Two examples are presented here – the EPL and the NFL.

English Premier League (EPL)

The EPL is a private company where the individual soccer clubs (currently 20) playing in that league in a given year are the "shareholders." Headquartered in London, England, the EPL is the organizing body of the Barclays Premier League that has responsibility for the related competition, the rules, commercial rights (sponsorship, merchandising, and licensing), and broadcast rights. The EPL has a board of directors with its own chairman and appoints a chief executive. The 20 clubs play a 38-game season, playing each other twice per season (home and away). The EPL negotiates central contracts with third parties, the largest of which are with media partners (such as contracts with television partners in the UK and in more than 100 other countries) and sponsors (such as naming rights to the league itself).

The EPL regularly distributes the central revenues it receives (net of its own costs) to each of the member clubs. There is much flexibility as to the ownership structure of the clubs. Examples observed in the EPL include the privately owned model, the publicly traded model, and the community-owned model. The EPL operates alongside multiple other soccer bodies, including:

1   FA (Football Association) – has responsibility for the English national team as well as other professional and amateur competitions including the lower-tiered English leagues such as the Championship League.
2   UEFA – the European body responsible for the sport in Europe, including the high-profile Champions League annual tournament.
3   FIFA – the global body responsible for soccer, including multiple world cups such as the men's and women's national competitions held every four years.

Many other countries around the world have professional soccer leagues similar to the EPL, such as La Liga (Spain), the Chinese Super League (China), and the A-League (Australia).

National Football League (NFL)

The NFL is equally owned by the individual clubs in the league (currently 32). Headquartered in New York City, USA, its published purpose is to "promote and foster the primary business of League members, each member being an owner of a professional football club located in the United States." The 32 clubs elect a commissioner who is the chief executive of the league. Of the 32 clubs, 31 are privately owned (all except the Green Bay Packers).[2] The NFL season includes 16 regular season games and a playoff series that culminates with the Super Bowl. The NFL negotiates central (or league-wide) contracts with its media partners and sponsors and distributes these revenues (net of its own operating costs) to each of the clubs. The NFL is the dominant commercial body in what is variously called American football, football, or gridiron. The sport has a very small global governing body (the International Federation of American Football, IFAF), based in France. The Canadian Football League (CFL) has nine clubs and plays a game similar to the NFL.[3] The CFL has a playoff series that ends with the Grey Cup.

Exhibit 3.1 highlights examples of multiple team-based leagues in different parts of the globe, including information on average regular season attendance per game.

3.1.2 Individual Sport Leagues

Two examples are presented here, the WTA and NASCAR.

Women's Tennis Association (WTA)

The WTA operates as a non-profit with headquarters in St. Petersburg, Florida. Its board of directors comprises eight members, including three player representatives, three tournament representatives, an International Tennis Federation (ITF) representative, and the chief executive officer (CEO). The CEO is appointed by the other seven board members. Registered professional tennis players elect the three player representatives. Members of recognized tournaments elect their three representatives. The ITF, which is

League	Sport	Countries	Teams	Founded	2013 Average attendance (approximate)*
National Football League	American football	United States	32	1920	68,000
Bundesliga	Association football	Germany	18	1903	42,000
Premier League	Association football	England	20	1888	36,000
Australian League Football	Australian rules	Australia	18	1897	32,000
Major League Baseball	Baseball	United States, Canada	30	1869	31,000
Canadian Football League	Canadian football	Canada	8	1958	27,000
La Liga	Association football	Spain	20	1920	26,000
Nippon Professional Baseball	Baseball	Japan	12	1950	26,000
Indian Premier League	Cricket	India	8	2008	24,000
Serie A	Association football	Italy	24	1898	23,000
Ligue 1	Association football	France	20	1932	21,000
Super League	Soccer	China	16	2004	20,000
Big Bash League	Cricket	Australia	8	2011	19,000
Major League Soccer	Soccer	United States, Canada	19	1996	19,000
National Hockey League	Ice hockey	United States, Canada	30	1917	18,000
National Basketball Association	Basketball	United States, Canada	30	1946	18,000
National Rugby League	Rugby	Australia, New Zealand	16	1997	17,000
National Lacrosse League	Indoor lacrosse	United States, Canada	8	1999	10,000
Women's National Basketball Association	Basketball	United States	12	1997	8,000
Liga ACB	Basketball	Spain	18	1957	6,000
Kontinental Hockey League	Ice hockey	Russia, Belarus, Kazakhstan, Latvia, Slovakia, Czech Republic	28	2008	6,000
Chinese Basketball Association	Basketball	China	17	1995	4,000

EXHIBIT 3.1 Examples of Professional Leagues for Team Sports

Note: This is not a complete list but a sample of leagues around the globe.

* For attendance estimates, reports vary by source so "approximate" average attendance is presented, rounded to the nearest 1,000.

Source: Various league websites, FIFA, *Forbes*, United Nations, *The Economist*

the global governing body for women's tennis with members from more than 200 countries, appoints its own representative. Similar to other leagues, the WTA collects central revenues, such as rights fees from media and sponsors, and makes distributions to the players and the tournaments. The WTA sanctions and governs women's professional tournaments in multiple countries. In 2014, the WTA published on its website that it had more than 2,500 players from 92 countries competing in more than 50 events with a prize purse of $119 million. The WTA's annual season culminates with BNP Paribas WTA Finals, the major year-end tournament that is held in Singapore and features the top eight ranked female players.

National Association for Stock Car Auto Racing (NASCAR)

NASCAR is a private company owned by the France family. Headquartered in Daytona Beach, Florida, NASCAR sanctions and governs multiple auto/motor racing competitions. It is predominantly a US-focused league with respect to (a) the locations of the tracks where races are held, and (b) the nationality of its drivers. Both US (e.g., Chevrolet and Ford) and non-US corporations (e.g., Toyota) have provided the cars used in its races. Further, NASCAR negotiates key contracts at the league level (such as for media rights) and retains 10 percent of central league negotiated revenues, with the tracks receiving 65 percent and the drivers/teams receiving 25 percent of the total central revenues. Both the tracks and the drivers/teams have their own revenue sources: tracks mostly from sponsorship and event-day revenues while for the drivers/teams it is mostly from sponsorship.

3.2 EXAMPLES OF LEAGUE-LEVEL DECISIONS

Sporting leagues provide the infrastructure within which individual clubs and athletes participate. Each league will have its own goals and objectives that it seeks to achieve. Exhibits 3.2 and 3.3 illustrate two leagues that publicly released their vision and mission statements.

Exhibit 3.2 relates to the National Basketball League (NBA), Exhibit 3.3 showcases the Australian Football League (AFL). Although individual leagues differ greatly on multiple dimensions, they all share the common belief that some central decision making is imperative for the viability of a league.

A series of examples of the decisions that most leagues face includes the following list.

1. **Health and welfare of athletes.** Multiple factors make this a decision of paramount importance for leagues. There is a genuine concern with the health and welfare of athletes around issues such as concussions, career-ending injuries, and complications from drug use. The importance of this decision is further amplified by the likely negative impacts on the league's brand and the resulting unwillingness of sponsors to support a sporting league where major health problems, injuries, or even deaths occur with some regularity. An additional factor is the potential negative impacts on youth participation levels in a sport where major injuries frequently occur, often resulting from parents removing their kids (or not enrolling them in the first place) due to health concerns.

2. **Integrity of performance outcomes.** One defining characteristic of sport is the uncertainty of outcome of any game, season, or playoff, where the results are not predetermined. Threats to the integrity of an uncertain outcome come from diverse sources. One threat is where an athlete agrees to perform below their potential so that they or their team loses or key events happen that affect

aspects of the game. The "Black Sox Scandal" refers to the 1919 World Series in baseball where eight players from the Chicago White Sox were alleged to deliberately lose to the Cincinnati Reds. All eight players from the White Sox received life bans from professional baseball. Betting syndicates have often been alleged to bribe players to affect outcomes on which betting occurs – such as the winner, the spread (the difference in scores), or an in-game event such as "the first scorer." Match-fixing allegations in soccer occur with some regularity. UEFA, for example, is devoting a large amount of resources to maintain the "integrity of the game." It works with government

- Our mission is to be the most successful and respected professional sports league in the world, guided by two principles:
  - We will grow and celebrate the game of basketball;
  - The game is our passion and at the heart of everything we do.
- Our teams and our players will be our focus, especially the excellence, history, and tradition of our franchises and the inspirational talents and achievements of our players.
- The ongoing emotional connection to our fans will be enhanced by the dynamic game and arena experience and the communication of that experience through all forms of media and entertainment.
- Participation in and education about the game of basketball will be developed and supported at every level.
- We understand that the popularity and visibility of our teams, players, and league obligate us to demonstrate leadership in social responsibility:
  - Our teams, players, and league office will be actively involved in improving the quality of life in their communities – and in all communities;
  - We will use our unique position to bring attention to important issues on a global scale and work to address them to the best of our ability; and
  - We recognize that the values of our game, including teamwork, sacrifice, discipline, dedication, and sportsmanship are worthy of broad application beyond our sport, and we will work diligently to promote their adoption.

Values

We have a commitment to excellence. We apply our passion for basketball to the activities that support the game and the businesses that grow from it. We do every task as well as it can be done, reflecting quality and attention to detail at every stage – from inception, to planning, to execution. We believe in equal opportunity to grow professionally and be empowered to make appropriate decisions. We also recognize the importance of job satisfaction and the need to balance the demands of work and personal life. We strive at all times to live by and work by the following values:

Teamwork: We work hard together in a true cooperative spirit and without regard for departmental lines or individual goals. Our priority is always to provide the best possible experiences, products, and services;

Innovation: We encourage entrepreneurship and innovative thinking. We create opportunities and do not merely react to those that come our way. We aim always to be on the cutting edge and ahead of all competition;

Integrity: We conduct ourselves in accordance with the highest standards of honesty, truthfulness, ethics, and fair dealing; and

Respect: We value our individuality and diversity. We are courteous and respectful to each other, to our fans, and to our business partners.

EXHIBIT 3.2 NBA Mission Statement
Source: Adapted from www.nba.com/careers/mission_statement_article.html

Vision Statement
To Be The Unassailably #1 Sports and Entertainment Offering in Australia

Strategic Themes:	
STRONG CLUBS	"18 strong and financially viable Clubs. Competitive balance – any team can win on any given day. Close games, exciting finishes. Every club has a great stadium deal, quality facilities and its own unique, vibrant identity."
SPECTACULAR GAME & EXCITING COMPETITION	"The most talented and best paid players, playing our extraordinary game. A great product that is well officiated and is exciting to watch. Our game played in the best stadia with the best at-game experience in every state and territory. A competition renowned for its integrity and reputation."
INDUSTRY REVENUE & DISTRIBUTION	"A strong industry economy. Industry revenue growth through a record media deal and collaboration between AFL and Clubs. Cost discipline and efficiency across the industry. Revenue reinvestment back to current and past players, Clubs, the community, and investment in stadium and media assets to set up for future growth."
COMMUNITY FOOTBALL	"Australia's game. Truly national, truly representative, truly connected to the community. Growth in community football Leagues, Clubs, and competitions across the country. Elite women's and 2nd tier competitions. One code across all States – national strategy, executed locally. A leader on social issues."
NEW FANS	"A diverse fan base that reflects the changing face of Australia. Our indigenous game to have an unassailable hold on the Australian Community – nationally – from the North to South, East to West, among women as much as men. Engaging kids to grow up to be our next generation of fans. Technology and new products drive new consumption of the game."
PEOPLE	"A highly engaged, talented and diverse industry workforce that reflects our community. An inclusive, high performance, values driven culture."

EXHIBIT 3.3 Vision Statement and Strategic Themes of the Australian Football League (AFL)

bodies, betting companies, etc. to detect unusual betting activity. The European Union Intelligence Unit provides training to players and other members of the "football family" to raise their awareness about this problem and has developed a mobile app (UEFA Alert) for people to report any suspicious activity.[4] Another threat to game integrity relates to the use of performance-enhancing drugs that disadvantage athletes who play fairly by the rules. Olympic sports such as swimming, cycling, weightlifting, and running have all had documented cases of athletes found to have used steroids. The result has typically been those athletes being stripped of their winning medals/trophies and given bans of differing length from participating in their sport.

3   **Eligibility of athletes.** Professional and collegiate bodies often have restrictions as regards participant eligibility. In some cases there are minimum age restrictions – such as the IOC requiring

gymnasts to be at least 16 years of age, the NBA requiring athletes to have a minimum one year after high school, or the NFL requiring a minimum of three years after high school. In other cases, the restrictions may be based on the athlete having "amateur status" – such as the NCAA in the US currently not allowing student athletes to be "paid to play." Athletes found violating these rules can be prevented from participating in that sport and their college subject to penalties.

4   **Structure of the competition and rules of the game.** Included here in team sports are decisions relating to the number of teams in a competition, the number of players on a team, the number of games, which teams play each other in a season, etc. The rules of the game include the equipment allowed for each athlete. Examples in individual athlete sports include the size of golf clubs and tennis rackets, and the composition of gloves used in boxing and mixed-martial arts. Decisions about equipment use can be motivated by health and safety risks of athletes as well as attempts to maximize the contribution of superior athlete ability to an outcome. Sporting and business rules can be split into different supervisory bodies. For instance, the sporting rules of Formula 1 and MotoGP are set by the corresponding international federations (FIA and FIM), while business rules are decided by the corresponding organizations (Formula 1 Management and Dorna). Similarly, the sporting rules of the game of soccer are set by the International Association Football Board (IAFB), while federations set rules such as transfer rights and the competition calendar.

5   **Revenue-sharing pools and allocation rules.** Many leagues negotiate so-called "league-wide" or "central" contracts and then distribute revenues to each of the clubs or participants. Key decisions here include both (a) what contracts are negotiated centrally, and (b) how the central revenues are allocated. The NFL negotiates media contracts centrally and allocates revenues equally among the 32 clubs. In contrast, the MLB allows each club to negotiate its own local media contract in addition to having a league-wide contract for an agreed number of games. Estimated total league revenues for each of the four major North American leagues and the five leading European soccer leagues are presented as Exhibit 3.4. In each league, the general pattern is increasing total league revenues over time.

6   **Relationships with players and player associations.** Decisions here include whether to have a collective-bargaining agreement (CBA) that includes the share of total league wide-revenues that players (in aggregate) receive, and whether to have either or both a maximum and minimum on the total salaries of individual clubs or the salaries of individual players. Chapters 5 and 6 discuss this pivotal aspect of sports business management.

7   **Enhancing and protecting the league brand.** This includes codes of conduct relating to league officials, players, coaches, and referees. Multiple examples illustrate how both on-field and off-field can diminish a league's brand. For example, in 2007, the NBA faced a scandal involving an official, Tim Donaghy, using inside information to bet on NBA games. Donaghy ended up pleading guilty following a police investigation and served time in prison. Increasingly, leagues in countries with sports gambling prohibitions are examining its legalization. In multiple countries where sports gambling is legal, leagues have worked with betting companies to better monitor gambling patterns and information on gamblers. In those countries, the leagues have explicit rules that prohibit gambling by players, coaches, and referees.

Leagues also can impose penalties on clubs and players for actions that they determine could diminish the game or league brand integrity. Box 3.2 illustrates the variety of actions the NFL has determined warrant loss of draft picks as all or part of the penalties imposed on their individual clubs.

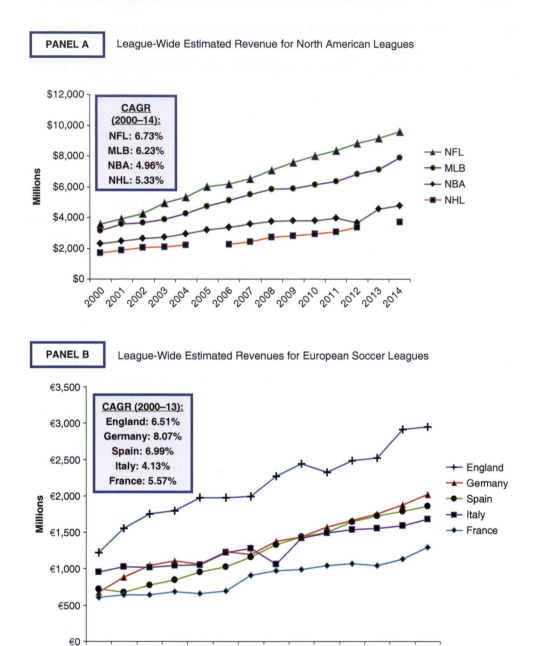

PANEL A League-Wide Estimated Revenue for North American Leagues

CAGR
(2000–14):
NFL: 6.73%
MLB: 6.23%
NBA: 4.96%
NHL: 5.33%

PANEL B League-Wide Estimated Revenues for European Soccer Leagues

CAGR (2000–13):
England: 6.51%
Germany: 8.07%
Spain: 6.99%
Italy: 4.13%
France: 5.57%

EXHIBIT 3.4 League-Wide Club Revenue in North America and Europe.
Panel A: North American professional sports leagues: *Forbes/USA Today* estimates of total league-wide club revenue ($M).
Panel B: European major soccer leagues: *Deloitte*'s report of total league-wide club revenue in "Big Five" leagues (€M).

BOX 3.2 NFL LOSS OF DRAFT PICKS ON CLUBS FOR ACTIONS VIEWED AS DIMINISHING ON-FIELD GAME INTEGRITY OR NFL BRAND INTEGRITY

Each year the NFL conducts a seven-round draft in which individual clubs take turns in selecting players from a pool of "rookies." In many cases, these players come from colleges and have been tracked by clubs on a very close basis for three or more years. Each of the 32 clubs chooses in a sequence based on their loss–win record from the most recently completed season. This process is repeated seven times (called "rounds"). Clubs invest sizable resources in identifying which players provide the "high expected value" to them, given their expected performance, their current roster, and the cost of each rookie selected.

The NFL has the disciplinary power to make an NFL club forfeit one or more draft picks. The contexts in which such disciplinary actions have been taken illustrate the many areas that the NFL views as serious threats to their game or brand integrity. Examples include:[5]

- **1980** Philadelphia Eagles lost a third-round pick for holding an illegal tryout.
- **1981** Denver Broncos lost a third-round pick for contract violations.
- **1986** New England Patriots lost a third-round pick for illegal use of the injured reserve list.
- **2001** Pittsburgh Steelers lost a third-round pick for exceeding 1998 salary cap.
- **2001/2** San Francisco 49ers lost a 2001 fifth-round pick and a 2002 third-round pick for salary cap violations.
- **2008** New England Patriots lost a first-round pick for what was labeled as "Spygate" – the Patriots videotaped the New York Jets defensive coach signals from their own sideline. The New England coach was also fined $500,000.
- **2011** Detroit Lions lost a seventh-round pick for tampering with Kansas City Chief players – this involved the Lions publicly announcing their interest in acquiring players under contract with the Chiefs and attempting to make impermissible contact with them or their agent.
- **2012/13** New Orleans Saints lost a second-round pick in 2012 and a second-round pick in 2013 for what was labeled as "Bountygate" – Saints players were alleged to be paying bonuses to each other for injuring players on opposing teams. In addition to loss of draft picks, there were other severe penalties – such as head coach Sean Payton being suspended for the entire 2012 season, and four players being suspended from playing for as few as three games up to the full 2012 season.
- **2016** Atlanta Falcons lost a fifth-round draft pick and was fined $350,000 for piping "artificial" noise into their home games at the Georgia Dome in the 2013 and 2014 seasons.

Leagues around the globe differ in the extent to which there is transparency in the way that "integrity allegations" are investigated, the evidence or testimony that is admissible, and the appeals mechanisms allowed for penalties imposed. Over time, there has been increasing concern by leagues about actions that threaten player health and safety.

3.3 LEADERSHIP AT THE SPORTING LEAGUE LEVEL

Most sporting organizations have a single individual that is viewed as the "head" and often major "face" of that organization. Titles for that individual vary and include commissioner, chief executive, chief executive officer, executive chairman, and managing director. Below the head executive is typically a management team, which can vary greatly depending on the size and financial capacity of the sporting league. The size and composition of the management team can also vary by the extent to which functions are executed at the league level, at the club, or by other organizations.

The management backgrounds, abilities, and styles of chief executives of leagues differ greatly across leagues and at different times. Internal surveys of league executives provided the following listing of important league CEO attributes given the context of "a new CEO being appointed for a league":

Strategic vision	Coalition builder
Integrity/personal values	Entrepreneurial capacity
Communication ability	Domain knowledge
Brand enhancer/brand protector	Risk manager
Decision making capacity	Charisma
Business/commercial acumen	Team builder

No one individual is expected to possess all these attributes. The attribute listing, however, does highlight the complexity of the role of a league CEO. The position has a combination of externally focused roles and internal management focused roles.

Many heads of high-profile sporting leagues have had extended tenures, longer than that observed for the CEOs of publicly traded companies. Research studies of *Fortune* 500 companies report the average tenure of CEOs to range between eight and ten years – for example, in 2000 it was ten years while in 2012 it was 8.1 years.[6] Consider the tenures of recent commissioners of major North American team-sport leagues:

- MLB: Bud Selig (1992/2015); Rob Manfred (2015–present)
- NBA: David Stern (1984/2014); Adam Silver (2014–present)
- NFL: Pete Rozelle (1960/1989); Paul Tagliabue (1989/2006); Roger Goodell (2006–present)
- NHL: Gary Bettman (1993–present)
- MLS: Don Garber (1999–present)

The tenures of some individual sport league heads have likewise been lengthy. For example, the last two commissioners of the PGA Tour (the organizer of men's professional golf tournaments) have been Deane Beman (1974/94) and Tim Finchem (1994–present). The heads of some major global bodies also have had long tenures. For example, the most recent two heads of FIFA are Joao Havelange of Brazil (1974/1998) and Joseph Blatter (1998–2015). These long tenures indicate that these individuals are very effective at building and maintaining a coalition of voters who first elect and then subsequently reappoint them.

Negotiating with players or their associations is a key role for the head of a team-based sports league. Many commentators portray such negotiations as between a group of homogeneous owners of clubs in that league and a group of homogeneous players. This is far from the case. There is much heterogeneity within the ranks of both owners and of players. For example, the owners of individual clubs in most leagues differ on multiple dimensions, including: (a) reasons for owning the club, (b) ownership style, ranging from a high level of personal involvement in most decisions to delegation to a professional management team, (c) family-owned versus investment syndicate-owned and the role of generations of family members, (d) wealth level of the owner and the percentage of total wealth associated with club ownership, (e) length of time owning a team, (f) level of outstanding debt associated with the ownership, (g) economic power of their local market, (h) brand strength of the club, (i) passion and style of the fan base, and (j) recent on-field success of the team. These differences can result in shifting coalitions of owners in a league in terms of what is the dominant position (votes in the room) on some key issues facing a league as regards its opportunities and challenges.

The management style of league heads can differ dramatically. Box 3.3 showcases how Jerry Reinsdorf, the owner of clubs in both the MLB (Chicago White Sox) and the NBA (Chicago Bulls), contrasts the management styles of two of the longest-tenured commissioners in professional sports.

BOX 3.3 CHICAGO WHITE SOX (MLB) AND CHICAGO BULLS (NBA) OWNER REFLECTS ON THE MANAGEMENT STYLES OF COMMISSIONERS BUD SELIG (MLB) AND DAVID STERN (NBA)

Jerry Reinsdorf is the owner of clubs in both the MLB and the NBA. He acquired the White Sox in 1981 and the Bulls in 1985. Bud Selig was commissioner of the MLB from 1992 to 2015 while David Stern was commissioner of the NBA from 1984 to 2014. Prior to becoming commissioner, Selig had major ownership of the Milwaukee Brewers of the MLB. Stern was outside counsel to the NBA prior to becoming NBA general counsel and then commissioner. Quotes from a 2013 interview[7] follow here:

MLB.com: As far as you're concerned, your career as an owner spans the tenures of two of the greatest commissioners in sports history. Let's start with Selig.

Reinsdorf: Bud without doubt is the best commissioner we in baseball have ever had. His ability to build consensus is amazing. If he weren't commissioner, he could have been a majority leader in the Senate. He's on the phone every day with everybody. We hardly ever have a vote that's not 30–0. And they don't start out that way. I've said to him sometimes, "What's wrong with 28–2?" He says, "No, I'm not bringing it up until it's 30–0." And look what's happened to the industry while he's been around: labor peace, revenues have grown by about six times since he started. He's just done an incredible job … Part of why he's so good is that he ran a team, so he understood the difficulties of running a team … He surrounded himself with good people, with Tim Brosnan, Tony Petitti, Rob Manfred and Bob Bowman, and he let them do their jobs.

MLB.com: How do you compare him with David?

Reinsdorf: They're both great. They both did fabulous jobs. When David Stern became NBA commissioner, the Finals were on tape delay. Now they're huge. But their styles are completely different. David is more autocratic than Bud. He gets teams to go along with him because they know he's so smart. He gets his votes in the meetings. He doesn't build consensus ahead of time. He's more of a corporate CEO, I guess. A corporate CEO doesn't have to deal directly with the shareholders. David doesn't really deal with his shareholders the way Bud does, but the results are the same. I don't think Bud could do it his way and David couldn't do it Bud's way. It's not David's nature to be romancing people and cajoling people.

3.4 ALTERNATIVE OWNERSHIP STRUCTURES OF SPORTING LEAGUES

Attempts to form new sporting leagues occur on a regular basis. A new league has a clean slate with which to decide the ownership structure. Two general models are typically considered by new league decision makers – the single-entity model and the distributed club ownership model. Each is described here. These two models are best viewed as ends of a spectrum, with some leagues having aspects of each model.

3.4.1 Single-Entity Ownership Model

A single group in the single-entity model owns the league and all clubs in the league. This single group can be an individual, an investor syndicate, or even another league. Each club can be viewed as operating a franchise with the single entity body being the franchisor. Several examples illustrate this model:

Example 1: ABL (American Basketball League – first game in October 1996; last game in December 1998) and WNBA (Women's National Basketball League – first game in June 1997; still operating). At the time of their debut, both the ABL and WNBA were professional women's basketball leagues that were structured as a "single-entity" model. A single entity in both cases owned the league and all clubs in that league. The ABL was owned by a group of investors (which included some players who received equity). The WNBA was owned by the NBA. Up to 2003, each WNBA club was required to be affiliated with an NBA club. In 2003, the Connecticut Sun club entered the WNBA as an independent franchise. The club was a "relocation" of the Orlando Miracle club that had been affiliated with the Orlando Magic of the NBA.

Example 2: XFL (Extreme Football League) – a 50/50 joint venture between the national television broadcaster NBC (National Broadcasting Corporation) and a professional wrestling league, the WWE (World Wrestling Entertainment). The league and all ten clubs were owned by the joint venture. The XFL launched in 2001 and only lasted a single season, due to poor attendance and rapidly declining television ratings.

Example 3: IPL (Indian Premier League) – owned by the BCCI (Board of Control for Cricket in India). The BCCI is the national governing board for cricket in India and dates back to 1928. It is the single most powerful national cricket body in the world, due in large part to cricket being such a dominant sport in a country of more than one billion people. For many years, elite professional cricket matches were played over either five days or one day. In the 2000s, in response to the demand for shorter games, a game lasting approximately three hours (called Twenty20) became more popular. Season one of the IPL was in 2009. Each of the initial eight IPL clubs (such as the Chennai Super Kings and the Mumbai Indians) were awarded franchises after a bidding process that was co-managed by the BCCI and IMG (a leading global sports management company). Over time, new franchises have been added by the BCCI and some have folded. Leading cricket players from around the world play for the IPL clubs.

There are multiple advantages of the single-entity model from the league owner's perspective:

■ Ability to place individual clubs in the preferred cities even where there may not be an investor willing to own a club in one of those cities.

■ Ability to assign individual players to teams, in a way to promote local fan enthusiasm. For example, the WNBA assigned two of its star inaugural signings to clubs close to their college teams. Lisa Leslie, a University of Southern California star, was assigned to the Los Angeles Sparks. Sheryl Swoopes, a star at Texas Tech, was assigned to the Houston Comets. Similarly, the BCCI gave five cricket players for the IPL "icon status" and assigned them to individual clubs with the requirement they be the highest paid player in that club. As an example, Sachin Tendulkar, widely recognized as one of the best cricket players in recent years, was assigned to his Mumbai Indians home side.

- Ability to promote competitive balance in the league by player assignments (and reassignments). A single-entity can assign players such that no club has a disproportionate share of individual stars.
- Ability to constrain player salary escalation. The single-entity model does not have individual clubs within the league bidding against each other for player talent.

The single-entity model potentially has the challenge of limited economic incentives to individual clubs. Much depends here on the willingness of the "central owning body" to allow the individual clubs to retain sizable parts of the commercial gains each club achieves through their own "local" activities. This is a classic problem with highly centralized organizations in general, and with franchise-based organizations in particular. It is important for the growth of a single-entity league that individual clubs that adopt innovative marketing practices or have superior on-field performance be able to capture a sizable part of the economic rents they create at their "local" level.

The single-entity model is frequently found in new startup leagues due in part to the risky nature of such ventures. A single entity can move relatively quick getting off the ground as well in relocating franchises that are not gaining traction in their current markets. If the league survives, there is often pressure over time to move to a more decentralized model (both in ownership of individual clubs and in league decision making rights).

3.4.2 Distributed Club Ownership Model

This is a common model in professional sport, where each individual club in the league has its own ownership group. This group can be an individual owner who owns 100 percent of the club, a company, or a syndicate where different entities own portions of the club. In many sporting leagues, individual clubs can and do change ownership regularly. Often approval by other club-owners is required before ownership changes in a league can be made.

Example 1: The National Hockey League (NHL) is the elite professional hockey league in North America. Headquartered in New York, it comprises 23 US-based clubs and seven Canadian-based clubs. Approximately 50 percent of the current players are Canadians, reflecting the broad base of the sport in Canada, where it is very much the national game. Each of the 30 clubs in the NHL has separate ownership. The individual club ownership groups include:

- family ownership (such as the Detroit Red Wings);
- investment syndicates (such as the Winnipeg Jets investor group); and
- corporations (such as the Philadelphia Flyers with Comcast being a major equity owner and the Toronto Maple Leafs with both Rogers Communications and Bell Canada being major equity owners).

Each of the 30 NHL clubs designates a voting representative at the owners' meetings. The NHL is a non-profit, tax-exempt organization that distributes revenues (net of its costs) to its 30 clubs. Decisions on change of ownership, the addition of new clubs, and club relocation all require a vote by the 30 owners. Over time, the NHL has added new clubs, such as going from 28 to 30 clubs in 2000 by adding expansion clubs in Columbus and Minnesota. A recent relocation was the Atlanta Thrashers becoming the Winnipeg Jets starting in the 2011/12 season. The 30 owners of NHL clubs elect the commissioner of the NHL.

Example 2: The National Rugby League (NRL), headquartered in Sydney, is the peak body running rugby league in Australia. Its governing body is the Australian Rugby League (ARL) Commission which is a corporate entity that has eight elected members. The Telstra Premiership is the premier professional competition and comprises 15 Australian-based clubs and one New Zealand-based club. There are 26 voting members of the NRL, who elect the members of the ARL Commission. Each club in the Telstra Premiership is a voting member of the NRL, as are the eight commission members. The two main sporting associations of the states of Australia where the sport has the most players (New South Wales and Queensland) are also voting members. The ownership structure for many of the 16 clubs is a community association football club that has many thousands of members who elect a board of directors for that club. Each club designates a voting member for decisions made at the NRL level. Several clubs are company-owned, either by a private group of investors (such as the Melbourne Storm) or are publicly listed (such as the Brisbane Broncos).

Soccer leagues across Europe often use a distributed ownership model, but can have different club structures within their leagues. Real Madrid and FC Barcelona in the Spanish La Liga are non-profit associations. Clubs such as Paris Saint-Germain, Chelsea, Manchester City, and Valencia are structured as companies. These four clubs have each been bought relatively recently by wealthy overseas investors. Other clubs have a large shareholder and multiple smaller shareholders. Finally, some clubs, such as Manchester United and Tottenham Hotspur from the EPL or AS Roma from the Italian League, are publicly traded in the stock market. Juventus has part of its ownership traded in the public markets with the Agnelli family having a controlling ownership.

3.5 COMPETITIVE BALANCE

"Competitive balance" or "parity" (as it is sometimes called) is a central concern to the administrators of many team-based leagues but not all. Competitive balance on-the-field can be defined at multiple levels – at the league level, at the game level, and at the national team (all-star team) level.

3.5.1 League-Level Competitive Balance

Competitive balance exists at the league level when as broad a set of clubs as possible have a realistic chance at the start of the season of winning the championship or at least making it to the playoffs. Evidence of competitive *imbalance* at the league level can include:

■ One club dominating the number one position over an extended period (a so-called "dynasty"). An extreme case is the St. George club in the Australian Rugby League competition where it won every Grand Final for 11 years in a row (1955/65)! The Boston Celtics won eight NBA Championships in a row from 1958/9 to 1965/6 and 11 of 13 from 1956/7 to 1968/9.

- Domination of the top end of a competition by the same clubs over an extended period. One example is La Liga, the Spanish Premier League where two clubs have dominated for many years – Barcelona FC and Real Madrid. Two clubs have likewise dominated the Scottish Premier League – Glasgow Celtic and Glasgow Rangers.[8]
- Domination of the bottom end of a competition by the same teams over an extended period. For example, at least eight MLB clubs have made the playoffs less than four times in the 20-year period from 1994/5 to 2013/14 – Chicago White Sox (three playoff appearances), Colorado Rockies (three), New York Mets (three), Milwaukee Brewers (two), Pittsburgh Pirates (two), Washington Nationals/Expos (two), Kansas City Royals (one), and Toronto Blue Jays (zero).

3.5.2 Game-Level Competitive Balance

Competitive balance at the game level means that with high probability the result of a game is not a "given" at the start of the game. Evidence of competitive *imbalance* includes:

- Large number of games with lopsided results ("blowouts").
- Large number of games where at a very early stage, one side has built a virtually unassailable lead.

At the game level, the key premise for seeking competitive balance is that fans expect an uncertain outcome that, in turn, will enhance their experience at the game. An extension of competitive balance at the game level, is the construct of "hope," where the game has increased importance if it can contribute to the team's potential to qualify for the post-season or win a championship. Both "uncertainty of outcome" and "hope" have been shown to encourage fan engagement with a given game.

3.5.3 National Team or All-Star Team Competitive Balance

Being on a national team (such as in soccer, basketball, rugby, or cricket) or on an "all-star" team is of high status to a player and his or her team/country. Competitive balance here means one club does not continuously dominate the composition of the national or all-star team over an extended period. All-star team-membership for players in leagues such as the NHL, NBA, and WNBA is often widely used in club marketing.

3.5.4 The Debate Over Competitive Balance

Competitive balance is very much a "religious mantra" in many leagues. Proponents of competitive balance at the league level argue that the uncertainty factor associated with multiple potentially strong teams promotes higher attendance, higher television ratings, and a broader set of sponsors. The idea is that fans of many clubs can genuinely believe their club at the start of the season can go "all the way." So, even if hope of the post-season or a championships is lost, having many games with uncertain outcomes right up to the end should reduce viewer "turn-off." Having a national or all-star team with players from many clubs adds to the stature of all those clubs, rather than just benefiting a small set of clubs in the league.

However, there is not universal embracing of competitive balance as a key pillar of league economic architecture. Many major soccer leagues have operated with vast payroll differences across clubs in any one season and often with only a few clubs having a realistic hope of winning a championship.

3.6 PROMOTING COMPETITIVE BALANCE AT LEAGUE LEVEL

Leagues have used multiple mechanisms in efforts to promote "competitive balance." Exhibit 3.5 summarizes some of these key mechanisms, which are further explained later on.

3.6.1 Player Assignment or Selection Mechanisms

The key aspect of this mechanism is that the better players in a league are spread across multiple clubs rather than on a small number of powerful or wealthy clubs. In single-entity leagues, a central body can assign or reassign individual players to clubs in an attempt to broadly spread high-quality players. Leagues with a distributed ownership model often have draft systems by which individual clubs select incoming players based on their perceptions of the "quality of incoming rookies." Several caveats are appropriate as regards the effectiveness of this mechanism. As discussed in Chapter 6, assessments of rookie quality are made under uncertainty. Not all highly ranked rookies deliver on their promise. Moreover, the role of coaches and team dynamics can mean that a team of individually lower-ranked players can outperform a collection of individual stars who underperform as a team.

Most player draft systems promoting competitive balance have clubs with lower ranking based on on-field performance in the most recently finished season given priority in selecting from the pool of eligible players. In the NFL, clubs select in exact reverse order to their win–loss record in the prior season. In the NBA, the draft gives highest priority to those clubs not making the playoffs in the prior year, but does not guarantee clubs select in reverse order to their prior-season win–loss record.[9]

1. **Player assignment or selection mechanisms**
   - Example: Draft system based on reverse order of on-field performance in the prior year.
   - Example: Supplemental player assignments (found in some single-entity leagues).
2. **Club financial constraint mechanisms**
   - Example: Maximum club hard salary level cap.
   - Example: Payroll tax on clubs exceeding soft salary cap.
3. **League "central" revenue-sharing mechanisms**
   - Example: Equal sharing of central revenues with high central revenues.
   - Example: Targeted extra allocations to lowest local revenue generating clubs.
4. **League redistribution of local club revenue mechanisms**
   - Example: Taxes on high revenue clubs that are redistributed to low revenue clubs.
   - Example: Taxes on home game revenues that are pooled centrally and redistributed to all clubs.
5. **Leagues with relegation/promotion mechanisms**
   - Example: Bottom clubs in terms of on-field performance relegated to lower league and higher clubs in lower league promoted to replace them.
   - Example: Heavy points deductions for clubs going into bankruptcy in leagues with relegation/promotion.

EXHIBIT 3.5 League Mechanisms to Promote Competitive Balance

Early draft picks can be especially valuable in sports where a dominant player can have great impact on subsequent team performance. Consider a sport such as basketball, where there are relatively few players on a squad. The Cleveland Cavaliers won the NBA 2003 draft lottery[10] and selected LeBron James. Subsequently, James more than delivered on his promise and played a key role in subsequent seasons for the Cleveland Cavaliers achieving a much higher win–loss performance and greatly increased television ratings. A series of poor seasons with multiple high draft picks can lead to a club building a nucleus of young talent that increases the likelihood of future NBA playoff success.

3.6.2 Club Financial Constraint Mechanisms

A characteristic of most leagues is that large differences will exist in the financial capacities of individual clubs or their owners in a league – see Chapter 4. If left unrestricted, the more wealthy clubs/owners with deeper pockets will have greater ability to invest in key players and better facilities. The result can be likely competitive imbalance. To counter this situation, many leagues have placed constraints on club spending, most often in the area of player spending. Examples include a "salary cap" and a "salary tax." These are restrictions or penalties on the maximum amount any club can spend on players. A hard player salary cap is where no club can spend more than a set amount on total player payroll. A soft salary cap is where the club can spend beyond a number but will receive penalties. A companion requirement is often a minimum salary payroll. The motivation for minimum salary caps is often to reduce the ability of clubs to spend minimally on players with the resultant higher likelihood that those clubs will be underperformers on the field. Chapters 5 and 6 further discuss decision making issues in this area.

BOX 3.4 AUSTRALIAN FOOTBALL LEAGUE BROADENS ITS FOCUS TO PROMOTE COMPETITIVE BALANCE TO NON-PLAYER FOOTBALL DEPARTMENT COSTS

The Australian Football League (AFL) is one of the major winter football codes in Australia, along with rugby league, rugby union, and soccer. In the 18-club elite level of the AFL, it consistently draws the highest average attendance per regular season game and draws the highest media contracts from broadcasters. Like most leagues around the globe, there are large differences across the clubs in their financial strength and challenges. The AFL has ten clubs in the larger Melbourne area, each of which has a long history in the current and a predecessor league. Within these ten clubs, four have major financial and brand strength (Collingwood, Hawthorn, Carlton, and Essendon). There are another eight clubs in the major metropolitan areas of Australia – two in Perth, two in Adelaide, two in Sydney, and two in Brisbane/Gold Coast. Within these eight clubs there are also major differences in financial and brand strength (with West Coast, Fremantle, Port Adelaide, Adelaide, Sydney, and Brisbane the strongest). Exhibit 3.6 presents a ranking of the 18 clubs in terms of 2013 operating revenues.

The AFL has a strong commitment to promoting competitive balance. A salary cap and a draft have been two important platforms the AFL has used to promote competitive balance across the 18 clubs. It has also made extra financial distributions to clubs that were in early stage of their heritage as part of the "grow the game" strategy of the AFL – notably to the two newest clubs (Gold Coast and Greater Western Sydney) that were competing in markets where there was limited prior exposure to the code.

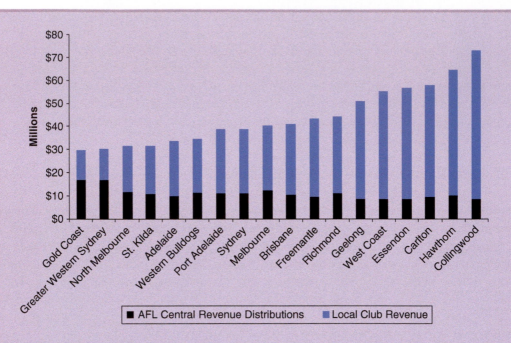

Panel B

Year	2006	2008	2010	2012	2014
Revenue (AU$M)	215.2	302.1	335.4	428.6	458.1
Operating surplus (AU$M)	140.1	207.4	230.4	295.7	315.7
Payments to clubs (AU$M)	96.6	131.8	142.0	200.3	215.9
Payments to AFPA (AU$M)	8.7	12.5	14.5	22.0	22.7
Total player payments (AU$M)	103.6	118.9	127.2	158.2	173.4
Total attendance (millions)	6.971	7.323	7.375	7.077	7.090
Number of clubs in league	16	16	16	18	18
Average number of members per club	32,445	35,881	38,391	39,312	44,693

EXHIBIT 3.6 Australian Football League Ranking of Clubs by 2013 Club Revenues and Summary Financials and Operating Information for League (2006/14)

A more recent area of concern as regards competitive balance has been the ability of the financially stronger clubs to invest disproportionately larger expenditures on "non-player football department costs." The proposed mechanism to address this area was a "soft cap per club" on non-player football department costs of AU$9.3 million in 2015 and AU$9.58 million in 2016. The proposed tax on expenditures above the "soft cap" is 37.5 percent in 2015 and 75 percent in 2016. Explicit guidelines were developed by the AFL as to what items were included in the cost categories of concern. Operating cost items included were:

- Employees – all those who are working in the football department "such as coaches, doctors, physiotherapists, trainers, conditioners, football IT and analytics employees, and recruitment."
- Football administrative costs – "apparel and clothing, supplements, sports drinks, all travel costs including overseas camps."
- Medical expenses – "doctors direct employment costs, medical consultants, and consumables."

Capital costs in specified categories were also included in the "non-player football department costs" using a depreciation schedule. These included "GPS equipment, heart rate monitors, general gym equipment, and altitude training equipment."

The AFL is very much operating in relatively unchartered waters in this area compared to other leagues around the world who have stayed focused on just "player payroll caps." However, there is little doubt that the competitive balance arguments advanced for having a salary cap apply equally to the "non-player football department cost" area. Likely the AFL will have much learning in developing and monitoring consistent protocols in this broader set of initiatives which seek to better level the football playing field across its 18 clubs.

Box 3.4 illustrates how the Australian Football League has expanded the focus of financial caps to include player-related expenditures for coaches as well as support areas in addition to player salaries. In leagues with club payroll restrictions related only to player payroll, the better financially endowed clubs have invested larger amounts in coaching and other supported areas than have many lesser financially endowed clubs.

3.6.3 League "Central" Revenue-Sharing Mechanisms

League sharing rules for central revenues can be an important competitive balance mechanism, depending on both (a) the relative magnitude of centrally collected revenues to total revenues, and (b) the sharing rule(s) adopted. Where the league is a non-profit organization (e.g., MLB, NBA), all central revenues (net of league costs) are typically distributed to the clubs. Where the league is a for-profit group, the league will often keep a percentage of the central revenue pool. NASCAR, for example, keeps 10 percent of its central television contract money and allocates the majority to the tracks and the racing teams. NASCAR is a private-for-profit league that is owned by the France family.

The major centrally generated revenues for many leagues come from league-wide media and league-wide sponsorship contracts. Leagues with a large percentage of central revenues to total league-wide revenues have the capacity to allocate the central revenues in ways that reduce the imbalance that could exist across clubs in a league. Much depends on the sharing and allocation rules. The two main alternatives that promote competitive balance are:

1   Higher allocations to the clubs with low local revenue-generating capability. This allocation rule reduces both the absolute and relative difference in total revenues across clubs. The Australian Football League (AFL) adopts this model when allocating central revenues to its 18 clubs. The two clubs with the lowest local revenues receive nearly twice the allocations that are paid to the two highest local revenue-generating clubs.

2   Equal allocation to all clubs in the league. This is the approach adopted by the NFL and more recently followed by the NHL. This allocation rule reduces the relative difference in total revenues across clubs.

In some cases, the rules for allocating central revenues can promote competitive imbalance rather than decrease it in a league. The EPL allocates its sizable central television revenue contract using a formula in which the better performing clubs on-the-field (which also happen to be the highest local revenue-generating clubs) receive the highest allocations. This allocation rule increases the absolute difference in revenues across clubs. (The rationale of the EPL here is to reward the performance of successful clubs as opposed to promoting competitive balance of clubs in the league. Some observers label the EPL as "raw capitalism" as opposed to the "socialism" they associate with the sharing rules used in North American leagues).

3.6.4 League Redistribution of Local Club Revenue Mechanisms

An alternative approach to reducing revenue imbalance in a league is to rank clubs on either local revenues or total revenues (after central revenue allocations) and then tax the higher revenue clubs and distribute the "taxes" to the lowest revenue ranked clubs. This approach is adopted in the MLB, where the high-revenue clubs pay a percentage of their revenues into a central pool that is then allocated only to the low-revenue clubs. High-revenue clubs such as the New York Yankees, the Los Angeles Dodgers and the Boston Red Sox have traditionally been taxpayers. Low-revenue clubs such as the Kansas City Royals, the Oakland Athletics, and the Pittsburgh Pirates have traditionally been beneficiaries of this mechanism. In some cases, the revenue redistribution payments have enabled low-revenue clubs to remain cash flow positive on a regular basis.

Some leagues "tax" local game-day revenues and include the "taxed" amounts in central revenues that are then distributed to some or all clubs. For example, in the NFL, the home club keeps only 66 percent of game-day ticket revenue with the remaining 34 percent going to the NFL and included as part of central revenue that is then allocated equally to all 32 clubs. This home-game ticket revenue tax effectively reallocates revenue from clubs with high home-game ticket revenue to clubs with low home-game ticket revenue. Home-game ticket revenue is a function of both the attendance levels in a stadium and the weighted average ticket prices in those stadiums.

3.6.5 Leagues Operating with a Relegation/Promotion Mechanism

Most North American leagues operate with what is known as a "closed club system." Here the same number and the same clubs appear in the league each and every year, with the exception of new clubs (expansion clubs) or relocated clubs. For example, since 1998, the same 30 clubs have appeared in the MLB. Attempts to reduce the number of MLB clubs (such as proposals in the early 2000s to eliminate the Minnesota Twins) have met with very strong opposition, especially from local communities and the MLB players' associations.

In multiple soccer leagues around the world, there is a promotion and relegation model where several weaker clubs in a major league are relegated (demoted) to a lower/minor league and several stronger clubs from the lower/minor league are promoted to the major league. Consider soccer leagues in England. The major league is the English Premier League. Below the EPL are three leagues administered by the Football Association. The EPL has 20 clubs playing each season. The next three leagues each have 24 clubs playing each season – the League Championship, League One, and League Two. At the end of each season, the bottom three clubs in the English Premier League are relegated to the Football League Championship, while three top clubs in the Football League Championship are promoted up to the Premier League.[11] This relegation/promotion feature aims to add stronger teams to the top tier league and shift the weaker teams to the lower tier league. It also creates drama (and "life/death" experiences!) for fans of clubs at the bottom end of the league ladder near the season's end. While the same number of clubs has been constant for many years in each of the four English soccer leagues, there has been much movement of clubs between the leagues. For example, from 1992/3 to 2014/15, only seven clubs have remained in the EPL each and every year – Arsenal, Aston Villa, Chelsea, Everton, Liverpool, Manchester United, and Tottenham Hotspur. More than 45 different clubs have appeared in the EPL in this same period. The relegation/promotion feature is effectively a "survival of the fittest" mechanism. It puts pressure on club management to remain competitive each and every year or else face the consequence of being relegated to a lower league where an immediate return to the more elite league is a very challenging hurdle.

One additional feature of some leagues with relegation/promotion is a heavy points deduction to a club that goes into bankruptcy (often called administration). The motivation here is that formal bankruptcy is a signal that the club will likely have severe financial constraints and will be even more disadvantaged in terms of fielding a competitive team. Clubs that go into bankruptcy during a season have a higher likelihood of being relegated at the end of the season, thus making way for a stronger club to take their place in that league.

3.7 EXAMPLES OF MAJOR MANAGEMENT INITIATIVES AT THE LEAGUE LEVEL

Leadership and strategy at the league level are important factors in understanding the initiatives underway and the challenges being addressed in different leagues. Increasingly, leagues are investing more resources into strategy analysis as part of their focus on growth opportunities, as illustrated in Exhibits 3.2 and 3.3. This section briefly highlights two key initiatives and challenges: value creation/sharing and globalization.

3.7.1 Value Creation (Growing the Pie) and Value Sharing

Almost all leagues are continually seeking ways to increase revenues from existing sources and create new revenue sources. Initiatives here are often part of efforts to "grow the game." Published reports show that all the major North American and European leagues have experienced significant revenue and cost growth over the past 20 years. On the revenue side, sponsorship, ticket sales, media rights, merchandising, and naming rights have all increased considerably, while on the cost side, player salaries, coaches' salaries, executive salaries, and facility costs have also increased over this period. Revenue growth and revenue-sharing are not always aligned. For instance, up to 2015 teams in La Liga still negotiated broadcasting rights individually. The blocking forces to joining rights and selling them as a package were the two most powerful teams in the league – Real Madrid and FC Barcelona believed that centralized negotiation and then sharing would mean lower revenues for each of them.

Included in value-creation initiatives are (a) the creation of league-related media assets (such as the MLB Advanced Media venture and the league-wide broadcast channels), and (b) investments by leagues in startup or early-stage ventures that use league assets as part of their growth strategies (such

---

BOX 3.5 MAJOR LEAGUE BASEBALL ADVANCED MEDIA (MLBAM)[12]

Major League Baseball hit a home run with the launching of Major League Baseball Advanced Media (MLBAM) in 2000. As the digital technology and live-streaming hub of Major League Baseball, MLBAM today is a multifunctional company that has modernized ticket sales, sponsorships, mobile applications, and merchandise sales for the league. In addition, and in possibly its most important contribution, MLBAM has expanded MLB's live-streaming applications. Being the first North American professional league to broadly market the live-streaming of games has led to benefits for MLB. As of 2015, MLBAM is live-streaming 400,000 hours of footage a year.

MLBAM was created through the joint funding of the MLB owners under the agreement that they would invest in it collectively and thus share the benefits equally (and the losses, if any occurred). MLBAM became profitable about 2003 and has been growing ever since. In 2014, *Forbes* reported that "MLBAM's rapid growth, top-shelf client portfolio and margins have enabled it to become bigger and more profitable than any other technology business in sports. MLBAM's revenue for 2013 likely came in slightly below $700 million and generated operating income in the neighborhood of $225 million … In a public offering, MLBAM would be worth somewhere around $6 billion to $8 billion."[13]

---

as the NFL taking equity in new ventures and developing premium hospitality experiences at NFL games). Box 3.5 illustrates the highly successful MLBAM venture of MLB.

3.7.2 Globalization

Global expansion represents a possible way for leagues to grow the base of their game, both on the field and off. Soccer is the most global of sports in terms of the number of countries with leagues with sizable revenues. No one country in soccer would have more than 30 percent of total global revenues. Global expansion for soccer can take multiple forms. For example, it still is not one of the dominant sports in key global market areas such as North America, China, and India. These markets represent growth opportunities for leagues in each country. Another area for soccer global expansion is sale of media rights. Elite European leagues, as well as UEFA, are investing resources in building their revenue from "overseas" media contracts. FIFA, the global sporting body for soccer, also is seeking revenue expansion from its running of world cups.

The four major North American professional team sports (football, baseball, basketball, and ice hockey) each dominate the global business aspect of their sport. This business domination opens up both opportunities and challenges in efforts to globally expand baseball revenues. Consider MLB, which has clubs in both the United States and Canada. The revenue base of MLB dwarfs that of leagues on other continents. One consequence is that players from multiple parts of the globe are attracted to play in the MLB and in the North American minor leagues. This provides MLB with the ability to increase its global revenue reach. Demand outside North America for MLB television broadcasts has been fueled by the desire to see locally developed talent play. Japanese interest in MLB games has been increased by the success of key Japanese-born and developed stars playing in MLB. A challenge for MLB is negotiating its role with other baseball leagues around the globe and with regional and global associations. MLB has been a partner in creating the World Baseball Classic, a World Cup-style event that attracts participation from other countries where baseball is played at a high level. One potential role for MLB is to be an investor in new leagues in other countries and to share its business development experience in building those leagues.

3.8 SUMMARY

This chapter introduces leagues and outlines some key decisions that league management have to deal with. While most examples provided are from the large leagues of North America and Europe, the concepts discussed are relevant to leagues of any size in any location. Across almost all leagues, "growing the game" and building new and enhancing existing revenue streams are imperatives that are constantly felt. Another universal challenge for leagues is building constructive working relationships across the many stakeholders discussed in Chapter 2. Later chapters provide further examples drawn from sporting leagues and clubs in many different sports in many different countries.

NOTES

1 The (a) and (b) classification scheme is best seen as ends of a spectrum. For example, some individual athlete-described sports have variants that involve more than a single athlete in a competition – such as doubles in tennis or the Ryder Cup in golf. Some motor sports have drivers/riders that enter a competition as part of a team. Moreover, in several key motor sports there are year champions for teams as well as for individual drivers – such as in Formula 1 and NASCAR.
2 The Green Bay Packers is a quasi-public corporate entity with shareholders and is the only NFL club that makes its financials publicly available.
3 Examples of differences include the number of players on the field and the number of downs. The teams in the CFL have 12 players versus 11 in the NFL. There are only three downs allowed to gain ten yards in the CFL versus four downs in the NFL.
4 For example, D. Hill and J Longman, "Fixed soccer matches cast shadow over World Cup," *The New York Times*, May 31, 2014.
5 P. Yasinskas, "History on lost draft picks," ESPN, March 21, 2012; A. Schefer and V. McClure, "Falcons fined $350K, lose draft pick," ESPN, March 30, 2015.
6 R. Feintzeig, "Study: CEO tenure on the rise," *The Wall Street Journal*, April 9, 2014.
7 B.M. Bloom, "Q&A with White Sox owner Jerry Reinsdorf," MLB.com, November 21, 2013.
8 Glasgow Rangers became a publicly traded company in 2000. It subsequently experienced several changes of majority ownership and much financial difficulty. In May 2011, Rangers was placed into "administration." It was then relegated from the Scottish Premier League, played in the Third Division for 2012/13, and then in the Scottish League One for 2013/14.

9	The NBA operates a "lottery" system in which balls for the 14 clubs who did not make the playoffs in the prior season are placed in an urn and three draws made to select the clubs with the first three picks. After that, clubs select in reverse order to their win–loss in the prior season.

10	The Cleveland Cavaliers won 29 games in the 2002/3 season, which placed them better than five other NBA clubs in terms of win–loss records. However, they were the first club drawn out of the 2003 NBA urn. In contrast, had the NBA operated with an exact reverse win–loss sequence Cleveland would have had the sixth pick after Chicago (21 wins), Golden State Warriors (21), Memphis (23), Denver (27), and Houston (28).

11	The three clubs relegated from the EPL are mechanically set as the three lowest clubs based on points earned during the 38-game season. The top two clubs in the League Championship, based on points earned are mechanically promoted to the EPL. The next four clubs go into a four-club elimination tournament with the club winning both rounds being the third club promoted to the EPL for the next season.

12	www.forbes.com/sites/maurybrown/2014/07/07/the-biggest-media-company-youve-never-heard-of; www.mlbam.com.

13	M. Ozanian, "MLBAM's home runs with Sony and WWE at CES set stage for IPO," *Forbes*, January 12, 2014.

4

CLUBS, OWNERS, AND MANAGEMENT

Clubs are the most recognizable entities for many professional sports. Players come and go, they are traded and they retire, coaches sometimes find success but more often are fired after a short tenure and the same can be said for general managers. However, the club typically endures, hopefully building a brand, an enduring fan base and a link to its local community. With the exceptions of very large markets or highly country-centric sports, a club typically is the only member of its league in its local market. The elite clubs – such as New York Yankees, Manchester United, Dallas Cowboys, Montreal Canadians, Bayern Munich, or Yomiuri Giants – have global fan bases, deep followings, and fans whose passion for the club runs deep. The fans of clubs with smaller followings or in smaller communities can have the same deep passion and commitment to their clubs. Indeed, in many smaller markets a sporting club can be an even more pivotal part of the community.

This chapter discusses decision making at the club level and the multiple factors that are part of the context in which those decisions are made. Chapters 5 and 6 provide further discussion of decisions relating to the player-side of leagues and clubs. In many clubs, costs related to the player-side are the largest and often the majority of total club costs.

4.1 DRAMATIC DIFFERENCES ACROSS SPORTING CLUBS IN KEY FINANCIAL VARIABLES

The norm in almost all professional team sports is dramatic differences in key financial variables at three levels: (a) across leagues of different sports, (b) across different leagues for one sport, and (c) across individual clubs within a given sporting league. This chapter discusses the factors that drive these differences with an emphasis on how club management decisions can either increase or decrease the observed differences. Information from two widely cited sources illustrates these differences – *Forbes'* annual studies of clubs in leading North American sporting leagues, and *Deloitte's Annual Review of Football Finance*.[1] As noted elsewhere in this book, the *Forbes'* numbers are "third-party" estimates and are not internally audited numbers. It is best to view them as approximations. The *Deloitte* financial numbers are based on audited financial statements.

4.1.1 Marked Differences Across Leagues of Different Sports

The league membership of a club in a given market is an important part of the context in which club decisions are made. As an exemplar, consider average club revenues across the four major North American professional team sporting leagues. Each year, *Forbes* publishes estimates of the revenues for each of the clubs in the NFL (32 clubs), MLB (30 clubs), NBA (30 clubs), and NHL (30 clubs). Panel A of Exhibit 4.1 shows the average club revenues as estimated by *Forbes* for each league since 2000.

For every year since 2000 the ranking across leagues has consistently been NFL with the highest average club revenues, then MLB, then NBA, and then NHL.

4.1.2 Marked Differences Across Leagues for One Sport

The country location of a league is also an important part of the context in which club decisions are made in a given sport. Consider soccer leagues around the globe. Each year, *Deloitte* in its *Annual*

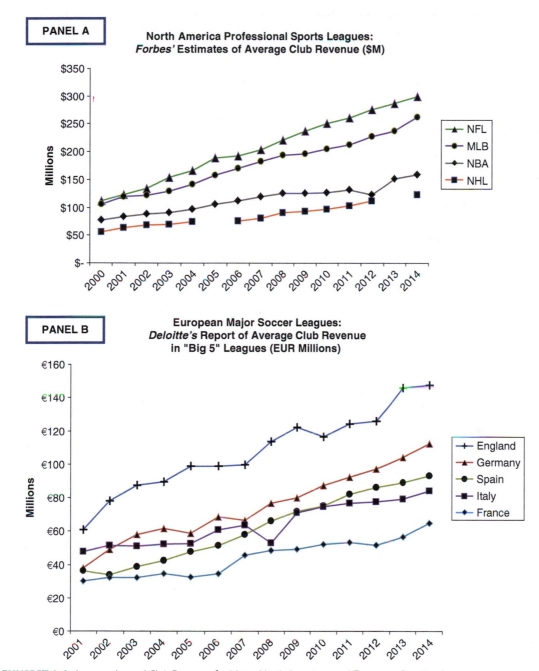

EXHIBIT 4.1 Average Annual Club Revenue for Major North American and European Sporting Leagues

Review of Football Finance reports the revenues of the elite professional soccer leagues in each of the five leading European countries. For the 2012/13 year, the average club revenues were (in euros) England's EPL at €147 million, Germany's Bundesliga at €112 million, Spain's La Liga at €93 million, Italy's Serie A at €84 million, and France's Ligue 1 at €65 million. The English EPL has average club revenues of approximately 2.27 times that of the fifth largest league, the French Ligue 1, and many times larger than the leading soccer leagues in numerous other countries! Panel B of Exhibit 4.1 plots the average club revenues since 2000 for the five leading European soccer leagues. The EPL has consistently had the highest average club revenue with the French league consistently the lowest.

4.1.3 Marked Differences Across Clubs for the Same Sport in the Same Region

Within a given league in a given sport, sizable differences across individual clubs in many key variables is the norm. The ratio of the revenues of the highest club to the lowest club in several leagues highlights these differences. In each of the four largest North American leagues, this ratio is over 2:1. Using *Forbes'* revenue estimates for 2013 for the highest and lowest ranked clubs, these ratios were:

	Highest revenue club ($M)	Lowest revenue club ($M)	Ratio
NFL	560 (Dallas Cowboys)	244 (Oakland Raiders)	2.30:1
MLB	461 (New York Yankees)	159 (Miami Marlins)	2.90:1
NBA	295 (Los Angeles Lakers)	109 (Milwaukee Bucks)	2.71:1
NHL	217 (New York Rangers)	80 (Arizona Coyotes)	2.71:1

Soccer clubs around the globe typically have less central revenue-sharing from their respective leagues than do North American clubs. This lower central revenue-sharing results in even more dramatic differences across clubs in the same league. As an illustration, consider the 2012/13 ratio for the highest revenue club to the lowest revenue for the two leading English soccer leagues. The EPL (with 20 clubs playing) has a ratio of 6.26: 1 while the Championship League (one level down, with 24 clubs playing) has a ratio of 3.88:1.

Exhibit 4.2 shows the ranking of clubs on estimated revenues for each of the leagues examined above.

Where a club is located in the hierarchy of clubs (on any number of dimensions) in a given league is also a key part of the context within which club decisions are made. For example, the opportunities and challenges facing a club such as the New York Yankees are very different than those facing a club such as the Miami Marlins. Consider the decision to acquire the playing contract of an elite player who is "demanding" a five-year, $20 million-a-year contract: in the MLB, these contracts are "guaranteed," meaning that even if the elite player loses form or becomes injured, the club still must meet the contracted payments. For the 2014 season, the Yankees had a team player payroll of $215 million compared to $48 million for the Marlins. The Yankees are far less impacted, in a relative financial sense, by the elite player underperforming than would be the Marlins. The $20 million contract is therefore a much higher risk for the Miami Marlins than for the New York Yankees.

This chapter now discusses decision making at the sporting club level. The discussion provides insights into why the marked differences noted above exist, and how these differences impact management decisions for individual clubs. A major factor that affects decision making at the club level is the chosen ownership model.

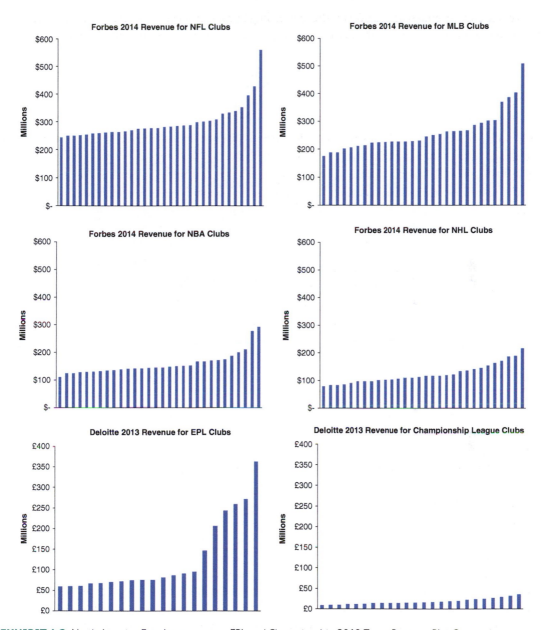

EXHIBIT 4.2 North America Four League versus EPL and Championship 2013 Team Revenue Plot Comparisons

4.2 ALTERATIVE OWNERSHIP MODELS OF SPORTING CLUBS

Exhibit 4.3 outlines five alternative models of sporting club ownership with examples from different leagues around the globe.

These alternative models can give rise to different objectives being pursued by the ownership group. As illustrated below, over time some clubs have changed their ownership model. Moreover, diversity within a given league can exist as regards the chosen ownership model of each club.[2]

Model	Examples
Private/single individual or family owner model	Chelsea (EPL) – Roman Abramovich Kansas City Chiefs (NFL) – Hunt family Los Angeles Galaxy (MLS) – AEG
Private/investment syndicate owners model	Boston Celtics (NBA) Los Angeles Dodgers (MLB) Winnipeg Jets (NHL) Maccabi Electra Tel Aviv (Israel Premier League Basketball)
Public traded company/multiple owners model	Manchester United (EPL) Celtic FC (SPL) Brisbane Broncos (NRL)
Subsidiary of publicly traded company model	Philadelphia Flyers (NHL) – Comcast majority owner Tohoku Rakuten Golden Eagles (Nippon Professional Baseball) – Rakuten owner FC Dynamo Moscow (Russian Premier League) – VTB bank owner
Association/cooperative model	Real Madrid CF (La Liga) FC Barcelona (La Liga) Collingwood Football Club (AFL, Australia)

EXHIBIT 4.3 Alternative Models of Sporting Club Ownership

4.2.1 Private/Single Individual or Family-Owner Model

In this model, an individual or family owns the sporting club. One route to this model is that the single owner was a foundation member or early investor in a nascent league. For example, several of the 32 NFL clubs still are (or still were until recently) owned by families of foundation investors in that league. For example, the Kansas City Chiefs of the NFL, owned from 1960 to 2006 by Lamar Hunt and his family, started as a foundation member of the American Football League (AFL). A similar example is the Buffalo Bills, which was founded in 1960 by Ralph Wilson as a foundation member of the same AFL. In this context, upon (or before) the death of the original founder, ownership is either passed onto other family members or sold to a different group. When Lamar Hunt died in 2006, ownership of the Kansas City Chiefs remained within the Hunt family. In contrast, when Ralph Wilson died in 2014, the Buffalo Bills were sold by the Wilson family to Terry and Kim Pegula for a reported $1,400 million. Often families who continuously own a foundation club over many decades and across several generations have a very large percentage of their wealth associated with the value of that club.

A second route to the private single-owner model is where a person acquires an existing club with inherited wealth or wealth acquired via non-sporting business activities. Several examples are illustrative of this route:

■ Mark Cuban, owner of the Dallas Mavericks in the NBA since 2000, accumulated wealth via his cofounding of MicroSolutions (sold to CompuServe in 1990) and cofounding of Broadcast.com (sold to Yahoo! in 1999).

- Steve Ballmer in 2014 acquired ownership of the Los Angeles Clippers of the NBA at a then-record $2 billion valuation. Ballmer in 2014 was the single largest owner of Microsoft and had a reported wealth of more than $20 billion. He joined Microsoft in 1980 and had been CEO from 2000 to 2014.
- Roman Abramovich in 2003 bought the high-profile EPL club Chelsea. Abramovich's wealth comes from the Russian energy sector during the privatization era in the 1990s.

A single private owner can decide to play a very active role in club decision making, or can adopt a very hands-off approach in which, after selecting key managers, they become a passive investor. These are two ends of the spectrum. Moreover, an owner may start at one end of the spectrum and change over time (either formally or informally). One characteristic of the private single-owner model is that the owner decides on the objectives of decision making for the club and the risks that they are willing to take.

BOX 4.1 WINNING IS A DIFFERENT PRIORITY FOR TWO NBA OWNERS IN THE SAME CITY! JERRY BUSS' LA LAKERS VERSUS DONALD STERLING'S LA CLIPPERS

Jerry Buss purchased the Los Angeles Lakers in 1979. The reported price of $67 million also included the Los Angeles Kings of the NHL and the Forum arena where both the Lakers and the Kings played.[3] He retained majority control of the Lakers until his death in 2013, when his ownership transferred to other members of his family. During this period, the Lakers' strategy placed a high premium on winning, including winning multiple championships. Part of this strategy was being willing to pay very high salaries to acquire and retain elite basketball players. The Lakers' alumni includes many superstars and many NBA Hall of Fame players – such as Kareem Abdul-Jabbar, Magic Johnson, Shaquille O'Neal, and Kobe Bryant. During the Jerry Buss era, the Lakers appeared in 16 championship series, winning ten. They rarely missed appearing in the playoffs. In a letter to his season ticket holders in 2007, after the Lakers lost in the first round of the playoffs, Buss stated: "You want to win. We want to win. We are on the same page. Merely qualifying for the playoffs is certainly an accomplishment; however, we all want more. That said, and we know this from experience, making it to the NBA finals is never easy, and winning it all is even harder … Our goal has been, and remains to be, to build the Lakers into a team that can regularly compete for championships. I believe that we have always shown a willingness to do what needs to be done and spend what needs to be spent to deliver you championship caliber basketball. We remain committed to that philosophy."[4]

Donald Sterling acquired ownership of the struggling and financially strapped San Diego Clippers in 1981 for a reported $12.5 million. In 1984 he moved them north to become the Los Angeles Clippers. Sterling lost ownership of the Clippers in 2014, which was associated with his making comments widely interpreted as being racially motivated. During his ownership, Sterling chose to operate with a player payroll much lower than the Lakers and many other NBA clubs. While an owner will rarely say "winning is not the driving factor," actions over an extended period can provide much insight. Sterling had the financial capacity to adopt the high player invest strategy followed by the Lakers. However, he appeared very comfortable with not aggressively pursuing the elite talent that the NBA clubs with frequent championship appearances or perennial playoff appearances acquire and retain. In the 33-year Donald Sterling era, the Clippers only went to the playoffs seven times, losing in the first round four times and losing in the second round the other three times. They never made the championship round even one year! One commentator stated: "Since 1981, Sterling's Clippers have compiled not merely the worst winning percentage in the NBA, but the worst winning percentage in all four major American sports."[5]

From a financial perspective, both the Lakers and the Clippers clubs have greatly appreciated in value since the late 1970s/early 1980s when both Buss and Sterling became NBA club-owners. The Lakers in 2014 were valued by *Forbes* at $1,350 million and the Clippers at $575 million. In an unusual acquisition setting, the Clippers were sold in August 2014 to Steve Ballmer for $2 billion. Both the Lakers in the Buss era and the Clippers in the Sterling era were reported to be operating at a positive cash flow level, unlike multiple other NBA clubs. One message here is that ownership motives may have very different objectives in one area (such as the paramount importance of winning), but may have similar objectives and results in another area (such as being profitable on an operating basis).

A family-run club can take a long-term perspective in its decision making, much as with many companies in other industries controlled or owned by individual families. While the press often takes an overly simplistic approach in characterizing the objectives or motives of individual club-owners, differences across individuals or families in their mix of objectives can be very marked. Box 4.1 illustrates this point by comparing the different strategies of two club-owners in the same league (NBA) playing in the same arena (Staples Center) – the Los Angeles Lakers/Jerry Buss ownership period (1979/2013) and the Los Angeles Clippers/Donald Sterling ownership period (1981/2014).

4.2.2 Private Company or Investment Syndicate Owners Model

Here a group of individuals pool their resources to acquire ownership of a club. The structure can vary and includes (a) an investment syndicate structure with partners, and (b) a private company structure with shareholders. Taxation, estate planning, and risk exposure considerations often are key factors in deciding on the specific private ownership structure.

One example of a syndicate is the current ownership of the Los Angeles Dodgers of the MLB. The Dodgers were purchased from the McCourt family for $2.15 billion in 2012 by Guggenheim Baseball Management LLC. This was a syndicate led by Mark Walter (CEO of Guggenheim Partners, a global financial services firm) and included Stan Kasten (the first CEO), Peter Guber, and Magic Johnson, among others. Another example of a syndicate is the Boston Celtics of the NBA who were purchased in 2002 for $360 million by Boston Basketball Partners LLC (BBP). BBP is a privately held investment syndicate with a four-member managing board, consisting of H. Irving Grousbeck, Wyc Grousbeck, Steve Pagliuca, and the Abbey Group, represented by Robert Epstein. BBP also has other founding investors who have a more restricted set of decision rights with respect to management of the Celtics.

An ownership syndicate, by definition, refers to groups of two or more owners, which can range in practice from two to many owners. A syndicate has a number of key elements that should be decided before the syndicate is formally created. Principal considerations in this regard include:

1   **Equity sharing:** the syndicate members determine how ownership is divided up, the processes in place if a member leaves or wishes to sell his or her portion, and other conditions related to equity.

2 **Profit/loss sharing:** the members determine what to do when a profit occurs (i.e., how profits are shared with the members and the club) or when a loss is the result (i.e., how the members cover the loss). "Capital calls" require owners to provide extra cash to retain their existing ownership, often in the event of an operating loss.

3 **Risk sharing:** the members determine processes to follow when faced with a high-risk situation, such as renovating the stadium, building a new stadium, or facing the prospect of a large financial loss.

An investment syndicate document will frequently outline the decision rights of different investors. In some cases, the syndicate will be led by a dominant individual who may appear to operate similarly to a single owner/private investor model. However, the other investors can always seek arbitration or take legal action if they believe improper actions are being taken by the dominant member of the syndicate. Legal disputes among members of a syndicate do occur and can sometimes be revealing about the internal challenges of maintaining an effective functional syndicate group.[6]

One example of a private company model for a sporting club is the current ownership group of the Winnipeg Jets of the NHL. The Jets ended its first era in Winnipeg (1972/96) when the club was relocated to Phoenix by an investment group led by Jerry Colangelo. True North Sports & Entertainment Limited was founded as a company in 2001, with the major investors being Toronto-based billionaire David Thompson and Winnipeg businessman Mark Chipman. It played a key role in building a new arena in downtown Winnipeg. In May 2011, True North purchased the Atlanta Thrashers from a private investment syndicate (Atlanta Spirit LLC) and relocated the club to start the second Winnipeg Jets era in the NHL.

Associated with the increasing valuations of clubs in many leagues has been a growing interest in groups of investors acquiring ownership rather than just individuals or families. Typically league rules will require the syndicate or corporation to nominate a single individual as the "voting member"/"governor" for league-wide decisions at a league owners' meeting.

4.2.3 Publicly Traded Corporation Model

This model is most often found in professional soccer leagues. Manchester United, one of the current leading soccer clubs in the world, has had two eras with this ownership model. It currently is in its second era as a publicly traded company. In 1989, Michael Knighton attempted to acquire a majority share of the club for £20 million, in what would have been the biggest takeover deal in the history of British football at that time.[7] Although his bid for control fell through, Knighton still ended up with a seat on the board.[8] Then in 1990, Manchester United was floated on the London Stock Exchange. By May 2005, the US-based Glazier family had acquired 98 percent ownership of the club by progressively purchasing the publicly traded shares of other shareholders in the club. In June 2005 the publicly traded vehicle was delisted and Manchester United once again became a privately held company. In August 2012, Manchester United had its IPO on the New York Stock Exchange. The shareholding is structured such that the Glazier family retains effective control. Prior to their acquisition by the BBP syndicate in 2002, the Boston Celtics of the NBA was a publicly traded company, although it was thinly traded as the Gaston family held majority of the stock.[9]

Several other leading soccer clubs in the world are also publicly traded. Current examples include Arsenal in England; Glasgow Celtic in Scotland; Roma, Lazio, and Juventus in Italy; and Borussia Dortmund in Germany.[10] Even though publicly listed, several of these clubs have very little "free floating" stock that is available for trading. For example, Arsenal has 66 percent held by Stan Kroenke (a

US-based investor with direct or related ownership of clubs in the NFL, NBA, NHL, and MLS) and 30 percent held by Red & White Securities. Both groups have not been sellers of their shares, which results in a low percentage of shares being available for day-to-day trading.

The publicly traded model is rarely found in the US for "stand-alone" sporting clubs. The Green Bay Packers of the NFL operates as a quasi-public company and is best viewed as a hybrid of a publicly traded company model and an association model (see below). It has issued shares that individuals purchase but operates as a non-profit company. It makes donations to many bodies and charities in Wisconsin. Effectively, purchasers of the shares receive a minimal set of rights and receive no dividends. There are limits on the percent held by any individual and protections against a third party making a takeover. The Green Bay Packers are the only one of the 32 NFL clubs with this model. All other 31 clubs are mandated by the NFL to be privately held and do not make their financials public on a regular basis. The Packers release an annual report that is the only independently audited set of club financials for an NFL club. The Saskatchewan Roughriders of the Canadian Football League operate with a similar structure to the Green Bay Packers.

4.2.4 Subsidiary of Publicly Traded Corporation Model

This model is found when the majority or total ownership of a sporting club is held by a larger publicly traded company. Often the motivation for owning the sporting club is to enhance the value of other assets held by the publicly traded company. This model was used for multiple MLB, NBA, and NHL clubs but is less observed now. Examples include:

■ Turner Broadcasting System and the Atlanta Braves/Atlanta Hawks. In 1976 Turner Broadcasting purchased the Atlanta Braves of the MLB. A key motivation was to "lock-up" content rights to showing Atlanta Braves games on its WTBS superstation. WTBS had broad cable distribution and enabled the Braves to build a strong nationwide brand, reinforced by a string of highly successful playoff-bound teams. The Braves are still often called "America's Team," dating back to its WTBS nationwide cable channel showing most Braves games live. Subsequent to Time Warner acquiring Turner Broadcasting, the Atlanta Braves were sold to Liberty Media in 2007. Turner Broadcasting acquired the Atlanta Hawks of the NBA in 1977, in part for similar "cable content rights protection" as with its earlier purchase of the Atlanta Braves. Time Warner sold the Hawks to the Atlanta Spirit investment syndicate in 2004.

■ News Corp and the Los Angeles Dodgers. In 1998 News Corp paid more than $300 million to acquire the Los Angeles Dodgers of the MLB. A key rationale was to pre-empt ESPN entering the LA regional sports network (RSN) market. In 2004, News Corp sold the Dodgers to the Frank McCourt family for more than $400 million with a related long-term rights agreement for News Corp's Los Angeles-based RSN to continue showing Dodgers games.

■ Walt Disney Co. purchased the Anaheim Ducks of NHL as an expansion team in 1992 and sold the team to Henry Samueli in 2005; the Anaheim Angels were purchased by Disney in 1995 and sold to Arte Moreno in 2003.

■ Comcast Spectacor (majority owned by Comcast since 1996) purchased the Philadelphia 76ers of the NBA in 1996. Comcast Spectacor founded the Philadelphia Flyers as an expansion NHL club starting in 1967 and still retains ownership. The Philadelphia 76ers were sold in 2011 to an investment syndicate led by Joshua Harris.

4.2.5 Association or Cooperative Model

This ownership structure is best viewed as a "member-owned cooperative" model where individuals purchase membership in the club and then elect a president who oversees a professional management team. Many amateur sporting bodies, such as private golf clubs, have aspects of this structure. Leading examples of the association model in professional team sports are found in soccer. Four examples in La Liga are Real Madrid, FC Barcelona, Athletic Bilbao, and CA Osasuna. These clubs have thousands of members and can support multiple sports. For example, while FC Barcelona – a premier soccer club – is the major revenue base of the "Barcelona cooperative," it also supports professional teams in basketball, handball, and roller hockey as well as amateur teams in sports such as volleyball, rugby, and men's and women's athletics. One advocate for this model quoted the UEFA president and then discussed its prevalence in Germany, which is the second largest soccer league in the world:

> Michel Platini, the UEFA President and French football legend said he "loved" the management structure of Real Madrid and Barcelona because the members remained responsible for the clubs and their decisions. "[Football] when you really come down to it, belongs in the sphere of human emotions. Real Madrid is a kind of religion for millions all over the world. You can't have that in the hands of one individual. It is as if the Catholic Church belonged to one person. It wouldn't be right," he said. Co-op ownership has also proven to be very successful in Germany … Thirty-three out of 36 clubs in the Bundesliga (top two leagues) are owned by their supporters and none of them have entered into administration over the past 42 years. Fans own at least 51 per cent of each club, which means that no individual can take control of the club. In the case of Bayern Munich, 130,000 fans own 84 per cent of the club.[11]

The association/cooperative model is also found in many of the 18 elite Australian rules clubs (playing in the Australian Football League), and some of the 16 elite rugby league clubs in Australia (playing in the National Rugby League).

4.3 OWNERSHIP MOTIVES AND MANAGEMENT DECISIONS

Management decisions are made within the context of the objectives being pursued by the ownership group. Much diversity exists as to why different groups acquire ownership of sporting clubs. This section outlines these different motives as a backdrop to examining the opportunities and challenges faced by the management of a sporting club.

4.3.1 The "Eight Ps" of Club Ownership

Exhibit 4.4 outlines what we call the "eight Ps" of club ownership motives – performance, profit, platform, pre-emptive, purpose, profile, power, and passion. Rarely is only one of these eight Ps the single or sole motive driving the owners of a sporting club. However, in many cases, a small subset of these motives is dominant.

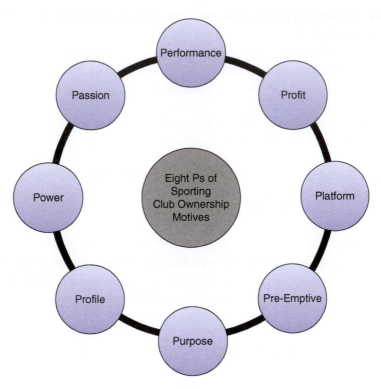

EXHIBIT 4.4 The Eight Ps of Sporting Club Ownership Motives

Performance: Winning on the Field

For many owners, achieving a winning performance on the field is an important motive. In some cases, winning itself is the core motive. In others, winning is viewed as important because it is believed to enhance motives such as profitability, profile, and power. Al Davis, long-term controlling owner of the Oakland Raiders of the NFL, was famous for his expression "Just win, baby."[12] One observer put it thus: "Winning is the ultimate deodorant. All teams have issues. The sweet smell of winning covers them all. The dire straits of losing allows them to seep out."[13]

There are many variants of this motive, including:

1   Winning one or more championships.
2   Consistently be in the contention of winning championships.
3   Consistently going to the playoffs.
4   Consistently winning at least a majority of regular season games.

Chapter 3 outlined various "competitive balance mechanisms" that some leagues have adopted to facilitate multiple clubs, rather than a very small number, having the "realistic hope" at the start of each season of being at least playoff-bound and even competing for a championship.

Not all owners place winning as a dominant motive. Box 4.1 illustrates how the owner of the Los Angeles Lakers (NBA) placed a very high priority on winning, whereas the owner of the rival Los Angeles Clippers (NBA) put relatively low emphasis on investing to build championship-challenging teams.

Profit

A sporting club is an asset to the ownership group and some owners put a premium on making a profit from that asset. Profits can come from two main sources:

1   Operating activities, where the revenues of the club exceed the total costs, including the often large player and coach compensation costs.
2   Capital appreciation of the sporting club.

A variant of the profit motive is the "loss avoidance" motive. Here, the ownership group may seek to pursue several motives, subject to the constraint that revenues at least cover operating costs. Investment syndicates that own a club making large losses often have to make "capital calls" on their syndicate members, which means that the members have to invest further money to retain their existing ownership percentages.

Platform

Sporting club ownership can be an important platform for an investor to enhance the value of other assets. There is growing interest in sporting clubs being a central part of a larger real-estate investment play. John Moores acquired ownership of the San Diego Padres in December 1994 and then co-developed with the city a new downtown stadium. The Padres ownership helped unlock sizable value increases in real estate projects surrounding the new stadium, in which Moores also had ownership interests.

Pre-emptive

Companies competing with each other in the non-sporting area (such as rival media companies) can be motivated to acquire a sporting club to pre-empt the rival acquiring and then adopting a platform strategy that disadvantages other media companies. In 1998, News Corp paid more than $300 million to acquire the Los Angeles Dodgers of the MLB. News Corp already owned regional sports networks in Los Angeles that carried Dodger games. One key motive for the Dodger acquisition was to prevent a mooted move by ESPN to set up a rival Los Angeles based regional sports network built around Dodgers live game broadcasts.

Purpose

Sporting clubs often play an important role in building the fabric of a community. Indeed, some individuals who legally own a club state they view themselves as being "the custodian of a community asset." A subset of investors have joined sporting club investment syndicates to either prevent a club relocating to another city or to bring a sporting club to a new city. In 1992, a syndicate was formed that included leading business people to acquire the San Francisco Giants (see Chapter 1). A pivotal motive for some members of the syndicate was to have the club stay in San Francisco as opposed to moving to Tampa Bay – it was an "investment in terms of civic pride as well as civic responsibility" rather than a pure financial investment. Charles Schwab was a leading financial figure in the city who joined the syndicate, but several years later was prepared to exit at a minimal value in large part due to his belief that the new Giants ownership was committed long-term to keeping the club in San Francisco.[14]

Profile

Ownership of a major sporting club often brings a stature and public recognition that ownership of other assets rarely provides. The owner of a sporting club is frequently in the media and can be the subject of much debate. Several Russian business tycoons have boosted their global profile by acquiring total or major ownership positions in leading sporting clubs outside of Russia – such as Roman Abramovich's purchase in 2003 of Chelsea in the EPL, and Mikhail Prokhorov's purchase in 2010 of 80 percent interest in the Brooklyn Nets of the NBA. Box 2.2 illustrates how Abu Dhabi has used its ownership of soccer clubs around the globe to promote its own global stature.

Power

Given the high profile of many sporting clubs, owners of those clubs can sometimes become influential figures in local politics and in the local business community. For example, they can be chosen to lead a city bid for a Summer or Winter Olympic Games to be awarded to the city by the International Olympic Committee. In a related way, they can play a major role within the sporting league of which the club is a member or a major role in the sport itself. For example, Jerry Colangelo has been able to lead positive change in the Phoenix community and Arizona by being part of the ownership group of the Phoenix Suns of the NBA, the Phoenix Mercury of the WNBA, and the Arizona Diamond Backs of the MLB. In 2014, the *Sports Business Journal* ranked Robert Kraft (lead owner of the New England Patriots of the NFL) as the third most influential person in sports business, stating: "No owner has more sway in NFL circles … But it's not just Kraft's role within the NFL that puts him at this spot, it's also his strong and deep relationships in political, cultural and entertainment circles."[15] Many media reports on sporting owners often overemphasize the ego-enhancement aspects of a power position and understate the many positive actions an individual with power can accomplish.

Passion

Passion as a motive can play out in several ways. One is passion for the sport itself. Ownership of a sporting club can enable that person to be closely involved with many aspects of the club and also to have the emotional connection to the sport taken to a heightened level. Some former athletes join ownership syndicates, in part as a way to remain engaged with a sport they love. Examples include Michael Jordan's ownership equity in the Charlotte Bobcats of the NBA, and Mario Lemieux's ownership equity in the Pittsburgh Penguins of the NHL. Another aspect of passion is the desire to be an owner in the sporting industry without that passion being linked to any single sporting league or sporting club.

4.3.2 Mixed and Changing Set of Motives

Individual owners and ownership groups typically will have combinations of several of the above motives. Moreover, within a single ownership group, individuals themselves can have different sets of motives. For example, some members of an investment syndicate "want to drive the bus, while others are very happy to just be on the bus and indeed have no desire to drive it." In some cases, differences in motives can lead to conflict within the syndicate members and even exits from the syndicate. Often the exit of a syndicate member is "sugar-coated in a press release as being mutual" when behind the scenes there has been a sizable fallout or even a brutal power play with one side a winner and the other side exiting.[16]

It is essential that the management group of a sporting club understand the key motivations of the ownership group (and the degree of agreement among the key members) when allocating resources. A challenge for the management of a sporting club can arise when ownership takes a different time horizon than is realistic and makes short-run decisions that perpetuate a "losing situation." The history of sports club management includes multiple owners who fire coaches or general managers on a very frequent basis in a futile search for immediate on-the-field success. Putting together the building blocks of a club that has sustained on-the-field high performance takes time, focus, and the commitment of resources. It is enhanced by the coach or general manager believing they have a reasonable timeframe to build on the field success.

4.4 JUGGLING THE MOTIVES OF MULTIPLE STAKEHOLDERS

Chapter 2 outlined key stakeholders in the sports ecosystem. Each of the stakeholders comes with its own set of motives, some of which may align with those of an ownership and some of which may conflict. Decision making by the owners of a sporting club is well-described as a juggling act where the owners/managers are considering both their key motives and how the motives of other stakeholders can be taken into account. Conflicts in the motives of different stakeholders are inevitable. Some examples are:

- **Club view versus league view.** Several legendary sports owners are applauded for taking actions that enhance the overall interests of their league, even at the expense of their own club. Many leagues have salary caps or revenue-sharing to constrain a small set of "rich" clubs spending many times the ability of other clubs in an attempt to win championships. Revenue-sharing rules are sometimes viewed by the high-revenue clubs sending revenues as penalizing their superior management abilities. Leagues have the ability to expel a club from a league if it takes actions that league management and other owners view as "detrimental" to the interests of the league.
- **Club view versus player view.** Conflict between owners and players can exist at both (a) the league level in collective bargaining negotiations, and (b) at the club level in individual player negotiations. Individual players will typically seek guaranteed high compensation over a longer term. Club management usually wants less guarantees, lower compensation amounts, and more flexibility over the contract length. While players and their agents are generally realistic as to the motives of both sides of the bargaining table, clubs can find themselves in very contentious negotiations that are played out, in part, in the public media.
- **Club view versus fan view.** Fans can place high premiums on the club being very competitive on the field. The media will often relentlessly criticize ownership of a club that has a long sequence of

losing seasons. Fans also prefer lower rather than higher prices for tickets, food, and beverages at the stadium. This conflict is highlighted when a club moves to a new stadium that has much higher price points for tickets, food and beverages, and – in the eyes of long-term season ticket holders – a shift to a "corporate focus" on high-paying club seats and suites.

■ **Club view versus city/government view.** Many clubs play in arenas or stadiums that are either owned or heavily supported by city/government funding. Examples of such support include financing in the construction stage, revenue-sharing (such as sharing of naming rights payments and parking revenues), and expenditure-sharing for ongoing facility maintenance and upgrades. Critics of city/government support for sporting clubs portray sporting owners as wealthy groups who have the capacity to pay for their own stadium or arena. While most operating agreements between sporting clubs and their city result in a shared sense of ownership of the arena or stadium asset, club management should always be alert to the need to build and nurture productive relationships with their host cities and governments.

4.5 CLUB DECISION MAKING WITH LEVERAGEABLE ASSETS AND INHERITED LIABILITIES

Sporting club management at a certain point in time rarely starts with a clean slate. Rather, they will have much that is in place that affects their opportunities and challenges. Exhibit 4.5 outlines some key parameters that impact club management decisions. It is important for management to identify how each parameter is either a growth accelerators or an inherited liability in the context of making key decisions.

Ownership

Many dimensions here have much impact on decisions. One dimension is the set of motives most important to the owner. As noted above, and in Box 4.1, sizable differences can exist across owners in this area. A second dimension is the financial capacity and willingness of the ownership to continually invest in building the sporting club assets. Having a wealthy owner is typically a positive, but that positive is enhanced if the owner commits to ongoing investment in the club. A third dimension is the reputation and network of the owner. Owners with stellar reputations and deep networks who can open doors are a great asset to management.

Owners that face financial challenges in other aspects of their business activities can be a liability to management if they place constraints on the spending of the sporting club that may have been unanticipated. For example, after the owners of the New York Mets of MLB suffered heavy losses in the Bernie Madoff financial scandal, they were reported to have cut back the Mets investment in acquiring new baseball talent.[17]

Management

A common research finding is that management talent is pivotal to the success of a company. A leverageable asset for a sporting club here is a management team that is broad-based across key areas, has at least some deep functional expertise, and a deep commitment to growth and innovation.

Factor category	Leverageable assets	Inherited liabilities
1. Ownership		
2. Management		
3. Country/Sport		
4. League and its infrastructure		
5. City/Region of club		
6. Arena/Stadium		
7. Team on-field performance		
Current		
Past		
8. Profiles of players/coaches		
Current		
Past		
9. Branding and sponsorship		
10. Fan base strength		
11. Media contracts and ownership		
12. Real estate		
13. Other factors		

EXHIBIT 4.5 Framework for evaluating the Leverageable Assets and Inherited Liabilities of a Sporting Club

Some sporting clubs have limited management talent, with few employees in the organization willing to innovate for fear of having a negative outcome. Being in management in the sporting industry is a dream job for many people. Unfortunately, this can result in some individuals being overly protective of their position and not willing to mentor others in the organization or give them appropriate credit. Effective senior management of a sporting club requires identifying and promoting the strong performers at all levels as well as either assisting the lesser performers to get much better or exiting them out of the club.

Country and Sport

Section 4.1 of this chapter highlighted the dramatic differences that can exist across countries and across sports in revenues per club. The stronger and larger the economy of the country where the club plays, the deeper the potential domestic revenue opportunities for that club. Where the sport of the club is a major one in the country, the more likely it is that potential sponsors will appreciate its capacity to engage with fans and be a platform for companies to partner with. Cricket in India is a classic example here, given its dominance of the total domestic sports spending. In contrast, managing a club for a nascent sport in a country requires education of potential sponsors and fans about the sport itself before efforts to deepen engagement of key stakeholders can occur. Cricket in North America is an example here – beyond a small number of people with a heritage in cricket-strong countries, little is known or cared about the game by most North Americans. Managing a club for a sport that has limped along with limited traction and growth in a country beyond a small set of die-hard players and supporters is especially challenging. When management accepts a position in a club of a given sport in a given country, many of the parameters in which club decisions will be made have been set.

League and its Infrastructure

Clubs have greater financial capacity when operating in a league with a strong economic underpinning and where there is a large amount of "central revenues" shared with the clubs. For example, Exhibit 4.2 shows the stronger revenue underpinning of clubs in the English Premier League vis-à-vis clubs in the lower-tier Championship League in the same country. The exemplar league as regards the sharing of a very large central revenue pool is the NFL.

Exhibit 4.6 presents summary financials from the audited financial statements of Green Bay. These financials highlight the very high percentage of total club revenues from "NFL central." For each of the 12 years to 2013/14, NFL centrally distributed revenues have increased (approximately doubling in this period). They have consistently been more than 50 percent of total Green Bay revenues. With a hard salary cap constraining player costs to an average of 52 percent of revenues over the 12-year period, Green Bay has always been profitable each year of this 12-year period.

The relegation structure of the English Premier League (and many other major elite soccer leagues) is an important constraint that management of soccer clubs face. The risk of relegation can dramatically shorten the time horizon of management decisions and can increase the uncertainty of projected future revenue streams. The evidence is that at least one of the three clubs promoted to the EPL each year is likely to be relegated back to the lower revenue Championship League the next year.[18] Being a recently promoted club in the EPL brings with it the inherited liability that many of the elite EPL clubs you will compete against will have revenues and player payrolls multiple times that of your club. From 1992/3 to 2013/14, only seven clubs have remained in the EPL each and every year.

City and Region of Club

This parameter brings with it both leverageable assets and inherited liabilities. One attractive asset of being a club in a large, metropolitan, commercially strong city is having fans that are likely able to pay high prices and a regional sports network likely willing to pay high amounts to show live games.

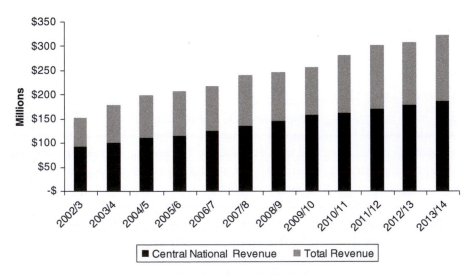

EXHIBIT 4.6 Green Bay Packers Summary Financials: 2002/3 to 2013/14

However, a related liability is that there are typically many other sporting clubs to compete against in that same market. New York City is the largest US market, but has three NHL clubs, two NFL, two MLB, two NBA, two MLS, and one WNBA club. Box 4.2 discusses the leverageable assets and the inherited liabilities of the New York Knicks in this highly competitive market.

An extreme example of city density of professional clubs is in the Australian Football League (AFL) where ten of the 18 clubs in that league are based in the greater Melbourne region. In the previous chapter, Box 3.4 includes an overview of the AFL.

BOX 4.2 THE NEW YORK KNICKS OF THE NBA – LEVERAGEABLE ASSETS AND INHERITED LIABILITIES AT SEASON'S END IN 2015

Assume you have been a highly successful CEO in several sporting clubs in the NBA and MLB. After a two-year break from sports management, you get a call from a leading executive recruiting company indicating that you are the lead target to become CEO of the New York Knicks. The Knicks are owned by the Madison Square Garden Company, with James Dolan as the chairman and controlling shareholder. As part of your analysis, you assess the leverageable assets and inherited liabilities of the Knicks. Although you have a very good sense of the issues, you still do an audit on available information and speak to multiple people before the planned meeting with the executive recruiter and Knicks ownership. Some useful background information includes the following:

- The Knicks were a founding member of the BBA in 1946, which in 1949 merged into the NBA. The club has won the NBA Championship in only two years (1970 and 1973). Over the 2000/1 to the 2014/15 seasons, it has only been to the playoffs five times, four of which it lost in the first round. In the 2014/15 season it had a win–loss record of 17 wins and 65 losses.
- The Knicks have consistently had one of the highest player payrolls in the NBA.
- The Knicks, along with the Los Angeles Lakers are the leading NBA clubs on both estimated valuation and estimated revenues. *Forbes* in January 2015 estimated the following:

	Los Angeles Lakers	New York Knicks	NBA Average
Estimated valuation ($M)	$2,600 (#1)	$2,500 (#2)	$1,106
Estimated revenues ($M)	$293 (#1)	$278 (#2)	$160
Estimated operating income ($M)	$104 (#1)	$53(#4)	$23

- *ESPN The Magazine* in their annual survey of fans from 122 clubs in the NBA, MLB, NFL, and NHL gave very low rankings to the Knicks on multiple variables including an overall ranking of second lowest (121 out of 122) in the 2014 survey. The only area where the Knicks ranked below 100 out of 122 was Stadium Experience (91st). Other areas include Coaching (108th), Ownership (118th), Affordability (121st), Players (122nd), and Fan Relations (122nd).

Leverageable Assets

Three major leverageable assets are at the league level, the city level, and the arena level. The NBA is a premier league with recently negotiated national broadcast contracts that have sizably increased the revenues distributed to each club. New York is widely viewed as one of the major sports markets in the globe. The Knicks have very high average ticket prices, which mean high game-day revenue but comes with fan pushback on affordability. The Knicks play at Madison Square Garden, which is one of the best-known arenas in the world. It has recently undergone a major upgrade. The Knicks brand is potentially a leverageable asset. It has historically been one of the strongest in the NBA despite the Knicks' recent below-average on-the-court winning record. One advantage here is that any sizable on-the-court turnaround will likely have quicker pick-up in brand strength vis-à-vis clubs that have had low relative brand recognition over their lifetime as a club.

Inherited Liabilities

The on-court struggles in the past 15 years are a major concern to a potential CEO. However, in a sporting club, much of the challenge here is appointing a quality general manager, a quality coach, and the Knicks being successful in player recruiting. It would be important to inquire how much say a new CEO would have vis-à-vis the owner on player-side decisions. The existing general manager (Phil Jackson) is one of the most storied coaches in the NBA. The existing coach (Derek Fisher) is a rookie. The Jackson–Fisher combination in their first year (2014/15) was a major disappointment.

The local media RSN contract for the Knicks can be viewed as a mixed situation. It is below the annual contract negotiated by the Los Angeles Lakers. However, the Lakers benefited from a bidding war in Los Angeles among existing RSNs and a new RSN backed by Time Warner. Such a bidding war is unlikely in New York, as the Knicks are shown on a RSN owned by the Madison Square Garden Company. Ownership is viewed by multiple outsiders as problematic for an incoming CEO. One television commentator (Keith Olbermann) referred to owner James Dolan as the "chief exasperating officer." At times, Dolan creates his own problems, such as in January 2015 when he responded to a fan's email in a way that enabled Dolan's critics to hammer and parody his judgment.[19] In addition, the New York press regularly targets Dolan. A new CEO should expect likewise to be targeted and potentially be the subject of media attacks.

Turnaround Opportunity with Upside?

A key issue to a potential new CEO for the New York Knicks is whether a turnaround on the court for the Knicks is likely given the current general manager and coach. Also included here would be the decision rights a new CEO would have vis-à-vis the owner in any subsequent appointments on both the playing and non-playing sides of the Knicks. The potential CEO has multiple additional factors to consider. One is financial. Can a contract be negotiated that has very heavy penalties to the Knicks if he is forced out in a very short time period or over personality issues with ownership? A second consideration is the potential upside and downside to his or her reputation and health from various scenarios should he accept the CEO position. A third consideration is the options the CEO candidate has from other sporting clubs and other areas. This is very much a position that a new CEO would accept with "eyes wide-open."

Cities vary greatly in their economic strength, the alternative forms of entertainment, and their sporting heritage. An example of an inherited liability in this area is a sporting club being located in a city with high unemployment and economic struggles with several key industries in decline. Cities also differ greatly in their attractiveness to players. New York City is frequently promoted to players as a place to maximize the non-playing income and better build their individual brand. Management of a sporting club in a small, low-profile city with little commercial ventures can face challenges in attracting players. The tax status of a city/state can also be an asset (low local income taxes) or liability (high local income taxes) to players considering clubs in different areas. Athletes based in Texas and Florida benefit from those states having no state income taxes, whereas athletes based in California will be paying an 11–13 percent state income tax rate.

Arena or Stadium Context and its Contract

Clubs with relatively new, state-of-the-art stadiums with multiple revenue streams (say from tickets, suites, naming rights, concessionaires, etc.) have leverageable assets that increase the options to further build the business and sporting sides of their clubs. In contrast, clubs with aging stadiums that have not been upgraded face a challenging context that can greatly constrain their options. As discussed in Chapter 18, the terms of the stadium/arena contract can also guide whether the stadium is viewed as a leverageable asset or an inherited liability.

Team On-Field Performance – Current and Past Strength

At any one point in time, there likely will be dramatic differences across clubs in the area of on-field performance. Club management for a current high-performing club will likely be seeking ways to reinforce this current strength. In contrast, management for a current low-performing club seeking a turnaround scenario will likely be evaluating a broader set of replacement players and coaches.

One key area where recent and current strong on-field team success can be especially advantageous is when a club moves from an aging stadium to a new stadium. In the new stadium, ticket prices and suites are very likely to be much higher priced. Winning on the field helps generate excitement to want to be at future games at the new stadium. The San Francisco 49ers of the NFL moved into a new $1.3 billion stadium for the start of the 2014 season. The club's stellar on-field success in the three years prior to 2013 is widely recognized as greatly helping the sale of many high-priced seat licenses as well as the selling out of stadium seats and suites with a very high revenue yield.

Profile of Players and Coaches – Current and Past Strength

Fan attachment to a club is often driven by – and heavily affected by – the status of its current and past players and coaches. Manchester United's ability to expand its sponsor and fan base in Asia was greatly assisted by the affection that many Asian fans had for individual players of the club, both past and current. It is important that clubs take substantive actions to promote positive contributions by players and coaches to their community and also increase awareness of those contributions. Box 4.3 highlights the various positive ways players and coaches of the San Francisco 49ers contribute to the Bay Area community and their broader fan base.

BOX 4.3 SPORTING PLAYERS AND THEIR CLUBS AS POSITIVE FORCES IN THE COMMUNITY – EXAMPLE OF SAN FRANCISCO 49ERS

Many media outlets are attracted to stories of sporting players behaving badly. Each year there is a predictable set of stories about professional athletes receiving DUIs, being charged with partner abuse, failing to make child support payments, and so on. The media, however, is less attracted to stories of players making positive contributions to society. Although most leagues and clubs have taken initiatives to develop programs for contributions to society and to give awards to help publicize these efforts, these initiatives and efforts rarely get much broad media coverage.

The San Francisco 49ers of the NFL illustrates efforts at the club level to have substantive community engagement. Bill Walsh, coach of the 49ers from 1979 to 1991, was an early and influential advocate for players to broaden their life beyond just the playing aspects of their career. Part of his focus was on encouraging athletes to be better prepared for their post-playing life through education. Another focus was making visits to organizations in the Bay Area where athletes could provide inspiration. An example in the 1980s was Walsh leading 49er athletes to visit patients at the cancer ward of Stanford University's Children's Hospital.

The areas of community engagement for the current 49ers include:

- Running the San Francisco 49ers Foundation. This is a non-profit organization that raises money via donations, events, etc. It supports development programs and activities. In 2014, it donated $4.6 million to Bay Area non-profits, including a $1 million gift to launch the new 49ers STEM Leadership Initiative, the Santa Clara Unified School District, and the Silicon Valley Education Foundation.
- Players and coaches visiting hospitals, schools, after-school programs, children-at-risk facilities, and camps to talk, read books, and lead athletic activities.
- Hosting Make-A-Wish and other charities at the training facility and at games.

The 49ers Annual Report states that "the organization, including 49er players, coaches, ownership, staff, and alumni donates over 2,500 hours of volunteer time to more than 130 community events and activities in the Bay Area each year." Joanne Pasternack, director of the 49ers Foundation and community relations states: "The Foundation is the embodiment of the 49ers commitment to being a force for change in the community. We do more than just play football – we use football as a platform to serve as role models and to making lasting change in the Bay Area."

Clubs that have a past history of "players behaving badly" as regards widely held social norms means management has to deal with inherited liabilities. Box 4.4 highlights how player behavior at the Portland Trail Blazers created "baggage" for club management, some of which was self-inflicted by very high-risk player signing decisions at that club.

Branding and Sponsorship

Sporting clubs differ greatly in the current and past strength of their brands. For major leagues, external surveys of sporting club brands and of individual factors driving brand strength are often published or

BOX 4.4 THE PORTLAND TRAIL BLAZERS EARN THE "JAIL BLAZERS" TAG

The Portland Trail Blazers of the NBA has had many highs and many lows in its franchise history. In 1970, the NBA granted Harry Glickman the rights to a new franchise based in Portland. After a "naming contest," the club chose the Trail Blazers name. In 1977, Portland won the NBA Championship, with Hall of Fame player Bill Walton playing a key role. Portland also appeared in the 1990 and 1992 NBA Championships.

In the late 1990s, the Trail Blazers built a squad that was high in talent but, based on past behavior, had a higher likelihood of off-court problems. Unfortunately for Portland, past behavior turned out to be very predictive of their behavior after joining the Portland Trail Blazers squad. Commentators started using the phrase "Portland Jail Blazers" to describe the club after multiple reports of off-field problems kept on surfacing. Comments made about the "Jail Blazers" included:

- "It seemed that Hades, the god of the underworld himself decided to create a basketball team in Portland that would bring so much disdain to the city. ... There hasn't been a collection of basketball players that have visited the Portland precinct [police station] more since the team was built by [the General Manager]. His knack for talent went along with his knack to find the troubled souls of the NBA."[20]
- *The New York Times* on May 8, 2003 reported the resignation of the Trail Blazers' general manager. The article cited three players "being cited for marijuana possession," one player "being arrested on suspicion of domestic assault," and another player "suspended for seven games by the league for threatening a referee after a game." The article noted that during the General Manager's tenure there had been "20 suspensions and 15 arrests of players."[21]
- Preston Waters in *The Jail Blazers: The Worst Behaved Team in Professional Sports History* cited one player being a registered sex offender, another player punching a teammate during practice and breaking his eye socket, one player with multiple marijuana charges and a DUI, and yet another player leaving mid-season due to cocaine and drug abuse.[22]
- Bonzi Wells, a player from 2000 to 2003 stated: "It was madness. I've never seen anything like it. You think some of the guys had off-the-court issues? It was ten times worse in the locker room."[23]

The player selection decisions by Portland were made with "eyes wide open" in that many of the character-challenged players had red flags at the time of their selection. By hiring so many off-the-field high-risk players, they took the extra risk that interactions between these players would add to what was already a combustible club environment. The Portland Trail Blazers of this era (late 1990s to early 2000s) has subsequently become the posterchild of what not to do as regards managing the risks associated with off-the-court high-risk players. The editor of the leading local newspaper (*The Oregonian*) stated at a conference that being the then-dominant sporting franchise in Portland meant that the "highs" of the club (such as when they won the NBA Championship) were magnified in the positive, but also that the "lows" of the club were magnified in the opposite negative direction. Clubs are increasingly under the media spotlight for "player behaving badly" off-field behavior, in part due to the greater monitoring of athletes on a 24/7 basis with mobile phones, social media, etc.

available from commercial services. Having a strong brand is a leverageable asset for the management of a sporting club in many areas – such as on the business side attracting fans, game attendees, sponsors, media contracts, and employees.

A strong portfolio of sponsors is an indication of the value of the club to a key stakeholder category. Sponsors can differ dramatically in the investment they are prepared to make in a club and the amount of activation they are willing to undertake. Elite clubs with a global brand typically have the ability to attract significant sponsor investments from blue-chip companies in many parts of the globe.

Fan Base Strength

Fans play many important roles in the life of a sporting club. Aspects of a fan base that can create leverageable assets for management of that club include the size of the fan base, the wealth level composition, the depth of emotional connection to the club, the demographics and its attraction to media companies and sponsors, and its geographical spread. Clubs that have large global and national fan bases, as well as local/regional fan bases, can leverage this broader reach via touring games, attracting more global sponsors, and being more attractive to potential young star players.

Media Contracts and Ownership

As will be discussed in Chapters 15 and 16, contracts between media companies and a sporting club vary greatly. Some media contracts certainly can be viewed as leverageable assets for the sporting club. An example would be the broadcast contract that the Los Angeles Lakers signed in 2011. This contract was at the time "the richest local television rights deal in the NBA. The 20-year contract with Time Warner Cable included the launch of two new regional sports networks – one English and one Spanish – and averages $200 million a year for a total worth of $4 billion. That amount could soar to $5 billion if a five-year extension option is exercised."[24] In contrast, many NBA clubs have annual media contracts less than $20 million a year. In some instances, new management of a sporting club is faced with a well below-market contract that still has five or more years to run. This would be the classic case of an inherited liability for which the new management team may have limited ability in the short run to change.

Ownership of, or equity in, media assets can be an additional leverageable asset if well managed. Chapter 16 discusses how multiple North American sporting clubs have negotiated to have equity positions in the regional sports networks (RSNs) showing their games. There can be financial returns here in the form of dividends. Their RSN may also expand their coverage to better showcase the club and its players and coaches.

Real Estate

Clubs differ in their ownership or control of real estate associated with the stadium or arena in which they play or their training facilities. In some cases, the real estate can be owned by the franchise for many years. Box 18.1, later in the book, outlines how the real estate surrounding Dodger Stadium of the Los Angeles Dodgers has been a long-term leverageable asset. Clubs constructing new stadiums may be able to negotiate with a city or county to include a rezoning of land as part of making the stadium a financially viable investment. The San Jose Earthquakes of MLS opened their 2015 season in the new Avaya Stadium. Construction cost was approximately $100 million. Included in the expected returns to the owners of the Earthquakes was rent from commercial and retail properties made possible from a rezoning ruling by the City of San Jose.

4.6 THE SPORT (ON-FIELD) SIDE AND BUSINESS (OFF-FIELD) SIDE OF A SPORTING CLUB

The two key sides of a sporting club are the sport side and the business side. Exhibit 4.7 provides examples of the functions often found in each of these two areas.

The size of club staff – or "head count" – will be affected by what activities are managed by the club. Exhibit 4.8 outlines the head counts of a sample of sport organizations. A club with stadium management responsibilities will have additional head count vis-à-vis a comparable club playing in a stadium managed by a city authority. Similarly, a club that also owns its own television network, restaurant, training facility, or that administers activations for its sponsors will have a larger head count.

Key decisions in each of the two sides in Exhibit 4.7 have consequences for the other side and for the club as a single entity with a brand, fan base, and many commercial partners. Decisions by a general manager to not renew players that in the past have been major contributors can result in much fan push-back and a reluctance by those players to stay engaged with the club later in their post-playing day activities. Box 4.4 shows how decisions on the playing side of the Portland Trail Blazers starting in the late 1990s led to much pushback from fans and the Portland press labeling the club the "Jail Blazers."

Exhibit 4.9 outlines a 2 × 2 matrix that captures four possible combinations of the on-field/off-field and success/failure categories. While these four combinations are very high-level characterizations, they do highlight some very different outcomes for a sporting club.

"Nirvana" is the ideal situation for a club with financial success and on-field success happening concurrently. Real Madrid, a leading club in La Liga, reported revenues of $797 million and profit of

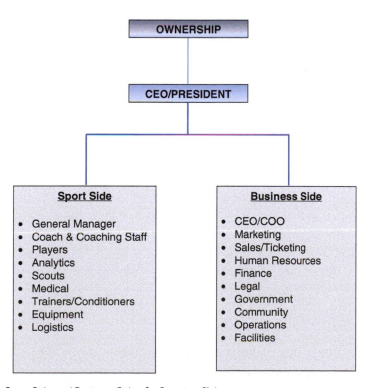

EXHIBIT 4.7 The Sport Side and Business Side of a Sporting Club

Team	Winnipeg Jets (NHL)	San Francisco 49ers (NFL)	Jacksonville Jaguars (NFL)	San Diego Padres (MLB)	New York Knicks (NBA)	Charlotte Hornets (NBA)	Chicago Fire (MLS)
Playing team (on-field) side							
Coaching staff	5	20	24	9	6	7	3
Personnel/scouting	26	21	34	22	32	15	2
Strength and conditioners	3	2	8	7	8	11	11
General management/ others	19	4	4	9	11	6	6
Subtotal	**53**	**47**	**70**	**47**	**57**	**39**	**22**
Business side							
Marketing/sales	10	20	54	95	124	98	38
Communications	3	28	9	21	34	3	2
Operations/facilities	6	16	14	26	—	14	3
Accounting/legal/HR	2	20	24	19	12	13	6
General management/others	8	33	5	17	3	8	2
Subtotal	**29**	**117**	**106**	**178**	**173**	**136**	**51**
Total	**82**	**164**	**176**	**225**	**230**	**175**	**73**

EXHIBIT 4.8 Sport Club Headcount Composition (Excluding Playing Squad)
Source: http://jets.nhl.com/club/page.htm?id=69827; www.jaguars.com/staffdirectory; www.49ers.com/team/front-office.html; http://tampabay.rays.mlb.com/team/front_office.jsp?c_id=tb; www.nba.com/knicks/front-office; www.arsenal.com/the-club/corporate-info/the-arsenal-board; www.chicago-fire.com/club/staff; www.nba.com/hornets/staff-directory

$50.9 million for 2013/14, a year in which the club won the UEFA Champions League. The Green Bay Packers have been to the NFL playoffs 75 percent of the time in the 2001/13 12-year period and won Super Bowl XLV in February 2011. At the same time, it was consistently profitable, was able to invest heavily in stadium upgrades, and consistently ranked high on external fan satisfaction surveys.

"Profit without winning" describes those clubs with impressive financial outcomes but ongoing on-field challenges. The Toronto Maple Leafs of the NHL is a prime example of this category. *Forbes* in 2013 had the Leafs as the most valuable club in the NHL at a $1.15 billion valuation based on estimated revenues of $142 million. *Forbes* reported a club profit of $48.5 million for 2013 and more than $500 million in profit over the decade up to and including 2013. On the ice, the Maple Leafs have been well below average. Each year 16 of the 30 NHL clubs make the playoffs. In the nine years since the 2004/5 lockout season, Toronto has made the playoffs only once (and then it was eliminated in the first round). They have not won the Stanley Cup since 1967. One word of caution here. The "pain" of not winning on the field is certainly felt by the fan base. In some cases, however, winning is not the driving motive of the ownership group.

"Expensive glory" is the opposite of "Profit without winning," where the club is performing well on the field but running large financial losses. Manchester City in the EPL was acquired by an Abu Dhabi owner in 2008. In the 15 years prior to 2008, City had many low performing years and had been relegated twice. Over the six seasons from 2008/9 to 2013/14, City moved from tenth in the EPL to winning in 2011/12 and 2013/14 and being second in 2012/13. The ownership group sanctioned the acquisition

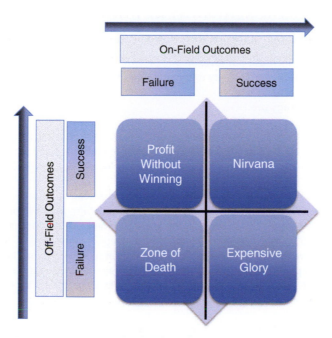

EXHIBIT 4.9 Club Management: On-Field/Off-Field Dynamics

of the contracts of multiple elite soccer players. Over this same six year period, City accumulated operating losses of more than £240 million (including 2010/11 with a loss of £81 million). These losses were only able to be covered because of its very wealthy owner. In the normal context, Manchester City would have become bankrupt as the club was not operating on a financially sustainable basis. Starting in 2011/12, the European governing soccer body (UEFA) instituted "financial fair play regulations" to constrain soccer clubs having very large losses in an attempt to achieve success on the field.

"Zone of death" is what we label clubs who are performing poorly both on and off the field. The Phoenix Coyotes of the NHL are a prime example of this category – where their on- and off-field performances are both low. The team missed the post-season in nine of the recent 15 seasons and, according to *Forbes*, has run a loss every year since 1999/2000, including periods of significant losses where the NHL was forced to take control of the club.

4.7 MULTIPLE AREAS OF ASSET-BUILD AT CLUBS

Sporting clubs are adopting multiple areas to build asset values. The following are illustrative:

1 **Sporting club asset-build.** The traditional focus by which asset-build has occurred for many sporting clubs is by building their on-field team performance and enhancing their attractiveness to fans and sponsors. Manchester United (see Exhibit 4.10 for their strategy) is a classic example where there has been major revenue growth from game-day revenues and sponsors over many years where it is now one of the most valuable sporting clubs in the globe. A major part of this strategy has been to build revenues from many parts of the globe.

2 **Stadium/arena asset-build.** Asset-build can occur here in multiple ways. The most direct way is related to the sporting team of the club. By building stadiums and arenas with greater revenue-generating

Vision: to be the best football club in the world both on and off the pitch

Business strategy: we aim to increase our revenue and profitability by expanding our high growth business that leverage our global community and marketing infrastructure.

The key elements of our strategy are:

1. **Expand our portfolio of global and regional sponsors:** We are well positioned to continue to secure sponsorships with leading brands. Over the last few years, we have implemented a proactive approach to identifying, securing and supporting sponsors. Global partners include AON, Bulova, Chevrolet, DHL, and Toshiba.
2. **Further develop our retail, merchandising, apparel, and product licensing business:** We will focus on growing this business on a global basis by increasing our product range and improving distribution through further development of our wholesale, retail and e-commerce channels. Our record-breaking kit deal with Adidas has £750 million minimum guarantee – ten-year contract expires 2025.
3. **Exploit new media and mobile opportunities:** The rapid shift of media consumption towards internet, mobile and social media platforms presents us with multiple growth opportunities and new revenue streams. Our digital media platforms, such as mobile sites, applications and social media, are expected to become one of the primary methods by which we engage and transact with our followers around the world.
4. **Enhance the reach and distribution of our broadcasting rights:** The value of live sports programming has grown dramatically in recent years due to changes in how television content is distributed and consumed. Specifically, television consumption has become more fragmented and audiences for traditional scheduled television programming have declined as consumer choice increased with the emergence of multi-channel television, the development of technologies such as the digital video recorder and the emergence of digital viewing on the internet and mobile devices.
5. **Diversify revenue and improve margins:** We aim to increase the revenue and operating margins of our business as we further expand into our high growth commercial businesses, including sponsorship, retail, merchandising, licensing and new media and mobile. By increasing the emphasis on our commercial businesses, we will further diversify our revenue, enabling us to generate improved profitability.

Business model: we review our revenue through three principal sectors

Commercial (£189 million in 2014: 20.8 percent compound growth per annum since 2008): Within the Commercial revenue sector, we have three revenue streams which monetize our global brand: sponsorship revenue; retail, merchandising, apparel & product licensing revenue; and new media & mobile revenue. We believe these will be our fastest growing revenue streams over the next few years.

Broadcasting (£136 million in 2014: 7.4 percent compound growth per annum since 2008): We benefit from the distribution and broadcasting of live football content directly from the revenue we receive and indirectly through increased global exposure for our commercial partners. Broadcasting revenue is derived from the global television rights relating to the Premier League, Champions League and other competitions. In addition, our wholly-owned global television channel, MUTV, delivers Manchester United programming to over 85 countries and territories around our world.

Match day (£108 million in 2014: 0.2 percent compound growth per annum since 2008): We believe Old Trafford is one of the world's iconic sports venues. It currently seats 75,635 and is the largest sporting club stadium in the UK. We have averaged over 99 percent of attendance capacity for our Premier League matches in each of the last 17 years.

EXHIBIT 4.10 Manchester United Vision, Business Strategy, and Business Model: From 2014 Annual Report

capacity for home games, asset-build will occur if the club is able to attract the fans and sponsors in a sustainable way. Creative management will seek to expand their revenue-generating focus beyond the home-team playing days. Most stadiums and arenas have many days in which capacity exists for additional events. For example, in the NFL there are only ten home games per year and possibly three playoff games. In many soccer leagues, there are only 25–30 home games. Arenas for basketball and hockey can have up to 60 home games. The result is much excesscapacity in most stadiums and arenas to host other events. These can include concerts, ice-shows, inspirational speakers, etc. By building a continuing pipeline of events in addition to the home games of a sporting club, asset-build can occur.

Where a sporting club has ownership of a stadium, the club has greatest flexibility to seek asset-build in this area. In cases where the ownership is held by a city or third party, much will depend on the operating agreement the sporting club has with the owner of the facility. Often where the club has much leverage, it will have a long-term agreement that provides much upside to the club from running additional events at the facility.

3 **Media-related asset-build.** An important source of asset-build for several clubs has been partial or full ownership of media assets. Chapter 16 describes how MLB clubs such as the New York Yankees and the San Francisco Giants have negotiated to acquire equity in RSNs showing their live games. The magnitude of the asset gains can, in extreme cases, result in the media company itself being more valuable than the sporting club.

4 **Real estate asset-build.** In many cities, the value of the land surrounding sporting facilities has markedly increased over time. One response here has been for clubs that are building new stadiums or arenas to take a broader equity interest in the surrounding real estate as well as the stadium itself. A notable example is the San Diego Padres when they planned the building of Petco Park in downtown San Diego. By architecting a broader development with residential, commercial, and a hotel, the Padres management was able to financially reap the benefits of the transformation that occurred in the area surrounding the new ball park.

5 **Specialized competence asset-build.** Some sporting clubs have sought to capitalize on the skillsets developed within their club. One example is the Dallas Cowboys who combined with the New York Yankees to create a consulting group (Legends) that provides multiple services to sports and entertainment ventures. Their areas of consulting include new venue planning, ticketing, hospitality, and fan engagement.

The five areas noted above illustrate how there is a premium on sporting clubs taking a broad perspective on the possible avenues to build asset value. Note that within each of the above areas, there are likely differences in the skillsets that management needs to acquire to fully exploit the opportunities in each area. Exhibit 4.11 shares another example of a club strategy, that of the Saskatchewan Roughriders of the CFL.

4.8 SUMMARY

This chapter highlights some of the multiple factors that are important for decision making management of a sporting club. Of central importance are the objectives of the ownership group. These objectives can differ across different owners and for the same owners over time. The leverageable assets and the inherited liabilities associated with the sporting club at the time key decisions are being made are also central to decision making.

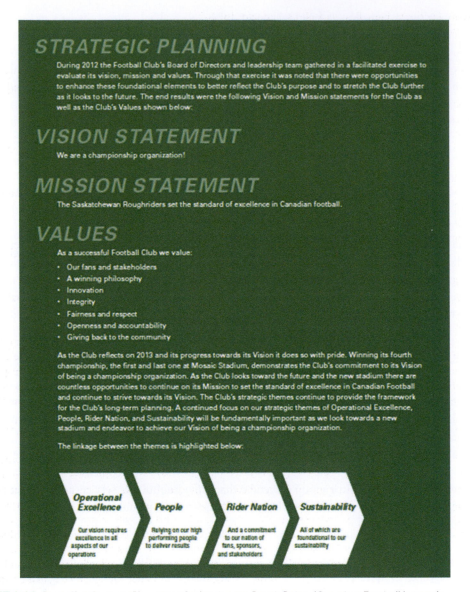

EXHIBIT 4.11 Sport Club Strategy Planning – Saskatchewan Rough Riders (Canadian Football League)
Source: Taken directly from annual report, www.riderville.com/page/ridersagm

NOTES

1 *Deloitte's Annual Review of Football Finance* is published annually and is based on financials reported by individual sporting clubs. *Forbes'* sporting club estimates are published annually at the start of each season and are estimates by the staff of *Forbes*. While there is often dispute over the specific numbers *Forbes* estimates, useful insights can be gained by the relative magnitude of differences across clubs.

2 The five club ownership models in Exhibit 4.3 are major ones found in the leading professional sporting leagues. Some other models are government-sponsored clubs (or even a league) – found, for example, in some "communist" country leagues – and university-sponsored clubs – found, for example, in some professional rugby competitions.

3 "Lakers owner Jerry Buss dies," Fox News, February 18, 2013.

4 M. Bresnahan, "Buss addresses season-ticket holders," LakersGround.net, June 17, 2007.

5 C.P. Pierce, "A fan's worst nightmare," *Grantland*, April 28, 2014.

6 An example is the dispute between Steve Belkin and other members of the Atlanta Spirit consortium. See K. Willis, "Atlanta–Spirit Group lawsuit settled, what does it mean for the Hawks?" *SB Nation*, December 26, 2010. See also B Baxter, "King & Spalding settles $195 million malpractice suit filed by Atlanta Spirit," *The AM Law Daily*, September 14, 2011.

7 "Man U sold in record takeover deal," BBC, August 18, 1989.

8 P. Davenport, "Knighton drops takeover but joins board," *The Times*, 12 October 1989.

9 G.W. Brown and J.C. Hartzell, "Market reaction to public information: the atypical case of the Boston Celtics," *Journal of Financial Economics* (2001): 333–70.

10 "Football clubs you can buy shares in," www.advfn.com, February 12, 2014.

11 A. Voinea, "Co-operative club Real Madrid is chasing another Champions League trophy," *Co-operative News*, May 12, 2014.

12 See, for example, G. Dickey, *Al Davis and His Raiders: Just Win Baby* (Harcourt, 1991).

13 "Winning is the ultimate deodorant," Warriorsworld.net, March 30, 2004.

14 J. Barnett, A. Dávila, G. Foster, and N. O'Reilly, *San Francisco Giants: Opportunity and Challenges in Different Eras* (Stanford Graduate School of Business, 2014).

15 *Sports Business Journal*, December 8–14, 2014, p. 22.

16 The San Francisco Giants in the 1990s had disagreements among syndicate members aired in public – see J. Barnett, A. Dávila, G. Foster, and N. O'Reilly, *San Francisco Giants: Opportunity and Challenges in Different Eras* (Stanford Graduate School of Business, 2014).

17 Observers maintained that the lead owners of the Mets (Fred Wilpon and Saul Katz) benefited from the early years of Madoff's fraud and were able to invest more into the Mets than had they invested money elsewhere at a lower and less consistent return. See B. Petchesky, "How Bernie Madoff's money ran the Mets," Deadspin.com, February 21, 2012. S.F. Kovaleski and D. Waldstein, "Madoff had wide role in Mets' finances," *The New York Times*, February 1, 2011, quotes a former employee of the Mets stating that "Bernie was part of the business plan for the Mets."

18 "Probability dictates that at least one newly promoted side will be relegated each season," B. Cohen, "Who will be relegated from the Premier League in 2014/15?" www.freebetsfreetips.com, December 9, 2014.

19 Dolan's email was reported as follows: "Mr Bierman, You are a sad person. Why would anybody write such a hateful letter? I am just guessing but ill bet your life is a mess and you are a hateful mess. What have you done that anyone would consider positive or nice. I am betting nothing. In fact ill bet you are negative force in every-one who comes in contact with you. You most likely have made your family miserable. Alcoholic maybe. I just celebrated my 21 year anniversary of sobriety. You should try it. Maybe it will help you become a person that folks would like to have around. In the mean while start rooting for the Nets because the Knicks don't want you. Respectfully James Dolan" T. Burke, "Dolan: 'Start rooting for the Nets because the Knicks don't want you,'" *Deadspin*, February 2,1015. Dolan later was reported as saying: "I get emails all the time … And I gener-ally don't respond to the bad ones, right? This time, it just caught me at the wrong moment, and I responded, sort of a tit-a-tat … I know I should not have done that, and I did it anyway because he made me angry," *The New York Times*, February 14, 2015.

20 https://blazersog.wordpress.com/2008/03/13/where-are-the-jailblazers.

21 "NBA Roundup: Blazers president quits, leaving troubled team," *The New York Times*, May 8, 2003.

22 http://elitedaily.com/sports/where-the-hell-are-the-portland-jail-blazers.

23 http://slumz.boxden.com/f16/bonzi-wells-releases-independent-report-on-jail-blazers-locker-room-culture-must-read-2067783.

24 C. Settimi, "The NBA's richest local television deals," *Forbes*, January 22, 2014.

5 PROFESSIONAL ATHLETES AND PLAYERS' ASSOCIATIONS/ UNIONS

This chapter and the one that follows examine key decisions that affect elite-level participants in sports. The first part of this chapter focuses on the ecosystem surrounding compensation negotiations for athletes. We then discuss players' associations with examples of major decisions that these associations make. Emphasis is often placed on looking at issues from the professional athlete's perspective. Chapter 6 looks at player evaluation from the club perspective as part of an analysis of the club player-side decision making process.

5.1 THE PROFESSIONAL SPORTS ATHLETE ARENA

A professional athlete is one who is compensated for their participation in a sport. In most cases, this compensation will include financial aspects. Other aspects can include in-kind compensation (such as vehicles, accommodation, and other lifestyle items). Athletes are assets in the professional sport business. They are drafted, signed, traded, and their contracts often sold. Elite athletes are pivotal assets for clubs and leagues due to their ability to provide on-field performance, to attract large revenues, grow fan following for a sport, and drive alternate revenue sources such as sponsorship, merchandising, and media rights fees.

A useful distinction when understanding the business of sports is between (a) athletes in *team sports* (such as Sidney Crosby in hockey, LeBron James in basketball, Marta and Lionel Messi in soccer), and (b) athletes in *individual sports* (such as Usain Bolt in athletics, Roger Federer in tennis, Danica Patrick in motor racing, and Maria Sharapova in tennis). Athletes in team sports often are surrounded by a larger economic infrastructure than those in individual sports.

5.1.1 Player Payroll Growth

Several patterns can be observed from a diversity of sources relating to professional athlete compensation in team sports. A caution here is that many of the surveys quoted are based on third-party estimates rather than audited numbers. However, general trends can be inferred from these surveys. Consider first average club payroll evidence for leading team sports:

1   Over time, compensation of professional team athletes for their on-the-field performance has generally increased since 2000 for major sports. Exhibit 5.1 shows the total club payrolls across the four North American leagues (Panel A)[1] and the five leading European soccer leagues (Panel B)[2] each year since 2000.

Note that in Exhibit 5.1, there are years for some leagues in which there have been declines in average payroll. For example, following the 2004/5 lockout in the NHL, there was a new collective bargaining agreement in which the level of salaries decreased in the 2005/6 season compared to those in the 2003/4 season. As a second example, the Italian premier soccer league in the 2001/2 to 2006/7 period declined.

The leagues in Exhibit 5.1 are at the elite level of professional team sports. In many other leagues, there are much lower average club salaries. For example, the premier men's soccer league in Australia is the A-League, This league has the following total salary cap per team[3] (in $AU millions):

Salary cap	2012	2013	2014	2015
Maximum	$2.400	$2.478	$2.500	$2.550
Minimum	$2.045	$2.107	$2.125	$2.168

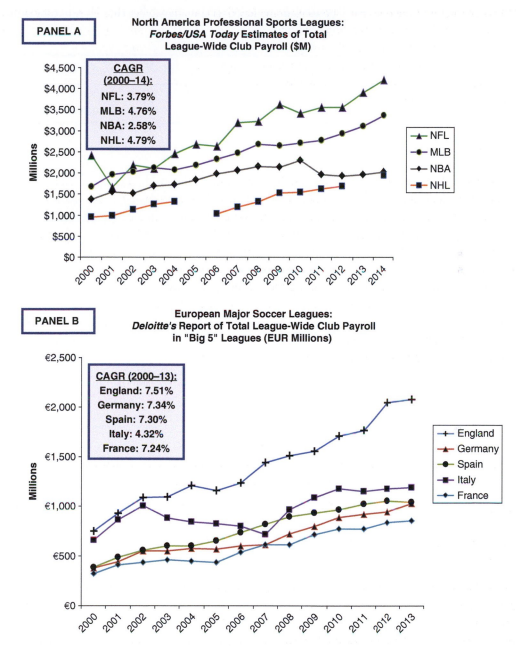

EXHIBIT 5.1 Total League-Wide Club Payroll Comparison for Major North American and European Sporting Leagues

The Hyundai A-League has a "soft" salary cap as clubs are allowed to spend outside the salary cap in certain circumstances. Specifically, clubs are allowed to sign two marquee players, one guest player, use an allowance of $150,000 on homegrown players, provide relocation expenses to a certain threshold and sign three contracted, under-20 players on the prescribed minimum remuneration which are all outside of the salary cap.

Similarly, the Women's National Basketball League (WNBA) in the US has the following maximum and minimum team salary caps[4] (in US$ millions):

Salary cap	2010	2011	2012	2013
Maximum	$0.827	$0.852	$0.878	$0.913
Minimum	$0.796	$0.819	$0.844	$0.869

Other things being equal, the league that a player is in plays a central role in average salaries. The low level of team compensation for professional women's team sports is one of the most challenging aspects of the sports industry. Professional athletes competing in women's team sports for many years have struggled to have salaries even close to their male counterparts. The much lower revenues associated with professional women's sports leagues is a major factor causing this differential between men's and women's team sport compensation.

2   Total league player compensation as a percentage of total league revenues has not consistently increased or decreased each year since 2000 for the major sports. In Chapter 2, Exhibit 2.3 plots these percentages for the same nine major leagues in Exhibit 5.1. Over time, the percentage of compensation for players has varied for each league, increasing in some years and decreasing in others. For instance, the Italian soccer league has the highest average percentage of all the nine leagues in Exhibit 2.3. Indeed, in 2001/2 this ratio is 99 percent. It is not surprising that many Italian clubs had large losses in the early 2000s. In subsequent years, the management (or lenders) of these clubs put constraints on salary levels in an attempt to reduce these losses.

5.1.2 Individual Professional Athlete Total Compensation Evidence

Consider now evidence on individual player total compensation (including sponsorships). Here, again we caution that these reported numbers are based on third-party estimates. Individual athletes rarely make public details of their actual compensation and its components.

1   Rankings of the elite highly compensated athletes show a mixture of individual sports athletes and team sport athletes. Consider *Forbes*' top ten ranked athletes over the decade from 2004 to 2013 – see Exhibit 5.2. There are 100 athlete appearances in Exhibit 5.2 (ten athletes each year for ten years). Athletes from team sports had 52 percent of the appearances while athletes from individual sports had 48 percent of the appearances. The leading sports are basketball (25 percent), golf (19 percent), soccer (17 percent), boxing (9 percent), NFL (8 percent), tennis (7 percent), and Formula 1 (7 percent).
2   Individual sport athletes top the *Forbes*' list each year from 2005 to 2014. Tiger Woods is #1 in eight of the ten years, while Floyd Mayweather is #1 in two years (2012 and 2014). *Forbes* estimated Mayweather made $105 million over the one-year period ending in July 2014 (almost all from boxing events with minimal sponsorship earnings).
3   Rankings of the top 100 compensated athletes show that a higher proportion come from team-based sports (basketball, football, etc.) as opposed to individual sports. Exhibit 5.3 shows

Panel A: Sport representation

Team sports		Individual sports	
NBA	25%	Golf	19%
Soccer	17%	Boxing	9%
NFL	8%	Tennis	7%
MLB	2%	Formula 1	7%
Total	**52%**	Moto GP	4%
		NASCAR	1%
		Cycling	1%
		Total	**48%**

Panel B: Players with two or more appearances

Team sports		Individual sports	
Players	Appearances	Players	Appearances
Kobe Bryant	10	Tiger Woods	10
David Beckham	8	Phil Mickelson	9
LeBron James	7	Roger Federer	6
Michael Jordan	5	Michael Schumacher	4
Cristiano Ronaldo	4	Valentino Rossi	4
Lionel Messi	3	Floyd Mayweather	3
Alex Rodriguez	2	Manny Pacquiao	3
		Kimi Räikkönen	3
		Oscar De La Hoya	2

EXHIBIT 5.2 Composition of *Forbes'* Top Ten Compensated Athletes: 2005/14 (Athletes With Two or More Appearances Recognized By Name)
Source: Forbes

the composition of *Forbes'* top 100 athletes for 2014 – MLB (27 percent), NBA (18 percent), NFL (17 percent), Soccer (15 percent), and Cricket (1 percent) collectively comprise 78 percent of the top 100 athletes.

4   Male athletes dominate the rankings of highly compensated athletes. The top female athlete in 2014 was Maria Sharapova (34th with $24.4 million). Only three of the 100 top athletes in 2014 were female.

5   US nationals have the highest percentage of the most highly paid athletes. For the top 100 on the 2014 list, 60 percent are US nationals. The remaining 40 percent are from 24 other countries, with the United Kingdom (five), Dominican Republic (four), Spain (four), Venezuela (three), and Germany (three) leading the remaining country representations.

Category/league	Percentage of Top 100	Percentage of earnings from salary	Percentage of earnings from endorsements
Team sports – 78% of Top 100			
MLB	27 %	95 %	5 %
NBA	18 %	76 %	24 %
NFL	17 %	89 %	11 %
Soccer	15 %	77 %	23 %
Cricket	1 %	13 %	87 %
Individual Sports – 22% of Top 100			
Tennis	6 %	27 %	73 %
Golf	5 %	34 %	66 %
Boxing	4 %	94 %	6 %
NASCAR	3 %	68 %	32 %
Formula 1	3 %	93 %	7 %
Track	1 %	1 %	99 %

EXHIBIT 5.3 Composition of *Forbes'* Top 100 Compensated Athletes in 2014
Note: Both cricket and track have only one athlete (1 percent of the 100 total athletes). For cricket, it is Mahendra Singh Dhoni, who has very large endorsement income. In track, the athlete is Usain Bolt, also a high earner in terms of endorsements.
Source: Forbes

6   Sports vary greatly in the percentage of earnings from (a) on-the-field salary versus (b) endorsements and related compensation. The last two columns of Exhibit 5.3 shows *Forbes'* estimate of the average percentage of total compensation from salary as opposed to endorsements/apparel/sponsorship. Of the four team sports with the highest representation in Exhibit 5.3, basketball (NBA) and soccer athletes have the highest percentage of earnings from the endorsements /apparel/sponsorship categories. Of the four individual sports with the highest representation, tennis and golf have the highest percentage of earnings from endorsements/apparel/sponsorship. Further discussion of this area (athlete endorsement) can be found in Chapter 12.

5.2 PROFESSIONAL ATHLETE COMPENSATION NEGOTIATIONS ECOSYSTEM

5.2.1 Some Key Factors in Compensation Ecosystem

While the expected ability of a player is the most important factor in compensation decisions, these negotiations do not occur in a vacuum. Rather, they take place within an ecosystem that has multiple influences. Decision makers who recognize and exploit the many aspects of this ecosystem are likely to be better informed in their negotiations. We use the context of a player compensation in a team sport to illustrate important aspects of this ecosystem:

Free Market versus Constrained Market Structure

Chapter 3 highlighted how team sport leagues around the globe differ greatly in how they embrace free market principles as regards player compensation. Some leagues operate with basically a free market structure while others have multiple constraints on free market forces being allowed to operate. The following can be found in different leagues on a spectrum that has free market setting at one end and a heavily constrained market setting at the other end:

Free Market Structure

An extreme version is where there are no constraints on both the total player payroll for each club and on the salaries of individual players in the league. Leading elite soccer leagues around the globe operated with the structure for many years. The result was often vast differences across clubs in both the total payrolls and in the salaries paid to individual players. Starting in 2011, each of the clubs in the European country soccer leagues can still operate with this free market structure with at least one important proviso. That proviso is called "financial fair play rules." These rules penalize clubs whose total revenues are below their committed outlays for player compensation and other sporting and business expenses.[5] Even within this proviso, European soccer clubs that generate high revenues still have great flexibility in regards to their total player payroll and how that is allocated across individual players.

Constrained Market Structure

The philosophy underlying the structures of many team sport leagues is that multiple constraints on payroll decisions need to be put in place to achieve objectives such as competitive balance in the league and financial stability of clubs. These constraints are typically determined as a result of bargaining between a league and the union that represents players in the league. They are codified in what is frequently called a collective bargaining agreement (CBA). Multiple constraints on player payroll decisions can be found in CBAs in different leagues around the globe. Examples include:

- **Constraints on maximum total player payroll.** An extreme constraint is a hard salary cap where no team can have a total player payroll above a set financial number. For example, the NFL in 2015 had a total team salary cap of $143.28 million per club. Australian professional team sports also have this hard salary cap model as regards the A-League (soccer), NRL (rugby league), and AFL (Australian rules league). A less extreme version allows for clubs to exceed a set financial amount, but imposes increasingly heavy taxes (luxury taxes) on clubs that exceed that amount. The NBA operates with this structure – see Box 6.2 for further discussion on this topic.
- **Constraints on minimum total team salary levels.** These constraints in CBAs are largely motivated by efforts to prevent owners who place profitability as their major objective and are willing to dramatically reduce team payrolls to achieve that profitability, irrespective of the likely decrease in on-field competitiveness of the club. Examples of this constraint exist in the NFL, the WNBA, and the A-League.
- **Constraints on individual player salaries.** There are many options here that are found across leagues. These include minimum and maximum salaries for rookies and minimum salaries for all athletes on a club. Maximum constraints on individual salaries can be dollar amounts or percent of total payroll. An example is the NBA individual player salary cap. Under the 2011 CBA, no player with six years or below in the NBA can receive more than 25 percent of a "soft" total team salary cap. For players with ten or more years in the NBA, no player can receive more than 35 percent of this cap.

Bargaining context resulting from the global stature of a sport and the flexibility of player transfers across leagues

A general principle in labor (and other) negotiations is that the broader the demand from different parties, the higher the salary will likely be. Situations where there is only one employment option for a player and many players bidding for that one slot typically do not provide a strong negotiating setting for the player. Sports that have multiple high-revenue leagues across the globe likely will have elite athletes with multiple bidders for their talent. Soccer is the showcase example of this situation. Leading soccer players such as Lionel Messi (Barcelona), Cristiano Ronaldo (Real Madrid), Zlatan Ibrahimović (Paris Saint-Germain), and Wayne Rooney (Manchester United) are global stars that can attract multiple offers from many clubs. The existence of at least five major European soccer leagues creates a competitive bargaining advantage for such soccer stars and their agents in their negotiations. Each of the four major North American sporting leagues (NFL, MLB, NBA, and NHL) do not have this extreme global bargaining dynamic, which reduces the ability of a player in one of those leagues to play off bids from non-North American leagues against bids coming from their own North American league.

This bargaining context factor has been highlighted several times in North America when new leagues have been set up to compete with an existing league. For example, from 1983 to 1985, the United States Football League (USFL) competed against the NFL, including bidding for elite players. Each year the Heisman Trophy winner out of the US college system is highly sought by NFL clubs. However, during each of the three years the USFL operated, the Heisman Trophy winner was bid away by USFL clubs who were offering much larger salaries than were available in the NFL.

Individual sports have different structures regarding their bargaining context. Where there is only one large body employing the athletes in that sport or providing a platform for them to perform, individual athletes will likely have less bargaining power than when there are multiple options for the individual to perform. This is the classic monopoly position that courts have penalized companies for violating anti-trust laws. Aspects of this are alleged to occur in several sports. For example, it has been argued that UFC, the leading mixed martial arts league, has used its dominant position to keep fighter salaries at a lower level than would be the case had two or more powerful mixed martial arts leagues existed. In boxing, greater competition across several broadcasters for elite talent has enabled several fighters to negotiate very sizable new contracts. Leading boxer Floyd Mayweather was able to negotiate a six-fight deal with Showtime for what *Forbes* estimates to be $200 million guaranteed with further earnings a possibility.[6]

General market factors affecting the revenue base of the sport in which the athlete plays

Chapter 3 on leagues highlighted the sizable revenue differences across sports in their revenue generation. The stronger the revenue base of a league, the greater the ability to compensate its players. Although the media often highlights the multimillion-dollar salaries of elite players in high-revenue sports, many professional athletes play in leagues with much lower revenue bases. Lower salaries are to be expected in these lower-revenue leagues.

In many countries and sports there is a tiering of leagues by revenues, and those athletes who play in the lower-tiered sporting leagues have to accept that average salary levels likely will be well below those paid to athletes in the higher-tiered leagues. Many players who aspire to play in the NFL are prepared to showcase their talents in much lower revenue leagues – these include the Arena Football League and the Canadian Football League. Salaries in these two lower-tiered leagues are many times lower than those found in the NFL.

Club's ability and willingness to compete heavily on salary for players

For some leagues, clubs can differ greatly in their total salary levels. MLB clubs such as the New York Yankees and the Los Angeles Dodgers, with their enormous revenue bases, have shown multiple times that they have both the capacity and the willingness to offer elite players very high salaries over long time periods. In contrast, a club such as the Oakland Athletics for many years has had a strategy of being in the lower tier of total club payrolls, not bidding for the highest-performing free agents, and not offering many long-term, financially risky contracts. Athletes and their agents who understand how the capacities and strategies of each potential club differ come to the negotiating table in a more informed way.

Negotiating skills and philosophies of parties in the negotiation

The parties in a salary negotiation are typically the club on one side (often represented by the general manager) and an agent (often alone and sometimes with the player). Both sides have a vested interest in understanding what the other side in the negotiation will "settle" for, although there is often incentive for each party to not reveal their "final position" early on in the negotiations. Agents can work in broad-based agencies (e.g., CAA, IMG, Octagon, and Wasserman Media Group), with sport-dedicated agencies (such as BDA/Bill Duffy in basketball, Boras Corporation/Scott Boras in baseball, and Peter Carlisle in action sports), in law firms, or as independents. Agents often have legal, business, and sport management backgrounds and expertise. Some are celebrities themselves (e.g., Jay Z with Roc Nation Sports), others are former players. In many cases, today, they are recruiting players at a very young age in the hope that they become professionals.

5.2.2 Some Differences in the Compensation Ecosystem

Some contrasts between the North American major professional sports and the elite European premier leagues (soccer/association football) illustrate how player compensation ecosystems can differ.

1   With respect to players' contracts, European markets for players are typically less regulated, and more "capitalistic." In the Bosman case (1995), European courts ruled that limits on European players moving freely across European clubs were illegal. The decision was based on the fact that markets for players should be no different from markets for other jobs, so teams should be free to hire any European player without restrictions. In contrast, North American leagues have numerous specific rules, such as minimum and maximum salaries or player composition. The Canadian Football League for example has a "Canadian content" rule, stipulating a minimum number of Canadian players that each club must have on their roster.

2　　Player movement (or "transaction rules") is typically different in Europe than in North America. In European football/soccer, transaction rules are set by international federations, such as FIFA for the premier leagues. These rules provide uniformity across countries and leagues (although labor and tax laws differ).[7] In the case of FIFA, there are two windows for players to move across teams. The typical contract specifies not only the salary and its structure, but also the length of the contract. This latter aspect becomes crucial. If another team wants to buy a player with a contract, they can only do so if it pays the buyout clause. For instance, in 2009 FC Barcelona upgraded Lionel Messi's contract by increasing the buyout clause to €250 million.

3　　Over time, North American players' associations (unions) have been able to gain more freedom for players and create more competition across teams for their services. Still, rookie players are bound to play their initial years on teams that draft them with a cap on the maximum salary. For instance, NBA players can only move and negotiate better salaries after playing at least three years. Some leagues such as the NFL do not have guaranteed contracts and teams can cancel a contract at will. This rule shifts the risk of a large injury to the player and to frontload contracts for good players who want to protect themselves from this risk. In contrast to European leagues, transfers in North America seldom include money but rather involve other players and draft picks.

4　　The North American and European leagues often differ on talent identification structure. European leagues rely on market mechanisms and allow teams to compete against each other to hire the best talent with minimal regulation constraints from FIFA.[8] Because transfers of star players are expensive in Europe, competition for talent has expanded with some clubs investing heavily in youth academies. Teams are competing by offering contracts to parents (because children cannot officially work until they are 18).[9] Teams in Europe often have their own schools where they nurture younger players in development leagues. This route is very attractive because those players that reach the main team through the development system come at lower costs rather than through the open market with its expensive transfer fees. In North America, talent selection is highly regulated through draft systems. The basic process is similar across the major North American leagues. Players who want to play in the league (and meet the league's requirements) sign up onto a list. Once a year, teams choose players from this list in a predetermined order. This order depends on various factors. The main factor is the teams' sporting performance the previous year. Teams that performed worst are the first ones to select.[10] This structure is meant to balance sporting talent, with weaker teams choosing the most talented rookies. This highly regulated talent selection comes together with contracting rules that limit players' moves across teams for several years. The NFL and NBA largely rely on college sports (and senior high school sports) to develop talent. In contrast, the MLB and NHL rely heavily on minor leagues as well as colleges to develop talent.

5.3　PLAYER RETIREMENT DECISIONS

5.3.1　Evidence on Active Playing Career Length

Most high-profile athletes in team sports have a relatively short playing career. In most team sports, it is rare that an athlete is still playing at the age of 40. Statistics on average playing career and average earnings for professional athletes differ by methodology. One widely quoted set of numbers is in Exhibit 5.4. In this Bleacher Report article, the average active playing career ranges from 3.5 years for the NFL to 8.0 years for EPL.

The studies underlying Exhibit 5.4 differ in years covered and in their definitions of what is an active athlete. For example, a study by the NFL focused only on athletes that were on the active roster at the start of the season, as opposed to a broader sample of NFL players that included those that may have be activated after injuries to players on the squad at the start of the season. The NFL study reported for this more restricted set of players an average playing career of six years as opposed to the 3.5 years reported in the Bleacher Report article.[11] The majority of studies on team-based "athlete playing careers" rarely report average professional career lengths exceeding ten years.

Individual sport athletes vary greatly in their playing career lengths. Olympic athletes in sports such as gymnastics, swimming, and track rarely are over 30 years old. In contrast, many elite athletes over the age of 30 can be found in sports such as golf and equestrian.

5.3.2 The Retirement Decision by an Athlete

One of the most difficult decisions for an athlete to either make or accept relates to retirement from being an active player. For some athletes, a severe injury basically leads to a retirement. In other cases, the decision is "forced" on the athlete when a club cuts the player on a roster or does not renew a contract and no other clubs are willing to add that player to their squads. In both of these cases, the retirement decision is effectively made for the player, regardless of how much that player is willing or unwilling to accept the decision.

Bill Walsh, the NFL Hall of Fame coach, counseled many active athletes on when to retire from being an active athlete. Exhibit 5.5 lists 11 factors Walsh listed as important in retirement decisions of professional athletes. Note that factors in the Walsh list include a mixture of on-field performance, on-field playing options, financial, personal motivation, and availability of post-playing time career options.

The buildup of knowledge about the physical and mental toll in high body impact sports is highlighting the dangers of very extended playing careers in those sports. However, players often are "in denial" about this growing evidence applying to themselves, simply rationalizing that it cannot or will not happen to them. This makes it especially important for leagues and players' association to develop ground rules for protecting players from exposing themselves to further risks of continued playing. This protection could be on a game-by-game basis (such as not allowing a player with concussion to re-enter a game where he has been concussed) or to a "final" retirement decision.

5.4 DECISION MAKING AT PLAYERS' ASSOCIATIONS

5.4.1 Examples of Players' Associations

Players' associations are an important stakeholder in the sports industry. In multiple sports, these player associations negotiate with a league on multiple factors that affect the health and viability of the league itself. Often, the result will be a collective bargaining agreement (CBA). This is an agreement between a league and its players that governs "working conditions." Examples of players' associations include:

- National Football League Players' Associations (NFLPA, formed 1956) – latest CBA covers 2011 to 2020.
- Major League Baseball Players Association (MLBPA, formed 1966 as a labor union) – latest CBA covers 2011 to 2016.

League	Average playing career	Average yearly salary	Average career earnings
NBA	4.8 years	$5.15 million	$24.7 million
MLB	5.6 years	$3.2 million	$17.9 million
NHL	5.5 years	$2.4 million	$13.2 million
NFL	3.5 years*	$1.9 million	$6.7 million
MLS	3.2 years	$0.16 million	$0.5 million
EPL	8.0 years	£0.676 million	£5.4 million

EXHIBIT 5.4 Player Average Active Playing Career and Average Salary
*NFL study based on players on active roster at the start of the season had average playing career of six years.
Source: S. Sandler, "NFL, MLB, NHL, MLS, and NBA: which leagues and players make the most money?" Bleacher Report, March 18, 2012; "Career by numbers: footballer," *The Guardian*, 2010

1   Existing physical health. Ability to retain health if continuing to play.

2   Possible salary offer and potential ability and willingness of club to meet salary level desired by player.

3   Personal desire to continue playing. Is the thrill still there?

4   Ability to handle media pressure if continuing; "old father time" comments.

5   Performance level. Is it declining? Is it competitive?

6   Desire of athlete. Go out on top? Stay on until cut?

7   Coaches'/management's likely intentions to use athlete. Is a transition already being played out?

8   Future prospects for team. Player avoiding the "big regret" if teams goes to top next year.

9   What post-retirement career options are available to athlete? Personal fulfillment? Financial? Has athlete already been planning for next year?

10 Financial capacity of athlete to retire. Fund saved or invested (how secure)? Likely lifestyle demands for cash (himself, family, entourage)?

11 Agent and agent's ability to negotiate future deals.

EXHIBIT 5.5 The Player Retirement Decision: Bill Walsh's Perspective on Factors for Players to Consider

■ National Basketball Players Association (NBPA, formed 1954) – latest CBA covers 2011 to 2021.
■ National Hockey League Players' Association (NHLPA, formed 1967) – latest CBA covers 2013 to 2022.
■ Major League Soccer Players Union (MLSPU, formed 2003) – latest CBA covers 2010 to 2014.

While many smaller leagues around the globe also have counterpart players' associations, they vary greatly in their management depth and their negotiating abilities. Examples of these include:

■ Professional Cricketers' Association (PCA, formed in England in 1967).
■ Rugby Union Players' Association (RUPA, formed in Australia in 1995).
■ South African Jockeys' Association (SAJA, formed in 1958).

FIFPro is the union for 65,000 soccer players around the world with 56 country unions. In contrast to its North American counterparts, FIFPro is just beginning to gain some relevance in the sport.

5.4.2 Key Decisions Where Player Associations Are Central Actors

As regards bargaining dynamics, there are several key issues on which major decisions are made:

Decision #1: Can an agreement be reached without a strike or lockout?

A strike occurs when the players refuse to play under the conditions offered. A lockout occurs when the league/owners shut down the operations on the pretext that the players will not agree to certain conditions that the owners have either offered them or are muted to be offering them. Strikes and lockouts can have severe economic impacts. Exhibit 5.6 outlines strikes and lockouts in four major North American leagues.

League	Year	Stoppage	Length (days)	Games lost	Main issues
NFL	1970	Strike	2	0	Minimum salaries, pensions, health benefits
	1974	Strike	40	0	Free agency, minimum salaries
	1982	Strike	57	0	Percentage of gross proposal
	1987	Strike	24	Other*	Free agency
	2011	Lockout	132	0	Free agency, salary cap, rookie compensation, minimum salaries, franchise tags
	2012	Referee lockout	118	0	Compensation, pensions
MLB	1972	Strike	13	86	Pensions
	1973	Lockout	17	30	Salary arbitration
	1976	Lockout	17	0	Free agency
	1980	Strike	8	0	Free-agent compensation
	1981	Strike	50	712	Free-agent compensation
	1985	Strike	2	0	Salary arbitration
	1990	Lockout	32	0	Salary arbitration and salary cap
	1994–5	Strike	232	920	Salary arbitration and revenue-sharing
NBA	1998–9	Strike	191	928	Salary cap, luxury tax
	2011	Strike	161	240	Salary cap, revenue-sharing
NHL	1992	Strike	10	Other**	Free agency, arbitration, pensions
	1994–95	Lockout	103	448	Salary cap, luxury tax, free agency
	2004–05	Lockout	310	1230	Salary cap, luxury tax, revenue-sharing, reform to league entry-level system
	2012–13	Lockout	119	510	Revenue-sharing, player contracts, free agency

EXHIBIT 5.6 Strikes and Lockouts in the Four North American Leagues
Note: * games played with substitute players; ** games rescheduled.

The 1994/5 MLB strike lasted more than six months and led to the cancellation of the World Series. The 2004/5 NHL lockout led to the cancellation of the whole regular season and the playoff series (see Box 5.1).

BOX 5.1 THE NHL LOCKOUT RESULTS IN THE LOSS OF THE 2004/5 FULL SEASON

Negotiations between the NHL and the NHL Players' Association (NHLPA) have long been contentious. There was a strike by players in 1992 (lasting ten days) and a lockout by owners in 1994/5 (lasting 103 days). A new CBA was on the table starting with the 2004/5 season. For many years, the NHL operated with minimal restrictions on the total player payrolls of individual clubs. Individual clubs competed heavily with each other for talented players. *Forbes* estimated that 20 out the 30 NHL clubs in 2003 were losing money. In February 2004, Arthur Levitt (a former chairman of the Securities and Exchange Commission) released a report that was financially supported by the NHL. The major conclusions of the report were that for the 2002/3 season, the NHL had combined operating revenues of $1,996 million, combined operating losses of $273 million, and player costs ($1,494 million) that were 75 percent of revenues. Not surprisingly, the NHLPA did not accept the numbers presented by the NHL-sponsored study.

For the CBA starting in 2004/5, the NHL owners wanted to implement a salary cap regime akin to what was operating in the NFL. A salary cap was strongly opposed by the NHLPA. In September 2004, NHL commissioner Gary Bettman announced a lockout, arguing that the financial stability of the NHL required the "cost certainty" that he argued came with a salary cap. In December 2004, the NHLPA led by Bob Goodenow offered a rollback in player salaries but refused to agree to a salary cap. After many failed efforts to bring the two sides together, Bettman announced in February 2005 the cancellation of the whole season. This was a first for the NHL. In July 2005, a new CBA was agreed to that included a salary cap with upper and lower limits on club player payrolls. Player salaries were set to be 57 percent of league revenues when determining the annual salary cap.

The 2014/15 period saw multiple ten-year reviews of the 2004/5 lockout. Comments from a *Grantland* article by S. McIndoe[12] included:

- **Salary cap.** The 2014/15 salary cap was $69 million compared to $39 million for the 2005/6 season. "By any reasonable measure, the [salary cap] system has worked as designed. The owners have their cost certainty, and the big markets can no longer dominate."
- **Franchise stability.** Only one club relocated post the 2004/5 (Atlanta Thrashers to Winnipeg) compared to four in the prior decade. "The hopes here have largely been realized … The Atlanta Thrashers situation was likely unsalvageable under any system."
- **Competitive balance.** Seven different clubs won the Stanley Cup in the first seven years after the 2004/5 lockout. "Overall there does seem to be more parity."
- **Player salaries.** The unintended negative consequence according to McIndoe was players negotiating excessively longer contracts that extended well beyond their likely playing years – "with their annual earnings artificially restrained, players found themselves asking for longer-term deals. And the teams gave in … Soon, contracts for star players were stretching into double-digit years … The situation became so bad that the league tried to institute a five-year limit … The league ended up settling [in the 2012 CBA] for an eight-year limit, which has become the de facto standard for star players."

The 2012/13 NHL season started with a repeat of the 2004/5 season, a lockout by owners. This third lockout resulted in the season being reduced from 82 games to 48 games. A key part of the new CBA was a further reduction of the percentage of total player payroll to total NHL revenues from 57 percent to approximately 50 percent. This further reduction sizably increased the profitability of the 30 NHL clubs.

Each of these four leagues has had multiple strikes or lockouts. The MLS Players Union threatened to strike in 2010, but signed a CBA days before the start of the 2010 regular season.

While there are multiple factors leading to the various strikes and lockouts, salary and revenue-sharing issues are typically central. Often where the players' association and a league are far apart in their negotiating positions, an arbitrator may be appointed in an attempt to bring the parties together. Moreover, in some cases politicians may insert themselves in the negotiations for either genuine or grandstanding reasons.

Decision #2: Should there be constraints on club total player payrolls, individual player payrolls, and player age minimums?

Chapter 3 highlighted the importance many leagues place on having maximum constraints on either club total player payrolls or on individual player salaries. Players' associations typically have opposed such constraints or sought to negotiate much looser constraints than the leagues propose in negotiations. These associations are more likely to support constraints or minimum total or individual player payments. The CBAs that several players' associations have negotiated include minimum age requirements – such as one year beyond high school for the NBA and three years beyond high school for the NFL.

Box 5.2 outlines the differing positions of the heads of the NBPA and the NBA/owners as regards key foundations of their existing CBA. In many sports negotiations, parties will put out statements that subsequently end up as extreme positions that are compromised in the final CBA.

BOX 5.2 NEWLY APPOINTED HEAD OF NBPA ATTACKS KEY FOUNDATIONS OF PRIOR COLLECTIVE BARGAINING AGREEMENTS[13]

From 1996 to 2013 Billy Hunter was executive director of the National Basketball Players Association (NBPA) and had negotiated several CBAs where salary caps were a foundation of the agreement. In 2013, a committee of NBA players unanimously voted to end Hunter's role as head of the NBPA. In July 2014, Michele Roberts was appointed as the new head of the NBPA. She came from outside the sport, having been a successful trial lawyer. She was the first woman union head of a major North American male players' association. Her early statements challenged the very foundations of many prior CBAs in the NBA and multiple other leagues. In a November 2014 interview she stated:

I don't know of any space other than the world of sports where there's this notion that we will artificially deflate what someone's able to make just because ... It's incredibly un-American. My DNA is offended by it. I can't understand why the [NBPA] would be interested in suppressing salaries at the top if we know that as salaries at the top have grown, so have salaries at the bottom. I contend that there is no reason why the union should embrace salary caps or any effort to place a barrier on the amount of money that marquee players can make.

Roberts also took issue with the minimum constraints on player age in the current CBA that Hunter had negotiated. There was a minimum age of 19 or at least one year of college after high school. Adam Silver, the new commissioner of the NBA had proposed further increasing the minimum age to 20. Roberts stated:

It doesn't make sense to me that you're suddenly eligible and ready to make new money when you're 20, but not when you're 19, not when you're 18. I suspect that the association will not agree that this is not going to be one that they will agree to easily. There is no other profession that says you're old enough to die but not old enough to play.

Roberts also suggested shortening the regular season, which would have negative effects on club revenues:

Every time a player gets hurt, I think, my God, they really are pushing their bodies. And back-to-backs, those are the ones I really find disturbing. So the answer, of course, is that everybody wants a shorter season. The tension is "will that mean less money?" And that's something we need to talk about and think about. I don't think it would hurt the game to shorten the season.

To no great surprise the NBA/owners disagreed strongly with Roberts' statements and even choose to issue a press release that included the following:

We couldn't disagree more with these statements. The NBA's success is based on the collective efforts and investments of all the team owners, the thousands of employees at our teams and arenas, and our extraordinarily talented players. No single group could accomplish this on its own. Nor is there anything unusual or "un-American" in a unionized industry to have a collective system for paying employees – in fact, that's the norm.

These opinions by the heads of the two main parties to the next CBA negotiations suggest there is a sizable gap to be closed between the NBPA and the NBA/owners before an agreement is reached.

Decision # 3: What is the revenue-sharing between the players and the league/owner?

Exhibit 2.3 of Chapter 2 presented some general patterns for both North American Leagues and European soccer leagues. The average percentage of estimated total player compensation to estimated total revenues in the four seasons from the 2011/14 period for the four North American leagues and 2011/13 for the five EPL leagues are:

NFL	MLB	NBA	NHL
42%	43%	47%	52%

England	Germany	Spain	Italy	France
70%	52%	58%	73%	72%

These percentages should be viewed as approximations as some are based on third-party estimates. However, they do highlight how the four North American leagues, where there are CBAs that constrain salaries, have lower average percentages of total revenues going to their players than do the five major European soccer leagues. European soccer leagues operate with much more adherence to a free-market approach to player compensation.

Decision #4: What protocols should be put in place to protect player health and welfare?

A prime responsibility of a players' association is taking a lead on protecting the health and welfare of their players. There are many aspects here. It can relate to on-field aspects such as equipment, penalties for dangerous play, and restrictions on injured /concussed players re-entering a game in which that injury/concussion occurred. It can also relate to off-field areas such as developing minimum standards for agents to be registered as able to represent players, and developing programs to help current players better prepare for their post-playing careers.

5.5 PLAYERS BEHAVING BADLY

5.5.1 Examples of Misbehavior

Leagues and players' associations continually are faced with player behavior issues that at a minimum attract negative press and in some cases result in arrests and subsequent convictions.

Below is a categorization of potential "athlete behaving badly" situations:

- Legal violations – such as driving under the influence, rape, partner physical abuse, or even murder.
- League-rule violations that may not be legal violations – such as a player taking drugs that are permitted to be taken in a region but precluded from use by a league (such as an NFL player in Denver or Seattle smoking marijuana).
- Club or coach rule/edict violations – such as a player consistently turning up for practice late, or not abiding by a NFL club rule that women are not permitted in hotel rooms the night before a game.
- Societal norm violations. This is a difficult area, as societal norms can vary across segments of society and over time. One example here was a coach who fined several players who turned up late for an agreed appearance at a charity fundraiser and then behaved in a way several sponsors viewed as "unacceptable" (such as not interacting with invited guests and not being willing to have photos taken with the invited guests). As mentioned, societal norms are ever-changing especially with breakthroughs in modern technology and increased usage of social media. Social media has forced many leagues to create rules against usage during game time, as well as educational programs involving "safe" social media usage.

5.5.2 Disciplinary Procedures

Two areas of continual debate between leagues and player associations are:

1 What procedures to take when allegations of player misbehavior occur. Included here are cases that involve the police where an arrest is made but no court case has occurred. There are differences

across leagues in whether the final decision on penalties is made by a league commissioner or an independent panel.

2   What levels of penalties to impose. One procedure is to outline in advance penalties for different behaviors and the consequence of repeat violations. An alternative procedure is to allow the person/panel deciding to have maximum flexibility as to penalties.

Given the high level of societal attention to player misbehaviors, there is a premium on having predictability and transparency in the both the disciplinary process and in the likely penalties of different player actions. There is also a premium on both leagues and players' associations making concerted efforts to not only have programs for athletes addressing these issues, but to also make concerted efforts to have those programs be effective. There is increasing recognition that leadership from players themselves can be very effective in making potential "at-risk players" better understand the consequences of their possible actions and the responsibilities they have to their other players, their club, and the league in which they play.

5.6 THE ROLES OF AN AGENT IN THE SPORTS BUSINESS

Agents are another actor in the business of professional sports. Ideally, agents complement athletes and often coaches in managing their business interests and often other aspects of their lives that require the voice of experience and knowledge. They can potentially be mentors, business representatives, and advisors. On the business side, the agent negotiates on behalf of the player about the economic conditions within the contracting rules of the particular sport. The relationship between a player and a team, if it is a team sport, or between the player and the sports community (events, fans, or sponsors) goes beyond a one-off meeting. The agent not only has to balance getting the best economic deal for the player, but also the long-term career ramifications of the contract. These considerations may include the fit of the player within the team, the impact of the athlete's actions on fans and sponsors, or how to best set up the athlete for the next round of negotiations for a future contract. Exhibit 5.7 describes the possible roles of an agent.

Sports services	Business services	Personal services
• Market the player to find the best team given the characteristics and preferences of the player • Negotiate contracts with teams including compensation, transfer fee, and duration • Negotiate appearance fees with events • Communicate with team managers • Assist the player to make informed career choices	• Identify licensing, endorsement and sponsorship opportunities for the player • Manage relationships with the media • Build and activate the player's brand through appearances in non-sporting events • Public relations • Manage the player's professional agenda • Manage social media presence	• Wealth management • Tax filing • Support the player with personal needs ranging from buying a home to moving around a foreign country • Legal work

EXHIBIT 5.7 Multiple Potential Roles of an Agent in the Sports World

There are differing viewpoints on how many of the roles in Exhibit 5.7 should be performed by a single agent. Wealth management is one area that has been identified by many as warranting a separate advisor distinct from the agent.

The business aspect includes endorsements, sponsorships, public relations activities, and building the player's brand. Oftentimes, agents for top-level athletes work with third parties who provide expertise on these aspects. Managing all the economic possibilities of star athletes is a challenging process, as is maintaining the balance between the playing and business interests.

An important element of the agent–athlete relationship is that sporting careers are often short and agents and players do not want to leave money on the table. However, many times a player's sporting preferences do not align perfectly with their (or their agent's) business interests. In order to maximize their revenue in a competitive environment, athletes and their agents must sometimes make concessions in return for less salary, such as job security, potential overall long-term value of the contract, or opportunities for marketing revenue external to the contract. An example of this is the 2014 contract of Andy Dalton (quarterback) with the Cincinnati Bengals of the NFL. Dalton signed a lucrative six-year, $115 million deal, with $22 million guaranteed. While this contract on the surface seems like a good one for Dalton, Dalton and his agent actually gave up a considerable amount of job security (guaranteed salary) in return for a potentially more lucrative contract. Contracts in the NFL are not fully guaranteed. Dalton's contract contains all of his guaranteed $22 million within the first year of the deal, making it essentially a one-year deal, with the club having the option to "pay as you go" based on Dalton's performance for the following years. Thus, if he performs, he will earn more salary, but if he does not or is injured, he will not be paid. The Cincinnati Bengals would likely view the front-ending in year one of the guaranteed amount as attractive as it insulates the Bengals from poor player performance by giving them the option to terminate the contract whenever they like with little financial impact, while still having the structure in place to reward exceptional performance. Box 6.1 in Chapter 6 provides one of the extreme examples of a player and his high-profile agent accepting a contract laden with unlikely-to-achieve incentives that (*ex post*) was beneficial to the New Orleans Saints.

Box 5.3 describes the issue of gender and player salaries in tennis, while Box 5.4 outlines a recent dispute around players' salaries in the Ultimate Fighting Championship.

BOX 5.3 GENDER EQUITY AND TENNIS PLAYERS' SALARIES

In 2007, Wimbledon finally relented its long-held policy of higher prize money for men and joined the other three tennis majors in awarding the same prize money for men's and women's events. The US Open was an early adopter of equal pay in 1973. In 2001, the Australian Open adopted this policy. In 2006, the French Open awarded the same prize money for men's and women's singles and in 2007 expanded this to all of its events.

Wimbledon had long defended its differential pay policy. For example, in 1999, the Chairman of Wimbledon commented:

We do surveys of all the people who come on a regular basis and, in three surveys over the past 10 years, 70% of the people say that first and foremost the thing they want to watch is men's singles. The women have every right to request, but to demand [equal pay] I think it is hurtful and damaging to Wimbledon. It implies that we treat them unfairly and that's obviously not true from the evidence. I think that the players enjoy playing Wimbledon and the prize money is only a small portion of their income.[14]

In a 2014 interview, Stacey Allaster, CEO of the WTA, gave insight into the lobbying behind Wimbledon's change in policy:

The women's prize money was at 93 percent of [men's] pay in 2006. We launched a public opinion campaign in France and Britain. We presented the data that showed our sponsorship revenues were very strong. We had a strong political campaign in business leaders like Richard Branson. Tessa Jowell, the minister of sport in Britain, was able to get [prime minister] Tony Blair on the House of Commons floor to say that Wimbledon should pay equal prize money. Our ace was Venus Williams. On the eve of the Wimbledon finals in 2007, Larry Scott [then CEO of the WTA] said to Venus, "I'd like you to talk to the All England committee about equal prize money. I'm just a suit." Venus, with her gift of diplomacy, was able to bring it over the line.[15]

Some male players continue to express opposition to the equal prize money policy. For example, Gilles Simon, a French professional player, was quoted as saying that "male players spent twice as long on court" at major championships and that "equality in salaries isn't something that works in sport. Men's tennis remains more attractive than women's tennis at the moment."[16] When pushed to explain his comments further, he later responded:

I am for equal pay in life, but not in entertainment. It's not about how hard you work. It's about the show. I believe men's tennis is more interesting than women's tennis. You have to be paid on that basis ... We have equal prize money because women's tennis at the time was as interesting as the men. Unfortunately most of those women stopped.

Simon has also pointed to the different prices for tickets to the men's and women's finals at majors to support his view.

In 2014, the BBC conducted a study of 35 global sports where men and women compete for prize money.[17] It reported that 25 sports pay equally and ten do not. Sports with the biggest disparity in prize money include:

- Football World Cup – men's (£22 million) versus women's (£0.63 million)
- Football Association Cup (England) – men's (£1.8 million) versus women's (£0.005 million)
- Cricket World Cup – men's (£2.5 million) versus women's (£0.047 million)
- Surfing World Champs tour – men's (£0.062 million) versus Women's (£0.037 million)

The Football Association was quoted as strongly defending its differential in prize money by saying that men's and women's football are incomparable, describing them as "polar opposites" in global reach. Kelly Simmons, the FA's director of the national game and women's football, said in 2014: "The men's game is a huge multi million pound industry so when you compare it to the women's game, which until three or four years ago was played by amateurs, the gulf is enormous."[18]

BOX 5.4 UFC MONOPOLIZATION ALLEGATIONS AND FIGHTER PAYMENTS

A key issue at the forefront of the sport industry relates to the assessment of the fair market value of athletes and the value they bring to the leagues that they participate in. For superstars, from LeBron James of the Cleveland Cavaliers to Sidney Crosby of the Pittsburgh Penguins, an informed argument can be made that they are worth much more to their leagues than their compensation currently dictates. Often salaries are restrained by salary caps or other league-wide regulations. Without these constraints, certain top-level athletes could potentially make much more money than they currently do. This issue is typified in a current legal dispute between the Ultimate Fighting Championship (UFC) and mixed martial arts athletes Jon Fitch, Nate Quarry, and Cung Le. In a lawsuit filed in December 2014, the fighters argue that the UFC is using its alleged monopoly power in mixed martial arts to suppress fighter payments. Specific allegations made in the lawsuit were publicly reported by one of the fighters' lawyers as follows:

The lawsuit alleges that the UFC has engaged in an illegal scheme to eliminate competition from rival MMA promoters by systematically preventing rivals from gaining access to ingredients critical to successful MMA promotions, including by imposing extreme restrictions on UFC fighters' ability to fight for rivals during and after their tenure with the UFC ... The UFC also takes the rights to fighters' names and likenesses in perpetuity. As a result of the UFC's scheme, we allege that UFC fighters are paid fraction of what they would earn in a competitive marketplace.[19]

The success of UFC inevitably has attracted an ongoing number of competitors, several of which appear to have relatively deep pockets. For example, Viacom – the parent company of CBS – acquired a majority interested in Bellator Fighting Championship in October 2011. Bellator subsequently has appeared on Viacom's cable channel, Spike TV. In February 2013, World Series of Fighting signed a three-year agreement with NBC Sports Network. The increased presence of Spike TV and NBC Sports Network has increased competition levels in the mixed martial arts market for fighters.

5.7 SUMMARY

This chapter outlines professional athletes and their unions/associations, including content on the main issues, decisions, and business aspects facing these two stakeholders. The chapter focuses primarily on professional athletes, with particular attention on the major sports. Specific detail on the payroll decisions in professional teams sports follows in Chapter 6.

NOTES

1 Club payroll numbers are taken from *USA Today*. Club revenue numbers are from estimates made by *Forbes*.
2 *Deloitte Annual Review of Football Finance*, June 2014.
3 www.footballaustralia.com website. See also "A-League clubs to see slight salary cap raise under new pay deal," ABC.net.au, June 30, 2013.
4 Altiusdirectory.com, WNBA Salaries 2015.

5 "Financial fair play: all you need to know," UEFA.com, February 28, 2014.

6 www.forbes.com/sites/kurtbadenhausen/2013/02/20/floyd-mayweather-hits-jackpot-with-new-showtime-ppv-deal.

7 It is not unusual for FIFA regulations to have to "accommodate" country/trading block labor laws. For instance, FIFA has been toying with the "6 + 5" rule where six of the players at the beginning of a game should be players eligible to play in the national team. The objective was to strengthen the national teams, forcing teams from the country to have players getting exposure to top level competition. Yet, the rule goes against labor laws in Europe, where workers with EU nationalities can work in any EU country without restrictions.

8 FIFA regulates the allocation of transfer money to the teams involved in bringing up a player. The original team has the right to a training compensation fee estimated based on the years the player has been at the club, the categories at which he played, and the ratio of players trained per professional player.

9 Transfer is granted if the transfer is for "non-football"-related reasons.

10 The NFL operates mechanically, with clubs selecting in the reverse order of their win–loss record of the prior season. In contrast, the NBA uses a lottery system for the first several picks that results in the lowest performing club in the prior year not automatically having the first draft pick.

11 "What is the average NFL player's career length? Longer than you might think, Commissioner Goodell says," NFL press release, April 18, 2011.

12 S. McIndoe, "The day the NHL died: how far have we come since the cancelled 2005 season?" *Grantland*, February 12, 2015.

13 The quotations in Box 5.2 are taken from P.S. Torre, "NBPA director: 'Let's stop pretending,'" ESPN, November 13, 2014.

14 "Wimbledon confirm move to prize money equality," *The Guardian*, February 22, 2007.

15 J. McGregor, "How women's tennis fought for equal pay," The Washington Post (September 5, 2014).

16 G. Moore, "Gilles Simon has another swipe at women… after losing," *The Independent*, June 29, 2012.

17 A. Thompson and A. Lewis, "Men get more prize money than women in 30 percent of sports," BBC Sports, October 28, 2014.

18 "www.hrcareer.net.au/news/few-game-to-fix-sports-gender-pay-gap"

19 T. Critchfield, "Class-action lawsuit filed against UFC by Cung Le, Jon Fitch, Nate Quarry," *Sherdog*, December 16, 2014.

CLUB PLAYER-SIDE DECISION MAKING

6.1 MULTIPLE INVESTMENT AND EXPENDITURE AREAS ON THE CLUB PLAYER-SIDE

The central product of sporting leagues, clubs, and events is the athletes and their competition. Underlying this product is often a large infrastructure and investment by sporting clubs and individual sport teams. Exhibit 6.1 outlines five decision areas where key investments are made relating to the player side of a club or team.

- **People:** While the on-field players attract most attention, multiple other people play a central role. Titles used by executives making player-related decisions are far from consistent. The phrase "general manager" will be used to refer to the executive(s) who make decisions about which players to contract for a club or renew. These contracts often have a multi-year time horizon. The term "coach" will be used to refer to the executive(s) who make decisions as regards who plays on a day-by-day basis.[1] An important growth area is analytics, where individuals with the ability to systematically analyze data and draw reliable inferences are playing important roles in club decision making.
- **Equipment:** Sports vary greatly in the equipment arena. Sports such as basketball and soccer are light in "game-day" equipment, relative to say NFL and college football and motor sports such as Formula 1 and NASCAR. Training and medical equipment is an area where advances can often come with high price tags.
- **Travel:** The geographic spread of a sport is one factor that affects the level of expenditure in the travel arena, as well as whom and what is transported. A global sport such as Formula 1 has extremely high travel costs. It has events in many continents and requires the shipment of multiple cars and other equipment as well as the drivers and their large teams. In high-revenue leagues, many clubs now use private charters for travel at a higher cost than regular airlines. One benefit here is that the players and coaches can travel as soon as they are ready, rather than fitting into commercial flight schedules. Lower-revenue sports, such as Minor League Baseball, have players travel on buses and stay in lower-cost hotels with much lower daily allowances.

People	Equipment	Travel	Technology	Facilities
Players	Player equipment	Accommodation	Hardware/devices	GM facilities
General manager	Training equipment	Transit to home	Software	Coach facilities
Head coach	Coaching equipment	Flights	Data acquisition	Assistant/specialty
Assistant coaches	Scouting equipment	Buses	Data	coach facilities
Specialty coaches	Analytics tools	On-Road incidentals:	analysis: expertise	Player facilities
Scouts	Medical equipment	per diems, food,	Data	Trainer facilities
Trainers	Hardware	taxis, etc.	analysis: software	Medical facilities
Medical staff	Game-day equipment	Scouting travel and	Data	Sport science
Recovery staff		incidentals	analysis: sampling	facilities
Team operations		Scheduling	Data analysis:	Exercise facilities
Sport scientists		Customs (if border	storage	Playing facilities
Analytics		crossed)		Recovery facilities

EXHIBIT 6.1 Some Key Decision Areas for Playing-Squad Side of Sporting Club

- **Technology:** A rapidly expanding cost area for many leagues and clubs is technology. For example, the NBA has installed multiple cameras in each NBA arena that provides data-feeds about all player and ball movements. This extensive additional data feed has spawned further investment by clubs in data analytics people and software. Tracking players in-game and training body movements and health has been facilitated by new investment in "wearables clothing." This type of clothing transmits data for devices to track and analyze (see Section 6.6.4). Safety is also being facilitated by equipment such as smart helmets that measure the impacts of hits on the head of a player.
- **Facilities:** The diversity across clubs and events in facilities for their athletes and support can be extreme. In the high revenue sports, investments of $20–50 million in new "training facilities" are occurring. In some cases, clubs are even offering sponsors naming rights to their training facilities – such as the MasterCard Centre for Hockey Excellence of the Toronto Maple Leafs (NHL) and the Atlantic Health Jets Training Center of the New York Jets (NFL). In sports such as equestrian, horse polo, and thoroughbred racing, there are "back-end" multimillion-dollar facilities housing the horses, which themselves may have cost or be valued in the millions.

This chapter examines some major decisions in these areas, recognizing that the overall topic is very broad and we can only highlight key decisions in several of these areas. Much emphasis will be given to decisions related to player compensation and analytics.

6.2 CLUB PLAYING-SQUAD TOTAL PAYROLL DECISION MAKING

Total player payroll decision making can be viewed as a multi-year portfolio challenge where a club's playing squad is viewed as a collection of individual player assets in the same way that an investment portfolio is built up from investments in individual stocks, bonds, and other assets. Increasingly, the emphasis is on examining the value to a portfolio that different athletes can bring. Value assessment here includes the expected costs incurred (salary, training support, etc.) as well as ability to contribute to winning and other aspects of a team (such as culture and reputation). Most individual player contracts are for multiple years rather than just for one year ahead. Total player payroll decisions in this arena have three critical areas – size, mix, and time horizon.

6.2.1 Size of Total Club Player Payrolls in a Specific Year

Exhibit 6.2 presents the estimates of the average club player payrolls for four North American leagues (NFL, MLB, NBA, and NHL) and five European soccer leagues (English Premier League, German Bundesliga, Spanish La Liga, Italian Serie A, and French Ligue 1).

Examples of average club payrolls from Exhibit 6.2 are:

League	2000	2004	2008	2012	2013
NFL	$75.4 million	$76.9 million	$100.8 million	$111.0 million	$122.3 million
MLB	$55.8 million	$69.0 million	$89.5 million	$98.0 million	$103.6 million
EPL	€16.20 million	€22.50 million	€30.95 million	€42.05 million	€43.10 million

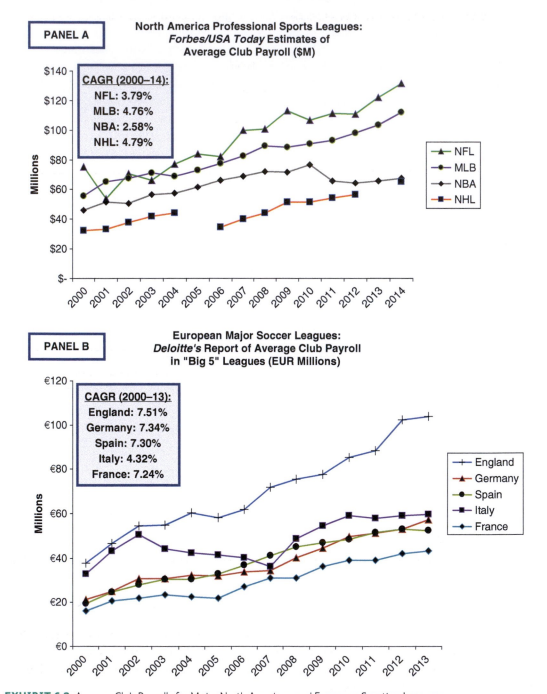

EXHIBIT 6.2 Average Club Payrolls for Major North American and European Sporting Leagues

While average player payrolls in the nine leagues in Exhibit 6.2 have increased over the 2000/13 period, there is not always a consistent year-to-year increase in each league.

Leagues differ in the variation across clubs in their average payrolls. Exhibit 6.3 shows the ranking of clubs by their 2014 team payroll for the four major North American leagues, and the 2013 payrolls for the top two English soccer leagues (the English Premier League and the Football Championship

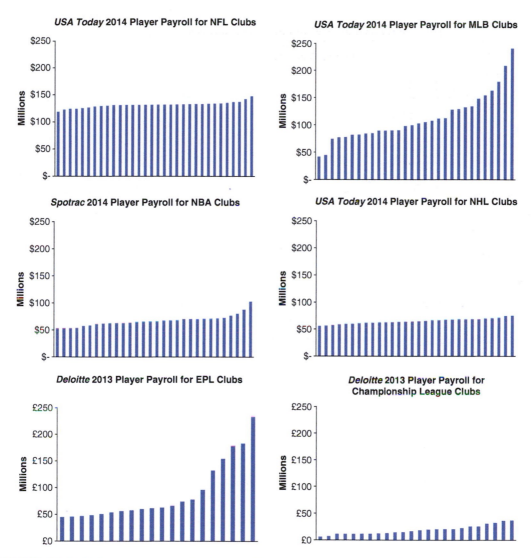

EXHIBIT 6.3 North America 4 League 2014 versus EPL and Championship League 2013 Club Player Payroll Plot Comparisons

League). A caution here: what third parties such as USA Today estimates for club payrolls can differ from what clubs report to their league using the "payroll accounting" rules of the league.

The highest and lowest club payrolls in each league for 2014 and the ratio of the highest to lowest payrolls for the North American leagues are:

League	Highest 2014 payroll	Lowest 2014 payroll	Ratio
NFL	$147 million (Buffalo Bills)	$118 million (New York Jets)	1.25
MLB	$241 million (LA Dodgers)	$41 million (Miami Marlins)	5.88

League	Highest 2014 payroll	Lowest 2014 payroll	Ratio
NBA	$102 million (Brooklyn Nets)	$53 million (Orlando Magic)	1.92
NHL	$75 million (Dallas Stars)	$56 million (Ottawa Senators)	1.34

Soccer leagues around the world likewise show large differences both across leagues and between the highest and lowest club payrolls in each league. La Liga in Spain has two dominant high payroll clubs. For the 2013/14 season, Real Madrid was #1 at €220 million (Barcelona was €195 million). Four clubs in La Liga were estimated to have payrolls of €11–14 million (including Levante – estimated at €12.5 million). The two highest leagues in England are the English Premier League (EPL, 20 clubs) and Football Championship League (24 clubs). The highest payroll club in the EPL in 2012/13 is more than six times the highest payroll club in the Championship League.

League	Highest 2013 Payroll	Lowest 2013 Payroll	Ratio
La Liga	€220 million (Real Madrid)	€12.5 million (Levante)	17.60
EPL	£233.11million (Manchester City)	£45.29 million (Wigan Athletic)	5.15
Championship	£37.42 million (Bolton Wanderers)	£6.21 million (Peterborough United)	6.03

With soccer leagues in most countries, many leagues operate with no club having a total payroll more than $1 million.

6.2.2 Mix of Total Club Payroll in a Specific Year

Large differences across clubs in a given league can often be observed in the mix of player salaries. Examples include:

- Percentage of total payroll taken by the highest paid player, top two paid players, top three paid players, etc. Consider the NBA in 2014 using Spotrac.com as the database. Examples of differences in the percentage of total payroll paid to the top paid player in 2014 are:[2]

Team (player percentage – player name)	
New York Knicks (41.1 percent – Carmelo Anthony)	Los Angeles Lakers (30.8 percent – Kobe Bryant)
Miami Heat (28.2 percent – Chris Bosch)	Oklahoma City (27.1 percent – Kevin Durant)
Golden State Warriors (20.7 percent – David Lee)	Philadelphia 76ers (15.0 percent – Jason Richardson)

- Higher percentages are typically associated with the highest paid player being one of the elite players in the league. They can also reflect some ex-elite players at the back end of their careers who had signed long-term contracts at very high salaries before they had a more recent decline in performance. There is a large "key man" risk when one or two players dominate the total player payroll. Injuries, loss of form, or loss of passion can result in those key players becoming minimal or even non-contributors, leaving the club with much less available payroll to recruit other players or retain current important contributors.

■ Percentage of total payroll taken by each position area. Consider the NFL in 2015. Examples of differences in the percentage of total payroll paid to the highest paid quarterback are:

Team (player percentage – player name)

Dallas Cowboys (19.1 percent – Tony Romo)   Denver Broncos (14.5 percent – Payton Manning)

Green Bay Packers (12.2 percent – Aaron Rodgers)   New England Patriots (9.4 percent – Tom Brady)

Indianapolis Colts (4.7 percent – Andrew Luck)   New York Jets (0.9 percent – Geno Smith)

Seattle Seahawks (0.6 percent – Russell Wilson)

■ These differences can reflect multiple factors, including differences in expected contributions to winning, differences in years since being drafted (due to a rookie salary cap), and differences in the importance clubs give to the quarterback position.

The literature on investment portfolio risk management provides useful lessons for sporting club salary risk management. Investment managers frequently look at factors affecting the diversification of the portfolio. A portfolio that is 90 percent invested in a single oil stock is very exposed to large losses if that stock declines (and very large profits if that stock increases). Having a broader base of individual assets in a portfolio means a lower downside risk to the returns of the portfolio. As noted above, a sporting club that heavily skews a very high percentage of the total payroll to one or two players is increasing its risk profile.

6.2.3 Time Horizon of Contracts

There are often dramatic differences across clubs within a given league as to the number of players on "long-term" contracts and the extent to which they commit a club to large expenditures for many years in advance. Exhibit 6.4 illustrates how the Los Angeles Kings in the NHL greatly differ from four other NHL clubs in the extent of their total payroll in future years being already committed. The NHL operates with a salary cap maximum ($69 million in 2014) and a salary cap floor ($51 million in 2014).

Exhibit 6.4 shows the number of NHL players in five clubs that have contracts in 2014 that extend beyond 2018. The Kings have eight players on contracts extending beyond 2018, at average annual payments from $4 million to $7 million. This represents a very large percentage of the total payroll committed many years into the future. The Kings won the Stanley Cup in 2011/12 and 2013/14 and have adopted a strategy of retaining many key members of their squad for multiple years out. This comes at a sizable loss in flexibility in later years, with many contracts extending five years beyond winning the 2013/14 Stanley Cup. The small number of long-term contracts in 2014 signed by each of the Anaheim Ducks, San Jose Sharks, Toronto Maple Leafs, and Vancouver Canucks highlights the relatively extreme long-term commitment to a set number of players that underlies the Los Angeles Kings total player payroll planning. A caveat here is that the Kings can trade players under long-term contracts. However, the trade value of an aging, lower-performing player at the back-end of a long-term contract often is much lower than on that player's contract.

Team	Player	Age	Average salary ($M)	Contract expiration year
Los Angeles Kings	Drew Doughty	25	$7.000	2019
	Slava Voynov	25	$4.166	2019
	Jacob Muzzin	26	$4.000	2020
	Marian Gaborik	33	$4.875	2021
	Alec Martinez	27	$4.000	2021
	Jeff Carter	30	$5.272	2022
	Dustin Brown	30	$5.875	2022
	Jonathan Quick	29	$5.800	2023
Anaheim Ducks	Corey Perry	29	$8.625	2022
	Ryan Getziaf	29	$8.250	2021
San Jose Sharks	Logan Couture	25	$6.000	2019
	Joe Pavelski	30	$6.000	2019
	Justin Braun	28	$3.800	2020
Toronto Maple Leafs	David Clarkson	30	$5.250	2020
	Dion Phaneuf	29	$7.000	2021
	Philip Kessel	27	$8.000	2022
Vancouver Canucks	Alexander Edler	28	$5.000	2019

EXHIBIT 6.4 Player Contracts in 2014 Extending Beyond 2014/18 for Five Selected NHL Clubs

6.2.4 A Value Perspective of Individual Players in a Portfolio

The portfolio approach to total player payroll planning highlights that even the most talented player has to be evaluated on a value basis as there is an opportunity cost to overpaying for talent. Astute payroll management seeks to identify players that are undervalued by the market, providing the opportunity to increase the aggregate talent in a club at a lower cost. The growing use of analytics has sought innovative ways of assessing talent with greater focus on seeking the most reliable evidence about: (a) the relative contribution of different areas of talent to winning, (b) the likely possession of different aspects of talent by individual athletes, and (c) the expected cost of acquiring different levels of talent.

6.3 KEY ASPECTS OF PLAYER CONTRACTS

Player contracts over time have become increasingly complex, in part due to CBA agreements themselves becoming increasingly complex. Some key concepts are:

■ **Guaranteed contracts.** In a guaranteed contract for a player, the other side of the contract (such as a club or a sponsor) takes the risk that the player will remain playing at the expected level for the duration of the contract. Player contracts in MLB have this feature. When an MLB club signs a player to a seven-year contract for a total of $126 million, they are required to pay the full $126 million irrespective of the players' subsequent performance, health, or attitude. In some leagues, player contracts are not fully guaranteed. When an NFL club announces a five-year player contract for a total amount of $40 million, that player is not guaranteed to receive the full $40 million. If the club wants to cut the player after year one, yearly payments for years two to five are not guaranteed and need not be paid. This inherently creates more financial risk to the player. However, as noted below, one response by players and their agents in this non-fully guaranteed contract setting has been to negotiate a higher percentage of the contract as guaranteed payments.

- **Signing bonus.** Player contracts for highly demanded players often include an up-front signing bonus. This bonus is an especially important component when the player contracts are not guaranteed over the life of the contract. By giving a bonus, the club also pays the player immediately (in most cases), which is typically a financial advantage to the player and the agent. In the NFL, players (and their agents) attempt to increase the percentage of the player contract that is classified as a signing bonus or guaranteed to insulate the player as much as possible from the risk of performance below expectation or injury. For example, in 2013 Aaron Rodgers, the quarterback of the NFL's Green Bay Packers, signed a five-year $110 million contract. *Spotrac* reported that the signing bonus was $33.25 million and that $54 million was guaranteed.[3]
- **Rookie salaries/contracts.** A recent evolution in professional sport contracting has been the advent of the rookie salary, whereby a rookie salary is capped or, in some cases, set by their draft order. For example, the NBA Rookie Salary Scale is a function of both rank in the draft pick and years in the NBA:[4]

Draft pick #	1st year salary	2nd year salary	3rd year salary
1	$4.592 million	$4.798 million	$5.005 million
2	$4.108 million	$4.293 million	$4.478 million
10	$1.998 million	$2.088 million	$2.178 million
20	$1.215 million	$1.27 million	$1.324 million
30	$0.911 million	$0.952 million	$0.993 million

For elite rookies, these rookie salaries are well below those that they could have commanded with an open market for all potential and current players.

- **Performance bonuses.** Star players and higher-risk players often have contracts that are laden with performance bonuses. In the case of the star player, this could include a cash award if they are named the most valuable player or if the team qualifies for the post-season or wins a championship. In the case of a risky player – perhaps a player late in their career or a player coming off an injury – the performance bonuses often are paired with a low (or very low) base salary to protect the club from the player not performing or getting reinjured. Box 6.1 highlights the downside to the player of the heavy incentive-based NFL contract signed by Ricky Williams, a Heisman Award-winning running back from the University of Texas.

- **Transfer fees.** When players under contract move from one team to another, the teams often exchange other aspects beyond just the player moving. North American leagues often limit the amount of money that teams can transfer to emphasize other assets such as other players or draft picks. In other parts of the world, notably in soccer, teams exchange money to buy and sell the contracts of players. A player's contract specifies the amount of money that the team receives if another team wants to buy a player under contract. For instance, Messi, one of the best players in the world, who has spent his entire professional career at FC Barcelona, has a clause in his contract specifying that if another team wants to hire Messi, it will need to pay FC Barcelona €250 million. This amount will get Messi to another team without the need for FC Barcelona to agree to the transfer. In most cases, the buying and the selling team negotiate a transfer fee lower than the amount in the clause.

BOX 6.1 RICKY WILLIAMS OPTS FOR A HIGH INCENTIVE-LADEN CONTRACT WITH THE NFL'S NEW ORLEANS SAINTS BUT EARNS LESS THAN 20 PERCENT OF THE NOMINAL $68 MILLION CONTRACT AMOUNT

Ricky Williams was a star running back at the University of Texas in the late 1990s. A Heisman Trophy winner, he was predicted to go very early in the 1999 draft for the NFL. The New Orleans Saints selected Williams with their fifth pick. Unlike most drafted players, Williams appointed a sports agency firm owned by Master P, a rap singer who had little experience in negotiating sport contracts. The contract Williams signed was nominally a seven-year $68 million one. However, the contract was heavily contingent on incentives. For example, a large bonus would be paid if he rushed for 1,600 yards each year in three of his first four seasons. At that time, no running back had achieved this feat. He would receive a $3 million bonus if he broke the league single-season rushing record of 2,105 yards. Another incentive was based on his playing 35 percent of all offensive plays. However, the coach makes these calls, not Williams! *The New York Times* reported that the contract

> includes an $8.840 million signing bonus and will be worth between $11.1 million and $68.4 million, contingent upon performance. If he performs in the NFL as he has performed in college, his contract will be the most lucrative ever given a rookie. If he fails to reach goals set in the incentive clauses, he will earn the league minimum for the next seven years: $175,000 in the first year, increasing annually to $400,000 in the seventh. Williams has agreed to either the best contract ever or one of the worst, depending on how his National Football League career plays out.[5]

Unfortunately for Williams he earned very little of the incentive-based components of his nominal $68 million contract. For example, in his first three years with the Saints he rushed for 884 yards (1999), 1,000 yards (2000), and 1,245 yards (2001). This was short of the 1,600 yards for three out of four years and well short of the 2,105 single-season record incentive. He was traded to the Miami Dolphins after the 2001 season. Williams' 1999 contract is frequently included in lists of the worst ever sports contracts. One commentator noted:

> The contract runs contrary to what every other agent knows: guaranteed money and base salary always trump incentives. Williams was tragically underpaid for the duration of his time with the Saints. Williams fired his celebrity agent, and then signed with heavyweight agent

Leigh Steinberg. But the damage was already done. Williams had taken on a contract with the potential for big bucks, but it was a trap. His deal is now a cautionary tale for young athletes, agents, and managers.[6]

The sports industry is one in which there is much second-guessing of decision making with after-the-fact "experts" who criticized decisions on the basis of outcomes rather than the quality of the decision process. However, the Ricky Williams 1999 contract had many "red flags" at the time it was signed. His appointment of an inexperienced agency firm was high-risk. Moreover, even at contract time, many experienced agents and general managers regarded the key incentives as extremely unlikely to be achieved.

6.4 MULTIPLE FACTORS AFFECTING PLAYER CONTRACTING

The many factors that affect the context in which player contracts are negotiated include (a) those that affect the general manager with regards to decisions relating to on-the-field abilities and contributions to team winning, and (b) those decisions that relate to the broader picture of the athlete as regards to their off-the-field character and behavior, as well as any personal branding that may or may not reinforce the club brand.

6.4.1 The General Manager Perspective

General manager decisions regarding the total payroll, its mix across players, and the horizon of contracts occur on a continuing basis. Every year is a new potential contracting cycle and within each year there are opportunities to restructure current player contracts or trade players. Section 5.2 on the professional athlete compensation ecosystem outlined some general aspects of this arena. Focusing on the general manager of a club in a given league, some more specific factors that affect general managers' decisions are:

- **Individual player abilities and contributions to winning on the field.** In general, this is a pivotal factor. Section 6.5 of this chapter discusses this central area of club management. Many success stories in club sports management have their foundations in astute player assessments and decisions. Likewise, many of the disaster stories in club sports management can be associated with poorly informed or researched player assessment and acquisitions. While it is important to recognize that such decisions are made under uncertainty, structured evidence gathering and analysis can reduce the likelihood of bad outcomes.
- **League-specific regulations.** General managers in many leagues face total player payroll maximums and minimums, luxury tax thresholds, tax rates, and so on. Exhibit 6.5 shows the annual salary cap of the NFL since 2001. This is a hard salary cap with penalties for clubs exceeding the cap. Clubs will often restructure some existing contracts of other players when proposed contracts will result in a potential salary cap violation. Box 6.2 discusses how the Brooklyn Nets incurred a luxury tax of more than $90 million for the 2012/14 seasons. This record luxury tax was associated with a change in the NBA luxury tax computation designed to heavily penalize clubs exceeding the salary tax threshold by large amounts over multiple years.

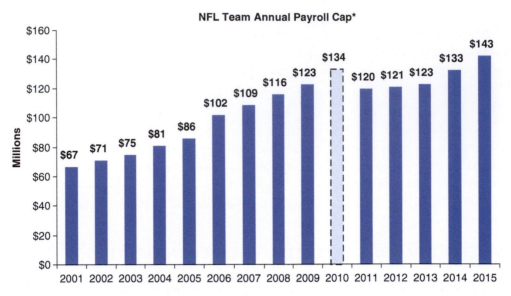

EXHIBIT 6.5 NFL Team Annual Payroll Cap

BOX 6.2 BROOKLYN NETS FACE A $90 MILLION SALARY LUXURY TAX AND A SECOND-ROUND PLAYOFF ELIMINATION AFTER SIGNING ONE-YEAR CONTRACTS WITH BOSTON CELTICS VETERANS

Starting with the 2012/13 NBA season, the Brooklyn Nets started playing at the Barclays Center in Brooklyn. From 1976/7 to 2011/12, the club had been called the New Jersey Nets and played at several arenas in New Jersey. A perennial underperforming club with a lower-tier status than its cross-town rival, the New York Knicks, the hope was that the shift to Brooklyn would kick-start a major upward shift in its stature in the New York sporting landscape. Another reason for hope was the change in majority ownership of the Nets in 2010 to Mikhail Prokhorov, one of the richest businessmen in Russia. Included in this box is player payroll information from *Spotrac* on the Nets in the 2012/13 to 2014/15 seasons. For the 2012/13 season, the Nets had the second highest NBA total payroll at $83.529 million, behind the Los Angeles Lakers at $99.847 million. For the regular (strike-shortened) 2012/13 season, the Nets had a disappointing record of 21 wins and 31 losses and were eliminated in the first round of the playoffs by the Chicago Bulls. In July 2013, the Nets acquired Paul Pierce, Kevin Garnett, and Jason Terry in return for "five players, three future first-round draft picks, and the right to swap spots in the 2017 draft."[7] Paul Pierce, after 14 years in the NBA (all with the Celtics), joined the Nets at a $15.333 million salary. Kevin Garnett, after 18 years in the NBA (12 years with Minnesota and six years with Boston), joined the Nets at a salary of $12.433 million. The result was that the Brooklyn Nets' total payroll at $102.928 million was the highest in the NBA. The New York Knicks payroll was second at $89.184 million. In February 2014, the Nets traded Jason Terry to the Sacramento Kings.

Prior to the start of the 2013/14 season, Howard Beck in *The New York Times* reported that "the free-spending Nets are guaranteed to shatter the league's luxury-tax record next season." His preliminary estimate was that after the Boston Celtics trade, they would trigger a luxury tax of $75 million. Beck concluded that "there is apparently no price that Mikhail D. Prokhorov, the Nets' billionaire owner, is not willing to spend in pursuit of a championship."[8] Prior to the start of the 2013/14 season, Billy King – the Nets general manager – stated:

> I think it's great for our fans and for our organization that we have an owner who is willing to spend the money and spend it wisely ... We didn't just spend the money to spend it, we feel like we've advanced our common goal to win a championship. When we did this [Boston Celtics deal] we mapped it out. We have a couple of years window to do what we've set out to accomplish and then we can reevaluate it.[9]

The 2013/14 season proved to have multiple disappointments, especially for a club with by far the largest total player payroll in the NBA. The regular season record of 44 wins and 38 losses was only sixth in the Eastern Conference and 14th in the NBA overall. The Nets won the first round of the playoffs over the Toronto Raptors (4–3) and then lost the second round to Miami (1–4). Financially, the 2013/14 season was record-breaking as regards NBA club after-tax losses. The NBA's luxury tax penalizes clubs for exceeding the salary tax threshold. Prior to the 2013/14 season, the luxury tax was dollar for dollar. This meant that the Nets 2012/13 payroll being $13.222 million excess of the salary tax threshold attracted a $13.222 million luxury tax. Starting with the 2013/14 season, the tax increased with the amount above the tax threshold – $1.50 tax per dollar spent above the threshold, over $5 million it increases to $1.75, over $10 million it increases to $2.50, over $15 million it increases to $3.25, and over $20 million it increases to $3.75 (and increasing $0.50 for each additional $5 million over).[10] The tax also increases with the number of years the club is above the threshold. ESPN reported at the end of the season that the Nets would pay $90.57 million in luxury taxes for 2013/14. Five other NBA clubs were also reported to be paying luxury taxes for the 2013/14 season – New York Knicks ($36.3 million in taxes), Miami Heat ($14.4 million), Los Angeles Lakers (8.9 million), and Los Angeles Clippers ($1.3 million).[11]

For the 2014/15 season, the Nets made efforts to scale back their total payroll. Prior to the start of the season, they did not re-sign Paul Pierce, who then signed with the Washington Wizards as a free agent at a two-year $10.848 million deal – the average $5.424 million being well below the $15.333 million Nets paid Pierce for his one year on the team. In February 2015, Garnett was traded by the Nets to the Minnesota Timberwolves.

The Boston Celtics trade highlighted the risks of acquiring aging talent at high prices in a short-run attempt to win a championship. The NBA's new luxury tax regime that started in 2013/14 increased the penalty to record levels for a club in the NBA. Beyond the additional luxury tax of $90 million and the more than $27 million salaries paid to Pierce and Garnett in 2013/14, there was the loss of three future first-round draft picks. In a league such as the NBA where high draft picks are highly valuable currency, it is little wonder that the Brooklyn Nets–Boston Celtics July 2013 trade is often used to caution efforts to dramatically increase player payroll in a short-run search for championship rings.

Brooklyn Nets (NBA) Player Payrolls 2012/13 to 2014/15

Year/season	2012/13	2013/14	2014/15
Total Brooklyn Nets payroll	$83.529	$102.928	$88.21
NBA luxury tax threshold	$70.307	$71.748	$76.829
Excess over tax threshold	$13.222	$31.18	$11.381
Players with salaries > $5 million	**2012/13**	**2013/14**	**2014/15**
Joe Johnson	$19.752	$21.466	$23.18
Deron Williams	$17.777	$18.466	$19.754
Brook Lopez	$13.668	$14.693	$15.719
Kris Humphries	$12.000	—	—
Gerald Wallace	$9.682	—	—
Paul Pierce	—	$15.333	—
Kevin Garnett	—	$12.433	—
Marcus Thornton	—	$8.05	—
Thaddeus Young	—	—	$9.16
Jarret Jack	—	—	$6.3

- **Owner-related aspects.** Owner aspirations, ability to spend, and willingness to spend are key determinants of player-related decisions. The Brooklyn Nets 2013/14 $90 million luxury tax was, in part, driven by an owner with a desire to win a championship in the short run and the ability to spend large amounts of money. Some investor syndicates who may desire to win a championship do not have the financial capacity to cover large losses with high-cost players being added to a playing squad. Most general managers operate with relatively tight financial bands within which they can spend in a given year. Another aspect of owner-related aspects is the budget horizon that an ownership group is willing to provide a general manager. Given that many contracts are for multiple years, owners that provide multi-year budget guidelines to general managers will help facilitate decision making. However, in some cases, owners only provide general managers with "hard numbers" one year ahead, which adds to the challenges faced by these general managers.
- **Club playing styles and general manager or coach priorities.** Some clubs build squads that have a "trademark" style that their fans find attractive. An example would be a basketball club that operates with a "fast break and transition offense" where there is a premium placed on moving the ball down the court via short passes. A somewhat differentiated style is called "run and gun" where the emphasis is on a large number of field goal attempts. Although not totally differentiated, other styles include a "Princeton offense" and a "dribble drive/Memphis attack." Depending on the chosen style, some players will be attractive hires while other players would be less attractive.
- **Changes in a general manager, coach, or a star player can lead to changes in the priorities given to signing different types of players**. Some NFL general managers prefer quarterbacks with short passing abilities whereas others value more highly the ability to make long passes. The

Atlanta Falcons of the mid-2000s built a playing and coaching style around the highly athletic and running ability of their star quarterback Michael Vick. Unfortunately, Vick was convicted in 2007 of dog fighting and a new quarterback recruited (Matt Ryan). The result was a substantial shift in playing style and offensive player selections at the post-Vick Atlanta Falcons.

■ **Current squad's perceived strengths and weaknesses.** General managers and coaches are continually assessing many possible changes to their existing squad. For example, goalkeepers in soccer teams play a central role in achieving on-field success. A general manager may conclude that the current #1 goalkeeper's reflexes have greatly slowed and that signing a new goalkeeper is high priority if the club is to win more games. In leagues where mid-season trades are possible, injuries to key players in the first part of a season can prompt trades to fill in gaps in the current squad.

■ **Current and likely future availability of players to contract**. Three possible sources of player pools to contract for a playing squad are a draft, player trading, and free agency. *Drafts* are frequently structured by leagues to facilitate the efficient assignment of new athletes to individual clubs in that league. While assignment rules differ by league, the most common rationale is to facilitate the lower on-the-field performing clubs having priority in selecting the higher ranked new athletes. *Player trading* is where one club acquires the contract rights for a player from another club. In many soccer leagues, player trades can be done with financial payments made by the club purchasing the player contract. In other leagues, trades involve player contracts on both sides and also often draft picks. *Free agency* is where a player has finished obligations under a current contract and is "freely" available to contract with any club in a league. General managers and their advisors have the ability to collect and analyze information about the strengths and weaknesses of the potential players in each of these three possible player pools. In some years, a given pool may have many highly talented players while in other years, the same pool may have very little talent.

■ **Progression plan philosophies.** Within a given club, astute general managers and coaches likely have well-developed progression plans for key positions. The execution of any given progression plan, however, can be very challenging. Consider the context of a general manager and the coach jointly having a progression plan for an elite player who is still the starting player but is declining in ability. Assume the planned replacement is progressing very quickly and approaching the end of his current contract. How quickly to start the transition process? Here we see differences in philosophies. Some general managers and coaches delay the transition much longer than others. Bill Walsh, one of the most respected NFL coaches (with the San Francisco 49ers) had the philosophy of "a year too early is better than a year too late." Walsh was subjected to much criticism when he followed through on this philosophy and did not renew multiple starting players who were still very much "brand names" of the 49ers. Financial considerations can add further complications. The current elite starter may love to play and be more than willing to sign a new contract with a lower salary, while the planned replacement may be demanding a very high new contract. Suffice it to say, decisions in this area will be second-guessed and criticized by many commentators and fans, and be the subject of endless comment on talk-back radio.

■ **Regulatory effects on player value estimates**. Chapter 5 and Section 6.3 of this chapter outlined how some leagues impose caps/maximum salaries for rookies acquired in a draft. Some commentators refer to such rookies as being available at "wholesale market" prices. In contrast, free agent players often have multiple bids and there is much knowledge about their abilities. The free agent market is often referred to as a "retail market." As a general rule, wholesale prices are lower than retail prices. Another example of a regulatory impact on player value assessment is leagues rules where minimum salaries for players increase the longer the years an athlete is playing in a league. Such a regulation reduces the value of an athlete with a constant ability level as that athlete ages as regards playing time in a league.

6.4.2 Factors Beyond On-Field Abilities and Contributions to Winning

General managers typically have value analysis and winning on the field as central focuses of their decision making. Additional factors can, at times, require a broader perspective on player-related decisions. Two examples are:

- **Premium placed on character.** Players vary in their likelihood of off-field character challenges. In some cases players with very high abilities can come with a higher likelihood of negative off-field issues such as alcohol, drugs, or partner physical abuse. They may even have a long track record of off-field problems. The ownership and executives at different clubs take varying positions as to how to balance the upside of on-field ability with the downside of off-field risks. Box 4.4 in Chapter 4 discusses how, starting in the late 1990s, the Portland Trail Blazers selected talented basketball players who, based on past behavior, had a higher likelihood of off-field problems. The consequence was that the club became known as the "Portland Jail Blazers" when past behavior turned out to be predictive of future behavior. At some clubs, ownership takes a very hard proactive stand against recruiting players with "questionable character traits." This hard stand does not mean such problems will not occur. However, the aim here is often to reduce the likelihood of "players behaving badly" and to send warnings to players that actions that the club views as "brand diminishing" can have serious negative consequences for their careers.
- **Player brand strength.** A small number of players have global or regional brands that bring benefits to a club beyond their on-field ability and their contributions to winning games. Some of the world's elite soccer players are the best examples, including David Beckham, Lionel Messi, and Cristiano Ronaldo. Beckham is the quintessential example. While never ranked as a #1 player in the world, his brand was #1 as regards elite soccer players. In the years prior to his retirement in 2013, Beckham's brand power translated to higher sales of merchandise, higher attendance at games, etc. at multiple clubs. When Beckham transferred from Manchester United (EPL) to Real Madrid (La Liga) in June 2003, there was a surge in sales of Real Madrid jerseys with his number 23 and name that more than paid for this transfer fee between the clubs (see Chapter 12 for a detailed review of this). Similarly, when Beckham transferred to the Los Angeles Galaxy of Major League Soccer (MLS) in 2007, there was a large uplift in Galaxy jersey sales. There was also an increase in attendance at Galaxy home and away games in MLS. From a business perspective, Beckham's brand consistently brought increased revenues and increased brand strength to the clubs for which he played.

6.5 BUILDING EVIDENCE ON THE ABILITIES OF PROFESSIONAL ATHLETES

When assessing athlete ability, it is useful to distinguish between athletes in individual sports and those in team sports. Two key dimensions are:

1   What is the ability level evidenced to date?
2   What is the expected ability level over the length(s) of possible contracts and beyond?

6.5.1 Individual Sport Athletes and Ability Assessment

For individual sports there are often well-respected and agreed indicators of ability to date for many athletes. For example, golf and tennis athletes show evidence of their abilities by where they position in tournaments. For athletes performing in the most elite tournaments, rankings can be developed from where the athlete is positioned relative to the "best" athletes in the world. Where the athlete is not competing against the "best in the world," adjustments need to be made for the quality of the opponent(s) when assessing ability evidenced to date.

The more challenging task is assessing the likely expected future performance over the length of a potential contract for an individual sport athlete. For many individual sport athletes, those contracting with the athlete could be a sponsor or an apparel/shoe company. There can be much uncertainty in this assessment. However, there is often quantitative evidence to predict expected performance as a function of age and other variables (such as past injuries) based on the performance of many other athletes over their playing lifespan. Individual athletes and their agents likely argue that they are the exception and that they will play at a higher level for a longer period than the statistics based on a large pool of athletes in their sport. It is here that negotiation skills can play an important role in negotiations.

One approach adopted here is to write contracts that shift much of the future performance uncertainty to the athlete. For example, at the end of each season global rankings of golf and tennis players are produced by the respective associations in those sports. Nike for example, could negotiate a long-term contract with a 34-year-old Serena Williams that has annual bonuses that vary based on her WTA ranking. Williams could receive a bonus of $20 million if she is ranked #1 in a given year, $15 million if ranked between 2 and 5, $10 million if ranked between 6 and 10, and so on.

6.5.2 Team Sport Athletes and Ability Assessment

For team sports, an athlete's "contribution to winning" is of pivotal importance. For some positions in sports, there is much agreement on how to quantify "contribution to winning." Consider evaluating pitchers in baseball. Over a season playing many different clubs, pitchers can be ranked on metrics such as wins and earned run average (ERA, which is the average number of runs given up per nine innings pitched). Similarly, in cricket bowlers can be ranked on wickets taken and average runs given up per wicket taken. Both baseball and cricket have a similar structure of a single individual being able to make significant contributions to winning in an identifiable way. In many other sports, there is more of a "joint contribution" by many players when key moments contribute to winning in a game. In a soccer game, a player may score few goals but be a central figure in setting up scoring opportunities. There is an ever-growing number of statistics to assist in the evaluation of past performance of athletes such as "contribution to winning."

No matter how many advances are made in developing metrics that give better insight into past "contribution to winning," the larger challenge of predicting the future expected "contribution to winning" remains. Chapter 1 highlighted this uncertainty as regards the decision by the San Francisco Giants of MLB in late 2006 to offer Barry Zito a seven-year then-record $126 million contract for a starting pitcher. Zito's win percentage in the seven years from 2000 to 2006 with Oakland Athletics was 61.8 percent with an ERA of 3.49 runs per nine innings. The Giants were hoping for a continuation of this stellar record in the next seven years. Unfortunately, Zito's performance in the 2007/13 period was well below what was expected – a 44.1 percent win percentage and a 4.81 ERA. This dramatic decline in performance highlights the uncertainty under which decisions to write contracts with players are made.

6.6 THE SPORTS ANALYTICS REVOLUTION – ANALYTICS GOES MAINSTREAM

The collection of data is a central part of scoring most sporting contests. Wins and losses are based on goals scored, runs hit, touchdowns, golf scores, etc. Over time, there has been a dramatic increase in using data to better understand key aspects of sports as opposed to just scoring sporting outcomes. Sports analytics is the structured and rigorous examination of data relating to the sports industry where the aim is to provide new insights and enable more informed debate and better decision making by key stakeholders.

This section gives a brief overview of multiple areas where analytic advances are being made. The greatest challenge in this area is increasing the quality of data analysis. While in many areas there has been a rapid increase in available data, there has not always been a commensurate increase in the abilities of analysts to draw the most reliable inferences from the data. Box 6.3 discusses the MIT/Sloan Analytics Conference that has been a key contributor to increasing both knowledge and awareness of the many areas where important advances have been made, as well as highlighting areas where future efforts could yield high returns.

BOX 6.3 MIT/SLOAN SPORTS ANALYTICS CONFERENCE HELPS BUILD AND SHOWCASE THE ANALYTICS REVOLUTION

The sports analytics movement in sports management is a wave that is affecting multiple parts of the industry. The MIT Sloan Sports Analytics Conference is an important annual event helping build the wave. This student-driven conference debuted in 2007. It was started by the MIT EMS (Entertainment, Media, and Sports) club with the guidance of Daryl Morey (general manager and managing director of baseball operations at the Houston Rockets) and Jessica Gellman (vice-president of customer marketing and strategy for the Kraft Sports Group). A forerunner of the conference was when Morley started teaching a MBA course at MIT on sports analytics in 2004. Over time the conference has built both its stature and its reach. It is one of the most impressive asset-builds in sports management.

The first three conferences were one-day events held at MIT, with the format of panels and key speakers. From the outset, thought leaders (such as Bill James) and league and club executives (such as Adam Silver, Mark Cuban, and Wyc Grousbeck) appeared on the panels or as keynote speakers. The attendance at the conference grew from 175 in 2007 to 550 in 2009. In 2010, the conference shifted to Boston Convention Centers to accommodate larger attendances, which grew to over 2,500 in 2013. Also starting in 2010, the conference moved to a two-day format. One addition to the two-day format starting in 2011 was "First Pitch," which is a sports business case competition open to student teams attending the conference. In 2015, 23 student teams participated. The top three teams present at the conference, with the winner being given an "Alpha Award."

The MIT Sloan Conference website (www.sloansportsconference.com) has a superb collection that enables a deeper perspective to be gained on the many areas where analytics are transforming the industry: (a) videos of the panels, (b) research papers and slide decks that highlight rich data analysis in both the on-field and off-field areas, (c) invited speakers, and (d) sponsored presentations.

This website should very much be the first port of call for those wanting to stay at the cutting edge of the sports analytics wave that is broadly impacting many areas of the sports industry. Morley, a mainstay of the conference since its start, stated: "The reason for [our] growth is simple. Analytics helps you make better decisions, which helps you win."[12] A word of caution here: many key sports analytic executives are either reluctant to speak at the MIT Sloan conference or only speak in generalities for concern that any "proprietary intellectual capital" they have developed will be quickly adopted by others attending the conference.

6.6.1 Player Selection and Contracting

Baseball was one of the first sports where extensive analysis of game-related statistics focused on evidence-based insights into player abilities and their contributions to winning. The term "sabermetrics" was coined in 1980 by an early pioneer (Bill James) to describe "the search for objective knowledge about baseball."[13] What has been developed is an increase in the number of statistics computed about different positions and players – such as "runs created" and "wins above replacement" (WAR).

The Oakland Athletics of MLB is widely recognized as an early adopter of sabermetrics starting with Sandy Alderson and Billy Beane. Beane's tenure as general manager of the Athletics started in 1997. He gained much recognition when he built an analytic unit that used extensive data analysis to identify both (a) those attributes of players that contributed to winning, and (b) those attributes that were relatively undervalued in terms of player salaries. Operating with one of the lowest payrolls in MLB, the Athletics regularly had more wins than most other MLB clubs. The publication in 2003 of a book titled *Moneyball* by Michael Lewis and then the release of a movie by the same name in 2011 brought data analytics into the general dialogue. Section 6.7 of this chapter provides further discussion on this topic.

Clubs in many other leagues are increasing their investment in analytics as regards player selection and contracting. The result has been an expansion in metrics that capture player contribution to winning. For example in basketball, new metrics include "offensive efficiency," "efficient offensive production," and "defensive stops gained."[14] Major leagues are now investing sizable resources in tracking many more aspects of games. The NBA has cameras in the ceilings of all its arenas with a resultant major increase in data available to all clubs for analysis. One potential result is more reliable evidence on the differential contributions to scoring of players on the court.

6.6.2 In-Game Decision Making

Many decisions are made within games on the basis of limited information and relying on past experience and intuition. The growth of rich databases on many aspects of games has led to insights about ways to increase the likelihood of better outcomes within games. For example, NFL coaches make decisions about what plays to call on each of the four downs they have to move the ball ten yards forward. Evidence based on thousands of plays involving key players in forthcoming games, can give insight into the likelihood of possible outcomes with different calls. As with all predictions, there is still uncertainty. However, the likelihood of a good outcome is increased by being better informed.

6.6.3 Health and Injury Prevention and Rehabilitation

An important challenge for a sporting club is having its athletes healthy and able to perform to their best abilities for as many games as possible. An athlete who is on a $10 million annual salary, but is only available 60 percent of the games can be very expensive and provide poor value for a club. A phrase often used by general managers and coaches is "the best ability of an athlete is their availability."

Research in this health and fitness area is occurring on multiple fronts, a large part of which involves rigorous data analysis. One area is identifying how different athletes vary in their likelihood of injuries. A past record of injuries has been found to increase the likelihood of future injuries. A second area is gaining early warning signals of an athlete's physical problems so that preventative measures can be taken to minimize the severity and duration of the injury. A third area is innovations in rehabilitation. For example, some knee injuries that previously would have required a long time out from playing now only require a three- or four-week rehabilitation period.

6.6.4 Training Programs and Wearables Clothing

Training routines for athletes have long had a strong data element. For example, swim coaches have programs based on doing set multiples of laps per training session. In recent years, there has been a growth in "wearables," which are clothing or devices that enable data about the wearer to be transmitted to computers. Wearables are now being used in many areas such as medical research, alcohol rehabilitation, and weight-loss programs. They are also being increasingly used in sports training programs. Sporting clubs can track speed over different distances, body temperatures, sweating, etc., associated with different training routines. Printouts can be produced for each athlete as they leave the training field. Databases with inputs from wearables can be built on many different athletes and many different training programs. Such databases can be the building blocks to gaining better insight into increasing the capacities of individual athletes and increasing the percentage of times they are available to play.

6.7 EVALUATING THE SUCCESS OF CLUB PLAYER DECISION MAKING

Chapter 4 outlined eight motives for club ownership: performance, profit, platform, pre-emptive, purpose, profile, power, and passion. The importance that individual owners place on these individual motives should guide how club player-side decision making is evaluated. We shall discuss two frequently cited motives and their link to how the club player decision making function in a club is evaluated:

- **Performance: winning on the field.** With this objective, there can be a tiering of benchmarks. The peak to many owners is winning the "championship." In many leagues, there is a clear "championship" to use as a benchmark. It is the Super Bowl in the NFL, the World Series in MLB, the NBA Championship in the NBA, and the Stanley Cup in the NHL. In many soccer leagues there are multiple "championships" in any one year. Consider the English Premier League. The major "wins" that are possible are the EPL Champion (based on points from 38 regular season games), the UEFA Championship League title, European League title, and two major domestic cups based on an knock-out tournament (the Capital Cup and the FA Cup). Short of winning a championship, another benchmark is consistently making the playoffs.

■ **Profit/cost per win.** One limitation of relying exclusively on such benchmarks is that they ignore the costs associated with winning. In leagues that put very tight maximum and minimum restrictions on total player payrolls, this limitation is not a major one. In leagues where clubs have very few payroll restrictions, the cost per win can highlight differences in efficiency across clubs with very different total player payrolls. The cost-per-win measure has attracted greater attention with the success of several clubs using sports analytics as a key aspect of their player decision making. As noted in Section 6.6, Billy Beane is highly associated with the Oakland Athletics adoption of analytics while working with one of the consistently lowest player payrolls in MLB.

Exhibit 6.6 shows the efficiency and effectiveness with which the Athletics have delivered on their low payrolls. Panel A of Exhibit 6.6 shows that over the 16-year period of 1998 to 2013, the Athletics

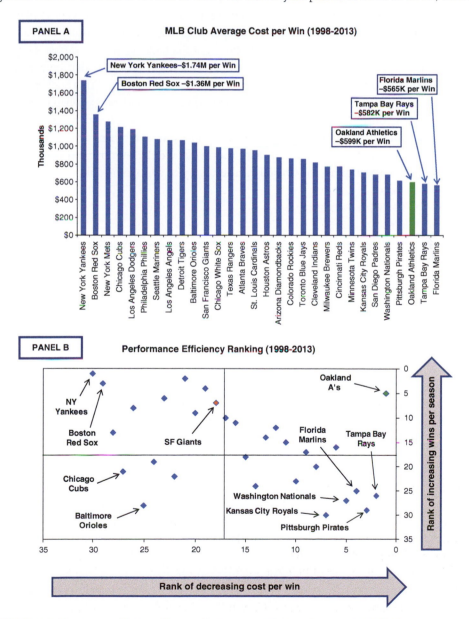

EXHIBIT 6.6 MLB Club Average Cost per Win and Performance Efficiency Ranking (1998/2013)

had the third lowest payroll cost per win. Panel B of Exhibit 6.6 combines the cost-per-win metric with the average number of wins per season. The vertical axis of Panel B ranks clubs in terms of the average number of regular season wins per season. The horizontal axis is the rank of cost per win. The upper right-hand corner of the graphic captures those clubs that had above average wins and below average costs per win. The Oakland Athletics are positioned in this upper right-hand corner, highlighting the club's highly effective player-side decision making.

6.8 SUMMARY

This chapter showcases the challenging area of club player-side decision making. A key underlying concept here is value analysis, where the focus is on identifying undervalued players so that the club can increase its likelihood of winning at a lower cost per win. A second key concept is viewing player payroll decisions for a team-based sport as a portfolio decision challenge where emphasis is placed on maximizing expected returns while understanding and choosing a risk level that ownership deems appropriate. A third key concept that has been stressed in multiple chapters of this book is uncertainty. There is uncertainty about expected player individual performance and in team-based sports uncertainty about expected contributions of individuals to team performance. The analytics revolution outlined briefly in Section 6.6 is reducing but not eliminating many areas of uncertainty. Making informed decisions about player contracting is an important way to reduce the number and magnitude of bad outcomes in what is in many sports the single largest category of costs for a club.

NOTES

1 Leagues and clubs differ in the titles for general managers and coaches. Other titles for the general manager function include "president of baseball (hockey, etc.) operations" and "director of player personnel." Other titles for the lead coach include "head coach" and "manager."
2 The denominator for these percentages is the total player payroll for active contracts. The percentages decrease when total payroll includes "dead money" which is payments made to players no longer on the active playing squad. For example, the New York Knicks has a total player payroll for active contracts of $54.419 million while its total payroll including dead money is $80.591 million. Carmelo Anthony's contract is 27.7 percent of the $80.591 million amount.
3 www.spotrac.com/nfl/green-bay-packers/aaron-rodgers.
4 www.basketballinsiders.com/nba-salaries/nba-rookie-salary-scale-by-draft-year.
5 "Pro football – New Orleans: Williams agrees to large deal," *The New York Times*, May 15, 1999.
6 A. Ellis, "What is the worst sports contract of all-time?" *Quora*, November 20, 2013.
7 Z. Cox., "Kevin Garnett trade cements Celtics–Nets blockbuster as one of worst ever," NESN, February 20, 2015.
8 H. Beck, "Record luxury tax looms for the Nets," *The New York Times*, July 9, 2013.
9 F. Blinebury, "Payroll not a taxing problem for nets," hangtime.blogs.nba.com, July 10, 2013.
10 L. Coon, "NBA salary cap FAQ – 2011 collective bargaining agreement," www.cbafaq.com/salarycap.htm#Q21, January 13, 2015.
11 B. Windhorst, "Nets to pay record $90 million luxury tax," ESPN.com, July 9, 2014. The NBA distributes a large percentage of the luxury taxes collected in a given year to the non-taxing paying clubs on an equal allocation basis.
12 J. Mirtle, "Sloan conference leading big data revolution in sports," globeandmail.com, February 27, 2015.
13 Society for American Baseball Research, *A Guide to Sabermetric Research*, (http://sabr.org/sabermetrics).
14 S.M. Shea, *Basketball Analytics: Objective and Efficient Strategies for Understanding How Teams Win* (Create Space Independent Publishing Platform, 2013).

7

GLOBAL SPORTING BODIES, FEDERATIONS, AND ASSOCIATIONS

This chapter examines not-for-profit organizations that play central roles in the global sporting world, in the management and production of events at many levels, and in how participants play their sport. Decisions by these organizations literally affect the lives of many professional athletes and many millions of amateur participants. While we discuss only a small number of organizations, those covered highlight the diversity and richness of the sporting landscape in this area. A word of caution: there are multiple abbreviations that exist in the sector of the sports world discussed in this chapter. Appendix 7A contains a list of abbreviations referred to in this chapter and their "full names."

7.1 CATEGORIES OF GLOBAL SPORTING BODIES AND FEDERATIONS

Exhibit 7.1 provides examples for each of three categories of these organizations that are discussed in this chapter.

- Global bodies overseeing multiple sports – Panel A of Exhibit 7.1. These are bodies where many sports are either showcased in global events (such as the IOC, IPC, IWGA, CGF, and FISU) or regulated (such as WADA).
- International federations (IFs) for individual sports that are IOC members – Panel B of Exhibit 7.1. These bodies regulate global aspects of an individual sport (or related set of sports) that is showcased in the Olympics.
- International federations (IFs) for individual sports not IOC members – Panel C of Exhibit 7.1. These bodies regulate global aspects of an individual sport (or related set of sports) that is not currently (as of 2015) showcased at the Olympics.

Individual sporting federations typically have both professional and amateur athletes and a vast number of participants who often start in that sport at a very young age. Decision making by the sporting bodies and federations can entail juggling very diverse and at times competing constituencies. It can also involve some public and more often private lobbying, political infighting, and compromises.

7.2 THE INTERNATIONAL OLYMPIC COMMITTEE (IOC)

The IOC is the global multisport federation (sometimes called a multisport organization, MSO) that organizes the Summer and Winter Olympic Games.[1] Both Games occur on a four-year cycle. The IOC is the leading authority and rights-holder for the Olympic movement. A not-for-profit organization, the IOC is a highly sophisticated organization in terms of sponsorship, media rights, and event management. It is also a leading proponent for the role of sport to make the world a better place. The IOC is organized into National Olympic Committees (NOCs) at the country level. These NOCs are responsible for the local actions of the Olympic movement and the governance of the IOC. When a Summer or Winter Olympics is awarded to a city, there is an organizing committee appointed – called the Organizing Committee for the Olympic Games (OCOGs). These committees take the name of the city as its first word. Examples are VANOC for the Vancouver 2010 Winter Olympics and LOCOG for the London 2012 Summer Olympics.

Exhibit 7.2 (Panel A) presents summary financials as reported by the IOC for three four-year periods 2001/4, 2005/8, and 2009/12. A four-year cycle is often used in IOC budgeting as it includes a

Panel A: Global bodies overseeing multiple sports

International Olympic Committee (IOC) – based in Lausanne, Switzerland. Founded in 1894.

International Paralympic Committee (IPC) – based in Bonn, Germany. Founded in 1989.

International World Games Association (IWGA) – based in Colorado Springs, USA. Founded in 1981.

Commonwealth Games Federation (CGF) – based in London, UK. Founded in 1930.

International University Sports Federation (FISU) – based in Lausanne, Switzerland. Founded in 1949.

World Anti-Doping Agency (WADA) – based in Montreal, Canada. Founded in 1999.

Panel B: International federations for individual sports with IOC membership

International Association of Athletics Federations (IAAF) – based in Monaco. Founded in 1912.

International Basketball Association (FIBA) – based in Mies, Switzerland. Founded in 1932.

International Federation of Association Football (FIFA) – based in Zurich, Switzerland. Founded in 1904.

International Ice Hockey Federation (IIHF) – based in Zurich, Switzerland. Founded in 1908.

International Boxing Association (AIBA) – based in Lausanne, Switzerland. Founded in 1946.

World Rugby/International Rugby Board (IRB) – based in Dublin, Ireland. Founded in 1886.

Panel C: International federations for individual sports not members of the IOC

International Automobile Federation (FIA) – based in Paris, France. Founded in 1904.

World Baseball Softball Confederation (WBSC) – based in Lausanne, Switzerland. Founded in 2013. Merger of former International Softball Federation (was based in Plant City, Florida, USA – founded in 1952) and International Baseball Federation (was based in Lausanne, Switzerland – founded in 1938).

International Cricket Council (ICC) – based in Dubai, UAE. Founded in 1909.

International Federation of American Football (IFAF) – based in La Courneuve, France. Founded in 1998.

International Surfing Association (ISA) – based in San Diego, California, USA. Founded in 1964.

World Squash Federation (WSF) – based in Hastings, UK. Founded in 1967.

EXHIBIT 7.1 Global Sporting Bodies and Organizations

Summer Olympics and a Winter Olympics. For the 2009/12 four-year cycle, the IOC reported revenues of $5,000 million. The three large distributions in this period were:

- $1,642 million to the two organizing committees in this cycle (VANOC and LOCOG),
- $735 million to the NOCs, and
- $729 million to the IFs recognized by the IOC. These IFs, in turn, distribute money to the national sport federations (NSFs), which are also called national sporting organizations (NSOs).

The IOC also distributes funds to other recognized organizations such as the World Anti-Doping Agency, the Court of Arbitration for Sport, the International Olympic Academy, and the Youth Olympic Games. Exhibit 7.2 (Panel B) highlights that sport organizations such as the OCOGs, NOCs, and NSOs also often receive financial support from government bodies.

| Panel A | Financial Distributions to Key Sporting Organizations from IOC ($Millions) |

| | Four-year cycle | | |
Selected distributions	2001–4	2005–8	2009–12
To OCOGs (Organizing Committees for Games)	1,517	1,811	1,642
To NOCs (National Olympic Committees)	321	437	735
To IFs (International Federations)	349	425	729
To recognized organizations (e.g., WADA)	85	102	102

| PANEL B | Graphic Overview of IOC Distributions with Funding Support from National Government Bodies Included |

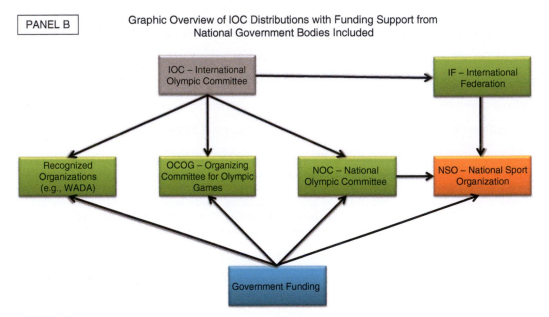

EXHIBIT 7.2 Financial Distributions to Key Sporting Organizations from IOC and National Governments
Note: Selected distributions do not sum to the total revenues and are shown to highlight key line items of the IOCs financial summary.
Source: IOC Factsheet, IOC Financial Summary (July 2014)

For many decades until the early 1990s, the Olympic Games were restricted to amateur athletes. Much of management was on a volunteer basis. For instance, Avery Brundage, IOC president between 1954 and 1974 spent part of his personal fortune on the Olympics and accepted no reimbursement for expenses. This attitude illustrates the traditional view of sports as a purely social activity rather than a commercial and business activity that underlies the founding values of the IOC and federations. The magnitude of the dollar amounts in Exhibit 7.2, however, highlight that professional management now is an essential component of the IOC infrastructure.

7.2.1 Examples of Important IOC Decisions

The IOC makes multiple important decisions, including:

- **Selection of the city where the Olympic Games will take place.** For this decision, the IOC runs a competitive bidding process among candidate cities. Over time, the IOC has made changes in its bidding processes to increase transparency and reduce the opportunities for corruption.
- **Selection of the sports that will be part of the Olympic Games.** There have been multiple high-profile decisions to both add sports and to drop sports. Examples of added sports include:
  - Tennis – added back in 1996. Was included as a sport from 1896 to 1924.
  - Golf – added back in 2016. Was included from 1900 to 1904.
  - Beach volleyball – added in 1996.
  - Snowboarding – added in 1998.
  - Half-pipe skiing – added in 2014.

  In a secret ballot in 2005, the IOC members voted to drop both baseball and softball after the 2008 Summer Olympics. Both sports had been included since 1992. One commentator stated: "The IOC have never specified exactly why the sports were dropped, the most commonly cited reasons are baseball's refusal to comply with all the World Anti-Doping Agency rules and the absence of Major League Baseball players from the Olympics."[2] The decision to add or drop a sport in the Olympics is especially important for smaller sports that do not have a marquee event (such as a world cup) of their own. For these sports, the Olympics are the largest event in terms of reach. Being an Olympic sport has also other important consequences including the financial gains from the IOC's distribution of the proceeds of the Games. As shown in Exhibit 7.2, the IOC distributes major parts of its revenue surplus from the Games to IFs and to NOCs.
- **Selection of broadcast partners.** Payments from broadcast partners are a major part of the revenue base of the IOC and have continually increased over each Olympic cycle of bidding. For the 2009–12 period, the IOC reported that broadcast revenues comprised 73 percent of the total revenues of $5,000 million, with sponsorship revenues the next largest category with 18 percent of total revenues. Chapter 15 on "Sports Broadcasting: Content and Distribution Decisions" includes discussion of network bidding for IOC rights. Exhibit 15.5 shows the sizable growth in summer and winter broadcast revenue since the 1960 Olympics. Box 15.4 provides insight into the IOC's decision in 2014 to extend the US broadcasting rights to NBC without a competitive bidding process being conducted.
- **Selection of the members.** Members of the IOC come from all continents and are voted in by the existing members. The process by which potential at-large members are identified, vetted, and then voted on is not transparent. Reforms to the IOC's structure in the early 2000s resulted in the setting of an age limit of 70 years for newly elected members. Those becoming members before 2000 have an age limit of 80 years. There were 102 members as of March 2015. The mix from different regions was:
  - Europe – 44 members
  - Middle East – six members
  - Africa – 13 members
  - North/Central America and Caribbean – 14 members
  - South America – five members
  - Asia – 15 members
  - Oceania – five members

- Members of the IOC include at-large members, as well as members associated with IFs, NOCs, and athletes. There is a maximum of 15 members from each of the IFs and the NOCs. There is also a maximum of 15 IOC members from athletes taking part in the Olympics. Participating athletes vote on their representatives in the IOC.
- **Selection of the president of the IOC.** The president of the IOC is selected by a voting process of its members. The terms of IOC presidents are now restricted to a maximum of 12 years – one term of eight years with a possible extension for another four years. Jacques Rogge of Belgium was the first president to have a length of tenure restriction – from 2001 to 2013. The first term as president of Thomas Bach of Germany started in 2013. Juan Antonio Samaranch of Spain was president from 1980 to 2001. During his tenure there was a rapid increase in the revenue base of the IOC, but also ongoing allegations of financial and other improprieties. Following an investigation of allegations associated with the Salt Lake City 2002 Winter Olympics, several IOC members were forced to resign their positions.

As with many areas of sports, the dramatic increase in the level of money associated with the IOC has led to both an increased level of management structure as well as ongoing criticisms that "money" has diminished the focus on Olympic sporting ideals.

7.2.2 National Olympic Committees (NOCs)

The IOC is organized into National Olympic Committees (NOCs) at the country level. NOCs are the rights-holders of the Olympic and Paralympic marks in their respective countries/jurisdictions. Examples include the British Olympic Association (BOA), the United States Olympic Committee (USOC), the Canadian Olympic Committee (COC), and nearly 200 others. The structure and operation of NOCs varies significantly by country and by Games (Summer or Winter). NOCs, by most accounts, are powerful federations who have considerable influence in the sport industry in their own jurisdiction, particularly with respect to the role that their country (jurisdiction) plays on the international sport stage. In many countries, governments have ongoing substantive relationships with their NOC.

NOCs are multisport not-for-profit organizations. They operate largely through the national sport federations (NSFs). NOCs manage the national Olympic teams (logistics, operations, etc.) and support NSFs in their objectives to advance sports and, specifically, to succeed at the Olympic Games. Their activities include:

- NOCs invest in and support the training and selection of elite coaches, athlete training, athlete post-career integration, competitions, legal, training facilities, training camps, sport science support, nutrition support, and medical support. Most of this is around or during Olympic Games with some support to targeted athletes pre-Games.
- NOCs coordinate and oversee Games-related operations including transportation, lodging, equipment, and security.
- NOCs through NSFs market and communicate the Olympic Games. They insure that all Games-related information gets to athletes, coaches, and other stakeholders. Included here is Olympic Game ticket allocations and their distribution. During the Games and around the Games, the NOC deals with media. Government relations in their home jurisdiction is also under the purview of an NOC (e.g., lobby efforts with sport funding).

- NOCs also engage in revenue-generation – via sponsorship, broadcasting, licensing, and fund-raising. This funding is then shared with national federations, other sports organizations, as well as athletes within each country. For example, the USOC receives considerable revenue from the sponsorship deals it signs around the Olympic Games. For example, at the 2012 London and 2014 Sochi Games, McDonald's had a sponsorship that was estimated to be worth $100 million every four years.
- Each NOC represents their country or jurisdiction on the IOC (IPC for NPCs), IFs, and other international sport federations.

In recent years, many NOCs have partnered with their governments on initiatives designed to improve the country's performance at the Olympic Games. For example, Canada's "Own the Podium" program is jointly funded by Sport Canada and the Canadian Olympic Committee (COC) to provide targeted, high-level investment, sport science, coaching, and training support to athletes who have a "decent" chance to win a medal. Australia (Australian Institute of Sports, AIS) and Britain (UK Sport) have done similar joint government/NOC partnerships. NOCs will also explore partnership with other associations (e.g., USOC and the NCAA on scholarships), municipal governments (e.g., a local training center), and corporations who wish to partner with Olympic-bound athletes. See Box 7.1 for a discussion of the German Sports Olympic Confederation and its many initiatives.

BOX 7.1 THE GERMAN SPORTS OLYMPIC CONFEDERATION

Germany has been one of the leaders in Olympic success in recent years. With 63 medals over the last two Olympics (2012 London, 2014 Sochi), Germany is certainly a force to be reckoned with in international competition. Behind the success of Germany, is their NOC, the German Sports Olympic Confederation (Deutscher Olympischer Sportbund, DOSB). The DOSB proclaims that it is responsible for safeguarding, promoting, and furthering the Olympic idea; it achieves this in many different ways, including sport development programs, education, and youth programs. For example, in an effort to promote and develop sport in Germany, the DOSB uses marketing campaigns with slogans such as "Sport is good for Germany" and "Trim action," which are widely known around the country. The campaigns are centered on various programs that promote sport to senior citizens, women, and families, among others. The DOSB also holds a great interest in promoting sport at the earliest ages and getting children involved early on. For example, in an effort to educate the German population about sports programs and sport in general, the DOSB has licensed about 500,000 people as certified coaches, exercise leaders, club managers, or youth leaders. This licensing program puts people in a position to help support the almost ten million children that are a part of the German Sports Youth program. The DOSB funds itself by its memberships, including more than 28 million individual members and more than 91,000 sport clubs, as well as receipt from lottery revenue and marketing licenses. In addition to this, the DOSB also receives substantial help from the government and third parties that help build and maintain facilities throughout Germany, this allows them to have such a large youth and development program.

7.3 INTERNATIONAL FEDERATIONS

An international federation (IF) is a not-for-profit organization governing and overseeing one sport (or several related sports) at the global level. Some of the most influential and important sport organizations in the world are IFs, such as FIFA (football), FIBA (basketball), ITF (tennis) and World Rugby (rugby). Box 7.2 provides information on FIBA.

BOX 7.2 FIBA – A HIGH-PROFILE INTERNATIONAL FEDERATION

The Fédération Internationale de Basketball (FIBA) is the IF responsible for the sport of basketball worldwide. FIBA is organized as five "FIBA zones": Africa, Asia, Americas, Europe, and Oceania. Its membership is comprised of 213 NSOs globally. The FIBA board of directors is responsible for FIBA international rules and regulations, as well as the FIBA World Cup and other global FIBA championship events. The FIBA central board, comprising 27 members, establishes the sports international regulations, and the assignment and organization of the FIBA World Cup. The central board members consist of a president, a secretary general, a treasurer, an NBA representative, a players' representative, 18 members representing different countries, and three co-opts. The current board of directors (as of October 2014), includes president Horacio Muratore from Argentina, secretary general Ingo Weiss from Germany, NBA representative Mark Tatum from the US, player representative Vlade Divac from Serbia, and co-opted members Julia Anikeeva from Russia, Manuel Pangilinan from Philippines, and Erick Thohir from Indonesia. Other members of the board are from Mali, US Virgin Islands, Qatar, Turkey, New Zealand, Mozambique, Benin, Paraguay, Canada, USA, Puerto Rico, China, Belgium, Spain, France, Sweden, Australia, and the Marshall Islands. There are also a number of commissions of FIBA, including: technical commission, competitions commission, legal commission, governance commission, finance commission, medical commission, support and development, advisory board, appeals panel, and the working calendar group.

Appendix 7B presents details of more than 80 IFs. Panel A of Appendix 7B shows IFs that are members of the IOC, which means they have events at either the Summer or Winter Olympics. Panel B of Appendix 7B shows IFs that are not members of the IOC but are recognized by the IOC. As noted in Section 7.1, some IFs that are not currently members of the IOC can and do make proposals to the IOC for their membership. Panel C of Appendix 7B lists other IFs that have some sporting aspect.

7.3.1 Role of International Federations

An IF is the global steward for its sport. In some cases an IF is a steward for multiple related sports. Exhibit 7.3 presents information on nine IFs that manage multiple related sports.

For example, FINA is responsible for swimming, diving, water polo and synchronized swimming. As part of its stewardship, each IF takes responsibility globally for its sports on all levels: development,

Summer Sports				Winter Sports	

Summer Sports

1 FINA: Aquatics
Diving
Swimming
Synchronized swimming
Water polo

2 ICF: Canoe
Slalom
Sprint

3 ICU: Cycling
Cycling BMX
Cycling road
Cycling track
Cycling mountain bike

4 FEI: Equestrian
Dressage
Eventing
Jumping

5 FIG: Gymnastics
Gymnastics artistic
Gymnastics rhythmic
Trampoline

6 FIVB: Volleyball
Beach volleyball
Volleyball

7 UWW: Wrestling
Greco-Roman
Freestyle

Winter Sports

8 FIBT: Bobsleigh
Bobsleigh
Bobsleigh skeleton
Skating
Figure skating
Short track speed skating
Speed skating

9 FIS: Skiing
Alpine skiing
Cross country skiing
Freestyle skiing
Nordic combined
Ski jumping
Snowboard

EXHIBIT 7.3 Examples of International Federations and Related Sports Managed

participation, competition, and performance. The members of an IF are NSFs, with one federation per jurisdiction (normally a single country). The NSFs elect the leadership (board of directors) of the IF at the organization's annual general meeting (AGM).

IFs play a vital role in the sport landscape. First, they decide the rules for qualification, the rules of the game, and the structure of world competitions such as world cups or the Olympics (where applicable). With a few high-profile exceptions such as soccer, the Olympic Games are the flagship event for IFs that are members of the IOC. Second, each holds the rights for the world championship(s) in its sports at all levels from elite to junior, male and female, and often also for the Paralympics. Third, each is responsible for the daily operations of its organization and any issues that arise (e.g., player misbehavior, etc.). Fourth, IFs work with its member NSFs to support and promote grassroots efforts that grow the sport across the world. Sport participation, in particular, is an increasingly higher priority as sport participation rates decline in many parts of the world. Fifth, each is charged with promoting and monitoring the integrity of its sport. Sixth, each leads efforts – along with WADA – on the anti-doping front for its sports including initiatives such as education programs to athletes and coaches. Seventh, IFs work with the IOC and global organizations (e.g., United Nations) to promote the positive benefits of sport to youth, including initiatives around diversity, fair play, and inclusion. Eighth, each IF takes the lead role in communicating and working with major global organizations, including the IOC, WADA, IPC, and the professional leagues (such as European soccer leagues, NFL, NHL, NBA, MLB, and MLS).

Some IFs have publicly released strategic plans to showcase to their various stakeholders their vision, values, and initiatives. Exhibit 7.4 presents the strategic plan of the International Cricket Council (ICC). The ICC, based in Dubai, manages multiple versions of the game of cricket. Two version of the game (one-day international (ODI) and Twenty20) have world cups in which national teams compete. The 2015 Twenty20 World Cup game between India and Pakistan, played in Adelaide Australia, was reported to set global viewership records for cricket games of more than one billion viewers.[3]

7.3.2 Role of National Sport Federations (NSFs)/National Sporting Organizations (NSOs)

National sport federations are governing bodies responsible for the overall administration and development of a given sport or sports in a particular country or jurisdiction. Their functioning is similar to the international federations but within their own geographic boundary. They also share a common objective, which is to develop and grow their sports nationally through participation, grassroots sports, and top-level competitions. They seek to achieve these objectives by working with participants, elite athletes, clubs, sport organizations, media, commercial partners, and government bodies. Box 7.3 uses Hockey Canada to illustrate the diverse activities of an NSO.

NSFs can be very different depending on factors such as the size of the country, its economy, and the relative status of the sport in that country. The Football Association (FA) in England is the governing federation for soccer in a region with a large and relatively strong economy. The FA was formed in 1863 and is reported to be the oldest football association in the world. Soccer is a major sport in England (where it is known as football) at both the professional and participant level. In this context, the FA operates with an extensive professional staff that has much functional expertise. In contrast, in the case of small economies or with minor sports in a country, the management of a federation may consist of only one or two full-time employees with several volunteers assisting in all different types of assignments.

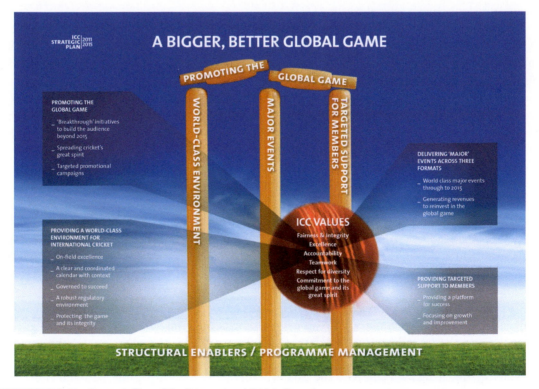

EXHIBIT 7.4 The Strategic Plan of the International Cricket Council

BOX 7.3 HOCKEY CANADA PLAYS MULTIPLE ROLES AS A LEADING CANADIAN NSO

In Canada, ice hockey is the national winter sport and is extremely popular. When the country's men's national team captured gold in a thrilling game to conclude the 2010 Winter Olympic Games (held in Vancouver, Canada), more than two-thirds of the country tuned into the game via television. A national celebration erupted following the thrilling finale to the game. The women's national team – who also captured gold in Vancouver with a television audience of more than a third of the population – regularly sells out its exhibition games in NHL arenas across the country. The NHL is the most popular professional sport and its televised *Hockey Night in Canada* every Saturday in the winter months is a national institution that dates back more than 50 years. More than 540,000 boys and nearly 85,000 girls play minor hockey.

Hockey Canada, the NSO for the sport in Canada, governs the sport nationally and is responsible for the growth and development of the game.[4] It manages programs from entry-level to high performance, names the national and Olympic teams, and represents Canada with the IF for the sport (International Ice Hockey Federation, IIHF). Hockey Canada partners with the Canadian Hockey League (CHL, major junior hockey) and Canadian Interuniversity Sport (CIS, university hockey) on various initiatives. A not-for-profit organization headquartered in Calgary, Alberta, with offices in other parts of the country, Hockey Canada was founded (under a different name) in 1914. Today, the NSO has a staff of more than 120 professionals. It is supported by more than a dozen blue-chip sponsors and has a highly successful merchandise program. Hockey Canada operates major events across the country and administers programs that support coaching, player development, and much more for men's hockey, women's hockey, and sledge hockey (Paralympic version of the game). Hockey Canada has 13 member provincial branches that operate more than 3,500 minor hockey associations with more than 634,000 registered kids and nearly 100,000 registered adults. Thousands more play informally. Hockey Canada also reports that there are 98,000 registered coaches and 32,000 accredited officials. It has more than 580,000 Facebook fans, the highest of any NSO in the country.

Hockey Canada's board of directors – all volunteers – are elected for four-year terms by the membership of the organization. The NSO then operates seven standing committees (national appeals, governance, audit and finance, human resources, risk management, program standards, and nominations) and five councils (minor, junior, female, development, and senior) that report to the board. Hockey Canada also has a foundation, the Hockey Canada Foundation, which supports its charitable efforts.

Typically, the leadership (CEO or executive director) of an NSO is responsible for a number of key tasks, including:

1   Setting the strategy and strategic plan for the organization.
2   Drafting and approving policies to guide the activities of the NSO.
3   Representing the sport's interests at the IF table.
4   Determining the qualification criteria and funding for national teams.

5   Organizing or sanctioning the rights to organize national championships, national events and national qualifying events.

6   Managing anti-doping in their country/jurisdiction.

7   Financing their sport.

8   Marketing their sport(s) and discipline(s).

9   Managing coaching and technical programs.

10   Hosting major events.

11   Growing sport participation.

12   Lobbying the federation and regional governments for more support.

13   Launching, operating, and funding national training centers or regional training centers.

A number of NSOs today are increasingly engaging in social media to pursue their marketing objectives. Since social media can be a powerful and cost-effective communication tool, it allows and enables NSOs to reach out and interact with their stakeholders directly and in real-time, with no borders and time barriers.

7.3.3 Conflicts and Differences Between Different Sporting Bodies

With many sporting bodies at the global, continent, and national levels, as well as powerful sporting leagues and clubs, it is not surprising that conflicts of interest and other differences can arise between two or more bodies. Several illustrations are:

- The IOC includes soccer as one of its Summer sports. Countries compete for the gold medal in men's and women's competitions. FIFA, the most wealthy IF, earns major dollars from its own global World Cup competitions. Exhibit 7.5 shows the revenues, expenses, surplus (revenues minus expenses), and reserves of FIFA from 2007 to 2014. Over a four-year cycle, FIFA's revenues are within 80 percent of the IOC's revenues. The FIFA Men's World Cup is FIFA's "jewel in the crown." To avoid the Olympic soccer medal competition being an equivalent World Cup, FIFA restricts the men's tournament to be effectively a tournament for those aged under 23.[5] This restriction means that most of the star soccer players in the world do not play in the Olympic Games.

- The IOC in 2005 voted to exclude baseball (a men-only sport) and softball (a women-only sport) from the Olympics after the 2008 Summer Olympics. The April to October playing season of US Major League Baseball, the leading professional baseball league in the world, clashes with the Summer Olympics' August time slot. MLB clubs were very reluctant to release their star players to appear in the Olympics. This meant that the best players in the world were not showcased at the Olympics. Some observers surmised that the conflict between the self-interested position of MLB and the self-interest of the IOC was important to many who voted to drop baseball as an Olympic sport. Note that if this was the case, there was an inconsistency in continuing to include men's soccer as an Olympic sport and discontinuing men's baseball. FIFA, with its strong European heritage, is viewed by many as being an insider to the "Olympic Club."

- Basketball game rules played in the Olympics are governed by FIBA, the IF in basketball (see Box 7.2). These rules are not the same as those that the NBA mandates in what is the leading professional league in the world. For example, FIBA has four ten-minute quarters versus four 12-minute quarters in the NBA.[6] Further, court length differs between FIBA (91' 10" × 49' 2.5") and the NBA

(94' × 50'), as does the distance for a three-point field goal (FIBA 20' 6.1" and NBA 23' 9").[7] USA Basketball is the national sport federation for basketball in the USA. Exhibit 7.6 shows the Revenues and Expenses of USA Basketball. Its revenues are less than 1 percent of the total NBA revenues.

Year	Revenues	Expenses	Surplus	Reserves
2007	$882	$833	$49	$643
2008	$957	$773	$184	$902
2009	$1,059	$863	$196	$1,061
2010	$1,291	$1,089	$202	$1,280
2011	$1,070	$1,034	$36	$1,293
2012	$1,166	$1,077	$89	$1,378
2013	$1,386	$1,314	$72	$1,432
2014	$2,096	$1,955	$141	$1,523

EXHIBIT 7.5 FIFA Financials: 2007/14 ($M)

USA Basketball

For the years ending September 30, 2013 and 2012

REVENUE	2013	2012
Licensing and marketing	$ 2,750,957	$ 7,083,525
Support from United States Olympic Committee	1,108,722	1,131,308
Investment income	768,413	1,379,108
Competition income	400,000	421,295
In-kind contributions	313,514	584,382
Sanction and letters of clearance fees	67,177	49,770
Other	79,306	57,025
Total revenue	5,488,089	10,706,413
EXPENSES Program services:		
Events: Senior National Team – Men	767,655	3,105,630
FIBA World Championship U19 – Men	433,173	
FIBA World Championship U19 – Women	378,131	
FIBA Americas U16 – Men	371,550	
Senior National Team – Women	316,862	1,990,613
World University Games – Men	308,493	
FIBA Americas U16 – Women	308,343	
World University Games – Women	299,560	
Hoop Summit – Men	252,984	237,798
3 × 3 Championships – Men	111,012	108,285
3 × 3 Championships – Women	105,869	109,460

EXHIBIT 7.6 (cont.)

FIBA World Championship U17 – Men		348,472
FIBA World Championship U17 – Women		318,969
FIBA Americas U18 Qualifying Tournament – Men		313,945
FIBA Americas U18 Qualifying Tournament – Women		296,372
Pan Am Games – Men		157,644
Pan Am Games – Women		107,289
Disabled events grants Youth Division	191,511	30,532
Other program services	53,911	23,271
Total program services	3,899,054	7,148,280
Supporting services:		
General and administrative	576,430	680,401
Fundraising	75,311	152,591
Total supporting services	651,741	832,992
Total expenses	4,550,795	7,981,272
CHANGE IN NET ASSETS	937,294	2,725,141
UNRESTRICTED NET ASSETS, beginning of year	15,225,856	12,500,715
UNRESTRICTED NET ASSETS, end of year	$ 16,163,150	$ 15,225,856

EXHIBIT 7.6 Revenues and Expenses of USA Basketball

7.4 DECISION MAKING AT SPORTS FEDERATIONS

Although there are vast differences in the resources available to different sports federations around the globe, there are some underlying similarities to some of the decisions made and the challenges faced.

7.4.1 Mix of Paid and Non-Paid Management and Boards

As not-for-profit organizations, sport federations are typically organized under a board of directors elected by the members of the organization. A typical NSO board is elected by its regional/state/provincial members at the NSO's annual general meeting (AGM), where the leadership board positions (president, vice-president, secretary-general, treasurer, member-at-large, etc.) are elected for an upcoming term, typically two to four years in length. Board positions in sport federations are largely unpaid positions (expenses paid), where the president takes on a stewardship role for the federation. The president with the support of the board then hires a chief executive officer (CEO) (often called an executive director, ED, in smaller federations) to manage and run the organization's day-to-day activities, with periodic reporting and evaluation back to the board. The CEO has broad responsibilities, covering activities such as those at the grassroots and championship levels, as well as business-related activities such as finance and marketing. Depending on the resource base of the federation, professionals will be hired to lead or work on these various functions. In very small federations, the volunteer board members often take on some of these functions. In large federations there can be hundreds of people in their staff with a high level of expertise in different areas. Box 7.4 provides an example of the governance structure sport in a country (Canada) where government plays a major financial support role via Sport Canada, a department of the federal government.

BOX 7.4 GOVERNMENT SUPPORT OF SPORT – THE CASE OF SPORT CANADA

In Canada, sport is governed at a federal level under the Ministry of Canadian Heritage under Sport Canada. Sport Canada is a branch of International and Intergovernmental Affairs that has three key elements: Sport Programs, Sport Policy, and Major Games and Hosting. The program activities of Sport Canada are mostly about distributing funds to Canadian NSOs (e.g., Basketball Canada), MSOs (e.g., Canadian Centre for Ethics in Sport), athletes, coaches, and events. The Sport Support Program provides funding to MSOs and NSOs based on performance and other standards, while the Hosting Program selects events (based on criteria) to support, and the Athlete Assistance Program is a direct support program for high-performance athletes. The policy work of Sport Canada provides the frameworks, guidelines, and rules that structure funding and MSO/NSO operations in Canada. Examples include the Canada Games, a federal and provincial partnership on a youth sport games. Specific policies include the Canadian Sport Policy (2002, 2012) and the Fitness and Amateur Sport Act of 1961, which kicked off government involvement in sport in the country.

In addition to the federal government and Sport Canada, each of Canada's 13 provincial and territorial governments take on the responsibility to promote and develop sport in their province or territory. Most provincial governments focus on the participation and development aspects, leaving facilities to the municipal (city) governments. The Canadian Sport Policy has been endorsed by the 13 federal, provincial, and territorial governments in Canada, the MSOs, and the NSOs. The current version of the policy sets directions for 2012/22 on participation, development, high performance, and capacity considerations in sport. A series of action plans are outlined with responsibility assigned.

7.4.2 The Politics of Revenue and Other Resource Allocations

The context for many federations of (a) members having large differences in how they contribute to the revenues of a federation, and (b) equal voting creates a predictable lobbying environment. There are incentives for leadership candidates to lobby for votes by shifting resources away from the few large contributors to the more numerous members making relatively small contributions to revenue generation. Consider UEFA, the European Soccer Federation. It brings together 53 federations from many countries and regions. Its president is elected every four years. Each European federation has one vote, whether it is a large country such as Germany or France or a small one such as Andorra, the Faroe Islands, or Gibraltar. This structure means that the vote of a country like Andorra – with a population of 80,000 people – is as important as the vote of the representative from Germany. This governance structure means that the UEFA president is likely to be very attentive to the demands of smaller federations that can be fulfilled at a lower cost.

The alternative to equal voting by member of a federation is where the more powerful have more votes than other members. Box 7.5 describes voting changes at the International Cricket Council (ICC) where there was a shift from equal voting for its ten full members to India (and to a lesser extent Australia and England) having a much larger say in the administration of the global cricket world. India is the global economic powerhouse in the world of cricket.

BOX 7.5 INDIAN CRICKET FLEXES ITS FINANCIAL MUSCLE TO RESTRUCTURE GLOBAL REVENUE-SHARING BY THE INTERNATIONAL CRICKET COUNCIL

Cricket is one of the most global sports, with many of the leading countries being members of what is now called the British Commonwealth. The title of the global cricketing body was the Imperial Cricket Conference from 1909 to 1963, the International Cricket Conference from 1964 to 1988, and since 1989 has been the International Cricket Council (ICC). The "Imperial" word in the 1909/64 title very much reflected the early British dominant role in global cricket decision making. The inaugural "test status" members of the ICC in 1909 were England, Australia, and South Africa, all three of which were members of what was then called the British Empire (later to be called the British Commonwealth). Over time more members were added – India, New Zealand, and the West Indies in 1926. After Pakistan became a separate country in 1947, it joined the ICC as a "test status" country. South Africa ceased to be a member in 1961 when it lost British Commonwealth membership due to its apartheid policy. Additional members added were Sri Lanka (1981), South Africa (re-admitted in 1991), Zimbabwe (1992), and Bangladesh (2000). Currently, these ten countries form the Tier 1 ("full") members of the ICC. There are also 38 countries as "associate members" and more than 50 countries as "affiliate members."

From its inception in 1909 to 2005, the ICC was headquartered at the Lord's Cricket Ground in London, which was viewed by many as the ancestral home of cricket. Decision making was strongly influenced by what the British viewed as "in the best interests of cricket." The British viewpoint was not always shared by other members, especially those from India. In the early 2000s, ICC revenues began to grow with more lucrative media contracts associated with various forms of cricket world cups. In 2005, the headquarters of the ICC was moved to Dubai in the UAE. While the move was nominally motivated to take advantage of taxation benefits Dubai granted to the ICC, a very substantive reason was being closer to India, which had become the economic powerhouse of global cricket. Cricket in India, a country with more than one billion people, is the national and dominant sport.

In 2014, a major economic shift in ICC revenue allocations was proposed that reflected India's economic power position in global cricket. Prior to 2014, an equal sharing rule was used to allocate global revenues among the ten "full members." One commentator, Atul Pande, estimated that pre-2014, the "full members" received 71.6 percent in total of the revenue pool, with each member receiving 7.16 percent.[8] Post-2014, three countries increased their decision making power and revenue allocations – India, England, and Australia. Pande reported that the proposed revenue allocations post the 2014 ICC restructuring would be:

1   India – 34.6 percent
2   England – 10.5 percent
3   Australia – 8.0 percent
4   Pakistan – 5.8 percent
5   South Africa – 5.7 percent
6   West Indies – 4.9 percent

7   Sri Lanka – 4.9 percent
8   New Zealand – 4.6 percent
9   Bangladesh – 4.1 percent
10 Zimbabwe – 4.0 percent

While the above percentages are an outsider's estimate, there is general agreement that the final allocation to India will be several times above that of any other country. Pande noted that "even after the new revenue share agreement, India still has lower than its share of the global revenue it generates." He estimated that India's value creation was "upwards of 75 %."

7.4.3 Major Decisions at the Federation Level

Major questions to be answered by the board or the top management of a federation include:

- **What are the objectives of the federation?** Ideally, these objectives will guide how resources will be allocated. Will the federation invest more resources in investing in elite athletes? Will it devote more resources to grassroots infrastructure? Priorities are either set in advance of decisions, or else become revealed when those decisions are executed.
- **Who should lead our federation?** Choosing the CEO that will run the day-to-day operations is a crucial decision for a federation as with most other organizations. The CEO is the board's line of communication to the organization and often becomes the "face" of the federation externally.
- **How do we grow our federation with minimal resources?** Many small NSOs, provincial sport organizations, regional sport organizations, and state sport organizations, have few staff. In these cases, the board will be doing some of the "heavy lifting." For example, Modern Pentathlon Australia, the NSO for the sport in Australia, receives funding of AU$25,000 from the Australian Sport Commission for 2014/15.[9] With such a limited amount of resources, the board is likely seeking ways to acquire additional funding sources in order to hire staff and professionalize the organization.
- **Which events/sports should be on the program?** Federations seeking to make their events more attractive to potential young participants and to attendees at events often experiment with new events. Astute decisions about specific experiments to run can have much upside. Where a federation has responsibility over multiple areas of a sport, decisions about the broadness of areas to include in events are required. For example, the International Ski Federation (ISF) has domain over alpine skiing, cross country skiing, freestyle skiing, Nordic combined, ski jumping, and snowboard. Should separate events be held in each area or should combinations of them be included in a mega-event?
- **How to allocate the budget?** In addition to setting the global strategy for the federation, the board also approves the budget each year. Typically the CEO/ED works with the treasurer (a board member) to draft a budget for board approval. This important decision allocates resources for the year in broad categories (e.g., high performance, youth development, marketing, etc.) which the CEO/ED then works within to pursue the strategy outcomes for the year.

7.5 BUILDING THE REVENUE AND RESOURCE BASE

A constant challenge for global sporting bodies and federations is continuing to build the revenue and resource base. The following illustrate the multiple platforms being used:

- **Global body and international federation distributions.** Global bodies and international federations can be important revenue sources for organizations within their domain. Exhibit 7.2 illustrates how the IOC distributes money to both its NOCs and IFs.

- **Media rights.** As noted in Section 7.2, media rights represent the single largest revenue source for the IOC – 73 percent in the 2009/12 period. Federations governing sports with large global interest, such as FIFA, also have large media contracts that are central to their total revenue model. Many other federations, however, are at the other end of the spectrum as regards potential media rights revenue potential. There is increasing interest by smaller federations who struggle to get broadcast television contracts to use internet-based media content platforms. Here the revenues could be some combination of subscription, advertising, and sponsorship – see Model #1 in Exhibit 15.1 of Chapter 15.

- **Sponsorship.** Much like any sporting league, federations have to design a sponsorship strategy with the number and types of sponsors as well as the sponsorship packages. Figuring out what is the federation's competitive advantage to attract corporate interest is a major challenge for all but the most prominent federations. Indeed, each sport or set of sports holds unique traits and has athletes with great stories. But the market is crowded (including properties in other areas, such as arts, festivals, charities, and events) that make sponsorship difficult. The CEO must decide what this competitive advantage is, seek to establish it, and leverage it appropriately. For example, a sport such as track and field has characteristics of power and quickness, which might be the right choice to attract sponsor interest from corporations interested in those attributes.

- **Event attendance-related.** This revenue source is driven by factors such as the number of attendees, the prices charged, the merchandise sold, parking, and so on. It is important that federations negotiate effectively with the rights-holders to the venue(s) where the event will be held. Events that can have many hundreds of participants and thousands of spectators will require a sizable infrastructure to be in place, beyond the physical facility itself – examples include concessionaires, security, policy, and volunteers. Chapter 9 further discusses this area.

- **Government.** Funding from governments at multiple levels in multiple countries plays a central role in the financial and often other operational areas of decision making for country-based National Olympic Committees or national sport federations. Where a country sees success at a global level in sports as part of country branding, politicians can allocate sizable funds to the national sporting bodies. One contrast in this area is between China and India. "China Inc." has invested large amounts in building its international sporting success at the Summer Olympics. Over a three-decade period, China has moved its ranking in overall gold medals at the Summer Olympics from #11 in 1988 to being #1 or #2 in 2004, 2008, and 2012. In contrast, "India Inc." has not made Olympic sports success a priority in government spending. India has consistently ranked 40th or below in various Summer Olympic medal counts over many decades.

7.6 GRASSROOTS SPORTS

Sporting federations across the board have a vested interest in promoting a high level of grassroots interest in their sport. Many federations have developed programs to promote grassroots activity. In recent years, corporations are seeing the support of grassroots sports through sponsorship or endorsement as an effective way to market their products and services and their commitment to the local communities. For example, Football Federation Australia has teamed up with Hyundai to develop an initiative called the Goals 4 Grassroots program. The program is designed to provide funding and help raise awareness for more than 154 junior football programs throughout Australia. Programs like this aim to increase participation at earlier ages and then keep high levels of participation as girls and boys grow into their teenage years and beyond.

One of the main challenges to grow a particular sport is having facilities where the sport can be practiced. As society becomes more and more urban, access to safe sport facilities and quality coaching is more and more challenging. For example, finding a soccer pitch, basketball court, or outdoor swimming pool in the heart of a major city is becoming harder. The other main challenge for federations' grassroots sports programs is to attract players and children. This endeavor is of interest for the government because sports are associated with a healthier society as well as a more cohesive one.

7.7 GOVERNMENTS AND SPORTS MANAGEMENT

Governments in multiple countries are becoming involved in sports, in part because of the values it communicates, the benefits for health, its entertainment value, and the social identity that it represents. Government efforts often happen through sporting federations. Government's objectives here can include:

1   **Sport communicates social values that society deems as important** such as teamwork, development of social skills, competition, talent, friendship, winning, and losing. Although there are certainly negative elements (e.g., athlete misbehavior, injury), the positive are seen as dominating those negative ones.
2   **Sports improve the overall health of society.** Sport is intimately related to physical health and physical literacy. People practicing sports at an amateur level have better health directly because of the practice of sports and indirectly because of the habits (such as eating habits) associated with sports.
3   **The performance of their national teams and athletes is important to citizens** of countries, as evidenced by the billions of viewers of the Olympic Games, FIFA World Cup, and IAAF Athletics World Championships. Sometimes this passion can turn for the worse. For example, after Argentina's loss to Germany in the 2014 World Cup, riots on the streets of Buenos Aires erupted as upset fans took to the streets.[10]
4   **Sport is a reflection of society.** In today's open world, with ease of communication, sport is a way in which societies interact and communicate. Although people may have different interests, occupations, etc., people in a culture can attend a sporting event and for at least that night have the same interests as one another and connect in a way that they otherwise would not have been able to.

5   **Sport is a proxy for war and politics.** As some sociologists tell us, sport has taken the place of war (historically) as the competition ground for countries. The Olympics is the best example of this; during the 1980 Olympics, a hockey match between the USA and the Soviet Union was often referred to as a major morale booster for American citizens. The match took place during the height of the Cold War and was used by many US citizens as a confidence booster when the severely overmatched US team miraculously won.

6   **Sport can bring a country together.** For example, the men's Olympic gold medal ice hockey game at the 2010 Vancouver Games was the most watched television broadcast (sport or non-sport) in Canadian history, with peak audiences estimated to be about two-thirds of the country.

7   **Sport is a passion point** for many people that can influence voting patterns. Politicians are quick at meeting the athletes and players that have succeeded internationally to associate their image to the image of the winners.

Typical government initiatives include athlete funding, NSO support programs, talent identification facilities, coaching programs, event hosting, and sport policies.

7.8 SUMMARY

Many not-for-profit organizations play important roles in different levels of the sporting world. The highest public profile roles are associated with major world events such as the Olympics and world cups where there are a relatively small number of athletes but billions of dollars of media rights, sponsorship, and at-event revenues. The highest level of physical engagement occurs at the participant level, which often starts at very young ages for children. Associated with this vast number of active participants are armies of committed volunteers who assist in many different ways to help make the participant experience a rewarding one. Governments also have many potential roles to play in the multiple arenas discussed in this chapter.

APPENDIX 7A ABBREVIATIONS USED FOR ORGANIZATIONS DISCUSSED IN CHAPTER 7

- AIS – Australian Institute of Sport
- BOA – British Olympic Association
- CGF – Commonwealth Games Federation
- COC – Canadian Olympic Committee
- FISU – Fédération Internationale de Sport Universitaire
- IF – International Federation
- IOC – International Olympic Committee
- IPC – International Paralympic Committee
- IWGA – International World Games Association
- LOCOG – Local Organizing Committee for Olympic Games
- MSO – Multisport Organization
- NOC – National Olympic Committee
- NPC – National Paralympic Committee

- NSO/NSF – National Sporting Organization/National Sport Federation
- UEFA – Union of European Football Associations
- USOC – United States Olympic Committee
- WADA – World Anti-Doping Agency

Note: Specific IFs are presented in Appendix 7B

APPENDIX 7B LIST OF INTERNATIONAL SPORTS FEDERATIONS (IOC MEMBERS AND NON-MEMBERS)

Sport	International federation name	Initial	Number of member NSOs*	Website
International federations who are International Olympic Committee members**				
Aquatics	Fédération Internationale De Natation	FINA	203	www.fina.org
Archery	World Archery Federation	WA	153	www.worldarchery.org
Athletics	International Association of Athletic Federations	IAAF	212	www.iaaf.org
Badminton	Badminton World Federation	BWF	177	www.bwfbadminton.org
Basketball	International Basketball Confederation	FIBA	213	www.fiba.com
Biathlon	International Biathlon Union	IBU	60	www.biathlonworld.com
Bobsleigh	International Bobsleigh and Skeleton Federation	FIBT	60	www.fibt.com
Boxing	World Professional Boxing Federation	WPBF	196	www.wpbf-usbc.org
Canoe/kayak	International Canoe Federation	ICF	162	www.canoeicf.com
Curling	World Curling Federation	WCF	53	www.worldcurling.org
Cycling	International Cycling Union	ICU	127	www.uci.ch
Equestrian	Fédération Equestre Internationale	FEI	132	www.fei.org
Fencing	Fédération Internationale D'Escrime	FIE	145	www.fie.ch
Football	Fédération Internationale De Football	FIFA	209	www.fifa.com
Golf	International Golf Federation	IGF	137	www.igfgolf.org
Gymnastics	International Gymnastics Federation	FIG	128	www.fig-gymnastics.com

APPENDIX 7B (cont.)

Sport	International federation name	Initial	Number of member NSOs*	Website
Handball	International Handball Association	IHF	190	www.ihf.info
Hockey	International Hockey Federation	FIH	128	www.fih.ch
Ice Hockey	International Ice Hockey Federation	IIHF	73	www.iihf.com
Judo	International Judo Federation	IJF	201	www.intjudo.eu
Luge	International Luge Federation	FIL	54	www.fil-luge.org
Modern Pentathlon	Union Internationale De Pentathlon Moderne	UIPM	115	www.pentathlon.org
Rowing	World Rowing Federation	FISA	142	www.worldrowing.com
Rugby	World Rugby	WR	38	www.worldrugby.org
Sailing	International Sailing Federation	ISAF	140	www.sailing.org
Shooting	International Shooting Sport Federation	ISSF	161	www.issf-sports.org
Skating	International Skating Union	ISU	88	www.isu.org
Skiing	International Ski Federation	FIS	118	www.fis-ski.com
Table Tennis	International Table Tennis Federation	ITTF	220	www.ittf.com
Taekwondo	International Taekwondo Federation	ITF	128	www.tkd-itf.org
Tennis	International Tennis Federation	ITF	210	www.itftennis.com
Triathlon	International Triathlon Union	ITU	119	www.triathlon.org
Volleyball	International Volleyball Federation	FIVB	193	www.fivb.org
Weightlifting	International Weightlifting Federation	IWF	188	www.iwf.net
Wrestling	United World Wrestling	UWW	174	www.unitedworldwrestling.org
International federations who are recognized by the International Olympic Committee***				
Air Sports	Fédération Aeronautique Internationale	FAI	86	www.fai.org
Automobile	Fédération Internationale De L'Automobile	FIA	140	www.fia.com
Bandy	Federation of International Bandy	FIB	29	www.worldbandy.com

APPENDIX 7B (cont.)

Sport	International federation name	Initial	Number of member NSOs*	Website
Baseball/ softball	World Baseball Softball Confederation	WBSC	193	www.wbsc.co (not.com)
Basque pelota	Fédération Internationale de Pelote Basque	FIPV	30	www.fipv.net
Billiard sports	World Confederation of Billiard Sports	WCBS	148	www.billiard-wcbs.org
Boules	Bowls Sports World Confederation	CMSB	Not Available	cmsboules.org
Bowling	Fédération Internationale Des Quilleurs	FIQ	139	www.worldbowling.org
Bridge	World Bridge Federation	WBF	46	www.worldbridge.org
Chess	World Chess Federation	FIDE	182	www.fide.com
Cricket	International Cricket Council	ICC	105	www.icc-cricket.com
Dance sport	World Dance Sport Federation	WDSF	92	www.worlddancesport.org
Floorball	International Floorball Federation	IFF	66	www.floorball.org
Flying disc	World Flying Disc Federation	WFDF	58	www.wfdf.org
Karate	World Karate Federation	WKF	188	www.wkf.net
Korfball	International Korfball Federation	IKF	66	www.ikf.org
Life saving	International Lifesaving Federation	ILSF	130	www.ilsf.org
Motorcycle racing	Fédération Internationale de Motocyclisme	FIM	90	www.fim-live.com
Mountaineering and climbing	International Climbing and Mountaineering Federation	UIAA	63	www.theuiaa.org
Netball	International Federation of Netball association	INF	75	www.netball.org
Orienteering	International Orienteering Federation	IOF	79	http://orienteering.org
Polo	Federation of International Polo	FIP	81	www.fippolo.com
Power boating	Union Internationale Motonautique	UIM	50	www.uimpowerboating.com
Racquetball	International Racquetball Association	IRF	106	www. internationalracquetball.com
Roller sports	Fédération Internationale de Roller Sports	FIRS	135	www.rollersports.org

APPENDIX 7B (*cont.*)

Sport	International federation name	Initial	Number of member NSOs*	Website
Sport climbing	International Federation of Sport Climbing	IFSC	80	www.ifsc-climbing.org
Squash	World Squash Federation	WSF	147	www.worldsquash.org
Sumo	International Sumo Federation	IWSF	84	www.ifs-sumo.org
Surfing	International Surfing Association	ISA	94	www.isasurf.org
Tug of war	Tug of War International Federation	TWIF	53	www.tugofwar-twif.org
Underwater sports	Confédération Mondiale des Activités Subaquatiques	CMAS	130	www.cmas.org
Wushu	International Wushu Federation	IWUF	147	www.iwuf.org
Other international federations****				
Aikido	International Aikido Federation	IAF	47	www.aikido-international.org
Beach Soccer	Beach Soccer Worldwide	BSWW	—	www.beachsoccer.com
Bodybuilding	International Federation of Bodybuilding & Fitness	IFBB	182	www.ifbb.com
Broomball	International Federation of Broomball Associations	IFBA	16	http://internationalbroomball.org
Cerebral palsy	Cerebral Palsy International Sport and Recreation Association	ICSF	62	www.cpisra.org
Croquet	World Croquet Federation	WCF	29	www.wcfcroquet.org
Darts	World Darts Federation	WDF	69	www.dartswdf.com
Deaf sport	International Committee of Sports for the Deaf	ICSD	109	www.deaflympics.com
Dragon boat	International Dragon Boat Federation	IDBF	74	www.idbf.org
Draughts	World Draughts Federation	FMJD	68	www.fmjd.org
Fishing	Confédération Internationale de la Peche Sportive	CIPS	115	www.cips-fips.com/cips/index_en.html
Fistball	International Fistball Association	IFA	36	www.ifa-fistball.com
Fives	Rugby Fives Association	RFA	123	http://rugbyfivesassociation.net
Flying disc	World Flying Disc Federation	WFDF	88	www.wfdf.org

APPENDIX 7B *(cont.)*

Sport	International federation name	Initial	Number of member NSOs*	Website
Foosball	International Table Soccer Federation	ITSF	46	www.table-soccer.org
Football (US)	International Federation of American Football	IFAF	71	http://ifaf.org
Go	International Go Federation	IGF	74	http://intergofed.org

* Refers to the number as of May 1, 2015 from IF websites or annual reports. Often members are classified differently by IF, so assumptions were made. In some cases, estimates were made, so numbers should be considered as approximate. All content in the table is taken as of May 1, 2015.

** IOC member IFs have sports on the program of the Summer or Winter Olympic Games (see www.olympic.org).

*** IFs recognized by the IOC are not members on the Olympic program but are recognized as IFs by the IOC (see www.olympic.org).

**** This is a list of other IFs that are not members of the IOC nor recognized by the IOC. They are sourced from Sport Accord lists (www.sportaccord.com) and other sources. This list is not to be considered complete in terms of all the IFs that exist.

NOTES

1 An important document as regards understanding the IOC is their Olympic Charter – see www.olympic.org/Documents/olympic_charter_en.pdf.

2 J. Linden, "Baseball-softball vow to fight on after Olympic rejection," *Reuters*, September 8, 2013.

3 A. Faulkner, "Billion eyes on most watched cricket match in history," The Australian (January 13, 2015). See also http://www.business-standard.com/article/beyond-business/india-pakistan-world-cup-match-created-history-in-digital-views-too-115021700415_1.html

4 http://cdn.agilitycms.com/hockey-canada/Corporate/About/Downloads/2014_dec_annual_report_e.pdf.

5 A maximum of three male players over 23 years of age are eligible to play in the finals of the Olympic medal competition in soccer.

6 http://basketball.about.com/od/internationalbasketball/tp/Olympic-Basketball-Vs-The-Nba.htm.

7 www.worldofbasketball.org/difference-between-nba-and-fiba-rules.htm.

8 A. Pande, "Momentous BCCI control just the beginning of real restructuring of cricket world and running of the game," *SportzPower*, February 21, 2014.

9 www.ausport.gov.au/__data/assets/pdf_file/0008/596123/Web_NSO_Investment_Sheet_2014-15_19_February_2015.pdf.

10 http://rt.com/news/172496-argentina-football-fans-clash.

8 COLLEGE SPORTS

College or university is a key stage in life for many people.[1] From the late teenage years into adulthood, many study in a variety of college fields to further their careers and learning. While for many students sport is an important element of the post-secondary (post-high school) education experience, the level of engagement varies dramatically school by school and student by student. Indeed, there are multiple aspects of the college lifestyle where college sports can play a role in student life (participant, social, special events, etc.). Further, many – including those who attended and those who did not attend – also engage in college sports later on in their post-college lives as alumni or fans of sport. This engagement takes on numerous forms:

- **Intercollegiate games and events.** Here student-athletes from one college compete with student-athletes from other colleges. At one extreme are games where there are national or regional broadcasts with large fan interest. In the United States, some college football games are played in football stadiums with more than 100,000 in attendance. Broadcasts of some college football "bowl games" (i.e., championship games) have attracted audiences that exceed those watching many MLB, NBA, and NHL championship games.[2] At the other extreme are intercollegiate games in lower-profile sports where there is much less media attention and where there may be more student-athletes competing than there are people watching (and often those watching are friends and family of the athletes participating).
- **Intra-college games and events.** In these cases, students within a college participate in games and events against other students in the same college – often called intramural sports. Participants in these games often follow the rules that are used in intercollege games or at comparable games in professional leagues. Intramural leagues are often managed by the college's athletics department or student associations.
- **Recreational activities.** These activities are informal in nature, where students use sporting activities to promote their mental or physical health. Rationales for competing include body image, social, and fitness. Colleges differ greatly in the investments they have made in the quality and quantity of infrastructure and commitment they have to recreational sports being an important aspect of student life. In some cases, recreational activities require significant infrastructure investment (e.g., swimming, weightlifting) while in others, only an area of grass is required (e.g., flag football, ultimate Frisbee).
- **Fan commitment/engagement with college games and events.** These fans attend intercollegiate games and events and can include current or past college students as well as many who did not attend college.

8.1 MULTIPLE LEVELS OF DECISION MAKING IN COLLEGE SPORTS

Although other countries support and invest in college sports, colleges in the United States have made by far the largest investments in sports, especially in intercollegiate games/events. Here, multibillion-dollar media contracts exemplify the high level of interest in elite college football and basketball games in United States colleges. Exhibit 8.1 provides an overview of three categories of institutions in the US college sports landscape.

At each level, there are many people in management positions who possess particular skillsets. Indeed, as the revenues associated with college sports have increased, there has been an expansion in the number and professionalism in college management ranks. These levels are described here:

- **Governing body level.** The National College Athletic Association (NCAA) is the leading US college sport governing body. The head executive of the NCAA is called the president.

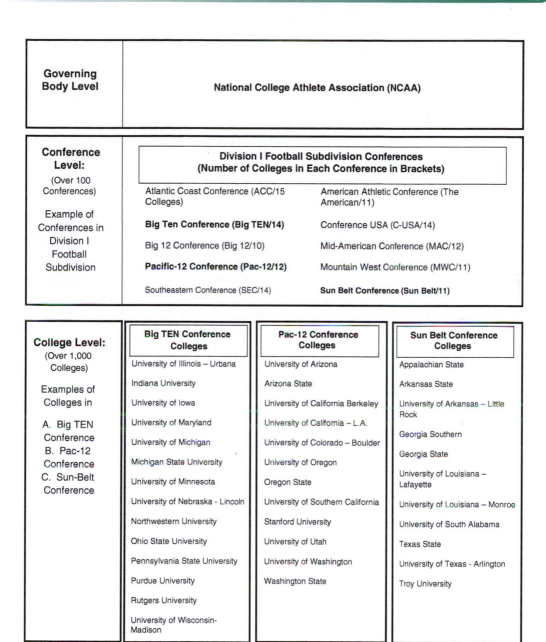

Governing Body Level	National College Athlete Association (NCAA)

Conference Level:
(Over 100 Conferences)

Example of Conferences in Division I Football Subdivision

Division I Football Subdivision Conferences
(Number of Colleges in Each Conference in Brackets)

Atlantic Coast Conference (ACC/15 Colleges)	American Athletic Conference (The American/11)
Big Ten Conference (Big TEN/14)	Conference USA (C-USA/14)
Big 12 Conference (Big 12/10)	Mid-American Conference (MAC/12)
Pacific-12 Conference (Pac-12/12)	Mountain West Conference (MWC/11)
Southeastern Conference (SEC/14)	**Sun Belt Conference (Sun Belt/11)**

College Level:
(Over 1,000 Colleges)

Examples of Colleges in

A. Big TEN Conference
B. Pac-12 Conference
C. Sun-Belt Conference

Big TEN Conference Colleges	Pac-12 Conference Colleges	Sun Belt Conference Colleges
University of Illinois – Urbana	University of Arizona	Appalachian State
Indiana University	Arizona State	Arkansas State
University of Iowa	University of California Berkeley	University of Arkansas – Little Rock
University of Maryland	University of California – L.A.	
University of Michigan	University of Colorado – Boulder	Georgia Southern
Michigan State University	University of Oregon	Georgia State
University of Minnesota	Oregon State	University of Louisiana – Lafayette
University of Nebraska - Lincoln	University of Southern California	University of Louisiana – Monroe
Northwestern University	Stanford University	University of South Alabama
Ohio State University	University of Utah	Texas State
Pennsylvania State University	University of Washington	University of Texas - Arlington
Purdue University	Washington State	Troy University
Rutgers University		
University of Wisconsin-Madison		

EXHIBIT 8.1 The Ten Conferences in the Division I Football Subdivision

- **Conference level.** Conferences comprise a group of colleges who collectively agree to be affiliated, play games with each other, and share revenues from those games. There are more than 100 conferences in the US, with a very broad spectrum in terms of multiple variables – such as revenues from intercollegiate sports, number of available student-athlete scholarships, and investments in physical sporting infrastructure. Exhibit 8.1 shows the ten conferences in the Division I Football Subdivision, which includes the largest colleges with regards to revenues, available scholarships, and investments in facilities. The number of individual colleges in a conference ranges from six up to a high of 16 colleges. The number of individual colleges in each Division 1 Football Conference in Exhibit 8.1 is shown for each conference – they number 124 in total.[3] The head executive at each conference typically is called the commissioner.

- **College level**. This level of the landscape includes active involvement by students in sports at individual colleges, in intercollegiate and intra mural games and events, and as attendees at games. There are more than 1,000 individual colleges in the United States. As an example, Exhibit 8.1 shows the 14 colleges in the Big TEN, the 12 in the Pac-12, and the 11 in the Sun-Belt Conference. The number of colleges in the ten Division 1 Conferences in Exhibit 8.1 range from a high of 15 for the ACC to a low of ten for the Big TEN. As discussed later in this chapter, there can be shifts in the individual colleges affiliated with a particular conference. At the high-revenue end of conferences, the trend has been to increase the number of colleges in a conference. The head executive for the sports department in a college normally is called the athletic director.

While other countries have more modest investments in college sports than in the United States, key games or events can attract national or regional attention in those countries. In Canada, Canadian Interuniversity Sport (CIS) is the governing body, with membership from many degree-granting colleges in Canada. Although smaller in scope, the CIS is structured like the NCAA, but with four conferences and more than 50 participating institutions. Unlike the NCAA, the CIS allows student-athletes paid by professional teams to participate in CIS governed college sports such as hockey.[4] In England, British Universities and Colleges Sport (BUCS) oversees sports for more than 150 member institutions.[5] Its vision is to "enhance the student experience through sport." At the more global level, the International University Sports Federation (FISU) promotes inter-country college games and events, including the World University Games. The FISU states that it "supports competitions which give students-athletes the opportunity to come together from all around the world in a spirit of understanding and peace, with a view to obtaining results at high technical level."[6]

8.2 THE COMPLEX LANDSCAPE OF COLLEGE SPORTS

The college sports landscape has a level of complexity that makes decision making and management in key areas relatively slow and often the result of many compromises. Exhibit 8.2 outlines some key stakeholders that play a role in the college sports landscape. Factors that contribute to this complexity are described in the following sections.

8.2.1 The Diversity of Goals Being Pursued by Different Stakeholders

Both within and across different stakeholder groups, there can be sizable differences in the goals being pursued. Exhibit 8.2 presents some key stakeholders and possible metrics that may be important in monitoring the health of college sports. Consider the student stakeholder in Exhibit 8.2. Some student-athletes view college as central to developing an academic foundation that will bring lifetime benefits. Metrics such as graduation rates and post-graduation employment metrics are important to such students. Other student-athletes view college as a platform to showcase their sporting talents to professional leagues and Olympic sponsors, etc., where sport is their primary focus – sometimes referred to as the "rent-a-college athlete." Metrics such as athletes in professional leagues from each college, and endorsements after their college days can be important here. Some professional leagues impose minimum age restrictions for athletes, which can result in a cadre of students attending a

Student/student family focus	Individual sport focus	Athletic department focus	University focus
• Student as "student" metrics • Student as "athlete" metrics • Scholarships available • Graduation metrics • Post-graduation employment metrics • Business metrics	• Acceptance rate for "target" admits • Admissions scores metrics • Scholarships available • National rank • National championships • Graduation metrics • Athletes in professional leagues/Olympics • Coach/trainer stature • Physical facility quality • Business metrics	• National championships • Athletic department rankings • Physical facility's quality • Business metrics	• President/administration • Deans, faculty & staff • National statures • Athlete vs. non-athlete scholarships • Alumni networks • Alumni metrics • Business metrics
Conference/NCAA focus	Media/sponsors focus	Donors/foundations focus	Government/regulations focus
• Conference rankings • Conference partner strength • NCAA compliance/sanctions • Business metrics	• Media exposure metrics • Media rating metrics • Media/sponsor contracts • Business metrics	• Endowment base • Annual donations	• Compliance with laws/regulations • Political network of university

EXHIBIT 8.2 Key Stakeholders in the College Sports Landscape and Examples of Metrics

college with the explicit goal of attending that college for the minimum number of years required and then seeking to become a professional athlete.

At the level of individual sports programs, coaches of some college programs measure their success by their national standings and number of college championships won. In these cases, winning on the field is central to their existence. They may aggressively recruit students knowing that the academic abilities and aspirations of those students are minimal. The coaches of other college programs for the same sport, however, may place much greater emphasis on having students graduate and develop life-long skills in addition to winning championships.

Colleges have multiple stakeholders in addition to students and sporting programs. Presidents, administrators, deans, faculty, and staff each can influence the role of sports in the college. The strategies of major colleges as regards sports differ dramatically. Colleges such as Duke University, Notre Dame, Stanford University, Ohio State University, and the University of Texas each operate with large athletic department budgets and a strong tradition of support at the university president level for intercollegiate sporting programs. At the other end of the spectrum is the University of Chicago that long ago decided that allocating large amounts of money to an athletic department was counter to the dominant academic culture that its leadership sought to build and maintain. It is a Division III school in the NCAA, which means that scholarships targeted for student-athletes are not available to applicants.

Adding to complexity here is the heterogeneity of many individual stakeholder groups. For example, there are strong differences across faculty as regards the role of sports in a college education. Even colleges that operate with large athletic department budgets have a subset of the faculty who actively criticize and openly oppose the recruitment of student-athletes whose academic credentials they perceive to be below that required of other accepted students in the college. Some faculties also criticize the use of university funds to support infrastructure and programs related to college sports, arguing that there are other more important university priorities than building athletic training facilities and stadiums.

8.2.2 Large Differences Across Colleges in their Revenues, Expenditures, and Funds Available to Invest in Athletic Departments and in Physical Sport Facilities

The large number of conferences in the United States play some role in grouping colleges that are more alike in their philosophies and financial capacities. However, even within a given conference, there can be large differences in revenues and endowments. Consider the ten conferences in the Division I Football Subdivision shown in Exhibit 8.1. Exhibit 8.3 (Panel A) reports – for 2013 – the highest and lowest revenue colleges in each conference. On average, the revenues of the highest revenue college is more than double that of the lowest revenue college across the ten conferences in Exhibit 8.3.

Across conferences, differences are even more dramatic. Multiple colleges operate with revenues and budgets well below $30 million a year. In contrast, the University of Texas at Austin had 2013 revenues of more than $165 million and expenditures of more than $146 million. Exhibit 8.3 (Panel B) shows the distribution of revenues for 230 college athletic departments in 2013 from the *USA Today* database. Of note, more than 50 percent of the 230 colleges have revenues under $30 million. These large differences across colleges in their revenues from sports and in their endowment bases can create tensions between the "rich and the poor" within the NCAA and within conferences. A NCAA ruling that student-athletes be allowed an extra $5,000 a year for parent visits to games can be embraced by the "rich" end of colleges as a recruiting tool but be viewed as a heavy burden for the financially strapped "revenue poor" colleges.

There are a number of reasons why budgets differ school-to-school by such a significant margin. Six of these are described briefly here. While some are beyond the direct control of the athletic director, others can be affected by decisions at this level:

1   **Alumni base local – attendance.** An important driver of ticket sales revenues for sports such as football, basketball, ice hockey, and volleyball is the number of alumni who live nearby. A second factor would be the location of the school. A college in a large, highly populated city has a potentially larger population base to draw on – however, it may also have many competing entertainment options.
2   **Alumni base wealth – donations.** Schools that have wealthy and supportive alumni that fund major projects and/or scholarships/endowments help build a larger budget capability.
3   **Size of football stadium and ability to fill it.** Providing the demand is there, a football stadium with many seats is a major driver of revenue.
4   **Priorities of school.** Some schools have sport as a priority (e.g., Ohio State), while others (e.g., University of Chicago) view athletics as a minor priority compared to academic outcomes.
5   **Media deal.** The strength of the conference media deal (e.g., Pac-12) or their own independent media deal (e.g., University of Texas) affects revenue inflows.
6   **Number of sports.** Some schools, such as Stanford and Ohio State, field teams in a large number of sports, while others, like the University of Texas, focus their resources on a smaller number.

Panel A: Division I football highest and lowest revenue conferences 2013 ($M)

Conference	Highest revenue ($M)	Associated expenses ($M)	Lowest revenue ($M)	Associated expenses ($M)
ACC	108.51 Notre Dame*	88.85	48.83 Wake Forest	46.74
Big TEN	149.14 Wisconsin	146.66	66.41 Northwestern	66.41
Big 12	165.69 Texas	146.81	72.92 Texas Tech	66.30
Pac-12	97.80 USC	97.80	47.19 Washington State	52.13
SEC	143.39 Alabama	116.91	61.12 Vanderbilt	61.12
AAC	96.19 Louisville	92.38	42.02 Houston	42.66
Conference USA	35.81 East Carolina	36.64	18.57 Louisiana Tech	18.44
MAC	28.71 Miami-Ohio	28.93	23.61 Bowling Green	20.70
Mountain West	39.21 San Diego State	42.85	23.68 Utah State	24.31
Sun Belt	27.61 Western Kentucky	27.71	11.23 Louisiana Monroe	11.44

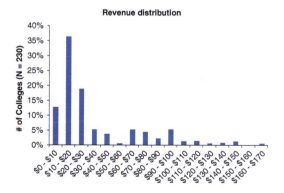

Panel B: Percentage distribution of revenue and expenses for 230 *USA Today* college database NCAA programs ($M)
Source: USA Today, for school year 2013, www.usatoday.com/sports/college/schools/finances

EXHIBIT 8.3 Institution Revenue and Expenses by Conference
* Although Notre Dame is independent in football, they compete in the ACC in all other sports.
Source: http://ope.ed.gov/athletics/GetOneInstitutionData.as

Outside of the United States, size and scope differences across college sports activities and investment also exist but at a relatively lower level. For example, in Canada and the CIS, there are some schools (e.g., Simon Fraser University) which participate in the NCAA Division II, others (e.g., Laval University, Queen's University, Western University) who play their football games in front of large, ticket-purchasing audiences, while most operate on very modest budgets with volunteer or part-time coaches.

8.2.3 Large Differences Across Sports in the Revenues from Sports Games and Events

While there are more than 30 different NCAA sports played in US colleges,[7] it is only a small number that generate sizable revenues that help cover the operating costs of athletic departments. The three largest revenue-generators are men's football, men's basketball, and women's basketball. Exhibit 8.4 reports on the top five sports in 2013 ranked by their median revenues for all the individual colleges playing that sport. For both men's football and men's basketball, the highest revenue programs can be four or five times the median revenues of other programs. While many sports have broad national participation, some have a very strong regional concentration of the elite programs. For example, the elite (ice) hockey programs in the United States are predominantly in the upper-midwest colleges and the northeastern colleges. In contrast, many of the elite water polo programs are found in the western states.

One consequence of a small number of sports generating revenues is that there is sizable cross-subsidization of many sports by the football and basketball programs. The costs of most sports programs are being underwritten by the surpluses provided by these football and basketball programs. This cross-subsidization can create tension in college sports management. An example is college coach salaries.

Men's sports	
Football	20.278
Basketball	5.580
Ice hockey	0.965
Lacrosse	0.650
Baseball	0.363
Women's sports ($M)	
Basketball	0.290
Ice hockey	0.238
Lacrosse	0.205
Equestrian	0.171
Gymnastics	0.110

EXHIBIT 8.4 Top Five Sports – Median 2013 Revenues ($M)
Source: NCAA.org

For example, consider a college where the football coach has a $5 million annual salary and the swimming coach, with multiple Olympic student-athletes has a $200,000 annual salary. Even the $200,000 salary for the swimming coach likely is subsidized by the football revenues, given the minimal swimming gate revenues and the high costs of operating college swimming programs.

8.2.4 Large Differences Across Men's and Women's Sports in Revenues from Sports Games and Events.

Men's sports are the dominant revenue-generators for college sports. The NCAA reports the largest and median amounts for total revenues and net revenues (revenues minus expenses) for three groupings of 23 different sports:

- Men-only sports – such as baseball, football, and wrestling.
- Women-only sports – such as bowling, field hockey, rowing, and softball.
- Coed gender sports where there are both men's programs and women's programs – such as basketball, cross country, fencing, gymnastics, (ice) hockey, soccer, swimming and diving, tennis, track and field (indoor), track and field (outdoor), volleyball, and water polo.

Exhibit 8.5 shows summary data for each of these three sport groupings for the 2011 to 2013 years.

Year	Largest total revenues				Median total revenues			
	Men's	Women's	Coed	Total	Men's	Women's	Coed	Total
2011	119.57	12.18	51.47	150.30	28.50	3.17	17.00	52.72
2012	131.38	16.36	55.41	163.30	29.46	3.34	17.43	55.98
2013	132.77	24.18	55.40	165.69	32.54	3.61	18.90	61.92

Year	Largest net revenues				Median net revenues			
	Men's	Women's	Coed	Total	Men's	Women's	Coed	Total
2011	4.29	−5.07	0.05	0.97	1.43	−6.94	−5.33	−10.28
2012	2.38	−5.42	0.00	0.46	0.00	−7.33	−5.94	−12.27
2013	2.83	−5.80	0.00	0.20	0.42	−7.45	−6.11	−11.62

EXHIBIT 8.5 Largest and Median Revenues and Net Revenues for Men-Only, Women-Only, and "Coed" Sports ($M)
Note: Men-only sports include football, baseball, and wrestling; women-only sports include field hockey, rowing, softball, and bowling; "coed" sports are where there is a separate men's competition and a separate women's competition for the same sport – for example, basketball, cross-country, golf, gymnastics, ice hockey, lacrosse, soccer, swimming and diving, tennis, track and field (indoor), track and field (outdoor), volleyball, and water polo.
Source: NCAA.org

Several men-only sports (especially football) have the largest revenues and can provide a surplus to cross-subsidize other sports. Women-only sports and the "Coed gender" sports have lower revenues and consistently negative median net revenues (as reported in Exhibit 8.5). Given the dominant role of men's sports in driving college revenues, a financial argument can be made that women's sports are benefiting from this cross-subsidization. A change in the revenues or expenses for men-only programs can have much impact on the resources available for women's programs in many colleges.

8.2.5 NCAA College Sports Regulations Prohibit Professional Athlete Status for Student-Athletes

A source of much tension in the college sports landscape in the United States is the prohibition by the NCAA of payments to athletes over and above tuition, board (housing), and some incidental expenses. The consequence is that in the major revenue sports, especially football and basketball, college athletes are in effect cross-subsidizing many other aspects of the landscape. College coaches in the high-revenue sports benefit from no direct payments being made to elite athletes as more resources are available to invest in coaches.

One view is that college sports programs in the United States operate as a "low cost" farm team for professional sports. The NFL, for example, draws its athletes largely from colleges and yet there is no revenue stream to the colleges from the NFL or its clubs. Even though the NBA only requires students to have at least one year of post-high school life prior to entering the NBA, colleges can play the role of enabling better screening of players as well as fostering skill development. Yet again, there is no cash flow from the NBA to the colleges who help "develop" the talent they draft to their clubs. In contrast, many major professional soccer clubs around the globe have academies that train youth and have player contracts that enable the professional clubs to capture some of the rents from the few graduates that join professional clubs (either as a free hire for their own senior team or from the sale of a player contract to another professional club). The Manchester United academy is renowned for its stunning set of "graduates" such as David Beckham, George Best, Bobby Charlton, Ryan Giggs, Mark Hughes, Gary and Phil Neville, and Paul Scholes As discussed later in this chapter, "pay for play" in US college sports will likely continue to be the subject of much debate and legal issues.

8.2.6 Role of Governments in the College Sports World

Given the important role of colleges in communities, it is not surprising that multiple layers of government can impact decision making in the college sports area. The political process that underlies much of government adds to the complexity and uncertainty of college sports management. In the United States, Title IX is an example of federal legislation that has had a major impact on college sports.

Title IX is part of the United States Education Amendments of 1992 law. The law states that "no person in the United States shall, on the basis of sex, be excluded from participation in, be denied the benefits of, or be subjected to discrimination under any education program or activity receiving federal financial assistance." This law requires that "athletic participation opportunities be substantially proportionate to the student enrollment." An example of compliance with this law would be a college with a male 48 percent/female 52 percent enrollment, having student-athlete scholarships allocated on the same 48 percent male/52 percent female basis. For many colleges with elite football programs (which have up to 85 scholarships per team), complying with Title IX has resulted in increased investment in scholarships for high-participation female team sports such as field hockey, soccer, softball, and water polo. Another consequence of Title IX has been some colleges cutting men-only sports in order to meet the Title IX requirements. Box 8.1 illustrates the reduction in men's wrestling programs by many colleges that took place after Title IX was enacted.

BOX 8.1 MULTIPLE COLLEGES DECIDE TO DROP MEN'S WRESTLING PROGRAMS TO COMPLY WITH TITLE IX[8]

The Title IX legislation, first passed in 1972, has led to continued monitoring of the balance of men's and women's programs in college sports. It has also led to decisions by colleges to add women's programs and drop some men's programs. In 2001, the Government Accounting Office (GAO) reported that between 1981/2 and 1998/9, the number of women's college teams had increased by more than 65 percent (from 5,695 to 9,479). In contrast the number of men's college teams had remained nearly unchanged at 9,149 in 1998/9, just 36 more than in 1981/2. The sport exhibiting the most increase was women's soccer. The sport with the most teams eliminated was men's wrestling. The GAO surveyed the reasons for discontinuing teams. For men's teams, the reasons cited were "insufficient student interest" (33 percent), followed by "gender equality goals/regulations" (31 percent), and "resources needed for other sports" (30 percent).

Two examples of decisions to cut wrestling programs were Marquette University and Bucknell University, as summarized here:

■ Marquette University (located in Milwaukee, Wisconsin) announced in June 2001 that it was cutting its men's wrestling program. The *Milwaukee Sentinel* commented: "Men's programs die out by the dozens in an ugly side effect of federal laws. NCAA wrestling alone has lost 56 teams in the last 20 years. It was an agonizing choice for the Marquette management, but the only practical one. So even though the wrestling was privately funded, even though these wrestlers brought in money to the school by paying their own way, even though the team was also an academic success, the sport was dropped because it skewed the male-to-female proportionality requirements of Title IX."

■ Bucknell University (located in Lewisburg, Pennsylvania) announced in January 2002 that it was cutting its men's wrestling and its men's crew (rowing) programs after a 1995 NCAA Review of Bucknell had found it was not in compliance with Title IX requirements. Despite subsequent efforts to achieve compliance (such as adding two new women's sports), Bucknell stated in January 2002 that "to achieve 'substantial proportionality' under Title IX guidelines, [we] chose to discontinue wrestling and men's crew as varsity sports." They then reclassified these sports as "Club-varsity, so that they would not draw any university funds." By 2003, Bucknell had reached full compliance with the Title IX requirements. In May 2004, Bucknell announced that William Graham, an alumni and former co-captain of the Bucknell wrestling team in 1962, was donating $5.6 million to bring back the men's wrestling program. However, the donation also covered women's sports. The $5.6 million was structured as two equal distributions – half to support men's wrestling and half to support a variety of women's sports, with an emphasis on women's crew. It was structured to provide an equal number of new varsity opportunities for both men and women, thereby helping maintain compliance with Title IX.

State-funded universities in the US rely, in part, on their state legislatures for funding. Given that many college athletic departments run at a deficit, it is not surprising that state budget decisions can greatly impact the funds available for college athletic programs. Athletic directors in these publicly funded state schools quickly become aware of efforts by many supporters and detractors of college sporting programs to lobby politicians to affect changes that they view as desirable. For example, college sporting programs with lower graduation rates for student-athletes are very exposed to public examination in state legislatures. Box 8.2 describes the fallout from low student-athlete graduation rates for the football program at the University of California at Berkeley. This fallout included a revised compensation contract for an incoming football head coach.

BOX 8.2 FALLOUT FROM UNIVERSITY OF CALIFORNIA AT BERKELEY'S LOW FOOTBALL GRADUATION RATE

The University of California at Berkeley ("Cal") is one of the most academically respected institutions in the world, with numerous Nobel Prize winners and very demanding entry standards for most students. One black cloud on its stellar reputation has been the low graduation success rates (GSRs) for its football program. *The Daily Californian* student newspaper reported on February 7, 2015 that between 2003 and 2007, the Cal football team had the lowest graduation rate among the 72 programs in six major college football conference.[9] Only 44 percent of Cal football players graduated in the six years after their undergraduate admission.

> This puts Cal nine points below USC, which had the second worst graduation rate in the Pac-12 … Adding salt to the wound, Stanford finished at the top of the Pac-12 this year with a 93 percent graduation rate. The Cal football team's embarrassment was shared by the men's basketball team with a 38 percent graduation rate, also the lowest in the Pac-12.

The Daily Californian also commented that "the football team's GSR, which has steadily declined over the past four years, was a major factor in the firing of former football coach Jeff Tedford." Sandy Barbour, the Cal-Berkeley athletic director from 2004 to 2014 commented: "as the Athletic Director, I accept responsibility for what has happened and responsibility to fix it."

On March 1, 2013, Cal announced Sonny Dykes as the new football head coach. Dykes' contract would run through the 2017 season and was valued at $9.7 million. ESPN reported that his "annual salary before bonuses will be $1.8 million this season and in 2014, and $2.0 million in

2015. If Cal makes the Rose Bowl, Dykes earns a $60,000 bonus. He gets $50,000 for taking the Bears to any other BCS bowl. There are also academic-based bonuses, including $23,000 for each annual team grade point average above 3.0."[10] Skeptics questioned whether a $23,000 bonus was more tokenism than substantive.

SF Gate, in June of 2014, reported that Cal athletic director Sandy Barbour was stepping down:

> Chancellor Nicholas Dirks announced that Barbour will leave her position, which she has held for nearly 10 years. Among the lows [in Barbour's tenure] was firing Tedford as the football program sagged on the field and in the classroom; enduring an embarrassing 1–11 season under new coach Sonny Dykes; and, of course, the report showing Cal's football team had the worst graduation rate among the nation's 72 major-conference schools. The report angered many high-powered alumni and donors; one source said flatly it led to Barbour's departure. Dirks reiterated that "the … academic concerns were a factor in Tedford's firing."[11]

The University of California at Berkeley is one of ten campuses in the University of California system. In September 2013, Janet Napolitano (a former governor of Arizona and the US secretary of homeland security from 2009 to 2013) was appointed system-wide university president. When Napolitano proposed making winning bonuses for college coaches at all campuses contingent on student athletes maintaining a 2.0 grade point average, the board of trustees did not vote to adopt her proposal. The opposition to her proposal included concerns that the 2.0 minimum academic standard was too low, as well as those who were happy with the current status quo. Not surprisingly, many college coaches have mixed reactions to academic benchmarks in their contracts. One commentator stated:

> Coaches want motivated athletes. They don't want to say to an athlete, "You should really focus on your studies more." That's not how we motivate athletes. We motivate them by saying, "Keep working hard and get in the weight room." There's this inherent logical contradiction with this policy where a coach is telling an athlete one thing, but being rewarded for another.[12]

Outside of the United States, many countries have post-secondary education systems that are heavily government funded (federal and state/provincial). In the case of the CIS in Canada, many of the sport programs at smaller universities are heavily funded from tax dollars and central university operating budgets, thereby limiting discretionary spending and increasing government and general population interest in decisions made by the CIS, its conferences, and athletic directors.

8.2.7 Legal Cases Continuing to Shift the Landscape

Legal cases often highlight grey areas in college sports. They can also cause or lead to shifts in the evolution of the sports landscape and affect decision making. Examples include:

- Should college athletes be able to be compensated for their images? The 2014 O'Bannon litigation versus the NCAA, held in Oakland, California, was about NCAA restrictions on student athletes sharing "revenues generated from the use of their names, images, and likeness in addition to a full grant-in-aid." In this case, the United States District Court decision ruled in favor of the student-athlete, which will likely be appealed by the NCAA.[13]

■ Should college players be able to form a union and collectively bargain to improve their "conditions of employment"? Several students from Northwestern University petitioned the National Labor Relations Board to rule that the demands placed on college athletes effectively make them employees and thus should be able to form a union.[14] Decisions here can change the current NCAA position that student-athletes are amateurs and should not receive financial compensation in addition to scholarships.

It is clear that there will be ongoing challenges to the current NCAA structure of college sports and that the court system will be an important venue in which some of these challenges will be played out.

8.3 GOVERNING BODY: NATIONAL COLLEGE ATHLETE ASSOCIATION (NCAA)

Exhibit 8.1 highlights the NCAA as the governing body and hence playing a central role in the administration of college sports in the United States. The NCAA is "a voluntary association of over 1000 colleges and universities, athletic conferences and sports organizations devoted to the sound administration of intercollegiate athletics."[15] The NCAA's origins date back to 1905, when representatives of 13 colleges met to propose football rule changes to make the game safer for students. On December 28, 1905, representatives of 62 schools met in New York City to found the Intercollegiate Athletic Association of the United States (IAAUS). The group changed its name to the National Collegiate Athletics Association (NCAA) in 1910.

8.3.1 NCAA Division Structure

The NCAA is a tax-exempt, non-profit organization. It is divided into three divisions: Division I, Division II, and Division III. Each division caters differently to the student-athlete and to its college members as a whole. Division I includes the highest-revenue college programs and attracts the most media attention for its sporting events. It is the playing ground for many athletes with legitimate aspirations for elite high-performance sport, such as to play professionally or to appear in the Olympic Games.

Division I is further divided into three subdivisions – DI-A, where minimum requirements for football spectator attendance must be met, DI-AA, where football exists but there are no attendance minimum requirements, and DI-AAA, whose members do not field a football team. Division II schools typically operate with much lower revenues, athletic budgets, and fewer scholarships than Division I schools. Division III schools are not allowed to offer athletic scholarships. Division III bylaw 15 states that a member college "shall not award financial aid to any student on the basis of athletics leadership, ability, participation, or performance."[16]

Membership in each division, as of September 2014, is:[17]

I-A	I-AA	I-AAA	II	III	Total
125	125	95	306	438	1,089

As intercollegiate athletics grew, concerns have grown that college sports would interfere with the academic mission of colleges. In 1989, after several years of highly public scandals in intercollegiate sports, *Time Magazine* characterized the problem as "an obsession with winning and moneymaking that is pervading the noblest ideals of both sports and education in America." *Time* then noted that the victims included both the athletes who, in their view, were not receiving a quality education, as well as "the colleges and universities that participate in an educational travesty – a farce that devalues every degree and denigrates the mission of higher education."[18]

In October 1989, the trustees of the Knight Foundation (a private independent foundation) funded a project known as the Knight Commission to propose reforms to college athletics. The first Knight Commission report was issued in 1991, and most of its recommendations were implemented by the NCAA. Ten years later, the commission revisited the issue, finding that "it is clear that good intentions and reform measures of recent years have not been enough – The Commission is forced to reiterate its earlier conclusion that 'at worst, big-time college athletics appear to have lost their bearings'. Athletics continue to 'threaten to overwhelm the universities in whose name they were established.'"[19]

8.3.2 NCAA Decisions as Regards Student-Athlete Focus and Financial Support

The NCAA has multiple rules in place that attempt to maintain some balance between the academic and the sporting lives of student-athletes. Decisions relating to maintaining minimum academic standards, having caps on maximum hours and calendar dates devoted to athletics, and prohibitions against financial payments illustrate the diversity of the NCAA rules.

Minimum Academic Standards

An example of such standards is the minimum academic standards that freshmen must meet in order to maintain their eligibility to compete.

> Beginning in 2016, freshmen will have to meet a new standard to be eligible to compete in their first year. Prospective student-athletes who achieve the current minimum initial-eligibility standard on the test score-GPA sliding scale with at least a minimum 2.3 core-course GPA would continue to be eligible for athletically related financial aid during the first year of enrollment and practice during the first regular academic term of enrollment. Student-athletes serving this academic redshirt year would have to successfully complete nine semester or eight quarter hours during their first academic term to be eligible for practice during their second term. For immediate access to competition, prospective student-athletes will be required to present at least a 2.0 GPA and an increased sliding-scale credential.[20]

Making minimum academic standard policies effective requires individual colleges to ensure that student-athletes take regular courses and that they are graded on a similar basis to other students in that college. Allegations of student-athletes being "channeled" to "soft courses with guaranteed grades" arise with some regularity. For example, reports of a 2012 academic fraud investigation at the University of North Carolina referred to "'paper classes' – independent studies requiring little work and no attendance. Athletes were able to get easy 'A's' without actually going to class."[21]

Caps on Maximum Hours Devoted to Athletic Practices

The NCAA has a 20-hour per week cap on the amount of time that student-athletes can spend in supervised sporting practices. Notwithstanding these formal caps, many athletes report longer times in actual practice (sometimes under the cover of "unsupervised practices"). A 2006 survey of NCAA student-athletes found that "football players in major college programs estimated they spent 44.8 hours per week on athletic activities."[22] Many student-athletes argue that in reality there are immense pressures on them to focus on their sporting activities. Richard Sherman, a Stanford graduate and subsequently a member of the Seattle Seahawks NFL club, stated:

> I don't think college athletes are given enough time to take advantage of the free education they are given. It's frustrating because a lot of people get upset with student-athletes and say you're not focused on school and not taking advantage of the opportunity you're given. I would love for a regular student, just for one semester, to have a student-athlete schedule during the season and show me how you balance that. Show me how you schedule your classes when you can't schedule classes from 2 to 6 o'clock on any given day. Show me how you're going to get all your work done when you get out [of practice and meetings] at 7.30 or so and have a test the next day and you're dead tired from practice and you still have to study and get the same work done. People say you get room and board and they pay for your education. But ... you're there to play football. Those are the things coaches tell you every day. Luckily I was blessed to go to Stanford, a school primarily focused on academics. But as the coach would attest, we were still there to play football.[23]

Amateurism – Pay-for-Play Prohibitions

Over its history, the NCAA has maintained a strong prohibition against student-athletes receiving financial compensation outside of scholarships to offset tuition and cost of living. On this point, the NCAA publicly states:

> Amateur competition is a bedrock principle of college athletics and the NCAA. Maintaining amateurism is crucial to preserving an academic environment in which acquiring a quality education is the first priority. In the college model of sports, the young men and women competing on the field or court are students first, athletes second. Amateurism requirements do not allow for contracts with professional teams; salary for participating in athletics; prize money above actual and necessary expenses; play with professionals; tryouts, practice or competition with a professional team; benefits from an agent or prospective agent; agreement to be represented by an agent; and delayed initial full-time collegiate enrollment to participate in organized sports competition.[24]

The NCAA has imposed strict penalties on colleges that are found violating this "amateurism" policy. In 1985, the NCAA announced what is called the "death penalty" on Southern Methodist University (SMU). An athlete reported receiving payments to sign with SMU and ongoing payments while playing. The payments came out of "supporter slush funds." SMU's 1987 football season was cancelled and there were no home games in 1988. In 2012, the NCAA imposed sanctions on the University of Southern California (USC) for payments made by an agent to the family of a recruit. USC received a two-year post-season ban and a reduction of 30 scholarships over a three-year period.[25]

8.3.3 NCAA Financials and Distributions – March Madness Media Contract as the "Key Revenue Pillar" for the NCAA

Exhibit 8.6 presents summary financials for the NCAA for the years ended August 31, 2009/13.

As Exhibit 8.6 reports, the single largest revenue stream for the NCAA comes from the broadcast contracts for the Men's Basketball Championship series often called "March Madness." In 2013,

	2009	2010	2011	2012	2013
REVENUES					
Television and marketing rights fees	597.377	645.691	690.314	708.861	726.391
Championships and NIT tournaments	76.364	71.922	93.412	101.910	110.631
Investment income	9.098	21.404	33.453	29.542	41.398
Sales and services	16.211	18.031	21.756	24.160	27.307
Contributions – other	2.654	0.239	0.190	0.058	0.058
Contributions – facilities	0.200	−10.468	6.823	7.155	7.074
Total revenues	701.904	746.819	845.948	871.686	912.859
EXPENSES					
Distribution to Division I members	391.759	434.648	480.012	503.798	527.432
Division I championships/NIT tournaments	63.630	67.662	74.375	85.744	97.407
Division II championships, distributions, and programs	28.246	28.510	31.696	32.493	35.650
Division III championships and programs	19.047	19.897	22.019	25.373	27.531
Association – wide programs	121.025	124.135	134.253	115.041	122.244
Management and general	32.016	32.37	35.706	38.319	41.785
Total expenses	655.723	707.222	778.061	800.768	852.049
SURPLUS	46.182	42.597	67.887	70.916	60.751
REVENUE FOR MEN'S BASKETBALL					
"March Madness" from Turner and CBS	568	617	653	666	681

EXHIBIT 8.6 NCAA Financials 2009/13 ($M): Consolidated Statement of Activities

Source: NCAA Annual Reports

the March Madness contract was approximately 74 percent of the total revenues for the NCAA, or $681 million out of total revenues of $913 million. The agreement "conveys exclusive television and other internet and multimedia broadcast rights to Turner and CBS for 14 years in connection with the Division I Men's Basketball Championship. In addition, the Men's Championship Agreements grant Turner and CBS marketing rights with respect to all NCAA Championships."[26] The total value of this contract was valued at $10.8 billion (averaging $771 million per year over the life of the contract). The previous agreement covered an 11-year period up to 2011 with an aggregate value of approximately $6 billion, thereby averaging $545 million per year in revenues over the course of that contract. The 40 percent increase in the annual payments by Turner/CBS for March Madness for the 2011/24 contract illustrates the media drawing power of elite college sports.

Exhibit 8.6 highlights that the bulk of the NCAA revenues are distributed to its member colleges. There are multiple buckets with different guidelines as to how the revenues are allocated to the conferences and colleges. Some allocations go to conferences. For example, as described in Section 8.4, funds in the so-called "Basketball Fund" bucket are distributed based on the number of appearances (games played) in March Madness that colleges from each conference play. This bucket is the single largest. Other allocations go directly to colleges. For example, the "Academic Enhancement" bucket for Division I colleges is distributed equally to every college in Division I.

8.4 CONFERENCES AS A PIVOTAL PART OF THE COLLEGE SPORTS LANDSCAPE

There are more than 100 college conferences in the NCAA and four in the CIS. Exhibit 8.1 outlines the ten conferences in the Division I Football Subdivision Conferences. By definition, a conference is a group of colleges who collectively agree to abide by conference rules, play games against each other, and share revenues.

8.4.1 Why Colleges Group in Specific Conferences

Multiple factors explain how and why colleges come together to be members of the same conference:

- **Geography.** This factor historically was central to determining what colleges came together under a conference umbrella. For example, consider the colleges in the Pac-12, where the initial eight colleges all came from the West Coast of the United States: University of California at Berkeley, University of California at Los Angeles, University of Oregon, Oregon State, University of Southern California, Stanford University, University of Washington, and Washington State. Subsequent additions to the conference were also schools in the western states: the University of Arizona and Arizona State in 1978, and the University of Colorado at Boulder and the University of Utah in 2011.
- **Travel time.** Given the student-athlete status, avoiding large travel times for student athletes when having "away games" has reinforced the geographic focus factor underlying conference membership. However, both faster air travel and economic factors have reduced the importance of this factor, especially for conferences with many high-revenue colleges.
- **Similar stature and values.** Each of the 12 colleges in the Pac-12 are leading colleges in their states. For example, the University of Utah is one of the two leading colleges in Utah. Brigham

Young University (BYU) is the other leading college in Utah. BYU is privately owned by the Mormon Church and has a much stronger religious element as opposed to the other colleges in the Pac-12. Moreover, BYU strongly opposes playing games on a Sunday, which is where games are frequently scheduled in the Pac-12. BYU operates as an "independent" in some sports (such as football) and as a West Coast Conference member in other sports.

■ **Economics/revenue implications of alternative conference membership.** This factor has become increasingly important and, in the eyes of some, is the dominant factor in recent conference membership changes. This economic factor operates at both the conference level and at the individual college level. Conferences with colleges that have strong brands and large alumni bases enable those conferences to have more negotiating power with media companies. Colleges in such conferences further benefit from larger revenue allocations from the central conference contracts. The increasing importance of college conference media contracts and college conference media networks has fueled some of the recent changes in conference affiliations.

8.4.2 The College Conference Membership Carousel

There has been considerable fluidity in both the number of conferences and in the membership of individual conferences over the history of the NCAA. There are many conferences that existed for some time and then later disbanded with the individual colleges then realigning with other conferences. Within surviving conferences, there have been multiple shifts in membership. One study reported that "since Nebraska moved to the Big TEN in 2010, there were 84 moves up to March 2014 affecting 21 Division I conferences."[27] Exhibit 8.7 outlines the changes in membership of the five major US college football conferences from 2010 to 2014. As shown in Exhibit 8.7, there was a net addition of eight colleges to these five conferences in this five-year period.

Why these changes? Increased revenue potential for a college appears to be a major factor, since adding more colleges can have several revenue enhancements for a conference. More colleges increases the number of attractive match-ups if the new additions are well-known college brands. A second reason is a NCAA rule allowing a final conference football playoff game if the conference has 12 or more colleges in its membership. This conference football playoff game also can raise the profile of the teams in that playoff and result in them playing in more attractive college bowl games.[28] A third reason is the increase in the revenue base of a college conference media network. For example, when Rutgers University and University of Maryland joined the Big TEN Conference in 2014, the number of within-conference subscribers to the Big TEN network was increased as both came from states that had no college in the Big TEN. Since Rutgers is in the 11th largest state by population and Maryland is the 19th largest state, the increased market reach for the Big TEN network was significant.

Dissatisfaction with the current conference affiliation is another prompt to a relocation decision. In 2012, Texas A&M left the Big 12 conference and joined the SEC Conference. Texas A&M had long been a key anchor college of the Big 12, and its rivalry with University of Texas at Austin provided banner events for both the conference and the national media. However, the University of Texas gained a more preferred revenue position when it established its own regional sports network, the Longhorn Network.[29] In a blog, the Texas A&M athletic director noted: "You all know the landscape of the Big 12 Conference was altered by the creation of the Longhorn Network."[30] Part of good management of a conference is keeping those colleges within a conference that have very high value. On this measure, the loss of Texas A&M to the SEC was a major one.

Conference	Adds	Leaves
ACC	University of Notre Dame (2013) University of Pittsburgh (2013) Syracuse University (2013) University of Louisville (2014)	University of Maryland (2014) – to Big TEN
Big TEN	University of Nebraska (2011) University of Maryland (2014) Rutgers University (2014)	—
Big 12	Texas Christian University (2012) West Virginia (2012)	University of Colorado (2011) – to Pac-12 University of Nebraska (2011) – to Big TEN University of Missouri (2012) – to SEC Texas A&M (2012) – to SEC
Pac-12	University of Colorado-Boulder (2011) University of Utah (2011)	—
SEC	University of Missouri (2012) Texas A&M (2012)	—

EXHIBIT 8.7 College Conference College Realignments: 2010/14 in Five Major Division I Football Conferences

8.4.3 College Conference Revenue Pillars

Conference revenues can come from several or all of the following sources, depending on the conference and its status:

1   **NCAA revenue distributions.** These outlays include general distributions to all NCAA members and specific distributions based on a particular conference and its colleges. An example of the latter is the Men's Division I Basketball Tournament ("March Madness") revenue distributions. There are 32 conferences in Division I. The champion of each conference qualifies for the tournament and the remaining 36 are "at-large berths" as selected by a NCAA selection committee. This pool of 68 is narrowed to 64 with a per-tournament four-game series between eight low seeds. Every college selected gets a point for each game played in the tournament. Each point is valued at more than $1 million. The more games played, the higher the revenues distributed to their conference. Thereby, the conference with the most number of games played in "March Madness" receives the highest allocation of revenues from the NCAA's Division I Basketball Tournament revenue pool.

2   **Conference media contract revenues**. Most major media contracts for football and basketball games are negotiated at the conference level. Exhibit 8.8 shows the current media contracts for the five "power conferences." The yearly average of the media contracts in Exhibit 8.8 ranges from $200 million to $250 million. Contracts with most other conferences are at much lower amounts due to the lower drawing power of games in those conferences.

Conference	Network	Contract total ($M)	Years of contract	End year	Average yearly ($M)
ACC	ESPN/ABC	$3,600	15	2026–7	240
Big TEN	ESPN	$1,000	10	2016–17	248
	Big TEN Network	$2,800	25	2031–2	
	CBS	$72	6	2016–17	
	Fox	$145	6	2016–17	
Big 12	ESPN/Fox	$2,600	13	2024–5	200
Pac-12	ESPN/Fox	$3,000	12	2023–4	250
SEC	ESPN	$2,250	15	2023–4	205
	CBS	$825	15	2023–5	

EXHIBIT 8.8 College Conference Network Contracts for Football/Basketball Games
Source: K. Dosh, "A comparison: conference television deals," ESPN, March 19, 2013

3   **Conference Network revenues.** College conference networks are recent additions to the regional sport network (RSN) industry. Chapter 16 provides an overview of developments in this area. In recent years, three conferences have launched successful RSNs, as follows:
  ● Big TEN network – launched in 2007 with Fox Sports as an equity partner. Fox now has 51 percent equity and 49 percent is held by the Big TEN Conference.
  ● Pac-12 network – launched in 2012 as a wholly owned subsidiary of the Pac-12 conference.
  ● SEC network – launched in 2014 with ESPN as the 100 percent equity owner.
  Each of these three conferences receives revenue streams from their college sports networks. These networks package a broad set of games covering many sports. Many of the major football games are not available for these college conference networks as they are included in the existing media contracts outside of the RSN's.

4   **Conference final games/tournaments.** Over time, conferences have expanded the "end of regular season" within-conference games with the potential to build extra net revenues. For example, Division I Football Conferences with 12 or more colleges now have conference "finals." The SEC Conference has 14 colleges, divided into an Eastern Division and a Western Division. The first SEC Championship Game was played at the Georgia Dome in Atlanta, Georgia on December 6, 2014 between the Eastern Division Champion (University of Missouri) and the Western Division Champion (University of Alabama). Conference final tournaments for men's and women's basketball now occur in many conferences as well.

5   **College Football Playoff (CFP) national championship revenues.** Post the regular college football season and the conference final games is the college bowl season, a staple on the United States sports calendar for nearly a century. Starting in 2014/15, the Division I Football Conferences launched a four-college playoff series culminating in a National Championship game. The "Power Five" conferences each receive a $50 million base allocation, while the "Group of Five" each receive a $10 million base allocation – see Box 8.3 for discussion of the revenue distributions associated with this new format.

6 **Contract bowl game revenues.** The "college football bowl" season starts after all the conference football games have finished. The six major bowls (Cotton Bowl, Fiesta Bowl, Orange Bowl, Peach Bowl, Rose Bowl, and Sun Bowl) are affiliated with the CFP series. There are more than 30 other bowls where typically two conferences agree for one of its colleges to appear in that bowl. For example, the Citrus Bowl (currently titled the Buffalo Wild Wings Citrus Bowl) is affiliated with the SEC and Big TEN Conferences. Both conferences contract with Citrus Bowl management (Florida Citrus Sports) to provide a team to play in a nationally televised game that is played in Orlando, Florida on January 1. The contract currently includes a payment to the SEC and Big TEN Conferences of more than $4 million each. Many other bowls have lower payments to their affiliated conferences.

BOX 8.3 NEW COLLEGE FOOTBALL PLAYOFF (CFP) LLC FORMS TO BUILD NATIONAL CHAMPIONSHIP GROUP OUTSIDE OF NCAA

For many years, NCAA football did not have a final playoff series akin to what many professional sports have in order to declare a "clear cut" national champion. While each year there were several rankings of college football teams (either by poll or computer), these did not always agree and were often referred to as "paper rankings." The opposition to having a final playoff series was often that it would prolong the already overly long football season and further disrupt student-athletes getting back to focus more on their academic studies. For many commentators, the extra revenue dollars available from having a football championship series made it a matter of "when, not if" it would eventuate. The college basketball post-season "March Madness" highlighted the revenue potential of such a series. The NCAA's basketball contract with its two broadcast partners (Turner and CBS) averaged $771 million per year over the 2011/14 period. This contract was central to the NCAA's financial capacity.

When discussions about a college football championship series became serious, the question quickly arose as to who would drive the decisions and who would be eligible to share in the revenues. During 2012, the commissioners of the ten Division I Football Conferences met to debate various formats. In April 2012, an eight-team and a 16-team "playoff format" were "taken off the table." In June 2012, the commissioners voted for a four-team format starting in 2014/15. A new LLC that was separate from the NCAA was created – College Football Playoff LLC (CFP). The CFP website (http://collegefootballplayoff.com/chronology) includes the following further details:

The presidents and chancellors also endorsed (1) rotating the semi-final games among six bowl sites and rotation of the championship game among neutral sites; (2) managing the championship game by the conferences; and (3) creating a selection committee that would rank the teams to play in the playoff, giving all the teams an equal opportunity to participate. Among the factors the committee would be instructed to value were win–loss record, strength of schedule, head-to-head results, and whether a team is a conference champion.

The presidents' group also decided to (1) play the semifinals New Year's Eve or New Year's Day; (2) create "Championship Monday" by setting the date of the championship game on the first Monday in January that is six or more days after the second semi-final game is played; (3) establish the new format to cover a 12-year term, from the 2014/2015 season through the 2025/6 season; (4) distribute revenue from games according to a formula that (a) rewards conferences for success on the field, (b) accommodates teams' expenses, (c) acknowledges marketplace factors, (d) rewards academic performance of student-athletes; and (e) eliminates the "automatic qualification" designation.

In November 2012, CFP and ESPN reached an agreement to "present the games for 12 years on an exclusive basis across ESPN platforms." The agreement was reported to be worth about $470 million per year through 2025 to the NCAA.[31]

The 2014/15 games had two January 1 games. First, the University of Oregon defeated Florida State (59–20) in the Rose Bowl, and then Ohio State defeated the University of Alabama (42–35) in the Allstate Sugar Bowl. Those two games comprised the first round of the playoff – the semi-finals. Then, on January, Ohio State defeated the University of Oregon (42–20) in the Championship game, where ESPN reported an "18.5 overnight television rating, the highest metered market ever for ESPN."

Revenue Allocations From College Football Playoffs

By creating a separate LLC outside of the NCAA, the CFP elected to not share revenues with the majority of the NCAA colleges. The ten Division I Football Conferences were divided into two groups:

- Five "Power Conferences" – namely ACC, Big TEN, Big 12, Pac-12, and SEC – would each receive a base allocation of $50 million.
- The "Group of Five" Conferences (i.e., American, C-USA, MAC, Mountain West and Sun Belt) each received a base allocation of $10 million.

Allocations were also made to individual conferences based on whether a college from that conference appeared in a specific bowl. For example, the ACC and the Pac-12 each received an extra $6 million allocation from their colleges appearing in the Rose Bowl. These revenue allocations highlight the growing use of "naked power" in how the higher revenue conferences are increasing further the revenue differences between themselves and the lower revenue colleges.

8.4.4 Conference Net Revenue Allocation Rules

The general pattern in many conferences is equal allocation of revenues among member colleges. Over time, some conferences that had unequal allocations of revenues have moved to an equal net revenue-sharing. For example, in the Pac-10 conference (the predecessor to the current Pac-12), the two Southern California colleges (USC and UCLA) had larger revenue allocations than the other eight colleges – a key rationale was the disproportionate role that the Southern California market contributed to the size of the media contracts. In 2011, a new Pac-10 commissioner negotiated major upgrades in conference revenues. With a sizable increase in the total conference revenue pie, USC and UCLA agreed to shifting to an equal net revenue-sharing model.

When new colleges join a conference, there is often a "vesting period" before they share equally in the conference revenues. For example, the Big 12 conference was reported to be sharing approximately $220 million in 2014 with its ten members. Eight "long-time" members (Baylor, Iowa State, Kansas, Kansas State, Oklahoma, Oklahoma State, Texas, and Texas State) will get approximately $23 million each. The two most recent members (Texas Christian and West Virginia) will get approximately $14 million each and will move to full equal sharing after a further two years.[32]

Selected colleges have used their strong negotiating power to position themselves in a stronger revenue position than that enjoyed by most other colleges in their conference. For example, the University of Texas has its own Longhorn Network, which is operated by ESPN. Starting in 2011, the Longhorn Network is a regional sports network showing University of Texas games and other content. It was reported that the contract with ESPN pays the University of Texas an average of $15 million a year.[33]

8.5 COLLEGES AS THE COALFACE OF COLLEGE SPORTS MANAGEMENT

Individual colleges are where the student-athletes are found and where many key decisions are made that shape the college sports landscape. Four examples of such decisions are the budget size and level of investment in infrastructure, the number of NCAA sports to support, the payments to be made to college coaches, and the business functions that are undertaken by third-party agencies as opposed to "in-house."

8.5.1 Budget Level and Investments in Infrastructure

Central to many decisions at the college level is the budget available to the Athletic Department. Exhibit 8.3 (Panel B) highlights the dramatic differences across the 230 colleges in the NCAA from the *USA Today* database. Notably, there were 13 colleges in this database with more than $100 million in revenues and more than $100 million in expenses in 2013. The major categories of revenues for a college include:

- **Game-day revenues.** Underpinning the revenue budgets of many of the large revenue colleges are football programs that play in large stadiums. Ticket revenues are typically the largest game day revenue item. Colleges can also receive revenues from food and beverage sold in the stadium, as well as parking and other in-stadium sources.
- **Distributions from conference net revenues.** Section 8.4 outlined key conference revenue sources such as media contracts and bowl revenues that are shared among member colleges.
- **Contributions from alumni.** Alumni or "boosters" are an important source of resources for many colleges and many programs. These can include "extra" donations to get preferred seating at games to general purpose donations to an athletic department. Major donors, in some cases, fund portions of new facilities or scholarships as well. For example, T. Boone Pickens was reported to have donated $165 million to Oklahoma State University (his alma mater) for athletic facilities.[34]
- **Sponsorship and advertising.** Corporate partners include team apparel providers (such as Nike and Under Armour), sport beverage companies (Gatorade, Powerade), auto manufacturers, and many more. These can take the form of both sponsors (those who enter into partnerships with the college) or advertisers (those who buy media space, such as sideline signage).

■ **Licensing of merchandise and other items.** Colleges with large followings (students, alumni, and fans) are able to generate revenue by licensing their marks to clothing companies who will in turn sell merchandise branded by college. The Collegiate Licensing Company (owned by IMG) is a major force in this area, representing more than 200 colleges and the NCAA in licensing arrangements.

■ **Income from endowments.** Alumni and supporters make what are often called "capital donations" with only the returns on the capital available for use in the annual operating budget. The proceeds (interest) from the investment of that capital can be used to fund various activities of the athletic department.

Colleges differ greatly in their mix of these revenue sources. In each of these areas, we see efforts by athletic directors and their management to increase revenues. Consider some examples as follows:

● **Building larger and upgraded stadiums and arenas.** In recent years, colleges with strong football or basketball programs have invested in expanding their stadium or arena to increase their capacity to grow revenues and have more fans attending their games. There are now multiple college football stadiums with 100,000+ seating capacities. Examples include the University of Michigan (109,000), Penn State (106,000), Texas A&M (106,000), and Ohio State (104,000).[35]

● **Shifting conference membership.** Section 8.4 illustrated multiple shifts. For example, the University of Utah has seen its conference revenue increase after shifting in 2011 from the Mountain West Conference to the Pac-12 Conference.

● **Signing major apparel deals.** An example is the 2014 contract between Notre Dame and Under Armour. ESPN reported that the ten-year contract was "the most valuable shoe and apparel contract in college sports history" with an estimated value of approximately $90 million over the ten years.[36]

8.5.2 Decisions by Colleges on the Number of NCAA Sports

Decisions about the number and type of NCAA sports to have in a college athletic department have very large consequences for the college as a whole and for the management of that college. Student-athletes applying to different colleges typically only choose among those that provide a viable program in their chosen sport. A decision by a college to not support, say, a NCAA men's soccer or a NCAA men's wrestling program will result in student-athletes in those sports not applying to that college.

Only a few colleges have decided to have a very large number of NCAA men's and women's sports programs. Exhibit 8.9 illustrates the diversity in program sizes in the ten Division I Football Subdivision Conferences.

Both Ohio State and Stanford have 36 sports, which requires large across-the-board investments in scholarships, coaches, and facilities. Both colleges take the position that having a large offering of men's and women's programs helps attract applications from a broad pool of high-school students and enhances the diversity of the student body. In contrast, the University of Texas has chosen only to support 18 sports, despite having the largest revenues and expenditures of all colleges. The University of Texas has decided that it will focus only on a subset of sports for which it can have an elite nationally ranked program. Box 8.4 discusses the role of Stanford's support of a large number of sports as one factor in its winning the Director's Cup every year from 1994/5 to 2013/14.

Conference/college	Men	Women	Total	Conference/college	Men	Women	Total
ACC				**The American**			
Boston College	13	16	29	Univ. of Central FL	6	9	15
Univ. of North Carolina	12	14	26	Univ. of Houston	6	9	15
Big TEN				**Conference USA**			
Univ. of Michigan	13	14	27	Old Dominion	9	9	18
Ohio State	18	18	36	Rice University	7	7	14
Big 12				**Mid-American**			
Univ. of Oklahoma	9	10	19	Akron Univ.	8	10	18
Univ. of Texas – Austin	8	10	18	Ohio Univ.	6	9	15
Pac-12				**Mountain West**			
Stanford	16	20	36	Boise State	7	11	18
Univ. of Utah	7	10	17	San Jose State	6	12	18
SEC				**Sun Belt**			
Univ. of Kentucky	10	11	21	Arkansas State	5	7	12
Texas A&M	7	9	16	Georgia State	6	9	15

EXHIBIT 8.9 Number of NCAA Sports Programs in Selected Colleges – 2015

BOX 8.4 STANFORD UNIVERSITY AND ITS 20-YEAR RUN OF WINNING DIRECTOR'S CUP

The Directors' Cup is a competition between college athletic departments that ranks each men's and each women's sport on the basis of on-field success (100 points for a national championship and lower points thereafter for lower rankings in that sport). At the Division I level, the top ten men's sports and the top ten women's sports in each college are eligible for scoring. The college with the most number of points is awarded the Director's Cup. The Director's Cup allows many low-revenue sports to make important contributions to the aggregate score. This has proved of great value to Stanford University. After finishing the 1993/4 year in second place to the University of North Carolina, Stanford won the cup for the next 20 years (1994/5 to 2013/14). A variety of colleges have come second during this 20-year period – such as UCLA (six times), the University of Florida (four times and a fifth with a tie), the University of North Carolina (three times and a fourth with a tie), and the University of Texas (three times).

Multiple factors contribute to Stanford's 20-year dominance of the Director's Cup. First, is the large number of sports in the program. Stanford funds 36 different sports, which allows sports with minimal or zero points in a particular year to not go into the scoring. For example, in 2012/13

Stanford had four women's sports with points (field hockey, lacrosse, rowing, and softball) but were below the points of ten other women's sports such as basketball and water polo. In contrast, a college such as the University of Texas with only 18 sports has no room to "eliminate" the scores of sports that have zero or low points in a given year.

Second, Stanford is well known for investing heavily in many lower-revenue sports (such as tennis and swimming) that can bring prestige to their university in ways such as Olympic berths. Points for many of these sports have helped boost Stanford's aggregate point score. Stanford's golf team has long been one of the premier programs in the country, winning a total of eight national championships and boasting an alumni base that includes PGA greats Tiger Woods and Tom Watson. It even has an 18-hole golf course on its campus. While many other schools limit their investment in low-revenue sports, Stanford does not.

Third, despite being a relatively small university (fewer than 8,000 undergraduate students), Stanford invests heavily in student-athlete scholarships at levels above or comparable to much larger colleges such as Ohio State University (44,000+ undergraduate students) and the University of Texas (39,000+ undergraduate students). Fourth, its alumni has both the capacity and a strong commitment to "giving back" that has enabled Stanford's athletic department to have the highest endowment base of all US colleges. Fifth, it has much "drawing power" for high-school applicants with very high ranked undergraduate programs, a powerful alumni network, its location in Silicon Valley, its warm climate, and a very sizable investments in physical facilities (sporting and non-sporting).

Despite many benefits when competing for the Director's Cup, Stanford faces multiple challenges to continue its 20-year run of success. First, its demanding academic standards for applicants is a barrier to recruiting in certain situations. Coaches have to be very particular in which high-school students they allocate energy to recruiting. Second, some applicants who pass the admission criteria may prefer to go to other colleges that have less academically demanding programs so as to more fully concentrate on maximizing their potential for a professional sports career. Men's basketball has proved especially challenging for recruiting, especially given the "one and done" attitude of some high-profile high-school recruits aiming to enter the NBA as soon as possible (the NBA requires at one year beyond high school before entering the NBA). Third, Stanford has a smaller stadium (approximately 50,000 capacity) and a smaller basketball arena (approximately 7,500 capacity) than many other high-profile colleges, so it receives much lower ticket revenues than most high-revenue schools. Fourth, Stanford operates with a lower athletic budget than many schools seriously competing for the Director's Cup. Stanford's athletic department budget is running at about 60–70 percent of the budgets of the largest college athletic departments. The overhanging question for many years has been "not if, but when" one of these larger higher revenue schools takes the Director's Cup crown from Stanford.

Title IX has had a major impact on the number of women's programs in colleges. In many colleges, there are more women's programs than men's programs, in part due to a men's football program having a large number of participants and scholarships. Of the 20 colleges in Exhibit 8.9, 17 colleges have more women's programs than men's with the other three having the same number of programs. Exhibit 8.10 provides summary financial statements for two universities – the University of Texas at Austin (Panel A) and the University of Virginia (Panel B).

Panel A: University of Texas Financial Report

University of Texas Financial Report

	2008/09	2009/10	2010/11	2011/12	2012/13
Revenue					
Ticket Sales, LASP, Building Use Fees	55,394,209	56,741,661	61,196,689	59,207,378	60,860,735
Game Guarantees	500,000	460,000	531,020	445,000	560,500
Contributions	37,291,370	37,110,293	37,337,126	40,747,347	37,386,271
NCAA, Conference Distributions	14,325,151	14,751,503	14,824,329	21,024,408	21,740,372
Concessions & Novelty Sales	3,892,527	3,697,206	4,521,490	4,157,017	3,610,072
Royalties, Advertising, Sponsorship & media rights	18,381,489	22,403,813	22,890,041	28,710,662	33,421,518
Sports Camps	4,523,133	4,791,827	5,221,011	4,162,420	4,157,893
Endowment & Investment Income	1,656,008	1,406,944	1,385,209	1,348,505	1,367,616
Other Income	2,806,144	2,192,108	2,389,011	3,492,418	2,586,509
Total Revenue	138,770,031	143,555,355	150,295,926	163,295,115	165,691,486
Expenses					
Athletic Student Aid	7,891,315	8,444,494	8,957,818	9,350,290	9,956,344
Game Guarantees	2,412,295	2,091,580	2,112,457	2,394,373	2,738,277
Coaches' Salaries & Benefits	19,701,681	22,395,654	22,230,725	22,795,664	24,415,065
Administrative Salaries & Benefits	24,631,000	25,119,486	27,681,115	30,730,186	30,823,731
Recruiting	1,322,464	1,257,768	1,470,389	1,457,857	1,405,178
Team Travel	7,624,343	7,695,570	7,120,566	7,215,950	7,276,677
Equipment, Uniforms & Supplies	2,694,512	2,788,333	2,302,543	2,671,921	1,398,943
Games and Event Expenses	18,500,104	18,885,378	23,611,532	22,352,875	25,486,020
Fund Raising & Development	8,393,475	7,536,591	6,336,345	5,401,098	4,798,655
Sports Camps	2,465,121	1,923,209	2,512,080	1,592,133	1,982,899
Facilities Expense	7,301,299	6,789,518	6,615,978	6,695,163	7,322,189
Debt Service	14,716,297	16,484,214	16,735,060	17,320,450	17,803,047
Spirit Group Expense	1,331,067	1,264,522	982,472	1,311,575	1,275,111

University of Texas Financial Report

	2008/09	2009/10	2010/11	2011/12	2012/13
Medical Expense	1,678,082	1,853,181	1,619,602	1,683,099	1,865,346
Membership Dues & Fees	338,195	360,339	332,777	372,152	449,122
Direct Support to Institution	3,932,480	3,760,275	9,026,363	8,285,714	9,201,066
Capital Outlay	4,758,454	6,249,655	7,046,198	8,027,966	9,268,804
Other Expenses	2,717,698	1,786,422	3,065,356	4,924,924	7,810,980
Total Expenses	132,409,882	136,686,189	149,759,376	154,583,390	165,277,454
Fiscal Year Net Income	6,360,149	6,869,166	536,550	8,711,725	414,032

LASP = Longhorn Ali-Sports Package

Note: University of Texas Annual Report labels what is reported as Revenues above as "Income and Transfers In" and Expenses as "Expenses and Transfers Out".
Source: University of Texas Athletic Department Annual Reports

Panel B: University of Virginia Financial Report

	FY 2012 Actual ($)	FY 2013 Actual ($)	FY 2014 Actual ($)
Revenue			
Operating revenue			
ACC distributions	13,204,774	16,406,066	17,700,302
Licensing royalties	415,707	374,741	392,775
Corporate sponsors	3,187,654	4,672,214	4,640,499
Facilities rental	180,850	120,500	385,401
Student fees	13,131,890	13,120,702	13,235,814
Post-season allowances	2,870,740	527,666	718,428
Ticket sales	12,192,687	11,926,316	15,072,925*
Concessions	987,424	928,190	1,020,567
Gifts: "friends of" and other	7,669,712	3,956,291	1,148,237
Virginia Athletics Foundation operational support	4,570,193	2,395,072	3,655,426
Virginia Athletics Foundation academic affairs support	860,037	882,578	1,030,003

Panel B: University of Virginia Financial Report

	FY 2012 Actual ($)	FY 2013 Actual ($)	FY 2014 Actual ($)
Virginia Athletics Foundation scholarship support	12,963,540	14,579,508	14,263,834
Smith Center Suite leases	4,784,721	3,003,344	2,453,784
Miscellaneous: clinics, entry fees, etc.	564,053	710,831	429,991
Student-athlete opportunity fund	0	0	507,209
Endowment income	1,349,198	1,898,050	4,062,869
Cash withdrawal from reserves	244,740	0	2,269,694
Total revenue	79,177,920	75,502,070	82,987,760
Expenses			
Salary			
Salaries and wages	25,267,357	25,083,367	27,042,979
Fringe benefits	5,327,887	6,103,557	5,942,182
Scholarships	12,800,494	13,311,913	14,444,793
Football and basketball guarantees	NA	NA	1,700,000
Services	9,572,458	9,971,084	10,303,203
Travel	6,579,260	5,957,377	6,361,193
Supplies and equipment	4,102,867	4,001,945	3,971,103
University overhead and contributions	1,712,300	1,927,780	2,520,380
Continuous charges	1,995,904	1,584,408	2,542,340
Debt service	6,487,013	3,627,298	4,505,657
Other transfers	5,332,380	2,969,981	3,653,931
Total expenses	79,177,920	74,538,710	82,987,760
Total operating income	0	963,360	0

Football ticket sales: $11,300,321

Basketball ticket sales: $3,273,306

Other ticket sales: $499,298

http://grfx.cstv.com/photos/schools/va/genrel/auto_pdf/2014–15/misc_non_event/FY14_Financials.pdf

EXHIBIT 8.10 Sample Financial Statements: Athletic Department Budgets

8.5.3 College Coach Salaries

The business model of many professional sports has athletes sharing 50 percent or more of the total revenues of the entire league. In these leagues, the elite athletes in most professional sports have salaries that are multiples of those paid to coaches. In college sports, the NCAA has an "amateurism" model where student-athletes receive zero to minimal compensation (beyond tuition and board). In turn, in high-revenue college sports, there is the financial capacity to pay large salaries to coaches. This situation can create a challenging context on campuses where there are very diverse opinions on what is an "acceptable compensation package" for an elite college coach. Despite the objections of some academics, college coach salaries in high revenue sports have continued to increase and can even be ten times that of some leading academics on the same college campus. In some cases, the football coach is the highest paid employee of the college.

Most publicity in this area occurs for football head coach salaries and men's basketball coach salaries. Exhibit 8.11 (Panel A) reports the top five head coach salaries in 2014 for college football and men's college basketball programs. The highest paid women's college coach in 2013 was Geno Auriemma, head coach of the Connecticut women's basketball team at $1.95 million in 2013 increasing to $2.4 million by 2017.[37] Exhibit 8.11 (Panel B) reports the sports with the ten highest median head coach salaries in 2013 for both men's and women's programs. The same pattern observed previously in this chapter is apparent in Panel B. The higher-money sports are more likely to have higher median head coach salaries. Men's head coach salaries are sizably above women's college head coaches for the high-revenue sports.

Focusing narrowly on revenue implications of having an elite football or basketball program, head coach salaries in the $5–10 million range may well still leave the programs as being net contributors to the college department financials. However, it leaves open the broader debate over the increasingly dominant role that revenue-generation plays in decision making in college athletics. There is increasing pressure by some colleges to look beyond revenue-generation and win/loss records when designing college coach salary packages. Box 8.2 examines the debate at the University of California at Berkeley over the low graduation rates of student-athletes on its football team, highlighting the challenges in making meaningful advances in this area.

8.5.4 Role of Agencies in College Sports Management

An important part of marketing at the individual college level is often subcontracted out to third parties who have the capacity to handle a broad base of functions. These include ticketing, hospitality, digital assets, event signage, live event radio, and television shows. Agencies providing these functions and services include:

- **IMG College.** Has contracts with more than 80 colleges. IMG has built up the colleges it represents by a combination of acquisitions (such as Host Communications and ISP Sports) and organic growth.
- **Learfield Sports.** Has contracts with more than 80 colleges. Also has partnerships with more than 1,200 radio stations.
- **JMI Sports.** A new entrant in this industry with the University of Kansas as its first college.

Each of these agencies provides employment opportunities for individuals in the sporting industry.

Panel A: Highest paid college coaches in football and men's basketball

Football	Annual salary ($M)	Men's basketball	Annual salary ($M)
University of Alabama Nick Saban	7.160	Duke University Mika Kryzewski	9.982
Michigan State Mark Dantonio	5.636	University of Louisville Rick Pitino	5.758
University of Oklahoma Bob Stoops	5.058	University of Kentucky John Calipari	5.511
Texas A&M Kevin Sumlin	5.006	University of Kansas Bill Self	5.960
University of Texas Charlie Strong	5.000	University of Florida Billy Donovan	3.905

Panel B: Median head coach salaries for 10 Division I Football Conference schools – 2013 ($M)

Men's Sports	Median Salary	Women's Sports	Median Salary
Football	1.904	Basketball	0.374
Basketball	1.201	Ice hockey	0.164
Ice hockey	0.373	Volleyball	0.145
Lacrosse	0.220	Lacrosse	0.139
Baseball	0.218	Gymnastics	0.135
Water polo	0.162	Softball	0.131
Soccer	0.157	Soccer	0.130
Volleyball	0.151	Field hockey	0.126
Wrestling	0.126	Crew	0.110
Tennis	0.117	Tennis/equestrian	0.105

EXHIBIT 8.11 Annual Salaries of College Head Coaches
Source: USA Today

8.6 SUMMARY

The many levels at which decisions are made in college sports and the strong differences in opinions on the criteria to judge the success of a college sports program or college athletic department make this area one of the most complex in sports management. While the continuing growth in revenues associated with college sports can increase the tensions between different stakeholders, one upside is the greater opportunities for students to have sports play an important role in their broader college experience and then subsequently as a source of employment.

NOTES

1 We use the term "college" to cover any post-secondary/high-school education. For example, it includes universities, military colleges, two-year colleges, and institutes.

2 R. Exner, "Most-watched college football games on television," Northeastern Ohio Media Group, January 12, 2015). The BCS title game at the Rose Bowl in 2006 between University of Texas and USC attracted 35.6 million viewers for ABC.

3 The count of individual colleges in each conference can vary depending on how you count colleges that are affiliated with a conference for some but not all sports. For example, the ACC count of 15 colleges includes Notre Dame, which has most sports playing in the ACC. Notre Dame football, however, is termed "independent," which means it is not affiliated with any conference. It negotiates its own media package with NBC for Notre Dame football.

4 Throughout this book, we use hockey to refer to the ice hockey version of the game. For other versions of "hockey," we use the more specific phrase – such as field hockey, roller hockey, and street hockey.

5 www.bucs.org.uk/homepage.asp.

6 www.fisu.net.

7 The NCAA ranks colleges for individual sports that have a "minimum" number of 40 colleges participating in intercollegiate games, www.ncaa.com/news/ncaa/article/2013-09-17/ncaa-rankings. Other sports have intercollegiate events, but are not included in NCAA rankings. An example is rugby, where a smaller number of colleges have programs with scholarships, paid coaches, etc. Women's rugby has been identified by the NCAA as an "emerging sport."

8 This box is an edited version of Case 5.2 "Marquette and Bucknell Wrestling Programs: Were They Pinned by Title IX?" in G. Foster, S.A. Greyser, and B. Walsh, *The Business of Sports* (Thomson South Western, 2006).

9 S.Y. Lee, "Despite improvement in mind, Cal's football graduation rates fall to national lows," *The Daily Californian*, October 28, 2013.

10 "Cal, coach Sonny Dykes finalize deal," ESPN, March 1, 2013.

11 R. Kroichick, "Cal athletic director Sandy Barbour leaves post with her head held high," *SFGate*, June 27, 2014.

12 J. New, "A real incentive or PR?" *Inside Higher Education*, February 6, 2015.

13 T. Farrey, "Ed O'Bannon: ruling is top of iceberg," ESPN, August,10, 2014.

14 B. Strauss and S. Eder, "College players granted rights to form union," *The New York Times*, March 26, 2014.

15 www.ncaa.org.

16 August 4, 2014 Memorandum from NCAA Division III Financial Aid Committee.

17 "Composition and sports sponsorship of the NCAA membership," www.ncaa.org.

18 *Time Magazine* statement quoted in foreword to *A Call to Action: Reconnecting College Sports and Higher Education*, report of the Knight Foundation Commission on Intercollegiate Athletics, June 2001.

19 *A Call to Action*, p. 8.

20 "What are the academic standards for freshman interested in participating in Division 1 athletics?" NCAA Degree Completion Award Program.

21 S. Ganim, "UNC fake class scandal and NCAA's response wind their way to Washington," CNN News, April 8, 2014.

22 J. Pope, "NCAA athletes work long hours, survey says," diverseeducation.com, September 4, 2009.

23 T. Blount, "Seahawks stars rant against the NCAA," ESPN, January 29, 2015.

24 "Amateurism," www.ncaa.org.

25 Real Clear Sports, Top 10 Infamous NCAA Sanctions, (May 17, 2013).

26 NCAA 2013 Annual Report, Footnote 11 (Televisions and Marketing Rights).

27 College Athletic Clips, Conference Realignment Graphic (Version #25, March 15, 2014).

28 This rule can be changed by the NCAA. It is likely that conferences with less than 12 colleges will seek to relax the 12 college requirement for a conference playoff game to be permitted.

29 Had the University of Texas joined other members in the Big 12 conference in establishing a conference-based network (like the Big Ten network) it would have been sharing the revenues with other conference members.

30 "Texas A&M wants to leave Big 12," ESPN, September 1, 2011.

31 "ESPN lands rights to college playoff for $470 million per year through 2015," CBSSports.com, November 21, 2012.

32 "Big 12 schools share a record $220M revenue for 2012/14, with most schools getting $23M," Fox News, May 30, 2014.

33 S. Wieberg, M. Hiestand, T. O'Toole, and E. Smith, "Texas Longhorn Network raising some concerns around Big 12," *USA Today*, July 21, 2011.

34 S. Wieberg, "Tycoon's $165M gift to Oklahoma State raises both hopes and questions," *USA Today*, February 21, 2007.

35 http://sportige.com/biggest-stadiums-in-college-football-08-21-2014.

36 D. Rovell, "Under Armour signs Notre Dame," ESPN, January 21, 2014.

37 "Geno Auriemma signs new deal," ESPN, March 27, 2013.

9 SPORTING EVENTS AND MEGA-EVENTS

The pinnacle of sports is the event itself. Whether it is a match, a race, or a sequence of events that configure a larger one such as the Olympics, sports become real when the actual event takes place. Events range from organizing a children's league or an amateur game at a local club to mega-events such as the FIFA World Cup or the Olympic Games that have more than a billion television viewers worldwide.

There is a veritable industry generating "top ten" lists in sports and the event space is a major part of this industry. Appendix 9A presents summaries of multiple "top ten event" lists. The FIFA World Cup in soccer appears frequently on such lists. The 2014 final of the FIFA World Cup in Rio de Janeiro with Germany defeating Argentina 1–0 attracted more than 500 million viewers. The month-long FIFA World Cup in Brazil was reported to have more than three billion interactions on Facebook and more than 670 million messages on Twitter.[1] The NFL's Super Bowl game is also a perennial on such "top ten event" lists. Since 2010, it has consistently attracted more than 100 million viewers in the United States each year.[2] Exhibit 9.1 provides a sample of a series of sporting events around the world in 2014 and their following via television viewership.

9.1 MULTIPLE DECISIONS IN RUNNING AN EVENT

Putting together a sporting event involves different decision makers at various decision points. The first aspect to consider is the type of event. Mega-events are complex projects involving numerous people, organizations, and decisions through extended periods of time.In contrast, small participant events such as a kids' soccer league are much smaller with much fewer decisions to consider.

Decision rights relating to events are often distributed among different parties. Event rights-holders typically decide early on who will be in charge of running the event. This decision can be structured in multiple ways. One way is for the rights-holder to open a bidding process much like what happens in the Olympics. Alternatively, it can choose an event organizer like European basketball teams have done with the Euroleague or FIA (International Automobile Federation) has done with Formula 1 and the World Rally Championship. The contract can extend through one realization of the event or through multiple years. The rights-holder can also transfer some decision rights to third parties. For example, it could negotiate media contracts directly, much like the IOC does, or it could delegate this negotiation to the event manager. A rights-holder can also run the event themselves, with their own staff and resources; this is often called an "owned event."

Events also include a myriad of actors who take several decisions. A central figure is the event manager or organizing committee, who typically get delegated a large number of decisions from the rights-holder. Other important actors include the players and athletes who decide whether or not to participate in the event, coaches and sporting staff, referees and technical staff, media, medical staff, fans, suppliers, leagues and federations, governments, and sponsors. Each one can make decisions that influence the running of the event and its success.

9.1.1 Timeline of Key Decisions

This section overviews six key decision areas, tracking an event along the timeline from event choice and location to the post-event evaluation. The context is one where the type of event has been chosen and decisions have then to be made on multiple ongoing fronts. As will be seen, the nature of the event

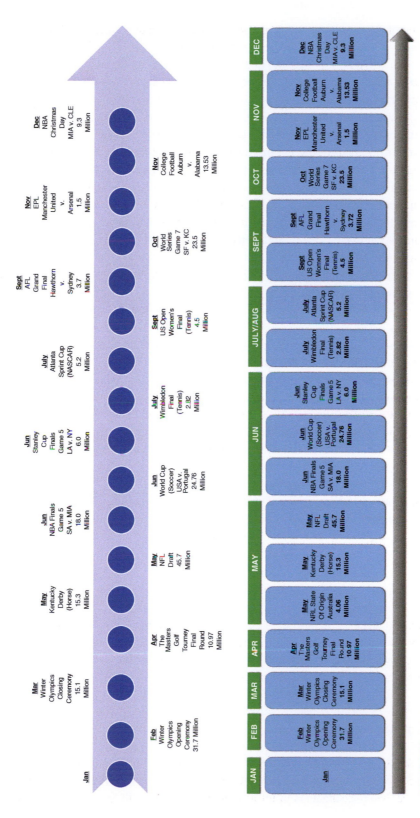

EXHIBIT 9.1 Television Viewing Figures for Sports Events 2014

Jan

Feb Winter Olympics Opening Ceremony 31.7 Million

Mar Winter Olympics Closing Ceremony 15.1 Million

Apr The Masters Golf Tourney Final Round 10.97 Million

May Kentucky Derby (Horse) 15.3 Million

May NFL Draft 45.7 Million

Jun NBA Finals Game 5 SA v. MIA 18.0 Million

Jun World Cup (Soccer) USA v. Portugal 24.76 Million

Jun Stanley Cup Finals Game 5 LA v. NY 6.0 Million

July Wimbledon Final (Tennis) 2.82 Million

July Atlanta Sprint Cup (NASCAR) 5.2 Million

Sept US Open Women's Final (Tennis) 4.5 Million

Sept AFL Grand Final Hawthorn v. Sydney 3.7 Million

Oct World Series Game 7 SF v. KC 23.5 Million

Nov EPL Manchester United v. Arsenal 1.5 Million

Nov College Football Auburn v. Alabama 13.53 Million

Dec NBA Christmas Day MIA v. CLE 9.3 Million

JAN	FEB	MAR	APR	MAY	JUN	JULY/AUG	SEPT	OCT	NOV	DEC

Jan

Feb Winter Olympics Opening Ceremony **31.7 Million**

Mar Winter Olympics Closing Ceremony **15.1 Million**

Apr The Masters Golf Tourney Final Round **10.97 Million**

May NRL State Of Origin Australia **4.06 Million**

May Kentucky Derby (Horse) **15.3 Million**

May NFL Draft **45.7 Million**

Jun NBA Finals Game 5 SA v. MIA **18.0 Million**

Jun World Cup (Soccer) USA v. Portugal **24.76 Million**

Jun Stanley Cup Finals Game 5 LA v. NY **6.0 Million**

July Wimbledon Final (Tennis) **2.82 Million**

July Atlanta Sprint Cup (NASCAR) **5.2 Million**

Sept US Open Women's Final (Tennis) **4.5 Million**

Sept AFL Grand Final Hawthorn v. Sydney **3.72 Million**

Oct World Series Game 7 SF v. KC **23.5 Million**

Nov EPL Manchester United v. Arsenal **1.5 Million**

Nov College Football Auburn v. Alabama **13.53 Million**

Dec NBA Christmas Day MIA v. CLE **9.3 Million**

itself affects many of these ongoing decisions. Sections 9.4 to 9.9 of this chapter further discuss these six decision areas.

- **Decision area #1: Selecting the event location.** This decision is most visible in rotating events such as world cups or national championships. For periodic events such as regular season league games, this decision is non-existent except under extreme circumstances such as closing of a stadium because of a penalty associated with problems in prior events.
- **Decision area #2: Creating the event and building the event brand.** The degrees of freedom vary between a standard event – such as a regular season league game where decisions are limited to regular stadium management issues – to events that have many more decisions, such as deciding the itinerary for the Dakar Rally or the halftime show at the Super Bowl. For larger events, the creation stage also involves creating and building the event brand as well as decisions on the organizational structure, processes, and functioning of the organizing committee.
- **Decision area #3: Planning the event.** This requires decisions on the objectives that the event is going to achieve. The event plan includes when certain milestones are expected to be reached in the planning and how the event will be financed.
- **Decision area #4: Preparing the event.** This is often the longest stage in event management. Many decisions regarding the operation of the event are made at this stage, including marketing, logistics, infrastructure, event impact, and process design. The event manager here could delegate tasks to different internal people in the organization or could contract to have external parties to take responsibility for them.
- **Decision area #5: Operating the event.** This happens during the actual running of the event. Good preparation will result in few decisions needing to be made during the operation of the event, as people will execute according to the design of each process and each scenario. Still, unexpected situations will happen for which people are not fully prepared. In these cases, people need to decide whether to refer to a more senior person in the organization or take the initiative themselves.
- **Decision area #6: Closing the event and post-event evaluation.** This involves all the actions happening after the event has taken place.

9.2 ALTERNATIVE CATEGORIES OF EVENTS

Exhibit 9.2 presents a categorization of different contexts in which events occur. Different event contexts greatly affect the decisions made in the six decision areas outlined in Section 9.1. Events take many forms, styles and sizes. There are regular mega-events that happen, say, every four years like the Olympic Games, FIFA World Cup, Commonwealth Games, continental games (such as the Pan American Games), or regional cups (like soccer's Copa America). Often these mega-events span through several weeks and rotate across different locations around the world. Potential city/country candidates go through a bidding and selection process to host and organize the mega-event. Shorter mega-events include annually run major end-of-season "grand finals" for sporting leagues such as the Super Bowl for the NFL and the Champions League Final for UEFA. Annual events such as Formula 1 Grands Prix, tennis and golf's grand slams, and the Tour de France also fall in this category.

	Stand-alone event with global interest that shifts each cycle	Event with global interest that is part of a broader league	National or regional event	Amateur events
Event run at an existing facility/ facilities	• Olympics • World cups in soccer, rugby, or cricket	• UEFA Champions League final • NFL Super Bowl • Formula 1 races at existing tracks • Indy 500 • Tennis majors	• PGA Golf events • Tier 2 tennis events	• High-school track events
Event run at a temporary facility with setup and strip-down	• Major cycling events such as Tour de France	• Elite marathons such as Boston, London, and New York • Formula 1 street races like Monaco	• "Sporting charity events" like marathons • Bay to Breakers running event in San Francisco	• Bike races in cities

EXHIBIT 9.2 Classifying Events by Facility Type and Global/Local Stature

North American league championships in the MLB (World Series), NBA (NBA Finals), and NHL (Stanley Cup) are structured as best-of-seven (first to win four games). These mega-events happen every year, and use the existing venues of the competing clubs. In contrast, marathon events (e.g., Boston Marathon, London Marathon) use temporary facilities that are then stripped down after the event. They take over the city and build temporary structures that then need to be stored until the following year. There are also mega-events that take place regularly, but not annually. For example, the Volvo Ocean Race – a premier yachting race that circles the globe – is held once every three years.

Many sporting events are of a "periodic event" nature without being classified as being of "mega" status. These events happen regularly through the year. These include the regular season games for team sport-based leagues – such as (a) the 162 games a year in MLB, (b) the 82 games in the NBA and the NHL, (c) the 38 games in the EPL, La Liga, Serie A, and Ligue 1, and (d) the 16 games in the NFL season. For these numerous events, the venue is fixed, there is no rotation, and no bidding to host takes place. Clubs in each of these leagues know at the start of each season the playing schedule and can plan well in advance for games that often differ in interest to their fans and other parties.

As the ratio of athletes (participants) to fans (spectators) increases, the nature of an event changes from one where the athletes are performing for spectators to one where the participants compete for enjoyment, health, and social benefit. In most cases, many of the aspects associated with professional events become less relevant and they are best defined as "participant events." While these events vastly outnumber the other types of events, they are comparatively small compared in terms of number of at-venue fans. Participation events can be divided into the following different classes, only the first of which is of high global or national interest:

■ **Global, high-profile participation events.** This class of event attracts participants from all over the world, typically thousands participate following some sort of qualifying process, and the events also include a high-profile competition for professional athletes. The Hawaii Ironman, the New York City marathon, and the Vasaloppet are examples of these types of events.

- **Festival-style participation events.** This class of participation event has emerged in recent years and is a combination of festival and run. Examples include Tough Mudder, Spartan Race, and the Mud Run. The competitive side of the race (e.g., determining a winner) is secondary to the physical challenge, fun, and team elements that dominate.
- **Amateur formal events.** This group includes any amateur event (e.g., state football championship, local ten-kilometer run, regular game in a women's volleyball league, etc.) where rules must be followed, an official is often involved, and a federation sanctions it.
- **Youth amateur formal events.** This category of events is the same as amateur formal events, but this category is focused on youth, sport development, and introducing new players to the sport. An aspect that further differentiates this from amateur formal events is the fact that parents are often a major stakeholder in these events. Examples would include a youth football/soccer league or an ice-skating championship.
- **Amateur informal events.** This includes any sport event that happens without major organization or sanction. These could include a learn-to-skate session, pick-up basketball games, etc.

9.3 EVENT STAKEHOLDERS

The planning and managing of events requires the effective coordination of a complex web of people for it to be become successful reality. These stakeholders include:

- **The event rights-holder.** As an illustration, any event that holds a specific designation as a world championship (e.g., the Sailing World Championships), national championship (e.g., the Chinese Table Tennis Championships), state/provincial championship (e.g., the California Surfing Championships), or a qualifier for one of the above, there is typically an organization that holds the rights to that event and the event's name. The rights-holder is often a federation (e.g., FIBA) but can also be a private organization (e.g., UFC, Ironman).
- **The organizing committee.** The organizing group is in charge of coordinating the different pieces for the event. This can be, for example, the hosting committee or a bid committee. Certain sports have a separate promoter such as in a boxing or mixed martial arts event.
- **Players/athletes/participants.** This stakeholder group is made up of those who play the sport. In some spectator events this can be very few, such as tennis with two players. In others there can be thousands, such as the New York City Marathon or Vasaloppet, both with 40,000+ participants.
- **Coaches.** In most events, the players/athletes/participants are directed, supported, or advised by a coach or a team of coaches. In some sports, such as American football, coaches are intimately involved in every play of the game and most teams have large staffs of coaches. In NCAA-sanctioned college football games, there is a limit of one head coach and nine assistant coaches. In NFL-sanctioned football games, there is no limit and some clubs have one head coach and more than 15 assistant coaches.
- **Referees/officials.** With the exception of informal events, most sporting events include this stakeholder group that is responsible for implementing the rules of the game and ensuring a fair and safe competition. For example, in basketball there are three designated referees in a NBA-sanctioned game, while in a FIBA-sanctioned game there are two referees.
- **Medical staff.** Events, particularly sanctioned ones, are responsible for providing medical support for cases of injury, exhaustion, dehydration, or other medical outcomes. Some players (or clubs)

will also have their own medical staff or support. A primary example would be a marathon or triathlon where a large number of medical experts will be present including physicians, chiropractors, physiotherapists, ambulance staff, and massage therapists.

- **Sport technical staff.** Events with strong high-performance elements engage sport technical staff as a stakeholder. Examples include sport scientists, event technicians (e.g., bobsleigh track), facility managers (e.g., lighting at a boxing match), and many more.

- **Spectators /fans.** This stakeholder group is often the largest group at major professional events, sometimes numbering 100,000 or more. The organizers are responsible for managing their experience from the first time they learn about the event through ticketing, accessing the venue, enjoying the event, exiting the venue, and recalling the experience. When media is present, fans extend to those experiencing the event remotely via television, online streaming, radio, or other mediums.

- **Suppliers.** Suppliers are the stakeholder group, mostly business-to-business, that bring into the event the products and services to enhance the fans' and/or participants' experiences. This group includes food suppliers, security firms, equipment providers, beverage providers, and many others.

- **Media.** Various media entities are involved in sporting events, ranging from international television to local newspapers, radio stations, and websites. Their importance grows as the event becomes larger and is consumed mostly by fans away from the venue.

- **Leagues and sport federations (international, national, state/provincial).** These sport organizations are relevant partners for most formal sporting events. Leagues and federations are the most important sporting organizations involved in events in terms of rules, participation, and sanctions. In some cases, the federation or league is the rights-holder to the event (e.g., national championship).

- **Governments.** National and regional governments are another important party to coordinate with in organizing many events. Governments give the right for an event to happen (such as marathons) but also act as suppliers providing services such as traffic management, safety and security, and even medical assistance.

- **Sponsors.** Corporations who invest in an event with financial or product/service resources are another stakeholder group in events. Sponsors range from *Fortune* 500 companies investing hundreds of millions of dollars in a mega-event to a local bike store offering a gift certificate to the winner of a local bike race. Sponsors provide a relevant part of the funding for an event and their satisfaction can impact the expected value of sponsorship rights in future editions of the event.

Some key stakeholders in running events are further explained in the following sections:

9.3.1 The Event Rights-Holder

Examples here include (a) the IOC with rights to the Olympics and its five rings, (b) the FIA, which holds the rights to several world championships including Formula 1 and the World Rally Championship, and (c) the NBA, which holds rights to the two leading professional male (NBA) and female (WNBA) basketball leagues in North America. In tennis, the rights to each event are often owned by a different party. This party can decide to move the tournament to another city or to sell the rights. Often, federations are the rights-holders in much the same way as with the FIFA (soccer) and FIBA (basketball) World Cups.

The holder of the rights to the event can decide to have another organization use the rights and organize the event or it can organize the event itself. For the Olympics, the IOC delegates the management of the event to a temporary organization such as the London Organizing Committee of the Olympic and Paralympic Games (LOCOG) for the 2012 London Olympics. In this particular case, the organization is temporarily set up as soon as the city is awarded the games and disbanded a few months after the closing ceremony of the Paralympic Games. Over this span of time, the organization grows from a few people into several thousands of employees and volunteers.

FIM (Fédération Internationale de Motorcyclisme) holds the rights to several world motorcycling championships with the MotoGP World Championship being the most famous one. For several years, FIM has granted the right to organize the Grands Prix that make up the championship to Dorna, a for-profit company. Dorna manages the entire operation, with FIM being involved only at the technical level. At each Grand Prix, Dorna partners with the local Grand Prix promoter to manage the event. The local promoter is typically in charge of local marketing, ticketing, traffic, and track management, while Dorna is in charge of publicity at the track, TV signal, global sponsors, and large parts of hospitality.

Some rights-holders organize events themselves, such as the UEFA Champions League, the Tour de France, Titan Desert, and Tough Mudder.

9.3.2 Sports Administrators and Organizations

The core of the operation of a sporting event is the management and the technical staff in charge of having the game operate within the rules of the sport. This includes the referees and officials, technical staff, medical staff, and representatives from the rights-holder and the organizing committee. For some sports, the event management only takes care of athletes when they arrive to the venue and leaves the rest of the logistics with the athlete or their own individual support teams. For example, a marathoner arriving at the Berlin Marathon will have to register, but most of the remaining elements of their preparation are of their own doing. Other organizations such as Dorna, the organizer of MotoGP, take a more active role. In particular, Dorna takes care of all the logistics of the material for Grands Prix happening outside of Europe. It flies the motorcycles and all the technical equipment from one Grand Prix to the next, facilitating the logistics that otherwise each team would need to set up.

Event management must also coordinate with technical staff from the rights-holder, usually a sport federation. For example, UEFA has strict procedures that need to be followed by any event organizer and it has its own people on the ground to make sure that these procedures are followed. The procedures range from having "clean stadiums" (meaning no non-UEFA sponsors are visible at the event) as well as removing any fans' signs that have comments considered offensive or misaligned with UEFA's values.

9.3.3 Spectators/Fans

The fans who are physically at the venue are a central part of managing any large event. This includes marketing the event to potential fans, then moving to ticketing and pricing, and finally managing the logistics associated with the whole "door-to-door" fan experience on event day (such as transportation to and from the event, the physical move into the stadium, around the stadium, and then out of the stadium).

Managing fans involves a large number of aspects. First and foremost is safety and security. This aspect ranges from minor issues that might happen during the event such as pickpocketing or verbal fights between fans from different teams, all the way to terrorist threats or even terrorist attacks. Sports in isolated but high-profile cases have suffered devastating fan-related tragedies. These include the terrorist attacks in Munich at the 1972 Olympic Games and the death of 39 soccer fans attending the European Cup Final between Juventus and Liverpool in 1985. Stadium design, security forces, coordination with the police, and risk management are all essential aspects to be considered when putting together an event.

Crowd management is another important aspect affecting fans' experience. It depends on the design of the venue, the number of people attending the event, and the ability of the event manager to influence their behavior. Enlarging the event beyond the game itself can help spread out the arrival of fans. Minor League Baseball teams have repositioned their events from just a baseball game to a family event where games and food are as relevant to fans as the game itself. This extended experience brings fans to the location at different times before the start of the game. Technology is also being developed to speed up fans' entry into the venue, facilitate purchases at the stadium, gather data about the fan for future marketing campaigns, and enhance the live and media experience.

Fans are segmented according to the different services that they purchase. Hospitality fans in suites have a different experience than regular fans. The event organizer also needs to plan and consider these different segments.

9.3.4 Suppliers

In contrast to fans, with whom contact happens mostly at the event date, suppliers are constantly coordinating with the event management organization through all the stages of the process. Where the organizations that manage events are temporary, there is often heavy reliance on subcontracting. Suppliers are often the main organizations carrying the learning from one edition of the event to the next. For example, various companies have emerged around the Olympic Games, specializing in every detail. Some companies specialize in the bidding process and advise cities interested in hosting the games on how to structure that bidding. Other companies specialize in security and have become the de facto repositories of security at the Olympic Games. Others specialize in athlete logistics and support, and still others in volunteer management. Such organizations exist for several reasons. One is because of their built-up expertise. Another reason is because of the lack of expertise within the organizing committee, which will in many cases be disbanded soon after the event closing.

Multiple suppliers play roles in event management, even when the event occurs on an ongoing basis. A case in point is technology companies. Advanced ticketing, telecommunications, broadcasting, or customer relationship management companies provide services and knowledge that an event manager typically does not have.

Event management organizations also rely on a myriad of suppliers that provide assets that the organization only needs temporarily or skills that suppliers can provide at a better cost or quality. Transportation is a case in point. Events require transportation during the event for athletes, VIP fans, or technical staff. This service is often subcontracted. Catering, security, ticketing, and hiring of part-time employees are examples of resources that are usually outsourced.

9.3.5 Media

The majority of fans of large events experience them through media such as television and mobile devices. Media revenues are central to the economics of many large events. Not surprisingly, media is a large revenue-generator. Broadcast revenues were more than 50 percent of the total NFL revenues in 2014 and 73 percent of the total IOC revenues in the 2009/12 period. Online media is playing an increasingly important role in fan engagement. Exhibit 9.3 highlights the growth in media exposure for events in recent years.

Where the rights to broadcast are sold to a third party, the event management organization will be involved in coordinating with the producer of the broadcasting signal. Some organizations – such as Dorna, in charge of MotoGP – have in-sourced media production because of the specialized skills required to produce high-quality motorcycle-racing media content.

Media coverage has important implications for an event. The quality of broadcasting affects viewership and the brand of the event. The value that sponsors derive from being associated with an event can be greatly affected by the broadness and quality of media distribution. The way networks integrate advertising also affects the experience of fans watching the broadcast. Rights-holders and event management organizations often like to sign longer contracts with media companies to align their interests in building a strong sports property.

Chapters 15 and 16 are devoted to the media aspects of the sport business.

9.3.6 Governments

Governments can play important roles in events of all sizes and interest. Government funding of community sports events is often associated with the important role that sport plays in society, especially in the health and development of children. Areas where governments support larger, more high-profile events include:

- **Funding** – governments can be an important facilitator of an event through a direct money contribution or by giving resources to the event for free.
- **Safety and security** – public services such as police and firefighters are pivotal for insuring the safety of the participants at the event.
- **Crowd management** – city governments can help facilitate crowd management around an event by helping with parking or special transportation.
- **Legal aspects** – certain events may require laws to be adopted for the event to take place. For instance, as part of the bidding for the Olympics, the IOC requires legislation to be passed at the country level to protect IOC sponsors from ambush marketing.
- **Logistics** – athletes, technical staff, and VIP guests can require special logistics arrangements that need to be coordinated with the local authorities.

In turn, hosting events can bring multiple positives to a city or country. These can include extra spending by attendees, employment for locals, and branding opportunities where the city or country uses the events to showcase itself to potential tourists or corporates.

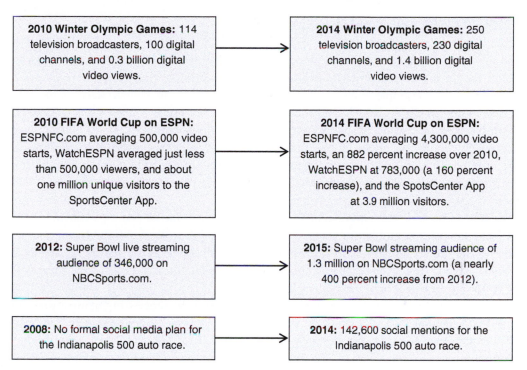

EXHIBIT 9.3 Evidence of Digital Media Growth in Events in Recent Years
Source: International Olympic Committee Marketing Fact File, 2014, ESPN Media Zone (http://espnmediazone.com/us/press-releases/2014/06/espns-fifa-world-cup-coverage-continues-significant-audience-growth/), Pew Research Center's 2015 Report on the State of News Media (www.journalism.org/2015/04/29/state-of-the-news-media-2015), CNN (http://money.cnn.com/2015/02/02/media/super-bowl-streaming-record), and Sprinklr (www.sprinklr.com/social-scale-blog/social-media-data-indy-500-coca-cola-600).

9.3.7 Sponsors

Sponsorship is often an important and, in some cases, a pivotal part of running an event. For example, sponsors such as Billabong, Nike, and Quicksilver have been an essential part of the economics of many surfing events. Good management of sponsors can help increase the value of sponsorship packages going forward. The value of sponsorship increases through exposure and activation. Exposure requirements are typically explicitly stated in the contracts and the event management organization needs to meet or ideally exceed their contractual obligations. For instance, a sponsor might have its brand on the boards of the stadium but fans may place their own flags on top, therefore blocking the board that the sponsor bought to display its own message. Good event management both reduces the likelihood of this happening by its board placement strategy, or makes the effort on game day to prevent fans blocking out the sponsor's visibility.

The activation of a sponsorship package depends, in part, on good coordination with the organizing committee. For example, if the sponsor has a tent where it gives away free samples or it collects fans' information, a good event manager will design the flow of fans in a way that it increases the number passing in front of the tent. Activation programs include a number of activities that require good coordination, such as sponsors bringing their top clients and having them experience the best event possible. Chapter 11 will further explore sponsorship.

9.4 SELECTING THE EVENT LOCATION

In multiple cases, there is considerable flexibility for a rights-holder as regards the event location. One approach by event-holders here is to have a bidding process by which cities make proposals to the rights-holder. An example is the Tour de France. The design of the different stages of the Tour de France combines having a balance between mountain and flat with stages finishing at particular cities. The Tour has been in England, Spain, Switzerland, and Belgium as part of the efforts of many cities to be associated with this flagship event. Individual cities bid and make proposals that can include police security, accommodation, and road closures to facilitate bikers not having to navigate cars and trucks. Formula 1, World Rallies Championship, MotoGP, and the Volvo Ocean Race also negotiate with cities for them to host a Grand Prix or a stage in a rally.

The IOC has a very structured bidding process by which countries and a chosen city submit a bid. Where there are multiple cities within a country wishing to make a bid, the National Olympic Committee will select the single city to bring forward to the IOC. For example, the city of San Francisco has sought to bid for the Summer Olympics multiple times. Each time it has failed to be chosen by the USOC as the city of choice to be voted on by the IOC.

The Super Bowl site selection is a multi-year process, with the process beginning a year or two prior to the actual award date. In general, the Super Bowl is awarded approximately four years in advance of the game. Host communities must treat the event like a "city-wide" convention, with massive commitment of sporting venues, convention venues, hotel rooms, transportation, public safety, and governmental support, as well as the sporting venue itself.

Criteria used by the NFL in making the city choice decision include:

- having an NFL team;
- having a stadium of a certain size (a minimum of 70,000 sellable seats);
- having certain warm weather conditions or a domed stadium (this rule was not binding for the decision to grant the 2014 Super Bowl to New York/New Jersey at MetLife Stadium);
- having a specified large number of hotel rooms, including percentages of "quality" hotel rooms within a 60-minute drive of the stadium;
- having several large ancillary venues per Super Bowl specifications (e.g., for the NFL Experience site).

If it is determined that a city will be able to bid on a specific game, then the city receives from the NFL the "Super Bowl Bid Specifications," which must be completed along with hotel and transportation contracts. Following submission of the preliminary bids, the NFL events department analyzes the information and does side-by-side comparisons with information from each bidding city. After the analysis is completed, the information is presented to the Super Bowl Policy Committee, comprised of three owners. All 32 owners then vote on the various city proposals using a structured process to determine the chosen city. A city that receives a three-quarters majority vote of the 32 NFL team owners is awarded the Super Bowl.

9.5 CREATING THE EVENT AND BUILDING THE EVENT BRAND

Once the selection of the location of the event has been decided, the organizing committee is formed according to the rules of the rights-holder. At the creation stage it defines the concept, the plan to get to a successful event, and its governance. The depth of the concept definition varies depending on the newness of the event. The first Dakar Rally involved a large amount of creativity to get the concept right. Dakar is the capital of Senegal, and is located on the west coast of Africa. Planning and execution for the first run of the event had many uncertainties. However, even after 36 editions, creation still plays a large role for the Dakar. In 2008, the race was cancelled because of security concerns; it was then moved to South America in 2009. Every year, the organizers come up with a different route and the regulations of the vehicles. The 2016 route travels from Lima, Peru to Rosario, Argentina.

As events move from amateur events to mega-events, creation plays a more important role. Every edition of an event ideally has some concept development that happens early on. The evolution of the Super Bowl and its brand illustrates how a successful brand had been continually refined to where it is now one of the major global events in the world.[3] Exhibit 9.4 provides a graphic of the evolution of the Super Bowl from a single game to a large-scale, multi-day mega-event.

Interestingly, the Super Bowl brand was not adopted until 1970, three years after the first AFL–NFL World Championship Game happened and the game itself was still relatively low-profile. In 1979, the NFL special events department was created to develop the Super Bowl. The former NFL senior vice-president of special events describes it as follows:

> By the late 70s, it became internally apparent that it was possible to market the game as a separate event rather than as part of the season. This is when merchandising increased and advertising (like program ads) and sponsorships were sold specifically for the Super Bowl as opposed to just the League brand.[4]

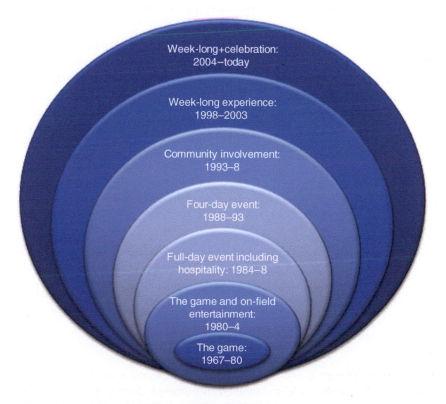

EXHIBIT 9.4 The Super Bowl: From Single Game to Mega-Event

Exhibit 9.5 builds on Exhibit 9.4 to illustrate the evolution of the event. The Super Bowl has become a recognized brand on its own within the umbrella of the NFL. The audience of the Super Bowl is multiple times larger than that of a regular NFL game. Exhibit 9.6 outlines the growth in Super Bowl viewership in the US since 1990 (Panel A) and the estimated growth in Super Bowl-related consumer spending since 2007 (Panel B).

In both panels, there is a strong upward trend, albeit not always on a year-by-year basis. Multiple reinforcing platforms explain this growth in the Super Bowl brand. For example, the organic creation and then programmed growth in ranking Super Bowl advertisements has meant that many viewers retain interest in watching the full four-hour coverage, even when there is a break from the game itself. Indeed, some viewers find rating the advertisements oncreativity more interesting and engaging than the game itself. This in itself is a remarkable outcome, given that many viewers now are increasingly seeking to watch televised programs on a tape-delay basis where they can "speed through" the advertisements. The halftime show is of high interest to many and features top entertainers such as U2, Paul McCartney, Britney Spears, and the Rolling Stones. The Super Bowl has mixed both sports and entertainment into a package that attracts a much broader viewership than its regular season and the early stages of its playoff season.

Years	Philosophy	Description
1960s–1970s	On the field	Emphasis on the spectacle of the three-plus hours of the game itself.
Early 1980s	On the field plus	Emphasis on the spectacle of the three-plus hours of the game and its accompanying on-the-field entertainment.
Mid-1980s	All-day event	Recognition that the game was not just the three-plus hours on the field plus entertainment, but a full day, including related activities and hospitality
Late 1980s/early1990s	Four-day event	With the advent of the four-night minimum stay requirement by hotels, recognition that there was a "captive" audience for four days – this led to the greater development of the local Super Bowl Host Committee
Mid-1990s	Community member	Recognition that the NFL, by virtue of the fact that it was so involved in the host city for several years, became a member of the community with its associated role of giving back – the first Super Bowl legacy, the NFL YET Center, was built in 1993 in Los Angeles
Late 1990s/mid-2000s	Week-long experience	League philosophy of maintaining the aura of the Super Bowl as the gold standard of events – the commitment to becoming bigger and grander each year, the best of the best (e.g., the Friday Night Party, the NFL Experience, etc.) – ensuring that the people who attend have a "once-in-a-lifetime" experience
Mid-2000s to present	One-week to two-week experience	Broad-based immersion of the city in the Super Bowl experience of which the game is put a part. Many activities available for local and visiting fans. Portfolio of high-end activities for sponsors and other league partners.

EXHIBIT 9.5 The Evolution of the Super Bowl to a Mega-Event

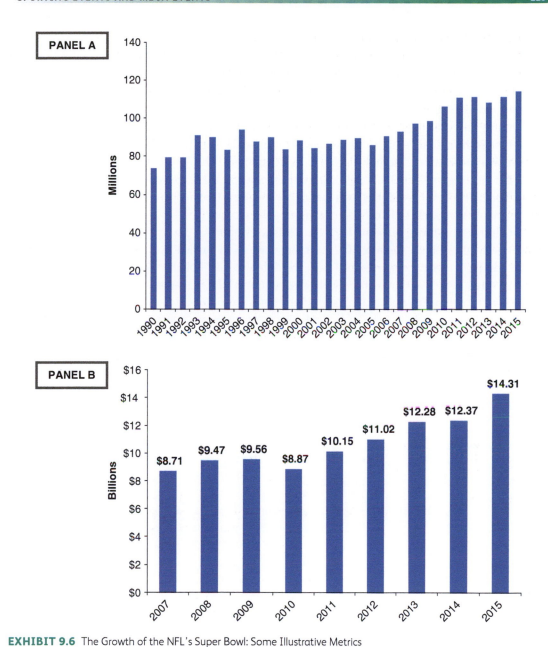

EXHIBIT 9.6 The Growth of the NFL's Super Bowl: Some Illustrative Metrics
Panel A: TV viewership of the Super Bowl in the United States from 1990 to 2015 (in millions).
Source: Nielsen; TV by the Numbers; Sports Media Watch
Panel B: Estimated Super Bowl related consumer spending in the US from 2007 to 2015 (in $ billion).
Source: National Retail Federation

The Super Bowl approach of building a brand based on an existing event exists elsewhere. Tennis tournaments such as Wimbledon (London) or Roland-Garros (Paris) have built their own strong brands within the brand of elite global tennis major tournaments. The Monaco Grand Prix has built its own brand that is related to the Formula 1 Championship brand, but exists as its own distinctive motor-racing event brand.

9.6 PLANNING THE EVENT

The more complex and unique an event is, the more planning it requires. The Summer Olympics is probably the most complex event in the sports world. Organizing committees start working as soon as they get the nomination, about seven to eight years before the Olympics happen for the selected city.

Planning an event requires agreeing on the objectives, including sporting ones, as well as those that sports can help come to life. City executives can now have sports event strategies that outline the events they want to attract and how they plan to attract them. The objective is not simply hosting the events, but creating a perception of the city through the people that experience these events. The legacy and sustainability of events are objectives that go beyond the actual happening of the event. Careful and astute planning increases the likelihood of achieving those objectives.

Beyond the objectives, planning involves a detailed outline of timelines and actions over time to achieve the final product. The mix of actions that need to be carried over depend on the objectives and the contracts that have been signed with the different stakeholders. City contracts, sponsorship contracts, venue agreements, or commercial agreements can all have explicit or implicit objectives. For instance, sponsorship contracts to tennis tournaments such as Roland-Garros or the Australian Open often demand heavy presence in the facilities of the tournament. Some high-end and high-paying sponsors invite their best clients to enjoy the event and demand elite-quality hospitality. The organizing committee needs to work closely with such sponsors to fully understand what kind of services they need and offer suggestions from their experience with other sponsors.

Box 9.1 outlines changes by UEFA in its country-based soccer league related to the objective of "improving the quality and standing of national team football."

BOX 9.1 UEFA'S EURO 2020

UEFA's European Championship (Euro) is an event among the top national soccer teams in Europe to decide the European champion. It happens every four years, halfway between FIFA World Cups. The event was not considered a major event in the European soccer calendar until the mid-1980s, when UEFA began to raise its profile.

The investment turned out to be successful and the Euro is now one of the top events in Europe. The format of the event up until the coming edition in France 2016 had a structure similar to the FIFA World Cup. Prior to the event, the 53 national teams that participate form groups of five to six teams and play in a round-robin structure to decide the 23 teams that participate in the final event of the Euro together with the host country. The 24 teams are assigned to six groups of four teams and the top two teams of each group together with the best thirds make it to the knock-out stage. Much like the FIFA World Cup, games are played in stadiums around the country.

Starting in 2020, UEFA decided to change the structure of the competition. Both the sporting and the structure side were changed. According to UEFA the objective was "to improve the quality and the standing of national team football … for more sporting meaning in national team football … associations, coaches, players and supporters increasingly of the opinion that friendly matches are not providing adequate competition for national teams."[5]

With the new sporting structure, there will be a competition called Nations League with four leagues each one composed of four groups of three or four teams. League A will have the top teams and League D the worst ones. The winners of each group in League A will move to the final while the last ones will be relegated and the winners from the next league promoted. The final four will decide the UEFA Nations League winner. The UEFA Euro will have ten groups and the top two of each team qualify for the final event. In addition each league in the Nations League will have a playoff, with the winners of each group in each league and the winners of each playoff qualifying for the last four places for a total of 24 teams in the Euro finals. If a winner has already qualified, then the next best ranked team will qualify.

The format of hosting the Euro in one country was replaced with having 12 cities around Europe hosting games and having the 2020 semi-finals and the final in London.

9.6.1 Risk Management

Comprehensive event planning includes risk management as a central component. For a smaller event, the main risk might simply be the weather. The plan could include a contingency plan that specifies alternatives in case the weather turns out to make the regular development of the event impossible. Mega-events have a multitude of variables that can negatively affect the event. Risk management likely cannot anticipate all occurrences, but game plans can be built over time based on experiences at many events and not just those of the existing rights-holder. For example, during the 2012/13 season of La Liga, one of Real Madrid's games had to be postponed because the lighting of the stadium failed. No contingency plan was in place and the game had to be rescheduled in an already tight calendar. Failure of lighting is now an event that has occurred multiple times across stadiums such that it is important to have a backup lighting game plan already in place for major events.

One of most important and very challenging areas of event risk management is threats of terrorism and attacks by extremist groups using the event to showcase their causes. The events at the 1972 Munich Olympics were an early warning in this area. The investments and organization required to reduce and manage this risk area has grown rapidly to where it can be in the tens of million dollars or more for mega-global events.

The financial plan is an essential part of the whole event planning process and of financial risk management. The financial plan details where money comes and goes and the timing of those flows. Often outflows come before inflows; investment in infrastructure and organizing the various aspects of the event are done well ahead of the scheduled date of the event. Inflows typically come later; ticketing happens as the event gets closer and merchandising also peaks at the event. To minimize these cash-flow issues, event managers often attempt to move forward some key cash inflows. Examples include selling media rights ahead of time, advanced ticket program sales, or having sponsors pay in advance. Formula 1 Grand Prix often offer tickets nine months ahead of the race at a discount to advance cash inflows. A mismatch between cash needs and cash inflows requires a financing plan with banks. The cash needs will be closely related to the resource plan of the event. Cash is required to be available whenever resources – whether employees or supplies – are needed.

Box 9.2 highlights several risks associated with team-based events that gave rise to games being played in front of no spectators (so-called "empty stadiums"). One set of risks related to the racial taunting of colored players by soccer fans in Eastern Europe. The second set of risks was associated with fan safety associated with civil unrest in the city of Baltimore.

BOX 9.2 TWO EUROPEAN SOCCER GAMES AND ONE U.S. BASEBALL GAME PLAYED IN "EMPTY STADIUMS"

Game-day revenues are an important revenue source for many events. For example, game-day revenues have averaged 24 percent of total club revenues over the 2009/13 period in three major European soccer leagues: the English Premier League (25 percent); German Bundesliga (23 percent); and the Spanish La Liga (25 percent). However, for several European soccer games and one U.S. baseball game, targeted events have occurred in "empty stadiums"/ "behind closed doors." This means no spectators were permitted in the venue. Playing a home game in an "empty stadium" has at least two potentially negative impacts – a loss of game-day revenue, and the loss of home-field advantage from a vocal supportive fan base in the stadium. The context between the European and U.S. "empty stadium" games was, however, very different. Both contexts highlight potential learnings for risk management.

European Soccer

In several cases, FIFA and UEFA have separately mandated that a home game be played in an "empty stadium." Both cases highlight the importance of clubs being proactive in taking all steps possible to eliminate "unacceptable and offensive behavior" at games.

- In November 2013, FIFA upheld an earlier ruling that the Ukrainian national team play its first home game during the 2018 World Cup qualifying tournament in an "empty stadium." FIFA's ruling was in response to Ukrainian fan behavior at a September 2013 game at the Arena Lviv stadium between the Ukraine and San Marino. Three areas of Ukrainian fan behavior were cited by FIFA: (a) displaying neo-Nazi banners/making Nazi salutes, (b) making "monkey noises and gestures" targeting a Brazil-born player, and (c) the use of pyrotechnics during the game. The Arena Lviv stadium was banned from hosting any 2018 World Cup qualifying matches. In addition, the Football Federation of Ukraine was also fined $50,000.[6]
- In February 2014, UEFA ordered the Russian Premier League club CSKA Moscow to play their next Champions League home match in an "empty stadium." UEFA stated: "CSKA must play their next UEFA club competition home game behind closed doors and pay a fine of 50,000 euros (£41,000) after supporters displayed a range of racist and far-right symbols during their 2–1 UEFA Champions League Group D defeat at FC Viktoria Plzeň December 10, 2013. The punishment reflects the fact the CSKA have previous records of racist behavior by supporters."[7] In a previous CSKA match against Manchester City, Yaya Touré of Manchester City was subjected to monkey chants by CSKA fans.[8] Touré is an Ivory Coast player who played with multiple elite clubs, including Barcelona, before joining Manchester City.

Major League Baseball

On April 29, 2015 the Baltimore Orioles played the Chicago White Sox in an Orioles home game at Camden Yards at which no fans were permitted to attend. The background was concerns about fan safety in the light of rioting associated with the death of an African-American who had been placed in a police van and suffered injuries that led to his death and subsequently much civil unrest in the city of Baltimore. On April 28, the Orioles released a statement that stated: "After consultation with Major League Baseball and city and local officials, tomorrow's game between the Orioles and the Chicago White Sox will be closed to the public." The Orioles three-game series against the Tampa Bay Rays for May 1–3 was transferred from Camden Yards to Tropicana Field in St. Petersburg, Florida.[9]

This Orioles "empty stadium" event highlights that in some cases there are factors that affect game-day event risk that are not directly controllable by a club. Note that in this context, suggestions were made that the Orioles should have approached the nearby Washington Nationals to have their April 29 game played at their stadium, where fans could have attended. From April 27 to May 3, the Nationals were on the road, playing games in Atlanta and New York.

9.6.2 Project Management Applications

The use of project management tools is an essential part of a well-managed event-planning process. The project plan details actions and milestones over time. The critical path indicates the actions that, if delayed, affect the delivery of the event. Actions outside the critical path can have delays without putting the delivery at risk. Project management plays around with three constraints: objectives (scope), time schedule, and budget. MotoGP races, like any other event, have milestones that need to be achieved for a Grand Prix to take place. The first milestone is setting the calendar for the championship, which is typically done a year in advance. Two weeks before the race, the operational team from Dorna that has been already working on the race back at headquarters is at the location. One week before the race, the entire team is on the ground at the racetrack to make sure that all aspects of the race are ready. Putting together a world motorcycle championship has hundreds of milestones related to the operations of the race itself. Box 9.3 highlights the complex nature of a boxing event.

BOX 9.3 EVENT COMPLEXITY: PACQUIAO VERSUS MAYWEATHER

In one of the most anticipated sporting events of the early 21st century, boxing stars Manny Pacquiao and Floyd Mayweather, both holders of world championship belts and Mayweather an undefeated champion, fought on May 2, 2015 at the MGM Grand Garden Arena. The event garnered global attention and set records with a reported record number of pay-per-views sold. The live event was sold out, with 16,800 fans purchasing tickets often at more than $2,000 each. Many areas of complexity and compromise in event planning and execution occurred during the journey to the May 2 fight occurring.

■ HBO and Showtime as co-producers. For many years HBO was the dominant force in the broadcasting of boxing events. More recently, Showtime had become an aggressive competitor.

Pacquiao was under contract to HBO for his fights. His manager was Bob Arum of Top Rank, who served the role as a promoter for many of the HBO fights. In February 2013, Mayweather announced he had signed a mega-deal with Showtime and was leaving HBO for a multi-fight deal that potentially could see out his active career. Articles at this time reflected the widely held opinion that this greatly reduced the likelihood of a fight. For example, the headline of one article was: "Now that Mayweather–Pacquiao is over, what's next for boxing?"[10] This headline was based on the expected inability of the two networks to form a partnership to make the fight happen. Underlying the expected impasse between HBO and Showtime were individuals who had worked at one company and then had joined the other company, not always on a voluntary basis. It was often reported that some key players in the two companies were well beyond the "not being on talking terms" animosity spectrum.

■ The boxers and their promotion companies. For multiple years, the two boxers had been paired as the "fight that should happen." However, there appeared to be limited urgency on the side of one or both to fight each other. Both were having lucrative individual fights with large purses. Mayweather's purses made him into one of the highest paid athletes in the world. Pacquiao had a sequence of fights with Juan Manuel Márquez that earned him very large purses. However Pacquiao's loss to Márquez in December 2012 appeared to reduce his bargaining power in a potential fight with Mayweather and may even have reduced the attractiveness of the fight itself. As each fighter got closer to a possible retirement, concerns started being expressed about whether the fight itself was as attractive to an audience as it may have been in 2011 or 2012. Were the two fighters each past their prime of fighting years? Mayweather and his advisors were well-known hard bargainers and suggestions that a 70/30 percent split in favor of Mayweather for a possible fight certainly made it less attractive to Pacquiao on both financial and ego terms. There was also a history of multiple possible agreements for a fight between the two fighters without an actual event occurring. The agreed split for the May 2, 2015 fight was reportedly 60 percent to Mayweather and 40 percent to Pacquiao.

The likelihood of a fight occurring started to increase in early 2015. A now-famous, very public on-court meeting between the two fighters at a Miami Heat home NBA game in January added to the rumor mill that a fight could be in the making. In the next three months there were increasingly signs that serious negotiations were taking place. The expected money associated with such a fight led to some unexpected bedfellows. HBO and Showtime co-produced the fight. It was their first formal boxing collaboration for a fight in more than a decade. The leading announcers from each company shared the announcing. The ring announcing was shared by HBO's Michael "Let's get ready to rumble" Buffer and Showtime's Jimmy Lennon.

Preparing the production of the event required a very different set of protocols than many other boxing events. Very few celebrities were given complementary tickets. Many "B" celebrities found out very quickly that they had to either pay a large amount to attend or stay at home. Executives associated with HBO, Showtime, CBS, etc. had to turn away requests for tickets (even paid tickets) from multiple high-profile friends. One executive sent out an email to all on his email list that simply said "DON'T ASK." The pre-event publicity saw many groups hyping the event. It quickly became called the "fight of the century."

Event day saw the broadcast side of the venture run into multiple problems. The fight was delayed for up to 30 minutes or more when cable and satellite systems struggled with an "electronic overload" due to many last minute pay-per-view buyers not being able to place their order. Several cable distributors reportedly had outages and they faced demands for refunds. Allegations about "massive piracy"[11] on video-sharing smartphones led to threatened lawsuits against companies facilitating the sharing.

Mayweather won the fight with a unanimous decision from all three judges (116–112, 116–112, and 118–110). Given the extreme hyping of the event, it was unlikely to live up to the expectations of some observers. Oscar De La Hoya, who had fought both boxers during his own career, sent out several tweets after the fight including: "Sorry boxing fans" and "Can't wait for some real action next week."[12] Some critics of the fight used colorful language. Chris Case in *USA Today* called it "the uber-bout that wasn't. The so-called fight of the century was a pay-per-snooze, a complete waste of everyone's time and money."[13] But one thing is for certain: the fight was not a waste of time for the fighters and their promoters. Varying reports soon after the fight suggested payments well above $100 million for each of the two camps. HBO and Showtime put aside their rivalry for a night and showed how the promise of the then biggest ever payday in boxing history could lead to "co-opetition" rather than 100 percent competition.

Each action in the project plan has an owner responsible for its execution and quality, a measurable output, a deadline, the resources required, place, and coordination with other actions happening at the same time. Coordination becomes more complex as the size of the event increases. Simple events such as organizing a kids' game requires little in terms of planning: specifying time and location, reservation of the location, and appointing an umpire that usually also fulfills the role of liaison with the local federation. More complex events involve a myriad of different outputs that need to be achieved and each one needs its own planning of actions. An event might include accommodation for athletes, press, authorities, and fans; catering; logistics and transportation; security; media operations; ticketing; sponsorship; ceremonies; cultural program; customer service; information technology; sport management; venue management; and management of volunteers. Each and every one of these factors requires its own specific plan as part of the master plan.

Events, especially those run for the first time or with a large amount of new aspects, are often stressful projects. Deadlines and optimistic plans lead to conflict, budget overruns, and pointing blame at others. Many global events suffer from poor planning and execution schedules. The result is often less-than-finished facilities by the event start date or very large cost overruns associated with overtime payments for workers operating for months on an around-the-clock basis. For example, the 2014 FIFA World Cup in Brazil was plagued with delays in the construction and renovation of stadiums, creating unease across all stakeholders.

9.7 PREPARING THE EVENT

The preparation phase for most events will take the largest amount of time and effort. The Olympic Games take seven to eight years of preparation for delivering 17 days of excitement. A Super Bowl is in the making for most of the 12–24 months before the actual game.

Preparing the event means executing the tasks described in the project plan that lead to the event. Here there will likely be ongoing unexpected situations that require a change in the plans or a revaluation of the project plan. Being quick at identifying and reacting to these situations is important. Managing the preparation of an event requires a constant monitoring to ensure that actions are being executed according to plan. Frequent meetings, often as frequent as daily, facilitate the coordination among different functions. Some of the unplanned occurrences can be beneficial: a cheaper than expected ticketing system or a volunteer training program growing faster than planned would be examples.

Red-flag deviations from plans are the negative ones leading to delays or cost overruns. Some of them can be identified before they hit the project and its measures. For instance, a supplier of technology can let the organizing committee know that the technology it was supposed to deliver will be two weeks late. Some deviations only affect a small part of the event, while others have implications for the overall event. Depending on the importance of the deviation, management teams at different levels need to evaluate the implications and the alternatives available. One aspect of sports event preparation that is fundamentally different from most applications of project planning is that the date of the event is typically fixed and close to impossible to shift backwards.

Risk management starts during the identifying event risks phase of planning the event. During both the planning and the preparation phases, contingency plans for many potential risks will be being scoped out and ideally have multiple "trial runs" practiced.

Preparing detailed operations manuals that describe the different processes leading to the event is an essential part of preparing the event. Once the event starts, there likely is little time to improvise, as a thousand different things will be simultaneously happening that seemingly require 100 percent of attention. The preparation phase also requires resources be devoted to outlining operating plans such as the protocol for the actual game, processes to collaborate with sponsors, crowd management, safety and security, and hospitality management procedures.

9.8 OPERATING THE EVENT

The most exciting, as well as the most exhausting, aspect of events management is likely the actual running of the event. During the event, multiple activities will be happening simultaneously and within short periods of time. Deadlines are critical and a flawed execution can have important implications in terms of stakeholders' satisfaction and revenues. The likelihood of an event externally appearing well-managed is increased by detailed, astute, and thorough planning. The schedule for the different activities is often detailed down to the minute, clearly detailing who is responsible for it, where it happens, and who needs to be coordinated. Rehearsing these plans enhances the operation of the event.

Difficult situations will inevitably happen. Some of them will have been considered in contingency plans and ideally the event management team can facilitate a quick and effective response. Other situations will be new and often unexpected. Responding to such unforeseen situations requires very good communication across the various levels of the organization to bring the right expertise and the right decision makers into the decision loop as soon as possible. It also benefits from a clear responsibility structure to understand who the decision maker is for these situations.

Unforeseen situations can be minor incidents that the various levels of the organization can directly handle, such as minor issues with the flow of fans through the venue, to problems in getting the supplies to the food concessions, or to minor interactions among fans. Major incidents require the reaction of higher levels of the organization and often the coordination of many functions. These major incidents can require crisis management approaches. Examples at the venue include major confrontations among fans that event security cannot adequately handle, a bomb scare, or the collapse of part of a seating structure. Unexpected issues can go all the way to kidnapping of athletes or terrorist attacks. The more the team has been trained to face these types of crisis, the faster and the more effective the reaction will be. Crisis management might even require transferring authority to the police. For instance, UEFA has a procedure specifying all the steps that need to be taken in case a stadium needs to be evacuated because of a terrorist threat, the collapse of part of the infrastructure, or the coming of a strong storm. While to date the majority of these procedures have not been required during any of the UEFA tournaments, it is astute event management to continue to invest heavily in maintaining and upgrading these capabilities.

9.9 CLOSING THE EVENT AND POST-EVENT EVALUATION

The task of the organizing committee is *not* finished at the end of the event. During the various stages of the event, the organization has gathered knowledge that can be useful to future events. The closing of an event includes steps to codify and transfer knowledge. At the Olympics, teams from the following Olympic city work closely with the organizing committee of the current Olympics to learn from their experience. The debriefing has to be as detailed as possible answering questions related to:

- what went well and why;
- what went not so well or even failed and why;
- what the organization learned from unexpected situations;
- what would be done differently; and
- what lessons were learned towards future event management.

The more detailed the post-event analysis, the greater the likelihood that more learning will be transferred to future events. UEFA's KISS platform (Knowledge and Information Sharing Scenario) is a digital repository of knowledge with documents and videos covering most aspects of event organization. It includes information from specific events as well as from the regular conferences and courses that UEFA organizes around the different aspects of association football (soccer).

Some events include data collection as part of the closing phase. Different stakeholders including fans and sponsors are interviewed or sent a questionnaire to get their view on the various aspects of the event. This data collection helps better understand the strengths and weaknesses of the event and how to improve going forward.

The final aspect of the closing of the event is to transfer the legacy of the event to the organizations that will manage it for the benefit of the city and its people. The legacy of mega-events often includes new sport and non-sports infrastructures. These infrastructures need to be managed to avoid having them become "white elephants."[14] A large part of the success of the legacy comes from good planning during the creation and preparation phases. Another component of legacy is the intangible benefits. Mega-events, but also smaller events, potentially create goodwill for the region. Much like activating sponsorship, the region needs to manage this intangible legacy to benefit from it. The event reinforces the brand of the region through brand awareness or brand recognition. Organizations responsible for managing this legacy have to activate this goodwill and transform it into increased tourism, more business, and better environmental, social, and economic status for its citizens. Without an active management of this legacy, the likelihood of a boost in goodwill out of an event can be greatly reduced.

9.10 VOLUNTEER MANAGEMENT

A large number of events from the Olympics to amateur games rely on volunteers. Attracting and managing volunteers becomes an important aspect of the organizing committee's efforts. Volunteers are community members that collaborate with the organization of an event to show their support and commitment to the success of the event. Volunteers, with rare exceptions, get no monetary compensation. For simple events such as children games, parents are often volunteers, fulfilling basic roles such as score-keeping and liaison with the little league. For larger events, they often get merchandising associated with the event such as T-shirts and tickets for events that are not sold out. Volunteers at Olympic Games events are a highly visible part of what occurs during the event. Here they help run a large portion of the games including working as drivers for the athletes, helping fans find their way around, helping the events themselves, or supporting medical needs.

For regions and cities with rather frequent events, volunteers get to accumulate experience that becomes handy as new events are organized. People that volunteer once tend to volunteer again and bring their prior knowledge to the event. A volunteer program starts with attracting people to work for the event with no financial compensation. People are motivated by a broad set of objectives other than money. Some of them love the sport and are willing to give their time and energy to promote the sport; others want to show the hospitality of local people and have visitors enjoy a great experience; still others hope to get to meet some of their idols; other volunteers love to be part of a unique experience; some volunteers see it as an opportunity to gain experience, get to know people, or even learn new skills. The organizing committee has to appeal to these different motivations and do so at different segments of the population to have a mix of volunteers in the pool. Volunteers have other professional activities in their lives and can bring this expertise to the event. Volunteers can fulfill a variety of roles and significantly reduce the cost of running an event.

A second important aspect in a volunteer management program is to select the right mix of volunteers for the needs identified in the master plan. Most volunteers work directly with fans and athletes, and their job is not necessarily highly skilled. Yet, some volunteers can have unique skills that make them very valuable for more sophisticated aspects of the event. High-profile events typically attract more volunteers than needed; some of them will not be recruited while others will join the organizing committee because their skills fit the needs.

The third aspect of a volunteer management program is training. Even for jobs that might look simple, there is often training involved. Fan-facing volunteers will often receive training around safety and security, customer service, or operations. Getting a certification can be part of the training program; not only might the certification be valuable for other purposes, but it also makes volunteers confident about their abilities to perform their tasks. Part of the training is to enhance the commitment of volunteers to the team and the event; team-building exercises and tokens of appreciation early on in the volunteer process are ways to get more committed volunteers that will deliver the best service.

During the actual operations, volunteers need to feel useful and deliver value that contributes to the event rather than feel like cheap labor that the event is taking advantage of. Having the tools and the training are important parts of this feeling of contribution to the project; the relationship with other volunteers, the feeling of being part of the group, and the respect and appreciation from the organizations are other aspects to carefully manage for the volunteer program to be successful. Frequent recognition and rewards, such as tickets, merchandising, access to athletes, or access to certain hospitality services, helps keep volunteers' commitment at a high and sustained level.

As part of the closing phase of an event, the event management organization evaluates the success of the volunteer program. Similar to any other aspect of event management, the organization collects data from volunteers, analyzes it, and evaluates strong and weak aspects of the program with the objective of documenting, learning, and improving future volunteer programs.

9.11 SUMMARY

This chapter introduces sport events and mega-events, a key aspect of the sport business. Management skills are essential in many aspects of the timeline of event activities described in this chapter. There are an increasing number of management tools that assist in these activities. Moreover, there are many areas where third parties have considerable expertise that can be harnessed to either increase the productivity of efforts in this area or to reduce the likelihood of occurrences negatively affecting the experiences of some or all of the stakeholders invested in having a successful event.

APPENDIX 9A THE CARAVAN OF TOP TEN SPORTING EVENT LISTS

Top ten sporting races by participants

Rank	Event name	Location	Date	Length	Participants
1	Kahit Isang Araw Lang Unity Run	SM Mail of Asia, Pasay, Philippines	January 22, 2012	10km, 5km, 3km	209,000
2	A Run for the Pasig River	Manila, Philippines	October 10, 2010	10km, 5km, 3km	116,086
3	Bay to Breakers	San Francisco, California, United States	May 18, 1986	12km	110,000
4	Cursa El Corte Ingles	Barcelona, Spain	June 5, 1994	11km	109,457
5	Broloppet/Broløbet	Malmö/ Copenhagen, Sweden/ Denmark	June 12, 2000	Half-marathon	92,266
6	City2Surf	Sydney, Australia	August 14, 2011	14km	86,696
7	Dam tot Damloop	Amsterdam, the Netherlands	September 20, 2009	10 miles, 4 miles and kids' runs	74,020
8	Hong Kong Marathon	Hong Kong, Hong Kong	January 15, 2015	Marathon, half-marathon, 10km, 10km wheelchair race, 3km wheelchair race	73,070
9	Round the Bays	Auckland, New Zealand	March 10, 2013	8.4km	70,000
10	Lilac Bloomsday Run	Spokane, Washington, United States	May 5, 1996	12km	61,298

Note: This is a sample of observed events, not an official list.

Top ten richest sports events (winners)

Rank	Event	Prize money*
1	UEFA Champions League/Soccer	$65 million
2	FIFA World Cup/Soccer	$31 million
3	UEFA Euro/Soccer	$29 million
4	World Series/Baseball	$19 million
5	UEFA Europa League/Soccer	$12 million
6	Super Bowl/NFL	$11 million
7	FedEx Cup/Golf	$10 million
8	World Series of Poker/Poker	$8.5 million
9	Dubai World Cup/Horse Racing	$6 million
10	FIFA Club World Cup/Soccer	$5 million

Source: *Forbes*

* Prizes are what the winners receive.

Top ten largest championship sporting events by spectators

Rank	Event	Sport	Championship	Attendance	Year	Venue	City, country
1	AFL Grand Final	Australian rules football	Australian Football League	99,454	2014	Melbourne Cricket Ground	Melbourne, Australia
2	FA Cup Final	Association football	FA Cup	89,345	2014	Wembley Stadium	London, UK
3	Football League Championship Play-off	Association football	Football League Championship	87,348	2014	Wembley Stadium	London, UK
4	College Football Playoff National Championship	American football	College Football Playoff	85,689	2015	AT&T Stadium	Arlington, USA
5	Copa del Rey Final	Association football	Copa del Rey	85,000	2013	Santiago Bernabéu Stadium	Madrid, Spain
6	NRL Grand Final	Rugby League	National Rugby League	83.833	2014	ANZ Stadium	Sydney, Australia

7	League Cup Final	Association football	League Cup	82,597	2013	Wembley Stadium	London, UK
8	Super Bowl	American football	NFL	82,529	2014	MetLife Stadium	East Rutherford, USA
9	All-Ireland Hurling Championship Final	Hurling	All-Ireland Hurling Championship	82,274	2012	Croke Park	Dublin, IRE
10	All-Ireland Football Championship Final	Gaelic	All-Ireland Football Championship	82,184	2014	Croke Park	Dublin, IRE

Note: This is a sample of observed events, not an official list.

Top ten sports by number of spectators

Rank	Sport	League	Country	Average attendance per game*	Total spectators per season (millions)
1	Football	NFL	United States	68,401	17.3
2	Soccer	Bundesliga	Germany	28,271	13.0
3	Soccer	Premier League	England and Wales	28,164	13.7
4	Australian rules football	AFL	Australia	27,316	6.9
5	Baseball	MLB	United States & Canada	26,380	74.0
6	Canadian football	CFL	Canada	25,572	1.9
7	Baseball	NPB	Japan	24,214	22.0
8	Soccer	La Liga	Spain	21,839	11.5
9	Cricket	IPL	India	21,678	1.4
10	Soccer	Serie A	Italy	21,402	8.4

Source: The Economist
* 2003 figures

NOTES

1 See "Cricket World Cup 2015 3rd most watched sports event in the world," *Total Sportek*, January 11, 2015 and "World Cup final sets US TV record," ESPN, July 15, 2014.

2 www.statista.com/statistics/216526/super-bowl-us-tv-viewership.

3 The following description of the Super Bowl draws heavily on a Stanford GSB case on "Super Bowl XL: Building and Managing a Mega-Event and a Mega-Brand" (2006).

4 Quote from Jim Steeg, reported in G. Foster, *Super Bowl XL : Building and Managing a Mega-Event and a Mega-Brand* (Stanford GSB Case, 2006), p. 15.

5 www.uefa.com/community/news/newsid=2079553.html.

6 M. Rachkevych, "FIFA upholds empty stadium order over racism, bans Lviv from hosting matches," *Kyiv Post*, November 27, 2013.

7 Quoted in "CSKA Moscow handed stadium ban by UEFA over racist conduct by fans," Sky Sports, February 18, 2014.

8 S. James, "City's Yaya Touré demands CSKA ban after racist chanting mars victory," *The Guardian*, October 23, 2013.

9 More examples of "empty stadium" games are in "Orioles aren't first team to play to empty seats," *The New York Times*, www.nytimes.com/interactive/2015/04/29/upshot/30up-empty.html?_r=0&abt=0002&abg=0.

10 See also D. Rafael, "Floyd Mayweather inks new PPV deal," ESPN, February 22, 2013.

11 M. Barr, "Mayweather–Pacquiao fight suffers massive piracy at hands of Twitter's Periscope," *Forbes*, May 3, 2015.

12 N. Schwartz, "Oscar De La Hoya blasts Mayweather–Pacquiao: 'Sorry boxing fans,'" *USA Today*, May 3, 2015.

13 C. Chase, "Mayweather–Pacquiao was a complete waste of time and money," *USA Today*, May 3, 2015.

14 A "white elephant" refers, in this context, to an expensive facility built for a particular event that now sits largely unused post-event.

PART III APPLICATIONS

10 SPORT MARKETING

As in most other businesses, aspects of marketing are central to many of the stakeholders in the sports ecosystem discussed in Chapter 2. PWC forecasts that the North American sports market is projected to grow from $56.9 billion in 2013 to $70.7 billion in 2018.[1]

Marketing is "an organizational function and a set of processes for creating, communicating and delivering value to customers and for managing customer relationships in ways that benefit the organization and its stakeholders."[2] Sport marketing is the specific application of marketing principles and processes to sport products and content and to the marketing of non-sports products and content associated with a sport.[3]

Exhibit 10.1 outlines the marketing path from a message or exposure to the target, acquiring awareness, and then that target becoming engaged with the message and its marketer. The final stage of the path is the target making a decision and hopefully the marketer seeing a desired outcome such as the sale of a jersey, the purchase of a ticket, or signing up to watch a pay-per-view boxing or mixed martial arts event. Examples of desired outcomes for participatory sports include enrolling children in a junior soccer league or signing up to run in a charity marathon fundraising event.

This chapter and the following four chapters cover multiple related areas of sport marketing, including sport sponsorship (Chapter 11), athlete endorsements (Chapter 12), sport event ticketing (Chapter 13), and fan engagement (Chapter 14). Many other chapters have frequent mention and linkage to sport marketing due to its central role in decision making in the sport ecosystem (see Chapter 2).

Box 10.1 provides an overview of observations made by many commentators on sports marketing. These observations give color to why sports marketing is such a high-profile topic to stakeholders.

EXHIBIT 10.1 Marketing and Steps to Desired Outcome

BOX 10.1 SOME COMMON COMMENTARY ON THE SPORTS INDUSTRY

Some commonly observed commentary on the sports industry provides an important backdrop to the sport marketing topics discussed in this and related chapters:

- Winning is highly important at the level of professional and elite sporting leagues and global events. In some instances (e.g., Olympic Games), winning (or at least a medal) is vital for any meaningful business outcome. In contrast, participation is the most important aspect of sport for many active amateur sport enthusiasts.
- Live sport remains the most important content for many TV and web streaming audiences. It is the last fortress for much must-see programming content.
- Sport content is "produced" for live at-event and media audiences, but it is not scripted and has no predetermined result(s). Uncertainty of the outcome is central to sports. This idea drives multiple leagues to fight against match-fixing. Professional wrestling in recent years has explicitly used the term "entertainment" rather than "sport" in the light of criticism that

their athletes often perform with predetermined outcomes. Many sports marketers see their major challenge as increasing the entertainment aspect of sports events while still retaining the integrity of the uncertainty of outcome aspect.

- Elite athletes, coaches, owners, and sports media personalities can be celebrities. Here the level of media attention on their 24/7 activities ratchets up to a very high level.
- Fans' and participants' passion for sport sets it apart from many other industries, opening amazing opportunities for being creative in sports marketing.
- Sport has very high-pressure moments and situations. Even the very best athletes in the world at their sport can crack under the pressure. Marketers sometimes use such moments to highlight the human aspect of athletes. Where the athlete reaches the pinnacle of success at a subsequent event, marketers have stories about resilience and determination to create emotive storytelling.
- A hardcore fan or devoted participant may spend sums of money or devote blocks of time on sport activities that others view as irrational. Fans can behave outside of their normal behaviors when their team wins or loses.
- National teams (Olympic Games, World Championships, FIFA World Cup) carry the hopes and aspirations of many of their citizens. Winning can bring surges of public patriotism. Not surprisingly, politicians spend time with athletes when they win.

10.1 MARKETING OF SPORT VERSUS MARKETING THROUGH SPORT

Sport marketing is now a recognized field of expertise and study. Two major related areas of activity in this field are marketing *of* sport and marketing *through* sport:

- **Marketing *of* sport** – the use of marketing strategies and tools by sporting organizations and athletes to market or co-market their own properties, services, facilities, events, and personas. In many cases, third-party intermediaries – such as "sports agencies," as well as the more general marketing agencies – play important roles in this arena. There are also many specialized companies that play complementary roles with the sports rights-holder – such as ticketing and consumer analytics companies. Brand-building, advertising, and merchandising are important activities that leagues, clubs, events, and athletes devote sizable resources to in their marketing *of* sport. Game- or event-day marketing activities, such as ticketing and hospitality, are also major marketing *of* sport activities for clubs and events.
- Panel A of Exhibit 10.2 shows the three major groups in the marketing *of* sport: the sports property, which is also the marketing investor in the "marketing *of* sport" situation; the intermediary agency; and the marketing target. Section 10.2 further discusses and illustrates each of these three groups.
- **Marketing *through* sport** – the use of marketing strategies and tools by non-sport organizations to market products and/or services through sport. Reasons for sports being a highly attractive platform for many companies and organizations to co-market include: (a) the high level of sports fan engagement and avidity, (b) the large number of fans that are interested in and identify with

Panel A: Marketing *of* sport

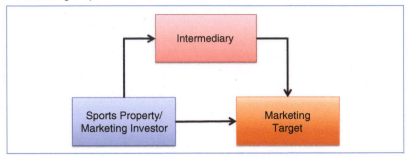

Panel B: Marketing *through* sport, *with* a partnership with the sports property

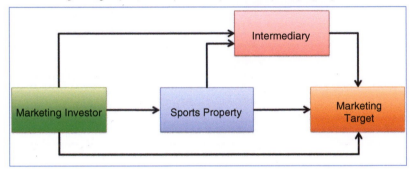

Panel C: Marketing *through* sport *without* a partnership with the sports property

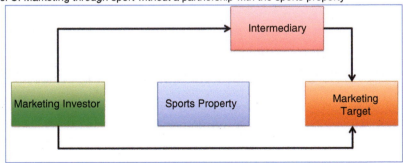

EXHIBIT 10.2 Alternative Marketing Contexts

leading athletes, and (c) the documented ability of live sports to draw and retain high viewer interest. Third-party agencies are often central in both strategy and execution in this area. Branding, sponsorship, advertising, merchandising, and hospitality are frequently found in the "marketing *through* sport" arena.

■ Panels B and C of Exhibit 10.2 show four major groups in marketing *through* sport: the marketing investor, the sports property, the intermediary agency, and the marketing target. Section 10.3 further discusses and illustrates each of these groups.

While there is much overlap between marketing *of* sport and marketing *through* sport, the major difference lies in who is making the investment. In marketing *of* sport, the sports property itself is making the investment. In contrast, in marketing *through* sport, the marketing investor is a body other than the sports property owner. Examples include a sponsor, an advertiser, or a potential suite-holder in a sporting facility. The key difference is that in the marketing *through* sport situation, the investor is not a sport organization. It is using sport to help market their non-sport products and/or services.

10.2 MARKETING *OF* SPORT

We now discuss the three key groups in Panel A of Exhibit 10.2 – the sports property, the intermediary, and marketing target. The focus here is on marketing strategy and execution decisions by the sports property itself.

Sports Property

Examples of this group include leagues, clubs, events, and athletes. Each group seeks to obtain financial and other types of resources to have the capability to conduct engaging sporting events that will attract and retain key parties such as fans, sponsors, media companies, and advertisers. The more attractive the sports property to these parties, the greater its ability to garner their support and commitment. For example, the IOC or the NFL can demand multimillion-dollar sponsorship rights fees in exchange for a partnership. In contrast, a local run may ask for $5,000 sponsorship in the form of products or services.

   Many sporting clubs have marketing and sales groups that seek to build and retain a large number of season ticket holders as well as promote ticket sales for individual games. These groups often exhibit much creativity as regards special promotions to attract different types of fans on different event days. These can include special giveaways (such as bobble-heads and T-shirts) as well as designated heritage days (such as Korean Heritage Night or Mexican Heritage Day). Box 10.2 illustrates the diversity of special promotions found in some Minor League Baseball leagues.

BOX 10.2 MARKETING IN MINOR LEAGUE BASEBALL – THE ENDLESS SEARCH FOR INNOVATIVE PROMOTIONS

Marketers for baseball clubs face the challenge of a very large inventory of games to sell to their fan bases. For example, Major League Baseball clubs play 162 regular season games each year as compared to NFL clubs who play 16 regular season games per year. Below the elite 30 MLB clubs are more than 150 Minor League Baseball clubs in North America. Game-day revenues are central to the economics of most of these clubs. Some of the most creative promotions to attract fans to games are found in Minor League Baseball. The following examples are from the "Top 10 Minor League Baseball promotions" listed on the Real Clear Sports website:[4]

10. *Office Space* Night. The Dunedin Blue Jays have movie-themed promotions where fans come dressed up as characters from a designated movie. One example was *Office Space* Night.

9. **Popsicle Night.** This night was promoted by the Bisbee Copper Kings to celebrate the life of Ted Williams, a famous MLB player. Williams had just died and his body was being kept frozen in liquid nitrogen "at a cryogenics laboratory in Scottsdale." The Copper Kings had the cool idea to give the first 500 fans free frozen popsicles. The Williams family was not amused by this promotion!

8. **Costanza Night.** This night celebrates the *Seinfeld* television show character George Costanza who decided in one episode to do everything the opposite of what was normal. The Fort Myers Miracle on this night did everything the opposite of what was normal at their park. Examples were the scoreboard running from the ninth to the first innings, the team wearing road uniforms, the men's and women's restrooms being switched, and players asking fans for their autographs after the game.

7. **A Chance to Win One Million Nights.** This promotion by the Nashua Pride was inspired by the television show *Who Wants to Be a Millionaire?* However, due to the restricted finances of the club, it was themed *Who Wants to Be a Turkish Millionaire,* which at the US dollar to Turkish lira exchange rate translated to no more than several dollars as the prize. Fans competed in a trivia contest on the field to win the prize.

6. **Pregnancy Night.** The Brooklyn Cyclones had pregnant women throw out the first pitch and run the bases. Lamaze classes were conducted on the field before the game and shown on the ballpark screens. However, the offer of a free season ticket to any women who gave birth that night in the ballpark was not taken up!

5. **Liposuction Giveaway Night.** The Mahoning Valley Scrappers had a fan competition where five finalists came on to the field and the winner was awarded a free liposuction from a nearby surgical center. The club ran the competition on their "All You Can Eat" regular Wednesday promotion night!

4. **Nobody Night.** The Charleston River Dogs intentionally locked fans out until after the fifth inning. Many fans could peer over the outfield fence with ladders. The club hosted a party outside the park with low-cost beer and food until the end of the fifth inning.

3. **Awful Night.** The Altoona Curve annually has its Awful Night with a "bevy of items that are not to be enjoyed." These included bad costumes, bobbing for onions, music by Milli Vanilli, and Spam sandwiches. Players were introduced with their "failure average" rather than their batting average.

2. **Silent Night.** The Charleston River Dogs promoted a game where during the first five innings no talking was allowed. Many fans duct-taped their mouth and held up different signs to indicate cheering or booing. Golf marshals lined the infield with "Quiet Please" signs.

1. **Auctioned-At-Bat Night.** The St. Paul Saints auctioned off the opportunity for a fan to make a plate appearance during the bottom of the eighth innings. The winner bid $5,601 for the opportunity, but unfortunately popped out to the catcher.

There is a veritable industry ranking the many promotions in Minor League Baseball. Other examples include:

- Top 12 Craziest Minor League Promotions – www.foxsports.com/southwest/lists/top-12-craziest-minor-league-promotions-081014.
- The 15 Best Minor League Promo Nights Happening in June – www.si.com/extra-mustard/2014/06/03/the-15-best-minor-league-promo-nights-happening-in-june.
- Crazy Promotions in Minor Leagues – www.usatoday.com/story/sports/mlb/minors/2013/07/03/second-amendment-gun-promotion-night-huntsville-stars/2484857.

Brand-building is an important part of marketing *of* sport for many organizations. One useful analogy for branding is to view a brand as a bank account where deposits and withdrawals are made. The strongest sport brands have often made many deposits to their brand bank account and can withstand a run of withdrawals and still maintain a strong brand presence. In contrast, weak sport brands have much less ability to withstand a sequence of negative events (brand withdrawals).

Intermediary

Intermediaries are third parties involved in sport marketing. They can play multiple roles. One role is to provide services to enhance the benefits to sports rights-holder, such as identifying and helping attract new sponsors. Another role relates to enhancing the benefits to the marketing target, such as the delivering of prizes to competition winners, the provision of tickets to fans, and providing online information about upcoming events. A third role is post-event fan and suite-holder satisfaction surveys. Examples of intermediaries include WME-IMG, Octagon, and Wasserman Media Group.

Marketing Target

Effective marketing requires the identification of and building knowledge about the target. One example of a large target group is a nationwide or even global fan base of a sports property. In such a situation, marketing could seek to build a high level of engagement via branding exercises, use of many information sources and platforms to keep a regular flow of interesting information, and the purchase of club memberships. Major soccer clubs such as Barcelona and Manchester United have global fan bases that are provided with a continual flow of information about the club, its players, special merchandise offers, online streaming programs, and the location of sports bars to see upcoming games. Social media has become a central part of many club fan engagement initiatives. A target group that is a subset of this larger group could be actual and potential attendees at game events, whether at the home stadium or when the club is playing "on the road." In recent years, several major clubs have played "friendlies" or pre-season games in different countries to sold-out stadiums with very sizable revenue yields for that club.

10.3 MARKETING *THROUGH* SPORT

This area of sport marketing includes a separate marketing investor that is not the sports property owner. Here the focus is on the strategy and execution of the sports investor and the interactions with the other three groups that were described in Section 10.2.

Panel B of Exhibit 10.2 illustrates one context of marketing *through* sport. Here the sports investor – often a corporation – has a formal relationship with the sports property owner that includes providing financial or other resources to the sports property. Examples include (a) Deutsche Telekom paying Bayern Munich an estimated annual €25 million to be the named shirt sponsor of the club,[5] and (b) Herbalife paying the LA Galaxy of MLS an estimated annual $4.4 million to be the named shirt sponsor of the club.[6] The arrows in Panel B capture the multiple interactions in this context.

Panel C of Exhibit 10.2 illustrates a different context of marketing *through* sport. Here the sports investor has no formal relationship with the sports property and provides no financial or other resources to that property. Examples include companies that run advertisements during the Super Bowl. For the

2015 Super Bowl, companies such as Victoria Secret and Universal Pictures (with its trailer for the *Fifty Shades of Grey* movie) paid the broadcaster (NBC) but made no payment to the NFL or the two individual clubs playing that game. The arrows in Panel C include no arrows to or from the sports property.

Advertising and sponsorship are two major areas of investment in the "marketing *through* sport" world. Kantar Media, part of the WPP marketing group, tracks advertising spending during network and cable sports programming. For 2014, it estimated the US total spend at $13.9 billion. Exhibit 10.3

Panel A: Industry categories of top 50 advertisers in sports programs

Category	Number of advertisers	Total spend ($M)
Automotive	15	1,870
Food and beverage	10	1,261
Financial services/insurance	8	918
Telecommunications	4	887
Electronics software/hardware	3	530
Entertainment	4	494
Pharmaceuticals	2	209
Retail	2	187
Airline	1	142
Internet	1	91
Total	**50**	**6,589**

Source: Kantar Media

Panel B: Top ten advertisers in sports programs

Advertiser	Total spend ($M)
Chevrolet	323
AT&T	310
Geico	292
Verizon	283
Budweiser	267
Samsung	208
Ford	201
Sprint	172
Subway	167
McDonald's	166

Source: Kantar Media

EXHIBIT 10.3　Top 50 Television Advertisers in Sports Programs

shows summary information for the industry categories of the 50 highest advertising spenders and the ten highest individual company advertisers. Chapter 11 provides multiple examples of companies that use sponsorship to market their companies and their products. Merchandising, another major category here, is discussed below in this section.

10.3.1 Marketing Through Sport With a Partnership With the Sports Property

In this context, as shown in Panel B of Exhibit 10.2, there are four main groups – the sports investor, the sports property, intermediaries, and the marketing target.

Sports Investor

GoDaddy, the internet domain register and web-hosting company founded in 1997, is an exemplar here. While it has invested heavily in both sponsorship and advertisement in multiple areas of sports, it is not a sports property owner. In some cases, its investment is an integral part of the sports "action" being broadcast. This is the case with its sponsorship of Danica Patrick in both the IndyCar motor car racing series (2005/11) and in the NASCAR Sprint Cup motor racing series (2012/15). Each race being broadcast showcases the GoDaddy brand with its distinctive neon green color on both Patrick's clothing and her car.

Sports Property

The sports investor in marketing *through* sport often will be directly interacting with sports property or properties. GoDaddy's investment in sponsoring Danica Patrick in the IndyCar and NASCAR motor series has involved it and its sports agency negotiating with Patrick, her agent, and with several of the racing teams in each league – such as Rahal Letterman Lanigan Racing and Andretti Green Racing in the IndyCar series and Stewart-Haas Racing in NASCAR. Negotiations here would cover the investment required and the conditions associated with that investment – such as the ability of GoDaddy to use Danica Patrick and the cars she drove in advertisements, and the number of her appearances at GoDaddy customer and employee events. It also involved GoDaddy and an intermediary working with individual racing tracks to facilitate GoDaddy activating its sponsorship at each track.

An important decision for the sports property is how much to subcontract to intermediaries. One extreme is to effectively contract with an intermediary company that offers for a guaranteed amount a "full service turn-key" model in which the sports property has a minimal role in execution of the event. Pros of this approach include the guaranteed revenue, the expertise level of the intermediary, and the minimal internal resources of the property owner needed to organize events. The cons include the potential lost revenue if the event is highly successful and the potential for conflict between the agenda of a sports investor and the agenda of the sports body. The first con can be reduced by having a contract in which there is revenue-sharing once revenues reach an agreed amount. The second con can be reduced by the sports property retaining decisions rights if events occur that (say) may diminish the reputation or integrity of the sports property. Many US colleges subcontract large amounts of their marketing efforts to intermediaries such as IMG College, Learfield Sports, and JMI Sports.

Intermediary

As discussed in Section 10.2, multiple agencies play differing intermediary roles. For example, WME-IMG has been the main agency representing Danica Patrick since 2009. An ESPN article noted:

> When Patrick signed with IMG in 2009, she took the rare step of turning her endorsement and contractual needs over to one company. [Mark] Dyer, IMG's senior VP/business innovation and a former NASCAR executive … became Patrick's liaison to NASCAR. … Patrick said, "He knows all the players, he knows the people, he knows the sport." … While Dyer focuses more on competition and team issues, Alan Zucker [of IMG] has been in charge of endorsement opportunities.[7]

Notably, there will be other agencies involved in producing a large scale marketing activity. For example, the GoDaddy Super Bowl advertisements involving Danica Patrick were developed by Deutsch New York.[8]

Marketing Target

The levels of investment by many companies marketing *through* sports typically brings much focus in decisions on the target audience. Consider Super Bowl advertisements. The Super Bowl has a very broad target audience with more than 100 million viewership in the United States in recent years – see Exhibit 10.4. The increasing advertising rates per 30 second slot reflect the elite status of the Super Bowl in attracting a large attractive and focused audience.

In contrast, advertisers for PGA golf tournaments have a much narrower demographic base. A 2015 article reported that the "television viewership for golf tournaments has remained the same over the past 10 years; white (87 percent), older (63 percent aged 55-plus), affluent (27 percent household

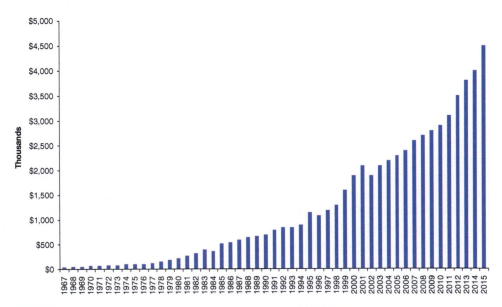

EXHIBIT 10.4 Super Bowl Estimated 30-Second Advertising Cost: 1967/2015
Source: NFL Research

income over 100k annually), and about two-thirds were male and 35 percent female."[9] This very narrow demographic results in a very different set of advertisers being associated with golf broadcasts (such as golfing equipment and high-end watches) than with Super Bowl broadcasts.

Governments, as well as companies, use sports to target specific market segments. An example is the National Guard in the US using motor sports to run advertisements for recruiting purposes. The advertisements aimed to "build strong brand awareness" with potential recruits. The National Guard sponsored Dale Earnhardt Jr., the long-time dominant NASCAR fan favorite, from 2008 to 2014. Earnhardt represented the down-to-earth American patriotic image that the National Guard was seeking in its entry class. The cost of this sponsorship for 2014 was estimated to be $32 million.[10] The National Guard was actively represented at multiple NASCAR events as part of this sponsorship.

10.3.2 Marketing *Through* Sport *Without* a Partnership With the Sports Property

The context here is where the sports investor does not have a contractual relationship with the sports property. As noted before, Panel C of Exhibit 10.2 highlights this context by showing no arrows associated to or from the sports property to other groups.

Many companies choose to advertise during or surrounding sporting broadcasts without having any relationship with the sports property. Rather the relationship is with the broadcaster. In some cases, the company may have no sponsorship or any other relationship with an existing sporting property rights-holders. The related decisions for the sports investor here include: (a) how to allocate a marketing budget, and (b) how much of the advertising budget to allocate to sports related broadcasts.

For some individual sports investment decisions in Panel C of Exhibit 10.2, the company may also be simultaneously having Panel B relationships for other sports investment decisions. GoDaddy's contractual relationships with IndyCar and NASCAR teams illustrate the Panel B context. GoDaddy's investment in Super Bowl advertising illustrates the Panel C context. GoDaddy's first Super Bowl advertisement was in the 2005 Super Bowl. For a company founded in 1997, this was an important decision as regards the allocation of its marketing budget. Exhibit 10.4 plots the estimated cost per 30-second slot each year from 1967 ($42,000) to 2015 ($4.5 million). These costs are just those that are paid to the Super Bowl broadcaster – CBS, Fox, and NBC in the case of GoDaddy in its sequence of Super Bowl advertisements. Other costs to GoDaddy would include both in-house costs of its marketing group as well as the costs of the agency that produces the advertisement. There are also the costs of third parties who monitor the effectiveness of its marketing investments.

A high-profile example of Panel C in Exhibit 10.2 is ambush marketing. Here a company markets *through* sport without paying the sports owner, while one of its competitors is paying that same sports owner for an "exclusive relationship." The IOC, when awarding an Olympics to a city, increasingly takes into account the willingness of the host country to pass new legislation protecting the "exclusive rights" paid for by the IOC's official sponsors.

Box 10.3 outlines the situation where Subway used ambush marketing to undermine the effectiveness of McDonald's sponsorship of the 2014 Olympic Games. McDonald's is a major competitor of Subway in many countries.

BOX 10.3 AMBUSH MARKETING: SUBWAY AND MCDONALD'S

The year 2014 showcased two major international sport events –the 2014 Sochi Winter Olympics and 2014 FIFA World Cup in Brazil. Television audiences for both events numbered in the billions. With such unique and potentially lucrative marketing opportunities, companies were very motivated to have their names attached to them. One of the biggest financial supporters of both events was the fast food restaurateur McDonald's, who spent an estimated $100 million on the Sochi Olympics, and another $25 million on the FIFA World Cup.[11] While the communications, activations, and status of McDonald's as both an Olympic sponsor and a FIFA sponsor were promoted around both events, a competitor of McDonald's was also successful in marketing around the 2014 Olympics and 2014 World Cup. This competitor is the popular sandwich chain Subway. But, how much did Subway pay for sponsorship rights fees for these two global events? Nothing. Considerably less than the $125 million invested by McDonald's.

Subway used athlete endorsements to ambush it. They were very creative in creating the illusion that they were an official sponsor of the games by hiring ex-Olympic athletes Michael Phelps, Apolo Anton Ohno, Nastia Liukin, and soccer legend Pelé, to endorse their sandwiches and create the illusion that they were in fact a major sponsor of both events. By using these athletes, Subway bypassed the IOC's "blackout period" where competing athletes cannot appear in advertisements in an approximate one-month window surrounding and including the Olympic event.

The 2014 fracas between McDonald's and Subway was not the first. During the 2010 Winter Olympics in Vancouver, Canada, Subway ran ads featuring Michael Phelps. A commentator described one such advertisement thus: "The commercials show Michael Phelps, the Summer Games star swimming 'where the action is this winter,' as an announcer says. From the animated map on which Mr. Phelps is swimming, it appears he is going someplace that begins with the letters 'C-A-N' – apparently an allusion to Canada." At an advertising conference after the games in 2010, Tony Pace, Subway's chief marketing officer, was asked about its alleged ambush marketing. His comment parodied a familiar line in McDonald's advertising when he commented: "My reaction to the fact that McDonald's is upset? I'm lovin' it."[12]

The effectiveness of Subway's ambush campaign was highlighted in the Global Language Monitor (GLM) Brand Affiliation index, which reported that Subway led all sponsors and non-sponsors (ambushers) during the first week of the Sochi 2014 Games. In fact, in the BAI report (published February 12, 2014), Subway has the highest rating (296.73), followed by four official Olympic sponsors (Samsung, P&G, Panasonic, and Coca-Cola). McDonald's – the official sponsor in Subway's category – was the 11th highest ranked corporation with an index score of 79.33. In the report, it is noted that "Subway, in turn, leads *all* Sochi Marketers with its unbridled, and some say outrageous athlete-focused commercials,"[13] which includes the Michael Phelps campaign noted in Box 10.3.

10.3.3 Licensing and Merchandising

Merchandising and licensing is an important revenue source in many sports. The sports property (athlete, club, league, federation, etc.) licenses its mark/logo out to the manufacturer of apparel, office products, automotive products, fitness equipment, sunglasses, and much more. In return, the manufacturer pays the sports property a fee for the right to use the mark/logo. Sometimes sport properties negotiate their licensing deals directly (e.g., the New Zealand All Blacks/Rugby New Zealand via their agency Velocity Brand Management) or other times the league does it centrally (e.g., NFL) and then shares the revenues amongst the clubs. Sales of licensed merchandise occur in the stadium, online, and in retail stores.

The merchandising deals of Manchester United illustrate the upper end of contracting in this area. Two companies pay to be associated with one of the great global sports club brands in the world. In a short time period, Manchester United changed both (a) the sponsor name on the uniform from Aon to Chevrolet, and (b) the uniform manufacturer from Nike to Adidas:

■ Starting with the 2014/15 EPL season, the Manchester United jersey showcases Chevrolet as its strip sponsor. The deal was reported to pay United at least £47 million annually.[14]
■ Starting with the 2015/16 EPL season, the uniform manufacturer is Adidas with an average minimum payment to United of £75 million per year. The 2014 Annual Report of Manchester United reported that the Adidas ten-year contract had a £750 million minimum guarantee – see Exhibit 4.10 in Chapter 4.[15] Nike, the previous long-term apparel partner, stated that "the terms that were on offer for a renewed contract did not represent good value for Nike's shareholders."[16]

Manchester United's £47 million jersey sponsor contract for the 2014/15 season was the highest in the EPL. Chapter 11 describes further jersey sponsor deals for all the clubs in the EPL for the 2014/15 season.

One of Manchester United's most celebrated former players is David Beckham. Box 10.4 highlights the global marketing prowess of Beckham in promoting the sales of Beckham numbered jerseys at multiple clubs at which he played.

BOX 10.4 THE MARKETING POWER OF BRAND BECKHAM: ON-FIELD SUCCESS AND OFF-FIELD CELEBRITY STATUS LEADS TO RECORD SHIRT SALES FOR MULTIPLE CLUBS

The building of "Brand Beckham" is one of the most successful stories in all of marketing. David Beckham played with multiple soccer clubs in his illustrious career, including Manchester United (1992/2003, 265 games), Real Madrid (2003/7, 116 games), LA Galaxy (2007/12, 98 games), AC Milan (on loan for short seasons in 2009 and 2010, 29 games) and Paris Saint-Germain (2013, ten games). The pillars of Brand Beckham included his on-field playing ability, his playing for highly successful clubs, his looks and boyish charm, his dating and marriage to Posh Spice (Victoria Adams) of the Spice Girls and their subsequent family, and Beckham's role in and appearance at many society events and charities.

The sale of soccer shirts carrying Beckham's name became an industry at each of the clubs at which he played. One estimate is that ten million Beckham shirts were sold in his 20-year playing career.[17] Some examples of the power of his brand as regards shirt sales are:

■ **Manchester United.** More than 50 percent of Manchester United's 2002 sales worldwide were from his number 7 shirt.
■ **Real Madrid.** Beckham took number 23 at Real Madrid as Zinedine Zidane already had number 7. (It was no accident that 23 was also Michael Jordan's number.) Real Madrid sold 8,000

Beckham replica shirts on Beckham's first day, beating the previous record of 2,000 when Ronaldo signed. By December 2003, sales had surpassed the million mark.

- **LA Galaxy.** The number of fans wearing Beckham shirts at LA Galaxy home and away games were something not seen before in MLS. Rankings of bestselling MLS shirts during his years at the Galaxy had Beckham consistently as the #1 seller.

- **AC Milan.** Beckham in 2009 and 2010 was on a short loan to AC Milan. The Italian club reported that Beckham jerseys were "selling at a rate similar to those of two-time world player

PANEL A

PANEL B

EXHIBIT 10.5 Electronic Arts Heat Map of FIFA 15 Online Game Users for Liverpool (EPL) and LA Galaxy (MLS)
Panel A: Liverpool Football Club of English Premier League
Panel B: LA Galaxy Football Club of Major League Soccer
Reference: EA Sports Internal Document

of the year Ronaldinho."[18] Ronaldinho was their star player from 2009 to 2011, after transferring from Barcelona.

- **Paris Saint-Germaine.** One article noted the PSG was expecting sales of more than 150,000 shirts when his short stay at the club was announced. "Despite retailing for £95, sales of Beckham 32 shirts have reached 'thousands' in the week since the former England captain announced he was signing for his new club."[19]

The MLS in North America also benefited from Beckham's global magnetism. MLS commissioner Don Garber noted, "There's arguably not a soccer fan on this planet that doesn't know the LA Galaxy and Major League Soccer, and David Beckham played a significant role in helping us make that happen. He was an unbelievable ambassador for the league, for the Galaxy."[20] Exhibit 10.5 shows a heat map that Electronic Arts develops to track the geographic spread of the online players of their EA Sports FIFA game.

The dots in Exhibit 10.5 show areas of high-density users. Panel A has the heat map for Liverpool FC of the EPL. This is one of the highest profile clubs in the world, with a worldwide fan base. Panel B has the heat map for the LA Galaxy. The pattern of spots in Panel B for continents beyond North America shows the contributions in recent years of Beckham and other star athletes that have played for LA Galaxy to building its brand at the global level. The Galaxy with Beckham built some of the global footprint observed for a high profile EPL club with a rich history and wide global presence.

Increased merchandising is but one of many aspects of the Beckham Brand success story in global marketing.

10.4 SPORT MARKETING BASICS AND CONCEPTS

Two key elements of marketing – the "exchange" and the "relationship" – are core to the marketing and the sport nexus. Spectator and participant involvement in a sport-related activity are examples of the core element of marketing theory called the *exchange*, where each party must receive something of value greater than what they invest. In these cases, the spectator/participant has an experience that exceeds the cost of the ticket/registration, while the sport organization receives the proceeds of the ticket/registration that is greater than its costs to provide the experience. Ideally, over time, the spectator becomes loyal to the club and the participant becomes loyal to the event or sport, thereby entering into multiple, reoccurring exchanges, or a *relationship*, another key marketing concept.

10.4.1 Sport Marketing Research

For a marketing investor, the first step often is understanding the setting in which the marketing effort will take place. Important questions are:

- Who is my target segment/target audience?
- What is the message to be conveyed? What do I want to tell them? What benefits do they seek that I offer/can offer? What values do I want to communicate? For example, do I want to raise brand awareness? Do I want to communicate a special new feature of my product?
- How differentiated is the value proposition? What special features do I have that people seek? How are they different from those of my competitors?

The above questions and sub-questions are generic to any marketing investment decision making process. For an investor in sport marketing, specific questions include:

1 Characteristics of the sports property fans. Who are they? What are their characteristics? How well do we know them?
2 Characteristics of the sport property. What kinds of value does the property convey? What makes it unique or at least differentiated relative to other alternatives available?
3 Integration within the existing group of companies working already with the sporting property. Are we looking for a new relationship or replacing an existing one? How does it fit with the companies we already work with?
4 The risks associated with establishing a relationship with a particular club or athlete. What risks should be considered and integrated in the deal?

In undertaking this market research, the sport marketer decides whether primary data is needed (i.e., specific surveys or focus groups are designed and administered) or if secondary data is enough (i.e., research already done by another party or internally, such as a database of syndicated study). Factors that are important here include the available budget, the timing of the decision, and the quality of the data available. Given the cost and time required to collect primary data, secondary data is often used. Some of this data could be available from government reports (such as census reports), from sport marketing research agencies, or from data that already exists at the organization (e.g., annual reports, employee surveys, financials, etc.).

If primary research is the chosen option, available approaches include: (a) a questionnaire online or in person; (b) interviews with the target market, online, on the phone, or in person; (c) expert interviews with leaders in the topic area; (d) small focus groups in sessions led by a facilitator; (e) an experiment where variables are controlled (like a lab) to assess the impact of one variable on another (others); and (f) observation where the researcher(s) go to key venues or markets and record the behaviors (with or without out interaction) of participants.

10.4.2 The Segmentation, Targeting, and Positioning (STP) Marketing Approach

The core idea of the STP approach is to identify reachable, homogenous market segments that allow for more effective marketing.[21] STP includes answering the following questions:

S How can we break our market down into homogeneous, reachable groups?
T Which of these groups (or group) should we commit our resources to reach?
P How do we want the selected target(s) to perceive our offering versus the offerings of our competition?

When Banco Santander, the Spanish banking group, decided to invest a significant portion of its marketing budget in Formula 1 (starting in 2010 for five years), they identified Ferrari as a very effective way to reach the largest proportion of their target market segment. Santander identified multiple advantages for the Ferrari sponsorship, such as:

- **Well-aligned brand attributes.** Ferrari's brand attributes included recognition, prestige, superior technology, leadership, innovation, strength, and trustworthiness.
- **Similarity in brand colors.** Both have traditional red as the brand color.
- **Audience overlap.** The Formula 1 middle- to upper-class audience fitted Santander's target audience.
- **The global reach of Ferrari and Formula 1.** Santander saw high value from Ferrari's high brand-awareness across different countries.
- **Minimal brand clutter on race cars and driver apparel.** Santander was able to negotiate (albeit at a high price) for its brand to be highly visible on the two Ferrari Formula 1 cars and their drivers with little clutter from other companies.

The first Santander contract with Ferrari was for the 2010/14 period. In 2012, Banco Santander extended the sponsorship through to the end of 2017.[22] The *Black Book 2014*, a respected industry source, estimated that in 2014 Santander was the second highest cash sponsor of Ferrari. The total 2014 cash-related revenues of the Ferrari team in Formula 1 were estimated to total $314 million. The top three cash sponsors in 2014 were Philip Morris International (estimated at $100 million), Santander ($40 million), and Shell ($36 million).[23]

Segmentation is used to break down the fans of a sport property, or the market of an advertiser, into smaller distinct segments. These segments can be established based on an array of different criteria – such as gender, age, interests, personality, wealth, occupation, participation rates, smoker status, marital status, or family status. For example, in segmenting the market for potential ticket-buyers for an NCAA D1 football team, bases such as "alumni status," "proximity of residence to the stadium," and "household income" have each been used by colleges in promoting different packages. Exhibit 10.6 illustrates this approach.

Targeting decides which of the segments identified is the prime target for the marketing effort. Criteria used here include size, reach, profitability, and measurability:

- **Size** identifies the total number of potential individual targets.
- **Reach** is simply "are we, with existing or new marketing tactics, able to reach this segment with our messages?" If, for example, a sports club only has the emails of the season ticket holders, many of which have multiple tickets, it cannot do an email blast during a game offering special rewards to each attendee in the stadium.
- **Profitability** asks if it is possible to achieve profit from this market segment, based on its size, reach and cost estimates to put the strategy in place.
- **Measurability** considers if reliable estimates can be made of key inputs for the marketing decision.

Positioning includes decisions about how the message of the marketing effort will be structured in order to be as effective and efficient as possible for the specific target segments. Positioning answers the question of how the selected target(s) should perceive the message. Is it based on price, luxury, quality, brand, or a particular association? For example, Red Bull differentiates on premium, brand, and edge. Volvo has long differentiated on safety. Omega positions itself based on precision timing. If the relationship is a sponsorship or an endorsement deal, the positioning establishes whether values and messages implicit in the sports property are consistent with the values and messages that the marketing effort wants to communicate. Chapter 11 further explores sponsorship decisions and Chapter 12 endorsement decisions.

Base 1 (athletics)	Alumni (former athlete)			Alumni (non-athlete)		
Base 2 (years since graduation)	1 to 3	4 to 15	15 or more	1 to 3	4 to 15	15 or more
Who are they?	Career starting, single, or early relationship	Career focus, relationship, kids possible	Established in career, relationship, grown kids	Career starting, single, or early relationship	Career focus, relationship, kids possible	Established in career, relationship, grown kids
What do they want?	Link to former team, link to coach	Nostalgia	Nostalgia, interest in giving back	Social experience, school pride	Social experience, school pride	Growing nostalgia for university (not sport)
Where do they buy?	Online, at gate, phone	Online, at gate, phone	Online, at gate, phone	Online, at gate, phone	Online, at gate, phone	Online, at gate, phone
Why do they buy?	"Living the dream"	"Missing the past"	"Booster"	Social experience	Nostalgia	"Booster"
How do they buy?	Single game	Single, multi-game	Season ticket	Single game	Single, multi-game	Season ticket
When do they buy?	A few days pre-game	Week or more pre-game	Pre-season	A few days pre-game	Week or more pre-game	Pre-season

EXHIBIT 10.6 Sample Segmentation Chart – Ticket Buyers to NCAA D1 Football

Positioning typically is based on one or more *attributes*. The cost attribute speaks to the price–quality association. Other ways to position an offering include by use (e.g., tennis racket specific for a serve-and-volley-style player), by benefit (e.g., an energy recovery drink scientifically proven to be better in a certain situation), by association (e.g., since Roger Federer endorses this watch, I should wear it), by market gap (e.g., a line of new shoes specific to a new sport or discipline), by usage environment (e.g., a ball specifically designed for inline hockey in the streets), and by "product of choice" status (e.g., "Gatorade is for athletes").

10.4.3 The Four Ps of Marketing – Product, Pricing, Promotion, and Place

Product, pricing, promotion, and place (the four Ps) are key elements of a marketing strategy. They are built from the market research undertaken and the results of an STP analysis. Product, price, promotion, and place have reached the status of being widely recognized by the phrase "the four Ps of marketing."

Product

Product defines the offer to the consumer. In the case of marketing *of* sport (Panel A of Exhibit 10.2), the product is the sporting event itself and everything that the sports organization builds around it.

The product goes beyond the physical elements of the event to include intangibles such as fans' experience at the stadium and fans' perception of a broadcast. For marketing *through* sport (Panels B and C of Exhibit 10.2), the product is the overall package offered to the company that buys the relationship/ association with the sport property. For a shirt sponsorship deal, it can include not only the placement of the brand in a prominent position on the shirt, but also VIP boxes, tickets, or special events to reinforce the relationship between the sporting property and the commercial brand. The company that sponsors the sporting organization is focused on how fans will change their perception and their buying behavior and not just the placement on the uniform.

Price

Price is the amount charged for the product. Price and willingness to pay are two factors affecting the perceived value of a sports product. Willingness to pay can vary for different fans and at different purchase dates. Price is the actual amount of money that a fan or company pays for the product. The sport marketer typically seeks to set the price sufficiently close to the perceived value so that the derived revenue is close to the maximum possible. The better the segmentation and the more diverse the distribution channels, the easier it is to charge different prices – this is called "price discrimination." Price discrimination is often easier for companies marketing *through* sport, because each deal is different enough that "apples to apples" comparisons are less transparent and clear-cut. In contrast, charging different prices is more problematic for simpler products. As discussed in Chapter 13, the advent of active secondary markets in ticketing is highlighting how some prices set by clubs have historically been very low relative to the perceived value to the consumer.

Promotion

Promotion is the set of tools available to communicate and adapt the product to different segments. These tools are included in the *promotional mix*, which includes sponsorship, public relations, advertising, sales promotions, publicity, and direct selling. For example, the promotional mix of Coca-Cola's global marketing strategy might include sponsorship of the Olympic Games and FIFA, the hiring of an agency to increase its public relations, the purchase of advertising time on prime-time television, a social media campaign, a buy-one-get-one-free promotion around the Olympic Games sponsorship, activities in pursuit of press articles about Coca-Cola's corporate social responsibility initiatives, and Olympic and FIFA branded Coca-Cola cans. Not surprisingly, the total budget for such a broad-based marketing campaign can be in the hundreds of million dollars.

Place

Place is the location or how the product offering is provided. For some sporting events, place can be a major differentiator. For example, the Masters golf tournament is held each year at the Augusta National Golf Club. This elite event takes place in an ideal golf course setting that the property owner invests large amounts in maintaining at the very highest level. In contrast, some football and baseball games are played in stadiums that have become substandard as regards the fan experience. There are several forces that reinforce the negative aspect of "place" for these substandard stadiums. One force is the large number of state-of-the-art stadiums that other football and baseball clubs have built and showcased to many stakeholders in their leagues. A second force is the continued advances in the "at home viewing experience" that even the most up-to-date stadiums face competition from. Both forces increase the potential spectator believing that the fan experience at the aging stadium is substandard at best and, in some cases, very poor value even at relatively low ticket prices. The place strategy differs in the case of sport retail products such as tennis balls or sport drinks, where the strategy is about getting the product to the consumer via retailers, wholesalers, and other mechanisms known as a "supply chain." In the case of a sport drink, such as Gatorade or Powerade, the supply chain includes grocery stores, gyms, vending machines, events, music festivals, and corner stores.

10.5 SPORT PROPERTY BRANDING

A brand is a visible symbol that showcases how a "product" has "strong, favorable and distinctive associations that differentiate it from its competitors."[24] Exhibit 10.7 presents rankings by *Forbes* of the 40 top brands in sports in 2014. The top ten brands in each of four categories are listed by *Forbes*: clubs, events, businesses (including apparel companies, media companies, and leagues), and athletes. These rankings cover many of the key stakeholders outlined in Chapter 2.

10.5.1 Branding Points of Competitive Advantage, Parity, and Disadvantage

Each attribute of a brand can be classified into one of three categories:[25]

■ **Points of competitive advantage** – these attributes are desirable, deliverable, and differentiating. "The points of difference often come into play in a brand's mantra. A brand mantra captures the essence of a brand in three to five words. It often helps to understand where the brand can and cannot go."
■ **Points of competitive parity** – these attributes are "where a brand breaks even with the competition and becomes close enough with competitors in the eyes of the consumer."
■ **Points of competitive disadvantage** – these attributes are where the attribute of a competitor's offering is better in the eyes of the consumer.

Branding strategy requires seeking to have as many points of competitive advantage that are important to the consumer, and as few as possible points of competitive disadvantage.

Consider the context of club marketing where there are multiple clubs from the same league available for a fan to support in the same market. For example, in the New York/New Jersey region there are two baseball clubs, two football clubs, two basketball clubs, three hockey clubs, and two MLS clubs to support. For this fan considering which club(s) to support, the league and the sport are points of competitive parity. However, from this same fan there could be multiple points of competitive advantage – such as the winning tradition of a club, the personas of its players, the technology capabilities of its stadium, and the past and current tradition of family members being loyal supporters of a particular club. In contrast, a point of competitive disadvantage could be the difficulty of public transportation to and from the venue, and safety concerns associated with areas surrounding the venue or the unruliness of the attendees at games.

2014 FORBES FAB 40

TOP TEAMS	2014 BRAND VALUE($M)	TOP EVENTS	2014 BRAND VALUE($M)
New York Yankees	521	Super Bowl	500
Real Madrid	484	Summer Olympics	348
Barcelona	438	Winter Olympics	285
Dallas Cowboys	404	FIFA World Cup	170
Manchester United	399	NCAA Men's Final Four	143
New England Patriots	351	UEFA Champions League	139
Bayern Munich	287	MLB World Series	113
Los Angeles Dodgers	279	WrestleMania	105
Boston Red Sox	260	Daytona 500	100
Los Angeles Lakers	254	Kentucky Derby	99
TOP BUSINESSES	**2014 BRAND VALUE**	**TOP ATHLETES**	**2014 BRAND VALUE**
Nike	19,000	LeBron James	37
ESPN	16,500	Tiger Woods	36
Adidas	5,800	Roger Federer	32
Sky Sports	4,500	Phil Mickelson	29
Under Armour	4,100	Mahendra Singh Dhoni	20
Reebok	880	Usain Bolt	19
YES Network	680	Cristiano Ronaldo	17
NESN	525	Kobe Bryant	15
MLBAM	520	Lionel Messi	12
UFC	440	Rafael Nadal	10

EXHIBIT 10.7 *Forbes* Fab 40 for Sports Brands – 2014
*Source: Forbes Publications

Part of club marketing in this context is to strengthen any important points of competitive advantage (such as having players use social media to further enhance the brand attractiveness of the club) and to diminish and ideally eliminate any points of competitive disadvantage (such as having very effective monitoring of potential fan misbehavior so that the venue is both family friendly and safe).

Fans often think about a brand as a name or a logo – Bayern Munich or Nike. However, the most important part of a brand is the intangible ideas and values that fans associate with it. The Dakar Rally is not about its logo but about the ideas of adventure, risk, toughness, and wilderness that the brand evokes on its fans. The All Blacks New Zealand rugby brand is not only about their logo but all the values that fans associate with their almost mystical tradition.

10.5.2 Multi-Brand Settings as the Norm in Sport Marketing

One essential characteristic of most sport marketing contexts is that marketing is done within a network of brands. For example, the Montreal Canadians brand is inherently linked to the brand of the National Hockey League as well as to past and current star players for that club. As a second example, the branding of European basketball depends on its federation (FIBA Europe), the separate European league (Euroleague), the individual clubs and their players, as well as the NBA brand that markets and plays some games on that continent, and it needs to carefully consider the work of the NBA in the continent. Important brand levels for team-based sports are often the league/federation brand, the club/team brand, and the player/athlete brand.

Leagues include such well-established brands as NBA, Formula 1, EPL, IPL, and NHL. Federation brands such as FIFA, FINA, and the USOC are equally well known. Each federation or league aims to build its own brand and create value for its partners, sponsors, events, and members. The larger revenue opportunities for leagues typically include television/media rights, league sponsors, and naming rights for a series. The stronger the league brand, the higher these rights are worth to fans and companies who want to undertake marketing *through* sport. For example, the NASCAR/Sprint title sponsorship that started in 2004 was reported to be a $70 million a year for ten-year deal.

Sport marketing decisions happen at multiple levels, with decisions taken at a higher level shaping the options available at lower levels. Also certain decisions influence each other but they are taken by organizations that are not necessarily "nested." For instance, an interesting split of decision rights happens in soccer. The choice of the apparel sponsor/supplier is a club decision while the shoe/boots choice is made by the individual player. Not surprisingly, conflicts can occur here when the companies sponsoring the apparel and the boots are different. Nike sponsors FC Barcelona, but Messi wears Adidas boots. Thus Messi can be in a commercial supporting Nike as player of the team, and then later be seen endorsing Adidas.

Motor sports have much complexity in branding due to their many levels:

■ League level – for example, Formula 1, NASCAR, IndyCar, NHRA.
■ Racing team level – for example, Ferrari team in Formula 1, Penske Team in NASCAR.
■ Driver level – for example, Lewis Hamilton, Dale Earnhardt Jr., Danica Patrick.
■ Track level – for example, Yas Marina Circuit in Abu Dhabi, Daytona Motor Speedway, Indianapolis Motor Speedway.
■ Event level – for example, Monaco Grand Prix, Daytona 500.

These multiple levels of marketing in motor sport have many sponsorship and activation opportunities for the various stakeholders involved but can create sponsor conflicts, ambush marketing issues, and potentially brand-clutter at individual events and in the broadcasts of those events. Chapter 3 further discussed important decisions as regards to league-related marketing.

10.5.3 Club/Team Brand

Clubs (e.g., Manchester United, Detroit Red Wings) and teams (Ferrari race team, Canadian national ice hockey team) also aim at enhancing the value of their brand. Major club and team names are global brands recognized across the world. Manchester United claims to have more fans that the entire population of the UK. Barcelona, Real Madrid, and Bayern Munich have similar global status as brands. Sporting clubs that have people across the world with an emotional connection to them are scarce and valuable to marketers. They can provide a platform for companies to communicate across geographies from North America to Asia, from Europe to Africa and Latin America. The elite clubs can afford to attract the top stars with high salaries, which increases their capacity to build high levels of engagement outside their domestic league base. In contrast, most sporting clubs have minimal national reach, which reduces their alternatives to build strong brands and afford top-quality players. While many clubs would like to build strong global and national brands, it takes a lot of investment, time, and most likely a period of sustained success.

Club- and team-level branding must be done within the framework of a league or federation. Coordinating these two levels can be challenging because they can differ in their objectives, resources, and marketing guidelines. They also differ greatly in terms of the aggressiveness and ability to leverage new platforms. For example, the NBA has embraced social media very aggressively. Having few players on the court, having players that are visible as opposed to wearing helmets/face gear, and having a strong celebrity aspect have all helped this effort. The NBA has built its own internal marketing arm (TMBO) into a highly respected marketing group whose role is to both build the brands and marketing strength of the individual NBA clubs as well as the brand of the NBA. At times, TMBO has also operated marketing operations for several clubs – such as with the New Orleans Hornets after Hurricane Katrina in its temporary move to Oklahoma (2005/7), and with the New Orleans team in 2010 when the NBA purchased the club from the then owners (George Shinn and Gary Chouest) due to their financial difficulties.

Chapter 4 also discussed important decisions related to club marketing.

10.5.4 Player/Athlete Brand

Most players in high profile sports have a "brand" but only the brand of top players has significant value beyond their on-field ability and their contributions to winning games. Locally, some players have brands with hometown followings. Minor League Baseball clubs highlight players who started/played for their club in their early years and then went on to play in MLB.

Players with valuable brands can create dilemmas for clubs when their on-the-field contributions are in decline while there brand strength remains strong or may even be increasing. From a sporting perspective, they should move to a lower tier team; however, their marketing value brings significant revenues to the team. Soccer leagues in the US have at times attracted major global soccer stars at the back end of their playing careers and have paid salaries at levels above what they would be paid had they stayed with clubs in the most elite leagues.

Chapter 12 discusses multiple issues regarding player branding and player decision making.

10.6 SPORT MARKETING DECISION MAKING

Key marketing decisions that sports investors and sports property owners face on an ongoing basis are highlighted in this section.

10.6.1 Sports Investor Decisions

How much to spend on marketing?

Marketing spending is a decision that is usually taken during the budgeting cycle. The decision depends on the expected return on marketing investments and on the amount of resources available at the company. These criteria depend on having a good understanding of the investment–return relationship for marketing. As part of this decision, results from previous years will be assessed and the input of the marketing director will be considered. In some cases, a company may decide to cut back its investments in sports marketing because new opportunities in other parts of its business increase in attractiveness.

What should the marketing mix be?

The decision on how much to spend on marketing is closely related to the decision about the marketing mix. This is how the company is planning to combine the various elements of marketing: advertising, promotion, channel management, etc. Sport marketing is one of the components of this mix and itself depends on its own mix including: sponsorship, sales promotions, hospitality, celebrity endorsement, experiential, owned event, advertising, public relations, etc. The marketing mix decision depends on the expected return on investment of each individual marketing effort but also on the combined effect of each individual effort; there are synergies across marketing initiatives – the value of an individual initiative depends on whether another initiative is also taken. Research and evaluation are vital to guide this decision and inform the decision makers. In the case of sponsorship, much has been made about (a) its rapid rise in spending over the past 20 years, up to around 20–5 percent of marketing communications budgets in North America, (b) poor evaluations (and often lack of evaluation) of its effectiveness, and (c) the rise of alternative property areas (e.g., festivals, events, arts) attracting marketing budgets.

What are the target market(s)?

Decisions on the mix and the marketing budget depends on the target market and how the company plans to address it. A large part of this decision is eliminating segments that will then not be pursued. This decision typifies the 80/20 rule (that 80 percent of your business typically comes from 20 percent of your customers), where the company needs to identify and target high-return segments and not try to reach too many segments and dilute the effort and the potential return. Box 10.5 discusses the challenge of marketing to millennials in the context of snow sports.

BOX 10.5 MARKETING TO MILLENNIALS: THE US SNOW SPORTS MARKET

A key element of market research for any sport or market is to determine the nature and characteristics of that market. A deep understanding of these facts can help in tailoring beneficial marketing programs leading to sales. The snow sports market, which includes snowboarding, alpine skiing, cross country skiing, and free-ski, is a growing market due to a number of factors such as the exposure from events such as the X Games and Winter Olympic Games, which has led to the creation of stars (e.g., Shaun White, Lindsey Vonn), increased participation, and a growth of new/cool events and disciplines on the programs of the Olympic Games and X Games.

Generation Y (15 to 30 years old as of 2015) are the main target of the snow sports growth. What characteristics does this segment have? Generation Y is also known as the millennial generation. In the United States, they number more than 70 million people in the United States born between 1985 and 2000. The majority (72 percent) of them own a smartphone, and 41 percent of those have made a purchase on their smartphone, yet they are the generation that is most resistant to marketers and require personalized, engaging content to get their attention. While snow sports may appeal to many within this demographic, geography, weather, and other factors make the availability of snow sports locally non-existent to many. Thus, only about eight million people, or 11 percent within this generation are snow-sport participants.

The top participation snow sports throughout this generation in order are alpine skiing, snowboarding, cross-country skiing, and freestyle skiing, with participation levels slightly skewed to male as opposed to females. The snow-sport market has a high correlation in ethnicity as well, where 61 percent of all Generation Y participants in snow sports are Caucasian (for comparison 62 percent of Generation X and 73 percent of Baby Boomers in the snow sports market are Caucasian). These facts note the challenges for snow-sport marketers attempting to reach this demographic.[26]

What are the values that the company wants its brand to have?

A brand encapsulates the meaning of the sport product (property) and drives its image in the marketplace. Thus, an investor must be careful and informed when they decide what sport or sport property to invest in. The sport property needs to be aligned with the brand and where it wants to go. A poor choice (such as endorsing an athlete who then behaves badly) can have major negative consequences for the brand.

10.6.2 Sport Property Decisions

Sport properties also face important decisions on the marketing front based on the concepts developed in this chapter.

How much is the sports property worth?

The sport property is typically seeking cash or contra products/services in return for the marketing value it possesses for an investor. Before going to market to seek these resources, the property needs to know its value to potential buyers. This process is known as "valuation."

What assets does the sports property have?

The next decision is how to support an investor to reach potential buyers. It involves choosing marketing tools, sales approaches, and distribution channels. Ideally, the efforts devoted to marketing and distributing the products of a sports property should be such that they maximize the revenues minus the incremental costs. Managers often rely on business plans and revenue-generation plans to decide how to go about this effort. This is often called a "revenue framework" and includes a range of products from ticket sales to media rights to sponsorship to public–private partnerships to fundraising to grants (government/federation) to sales of advertising to event hosting and more. For each product, managers assess what is possible (based on previous year's data and forecasted future potential) and a plan is developed.

How to structure the sport properties to maximize marketing value?

Many sport properties have multiple assets and limited resources. Consider a federation with multiple events, titles to sanction, and athletes to market. For these properties, an important decision is to determine how to structure these offerings. For example, the property holds the sanction rights to world championships, a national championships, or an Olympic qualifier. A key decision for the sports property is whether to commercialize these products directly or auction the rights for other organizations and intermediaries to exploit (as the FIA has done with Formula 1 or the World Rally Championship, or the FIM has done with MotoGP). Section 10.3 of this chapter discussed decisions in this area.

10.7 INDUSTRY EXAMPLE: ARIAT

Ariat has its genesis in the early 1990s in the manufacturing and marketing of high-performance riding boots for equestrians.[27] Through a very focused strategy of building a brand that emphasizes superior performance, fit, style, and an authentic equestrian heritage, it has grown to be the global leader in Western and English footwear for riders. In the early 2000s, it broadened its product line to include Western and English apparel.

Exhibit 10.8 presents the key marketing categories of Ariat and the types of marketing investments in each. Performance marketing targets consumers who are active with equestrian activities. It would classify as marketing *of* sport in the language of Exhibit 10.2. Investments here cover equestrian sports-related sponsorships as well as traditional advertising and digital and print communications. Equestrian sports-related investments include:

- **Sponsorship of equestrian federations.** It is the official supplier of apparel and footwear of the Fédération Equestre Internationale (FEI) and the official supplier of footwear for the US Equestrian Federation (USEF). US riders compete in many international events, including the Summer Olympics.
- **Sponsorship of events.** These include the Pro Bull Riding (PBR) tour as well as other rodeos and English horse shows. PBR events take place in metro areas around the country, and are the televised in the US. The PBR is owned by William Morris/IMG, the largest sports management firm in the world. Ariat also develops PBR promotions that drive PBR fans to locate Ariat retailers.
- **Athlete endorsements**. Ariat sponsors more than 50 athletes, many of whom compete globally. For example, it sponsors Beezie Madden in show jumping, who won the 2013 World Cup of Show

Jumping and won gold medals in both the 2004 Athens and 2008 Beijing Summer Olympics. Madden is a four-time USEF Equestrian of the Year winner. Ariat-sponsored riders compete in Ariat-branded coats in equestrian events. Ariat seeks to identify riders at an early stage of their career and builds strong brand relationships over time to maximize sponsorship value and credibility.

Exhibit 10.8 also highlights Ariat's lifestyle marketing. This is an example of marketing *through* sport, where Ariat markets to a broader consumer base by promoting the association of its products and its heritage with the authentic aspirational Western lifestyle showcased in equestrian activities. One example is product placement in movies. For example, the lead actor in *The Longest Ride* (2015) portrayed a bull rider who wore branded Ariat apparel. Ariat was a sponsor of the Hollywood premiere of the movie and was integrated into its promotional material. Ariat also sponsors country music singers and programs as part of its investments to both deepen its relationship with its existing customers as well as build engagement with the larger number of people who "live their lives in boots and jeans."

Marketing category	Marketing type	Ariat consumer segments	Description
Performance marketing	Associations Sponsorhips	English and Western	US Equestrian Federation (USEF), Fédération Equestre Internationale (FEI)
	Event Sponsorships	English and Western	Professional Bull Riding (PBR), Winter Equestrian Festival (WEF), Central Park Horse Show, Washington National Horse Show,
	Athlete Endorsements	English and Western	>50 global athletes, all disciplines
	Traditional advertising	English, Western, and Work	Print, billboard, co-op television (with retailers)
	Digital and print communications	All categories	Product technology communication, photography, website/digital communications
Lifestyle marketing	Digital marketing	All categories	Website, PPC, SEO, re-targeting, display advertising
	Social media	English and Western predominately	Facebook (600,000 fans), Instagram (50,000), bloggers
	Partnerships	Western predominately	Country music festivals and singers, film partnerships, etc.
	Public relations	English and Western-inspired fashion	Digital media, bloggers, print publications, broadcast
Retail marketing	Retailer shop-in-shops and event retail	English, Western, Farm, Lifestyle	Denim and apparel fixtures as well as branded footwear walls, table-top displays

EXHIBIT 10.8 Marketing Categories of Ariat

10.8 SUMMARY

Sport marketing is the application of marketing to the sporting context. It frequently involves inter-action between marketing investors, sports properties, intermediaries, and the marketing target. It is important to view sport marketing as an integral part of sports management and to continually build on marketing advances in many contexts from many industries.

NOTES

1 PWC, "Outlook for the sports market in North America through 2018," www.pwc.com/us/en/industry/entertainment-media/publications/sports-outlook-north-america.jhtml, November 2014.

2 www.ama.org.

3 M. Shank, *Sports Marketing: A Strategic Perspective*, 3rd edn (Pearson-Prentice-Hall, 2005).

4 www.realclearsports.com/lists/top_10_minor_league_promotions/intro.html.

5 "Bayern Munich extends sponsorship deal with Deutsche Telekom through '17," *Sports Business Daily*, August 23, 2012.

6 www.lagalaxy.com/news/2012/03/la-galaxy-and-herbalife-announce-record-10-year-extension.

7 B. James, "Danica Patrick's inner circle small, efficient," ESPN, July 13, 2012.

8 S. Elliott, "A 'grown up' GoDaddy hires an ad agency," Media Decoder, *The New York Times*, June 12, 2012.

9 www.wisgolfer.com/Blogs/Guest-Blogger/January-December-2014/Golf-advertisers-follow-the-money-and-the-demographics.

10 Associated Press, "National Guard wants to end Earnhardt sponsorship; Hendrick cries foul," Fox Sports, August 7, 2014.

11 C. Smith, "The biggest sponsors of Brazil's 2014 World Cup spend big to engage with fans," Forbes, June 12, 2014.

12 I. Boudway, "Does a $5 footlong make you think of the Olympics?" Bloomberg, February 3, 2014.

13 www.languagemonitor.com/olympics/sochi-ambush-marketing-race-is-in-the-books.

14 M. Ogden, "Manchester United's £53m shirt deal with Chevrolet unaffected despite likely absence of Champions League," *The Telegraph*, February 12, 2014.

15 "Manchester United agree new £750 million sponsorship deal with Adidas," *The Telegraph*, July 14, 2014.

16 "Nike ends Manchester United kit deal after 13 years," BBC, July 8, 2014.

17 A. Miller, "Beckham's shirt and boot sales stand at a staggering £1 billion... and PSG expect to bank £15m," *Daily Mail*, February 9, 2013.

18 A. Poggi, "Beckham shirt sales rival ex-World Player of Year, Ronaldinho," Bloomberg, February 5, 2009.

19 Miller, "Beckham's shirt and boot sales."

20 Associated Press, "David Beckham: he came, he sold, he conquered the USA," *USA Today*, December 2, 2012.

21 See Norm O'Reilly and Benoit Séguin, *Sport Marketing: A Canadian Perspective*, 2nd edn (Nelson Education, 2014).

22 "Inside Banco Santander's global sponsorship strategy," *IEGSR*, September 16, 2013; "Ferrari, Santander extend sponsorship deal," Crash.net, September 10, 2012.

23 D. Cushnan and E. Connally (eds.), *Black Book 2014: Formula One Racing: The Independent Business Companion to the Formula One Industry* (Sports Pro Media, 2014), p. 33.

24 There are many definitions of a brand. The definition presented in this chapter, is taken from Kevin Keller, one of the leading brand-thinkers –www.trendhunter.com/keynote/brand-planning-keynote.

25 www.trendhunter.com/keynote/brand-planning-keynote.

26 www.snowsports.org/gatekeeper/files/SIA_Engaging_GEN-Y_in_Snow_Sports.pdf.

27 The Ariat name comes from the last five letters of Secretariat, the 1973 Triple Crown winner in thoroughbred horse racing.

11 SPORT SPONSORSHIP

C hapter 10 distinguished marketing *through* sport from marketing *of* sport. In marketing *of* sport, it is the sporting property (such as a league, a club, or an event) that makes the market- ing investment. In marketing *through* sport, it is a third party – typically a corporation – that makes the marketing investment. Sport sponsorship is a major area of marketing *through* sport. Sport sponsorship involves a third party (called the sponsor) investing in activities that promote its brand or stature (financial or otherwise), through associating with a sports property (called the sponsee), and using that association to access, ideally in a compelling way, stakeholders of the sports property.

Examples of the stakeholders sought by sponsorship include the fans of a league or sporting club, participants in an event, or viewers of a digital sports media platform. Effective sponsorship occurs when this association with the stakeholders of a sporting property enhances the finances, brand, or stature of the sponsor in a cost-effective way. This chapter focuses on sport sponsorship activities as a general topic. Chapter 12 examines the related high-profile area of athlete branding and endorsements, which is the specific case of the sponsorship of an athlete.

Exhibit 11.1 provides an overview of the two key areas where the sponsor makes investments:

1 **Direct investment** – financial payments or provision of resources to the sponsee. Typically there will be a formal sponsorship agreement. These agreements vary in detail and complexity, often depending on the sophistication of the negotiating parties and the size of the investment.
2 **Indirect investments** (also called activation investments) – payments or provision of resources to agencies, companies, individuals, media companies, etc. with the purpose to deepen the impact of the sponsorship with the sponsorship target. The ratio of activation investments to the direct investment is often called the activation ratio.

For example, consider the sponsorship agreement between Nike and the Chinese Football Association (FA). Starting in 2015, this 11-year agreement averages an annual $16 million payment by Nike to the Chinese FA. Nike will also provide in-kind items such as equipment to multiple levels of Chinese soc- cer, including the Chinese national team, the Chinese Super League, and the Super Cup competition. Activation payments would include many activities that Nike would undertake to exploit its associ- ation with the Chinese FA. Examples of activation could include Nike entertaining major retailers and competition-winners at games played by the Chinese national soccer team, Nike promotional material at retail stores where Chinese soccer apparel is sold, and advertising on media outlets highlighting the association between Nike and Chinese youths playing soccer.

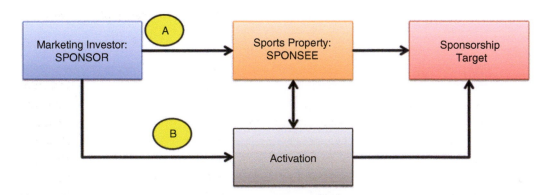

EXHIBIT 11.1 Direct and Indirect (Activation) Investments in Sport Sponsorship
A: Direct sponsorship investment
B: Indirect (activation) sponsorship investment

11.1 MAGNITUDE OF TOTAL SPONSORSHIP INDUSTRY

Sponsorship is a major source of revenue for sport properties and a powerful marketing tool for corporations. The world sponsorship market is estimated at $55 billion (2014) for sponsorship rights and another $85 billion spent on activating these sponsorship deals.[1] The North American sport market is estimated at nearly $65 million in size with approximately 25 percent coming from sponsorship.[2] The sponsorship market is not only sizeable but growing. In Canada, sponsorship spending (rights fees plus activation) hit CDN$2.85 billion in 2013, up nearly 40 percent from 2006.[3]

11.1.1 Major Sports Sponsor Industries and Companies

Exhibit 11.2 depicts information about major sports sponsor industries and companies for 2013 in the United States. This data is from the IEG Sponsorship Report, published by IEG, a leading advisory and commercial company with a long record of tracking sponsorship trends. IEG has much experience and expertise in collating company and industry information in a context where individual companies do not consistently report breakdowns of the direct investments in sponsorship. The information presented in Exhibit 11.2 covers only direct investments in sports sponsorship. Information about associated activation investments is much less available on a consistent and broad basis across many sponsors.

Panel A: "The big four" industries in sports sponsorship in the United States

Industry	2013 amount spent ($M)	2012 amount spent ($M)	Trend
Beverage	1,135	1,065	Increasing
Automotive	575	550	Increasing
Telecommunications	415	385	Increasing
Banking	395	355	Increasing

Panel B: Top 25 companies in sponsorship spending in the United States

2013 rank	Company	Industry	2013 amount spent ($M)	Trend
1	Pepsi	Beverage	355	Neutral
2	Coca-Cola	Beverage	295	Neutral
3	Nike	Apparel	265	Increasing
4	Anheuser-Busch	Beverage	260	Decreasing
5	AT&T	Telecommunications	180	Neutral
6	General Motors	Automotive	180	Neutral
7	Toyota	Automotive	160	Neutral
8	Ford	Automotive	150	Neutral
9	Adidas	Apparel	125	Increasing

EXHIBIT 11.2 (*cont.*)

2013 rank	Company	Industry	2013 amount spent ($M)	Trend
10	MillerCoors	Beverage	120	Decreasing
11	Verizon	Telecommunications	115	Neutral
12	FedEx	Courier	95	Neutral
13	Procter & Gamble	Consumer Goods	90	Neutral
14	Bank of America	Banking	80	Increasing
15	Sprint	Telecommunications	80	Decreasing
16	Berkshire Hathaway	Conglomerate	75	Neutral
17	Microsoft	Computer	75	Increasing
18	UPS	Courier	70	Decreasing
19	Citigroup	Banking	65	Decreasing
20	J.P. Morgan Chase	Banking	65	Neutral
21	State Farm	Insurance	65	Neutral
22	Target	Retail	60	Decreasing
23	Lowe's	Retail	55	Neutral
24	Visa	Financial Services	55	Neutral
25	Mercedes Benz	Automotive	55	Decreasing

EXHIBIT 11.2 IEG Estimates of the Top Industries and Companies for Sport Sponsorship Spending in the US
Source: IEG Sponsorship Report, May 27, 2014

Panel A of Exhibit 11.2 shows that beverage, automotive, telecommunications, and banking are the four largest categories of sponsors by investment levels. Panel B outlines the top 25 individual companies who invest in sponsorship and their industry. Sponsees differ sizably in how many categories of "official sponsors" they recognize. For example, the beverage category in Panel A includes several subcategories that some sponsees carve out as separate "official sponsor" groups, such as hard liquor, beer, carbonated non-alcoholic, energy drinks, fruit juices, and water. The companies in Panel B include those with large global footprints of customers (such as Coca-Cola, Nike, Microsoft, and Visa). By contrast, they also include companies with a predominant North American or even US customer base (such as AT&T, MillerCoors, and State Farm).

11.1.2 Major Sponsees Receiving Sponsorship Investments

Major sport properties are the beneficiaries and partners of sponsorship investors such as those in Exhibit 11.2.

■ The Olympic Games, and its well-established sponsorship program – known as "TOP Sponsorship" – is reported to have generated more than $950 million for the 2009/12 quadrennial from its 11 sponsors. Section 11.8 of this chapter describes the many companies that have been part of this program.[4] Each Olympic Games also has its own set of national-level sponsors. For example, the 2012 Summer Olympic Games in London raised $1.15 billion from its domestic sponsorship program and the 2014 Winter Olympic Games in Sochi, Russia raised an additional $1.3 billion through its domestic sponsorship program.[5]

- The NFL's sponsorship revenues (i.e., the league plus its 32 clubs) were reported to be $1.15 billion for the 2014 season, a 7.8 percent growth over 2013 and an increase of about $250 million since 2010. The league added several new sponsors in 2014, including Dannon, TD Ameritrade, and Nationwide Insurance. Gatorade sponsors 100 percent of the league and all the NFL clubs, while Anheuser-Busch sits at 91 percent of NFL properties (league plus clubs).[6]

- In its 2013/14 season, total sponsorship revenues for the NHL were reported to be more than $400 million for the NHL and its 30 clubs, nearly a 5 percent growth from 2012/13 and up more than $80 million since 2009/10.[7] The two key drivers of much of this growth were (a) the league's new assets, such as its outdoor stadium series, and (b) new blue-chip league sponsors, including Advil, L'Oréal, and Crown Royal. Some sponsors are highly vested in the NHL, such as Reebok who sponsors the NHL and 100 percent of its clubs.

- Major European soccer leagues have sponsorship and other commercial revenues as the second (or equal second on average) league revenue source. For example, *Deloitte* reported the following percentages and total amounts for 2013:

League	Media	Game Day	Sponsorship and Other Commercial	Total Revenue (€M)
England – EPL	47 %	23 %	30 %	2,946
Germany – Bundesliga	31 %	23 %	46 %	2,018
Spain – La Liga	48 %	22 %	30 %	1,859
Italy – Series A	59 %	11 %	30 %	1,682
France – Ligue 1	49 %	11 %	40 %	1,297

Chapter 15 discusses broadcast revenues. Chapter 13 examines ticketing revenues.

11.1.3 Differences Across Sponsorship Revenues Within the Same League

In many chapters of this book, differences across clubs along multiple dimensions have been documented and discussed. Club sponsorship is yet another area of difference. Most clubs do not report financial information about their individual revenue categories such as sponsorship. Some insight comes from estimates made by Bloomberg of revenues for multiple individual categories of the 30 MLB clubs for 2013.[8] In the Bloomberg work, four clubs were estimated to have sponsorship revenues greater than $30 million – New York Yankees ($84 million – 14.7 percent of estimated revenues), New York Mets ($55 million – 20.1 percent), Boston Red Sox ($40 million – 9.9 percent), and Los Angeles Dodgers ($39 million – 12 percent). The average sponsorship revenue per club was $25 million. With the median sponsorship revenues being $20 million per club (#15 ranked club is $20 million and #16 is $20 million), 14 of the 30 clubs were estimated to have sponsorship revenues less than $20 million. Across the 30 clubs, the average percentage of estimated sponsorship revenues to total estimated revenues was 11 percent. Not surprisingly, many of the clubs with the largest estimated revenues came from those located in larger cities.

11.2 DIVERSITY OF INDIVIDUAL SPORT SPONSORSHIP DEALS

Companies differ greatly in the details they provide on their sport sponsorship deals. *Sports Pro*, a leading monthly sports business magazine with broad-based coverage of many sports, regularly provides information on a diverse set of recently announced sponsorship agreements. Where possible, *Sports Pro* uses information from public releases by the sponsor or the sponsee. In other cases, it relies on its own internal research and reputable sources, including those quoted in the media. Appendix 11A provides summary information on the direct investments of 42 sponsorship deals drawn from a larger number described by *Sports Pro* in its April 2014 to April 2015 issues. The sponsorships are ranked from the highest to the lowest in terms of average annual sponsor investment. The 42 examples shown in Appendix 11A are drawn from all continents, showcasing that sponsorship is a part of the sports business world in many parts of the globe and providing an extensive sample of what sponsorship deals can look like. The vast diversity in the sponsorships summarized in Appendix 11A is found in multiple areas, described here:

- **Geographic location of "events."** Some sponsorships relate to leagues with globally dispersed events (such as Formula 1 and cycling), while others have a very regional event location (such as a title sponsor for a single PGA golf event). Note here that there can be extensive global media coverage even for a single regionally located event.
- **Type.** These examples include: (a) naming rights to leagues, clubs, stadiums, arenas, and motor racing series; (b) official category sponsors (such as the banking, beverage, and betting partners); and (c) technology providers.
- **Financial magnitude.** The largest sponsor deal in Appendix 11A is $128 million for each year of the ten-year apparel deal between Adidas and Manchester United. The smallest is $100,000 for Hyundai Construction to sponsor a NASCAR Camping World Truck Series event at Atlanta Motor Speedway.
- **Time length.** The length of the contracts range from 11 years (the Nike–Chinese FA deal) down to a one-year contract for a single weekend event (such as KFC's one year sponsorship of David Ragan in the Daytona 500 NASCAR race).
- **Industry of sponsors**. Banking, beverage, apparel, airlines, car, tire, and telecommunication industries all have more than two industry representatives in Appendix 11A.
- **Global versus national versus regional footprint of sponsor.** Companies such as Emirates, Nike, Adidas, and Fujitsu, with their global footprint of customers, see much benefit from their images being showcased on globally broadcast games and events. Other sponsors have a much narrower footprint of customers. An example is M&T Bank, the naming rights sponsor of the Baltimore Ravens stadium. M&T Bank is a US northeast-based regional commercial bank.

This diversity highlights that sponsorship agreements and their activation are likely to differ on a case-by-case basis. The following discussion is focused on a more general decision making approach to sponsorship agreements, their activation, and their evaluation.

11.3 SPONSORSHIP AS PART OF AN INTEGRATED MARKETING STRATEGY

Exhibit 11.3 shows the marketing path to a desired decision/outcome by the target from Exhibit 10.1 (Chapter 10) adapted to sponsorship.

The challenge of marketing is to achieve the desired decision and outcome by the target in a cost-effective way. There are multiple possible marketing approaches only one of which is marketing *through* sport, and then as a sub-part of that, sport sponsorship. The decision whether it is desirable or cost-effective to market *through* sport is an important first consideration for a marketing investor. For some target markets, sport in general or some specific sports may not have the ability to build engagement and mindshare in the target decision maker. For example, the marketing of highly engineered aerospace parts is effectively a technical person-to-technical person decision context. Here, there is a premium for safety reasons on choosing the very best technical choice. Marketing *through* sport likely would not be part of the marketing options chosen.

Assume the decision is made that an association with, say, soccer is a potentially effective way for a beverage company to market a new drink to a predominantly Hispanic community. The alternatives in such a situation would include:

- Sponsorship of a soccer club.
- Sponsorship of a soccer stadium.
- Sponsorship of one or more players that analysis suggests create strong positive reactions by members of the target community.
- Social media campaigns that highlight to target markets the benefits of the new product.
- Paid tweets by sporting and media personalities.
- Advertising when soccer games are being played.
- Digital marketing using online soccer websites.
- Imbedded advertising in electronic soccer games.
- Product placements in reality television shows.

Increasingly, decisions made by marketers relate to which combination of two or more of the above and others is the preferred mix of marketing tools to use. There is a premium on choosing individual marketing tools as part of a broader integrated marketing package rather than considering each one as an isolated decision.

The following discussion assumes that the decision maker has chosen to incorporate sponsorship into their marketing mix. Key areas that we now examine are:

1   Structuring the sports sponsorship decision, including the deliverables and the financial and other commitments (Section 11.4).
2   The activation plan and execution associated with the chosen package (Section 11.5).
3   The measurement and evaluation approaches that will be used to assess the effectiveness of the sponsorship and related marketing tools (Section 11.6).

EXHIBIT 11.3 Sponsorship and Steps to Desired Outcome

11.4 STRUCTURING THE SPORT SPONSORSHIP DECISION

11.4.1 Sponsorship Objectives

Having clear objectives early in the sponsorship process is helpful in designing all three aspects of the sponsorship arena – the upfront decision analysis, its activation, and the measurement and evaluation of its effectiveness. Examples of objectives drawn from the analysis of different sponsorships include (see next page):

EXHIBIT 11.4 MasterCard Sports Sponsorship Objectives and Platforms
Panel A: Sponsorship objective of MasterCard
Panel B: Segmentation of marketing platform

- **Build brand image:** Increase brand recognition in the mind of the consumer, potential consumer, or other marketing target(s).
- **Increase brand loyalty:** Promote the product by associating it with certain activities, sports, leagues, events, players, clubs, etc.
- **Stimulate sales:** Increase sales from existing consumers or attract new ones.
- **Gain access to a community of potential consumers:** Gain access to a new segment of the consumer base.
- **Create exclusivity:** Block competitors from positioning themselves in the same space in the mind of the consumer.
- **Motivate employees:** Promote loyalty and effort among employees.
- **Support the community:** Position the company as being involved in the community through the support of events and clubs that most members of the community are emotionally attached to.
- **Showcase a country** or as part of country brand-building, the benefits of which can include increased business investment and increased tourism.

MasterCard, a major global investor in sponsorship, has multiple objectives for its investments in sports and entertainment such as football, music, golf, rugby, baseball, tennis, hockey, and the NFL. Exhibit 11.4 outlines seven objectives of its extensive sponsorship properties.

Three main questions are examined by MasterCard in its property selection:

1 Who do I reach?
2 How can/can't I use assets?
3 What impact will it have?[9]

As a related illustration, Box 11.1 illustrates how Emirates Airlines, the government-owned airline of Dubai, UAE, has built a global portfolio of sporting sponsorships, as part of a global branding strategy for Dubai.

BOX 11.1 DUBAI USES SPORT SPONSORSHIP BY EMIRATES AIRLINES AS PART OF A GLOBAL BRANDING STRATEGY

Dubai is ideally placed on global airline routes to be a bridge between Europe and Asia as well as a hub with the Middle East and the surrounding countries. However, unlike several other Middle Eastern countries or Emirates, Dubai has minimal oil reserves. Its impressive growth has been built on its investing in becoming a major economic hub of the globe. Emirates Airlines, Dubai's national carrier, has been an important part of building its economic presence on the global stage. Dubai started Emirates Airlines in 1985. It has grown to be a leading airline internationally, with flights to more than 70 countries in six continents. It is a frequent winner or top-tier placer in numerous awards ranking global carriers on many areas.

Sports sponsorship has been an important pillar of Emirates' branding strategy. Global sports are especially attractive for its global branding strategy. Soccer is a major area of its sponsorship.

In 2004, Emirates signed the biggest club sponsorship in the English Premier League (EPL). The deal included naming rights to Arsenal's new stadium. In 2007, it reinforced the Arsenal partnership with an eight-year shirt sponsorship. Other soccer partnerships include the Asian Football Confederation, AC Milan, Paris Saint-Germain, Hamburger SV, Real Madrid, Olympiacos, and the Zain Saudi Professional League. Rugby sponsorships include USA Rugby and the Rugby World Cup. Tennis has been a major area of investment, in part due to its attractive demographics for an airline. Sponsorships include Emirates Airline US Open Series, Dubai Championships, US Open, Barcelona Open, Roland-Garros, and the ATP World Tour. Horse racing is a special target due to the ruler of Dubai, Sheik Mohammed bin Rashid Al Maktoum, having a total passion for the horse racing industry. Through several platforms, Emirates has invested heavily in horse racing. It sponsors Godolphin Racing, Maktoum's thoroughbred horse racing operations with its stables in Dubai, England, Ireland, US, and Australia. It also sponsors major horse racing events, including the Dubai Cup, which is the richest race in world horse racing, as well as the Melbourne Cup Carnival and the Singapore Derby. For cricket, Emirates sponsors the Elite Panel of ICC Umpires as well as being an official partner of the International Cricket Council. It is a global partner of Formula 1, where its branding is displayed on circuit bridges as well as hospitality suites at multiple events.

Emirates has exited as well as added to its portfolio of sports sponsorships. In 2014, Emirates announced that it would not renew its sponsorship of the 2018 (Russia) or 2022 (Qatar) FIFA World Cup tournaments. Some industry observers linked this exit with ongoing allegations of bribery at FIFA associated with the bidding and decision making for the 2018 and 2022 World Cups. The airline officially stated that "Emirates can confirm that … the decision was made of FIFA's contract proposal which did not meet Emirates' expectations." A senior executive of the airline was reported by Sky News as stating they were dissatisfied with FIFA's less than aggressive position in addressing the bribery allegations – "As a sponsor you expect they will come and write to you in the middle of the issue or at the end of it. To them they act as if it's nothing for sponsors. For us, in our history of sponsorship, it is the only event that when it happened our clients started writing to us saying 'why do you support this organization.' "[10] Four other FIFA sponsors also exited their FIFA sponsorships in 2014/15; Sony, Castrol, Continental Tyres, and Johnson & Johnson. FIFA's marketing director commented on these exits as follows: "Rotations at the end of a sponsorship cycle are commonplace in the sports industry and have continuously occurred since the commercialization of the World Cup began. It is natural that as brand strategies evolve they reassess their sponsorship properties."[11]

Dubai and Abu Dhabi are the two major Emirates in the UAE. In Chapter 2, Box 2.2 discusses how Abu Dhabi and its national airline (Etihad) have also used sports as part of its global branding strategy. However, in contrast to Dubai, Abu Dhabi has invested heavily in soccer club ownership.

11.4.2 Multiple Decision Areas

Making an informed sponsorship decision benefits from an analysis of the following areas, each presented in detail in the subsequent subsections.

Value Transfer

What values will be attached to the commercial brand if a particular sports property is sponsored? The fan–sports property relationship means that the values that fans attach to the sports brand migrate to the commercial brand. This value transfer enhances the perception that fans have of the commercial brand, increasing their willingness to buy that particular brand. For example, Gatorade's long-standing partnership with the Hawaii Ironman triathlon aided in attributing images of endurance, challenge, and fuel for athletes to Gatorade. Exhibit 11.5 depicts this sharing of brand value attributes from the sponsee to the sponsor.

The marketing manager needs to have a very clear understanding of the target population that the sports brand speaks to, as well as the values that it communicates to its fans. For instance, a sport like mixed martial arts speaks to a very specific demographic with a very particular set of values. Thus, the marketing manager needs to evaluate whether she wants to speak to this demographic and whether she wants to have the values that fans associate with mixed martial arts transferred to her brand.

The potential for successful alignment between the sponsor and the property increases when the marketing manager takes into account the values the sports property communicate as well as the visibility of the sports' images. For example, two Canadian Olympic athletes at the 2014 Sochi Olympic Games (figure skater Patrick Chan and ice hockey player Drew Doughty) were sponsored by McDonald's. Both the athletes and the sponsor were criticized for supporting food choices that some argue are inconsistent with a healthy lifestyle and the reduction of obesity in children.[12]

Risk of a Negative Outcome

What is the risk of negative outcomes that would damage the commercial brand? Given the high-profile nature of sports in the media, negative press at some stage(s) about any sports property is to be expected. It is important when evaluating a sports property to consider the different types of possible negative press and the likelihood of some contexts being a serious problem for the sponsor. Box 11.2 describes how in November 2013 Indra Nooyi, the chairperson and CEO of PepsiCo, publicly cautioned the

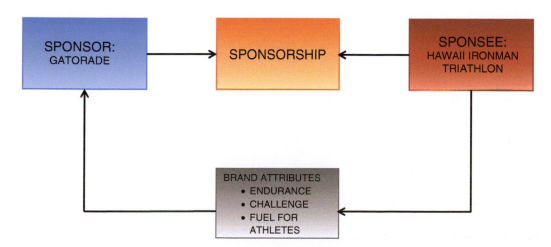

EXHIBIT 11.5 Sponsorship and its Sharing of Brand Attributes of Sponsee with Sponsor for Hawaii Ironman Triathlon

Indian Premier League (IPL) about gambling and other controversies long circling the IPL. PepsiCo invested more than $70 million in its high-profile title sponsorship of the IPL at the start of Season 6 in April 2013.

BOX 11.2 PEPSI SENDS THE INDIAN CRICKET BOARD A PUBLIC WARNING OVER PEPSI'S SPONSORSHIP OF THE INDIAN PREMIER LEAGUE

The Indian Premier League is one of the most successful new startup leagues in the history of sports. Season 1 was in 2008. It is a six-week league in which the best cricket players in the world play in the Twenty20 short-form of the game, with matches lasting approximately three hours. Allegations of financial improprieties, match-fixing, and less than transparent decision making have been an ongoing part of the IPL for much of its existence. A web search using terms such as "IPL," "scandal," "corruption," and "spot-fixing" brings up many items spread over multiple seasons of the league. The *Hindu Business Line* has part of its website devoted to its many articles on the "IPL spot-fixing scam." Spot-fixing is where there is betting on specific events occurring within a game in which those events have been "fixed" in an illegal way.

For its first five years (2008/12), the title sponsor of the league was the DLF Group, a leading Indian property developer. Starting in 2013, the league was titled the Pepsi Indian Premier League. Cost of the sponsorship was more than $70 million over a five-year period, with PepsiCo, the parent of the Pepsi product line, seeing sponsoring the IPL as a way to associate with India's twin loves of cricket and Bollywood. The IPL was not only a high-profile television ratings winner in India, but was appointment viewing for many cricket fans around the world. PepsiCo's chairperson and CEO was Indra Nooyi, an Indian-born executive who is frequently included in lists of the most respected business leaders. Nooyi was born in and received early education in Chennai, India, and had graduate education at the Yale School of Management. PepsiCo is headquartered in Purchase, New York.

Pepsi's first year of sponsorship saw betting allegation improprieties reach to the family of a senior IPL decision maker, and co-owner of the Chennai Super Kings. The Kings were a leading club in the IPL, having won the trophy in two of the first seven years and been runner-up in three other years. One blogger (www.vaishwords.com) choose to write an open letter to Indra Nooyi expressing his concerns:

Dear Ms. Nooyi,

I have a great deal of respect for you and it is in large part the reason I am sending this open letter to you. I believe integrity, honor and doing the right things are important to you, and that these are values you hold more dearly than those of simply pursuing and delivering bottom-line results, at all costs. Under your stewardship, PepsiCo's corporate philosophy seems to be more than words on your website: *we believe acting ethically and responsibly is not only the right thing to do, but also the right thing to do for our business."*

PepsiCo recently became the main sponsor of the Indian Premier League (IPL), reportedly signing a Rupees 396.8 core deal for a five year sponsorship of the IPL (source: Wikipedia). The IPL and its owners, the Board of Control for Cricket in India (BCCI) are currently engulfed in a massive illegal betting and match-fixing scandal that has tainted this tournament, the sport and distressed its loyal fan base. Worse than the unfolding scandal has been the spineless response to the crisis from its governing body, the BCCI. The President has refused to resign unconditionally, even though his son-in-law (CEO of one of the main IPL teams) has been directly implicated. The farce that is currently being orchestrated is not only shameful but also blatantly unethical. And it is now clear that there will be no "real" attempt made by the BCCI to get to the bottom of the scandal or cleanse this great sport. Instead, they seem to believe that by trying to pull the wool over our eyes they will be able to keep their purse strings intact and continue to fill their coffers. This without any consideration for the reputation of the sport they are charged with stewarding or any shred of respect for the fans that fill those coffers.

This is why I am reaching out to you, to implore you to do the right thing and disassociate your company and this great brand and sever all ties with Indian cricket. PepsiCo should terminate its IPL sponsorship immediately and unconditionally; until such time as there is has been an unbiased, fully transparent and ethically conducted investigation into the improprieties and an effort made to rid the sport of this cancer. Show us that PepsiCo is willing to stand by its stated corporate values, ethics, and integrity and do the socially responsible thing in India. Show us that even when the financial stakes are high for the company that you will follow your own guiding principle that states: ***Speak with truth and candor:** We tell the whole story, not just what's convenient to our individual goals."*
Sincerely,
Mr. Vaish[13]

Vaish received a response from a consumer relations associate supervisor of PepsiCo that he interpreted as a "standard form letter." It included the comment, "We appreciate the time you took to share your sincere feelings regarding this topic and for the constructive spirit in which they were offered. Please know that I've shared your concerns with our senior management to be sure that they fully understand your position."

Behind the scenes in 2013, Pepsi management likely was working to understand the ongoing allegations and to seek ways to mitigate their impact on the Pepsi brand. In an unusual response, Indra Nooyi in a November 2013 interview was very direct in her comments: "We are a highly ethical and principled organization. So we want to associate with organizations that are principled and ethical. We hope the current problems of the IPL are short term and they are addressed. But if they are not we will have to go back and rethink."[14] In October 2015, PepsiCo decided to exit the IPL title sponsorship after three years.

Chapter 12 discusses potential brand damage to sponsors associated with "players behaving badly" on and off the field.

Demographic Alignment

How do the property's demographics align with the commercial brand's target population? Commercial properties can choose to sponsor a particular sport property for various reasons. It might want to communicate with their existing consumers and the overlap between them and the fans' base is crucial. Or it may want to raise brand awareness among a new target segment. If this is the case, then the overlap between the fan base and the new target segment is critical to the purpose of the sponsorship investment. A sport such as golf in the United States has a very different demographic than does soccer in the country. Golf participants and fans are, on average, older, wealthier, and more likely to be a male than are those in soccer.

Clutter

How much clutter is there in the sporting property? In evaluating a sponsorship package, marketing directors evaluate the potential impact of the deal. Part of this impact on the behavior of fans depends on the visibility of the brand itself. Another aspect is the ability to activate the association. This second part is examined later in the chapter. In terms of visibility, a sponsorship package where the commercial brand has a prominent role and has few other brands competing for space is more valuable than one with many brands competing for the attention span of the viewer. Over time, some sports properties have moved from having numerous sponsors to a few. The idea is to create scarcity so that sponsoring the property is an exclusive privilege with little competition from other brands for space. Chapter 10 noted that one of the attractions to Banco Santander of sponsoring the Ferrari Formula 1 racing team was the minimal clutter on the two cars and their drivers. In contrast, some motor sports have more than ten sponsor logos on different parts of individual racing cars with the result that no one sponsor is conveyed in a clean and clear way when fans and viewers look at cars racing in those leagues.

Frequency and Reach

What is the frequency and reach of the sponsored property? Sponsoring the America's Cup sailing race series means visibility only when that series is run. Over the last ten series, the timeframe between successive America's Cup series has been far from consistent – it has ranged from three to five years apart. Moreover, races do not always occur at the times set, which creates problems for media broadcasting and for fans tracking the coverage. Races can be cancelled due to lack of wind or to too much wind. Even if the property tries to be at the forefront of attention in between races, it is hard to attract attention if the competition is years or even months away. In contrast, sponsoring MLB means almost daily exposure during the season, heightened daily exposure during the playoffs, and some interest during the off-season.

Sponsorship Package Inclusions

What are the different parts of the sponsorship package? The structure of sponsorship packages is as diverse as marketing managers' imagination. It ranges from the traditional brand exposure on the court or the players' shirt to include VIP access, free tickets, access to players, promotional campaigns at the venue, etc. This variety comes from the imagination of marketing managers at both the commercial brand and the sport property. For instance, Visa uses its Olympic sponsorship package to introduce new products at the Olympics with the objective of not only trying new products but highlighting their association with the five Olympic rings. Sponsorship is increasingly moving from exposure, such as the logo on the court, to having people experience the product through activation campaigns. Imaginative marketers aim to create a unique experience that will attract fans' attention and enhance the impact of the sponsorship investment.

Value to Sponsor

What is the value of the sponsorship to the sponsor? Two examples of areas that can create value to a sponsor are:

1   Impact on decisions made by the marketing targets – see Exhibit 11.3. These could include acquisition of new customers, a higher share of wallet by the existing customers, better partnerships with key suppliers, and higher levels of commitment made by employees. Estimates here are likely to be far from exact. However, it is important to directly address this area if the sponsorship decision is to be heavily driven by economic analysis. In recent years, demands within companies to conduct systematic return on investment (ROI) studies to justify sponsorship investments have increased greatly.

2   Impact on brand enhancement and potential brand damage. This category is related to decisions made by the marketing targets, but takes a broader perspective about how the multiple stakeholders of the sponsor view its brand resulting from the company's association with the sports property.

Sponsors are making advances relating to each of these areas in their quantitative and qualitative analysis of the benefits and costs of sponsorship investments.

11.4.3 Sponsorships as a Partnership

Consider a situation where the sponsor is entering into a partnership with the sports property. As with most negotiations, much is to be gained by each side considering the values and objectives of the other side as well as their own in building a sponsorship deal. Often, it is the sports property, or their agency or intermediary working on their behalf that will approach sports sponsors. Large sports sponsors have a structured approach to handle the literally hundreds of sponsorship proposals that they receive each year.

The sports property ideally should have done substantial analysis about the potential sponsor and the upsides and risks of a partnership before they start negotiations. Two examples of such an analysis are as follows:

1   Possible future changes in fans' perceptions of the brand and its attributes. Sports properties should anticipate how brand associations with sponsors over time may become negative as part of its risk mitigation analysis. Sports properties took very different attitudes as regards their fan base accepting tobacco sponsorship as momentum built on punitive tobacco legislation. Some sports exited or turned down lucrative tobacco sponsorships well before many countries passed legislation prohibiting tobacco advertising. Other sports, such as Formula 1, continued with tobacco sponsorship for much longer, in part due to the high magnitude of tobacco sponsorship in that sport. Box 11.3 describes the sponsor base of Formula 1 and issues associated with tobacco sponsorship. Placing

great weight on short-term financial factors can result in damage to the brand value of a sports property and create tension points with its other sponsors.

BOX 11.3 PHILIP MORRIS DOUBLES DOWN ON ITS MARLBORO SPONSORSHIP OF FORMULA 1'S FERRARI RACING TEAM

The Formula 1 automobile racing series has long attracted many global sponsors. The series has race weekends in Australia (one race), Asia (four races), Europe (eight races), Middle East (two races), North America (three races), and South America (one race). The *Black Book 2014*,[15] an annual independent Formula 1 industry review, provides the following estimates of the 2014 sponsorship revenue of each of its 11 racing teams:

Team	Sponsorship revenue*	Number of sponsors	Largest sponsor	Second largest sponsor
Ferrari	$219 million	23	Philip Morris ($100M)	Santander ($40M)
Red Bull Racing	$217 million	14	Red Bull ($110M)	Infiniti ($31M)
Mercedes	$162 million	16	Mercedes-Benz ($100M)	Petronas ($42M)
McLaren	$100 million	26	Mobil ($35M)	Johnnie Walker ($20M)
Lotus	$92 million	25	PDVSA ($30M)	Total ($28M)
Toro Rosso	$62 million	12	Red Bull ($50M)	CEPSA ($5M)
Sahara Force India	$57 million	18	Sahara ($33M)	Roshfrans ($6M)
Marussia	$56 million	16	Marussia ($45M)	InstaForex ($3M)
Williams	$53 million	17	Martini ($15M)	Banco de Brasil ($13M)
Caterham	$50 million	23	GE ($30M)	Safran ($6M)
Sauber	$42 million	19	Telmex ($15M)	Cuervo Tequila ($5M)

* Estimated total from numbers presented in the Black Book 2014.

Philip Morris' association with Formula 1, via its Marlboro tobacco brand, showcases the interaction between the imperative of Formula 1 teams attracting high dollar sponsorship with changing social norms and government policy. Formula 1 was one of the slowest industries to have tobacco sponsors exit their industry. Indeed, when individual countries with F1 events differed on the timing of their legislative bans on tobacco advertising, F1 events were still running with cars featuring tobacco product signage where it was still not banned by legislation. This rolling exit from tobacco advertising was labeled by some as the lure of tobacco money driving the Formula 1 league to the bottom in terms of social responsibility. The Ferrari team, with its Marlboro sponsorship since 1996, was a poster child for some in this "race to the bottom" commentary.

Philip Morris' early Formula 1 sponsorships using its Marlboro brand were short-lived, covering the 1972/4 period, the British Racing Motors (BRM) team and the Iso Marlboro-Ford team. From 1974 to 1996 Marlboro was a major sponsor of the McLaren team. This team had much track success with champion drivers Emerson Fittipaldi, Alain Prost, and Ayrton Senna. In 1997, Philip Morris' Marlboro became the title sponsor of the Scuderia Ferrari Marlboro team. As more countries banned tobacco advertising, the challenge for Marlboro was how to keep it its association with the very high-profile and successful Ferrari cars and drivers. There have been ongoing allegations that Philip Morris has adopted a "subliminal advertising" strategy in several areas, such as:

- **The Ferrari team color** – races in a red color similar to the color on a Marlboro cigarette pack. A neuro-marketing consultant argued that "Marlboro is sending indirect, subconscious signals that are talking to the brain without explicitly telling it we are being sold to – just by showing me a red Ferrari car."[16]
- **The "barcode" design of the cars** – "the design is a red, black and white barcode-like design on the canopy of the vehicles as well as on the uniform of the drivers. Up close it looks like a cool aesthetic touch but from a distance it appears to resemble [a Marlboro pack]."[17] In 2010 Ferrari agreed to drop the barcode logo.

Ferrari's corporate response to these allegations was both direct and blunt. In April 2010, it stated that none of the arguments about the choice of the red color and the barcode graphics "have any scientific basis, as they rely on some alleged studies which have never been published in academic journals. But, more importantly, they do not correspond to the truth … The partnership between Ferrari and Philip Morris is now only exploited in certain initiatives, such as factory visits, meetings with drivers, merchandising products, all carried out fully within the laws of the various countries where these activities take place. There has been no logo or branding on the race cars since 2007, even in countries where local laws would still have permitted it."[18] The Ferrari team name up to 2011 was "Scuderia Ferrari Marlboro." In 2011, a Ferrari spokesman stated that "Marlboro will no longer be a part of the team name. Whilst we do not agree with the concerns raised, our decision has been taken in line with our history of responsiveness on similar issues and to avoid what would have been an unnecessary and unproductive debate."[19] Despite the many bans on tobacco advertising in sports, Philip Morris renewed its Ferrari sponsorship from 2011 to 2015 at an estimated cost of $100 million a year. This renewal prompted health bodies – such as the Royal College of Physicians – to lobby the Formula 1's governing body to investigate the sponsorship for violating the intent of anti-tobacco legislation.

2   Proposals by a sponsor that may be difficult for the sponsee to consistently deliver on at the expected level. Sponsors typically see great value in having access to players, athletes, and the team coaches as part of their sponsorship agreements. The track record in this area for team sports has, at several high-publicity events, been under-delivery of commitments made by sporting properties in a sponsorship agreement. Sponsors may set up events at which players are expected to appear and then one or more of the following occur: players do not turn up, *or* players turn up late, *or* the players that turn up are more back-up players than starting players, *or* the players that do turn up do not interact well with the guests, *or* some players that do turn up consume too much liquor

and become abusive to the guests at the event. While in most cases players are great ambassadors for a sports property at sponsor events, it is typically the negative experiences that gain the most attention and can adversely impact the sponsor's brand.

11.4.4 Sponsor Agreements and Their Growing Complexity

The growth of sponsorship, and the increasing magnitude of individual sponsorship investments, is resulting in sponsorship agreements becoming increasingly lengthy and more complex. The sponsorship contracts of companies investing heavily in this area will often include:

■ Recognition of the deliverables to be provided to the official sponsor, such as name association recognition (e.g., official sponsor, title sponsor), sport association recognition (e.g., official sponsor of the British Tennis Association), and athlete association recognition (e.g., endorsed by Rory McIlroy).
■ Placement location of the logo – size and position – on the equipment, online, at the event and surrounding promotion banners and highway advertisements.
■ Visual image deliverables at the event site, at event surroundings, on direct transmission (television/streaming/radio) of the event, on replays (television/streaming/radio) of the event, and in advertisements and other promotions.
■ Suite and ticket allocations – such as four seats on the floor for an arena title sponsor.
■ Hospitality options, including levels of food and beverages and appearances by retired athletes and cheerleaders at suites.
■ Access to athletes, coaches, and team mascots.
■ Endorsement by athletes or appearances by athletes or the team in advertisements.
■ Access to non-open public areas – such as passes to pit row at motorsport events.
■ Use of facilities/suites on non-event date.
■ Ambush marketing protection – Box 10.3 discussed ambush marketing by Subway while McDonald's was the official sponsor of the 2014 Winter Olympics.

It is essential that each party to the contract be aware of the various clauses at the time the contract is being negotiated and then signed. There are instances where disagreements have occurred and one side of dispute first learns about the existence of specific clauses at the time of the dispute. Some clauses in sponsorship agreements have their origin in prior disputes between parties to a sponsorship agreement or where one party believes there was ambiguity over the deliverables in the agreement.

11.4.5 Sponsorship Categories and Exclusivity

Sponsorship properties need to decide on the various levels of sponsorship and sponsorship categories. Terminology differs across sports properties. Some use the levels of gold, silver, and bronze, while others divide by sponsors and suppliers, where the higher levels have more rights and activation opportunities than lower ones. Still others are moving to more creative classifications or basing their terminologies on the value provided to the sponsor (e.g., activation sponsor, presenting sponsor). The top-level sponsor for leagues and events is often referred to as the "title sponsor." Examples from Appendix 11A include

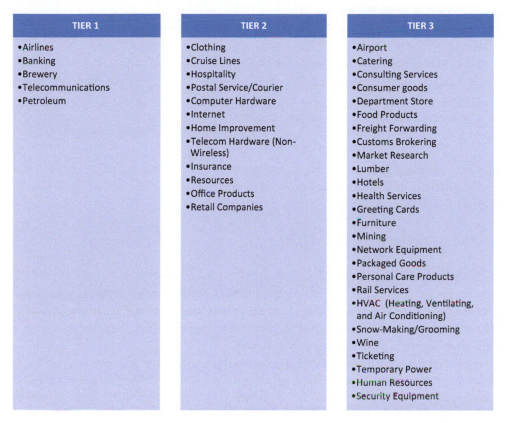

TIER 1	TIER 2	TIER 3
•Airlines	•Clothing	•Airport
•Banking	•Cruise Lines	•Catering
•Brewery	•Hospitality	•Consulting Services
•Telecommunications	•Postal Service/Courier	•Consumer goods
•Petroleum	•Computer Hardware	•Department Store
	•Internet	•Food Products
	•Home Improvement	•Freight Forwarding
	•Telecom Hardware (Non-Wireless)	•Customs Brokering
	•Insurance	•Market Research
	•Resources	•Lumber
	•Office Products	•Hotels
	•Retail Companies	•Health Services
		•Greeting Cards
		•Furniture
		•Mining
		•Network Equipment
		•Packaged Goods
		•Personal Care Products
		•Rail Services
		•HVAC (Heating, Ventilating, and Air Conditioning)
		•Snow-Making/Grooming
		•Wine
		•Ticketing
		•Temporary Power
		•Human Resources
		•Security Equipment

EXHIBIT 11.6 Vancouver 2010 Olympics Three Levels of National Sponsors Open to Canadian Companies

the Turkish Airlines Euroleague, the Verizon Indycar Series, M&T Bank Stadium, and the Barracuda Championship Reno-Tahoe event on the PGA golf tour.

Exhibit 11.6 shares the three levels of sponsorship categories at the Vancouver 2010 Winter Olympics. Tier 1 sponsors made the highest investment and received the most rights. Four of the five industry groups in Exhibit 11.6 are traditional high-revenue-generating sponsors for many sporting properties – airlines, banking, brewery, and telecommunications. The fifth Tier 1 industry of petroleum reflects its economic importance to Canada and hence was seen as a potential high-revenue sponsorship candidate.

A sponsorship category is the industry classification that defines the sponsor's background. In cases of exclusive categories, only one sponsor per category is allowed. For example, BBVA is the official bank of the NBA. This is an exclusive category that enables BBVA to associate its brand with the NBA, such as use of the NBA logos, and hospitality and tickets at NBA events. BBVA has a four-year contract in which it pays $30 million each year to the NBA for the rights to be the exclusive bank in this category. This means that no other bank or financial institution can explicitly associate with the NBA.

Categories can differ across sporting properties. Some properties choose to have a large number of categories. An example is the Air Canada Centre in downtown Toronto, with four different food category sponsors: donuts (Tim Hortons), burgers (McDonald's), pizza (Pizza Pizza), and sandwiches (Subway).

Sports properties typically charge more for exclusive categories than for non-exclusive categories. Potential value-adds from being an exclusive sponsor in a category include:

- Reduced clutter by having one sponsor per category.
- Potential increase in sales, such as Anheuser-Busch being the only beer company permitted to sell its brands at an arena.
- Positive associations between sponsor and property.
- Reduced effectiveness/potential of ambush marketing via improved consumer recognition of official sponsors versus non-sponsors, and
- Increased consumer knowledge of sponsor contribution to society, such as recognition that the sponsor supports the Olympic and Paralympic team athletes.

11.5 SPONSORSHIP ACTIVATION

Once a sponsorship deal has been signed, servicing occurs to ensure that all elements of the sponsorship contract are delivered upon. This could range from inviting the sponsor to key events, ensuring the tickets and access passes are ready on-site or sent beforehand, having signage of certain size or in particular locations, working with athletes to "lock-down" commitments to appear at events, regular communications throughout the partnership, and more.

Many sponsorship deals and their execution are facilitated by sports agencies such as WME/IMG, GMR Marketing, Wasserman Media Group, Momentum Worldwide, WPP, or Octagon. Globally, there are numerous agencies of different sizes and specializing in different sports and types of sponsorship. These include large global agencies (e.g., IMG, GMR, Wasserman, etc.) who have thousands of staff and operate in dozens of countries of the world down to individual single-person shops who provide expertise to a single (or small number of) client(s) on a particular aspect. Some of them deal with the entire sponsorship process, from finding the right partners for activation and measurement, while others specialize in some smaller aspect of sponsorship. The complexity of sponsorship means that a lot of the relevant knowledge is not available in-house at the sponsors themselves.

Box 11.4 provides an example with outcomes of a successful sponsorship activation.

BOX 11.4 SPONSORSHIP AND DIGITAL ACTIVATION

To be successful, sponsorship requires creative, value-adding activation. Today, these activations need to include both traditional elements (e.g., packaging, VIP appearances, etc.) and non-traditional elements (e.g., social media integration, digital assets). An informative example of an effective sponsorship activation program that touches on both aspects with very strong digital elements is the Kraft Hockeyville campaign. Hockeyville was launched in Canada in 2006 and the United States in 2015. The campaign is a competition that is sponsored by Kraft, supported by the National Hockey League, the National Hockey League Players' Association, and a television network (CBC in Canada, NBC Sports in the United States).

The title sponsor, Kraft Foods, is a multibillion-dollar North American manufacturer of grocery products headquartered in Chicago. The core idea of the activation is a competition where communities compete for a $150,000 prize towards renovating their local arena, hosting a pre-season NHL game the following season, and being profiled during NHL telecasts in Canada (formerly CBC, now Rogers Sportsnet) or the United States (NBC Sports). For example, Johnstown, Pennsylvania won the 2015 Kraft Hockeyville USA with the rewards of a $150,000 arena upgrade and a September 29, 2015 pre-season game between the Pittsburgh Penguins and Tampa Bay Lightning.[20]

The engagement of consumers in the campaign is done as follows. Municipalities are invited to put forward a bid for the award. Typically, more than 200 towns or cities put forward an application. If a municipality decides to bid, a bid committee is formed who then must put together a program on which people vote (via the website, phone, text, or social media). The recipient with the most votes wins.

Kraft Hockeyville has been awarded a number of accolades as a sponsorship activation program including the 2010 "Best Sponsorship Campaign" at the 2010 Globes Worldwide Marketing Awards.

The Sponsorship Report published some highlights of the 2011 Canadian version of Kraft Hockeyville that outline the impact. Consider that Canada has a population of just over 30 million.

- 17.3 million votes were cast;
- 227 communities bid;
- a total of 37,307 people were members of bid committees in those 227 communities;
- 7,861 videos uploaded to YouTube;
- 43,000 Facebook fans.

11.5.1 Activation Ratios

Activation is the further investment – beyond the rights fee – on various related activities (e.g., television commercials, accompanying web-based efforts, social media content, new packaging, etc.) to enhance the impact of the sponsorship. Although the sponsor (and its intermediaries) typically activates, collaboration between the sponsor and sport property is crucial. For example, the local organizing committee host body of each Olympics Games needs to assist Visa to set up money-access points at Olympic events and to ensure that other credit/debit card companies are not on-site. Recent studies show that sponsors invest anywhere from 70 to 170 percent of their rights fees investment in activation, while the sporting properties themselves often invest up to 10 percent of the rights fees they receive towards activations.[21] Many examples of underperforming sponsorships are due to poor activation rather than the property itself being a poor platform to showcase a product or service.

Activation ratios (activation investment relative to direct sponsorship investment) are useful during budgeting to highlight the overall investment required, rather than myopically looking only at the sponsorship investment. Deciding on the appropriate ratio can be very context specific. Cases of successful sponsorships can have widely varying ratios, ranging from as low as 1:1 to has high as 5:1 or more.[22] For example, the sponsorship of a sports property that has limited inherent assets or the need for massive activation, may have a ratio as high as 5:1 (e.g., C-level hospitality at a golf tournament) while others can work well with activations at 1:1 or lower, if limited additional work is needed (e.g., a naming rights deal for an arena).

11.5.2 Diverse Areas of Activation

Traditional and online advertising – where the sponsor uses the sports property's logo in its commercials or the theme of the commercials is related to the sports property – is a typical activation lever. In-store advertising and direct marketing approaches are also common in activation. Activation is often related to promotions such as prizes and sweepstakes. Tickets in a sponsorship package can be used to run special promotions where the winners get the tickets to an event and meet some players. Social media activation often involves the sponsor and the sports property working together. Hospitality examples include seating in VIP boxes and access to restricted areas at the venue such as "pit row" before a motorsport race. Sponsors usually invite their top clients to hospitality events to spend time with them and establish a deeper relationship with the hope of getting additional business.

An alternative activation strategy is to add sponsorships of other sporting properties that complement the main one. For instance, Banco Santander's main Formula 1 sponsorship investment was Ferrari. However, they were also title sponsors of various Grands Prix and secondary sponsors of other teams. The objective here of these additional sponsorships was to enhance the returns to the main investment and establish synergies between them. This sponsorship portfolio approach is often used when global sponsorships are reinforced through regional deals.

Examples of activations are many and include:

- **Mass market awareness:** advertising (TV, radio, print, outdoor), event signage, public relations, banners, uniform logos, offsite events/promotions, vehicle signage.
- **Spectator/participant awareness:** PA announcements, logo placement, scoreboard promotions, on-site activations, direct marketing.
- **Digital:** social media, mobile, digital promotions, blogs, websites.
- **Experiential:** product sampling, hospitality, VIP passes/entertainment, product demonstrations.
- **Retail:** point of purchase (POP) displays, sales promotions, contests to drive in-store traffic, coupons, in-store displays.
- **Image transfer:** licensing, merchandising, sweepstakes, games/video games, player/athlete sponsorship, coach sponsorship, league sponsorship.
- **Sponsor internal:** employee programs, staff rewards/hospitality, contests.

11.5.3 Industry Example of Activation: The NBA All-Star Weekend

The NBA All-Star Weekend is a showcase of sponsor activation as well as a showcase of the NBA elite athletes and their skills. This is a three- to four-day event held mid-season. The city changes each year and is known several years in advance.

One area of *pre-event activation* can include promotions such as prizes and sweepstakes. Official NBA sponsors such as Taco Bell and Foot Locker can run in-store special promotions where the winners get a NBA All-Star package that includes economy airfare, accommodation, and tickets to several All-Star events and games. Similar packages can be provided for employees of their retail outlets. Official sponsors such as Anheuser-Busch InBev and Coca-Cola can have supermarket presentations where marketing of new products is showcased with NBA All-Star banners and the logos of the local NBA club.

A second area is *at-event activation*. The All-Star Weekend includes many opportunities for sponsors to activate. Official sponsors such as Cisco and SAP could invite C-level executives from its major existing and potential customers to a two-day golf and conference event at elite courses on the

Wednesday and Thursday prior to the weekend activities. For fans, there is NBA House presented by BBVA Compass. This is "an interactive basketball experience that allows fans of all ages the opportunity to be part of the NBA All-Star excitement." On the Friday, the NBA runs a Technology Summit, where its sponsors and their guests are invited to participate. This has presentations by cutting-edge companies and thought leaders on many aspects of how technology is changing the business landscape of the sports and entertainment industry. The Friday, Saturday, and Sunday broadcast events give official sponsors much exposure, both at the arena and on national media. It is sponsorship on steroids! Friday night has the Sprint NBA All-Star Celebrity Game and the BBVA Compass Rising Stars Challenge. Saturday night is the State Farm All-Star Saturday Night with the Taco Bell Skills Challenge, the Foot Locker Three-Point Challenge, and the Sprite Slam Dunk. Sunday afternoon has the NBA D-League All-Star Game presented by Kumho Tire, and the Boost Mobile NBA D-League Slam Dunk Contest. The Sunday night has the Sprint Pre-game Concert and Inside the NBA presented by Kia. Night-life over the All-Star Weekend includes multiple parties. For the 2015 weekend, www.PartyFixx.co called itself "The official website for celebrity hosted parties and nightlife events NBA All-Star Weekend 2015 in New York City." Celebrities are advertised as headliners at many of these parties. Sponsors can buy tickets to many of these parties and have areas where they have their own hospitality within the party venue itself.

11.6 SPONSORSHIP MEASUREMENT AND EVALUATION

The third area of decision making in sponsorship relates to the measurement and evaluation of the sponsorship investment. Sponsorship is just one of the marketing alternatives open to a commercial company, so a major part of its justification relies on showing better returns than other alternatives. The size of some of sponsorship deals makes this need even more acute. Indeed, as sponsorship investments have grown in size in the past decade, attention to their evaluation from senior executives has also increased. Section 11.8 on Olympic sponsorship shows that over the eight cycles (of four years each) of the Olympic TOP sponsorship program, only three out of 28 companies were on board each and every cycle. One message here is that the vast majority of these 28 large companies at some stage made the decision to exit from a very high-cost sponsorship.

The framework in Exhibit 11.3 highlights some key areas where evaluation of sponsorship can be made going from message/exposure to awareness to engagement to the desired decision and outcome by the sponsorship target(s).

11.6.1 Message/Exposure Metrics

Brand exposure metrics are standard inputs into many sponsorship evaluations for categories such as naming rights and signage. Joyce Julius and Associates, a leading advisory firm in this area, tracks exposures and then converts them into an estimated value equivalence of the exposure. Joyce Julius describes their methodology as follows:

> Accurate, timely, detailed and verifiable, our approach delivers premium, yet cost-effective in-broadcast exposure research. Armed with *Image Identification Technology* (IIT) powered by Magellan, our veteran research staff digitally measures all clear and in-focus exposure time a sponsoring brand receives during the broadcast(s) in question...Joyce Julius also monitors and tabulates

each verbal mention received by the brand throughout the telecast. Once all of the in-broadcast visual and/or verbal exposure has been tabulated, a value for the brand's exposure is first calculated by comparing the on-screen time and mentions to the non-discounted cost of a commercial, which ran during the program in question.[23]

Exhibit 11.7 is an example of a Joyce Julius report. Sponsors activating at this NASCAR event can use the Joyce Julius reports as an important input in building a broader evaluation of the impact of their sponsorship.

When preparing a report such as Exhibit 11.7, Joyce Julius puts an emphasis on what it calls "Recognition Value" (see column in Exhibit 11.7), which goes a step beyond the commercial sport equivalency values, and takes into consideration elements such as size and location of the identity on screen, brand clutter, and any relevant brand integration into the action of the telecast. The

Driver	Exposure time	Mentions	Sightings	Recognition value
1 Jeff Gordon	52:26:00	198	52,169	$112,676,030
2 Kevin Harvick	43:49:25	330	41,850	$111,695,850
3 Jimmie Johnson	39:46:24	177	38,681	$106,184,650
4 Brad Keselowski	41:12:40	262	42,772	$97,416,455
5 Dale Earnhardt Jr.	30:58:13	161	28,699	$97,112,730
6 Joey Logano	38:06:53	245	41,505	$78,961,960
7 Kyle Busch	20:50:45	146	20,583	$67,449,280
8 Hamlin/Hornish	22:21:12	148	22,329	$65,287,105
9 Kyle Larson	23:51:19	83	24,331	$52,758,315
10 Matt Kenseth	19:49:21	143	19,821	$50,312,545
11 Kurt Busch	19:50:53	94	21,283	$47,611,285
12 Nemechek/Waltrip	19:05:26	10	3,594	$44,904,930
13 Clint Bowyer	15:13:25	69	15,477	$44,882,055
14 Tony Stewart	15:15:58	57	13,370	$43,443,810
15 Carl Edwards	15:59:19	120	15,540	$41,106,320
16 Ryan Newman	18:15:55	118	17,815	$40,986,575
17 Jamie McMurray	18:05:23	67	20,545	$39,251,735
18 Kasey Kahne	16:18:27	89	17,639	$38,633,810
19 Greg Biffle	13:02:36	55	12,970	$30,069,260
20 Danica Patrick	8:55:40	31	9,252	$29,991,750

EXHIBIT 11.7 2014 Driver-Related Sponsorship Results (TV)
Source: Joyce Julius & Associates

analyses that Joyce Julius undertakes measures non-event television programming, print media and internet news coverage, television coverage, on-site element analysis, and sponsorship exposure measurements stemming from promotions and advertising, as well as social media monitoring and fan surveying.

11.6.2 Awareness /Engagement Metrics

Exhibit 11.3 highlights that a key aspect of sponsorship activation is converting exposure into awareness. For some cases of sponsorship there likely will be a direct and known link to a target decision maker. For example, where SAP provides All-Star Weekend game tickets to C-level executives and an all-expenses-paid, high-end, two-day golf and conference event prior to the weekend, it is highly likely that the executives know the invitation is coming from SAP and that the purpose is to further strengthen or start a deep business relationship. In other cases, there is much more uncertainty over whether the intended recipients of the sponsorship messaging actually made the connection to the sponsor, let alone were prompted to make the decision the sponsor would view as desired (such as increased beverage purchases of the sponsors products).

Turnkey Sports & Entertainment is a leading custom research firm that has developed awareness methodologies that sponsors often use as part of their measurement and evaluation activities. For example, in a 2014 Turnkey survey of more than 400 members of an online panel, respondents were "asked to identify official NASCAR sponsors from a field of companies and brands that were provided to them for each business sector."[24] Respondents were classified as either "avid fans" or "casual fans" based on their frequency of tracking NASCAR race and driver information. The sample was individuals with some interest in NASCAR. The survey was conducted near the end of the 2012, 2013, and 2014 seasons, in the middle of the ten-race Chase for the Sprint Cup. Exhibit 11.8 reports on the percentage of respondents identifying what they believe was an official NASCAR sponsor.

These percentages reported in Exhibit 11.8 highlight several of the challenges of sponsorship in general, and NASCAR in particular. No category had more than 75 percent of respondents correctly identifying the official sponsor. For the beer, credit card, and banking categories, this percentage was less than 50 percent in every year for both sets of fans. In 2014, more respondents thought Anheuser-Busch was the official NASCAR sponsor than those who thought correctly that it was Coors Light. One of the challenges of NASCAR sponsorship is the potential for fans to misidentify official sponsors. This is complicated by the fact that there are multiple levels of sponsorship available to companies below the official NASCAR level – such as sponsorship of racetracks, races, racing teams, and drivers. Kevin Harvick, the 2014 Sprint Champion series winning driver in his #4 car, is sponsored by Anheuser-Busch. Dale Earnhardt Jr., the most popular NASCAR driver, was also sponsored in his #8 car by Anheuser-Busch. Little wonder that even avid fans may have trouble identifying the official NASCAR beer sponsor in 2014 as Coors Light!

For many years, the two leading NASCAR stock car series were the top-tier NASCAR Sprint Cup Series (starting in 2004 resulting from a direct investment by Sprint of $70 million per year) and the second-tier NASCAR Nationwide Series (starting in 2008 at a direct investment by Nationwide Insurance of $8 million a year). In December 2014, it was announced that Sprint would not extend its title sponsorship beyond 2016. The press release stated that "significant changes within Sprint and the highly competitive business environment" led to the decision.[25] Earlier, in September 2013, Nationwide had announced it was switching its investment after the 2014 season within the NASCAR world. The chief sales officer of Nationwide stated that "being a series sponsor was the right thing at

	Avid Fans			Casual Fans		
TIRE	2012	2013	2014	2012	2013	2014
Goodyear-SPONSOR	74.0%	70.0%	64.5%	60.3%	56.5%	58.7%
Bridgestone	6.0	8.5	12.0	6.5	7.0	7.0
WIRELESS						
Sprint-SPONSOR	55.5%	54.0%	52.0%	40.2%	40.5%	44.3%
AT&T	13.5	11.0	13.5	9.5	10.5	10.4
SOFT-DRINK						
Coca-Cola-SPONSOR	62.5%	53.5%	54.5%	44.2%	44.0%	37.3%
Mountain Dew	10.0	11.5	11.5	8.5	15.0	14.4
INSURANCE						
Nationwide-SPONSOR	54.0%	48.5%	43.5%	29.1%	35.0%	32.8%
Geico	9.0	7.0	7.0	11.6	6.5	16.4
BEER						
Anheuser-Busch	40.5%	35.5%	35.0%	37.7%	28.5%	34.8%
Coors Light-SPONSOR	25.5	34.5	23.5	26.1	32.0	23.4
CREDIT CARD						
VISA-SPONSOR	39.0%	41.5%	33.0%	35.7%	34.5%	30.3%
MasterCard	9.5	15.5	13.0	10.1	13.5	11.9
BANK						
Bank of America-SPONSOR	39.7%	36.0%	29.5%	35.2%	35.5%	29.9%
Citibank	7.5	9.5	10.5	8.0	7.5	5.5

EXHIBIT 11.8 Official NASCAR Sponsor Recognition by Avid Fans and Casual Fans
Source: Turnkey Sports & Entertainment, as reported in *Sports Business Weekly*, November 24–30, 2014

that particular time [2008] but we see Sundays [for Cup races] as the next step. You'll see us lean into this even more at the Cup level … I will spend more money in 2014 and 2015 [in NASCAR] by redirecting assets around a bit."[26] Nationwide's ongoing investments include sponsoring the Roush Fenway Racing driver Ricky Stenhouse Jr. in his # 17 car, as well as running advertisements during races featuring Danica Patrick and Dale Earnhardt Jr. As with many corporate exits or changes in sponsorships, there is often much second-guessing as to the "real" reasons for a change in investment as opposed to the stated reasons. For example, NASCAR replaced Nationwide with Comcast's Xfinity as the title sponsor of its second-tier series. The Xfinity sponsorship starting in 2015 was reported to be a ten-year deal for $200 million.[27] Nationwide may have been unwilling to lock themselves into a ten-year deal with NASCAR at an amount well above its earlier $8 million a year contract.

11.6.3 Desired Decision and Outcome

Sponsorships differ greatly with respect to the ability to associate investment spending and decisions/outcomes by the targets of the sponsorships. The increasing use of digital marketing is partly motivated by its greater ability to track linkages in Exhibit 10.1 (and its sponsorship equivalent Exhibit 11.3) between the message/exposure and the desired decision/outcome. For example, sporting properties that sponsor websites offering merchandise sold by the sporting property can track how different types of promotions lead to changes in purchasing behavior. Many sporting properties now seek to build databases of their fans and followers by sponsoring third-party content websites and offering prizes for individuals who digitally respond to their "free promotions." Such digital databases are potentially rich assets that can subsequently be the basis of multiple marketing and sales campaigns.

For many years sponsors have emphasized the importance of return on investment (ROI) as a key criterion for sponsorship decisions. Major sporting agencies have made advances in tracking the linkages in Exhibit 11.3, but for many large sponsorship investments, analysis of ROI is still a major challenge. However, improved evaluation of ROI is becoming more commonplace in the industry. For example, Exhibit 11.9 reports on a sample of the sponsorship evaluations completed by global sponsorship agency, IMI International, which specializes in assessing the effectiveness of sponsorships and activations.

Don Mayo, global managing partner of IMI, stressed in an interview that "it is of vital importance to activate a sponsorship in an innovative and aggressive way. Then, we must evaluate the ROI from the effort."

Exhibit 11.9, Panel A, presents two graphics from IMI's work around the 2014 Sochi Olympic Games related to ROI from sponsorship elements. The first graphic reports on TOP sponsor McDonald's impressions and Twitter analytics from the launch of the torch relay (October 2013) through to the end of the Games (February 2014), while the second provides a multi-level assessment of the TOP sponsors' ROI, highlighted by the finding that 11 million people noted an increase in their intent to purchase sponsors' products.

Panel B in Exhibit 11.9 reports on another IMI study, this one regarding ROI from sponsorship of the South African 2010 FIFA World Cup in Canada. Here, the first graphic reports on a number of positive impacts of sponsorship of the 2010 World Cup on Canadians including more than eight million Canadians feeling "more favorable" to at least one World Cup sponsor. The second graphic provides more detailed data by analyzing sponsoring organizations from the 2010 World Cup on four levels of outcomes: percentage who saw the promotion, percentage who now view the sponsor more favorably, proportion impacted, and total number of Canadians impacted. Coke, Adidas, Gillette, Canon, Budweiser, CBC, and Rogers were all impacted extensively by the sponsorship.

Panel A: Measurement of Sochi 2014 sponsorship

Panel B: Measurement of FIFA 2010 World Cup sponsorship

EXHIBIT 11.9 IMI International – Sponsorship Evaluations of ROI

11.7 INDUSTRY EXAMPLE: SHIRT SPONSORSHIP IN THE ENGLISH PREMIER LEAGUE

In many parts of the globe, except North America, a major part of investment in team sports is investing in a company name or brand appearing on the front center of the jersey. This a highly visible sponsorship at games and during broadcasts of games. Moreover, sales of jerseys to fans means that these fans then become walking advertisements for the brand when they wear the jersey.

Exhibit 11.10 shows jersey sponsorship estimates for each of the 20 EPL clubs in the 2014/15 season. The amounts reported in Exhibit 11.10 are sometimes third-party estimates and should be viewed as informed but not always figures from the actual contracts.

Exhibit 11.10 highlights multiple aspects of sports marketing. One aspect is the extreme tiering of deals across the 20 clubs playing in the EPL. Notably, the Manchester United deal is more than 60 times that of the Crystal Palace deal. The leading brands in most leagues are typically much stronger than the brands of many other clubs in the same league. A second aspect is the global nature of some of the companies investing in jersey sponsorships. The six largest deals reported in Exhibit 11.10 are for companies or brands with global customers and from different parts of the world – Chevrolet/General Motors from the US, Emirates from Dubai, Standard Chartered from the UK, Etihad from Abu Dhabi, Samsung from South Korea, and AIA from Hong Kong. Clearly these six companies see an association with the most global of all professional sports in one of its highest profile leagues as a good investment. A third aspect of Exhibit 11.10 worth discussing is the presence of four gambling/online betting companies who have purchased jersey sponsorships. These four sponsors include one based in the UK (Bet365) and three based in Asia (Dafabet, 12BET, and Fun88). Sports gambling is legal in the UK and in other countries such as Australia and New Zealand. Betting on EPL games is one pillar of fan avidity in that league.

Panel A: Industry composition of EPL Club Shirt Sponsors

Industry	Number of Clubs	Total Value (£M)
Airlines	3	52.50
Financial Services	6	49.75
Automotive	1	47.00
Electronics	1	18
Gambling/Online Betting	4	10.60
Beverage/Food Services	2	10.30
Technology	2	2.20
Travel Services	1	1
Grand Total	**20**	**191.35**

EXHIBIT 11.10 (*cont.*)

Panel B: EPL Club Shirt Sponsors

Club	Named sponsor	Industry	Value (£M)
Manchester United	Chevrolet	Automotive	47
Arsenal	Fly Emirates	Airlines	30
Liverpool	Standard Chartered	Financial Services	20
Manchester City	Etihad	Airlines	20
Chelsea	Samsung	Electronics	18
Tottenham	AIA	Financial Services	16
Newcastle	Wonga	Financial Services	6
Aston Villa	Dafabet	Gambling/Online Betting	5
Everton	Chang Beer	Beverage	5.3
Sunderland	Bidvest	Food Services	5
Swansea	GWFX	Financial Services	4
Stoke	Bet365	Gambling/Online Betting	3
West Ham	alpari	Financial Services	3
Queens Park Rangers	AirAsia	Airlines	2.5
Hull	12BET	Gambling/Online Betting	1.6
West Bromwich	Intuit/Quickbooks	Technology	1.2
Burnley	Fun88	Gambling/Online Betting	1
Leicester	King Power	Travel Services	1
Southampton	Veho	Technology	1
Crystal Palace	NETELLER	Financial Services	0.75
Grand total			**£191.35**

EXHIBIT 11.10 Shirt/Kit Naming Sponsorship Deals in English Premier League for 2014/15
Source: Based on A. Miller and N. Harris, "Manchester United's Chevrolet deal pushes Premier League shirt values to £191 million," *The Independent*, July 29, 2014

11.8 INDUSTRY EXAMPLE: ADDS AND DROPS BY IOC TOP SPONSORS

In the early 1980s, the IOC expressed interest in revenue-generation outside of television as the 1984 Los Angeles Games approached. For the 1976 Montreal and 1980 Moscow Games, sponsorship revenues (cash total value) had been low but the total number of sponsors had been very high, numbering in the hundreds of companies associated officially with each of the two Games. With the success of the

1984 Games in LA and growing interest in sponsorship from major corporations, the IOC revamped its sponsorship framework. It introduced The Olympic Program (TOP), which is based on the premises of fewer sponsors, exclusivity and high levels of servicing. Sponsors commit to a four-year period covering one Summer Games and one Winter Games.

Panel A of Exhibit 11.11 summarizes information on the first seven cycles of TOP. Panel B shows the individual companies who were sponsors for eight cycles with the 2013/16 cycles added.

There has been an approximate ten times increase in the revenues the IOC receives from this program over the first seven cycles. The number of sponsors has been between nine and 12 for each cycle.

Panel A: Successive editions of TOP

Edition	Years	Participating NOCs	Sponsors	Revenue
TOP I	1985–8	159	9	$96 million
TOP II	1989–92	169	12	$172 million
TOP III	1993–6	197	10	$279 million
TOP IV	1997–2000	199	11	$579 million
TOP V	2001–4	202	11	$663 million
TOP VI	2005–8	205	12	$886 million
TOP VII	2009–12	205	11	$957 million

Panel B: Companies who have been members of TOP

TOP	I	II	III	IV	V	VI	VII	VIII
Years	1985–8	1989–92	1993–6	1997–2000	2001–4	2005–8	2009–12	2013–16
Winter Games	Calgary	Albertville	Lillehammer	Nagano	Salt Lake	Turin	Vancouver	Sochi
Summer Games	Seoul	Barcelona	Atlanta	Sydney	Athens	Beijing	London	Rio
TOP sponsor for that quadrennial?								
3M	Yes	Yes	No	No	No	No	No	No
Acer	No	No	No	No	No	No	Yes	No
Atos Origin	No	No	No	No	Yes	Yes	Yes	Yes
Bausch & Lomb	No	Yes	Yes	No	No	No	No	No
Brother Industries	Yes	Yes	No	No	No	No	No	No
Coca-Cola	Yes	Yes	Yes	Yes	Yes	Yes	Yes	Yes

EXHIBIT 11.11 (cont.)

TOP	I	II	III	IV	V	VI	VII	VIII
Dow Chemical	No	No	No	No	No	No	Yes	Yes
Federal Express	Yes	No	No	No	No	No	No	No
General Electric	No	No	No	No	No	Yes	Yes	Yes
IBM	No	No	Yes	Yes	No	No	No	No
John Hancock	No	No	Yes	Yes	Yes	No	No	No
Johnson & Johnson	No	No	No	No	No	Yes	No	No
Kodak	Yes	Yes	Yes	Yes	Yes	Yes	No	No
Lenovo	No	No	No	No	No	Yes	No	No
Manulife	No	No	No	No	No	Yes	No	No
Mars	No	Yes	No	No	No	No	No	No
McDonald's	No	No	No	Yes	Yes	Yes	Yes	Yes
Omega	No	No	No	No	Yes	Yes	Yes	Yes
Panasonic	Yes	Yes	Yes	Yes	Yes	Yes	Yes	Yes
Phillips	Yes	Yes	No	No	No	No	No	No
Proctor & Gamble	No	No	No	No	No	No	Yes	Yes
Ricoh	No	Yes	No	No	No	No	No	No
Samsung	No	No	No	Yes	Yes	Yes	Yes	Yes
Sema	No	No	No	No	Yes	No	No	No
Time/Sports Illustrated	Yes	Yes	Yes	Yes	Yes	No	No	No
US Postal Service	No	Yes	Yes	Yes	No	No	No	No
Visa	Yes	Yes	Yes	Yes	Yes	Yes	Yes	Yes
Xerox	No	No	Yes	Yes	Yes	No	No	No

EXHIBIT 11.11 The Olympic Program (TOP) of the IOC

Source: www.olympic.org/Documents/IOC_Marketing/OLYMPIC_MARKETING_FACT_%20FILE_2014.pdf; http://olympicstudies.uab.es/lec/pdf/puig.pdf

Only three companies have been a TOP member in all eight cycles of the program's history: Coca-Cola, Panasonic, and Visa. There has been much change in the company membership of TOP, with many adds and drops over the cycles. Seven companies lasted only one cycle before exiting, namely Acer, Federal Express, Johnson & Johnson, Lenovo, Mars, Ricoh, and Sema. Another five companies exited after two cycles: 3M, Bausch & Lomb, Brother Industries, IBM, and Philips.

One experienced Olympic sponsor executive – David D'Alessandro of John Hancock – would argue that there is much pressure for companies to continue with high-cost programs. Part of his argument was that even more companies might have exited TOP if the decision to continue was based on ROI rather than also being influenced by corporate politics. In an interview, he stated:

> If you've got six to eight years invested in it ... that's $300 million to $400 million invested in [Olympic Sponsorship], including advertising. So I'm going to drop it? Really? If a company drops a sponsorship, that guy who pushed it is dead: a dead man walking inside the company. What am I supposed to do? ... Say "I" made a mistake? You stick it out.[28]

Some sponsors use "independent" agencies to give feedback on the effectiveness of their programs to reduce any in-house biases in favor of continuing existing programs.

11.9 SUMMARY

Sponsorships come in all shapes and sizes. Appendix 11A highlights much of this diversity. Companies have many different objectives when investing in sponsorship deals. One important common denominator, however, is the strategy of the sponsor seeking to promote its objectives by building an engaging association with the attributes of the sponsee. There is a growing sophistication in all three of the areas of pre-sponsorship decision analysis, activation, and post-sponsorship evaluation and measurement. Moreover, the growing use of digital tools in activation is helping progress in the challenging area of building reliable evidence about the link between sponsorship investments and the desired decisions by the sponsorship targets and their outcomes.

APPENDIX 11A EXAMPLES OF SPONSORSHIP DEALS AS ANNOUNCED IN *SPORTS PRO*

Sports Pro is a leading sports business magazine. It is published in London and covers in a substantive way all major sports around the globe. Each issue reports a "Directory of sponsorship deals." Information on amounts/life of deals is sometimes based on official announcements, while other cases feature estimates based on a diversity of reports.

Sport	Sponsor	Sponsor agreement	Country of sponsor	Total contract ($M)	Years of Contract	Avg. Annual Contract ($M)
Soccer	Adidas (apparel)	Global licensing deal with Manchester United (EPL)	UK	1,280	10	128
Olympics	Toyota (automotive)	TOP tier sponsor for IOC	Global	835	9	92.78
Soccer	Yokohama Rubber Co. (tires)	Shirt sponsor on front of jersey for Chelsea (EPL)	UK	300	5	60
Olympics	Bridgestone (industrial)	TOP Worldwide partnership with IOC	Japan	350	10	35
Football	Dr. Pepper (beverage)	Presenting sponsor for "climatic game" of College Football Playoff Series (CFP)	USA	210	6	35
Basketball	BBVA (financial services)	Official bank of the NBA	USA	120	4	30
Soccer	Emirates (airline)	Shirt and training kit sponsor of AC Milan (Serie A)	Italy	125	5	25
Olympics	Canon (technology)	Tokyo 2020 Olympics	Japan	128	6	21.3
Soccer	Nike (apparel)	Kit sponsor of Chinese national soccer team	China	176	11	16
Motorsports/ Formula 1	Martini (beverage)	Naming rights to Williams Martini Racing	Global	75	5	15
Motorsports/ Formula 1	Unilever (consumer)	Rexona brand on Williams Formula 1 cars and media platforms	Global	30	2	15
Motorsports/ NASCAR	Miller Lite (beverage)	Primary sponsor of Brad Keselowski/Penske Racing for 24 races	USA	48	4	12
MMA	Reebok (apparel)	Exclusive uniform deal with UFC	USA	70	6	11.67
Soccer	Caixa (financial services)	Shirt sponsor of Corinthians	Brazil	10.4	1	10.4
Motorsports/ IndyCar	Verizon (telecom)	Naming rights to IndyCar racing series	North America	100	10	10
Soccer	Heineken (beverage)	Beer partner of MLS	USA	40	4	10
Cycling	Orica (industrial)	Naming rights for Orica-Green Edge cycling team	Global	18	2	9
Australian rules football	BetEasy (betting)	Official betting partner of AFL	Australia	42.5	5	8.5
Soccer	Under Armour (apparel)	Kit sponsor of Sao Paulo (Serie A)	Brazil	41.2	5	8.24
Motorsports/ Formula 1	Pirelli (industrial)	Title sponsor of Spanish and Hungarian F1 Grand Prix Title	Spain/Hungary	8	1	8
Soccer	Microsoft (technology)	Strategic technology partner of Real Madrid	Spain	30	4	7.5
Football	M&T Bank (financial services)	Stadium naming rights for Baltimore Ravens (NFL)	USA	60	10	6
Boxing	Tecate (beverage)	Official beer of Mayweather–Pacquiao boxing match	USA	6	1	6

Sport	Sponsor	Description	Country			
Soccer	Commerzbank (financial services)	Stadium naming rights of Frankfurt/Bundesliga	Germany	27	5	5.4
Basketball	Turkish Airlines (airlines)	Title sponsor of Euroleague	Europe	26.8	5	5.36
College	Adidas (apparel)	Apparel and footwear sponsor of Arizona State University teams/athletes	USA	33.8	8	4.225
Cricket	Usha International (consumer)	Shirt sponsor on front of jersey of Mumbai Indians (IPL)	India	6	2	3
Motorsports/NASCAR	Snap Fitness (apparel)	Five race car sponsor of driver (Landon Cassill)	USA	2.5	1	2.5
Soccer	Avaya (technology)	Stadium naming rights of San Jose Earthquakes (MLS)	USA	20	10	2
Gaelic Sports	AIB Bank (financial services)	Banking sponsor of Gaelic Athletic Association	Northern Ireland	5.1	3	1.7
Soccer	MTN (telecom)	Sponsor of Zambian national soccer team	Zambia	3	2	1.5
Golf	Barracuda Networks (technology)	Title sponsor of Reno-Tahoe Open on PGA Tour	USA	4	4	1
Soccer	NRMA Insurance (insurance)	Shirt sponsor of Sydney Wanderers (A-League)	Australia	3.4	4	0.85
Rugby Union	Kingspan Group (industrial)	Naming rights to Ravenhill Stadium of Ulster Rugby	Ireland	8.4	10	0.84
Australian rules football	Virgin Australia (airline)	Shirt sponsor of Greater Western Sydney Giants (AFL)	Australia	3.8	5	0.76
Soccer	Opel (automotive)	Second-tier sponsor for SC Freiburg (Bundesliga)	Germany	1.36	2	0.68
Soccer	Deutsche Post (postal)	Second-tier sponsor for FC Koln (Bundesliga)	Germany	1.43	2.5	0.572
Motorsports/NASCAR	KFC (food)	One race sponsor (Daytona 500) of driver (David Ragan)	USA	0.4	1	0.4
Rugby league	Lumo Energy (energy)	Branding on "back of the playing shorts" of Melbourne Storm (NRL)	Australia	0.98	3	0.33
Field hockey	Kyocera (technology)	Shirt sponsor of German men's and women's national field hockey teams with German Hockey Association	Germany	0.115	1	0.115
Motorsports/track series	Hyundai Construction (industrial)	Title sponsor of Atlanta Motor Speedway Camping World Truck Series event	USA	0.1	1	0.1
Swimming	Yakult (beverage)	Healthy drink partner of Singapore Swimming Association	Singapore	0.26	3	0.087

NOTES

1 Estimated by sponsorship agency IEG.

2 PwC Sports Outlook, *At the Gate and Beyond: Outlook for the Sports Market in North America through 2018* (October, 2014)

3 The Canadian Sponsorship Landscape Study (CSLS, 2014)

4 International Olympic Committee, *Factsheet IOC Financial Summary Update* (July 2014)

5 International Olympic Committee, *Factsheet*.

6 IEG, *IEG Sponsorship Report*, April 6, 2015.

7 IEG, *IEG Sponsorship Report*, May 19, 2014..

8 "Major League Baseball franchise valuations," Bloomberg, October 23, 2013, www.bloomberg.com/infographics/2013-10-23/mlb-team-values.html.

9 Presentation by M. Robichaud, "Unleashing the passion: sports marketing in a changing world," Business of Sports Summit, Sydney, Australia, March 2015.

10 P. Kelso, "Emirates ends FIFA World Cup sponsorship," Sky News, November 3, 2014.

11 O. Gibson, "Scandal-hit FIFA lose three more major sponsors," *The Guardian*, January 23, 2015.

12 C. Weeks, "Olympic athletes urged to cut ties with sponsors like McDonald's and Coke," *The Globe and Mail*, February 21, 2014.

13 www.vaishwords.com/2013/06/open-letter-to-indra-nooyi-chairman-and.html.

14 "Pepsi threatens to withdraw sponsorship if IPL mess not cleaned up," *Rediff Cricket*, November 12, 2013.

15 D. Cushnan and E. Connally (eds.), *Black Book 2014: Formula One Racing: The Independent Business Companion to the Formula One Industry* (Sports Pro Media, 2014).

16 R. Gillis and J. Clegg, "Ferrari scraps barcode logo," *The Wall Street Journal*, May 9, 2010.

17 www.graphicology.com/blog/2010/4/28/292-the-sneakiest-design-ever.html.

18 www.formula1blog.com/f1-news/ferrari-lights-up-a-response-to-marlboro-ad-attacks.

19 K. Collantine, "Ferrari drops 'Marlboro' from official team name," F1Fanatic, July 8, 2011.

20 D. Molinari, "Johnstown named first 'Kraft Hockeyville, USA,'" *Pittsburgh Post-Gazette*, May 2, 2015.

21 IEG, *IEG Sponsorship Report*, March 31, 2014; N. O'Reilly, E. Beselt, and A. DeGrasse, *8th Annual Canadian Sponsorship Landscape Study* (2014).

22 N. O'Reilly and D.Lafrance Horning, "Leveraging sponsorship: the activation ratio," *Sports Management Review*, 16(4) (2014): 424–37.

23 www.joycejulius.com/inbroadcasttelevision.html.

24 Summary information from "Which of the following is an official sponsor of NASCAR?" *Sports Business Journal*, December 1–7, 2014.

25 "Spirit, NASCAR partnership to end after 2016 season," NASCAR.com, December 16, 2014.

26 Press release, http://racingroundup.com/nationwide-to-exit-nascar-series-sponsorship-but-stay-in-sport.

27 J. Gluck, "Xfinity ro become title sponsor of NASCAR's Nationwide Series," *USA Today*, September 3, 2014. *USA Today* reported that part of the $200 million Xfinity sponsorship was "$10 million a year in marketing Comcast was already obligated to spend through its share of a 10-year $8.2 billion TV contract (along with FOX)."

28 A.D. Madkour, "The unplugged David D'Alessandro," *Sports Business*, February 3, 2014.

12 ATHLETE SPONSORSHIP, ENDORSEMENT, AND BRANDING

A thletes are a central part of the sporting world both on the field and off. For a professional athlete, the battle on the field can attract many spectators to watch in person, and many millions to watch through any number of television and digital devices. Importantly from a business angle, this on-the-field action also can be part of a platform that enables both the athlete and potential partners to pursue their own business and other objectives. Many corporations are seeking to build their own brands and promote their financial and other interests through sponsorship/endorsement partnerships with athletes.

This chapter extends the discussion in Chapters 10 and 11 on marketing and sponsorships to explore marketing and sponsorship partnerships with athletes.

Exhibit 12.1 extends Exhibits 10.1 and 11.1 to incorporate the three major stakeholders that in most cases have roles in the planning and execution of an athlete sponsorship/endorsement partnership:

- the sponsoring company (the sponsor);
- the athlete doing the endorsement (the endorser); and
- the governing body of the athlete's sport.

This chapter also includes the related topic of player branding and the opportunities and challenges that athletes face in building their own brands. One fascinating aspect here is that athletes are also competing off the field. In their activities to build their own brands, they effectively compete with each other for the passion and mindshare of the many fans of their sport. The chapter ends with a discussion of amateur athlete endorsements.

12.1 THE LANDSCAPE OF ATHLETE ENDORSEMENTS

For a select number of elite athletes, endorsement income is a significant part of their total compensation. In Chapter 5, Exhibit 5.3 shows the percentage of endorsement earnings to total compensation

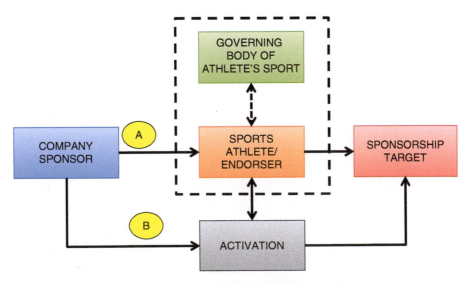

EXHIBIT 12.1 Key Stakeholders in Athlete Sponsorship/Endorsement Agreements
A: Direct sponsorship investment
B: Indirect (activation) sponsorship investment

for individual and team sports for *Forbes'* top 100 most compensated athletes in 2014. Tennis (73 percent) and golf (66 percent) have the highest percentages for sports with multiple athletes on the list. Basketball heads the team sport with the 18 NBA athletes in the Top 100, averaging 24 percent of total compensation from endorsements.[1]

Exhibit 12.2 reports the top 25 most compensated athletes from the 2014 *Forbes*. The highest compensated athlete (Floyd Mayweather) is reported by *Forbes* to have zero endorsement income. Explanations here include (a) the athlete not having any interest in seeking and delivering on contracts with companies, and (b) the athlete's past personal problems – including female assault charges and being jailed – make him an unattractive target for sponsorship. The extreme tiering of endorsement income to tournament winnings for the highest paid golf and tennis players reflect in part the high-wealth market segments that these sports attract in attendance, viewing, and purchasing behavior.

Athlete	Sport	Total earnings	Salary/winnings	Total endorsements	Percentage from endorsements
Floyd Mayweather	Boxing	$105 million	$105 million	$0	0%
Cristiano Ronaldo	Soccer	$80 million	$52 million	$28 million	35%
LeBron James	Basketball	$72.3 million	$19.3 million	$53 million	73.3%
Lionel Messi	Soccer	$64.7 million	$41.7 million	$23 million	35.5%
Kobe Bryant	Basketball	$61.5 million	$30.5 million	$31 million	50.4%
Tiger Woods	Golf	$61.2 million	$6.2 million	$55 million	89.9%
Roger Federer	Tennis	$56.2 million	$4.2 million	$52 million	92.5%
Phil Mickelson	Golf	$53.2 million	$5.2 million	$48 million	90.2%
Rafael Nadal	Tennis	$44.5 million	$14.5 million	$30 million	67.4%
Matt Ryan	Football	$43.8 million	$42 million	$1.8 million	0.04%
Manny Pacquiao	Boxing	$41.8 million	$41 million	$800k	0.02%
Zlatan Ibrahimović	Soccer	$40.4 million	$36.4 million	$4 million	9.9%
Derrick Rose	Basketball	$36.6 million	$17.6 million	$19 million	51.9%
Gareth Bale	Soccer	$36.4 million	$25.4 million	$11 million	30.2%
Radamel Falcao	Soccer	$35.4 million	$32.4 million	$3 million	8.4%
Neymar	Soccer	$33.6 million	$17.6 million	$16 million	47.6%
Novak Djokovic	Tennis	$33.1 million	$12.1 million	$21 million	63.4%
Matthew Stafford	Football	$33 million	$31.5 million	$1.5 million	4.5%
Lewis Hamilton	Auto racing	$32 million	$29 million	$3 million	9.4%
Kevin Durant	Basketball	$31.9 million	$17.9 million	$14 million	43.9%

EXHIBIT 12.2 The Top 25 Earning Athletes of 2014
Source: Forbes, www.forbes.com/lists

12.1.1 Increasing Magnitude of Athlete Endorsement

Several publicly traded companies with significant long-term contracts with athletes report the amounts of base compensation and minimum guaranteed royalty fees to their sponsored athletes. In May 2004, Nike reported this minimum to be $1,700 million. By 2014, this amount had grown to $4,704 million. Panel A of Exhibit 12.3 presents the 2014 disclosure in Nike's 10K Report. Of the $4,704 million outstanding in 2014, $1,381 million relates to obligations in years 2020 and beyond. This illustrates the long-term nature of several of Nike's large contracts with elite players.

12.1.2. Illustrative Criteria Used by Nike to Identify Potential Sponsorship Candidates

The attributes that Nike uses when evaluating the attractiveness of different athletes for sponsorship is presented in Panel B of Exhibit 12.3. Examples of current athletes with endorsement contracts with Nike include:

- **Golf:** Tiger Woods, Rory McIlroy, Michelle Wie
- **Tennis:** Serena Williams, Maria Sharapova, Eugenie Bouchard, Roger Federer, Rafael Nadal
- **Basketball:** LeBron James, Kevin Durant, Kobe Bryant, Carmelo Anthony, Chris Paul, Brittney Griner, Maya Moore
- **Soccer:** Cristiano Ronaldo, Wayne Rooney, Hope Solo

However exhaustive the due diligence, endorsement contracts have much uncertainty. There are no guarantees that the highest level of performance on the field will be sustained or that there will be no falls from the expected stellar personal behavior off the court.

12.1.3 Multiple Deliverables to Endorsing Athletes

The main areas of deliverables to an athlete in an endorsement agreement include:

1 Annual financial payment. For example, Maria Sharapova was reported in 2010 to have signed a $70 million eight-year contract with Nike.[2] This would amount to $8.75 million a year if the payment was in equal amounts. In some cases, there will be a larger upfront signing bonus with lower payments in the remaining years of the contract. Often there can be additional bonus payments for the athlete achieving major accomplishments in a specific year. Thus, Sharapova's contract could, for example, include additional payments if she achieved #1 ranking in the world or won two or more of the four major tournaments (the Australian, French, Wimbledon, and US Opens).

2 Revenue share of merchandise that carries the athletes name or brand. *Forbes* reported the 2012 US retail sales for athlete co-branded shoes by active NBA playing athletes to be LeBron James (Nike, $300 million), Kobe Bryant (Nike, $50 million), Carmelo Anthony (Jordan/Nike, $40 million), Derek Rose (Adidas, $25 million), John Wall (Reebok, $5 million), and Dwight Howard (Adidas, $5 million).[3] The percent of this revenue was not disclosed, but likely varied across athletes. Very few contracts have this revenue-sharing aspect.

Panel A: Summary of athlete endorsement: financial contracts from Nike 10-K annual report disclosures

Year	As of May 31, 2012 ($M)	As of May 31, 2013 ($M)	As of May 31, 2014 ($M)
2013	856	—	—
2014	804	909	—
2015	686	790	991
2016	491	586	787
2017	363	450	672
2018	—	309	524
2019	—	—	349
Thereafter	628	559	1,381
Total	**3,828**	**3,603**	**4,704**

Note: The amounts listed for endorsement contracts represent approximate amounts of base compensation and minimum guaranteed royalty fees Nike is obligated to pay athlete and sport team endorsers for use of its products. Actual payments under some contracts may be higher than the amounts listed, as these contracts provide for bonuses to be paid to the endorsers based upon athletic achievements and/or royalties on product sales in future periods. Actual payments under some contracts may also be lower as these contracts include provisions for reduced payments if athletic performance declines in future periods (2014 10-K Annual Report, p. 36).

Panel B: Excerpts from Nike's athlete endorsement strategy

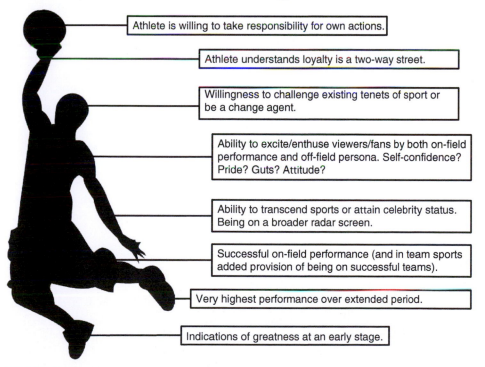

EXHIBIT 12.3 Nike Athlete Endorsements Summary
Source: Adapted from Nike public documents

3   Appearance money. Some endorsement contracts include specified amounts for the athletes to appear at designated events.
4   Apparel and equipment. A standard clause in the case of sports equipment, shoe, and apparel sponsors is the provision of "in-kind" merchandise from the sponsor.
5   Support "while on the road" at tournaments. For example, Nike rents out a "rest house" near the Wimbledon tennis grounds where Sharapova and other Nike athletes can rest in comfort and seclusion before and after matches.

Many athletes with endorsement contracts receive only apparel and equipment. Promising young athletes are often provided "free" apparel and equipment by manufacturers, typically before a formal contractual relationship has been signed.

12.2 SPONSOR DECISION MAKING

Exhibit 12.1 shows the company sponsor as one of the three key stakeholders in an endorsement agreement along with the athlete and the governing body of the athlete's sport. "Company" in the following discussion is a generic term for the "party" that pays the athlete. In most cases, the payer is a commercial company such as Nike, Under Armour, or Gatorade. However, it could also be a government body or a not-for-profit. For example, Dale Earnhardt Jr. and his racing team in NASCAR received a large part of the $32 million the National Guard spent on Sprint Cup sponsorship in 2014.[4]

The athlete endorsement decision by a sponsor is one of balancing the potential benefits with the potential risks. Aspects of both are now examined.

12.2.1 Potential Benefits to Sponsor

The potential benefits to the sponsor of using athlete endorsements include the following:

■   Athlete endorsements have the ability to drive corporate revenues by attracting sales from people who positively identify with the chosen athlete. Box 10.4 (Chapter 10) illustrates how David Beckham has generated major jersey sales at multiple soccer clubs in England, Spain, the US, Italy, and France. At the local level, businesses (e.g., car dealerships, insurance companies, local restaurants, etc.) may sponsor a hometown athlete in their city to endorse their product because potential customers will better identify and be drawn to that product because of their local sports hero's association with it.
■   Athlete endorsements have an advertising aspect, especially for star athletes with strong brands and high brand equity. For example, in 1995, Salton Inc. used boxer George Foreman as a spokesperson for their electric grill of the time, called the "Lean, Mean, Fat-Reducing Grilling Machine." It leveraged the strong following that Foreman had at the time for his larger-than-life personality and ability to box at a high level into his 40s. Foreman's endorsement of the grill helped build the Salton brand into one of the most recognizable in the grilling market and, by 1998, Salton had sold $200 million worth of the grills.[5]

■ The endorsement of the right athlete can allow a corporation to reinforce or reposition their brand by transferring images from the selected athlete to their brand. Since some athletes have very clear and established images in people's minds, this can be more pronounced than the image transfer from a league or club that is often less sharp. Box 12.1 illustrates how Maria Sharapova has chosen multiple corporate partners that align well with her brand attributes of high performance, style, fashion, and visual attractiveness.

BOX 12.1 MARIA SHARAPOVA NEGOTIATES TO SHARE IN THE UPSIDE OF HER ENDORSEMENT DEALS

Tennis player Maria Sharapova is one of the most followed athletes on the planet. She possesses key attributes that sponsors typically seek, including top on-court performance, charisma, good looks, and a willingness to spend time in front of fans and clients of sponsors. Her sponsors include Nike, Porsche, Samsung, Avon, and Tag Heuer. The CEO of Porsche stated that "Maria is the perfect choice. Her profile and charisma are an ideal fit for Porsche."[6]

For the year 2014, *Forbes* reported that Sharapova had endorsement revenues of more than $22 million. Her career endorsement earnings are estimated to be in excess of $100 million. In 2015, Repucom reported that Sharapova had the highest awareness of any women athlete in the global sample used for its "Celebrity DBI powered by Repucom." The next two female athletes were Serena Williams and Danica Patrick.

Nike is Sharapova's longest-standing corporate partner. Nike started the relationship with the provision of equipment and apparel when as a young teenager she had been identified as a talented junior athlete. The growing dimension of this relationship illustrates the ability of both parties to work and benefit together.

For the very elite, high brand value athletes, Nike has four basic stages of an evolving relationship:

■ Stage One: Provision of apparel and equipment + relationship-building.
■ Stage Two: Stage One deliverables + support at tournaments + continued relationship-building.
■ Stage Three: Stage Two deliverables and a financial agreement, typically over multiple years + focused relationship maintenance.
■ Stage Four: Stage Three deliverables, a revenue-sharing agreement on targeted products + focused and deep relationship maintenance.

Very few athletes reach Stage Three and have multiple contracts over an extended period. In the case of very select athletes, Nike is prepared to move to Stage Four.

In January 2010, it was reported that Sharapova had signed a new $70 million eight-year contract with Nike. Included in this contract was an agreement relating to a line of dresses designed by Sharapova. Her agent at IMG Tennis, Max Eisenbud, was reported as saying Sharapova might drop some of her nine endorsements "in favor of agreements that give her a percentage of sales. She already has an equity agreement in place with Cole Haan, a Nike subsidiary and US clothing, shoe, handbag and accessory designer."[7]

A high-profile extension of Sharapova's shift to an equity-sharing sponsorship model leveraging her brand is the Sugarpova candy line. This brand was launched in 2012 and has sold in more than 30 countries.[8] Part of her time commitments around tennis tournaments now include promotions at retail outlets where the candy is sold.

Observers view the relationship between Sharapova and her IMG agent as one of the most productive ones in the sports world. Sharapova commented: "Max is half family, half agent. He has been with me and believed in me from the beginning. I can be guarded around new people, but with Max, because of our history, there is a special level of trust."[9] Eisenbud singles out Sharapova's 2004 Wimbledon win over the heavily favored Serena Williams as catapulting the then 17-year-old girl onto the global awareness stage, including being on the cover of *Sports Illustrated*.

Box 12.2 describes how sponsors of Ricky Ponting, the highly successful Australian cricket captain, sought to align with his brand attributes of winning, high-quality performance, reliability, and leadership.

BOX 12.2 SWISSE WELLNESS LEVERAGES BRAND AMBASSADORS FROM THE SPORTING AND ENTERTAINMENT WORLDS IN A "360 DEGREE MARKETING STRATEGY"

Ricky Ponting was captain of the Australian cricket team from 2004 to 2011, during which time both the team and he achieved much international success. He is one of the most recognized and respected sportsmen in all countries where cricket is played. Both during his playing career and afterwards he has attracted sponsorship from multiple companies. For example, in 2003, CricketNext announced that Ponting would become its brand ambassador until the end of the Cricket World Cup in 2007. It stated: "Ricky Ponting was an effortless choice for us as a Brand Ambassador – a dynamic, dashing and daring player. We believe both Ricky Ponting and CricketNext are a manifestation of one unique brand property – a winner's spirit."[10] In 2013, Valvoline announced Ponting as their ambassador. It stated: "Valvoline today stands for superb performance and reliability. Ricky Ponting epitomizes the Valvoline brand's ideology of high performance, reliability and leadership."[11]

In 2006, Ponting became the first brand ambassador for Swisse Wellness, which markets vitamins, minerals, and supplements. A key theme of the Swisse Wellness message is "making people healthier and happier." Panel A of Exhibit 12.4 presents the Swisse Wellness "360 Degree Marketing Model." Ambassadors are an important part of this marketing model. These ambassadors include:

- Sporting athletes Ricky Ponting (former Australian cricket captain); Liz Cambage (former Australian basketball player/Olympic medalist); John Eales (former Australian rugby union captain); Tom Harley (former Australian rules football captain/television commentator)
- Nicole Kidman (internationally acclaimed Australian actor)
- Karen Martini (television presenter and writer)
- Timomatic (singer-songwriter and dancer)
- Ash Hart (model and yoga teacher)

Panel A: 360-degree marketing model

Marketing model highlights

1. Exclusive retailer promotions – promoting their brand via TV advertising, and creating campaigns that align with thier brand/shoppers

2. Strong marketing activity leads to increased number of SKUs on shelf

3. Increased shelf space and new product innovation to drive growth

4. Two waves of new product development per year

5. Discounting strategy

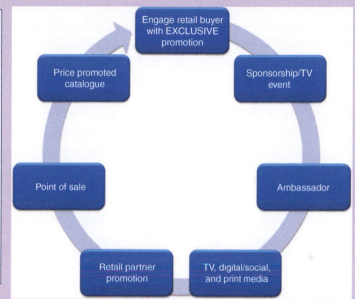

Panel B: Ricky Ponting in Swisse Wellness commercial

EXHIBIT 12.4 Swisse Wellness Example
Source: Swisse Wellness Internal Document

Panel B of Exhibit 12.4 is taken from a Swisse television commercial where Ponting is playing golf (he has a +1 handicap) and showcasing the benefits of a healthy lifestyle. The advertisement is one of five advertisements that are integrated into a campaign that also includes a suite of digital, point-of-sale, and print assets. Ponting is shown hitting a superb drive and then stating: "I retired from international cricket, but I still have that competitive drive. For the energy I need to perform I take Swisse Men's Ultivite every day."

A corporation can involve an endorsing athlete into its product development process and share that involvement externally. Endorsers of products related to on-field performance – including equipment, nutrition, recovery and medical – can have the athlete test or use the product in their training or competition. They can share the story with fans or sport participants to showcase how that product is working for and was developed with input from a star athlete they follow and respect. Gatorade promoted the involvement of top athletes – such as Sidney Crosby in ice hockey, Georges St-Pierre in mixed martial arts, and Derek Jeter in baseball– as part of their scientific process to better the impact of their sports drink.

An athlete endorser can support the corporation's ability to target other athletes in the same sport to use their products by leveraging the existing athlete in marketing efforts. For example, Wilson uses Roger Federer to endorse its tennis racquets. This provides players of all levels with more confidence and a feeling of attachment to Federer when they purchase a tennis racquet he has endorsed. From the perspective of the athlete, a young basketball player that strives to play professionally may look at the products that their favorite players use and think that since the athletes that they strive to be like use that product, they can become more like them if they use it as well.

Endorsement of commercial sporting goods brands can add significant credibility to the product. Top athletes are opinion leaders and people practicing the sport look up to them to decide what the best performing sports gear is. Use by an athlete can allow that company to break through the clutter and send a clear message about some product feature that is important to the target market. For example, Rickie Fowler, sponsored by Titleist, is one of the young exciting golfers on the PGA Tour. In 2010 he was named PGA Tour Rookie of the Year. Titleist provides full details of Fowler's golf equipment such as his chosen drivers, irons, wedges, putter, and balls. Young players starting golf in a serious way are much more likely to associate with Rickie Fowler than with many older PGA players, so Titleist is able to better market to the new generation of youth golf players by showcasing in its advertisements and promotional material its endorsement by Rickie Fowler.

Endorsement of global star athletes allows sponsors to reach markets globally. Global athletes such as Roger Federer, Lewis Hamilton, or Lionel Messi offer powerful global platforms due to the passion of their follower base in many countries. Yao Ming, the Chinese and Houston Rockets basketball player, was well known in many countries due to his basketball skills, height, and joyful persona. McDonald's used Yao in the 2000s as a key part of many advertisements that had a strong humor element. The global chief marketing officer of McDonald's stated: "Yao Ming personifies what the McDonald's brand is all about – a youthful, fun, dynamic spirit which connects to today's customers and cultures." Yao was a central part of advertisements in McDonald's "I'm lovin' it" campaign. For the 2004 All-Star Game balloting, Yao was #1 on visits from outside the US to the NBA websites, with more than half the total visits.[12] With the Rockets NBA games attracting large television audiences, other players on the team benefited from their association with Yao. Players such as Shane Battier and Luis Scola became well known in China and were able to make multiple visits to the country and endorse Chinese products. The expression "the Yao Ming bonus" was used to refer to players riding on Yao's coat-tails to make their own endorsement deals outside the US.[13]

12.2.2 Potential Risks to Sponsor

The risks to the sponsor of using athlete endorsements from the side of the athlete include:

■ **Decrease in ability to perform.** Research on the effect of age on the hitting ability of baseball players documents a significant drop off in hitting ability as the player ages beyond 30 years.[14]

Companies sponsoring star baseball players older than 30 have a much higher performance risk than when sponsoring a 25 year old hitting "phenom."

- **Reduced passion.** The athlete is no longer fully committed to the hours and mindshare required to stay at the elite level.
- **Injury risk.** Athletes can sustain serious playing related risks during actual games or in practice sessions. Players with a history of past injuries have a high likelihood of not playing most games in a season. Reduced playing time means the athlete is a less attractive endorser if a major part of the sponsor's target audience is fueled by the player's stellar on-field performances. Injury risk can also occur in the athlete's non-sport-related playing or training. Some playing/endorsement contracts have restrictions on the activities that the athletes/endorser can engage in their "summer," when leagues are not playing. Downhill skiing, water-skiing and bungee jumping are examples of non-permitted activities in some contracts. One related area of injury risk is the normal day-to-day risks people face in their regular lives – such as a car accident or cutting their hand on broken glass.
- **Off-the-field "bad" behavior.** Many examples from actual athletes are well documented and can be considered in deciding the risk profile of the athlete being evaluated. A high-profile example from player contracting is MLB's Josh Hamilton. As a Tampa Bay Rays Minor League player, Hamilton was reported to have "failed at least six drug tests."[15] During his first time at the Texas Rangers he had high-quality performance on the field, but also examples of bad behavior off the field. For example, in 2009 Deadspin.com showed pictures that Hamilton admitted were authentic of him "seemingly drunk" at a bar. Hamilton openly admitted he struggled greatly with alcohol problems. He commented that: "Obviously I eat at restaurants that have bars in them … Can I have a drink? Obviously, I can't."[16] In December 2012, Hamilton signed a five-year, $125 million guaranteed contract with the Los Angeles Angels of Anaheim. The outcome was not good for the Angels, either with his on-field hitting and attitude or his staying drug- and alcohol-free. In April 2015, the Angels traded Hamilton back to the Texas Rangers, with the Angels agreeing to "pay most of the remaining $80 million Hamilton is owned under the contract, which runs through 2017."[17] The money paid by the Angels to the Texas Rangers is called "dead money" in MLB language. To make it more painful to the Angels, the Rangers compete against them in the same West Division of the MLB's American League.
- **Other risks.** Additional areas of off-the-field risk include arrests for drunken behavior or DUI, partner abuse, and carrying arms without a permit. Sports-related "bad" behavior include taking of banned steroids, targeting opposing players with intent to inflict physical harm, and "fixing" games associated with payments from gambling syndicates. Box 12.3 describes the extended use of steroids by Lance Armstrong and the rapid sponsor fallout in October 2012 when the US Anti-Doping Agency filed charges against him. Exhibit 12.5 shows the celebrity DBI chart for Armstrong described in dection 12.5.1 of this chapter.

BOX 12.3 LANCE ARMSTRONG'S FALL FROM GRACE

Stories about "athletes behaving badly" attract much media attention. However, these same stories can have severe negative impacts on the brands of the companies sponsoring that athlete. In some cases, the negative behavior by an athlete can be a sudden event, such as the arrest of an athlete for partner abuse. In other cases, there can be a long period of "question marks" hanging over an athlete's behavior. The Lance Armstrong saga has elements of both. It is also a "Greek tragedy" in that, while the ending was devastating for multiple stakeholders, it had many moments of high theater along the various stages.

Lance Armstrong was one of the most celebrated American athletes of all time. After undergoing treatment for advanced testicular cancer that spread to his brain and lungs in 1996, Armstrong went on to win seven consecutive Tour de France titles, considered one of the most physically demanding events in the world and certainly the most famous cycling event globally. Through this performance, his story, and his charismatic personality, Armstrong attracted more than an estimated $200 million in endorsements.[18] During this time, Armstrong was also heavily involved in philanthropic efforts, most notably the founding of his non-profit organization the Lance Armstrong Foundation (now known as the Livestrong Foundation), which raised more than $500 million and supported more than 2.5 million people affected by cancer.[19]

Armstrong was idolized by many for his perseverance, character, and trustworthiness during his career. However, as time went on, he was increasingly accused of using performance-enhancing drugs by teammates and various others. In each case, he aggressively denied the claims, even going as far as filing lawsuits against his accusers. In October 2012, charges were filed against Armstrong for doping and drug trafficking by the US Anti-Doping Agency (USADA). These charges and the nature of his past denials of steroid-use led to a lifetime ban from sport and forced him to step down as chairman of the Lance Armstrong Foundation. Armstrong's top sponsors all exited from their sponsorship with Armstrong after the USADA filings. Examples were: Michelob, Trek, RadioShack, 24-Hour Fitness, Nissan, Oakley and Nike.

Comments made by sponsors at several stages of their relationship with an athlete that "brings the brand into disrepute" highlight the roller-coaster nature of such a relationship. An example is Anheuser-Busch, the global brewing company. Its Michelob ULTRA product line sponsored many cycling events to promote an association between the active lifestyle positioning of the ULTRA brand with participatory cycling events and cyclists. The following three public announcements by Michelob capture the changing landscape of its relationship with Armstrong:

- October 2009: Michelob announced the signing of a "three year agreement to become the brand's new spokesman and ambassador. 'Lance Armstrong is an ideal ambassador for this brand and we are honored to have him represent Michelob ULTRA,' said the Vice-President of marketing at Anheuser-Busch. 'Having dominated a sport that requires such a physical commitment, Lance is the perfect athlete to connect with adult beer drinkers who lead active lifestyles.'"[20] As part of its activation, Armstrong appeared at multiple cycling races across the US that were sponsored by Michelob.
- August 2012: After the USDA announced preliminary moves to ban Armstrong from cycling competitions for life, the Michelob vice-president of US marketing stated: "Our partnership with Lance remains unchanged. He has inspired millions with his athletic achievement and his commitment to helping cancer survivors and their families."[21]
- October 2012: The vice-president of US marketing said: "We have decided not to renew our relationship with Lance Armstrong when our current contract expires at the end of 2012. We will continue to support the Livestrong Foundation and its cycling and running events."[22]

Nike, a sponsor of Armstrong since 1996, was more descriptive in its reasons for terminating its contract with Armstrong. It stated: "Due to the seemingly insurmountable evidence that Lance Armstrong participated in doping and misled Nike for more than a decade, it is with great sadness that we have terminated our contract with him. Nike does not condone the use of illegal performance-enhancing drugs in any manner."[23]

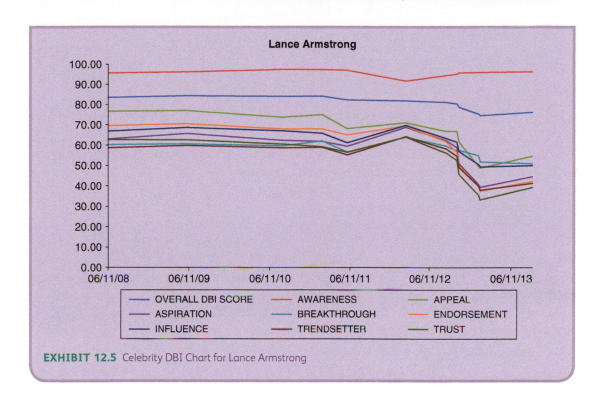

EXHIBIT 12.5 Celebrity DBI Chart for Lance Armstrong

There are also risks to the sponsor of using athlete endorsements that come from the side of the sponsor. Two examples are:

- **Change in company strategy making the sponsorship agreement less attractive.** Assume a company has a strategy focused on "final" consumers (known as a business-to-consumer (B2C) strategy) at the time the sponsorship agreement is signed. A specific athlete may be well suited to this strategy. Suppose now the company subsequently changes its strategy to focus on high-end corporate customers (called a business-to-business (B2B) strategy). In this new context, it could well be that either a different athlete is better suited to activate the B2B strategy or even that any athlete endorsement spending is not the best use of marketing investments.
- **Poor execution by the company or its agencies.** Not all companies activate their sponsorships effectively. Working productively with athletes who by their very achievements have had to be highly focused, and at times singularly focused, requires skilled and experienced people. For example, there are inappropriate as well as appropriate times to expect athletes to engage with and have their photos taken with the customers of a company. There are multiple instances of poor execution of an endorsement contract when the athlete has been placed in the wrong situation at the wrong time, with the predictable result that the athlete appears to be less than enthusiastic and supportive of the sponsoring company. Asking a NASCAR driver to have multiple photos taken with, and engage in substantive conversation with, the customers of a sponsor five minutes before the start of a race is poor execution on the sponsor side! There are multiple such examples of "self-inflicted" wounds by sponsors. Many times sponsors use agencies to help activate their sponsorships. It is imperative that these agencies understand not only the goals of the sponsor but also the appropriate protocols when working with the sponsored athletes. These protocols can vary by sport and can even differ greatly across athletes of the same sport.

Companies should both (a) be engaged in very careful risk assessment before signing a contract, and (b) then invest resources in risk monitoring and ideally risk-reducing activities with its player endorsement contracts.

12.3 ATHLETE DECISION MAKING

Exhibit 12.1 shows the athlete as a central party between the company sponsor and the sponsorship target. The first two decisions facing athletes or their agents are:

1   Is sponsorship/endorsement of interest?
2   Is sponsorship/endorsement highly unlikely even if of interest?

As noted with Floyd Mayweather being #1 listed in Exhibit 12.2, it is likely that he either had little interest in sponsorship deals or his own personal life had multiple red flags for potential sponsors. The leverageable assets and inherited liabilities framework used elsewhere in this book can assist the athlete understand the context of any possible negotiations. It can also provide directions that the athlete should take if the agenda is to become more attractive to companies leveraging their marketing via athlete endorsements.

12.3.1 Athlete On-Field Attributes

Performance Success

The main dimension (leverageable asset) for the endorsement value of most athletes is superior on-field performance. For example, Kevin Durant of Oklahoma City Thunder is one of the best players in the NBA. He is a relatively young/new star and won the 2014 NBA MVP. But he plays in the small-market Oklahoma City, where endorsement opportunities are more restricted than in cities such as New York and Chicago. However, due to his on court success, likeability, and league-wide following, he is among the highest paid athletes from endorsements in the NBA. Nike, for example, signed Durant to a deal in 2014 that could reach $30 million a year.[24] Interesting exceptions happen to this criterion. David Beckham, an England national team player, was never a FIFA Gold Boot or among the very top players of his generation, yet he outperformed in other dimensions to become one of the most highly marketable athletes ever. Box 10.4 in Chapter 10 outlines Beckham's impact on shirt sales at successive soccer clubs he played with over his career.

Potential for Future Success

Potential is a reason why many companies are looking to sponsor an athlete before they become a major star. This could mean entering into a contract with the athlete before they play professionally or prior to a major event (e.g., Olympic Games) where they might succeed. While signing an athlete to a lucrative contract before they play a professional game can be risky, the cost of signing a fast-rising star to a long-term endorsement contract can increase exponentially as promise is converted to high-profile success. For example, Andrew Wiggins, the first overall pick in the 2014 NBA draft, signed a shoe deal with Adidas for a reported $10–12 million five-year contract before playing in his first professional game.[25] The objective here is not as much the current value of the endorsement as the value the player will have if he or she becomes a star. Apparel companies are known to track young tennis and golf players even before their teenage years with the aim to build early associations that can later be converted to higher levels of loyalty from the athlete. In the early years it will be "free" equipment that will be provided and sometimes hospitality at major tournaments where the young athletes can meet their idols.

The absence of expected superior on-field performance is very much an inherited liability when a player/agent is negotiating a potential endorsement contract. An aging athlete with rapidly declining performance is not in the strongest bargaining situation with a potential sponsor.

Sport Specificity

Certain sports hold more weight/leveragability in terms of television exposure, visibility of the athletes' faces, interaction with the media, and global reach. For example, successful athletes in individual, global sports can potentially earn more endorsement money than those in team sports. These athletes receive more exposure and camera-time than do athletes in team sports. Golf and tennis here are "gold" endorsement properties. Tiger Woods, Roger Federer, Phil Mickelson, and Rafael Nadal are all in the top ten most highly compensated athletes in the 2014 rankings in Exhibit 12.2. Basketball showcases its athletes better than most other team sports, as there are only two teams of five players on a court, and no helmets to obstruct viewers seeing the emotions of players during the game. In contrast, ice hockey athletes from the NHL come with the inherited liability of broadcasts of their events rarely showing the faces of individual athletes during a game.

Playing Style

While on-field success is a big indicator of marketability, the manner in which athletes achieve this success may also be a major contributor to their value as an endorser. Specifically, players who are more noticeable because of their position or style are more likely to draw increased attention and exposure. Different styles can attract different sponsors. A classic example is Roger Federer and his smooth style and polished personality that luxury sponsors (e.g., Rolex) value. In contrast, Rafael Nadal's more aggressive style is a better fit for brands speaking to a younger audience.

12.3.2 Athlete Off-Field Attributes

Athlete's Character – Role Model versus Track Record of Problems

The character of an athlete is a pivotal factor in endorsement decisions. Several high-profile instances of highly endorsed athletes having large "falls from grace" have heightened sponsor due diligence in this area. Discussed elsewhere in this chapter are the sagas of Tiger Woods (Section 12.5.3) and Lance Armstrong (Box 12.3). Some athletes have strong track records that give sponsors high levels of confidence that any downsides due to personal problems are minimal. An example is Peyton Manning of the NFL. Over many years, his on-field success, self-effacing mannerisms, and highly publicized community service efforts have made him one of the highest paid endorsers of products.

Personality

Because top athletes are often seen as role models and even heroes, many fans want to know about their personal lives and feel a connection to them beyond just what they see on the field. Chapter 14 provides examples of athletes using social media to develop large followings by fans who seek to have emotional connections with them.

Physical Attractiveness

Physical attractiveness is a controversial yet important characteristic when it comes to athlete endorsements. Often considered with female athletes (e.g., Danica Patrick in motor sports and Maria Sharapova in tennis), the attractiveness factor is also evident in male athletes (e.g., Tom Brady in football, David Beckham in soccer). Physical attractiveness is a consideration for many potential endorsers as it can convey attributes such as elegance, sexiness, and toughness to their brand(s). Anna Kournikova in tennis is a classic example of leveraging this trait. While her on-court performance never put her in the top tier of tennis players, her attractiveness and personality gave her enlarged capacity to attract endorsements, media interest, and a large fan following.[26]

Unique Attributes

Sometimes an athlete can leverage a unique attribute that they have, either physically or socially, in a way that drives sponsors to them. For example, Troy Polamalu, a safety for the Pittsburgh Steelers of the NFL, is known for his massive head of hair. While defensive players in the NFL typically aren't big sponsor targets, Polamalu leveraged this physical trait into a lucrative endorsement deal with Procter & Gamble's haircare brand Head & Shoulders. Through the endorsement of Head & Shoulders, Polamalu appears in commercials claiming that he uses Head & Shoulders because it is "formulated to give you thicker looking hair in one week,"[27] a claim that his hair fully embodies in a way that not many other public figures can.

12.3.3 Other Factors

Multiple other factors also will influence the sponsors decision over and above the athlete's own on-the-field and off-the field attributes.

Being on a Winning Team

For team sports, the best combination for an athlete is to perform well individually and also for the team to be a winning one. Winning teams attract more media coverage and often more national broadcasts of their games. In leagues with extended playoff series, such as the NBA and NHL, being an athlete on a championship-winning team can mean continued playing time well beyond the regular season into the playoffs, when the media ratings and excitement are highest. Both the NBA and NHL have four-round playoff series, with up to seven games per series. Athletes that bring championship rings to sponsor events generate much extra positive feeling and vibe at those events.

Track Record of Athletes from League

The media gives much coverage to players that have off-field problems such as drunk driving, partner abuse, and illegal use of firearms. Over time, narratives are created (rightly or wrongly) that some leagues have a higher likelihood of such problems than others. For example, the NFL is portrayed as having a higher risk of off-field player behavior problems than does then NHL. The result is that sponsors may be extra cautious about signing a long-term sponsorship with an NFL athlete because of general negative press at the league level, irrespective of the character of the individual athlete.

Market Size and Influence

The market in which the athlete plays and is known also has a major impact on endorsement possibilities. Consider Cristiano Ronaldo, winner of multiple awards such as FIFA World Player of the Year and UEFA Best Player in Europe. His senior soccer career started with Sporting CP in the Portuguese Football League. Sporting CP was a strong #3 club in that league, but of lower stature than the two leading clubs of Benfica and FC Porto. *Deloitte* in 2014 ranked the Portuguese league ninth in Europe in teams of total revenues (€285 million in revenues in 2012/13). In contrast, the English Premier League was #1 (€2,946 million in revenues), the German Bundesliga #2 (€2,018 million), and the Spanish La Liga #3 (€1,859 million). Ronaldo lasted one season at Sporting CP before transferring to Manchester United in the EPL. The EPL was more than ten times the size of the Portuguese league and had global distribution of games. The EPL provided a platform for Ronaldo to compete at the very highest level and attract multiple high-value endorsements from global companies. In 2009, Ronaldo transferred to Real Madrid, one of the top three clubs in the world, playing in the #3 league. Had Ronaldo stayed playing in the Portuguese league, his global stature and endorsement income likely would have been much less than it became by playing for two of the three biggest clubs in the world in two of the three largest soccer leagues in the world. One newspaper referred to Ronaldo as the "£26.5 million walking billboard" with endorsements with major global companies such as Nike, Samsung, and Emirates.[28]

In some cases athletes with "baggage" may accept sponsorships that in the short run provide compensation, but in the longer run add to their "baggage." Consider disgraced Canadian 100m sprinter Ben Johnson, who was stripped of his Olympic Gold medal and world record following a positive test for steroids in 1988. Johnson later endorsed an energy drink called Cheetah. In advertisements, Johnson stated "I Cheetah all the time," reminding viewers of his cheating as an athlete.[29] Clearly, the athlete needs to be smart and think about more than just the payment amount available in the short run.

12.3.4 The World's Most Marketable Athletes – a Look into the Future by *Sports Pro*

Each year since 2010 *Sports Pro* has published a list of the world's 50 most marketable athletes. *Sports Pro* is a leading sports business magazine. It is published in London and covers in a substantive way all major sports around the globe. The focus of this list is marketing potential over a three-year period, looking ahead. The criteria used for inclusion include:

1   Value for money
2   Age
3   Home market
4   Charisma
5   Willingness to be marketed
6   Crossover appeal

The editorial people who develop the list noted that "putting the list together is an exercise in assessment and projection, balancing objective reasoning with subjective intuition." A key factor in their ranking was value for money, which meant that there is a bias against including established elite athletes who they perceive as already having endorsement contracts that are "fully priced."

Exhibit 12.6 shows the list of the top ten athletes from the 2012 to 2015 June editions of *Sports Pro*.

Focusing on the top ten athletes listed each year from 2010, the composition of the 60 listings is:

Rank	Sport	Number of listings	Rank	Sport	Number of listings
1	Soccer	13	6	Golf	5
2	Tennis	9	7	Cricket	4
3	Basketball	8	8	Football	3
4	Athletics	7	9	Swimming	3
5	Motorsports	7	10	Boxing	1

Young athletes with early successes on the field have been included on the lists on a regular basis. These include:

Athlete	Country	Sport	Age and Year of Appearance
Missy Franklin	USA	Swimming	19 when on 2014 List
Neymar	Brazil	Soccer	20 when on 2012 List
Sloane Stephens	USA	Tennis	20 when on 2013 List
Caroline Wozniacki	Denmark	Tennis	21 when on 2011 List
Eugenie Bouchard	Canada	Tennis	21 when on 2011 List
Jordan Spieth	USA	Golf	21 when on 2015 List

There is a premium on sponsors building skills at early identification of talent that is highly marketable for attributes off the field as well as on the field. *Sports Pro* makes extra efforts to seek out these young athletes when developing their rankings.[30]

2012

Rank	Athlete	Sport	Country
1	Neymar	Soccer	Brazil
2	Rory McIlroy	Golf	Northern Ireland
3	Lionel Messi	Soccer	Argentina
4	Usain Bolt	Athletics	Jamaica
5	Cristiano Ronaldo	Soccer	Portugal
6	Blake Griffin	Basketball	USA
7	Novak Djokovic	Tennis	Serbia
8	Sebastian Vettel	Motor racing/F1	Germany
9	Tim Tebow	Football	USA
10	Yani Tseng	Golf	Taiwan

2013

Rank	Athlete	Sport	Country
1	Neymar	Soccer	Brazil
2	Lionel Messi	Soccer	Argentina
3	Rory McIlroy	Golf	Northern Ireland
4	Robert Griffin, III	Football	USA
5	Usain Bolt	Athletics	Jamaica
6	Novak Djokovic	Tennis	Serbia
7	Lewis Hamilton	Motor racing/F1	UK
8	Cristiano Ronaldo	Soccer	Portugal
9	Sloane Stephens	Tennis	USA
10	Blake Griffin	Basketball	USA

2014

Rank	Athlete	Sport	Country
1	Lewis Hamilton	Motor racing/F1	UK
2	Virat Kohli	Cricket	India
3	Robert Griffin, III	Football	USA
4	Cristiano Ronaldo	Soccer	Portugal
5	Grigor Dimitrov	Tennis	Bulgaria
6	Usain Bolt	Athletics	Jamaica
7	Neymar	Soccer	Brazil
8	Missy Franklin	Swimming	USA
9	Blake Griffin	Basketball	USA
10	Sloane Stephens	Tennis	USA

2015

Rank	Athlete	Sport	Country
1	Eugenie Bouchard	Tennis	Canada
2	Neymar	Soccer	Brazil
3	Jordan Spieth	Golf	USA
4	Missy Franklin	Swimming	USA
5	Lewis Hamilton	F1	UK
6	Virat Kohli	Cricket	India
7	Stephen Curry	Basketball	USA
8	Kei Nishikori	Tennis	Japan
9	Katarina Johnson-Thompson	Athletics	UK
10	Usain Bolt	Athletics	Jamaica

EXHIBIT 12.6 *Sports Pro* List of the World's Ten Most Marketable Athletes
Source: *Sports Pro*. The published list each year reports the world's 50 most marketable athletes

12.4 GOVERNING SPORTING BODY DECISION MAKING

The third stakeholder in Exhibit 12.1 is the governing body of the athlete's sport. This body can play several roles in what endorsement contracts are negotiated, how they are activated, and how potential conflicts are to be managed. This body can also play a positive role in guiding both players and their sponsors in how to most effectively leverage their endorsement partnership.

12.4.1 Constraints on Endorsement Contracts and their Activation

In some extreme cases, leagues may place prohibitions on individual categories of companies that athletes in their league may have partnerships with. An example in some countries is prohibitions against athletes signing endorsement contracts with gambling bodies.

In most cases, the role of the league is placing boundaries on athletes and how they and their sponsors can activate on event days. Examples include:

- **League exclusives with partners.** An extreme case is the PGA's exclusive relationship with Getty Images. Getty is the only company permitted to take photos of golf players at the elite level of golf tournaments. Companies sponsoring golf players cannot take photos of players and send them out as part of a social media campaign. Nor can spectators on the course take photos and share them with their friends. These restrictions reduce the number of exposures that player-related sponsor logos visible at the course get from being transmitted to a much larger audience.
- **League or club sponsors having exclusives over player sponsors.** For example, if Nike is the shirt sponsor of the NFL, athletes with sponsorship relationships with Adidas, Puma, and Under Armour cannot wear apparel with their own sponsor's logos during the game. Similarly, Bose is the official partner of the NFL, with the result that NFL athletes cannot wear Beats by Dre headphones on the field or in game-day interviews. The more restrictions that a league or a club places on activation, the less valuable a sponsorship relationship with an athlete in that league becomes.
- **League protocols on use of social media.** Fans typically have an insatiable appetite for player comments and humor during the game itself. However, many leagues have very tight restrictions on the use of mobile devices, say, from the 30-minute period before the game, during the whole game, and the 30-minute period after the game.

12.4.2 Conflicts Between Growing the Pie and Sharing the Pie

Difficult situations can arise when compensation from the sponsors of athletes forms a major part of athlete total compensation and conflicts with the sponsors of the governing body arise. In the case of a sporting federation, any potential conflict can create tensions. For example, the British Triathlon Association (BTA) seeks sponsors to fund its programs and activities to grow triathlon in Britain. The total sponsor pie in triathlon is relatively small and its athletes often have minimal income. The BTA must also allow its top athletes to generate their own endorsements to support their training, racing, and triathlon-related activities. For example, the Brownlee brothers (Alistair and Jonathan) are two of the leading triathletes in the world and generate interest from sponsors for themselves as well as the BTA. The BTA needs to have a national team contract that both protects their sponsors (and ability to attract sponsors) and supports (or allows enough endorsement opportunities) the Brownlees' pursuit of their own sponsors.

Sponsorship and endorsement conflicts illustrate the classic conflict between growing the business (growing the pie) versus sharing the business generated (sharing the pie) among multiple stakeholders. At one extreme, having a single sponsor at all levels (with exclusivity) has the benefit of providing clear benefits to the single sponsor. However, the challenge here is deciding how to allocate the pie between the many stakeholders such as the league, teams, and athletes. The other end of the spectrum is where there are many sponsors, each at different levels, including at the athletes' level. Here protocols have to be put in place to guide the rights of the various sponsors and how they interact with each other.

12.5 ATHLETE BRAND ATTRIBUTES AND SPONSORSHIP ENDORSEMENTS

Chapter 10 introduced several topics related to the branding of sports properties. A brand was defined as a visible symbol that has strong, favorable, and distinctive associations that differentiate it from competitors.[31] There is growing interest in identifying player brand attributes and how players can build or destroy the value of their own brands.

12.5.1 Celebrity DBI Analysis

The Celebrity Davie-Brown Index (DBI) is an "independent index that quantifies and qualifies consumer perceptions of celebrities."[32] It provides much insight into how different attributes of targeted people are perceived by a large consumer panel. It is researched by and made available by the Marketing Arm, which is a consumer engagement agency. The DBI tracks a broad range of celebrities that includes athletes as well as actors, music artists, media personalities, and business people. At relatively short intervals, information is collected about how a large consumer panel responds to questions on eight attributes of each person being analyzed. Exhibit 12.7 shows and describes the eight attributes that are aggregated into an Overall DBI Score:

1   Awareness
2   Appeal
3   Aspirations
4   Breakthrough
5   Endorsement
6   Influence
7   Trendsetter
8   Trust

While the "awareness" variable is the most heavily weighted one, the exact weights for these eight attributes in the overall DBI score are kept confidential.

The DBI analysis has several strengths for insight into the attributes that a sponsor may want to explore when considering or negotiating an endorsement contract:

1 Awareness: Indicates the percentage of people who are aware of the celebrity either by name or face. Awareness is the baseline. Are you aware of this person? Image and name provided.

2 Appeal: Measures likeability of the celebrity. How much do you like or dislike this individual? (Dislike a lot, dislike, dislike a little, like a little, like, like a lot.)

3 Aspiration: Measures the degree to which people feel the celebrity has a life to which they would aspire. This individual leads the ideal life, one that others aspire to have. (Strongly disagree, disagree, slightly disagree, slightly agree, agree, strongly agree – same categories of responses for the remaining questions as well.)

4 Breakthrough: Indicates the degree to which people take notice of the celebrity when they appear on TV, film or print. If I come across this person in the media (TV, print, radio, etc.), I tend to pay attention.

5 Endorsement: Reflects the degree to which people identify the celebrity as being an effective product spokesperson. If this celebrity endorses a product, people will be more likely to consider purchasing that product. This individual would make a good product spokesperson for the right product.

6 Influence: Measures the degree to which people believe the celebrity is an influence in today's world. This individual is influential with today's audience. Other people are interested in what this person says and does.

7 Trendsetter: Reflects opinion on the celebrity's position with regards to trends in society.This individual is a trendsetter with today's audience.

8 Trust: Indicates the level of trust that the people place in the celebrity's words and image. If we were acquainted, I would trust this individual to consider my interests. When this individual speaks, people will believe what they say.

EXHIBIT 12.7 Davie-Brown Index (DBI) Eight Attributes of Celebrities
Source: Repucom internal document

- It is a structured approach to gaining insight into multiple attributes.
- Information on individual attributes is provided so analysis can be focused on the subset of the eight variables that are most relevant.
- Analysis can be done for targeted segments of their respondents as well as looking at factors that may affect individual celebrities.

Two examples relating to athletes will be used to illustrate the insights available with the DBI – LeBron James and Tiger Woods.

Exhibit 12.8 presents DBI charts pertaining to each of these two athletes. Box 12.3 includes DBI information in the context of examining Lance Armstrong's fall from grace associated with his denial and later admission of the use of performance enhancing drugs while competing in cycling events (Exhibit 12.5).

12.5.2 Analysis of Uplift in LeBron James Brand

The Cleveland Cavaliers selected LeBron James with its first overall pick in the 2003 NBA draft. He was a standout in his Akron, Ohio high-school years and was heavily hyped. In his senior year at high school he was given a two-game suspension for violating Ohio High School Athletic Association rules by accepting gifts valued above the maximum allowed. His Ohio background was a major boost to the fan base of the Cavaliers. He played with the Cavaliers for seven seasons from 2003/4 to 2009/10. Television ratings for Cavalier games dramatically spiked upwards when James joined the club. During this time he established himself as a superstar on the court, but was self-absorbed off the court. Each year his hope of winning the NBA Finals were dashed and he was viewed as a sore loser. One example

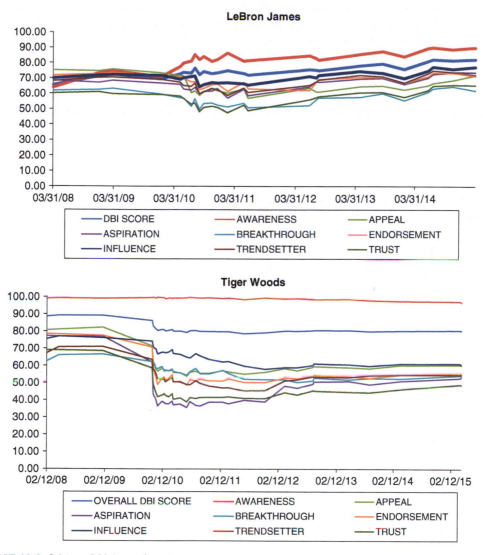

EXHIBIT 12.8 Celebrity DBI Charts for LeBron James and Tiger Woods

was in the final game of a 2009 playoff series loss when he walked off the court without shaking hands with the winning Boston Celtics. James became a free agent at the end of the 2009/10 season. In July 2010, ESPN broadcast a special called *The Decision* in which James took an eternity to announce that he was going to the Miami Heat. The program received much negative press. Retired NBA players Michael Jordan and Magic Johnson criticized James for approaching All-Stars Dwayne Wade and Chris Bosh as part of his decision making with the aim of building a Miami Heat "super team" that could win the NBA playoffs.

James' reputation when he joined Miami for the 2010/11 season was an all-star on the court but self-absorbed off the court, with a "winning is all that matters and not how you win or behave" attitude. Over his four years with Miami Heat, several positive changes occurred from a branding perspective. On the court, Miami Heat won back-to-back NBA championships in 2012 and 2013. Off the court, he engaged in more public service work and in 2013 he married his high-school girlfriend with whom he has had two sons. He also played a leading role in the National Basketball Players Association. After four years with Miami Heat, he returned to the Cleveland Cavaliers on a two-year contract.

Clearly LeBron James has matured as an individual since 2003 and has become a more marketable athlete. His chart in Exhibit 12.8 shows the DBI overall score and its eight components over the March 2008 to March 2015 period. Charts like this are available to potential sponsors on an ongoing basis. Consider a sponsor who in August 2010 was interested in an endorsement deal with James. However, she wanted quantitative evidence on the potential impact of the 2010 *The Decision* broadcast and his leaving Cleveland to search for NBA gold. In the March to September 2010 period, the only variable tracking higher was "awareness." However, this awareness increase is a negative, as is evidenced by the declines in variables such as "appeal," "endorsement," and "trust." Consider now a sponsor in early 2015 wanting confirmation that James' marketability had indeed grown considerably. Tracking the DBI variables in Exhibit 12.8 provides strong evidence of the positive uplift across the board in key variables.

12.5.3 Analysis of the Impact of Tiger Woods' Fall From Grace

The credibility of key marketing indicators can be increased or decreased when unexpected events that are widely recognized as impacting a brand in either a positive or negative way quickly show up in tracking variables. Exhibit 12.8 shows the DBI sheet for Tiger Woods covering the February 2008 to February 2015 period. Woods' golfing accomplishments up to 2009 are legendary. Exhibit 12.9 shows his yearly winnings and endorsements as reported by *Golf Digest*.

The weeks of late November/early December 2009 are a defining period in the career of Tiger Woods:

- November 25: The *National Enquirer* reports a story about Tiger Woods having an affair with a nightclub manager.
- November 27: Woods drives into fire hydrant outside his Florida home.
- November 30: Woods announces that he will not be playing in golf tournaments for the rest of the season.
- December 1: Another female goes public about having an affair with Woods. Woods releases a statement saying "I have let my family down and I regret those transgressions."
- December 11: Woods releases statement that he is taking indefinite leave from the game.
- December 14: Accenture is the first sponsor to drop Woods, stating he was "no longer the right representative … after the circumstances of the last two weeks."
- December 31: AT&T announces "We are ending our sponsorship agreement with Tiger Woods and we wish him well in the future."

Exhibit 12.8 highlights the sudden drop in multiple metrics tracked in the DBI. This rapid capture of an unexpected negative as regards Tiger Woods reinforces the credibility of the DBI metrics. From a sports sponsor perspective, the dramatic drops in the "endorsement," "aspiration," and "trust" variables are of high interest. The chart shows that in the 2010 to February 2015 period, the DBI variables have remained relatively flat, indicating that the consumer panel have not moved their perceptions of Woods back upwards to their mid-2009 levels. Exhibit 12.9 shows that Woods' endorsement income also has not returned to the 2008 and 2009 levels.

Year	Winnings	Endorsements	Total
1996	$894,060	$12,250,000	$13,144,060
1997	$2,380,831	$19,500,000	$21,880,831
1998	$2,927,946	$27,000,000	$29,927,946
1999	$7,681,625	$27,000,000	$34,681,625
2000	$11,034,530	$38,000,000	$49,034,530
2001	$7,771,562	$56,000,000	$63,771,562
2002	$8,292,188	$67,000,000	$75,292,188
2003	$6,700,288	$77,000,000	$83,700,288
2004	$6,370,407	$83,000,000	$89,370,407
2005	$11,992,739	$75,000,000	$86,992,739
2006	$11,941,827	$87,000,000	$98,941,827
2007	$22,902,706	$99,800,000	$122,702,706
2008	$7,737,626	$109,600,000	$117,337,626
2009	$21,015,196	$100,900,000	$121,915,196
Tiger Woods infidelity scandal breaks on November 25, 2009			
2010	$2,294,116	$72,000,000	$74,294,116
2011	$2,067,059	$62,000,000	$64,067,059
2012	$9,124,386	$77,000,000	$86,124,386
2013	$12,091,508	$71,000,000	$83,091,508

EXHIBIT 12.9 Tiger Woods' Career Earnings
Source: *Golf Digest*'s "Top 50 Earners" list. Figures for the list were compiled through *Golf Digest* interviews with agents, players, executives of companies involved with endorsements, industry analysts, and through the official money lists of the professional tours.

12.6 THIRD-PARTY OWNERSHIP OF PLAYERS' RIGHTS

A hybrid type of endorsement that is quite common in soccer is third-party ownership. Kids that show promise to become professional players are offered endorsement from wealthy individuals or investment funds. The endorsement happens as a salary to parents or any other kind of support such as paying for trips, buying apparel, or any other type of expenses. The player gives the fund the rights to all or part of his future transfer rights. This is called third-party ownership of a player's rights.[33]

Transfer of players in soccer involves teams exchanging payments associated with the rights. For instance, if a soccer team wants to buy the contract of a player currently under contract with another team, the buying team needs to purchase the contract held by the player's current team. The value of these rights is negotiated between the teams. Often there will be a maximum specified in the contract – this maximum allows the player to be transferred without the current team agreeing as long as the maximum transfer fee specified in the contract is paid. For instance, Bayern Munich bought Thiago Alcântara from FC Barcelona for a transfer of €25 million. Cristiano Ronaldo transferred from Manchester United to Real Madrid for almost €100 million. Messi's transfer is estimated to be close to €250 million.

Third-party ownership means that these rights are not owned by the team of the player but by the investment fund that sponsored the player through his junior years. Thus, when the player is transferred, the transfer fee does not go to the team, but to the investment fund. Out of 100 players that they sponsor, just a few become professional with a substantial transfer fee. The fund makes money from having these few "home runs." The fund is interested in promoting its players as hard as possible, so it is deeply engaged in the careers of its players. One alternative to promote them is to lend them to top-level teams, where the player is showcased and attracts the attention of rich teams who may want to get him. This lending strategy has allowed teams such as La Liga's Atlético de Madrid to access talent that its budget would not allow getting on the pitch. Having a relatively modest budget, Atlético has lined up talented players that have then been transferred to teams such as Chelsea or Manchester City. Third-party ownership helped Atlético to win La Liga in 2014 and also to reach the 2014 Champions League final against superpower Real Madrid.

Third-party ownership of a player's contract can create many tensions for a club. Owners of the contract mostly want the players to play as much as possible so they are seen by potential employers. They also have an incentive to push the coach to line them up, even if it is not in the best interest of the team.

The English Premier League has banned this type of ownership in its league. One EPL club, West Ham, was investigated when it appeared that it shared third-party ownership of an elite player, Carlos Tevez, when he transferred to West Ham. The context was very high-profile, as Tevez played a key role in helping West Ham avoid relegation from the EPL to the Championship League in the year he transferred.[34]

12.7 SUMMARY

Player endorsements are frequently observed in many sports. Indeed, in sports such as golf and tennis it is the main source of income for most professional athletes. Effective endorsement contracts require a close correspondence between the brand attributes of the sponsor and the brand attributes of the player. While there is much upside when this close correspondence is widely appreciated by the sponsor's target market, it is important to both assess and manage the risks associated with these contracts.

APPENDIX 12A   AMATEUR ATHLETE ENDORSEMENTS

Amateur athletes range from world champions to the pick-up beer league hockey team and everything in between. This group includes all those who participate in sport at any non-professional level. Some athletes in this group pursue endorsements, often with the support of federations, coaches, minor professional clubs, and leagues. An amateur athlete, by definition, is any participant in any sport who is not being paid a salary to play. Salary does not include athlete assistant programs run by governments or clubs that provide "living stipends" or "athlete carding" support in the form of a financial payment to the athlete.

The vast majority of amateur athletes have little likelihood of becoming professional athletes. For example, if one considers ice hockey in Canada (where it is the most popular sport), approximately 500,000 boys and 150,000 girls are registered players, while there are about 350 men in the NHL and around 25 women on the national team. A few thousand others play in minor leagues or collegiate/university leagues, but they still represent less than 1 percent of the total registered players.

Endorsement for amateur players requires careful working on offering value to potential sponsors. One option is to follow these steps:

- **Step #1: Focus on performance.** Endorsement value comes foremost from on-field performance. Thus, the first task of an amateur athlete is to demonstrate her sporting value. Delivering this performance often requires focusing the energy on sports, and having a friend, family member, or club to work on endorsements.

- **Step #2: Engage institutional support.** Sports have important institutions that support athletes both on the sporting side and the economic side. These institutions often have professionals working on endorsements that can help athletes. Federations at the various levels, clubs, National Olympic Committees (NOCs), and international federations (IFs) all are important sources of support.

- **Step #3: Develop a brand.** An athlete, even at an amateur level is potentially a brand with its values and the perceptions that it generates among the fans of the sport. The athlete needs to be aware of it and consciously manage it. She rarely can change her basic character, personality, or attitudes. But she can work on her image, interaction with people, and shaping her core characteristics according to the brand that she is building. The aim is to match the player with potential sponsoring companies whose own values and brand are well aligned with the values and brand of that player. This working on the brand goes beyond sporting performance to include how she dresses, behaves, and talks, the way she speaks to fans and media, and what her personal life is like. For each of these aspects, the athlete can seek professional experts who can help her become better at these different means of interaction. The process of creating equity in that brand begins with awareness (i.e., making sure that target audiences know of the athlete), exploring opportunities to build the brand, and delivering when these opportunities become available. As part of building a brand, an athlete can choose to focus her efforts on a particular aspect such as advocate of her local community, champion of national pride, or role model for future athletes. She can also develop relationships with local media interacting with journalists and bloggers providing them with time and content.

- **Step #4: Identify sponsorship opportunities.** This includes listing potential sponsors, partners, fundraising opportunities, and other sources of support both in terms of money and in-kind contributions (e.g., running shoes, energy bars, sport equipment, etc.). Consider also activities that will indirectly help drive resource generation. Examples include (a) being active on social media, radio, and TV, and (b) creating a local event (in hometown or current place of residence) that is the athlete's own event and can provide future opportunities. An example would be a 5km fun run that a national-level marathon runner organizes in their hometown each year.

- **Step #5: Talk to potential sponsors, fundraisers, and donors.** Set up a committee of supporters to help arrange for meetings and events (e.g., "meet and greet") to start connecting. Focus initially on local companies who can provide items of value (e.g., travel agent, law firm, retailer) and grow from there. At some point, the athlete may want to consider entering into a contract with a sports agent who can represent them. This will only arise if significant potential emerges and strong on-field performance happens.

- **Step #6: Make some noise.** This step involves undertaking some activities to get attention, create a buzz, engage with the athlete's hometown and build relationships with key stakeholders (e.g., mayor, owner of local restaurant, media personalities, etc.). Sporting organization partners (such as an NOC) can help provide guidance on how to increase reach, authenticity, credibility, and access.

NOTES

1 Male athletes dominate the top 100. The three female athletes on the 2014 list were all tennis players – Maria Sharapova (#34), Li Na (#41), and Serena Williams (#55).

2   D. Rossingh, "Sharapova said to renew Nike contract for 8 years, $70 million," *Bloomberg*, January 11, 2010.

3   K. Badenhausen, "LeBron James is the NBA's leading shoe salesman," *Forbes*, May 22, 2013.

4   In 2015 the National Guard announced that after that season it was ending its NASCAR sponsorship as part of the overall "Budget cutback of the Guard's sports sponsorship program," www.nascar.com/en_us/news-media/articles/2014/8/7/national-guard-sponsor-dale-earnhardt-jr-hendrick-motorsports.html.

5   D. Rovell, "Foreman's grill deal: best in sports marketing history?" *CNBC*, August 11, 2010.

6   D. Rovell, "Maria Sharapova, Porshe reach deal," *ESPN*, April 22, 2013.

7   http://tennisinfoblog.com/maria-sharapova-signs-70-million-nike-deal.

8   W.L. Adams, "Brand Sugarpova: how Maria Sharapova became the world's highest-paid female athlete," *Newsweek*, June 30, 2014.

9   P. Lattman, "Dealmaker for the shotmakers," *The New York Times*, August 26, 2012.

10   www.rediff.com/money/2003/nov/04ponting.htm.

11   www.valvoline.com.au/about-valvoline/news-and-events/Valvoline-brand-ambassador-Australian-cricketer-Ricky-Ponting.

12   K. Macarthur, "McDonald's signs NBA star Yao Ming," *Advertising Age*, February 12, 2004.

13   J. Feigen, "Rockets enjoy Chinese endorsement deals due to Yao," *Houston Chronicle*, October 13, 2010.

14   J.C. Bradbury, "How do baseball players age?" *Baseball Prospectus*, January 11, 2010.

15   "Angels Of John Hamilton will not be suspended by MLB," SI.com, April 3, 2015.

16   J. Lee, "Texas Rangers' Josh Hamilton admits to January relapse; says, he's human," ChooseHelp.com, August 9, 2009.

17   "Rangers GM: bringing back Josh Hamilton was an 'easy decision,'" *ESPN*, April 28, 2015.

18   M. Levinson and E. Novy-Williams, "Armstrong's cheating won record riches of more than $218 million," *Bloomberg*, February 21, 2013.

19   www.cnn.com/2013/01/17/us/lance-armstrong-fast-facts.

20   "Lance Armstrong signs deal with Michelob Ultra," *Velo News*, October 6, 2009.

21   http://sportsbizusa.com/blog/michelob-ultra-stands-behind-lance-armstrong.

22   T. Rotunno, "Armstrong loses eight sponsors in a day," *CNBC*, October 18, 2012.

23   Rotunno, "Armstrong loses eight sponsors in a day."

24   E. Matuszewski, "NBA's Kevin Durant said to sign $300 million, 10-year Nike deal," *Bloomberg*, September 2, 2014.

25   K. Helin, "Report: Andrew Wiggins signs $10–12 million shoe deal with Adidas," *NBC Sports*, July 9, 2014.

26   M. Lawrence Corbett, "Anna Kournikova is the best and worst thing to happen to women's tennis," *Bleacher Report*, June 17, 2013; C. Isidore, "Anna can keep winning off the court," *CNN Money*, July 8, 2002.

27   D. Rovell, "Polamalu spots work for Head & Shoulders," *ESPN*, August 23, 2012.

28   "How Ronaldo became the £26.5 million walking billboard," *Daily Mail*, October 21, 2014.

29   "Cheetah: drink of a cheater," *Chicago Tribune*, March 26, 2006.

30   www.eurweb.com/2014/10/nfl-throws-block-on-dr-dres-beats-headphones-opens-door-for-bose-era.

31   This definition is from Kevin Keller, www.trendhunter.com/keynote/brand-planning-keynote.

32   http://repucom.net/celebrity-dbi/case-study.

33   Further discussion of third-party ownership is in www.businessofsoccer.com/2013/04/18/the-realities-of-third-party-ownership.

34   www.soccerphile.com/soccerphile/premier-league/carlos-tevez-2.html.

13

TICKET PRICING AND VENUE-RELATED REVENUE STREAMS

Venue-related revenue streams – such as tickets or food and beverage – are, for most sports, in the top three revenue streams of clubs and events (along with media revenues and sponsorship revenues). Indeed, for some sports and events, venue-related revenues are still the dominant revenue streams, such as the many Minor League Baseball clubs and multiple amateur participant events. Exhibit 13.1 provides an overview of three major categories of venue-related revenues. This chapter focuses on two of these three categories – regular seat-related revenue streams and suite-related revenue streams. Special emphasis is given to ticket pricing. Chapters 10–12 discussed marketing, sponsorship, and advertising topics that cover the third (right-hand side) revenue stream in Exhibit 13.1.

Developments in sports ticket pricing are part of the more general topic of pricing in industries with perishable inventories such as airlines and hotels. Here, there is a timing aspect such that an unused seat or an unused hotel room on a given day cannot be inventoried and transferred for use on another day. Many important and potentially transformative developments are occurring in this more general pricing area. The change occurring in the sports ticket pricing arena is being driven by accumulated knowledge in ticketing companies working in both the sports and non-sports areas of pricing. There are also many entrepreneurial startup ventures that are developing new products that enrich the ticketing options and knowledge available to sporting executives charged with pricing decisions.

The ticketing arena for sports executives is one where major investments in new skillsets are required. There is increasing use of multiple large databases with the challenge of integrating them. There is also growing use of sophisticated pricing algorithms that incorporate both quantitative and qualitative data analysis with skillsets akin to those found in the leading technology companies such as Google and Facebook. In some cases, the new skillsets are acquired via partnerships that require sports executives to be excellent negotiators of partnership agreements and be able to work effectively with those partners. A key asset in negotiation with these partners is information about the ticket holders and fans of sporting clubs and events. This information has high value to many interested companies. It is important that sporting organizations benefit from the rich information they may share with multiple third parties in the new technology-driven/data analytics world of sports ticketing and marketing. Privacy issues such as the sharing of information also have assumed a higher profile in decision making in this area.

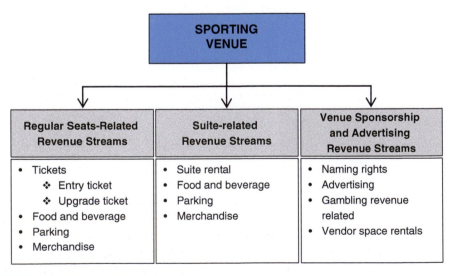

EXHIBIT 13.1 Multiple Revenue Streams for a Sporting Venue

13.1 MULTIPLE OBJECTIVES OF TICKET PRICING

Sporting executives making key pricing decisions typically have one or several of the following object-ives guiding their decisions. These objectives can conflict with each other (at least in the short run), so that often decisions will involve some weighting of two or more of these objectives.

13.1.1. Maximize the Expected Revenue Yield

This is a lofty objective that has much complexity. One dimension is determining the timeframe. Many clubs take at least a yearly perspective on ticket pricing and accept that some individual games in iso-lation could have been priced to yield a higher revenue number. However, setting prices focused on a single or a couple of games could set expectations about the pricing of other games in the season such that the overall annual revenues of the club would not have been maximized. The setting of sea-son ticket prices typically has a multi-year perspective so that any large repricing upwards is typically spread over several years rather than in just one year.

There is often much uncertainty about the sensitivity of demand to different ticket pricing regimes. The objective of maximizing the expected revenue yield in this uncertain and complex context is best viewed as seeking the approximate range of highest possible revenues. One aspect here is avoiding "obvious" cases where there is likely sizable underpricing for seats in games where customer pushback about high prices is likely to be minimal. The underpricing of very high-end seats at championship games is an example where many leagues and clubs have left much "money on the table" in the past. The consequence has been that third parties, such as brokers, have reaped large benefits from the league or club underpricing when these brokers were able to resell the tickets at market prices well above those set in the primary market.

13.1.2 Attract a Large Spectator Base to a Game or Event

There are multiple benefits to a club or event from having multiple sellouts or near-sellouts at their venue. One is that more fans are being touched by the game-day experience than when venues are only partially filled on game day. A second benefit is the likely increase in non-ticket game-day revenue streams such as parking, food and beverage, and merchandise sales. Clubs that operate with sales of season tickets being close to the venue capacity can reduce their efforts during the season on selling tickets and concentrate more of their resources and energies on general fan development.

13.1.3 Having a Great Game-Day Atmosphere

Games and events played before venues with sparse crowds generate little atmosphere for those playing on the field as well as those in the stands. Broadcasters much prefer to showcase games with high cap-acity utilization, as it implies many fans view the game or event to be important. One interesting trend has been to reduce the size of venues that had large amounts of unused capacities. One of NASCAR's premier racetracks is Daytona International Speedway. Up to 2015, the venue held more than 140,000 spectators. Under a major $400 million revamp of the racetrack (called "Daytona Rising"), the capacity will be reduced to 103,000 to build a better crowd atmosphere and to create more of a scarcity factor for tickets to its premier events such as the Daytona 500 (the opening race of the NASCAR season) and the Coke Zero 400 (the July 4th weekend event).

13.1.4 Attracting Targeted Groups to the Venue via Ticket Allocations at Low Ticket Prices (or Even Complementary Tickets)

Examples of groups that executives may want to target include:

- Introduce potential "new" season ticket holders to the game-day experience – such as fans on a wait list, or single game attendees in past years. Also included here are complementary upgrades in seating for a given game to existing season ticket holders. The aims here include attracting new season ticket holders or having existing ticket holders upgrade their packages to higher-priced packages.
- Increase the number of millennials to the fans in attendance to help build the future fan base – especially important in clubs with aging season ticket holder bases.
- Allow lower-income fans from the local community to attend games – especially important in cities or counties that have contributed high percentages of the funds required to build the venue via extra taxes.
- Reward volunteers and juniors at the grassroots level of the sport being played in the venue – such as a MLS soccer club inviting without charge coaches and junior players to the venue and to be on the field at halftime to showcase the grassroots activity of the local clubs.

13.2 LARGE DIFFERENCES ACROSS CLUBS IN GAME-DAY TICKET REVENUES AND AVERAGE TICKET PRICES

This section provides insights into the potential magnitude and composition of game-day revenues for the first pillar in Exhibit 13.1. We also show average ticket price differences across leagues and across clubs for the NFL, MLB, NBA, and NHL.

13.2.1 Estimated Differences Across MLB Clubs in Capacities, Average Attendances, and Ticket Revenues

Game-day gate revenues are a function of both the attendance level and the average price paid by each person attending. Exhibit 13.2 provides some insight for the 30 Major League Baseball clubs in 2013. MLB has the largest number of games per club each season (162 in the regular season) across the major team sporting leagues.

Exhibit 13.2 highlights some differences across the 30 clubs in several areas as regards capacity and attendance:

- Stadium capacities per game – from a high of 56,000 for the Los Angeles Dodgers to a low of approximately 35,000 for the Oakland Athletics.[1]
- Stadium average attendance per game – from a high of 46,216 for the Los Angeles Dodgers to a low of 18,645 for the Tampa Bay Rays.

Team	Stadium capacity	Stadium 2013 average attendance	Stadium% utilization	Estimated team revenue ($M)	Estimated gate receipts revenue ($M)	Estimated concessions revenue ($M)	Estimated parking revenue ($M)	Total% gate, concessions, parking of total revenue
Arizona Diamondbacks	48,500	26,355	54.34 %	195	41	12	23	28.72 %
Atlanta Braves	50,062	31,465	62.85 %	225	52	20	22	34.22 %
Baltimore Orioles	45,971	29,105	63.31 %	210	52	14	18	32.38 %
Boston Red Sox	38,928	34,979	89.86 %	405	174	36	40	51.85 %
Chicago Cubs	38,765	32,625	84.16 %	320	128	30	18	50.31 %
Chicago White Sox	44,321	22,105	49.87 %	225	59	17	25	37.78 %
Cincinnati Reds	45,000	31,288	69.53 %	205	54	15	19	36.59 %
Cleveland Indians	42,800	19,661	45.94 %	190	30	10	18	21.05 %
Colorado Rockies	50,000	34,491	68.98 %	195	46	22	18	36.41 %
Detroit Tigers	40,000	38,066	95.17 %	245	95	19	21	49.80 %
Houston Astros	42,000	20,393	48.55 %	205	45	12	23	27.80 %
Kansas City Royals	40,625	21,614	53.20 %	180	37	11	14	28.89 %
Los Angeles Angels of Anaheim	45,050	37,277	82.75 %	275	78	24	27	39.64 %
Los Angeles Dodgers	56,000	46,216	82.53 %	325	81	29	39	36.92 %
Miami Marlins	37,000	19,584	52.93 %	200	65	12	10	38.50 %
Milwaukee Brewers	42,500	31,248	73.52 %	205	64	18	18	42.93 %
Minnesota Twins	42,000	30,588	72.83 %	215	87	18	25	48.84 %
New York Mets	42,500	26,695	62.81 %	265	72	26	55	40.38 %
New York Yankees	52,325	40,488	77.38 %	570	265	53	84	55.79 %
Oakland Athletics	35,067	22,337	63.70 %	175	33	9	12	26.86 %
Philadelphia Phillies	43,000	37,190	86.49 %	315	142	28	26	56.83 %
Pittsburgh Pirates	38,000	28,210	74.24 %	185	39	14	15	28.65 %
San Diego Padres	42,000	26,749	63.69 %	195	34	14	20	27.18 %
San Francisco Giants	40,800	41,584	101.92 %	300	126	26	28	53.67 %
Seattle Mariners	47,000	21,747	46.27 %	225	48	17	29	30.67 %
St. Louis Cardinals	46,861	41,602	88.78 %	250	105	25	26	52.00 %
Tampa Bay Rays	45,000	18,645	41.43 %	175	30	8	14	23.43 %
Texas Rangers	49,178	38,795	78.89 %	260	79	22	19	41.15 %
Toronto Blue Jays	51,000	31,315	61.40 %	210	44	12	17	27.62 %
Washington Nationals	41,222	32,745	79.44 %	230	85	20	18	48.26 %
Grand Total	—	—	—	7,375	2,290	593	741	—
Average	44,116	30,505	69.23 %	246	76	20	25	38.50 %

EXHIBIT 13.2 MLB Club Stadium Related Information on Capacity, Average Attendance, and Venue-Related Revenue ($M) in 2013

Source: RSV Database; Bloomberg Media (www.bloomberg.com/infographics/2013-10-23/mlb-team-values.html)

- Stadium average capacity utilization – from a high of 101.92 percent for the San Francisco Giants[2] to a low of 41.43 percent for the Tampa Bay Rays.

Bloomberg in 2014 made estimates of total 2013 club revenues as well as select individual categories of revenues for each of the 30 MLB clubs – including gate receipts, concessions, and parking. Exhibit 13.2 also reports several of these Bloomberg estimates. The highlights for 2013 include:

- Annual gate revenues – from a high of $265 million for the New York Yankees (with the Boston Red Sox #2 as $174 million) to lows of $30 million for each of the Cleveland Indians and the Tampa Bay Rays.
- Annual concession revenues – from a high of $53 million for the New York Yankees to a low of $8 million for the Tampa Bay Rays.

Exhibit 13.2 highlights how the regular seats-related revenue series in Exhibit 13.1 include key contributions from parking and concessions. Average estimated concessions per club are $20 million and average parking revenues are $25 million compared to average gate revenue of $76 million.

It is important to emphasize that the Bloomberg numbers are estimates without access to the actual contracts that govern revenue creation and revenue-sharing at venues. There is much heterogeneity in these contracts. Some clubs, for example, capture 100 percent of parking revenues created, while other clubs may have contracts that require sharing of parking revenue with a city or county. The role of Exhibit 13.2 is in highlighting generaldifferences across clubs without asserting that every number is precisely in accord with audited financials.

13.2.2 Estimated Differences Across Leagues and Across Clubs in Average Ticket Prices

The Team Marketing Report has for many years consistently tracked stadium-related costs for fans across the NFL, MLB, NBA, and NHL. The standard report for each year includes the average ticket price per game, which is computed as "a weighted average of season ticket prices for general seating categories, determined by factoring the tickets in each price range as a percentage of the total number of seats in each venue."[3] Appendix 13A summarizes average ticket prices per league over the 1995/2014 period and the distribution across clubs in each of the four leagues in 2014. See also the related Exhibits 13.13 and 13.14.

Some summary information that highlights the multiple areas of differences in the average ticket prices for 2014 are highlighted below:

League	Average ticket price	Highest average ticket price	Lowest average ticket price	Ratio of high/low
NFL	$84.41	$122.00 (New England Patriots)	$54.20 (Cleveland Browns)	2.25
MLB	$27.93	$52.32 (Boston Red Sox)	$16.37 (San Diego Padres)	3.2
NBA	$52.50	$129.38 (New York Knicks)	$26.87 (New Orleans Pelicans)	4.82
NHL	$61.62	$122.20 (Toronto Maple Leafs)	$37.28 (Dallas Stars)	3.28

The NFL has the highest average ticket prices in 2014 with the MLB having the lowest average prices by a large margin. Within each league, the ratio of the highest to the lowest average ticket price ranges from 4.82 for the NBA to 2.25 for the NFL. The NFL benefits from being the most popular professional sport in North America (a demand factor) and having the fewest number of regular season games (a scarcity of supply factor).

13.3 KEY TERMINOLOGY

The ticketing area is one where terms are often used with differing meanings. It is also one where the proliferating new companies in this area are creating new names for areas they are developing new products or services. To ease the exposition, this section outlines the meanings we give to some key terms. Two key terms central to the flow of this chapter are "primary ticket market" and "secondary ticket market." Exhibit 13.3 presents a graphic of these two markets:

- **Primary ticket market.** This is the market where the ticket is sold for the first time and the seller is the entity with the original property rights to that ticket. An example would be the New York

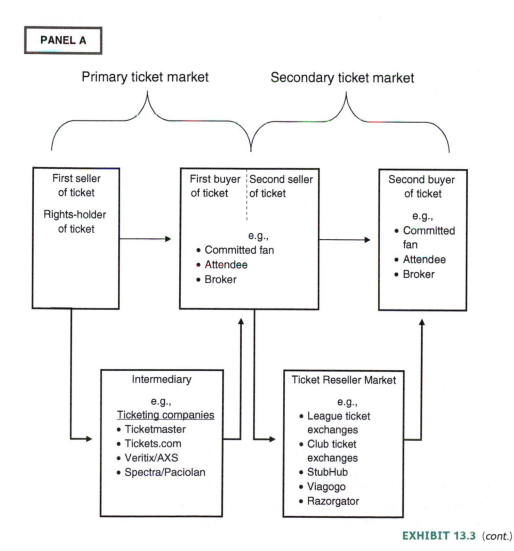

EXHIBIT 13.3 (*cont.*)

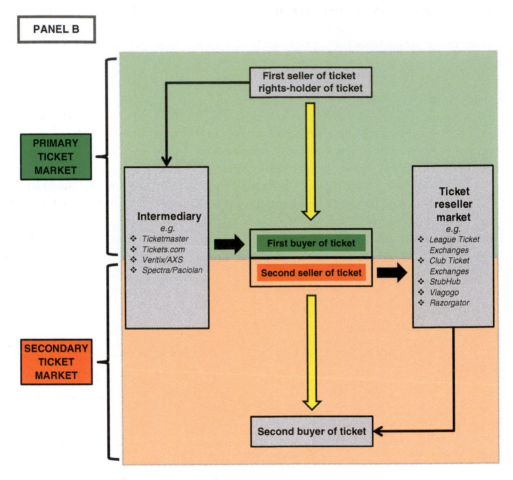

EXHIBIT 13.3 Primary and Secondary Markets for Tickets

Yankees being the seller of a full season of home game tickets package or the seller of a single-game ticket at Yankee Stadium. In some cases, the seller may have an agent that conducts the sale for either or both season ticket or individual game tickets. Major ticketing companies that act in this role include Ticketmaster, Tickets.com, Veritix/AXS, and Spectra/Paciolan.

■ **Secondary ticket market.** This is the market where a ticket that was already sold by the entity with the original legal rights to that ticket is resold a second (or third, etc.) time. In most cases, the seller will be different from the original property rights-holder. However, in some cases (such as Wimbledon and its Debenture Program) the property rights-holder may buy back the ticket and then sell it a second time (typically at a different price than in the first sale).[4] The term "on-selling" is sometimes used to describe the reselling of a ticket previously purchased but not used. The secondary marketplace can be an organized market (such as StubHub in the US and Viagogo in the UK) or it can be an informal market. In some countries or states, it is illegal to resell a ticket at a higher price than face value.

Other terms that are important to define include:

- **Face value of a ticket.** This is the price the ticket is listed on the primary market by the seller. Ticket prices transacted on the secondary market are often expressed as a percentage of the face value that is described as the mark-up percentage. Face values are typically expressed before any service charges of a ticketing company.
- **Black market for a ticket.** In countries or states where it is illegal to resell tickets above their face value, transactions that do occur are referred to as occurring on the "black market."
- **Price tiering of a venue.** This is where there is more than one ticket price point for the regular seats in a venue. The most desirable seats (such as seats closest to the action, or with the best views) are priced highest and tickets in other regions priced lower. The phrase "number of price points" is often used to describe the number of separate prices at which tickets are sold for an event in the venue.
- **Variable pricing.** This is a ticket pricing regime where primary market ticket prices set by a rights-owner do not have the same price for the same seat at each and every regular season game or event. There is typically one pricing round for a season, so that the initial price set for each seat at each game is unchanged during the season. Different prices for the same seat across different games can be due to multiple factors such as the attractiveness of the opponent, and the day of the week when the game is being played.
- **Dynamic pricing.** This is a ticket pricing regime where changes in the listed ticket prices can occur multiple times due to shifts in demand for and supply of tickets for a game or event. Recently, some clubs and events that had adopted variable pricing subsequently shifted to a combination of variable pricing pre-season and then dynamic pricing with the potential for continuous revisions to the initial round of prices set to reflect changes in the demand and supply conditions that occur after the start of a season.
- **Paperless ticket.** A ticket that is sold and digitally provided to the buyer without a hard copy physical ticket being sent. An extreme is that entry to a venue is only provided to ticket holders who provide their own digital address. A less extreme version is that at least one person entering the venue has provided a digital address – such as that of the original purchaser or via a digital transfer from the original purchaser to the person attending via an exchange platform controlled or accessed by the original seller.
- **Personal seat licenses (PSLs).** These are the rights to buy individual season ticket packages for a sporting club. In most cases, these rights can be traded. Many clubs that build new venues issue PSLs as a way to finance the construction cost. Chapter 17 describes and illustrates PSLs.
- **Broker.** This is an individual or company that buys tickets with the intention of reselling the tickets at a profit rather than attending the event. The broker carries what is called "inventory risk," which is the outcome where either they cannot on-sell the ticket or they on-sell the ticket at a selling price below their own earlier purchase price.

13.4 DETERMINANTS OF TICKET PRICES AND TICKET PRICE DIFFERENCES

This section overviews some basic factors that help explain the dramatic differences in the average ticket prices documented above. We first look at two factors in the context of ticket prices at a NBA basketball game.

13.4.1 Opponent Attractiveness and Seating Attractiveness Combinations

Exhibit 13.4 shows a 3 × 3 matrix where the two variables are:

- **Attractiveness of the opponent.** We distinguish between an AAA highly attractive opponent, a BB attractiveness opponent, and a C-level attractive opponent.
- **Quality of seating.** The seating ranges from "best seats in the house" (courtside) to average seat in the lower bowl of the arena to the "worst seats in the house" (in the upper bowl at the very back).

The highest demand will be for the AAA opponent/courtside seating pairing. In many NBA arenas, this combination can have ticket prices of $1,000 or more for a regular season game. NBA clubs over time have become more aggressive at raising ticket prices for the pairing in upper right corner of Exhibit 13.4 with little effect on demand. There is a very high scarcity factor with front row seats on the court, especially against an AAA opponent. The other extreme is in the bottom left of Exhibit 13.4 – a C-level opponent/upper tier seating pairing. Here the NBA club may well have trouble in selling out the upper tier section of the arena, even if it sets prices at a very low level. The potential attendee is looking at negatives on both opponent and seating and may well decide that there are many better alternative uses of her time and money. A club that decides to drastically decrease upper tier ticket prices to boost demand may well find that aggregate revenues decline, as the percentage increase in tickets sold is less than the percentage decrease in the ticket prices.

13.4.2 Broad Number of Factors Affecting Ticket Prices

Exhibit 13.5 outlines ten potential factors that affect ticket prices, including the two just discussed. There is growing use of rigorous quantitative modeling in the setting of ticket prices in general and sports ticket prices in particular.

Opponent/Seating	C-Level Opponent	BB-Level Opponent	AAA-Level Opponent
Courtside Seating			
Lower Tier Seating			
Upper Tier Seating			

EXHIBIT 13.4 The Demand for Tickets: Quality of Opponent versus Quality of Seating Matrix

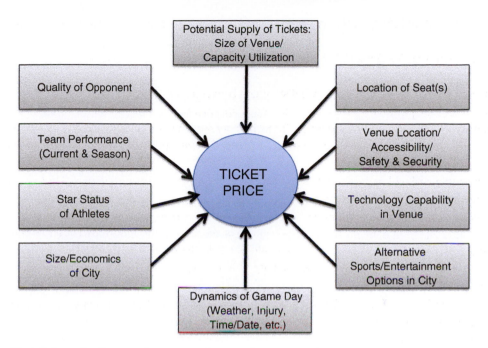

EXHIBIT 13.5 Some Key Factors Influencing the Demand for and Price of a Ticket

Some factors in Exhibit 13.5 relate to demand factors – such as the team performance, star athletes appearing, and the size and economic strength of the city. For example, the cities/regions with the highest ticket prices in Section 13.2.1 (New England/Boston, New York, and Toronto) are larger than those with the lowest ticket prices (Cleveland, San Diego, New Orleans, and Dallas). Other factors in Exhibit 13.5 relate more to supply factors – such as the capacity of the venue and its utilization, and the supply of alternative sports/entertainment options at the same time as the sporting event whose ticket prices are being examined.

It is essential that executives making primary market pricing decisions consider the perspective of ticket buyers. Some economists have argued that potentially every seat in a venue should have a different price. However, ticket buyers in many cases would be overwhelmed by seeing thousands of different ticket prices for a forthcoming event in a venue. Pricing executives aware of potential buyer pushback to seeing a multitude of available primary market prices often restrict the number of price points in a venue to a relatively small number. The perspective of the media is also important to consider. Companies that win a championship after many losing seasons are often tempted to greatly increase ticket prices for the next season. However, they may choose to announce a lower increase in price than desired to reduce the ability of the media to portray the club as a price-gouger and being disloyal to long-term season ticket holders who suffered through many losing seasons.

13.5 THE PRICING OF TICKETS ON THE PRIMARY MARKET

Panel A of Exhibit 13.6 outlines five eras of primary market pricing for tickets. The primary market is where the ticket is sold for the first time and the seller is the entity with the original property rights to that ticket.

Panel A: Primary market ticket eras for games and events

ERA #1: Uniform pricing regime	Tickets for all seats and all games priced the same.
ERA #2: Tiered pricing regime	Venue is tiered into sections based on the different attractiveness of the ticket area to buyers. Same seat has identical price for every regular season game.
ERA #3: Variable pricing regime combined with tiering	The primary market ticket price set by a rights-owner does not have the same price for the same seat at each and every regular season game or event. There is typically one pricing round for a season so that the initial price set for each seat at each game is unchanged during the season.
ERA #4: Dynamic pricing regime	Changes in the listed ticket prices can occur multiple times due to shifts in the demand for or supply of tickets for a game or event. After the initial round of prices are set, subsequent prices of tickets per game can change based on factors such as recent record of two teams playing, likely individual players appearing (such as the starting pitchers in MLB), and likely weather for the game. Supply and demand factors are allowed to drive potentially large shifts in prices set for individual games.
ERA #5: Inside-the-venue mobile upgrade ticket pricing regime	Venue attendees can access apps that showcase multiple unsold tickets in preferred seating that can be purchased and used for the remainder of a game or event

Panel B: Secondary market ticket eras for games and events

ERA #1: Disorganized offline marketplace for reselling of sporting tickets	Market populated with lack of guarantees as to ticket authenticity. World of hard-copy paper tickets creates challenges in rapid transfer of tickets.
ERA #2: Online market for reselling tickets emerges with minimal transparency as to sellers	Craigslist is an exemplar. It provides an online platform for buyers and sellers that previously were available in classified pages of print media.
ERA #3: Online marketplace for tickets with sophisticated classifications and with greater transparency into sellers	eBay opens in 1995 and has sporting tickets traded. StubHub starts in 2000 as an early dedicated online ticket exchange.
ERA #4: Leagues, clubs, and events play active roles in the secondary markets	Ticketing companies, in addition to third parties such as StubHub, form partnerships with leagues and clubs on either a revenue-sharing basis or a sponsorship model.

EXHIBIT 13.6 Ticketing Eras for Games and Events

Clubs have often moved through several of the eras in Exhibit 13.6, such that there is a cumulative increase over time in the options available to pricing executives.

13.5.1 Era #1: Uniform Pricing Regime for Primary Market

The simplest approach to ticketing is to have a single price for all seats and all games. While this may now seem simplistic, this approach has been observed. The San Francisco 49ers for many years had a single ticket price for all seats at Candlestick Park for each regular season game. The allocation of seats to fans was done on the basis of years as a season ticket holder. The fans on the 50-yard line on the lower deck of their stadium were those who had the longest number of years as a season ticket holder. This created high incentives for long-term season ticket holders to buy the season ticket package even if they moved out of town, as there were many "friends" willing to pay them above the face price for the "best seats in the house." It was even reported that some long-term ticket holders were "buying" their tickets several years after they had died!

A variant of this approach is when many NFL clubs priced all games equally, including the two pre-season home games and the eight regular home games. The pre-season games are widely acknowledged to be of lower quality, but for many years were not recognized in the prices set for those games by most clubs.

13.5.2 Era #2 Tiered Pricing Regime for Primary Market

Clubs and event-owners seeking to increase their revenues well understand that the Era #1 approach ignores the fact that all seats in a venue are not of equal attractiveness to buyers. To most people, the experience of sitting in courtside seats at an NBA game is much better than sitting in the back row of the highest deck of the arena. The first move away from Era #1 of a single price for all seats in a venue was moving to a tiered pricing of seats within a venue, where higher prices are charged for different seats based on their perceived attractiveness to potential buyers. Era #2 is where there is tiering of tickets prices for each game but that the same price for a seat in a given tier is set for all games in the season. For many years, most sporting clubs that sold packages of season tickets in different parts of a venue priced them differently, but for a given package the same price was charged for every home game. Thus, an NBA club that has 41 home games could offer four season ticket packages with:

Package A: Courtside $20,500, with each game priced at $500 per ticket
Package B: Sideline Club $8,200 with each game priced at $200 per ticket
Package C: Lower Deck $4,100 with each game priced at $100 per ticket
Package D: Upper Deck at $2,050 with each game priced at $50 per ticket.

This NBA club would be described as having four pricing tiers for a given game.

Many clubs used the Era #2 approach when pricing tickets to individual games in a given price tier for a season. Despite the fact that games differed greatly in their attractiveness (as evidenced by, say, large attendance differences in prior years across individual opponents), the same seat was priced the same amount for each and every game. Club executives adopting Era #2 were often criticized for creating incentives for black markets to develop, where tickets to high-demand events were later sold on secondary markets for well above their face value. Brokers benefited greatly by this primary market approach to pricing all games the same for a given tier.

13.5.3 Era #3: Variable Pricing Regime Combined with Tiering for Primary Market

Ticketing Era #3 – variable pricing – refines the Era #2 approach. Variable pricing is a ticket pricing regime where different prices are set for the same seat across different games. Increasingly sporting clubs are

2015 SAN FRANCISCO 49ERS

PRIME
(BAL, ATL, AZ, STL)

	SBL	SEASON	SINGLE
CLUB	$80k	$375	$475
	$30k	$350	$450
	$20k	$325	$425
RESERVED	$12k	$200	$300
	$6k	$150	$225
	$6k	$125	$180
	$5k	$125	$175
	$5k	$100	$145
	$4k	$100	$140
	$2k	$95	$130
	$2k	$85	$110

PRESEASON
(DAL, SD)

	SBL	SEASON	SINGLE
CLUB	$80k	$187	$187
	$30k	$174	$174
	$20k	$163	$163
RESERVED	$12k	$100	$100
	$6k	$74	$74
	$6k	$63	$63
	$5k	$63	$63
	$5k	$50	$50
	$4k	$50	$50
	$2k	$47	$47
	$2k	$43	$43

MARQUEE
(MIN, GB, SEA, CIN)

	SBL	SEASON	SINGLE
CLUB	$80k	$469	$569
	$30k	$438	$538
	$20k	$406	$506
RESERVED	$12k	$250	$350
	$6k	$188	$263
	$6k	$156	$211
	$5k	$156	$206
	$5k	$125	$170
	$4k	$125	$165
	$2k	$119	$154
	$2k	$106	$131

EXHIBIT 13.7 San Francisco 49ers Tiered Pricing for Season Tickets
Source: San Francisco 49ers season ticket webpage

adopting variable pricing when setting primary market ticket prices at the start of each season. To illustrate variable pricing, we first use the example of primary market ticket prices announced at the start of the 2015 season by the San Francisco 49ers of the NFL for Levi's Stadium. The NFL season has four pre-season games and 16 regular season games – this means for each club there are two pre-season home games and eight regular season home games. This relatively low number of games per season, coupled with the high popularity of NFL games, has created a scarcity factor that has resulted in high average ticket prices and in many games being sold out. Exhibit 13.7 presents the categories of primary market ticket prices available for Levi's Stadium. There are three variables that the 49ers use to set the prices laid out here:

1   **Season ticket prices versus single ticket prices.** The 49ers have set lower prices for regular season games when all ten games are purchased (two pre-season and eight regular games) than when single tickets are purchased. For example, tickets in Section 126 (bottom tier end zone) for the Green Bay Packers game (classified as a "marquee" game) cost $156 as part of a season ticket package and $211 as a single ticket. Single-game tickets for a primary market game are in relatively small supply for many NFL clubs.

2   **Price tiering.** When building Levi's Stadium, the 49ers used personal seat licenses (they call them stadium builders licenses or SBLs) to help finance its construction. The stadium was tiered into 11 categories. The right to buy the best seats in the house, which were on the 50-yard line and labeled Club VIP (Sections 115 and 138), cost $80,000 per SBL. The lowest SBL cost was $2,000 for the right to buy seats in the Upper Deck corners. Section 126 season ticket holders paid $6,000 for each SBL. For the Green Bay Packers game (classified as a "marquee" game), season ticket holders with different SBLs had 11 different price points ranging from $469 to $106. Section 126 cost $156 as noted above.

3   **Variable pricing.** The ten home season games in 2015 were classified into three categories with progressively higher prices for the same seat.

   - Pre-season games (two games: Dallas and San Diego).
   - Prime games (four games: Baltimore, Atlanta, Arizona, and St. Louis).
   - Marquee games (four games: (Minnesota, Green Bay, Seattle, and Cincinnati).

Ticket prices in our Section 126 season ticket package example were $63 for the two pre-season games, $125 for the prime games, and $156 for the marquee games. Factors such as the assessed relative strength of the eight visiting clubs in 2015, the potential star athletes on each visiting club, and the past history of games between the 49ers and each of the visiting clubs in 2015 were included in setting the prices of each of the three tiers.

Under the variable pricing approach in Exhibit 13.7, the 49ers have to wait for the NFL to release their final schedule of games for 2015 before announcing which games fall into which of their three categories. Use of just three categories to classify games for variable pricing keeps the primary market pricing schedule relatively straightforward to a buyer. The other end of the spectrum, not chosen by the 49ers, would have been for each of the 11 tiers to have different primary market ticket prices across the ten games. Had this been chosen, it is likely that the Green Bay and Seattle games would have been priced higher than the Minnesota and Cincinnati games, as well as the other six home games. This use of a relatively small number of price categories illustrates the comment that ticket pricing has "some art and some science, and has to be comprehensible to the buyer."

Major League Baseball has been very proactive in adopting variable pricing. Section 13.8 illustrates the extensive use of variable pricing by the Oakland Athletics for their season ticket holders. The Athletics have adopted both price tiering and variable pricing when setting primary market prices for full season packages of 81 home games. Games are classified into three categories – gold (highest priced), green, and white (lowest priced).

13.5.4 Era #4: Dynamic Pricing Regime for Primary Market

Season ticket holders purchase a package of tickets in which the prices on individual games are preset at the start of the season. For many clubs this leaves a large number of unsold tickets. The airline and hospitality industries have long embraced what is now called "dynamic pricing." In the sporting industry, there is a growing adoption of dynamic pricing in the primary market for tickets not sold to season ticket holders. Dynamic pricing is a ticket pricing regime where changes in the listed ticket prices can occur multiple times due to shifts in demand for and supply of tickets for a game or event.

Most sporting clubs do not have the in-house capability to conduct the extensive demand and supply analysis that enables better prices to be reliably developed. "Better" in this context means prices that result in increased revenues vis-à-vis previous pricing regimes such as variable pricing. Several pricing advisory companies emerged in the 2007/12 period that built multiple sporting clubs as clients. These include Qcue, Digonex, StratBridge, and MarketShare (with Ticketmaster as a partner). These companies build large databases of multiple variables that have reliably made predictions about the level of demand or changes in demand for sections of sporting venues as well as overall venue demand on a game-by-game basis. In some cases, dynamic pricing algorithms will recommend sizable increases in primary market ticket prices vis-à-vis what a club have used with variable prices set at the start of a season and not adjusted for subsequent shifts in demand or supply – such as a MLB club making a stronger-than-expected run for the playoffs in the last ten games of the season, leading to very large increases in demand for tickets. In other cases, dynamic pricing algorithms may recommend major drops in primary market ticket prices are necessary to boost demand when negative events occur affecting demand – such as a MLB club losing their top two starting pitchers or their leading hitter to season-ending injuries.

Support for dynamic pricing enabling increased revenues vis-à-vis prior pricing regimes comes from multiple executives of clubs that have shifted from a variable pricing regime (Era #3) to a dynamic pricing regime (Era #4). Box 1.2 describes how the San Francisco Giants trialed dynamic pricing in 2009 to sell outfield and upper-deck seats that were sold on a game-by-game basis. In 2010, dynamic pricing was expanded to all tickets sold on a game-by-game basis. Russ Stanley, managing vice-president of ticket sales and services, estimated "about an $8,000,000 increase in revenue year-over-year in 2010 from 2009" from their adoption of dynamic pricing. He noted that "we had a great year in 2010 that came down to the wire and we won the World Series. Had we not been able to be nimble and react to market value shifts, we would have left that money on the table."[5] Section 13.8 describes how the Oakland Athletics evolved its use of dynamic pricing, also partnering with Qcue for non-season ticket holder tickets.

13.5.5 Era #5: Inside-the-Venue Mobile Upgrade Ticket Pricing Regime for Primary Market

Ticket pricing for many decades stopped once those attending went through the turnstiles of the venue. But now, a rapid number of innovative software products for mobile electronic devices is creating enhanced revenue opportunities for attendees within the venue. Chapter 17 illustrates the use by clubs of apps that facilitate food and beverage delivery to individual seats in the venue. A new revenue stream related to ticketing is called "mobile upgrade ticket pricing." Several technology companies, including

Experience and Pogoseat, provide the software systems for clubs to capture this new revenue source. In its most simple form, current ticket holders at the venue, can see online what seats are not sold, and purchase an upgrade option.

MLB Advanced Media, who partner with Experience to facilitate mobile seat upgrades, included the following comments in a March 13, 2013 press release:

> MLB Advanced Media, L.P. (MLBAM), the interactive media and internet company of Major League Baseball, and Experience (findexp.com), the fan experience mobile technology company, today announced a partnership to deliver seat and experience upgrade technology at participating ballparks.
>
> The Arizona Diamondbacks, Atlanta Braves, Minnesota Twins and Oakland Athletics will be the first clubs to launch the service in April. During the 2012 season, the Braves, Experience and MLBAM successfully piloted a test of the mobile seat upgrade feature at Turner Field.
>
> The "At the Ballpark" app … accurately identifies the most desirable seat and experience for each fan, visualizing up-to-the-moment available inventory and completing the upgrade purchase through a safe and reliable mobile-optimized system.[6]

More complex versions of clubs selling unsold inventory of seats in desired locations are also potential products. For example, season ticket holders could be given the option of reselling their unused tickets as part of a mobile seat upgrade program. This would be a secondary market sale for which charges to season ticket holders could be made by potentially the technology provider and the club itself.

13.6 THE PRICING OF TICKETS ON THE SECONDARY MARKET

The secondary market is the market where a ticket that has already been sold by the entity with the original legal rights to that ticket is then resold a second (or third, etc.) time. In most cases the seller will be different from the original property rights-holder – see Exhibit 13.3. Exhibit 13.6, Panel B, outlines several different eras of the secondary market for tickets. As with several areas related to ticketing, both technology developments and changes in attitudes towards the ticketing market (legal and otherwise) have led to major transformations in the depth and transparency of the secondary market.

13.6.1 Era #1: Disorganized Marketplace for Reselling of Sporting Tickets

For many decades, the resale of tickets occurred on informal markets or "under-the-table" markets. There were multiple reasons for this market staying relatively disorganized for a long period:

1   Legislation in many countries or states prohibited the resale of tickets above their face value.
2   The original rights-holders to the tickets (such as leagues or clubs) taking a very negative viewpoint on the secondary market, viewing it as being competitive with the primary market that they controlled.
3   Fake tickets – there was a lack of assurance that tickets sold on the secondary market were authentic. In some cases, tickets purchased on the secondary market turned out to be fakes with the buyer having no recourse to the original rights-holder to obtain a valid ticket.
4   Information about availability of tickets and the sellers was very limited.

5   The inefficiency of trading in this disorganized market. Tickets were only available in physical form and buyers often had to go the seller's address to pick them.

Over time, reductions have occurred in each of the above friction points to an active secondary market developing.

13.6.2   Era #2: Online Secondary Market for Ticket Reselling Emerges, but has Minimal Transparency as to Sellers

The growth of the web in the early 1990s allowed sellers of tickets to increase the visibility of what they were selling to a broader community in a more efficient way. An example of one type of marketplace was Craigslist. Over time Craigslist has increased in the ease in which buyers could locate information about the tickets available for sale. However, these sites were best described as the classified advertisement sections of print newspapers that had been shifted to the web. Rich information about the sellers and their transaction history was typically not available on these websites. Nor were large investments made in building state-of-the-art technology.

13.6.3   Era # 3: Online Secondary Marketplace for Tickets With Sophisticated Classification and Greater Transparency into Sellers

eBay, one of the earliest growth companies that pioneered a marketplace with sophisticated classification of items for sale, started in the mid-1990s. A key pillar in its growth was having a reputation index about the sellers with feedback from buyers. Potential buyers could look at the satisfaction of past buyers and whether any concerns had existed about tickets not being authentic. An early dedicated site was StubHub, which was founded by two Stanford University MBA students in 2000. In the early years, StubHub was very much opposed by the leagues and clubs on the premise that they were cannibalizing their primary market tickets sales. In some cases tickets to a game that was not sold out were listed by a reputable seller on StubHub at a price below that on the primary market.

13.6.4   Era #4: Leagues, Clubs, and Events Play Active Roles in the Secondary Ticket Market

During the mid-2000s there was a gradual shift in the attitudes of primary markets rights-holders, such that increasingly many leagues, clubs and events embraced rather than opposed the secondary markets. For example, the MLB season has 81 home games. Buyers of the full season ticket package benefited greatly by having an efficient and transparent market in which to resell some of their large inventory of tickets rather than let them go unused. Unused tickets are often a prompt to season ticket holders deciding not to renew the package the following season. StubHub initially started working with some clubs on a revenue-sharing basis. They subsequently also gave clubs an option where they became an official sponsor for a set dollar amount for the right to resell the club's tickets with a window on the club's official ticketing page. This was a dramatic shift from the early 2000s, where the secondary market was viewed in a hostile way by many ticketing executives in the industry. One high-profile advantage leagues and clubs promote for their active involvement in the secondary market is that authenticated tickets to "any game" are available by going on the club website. Box 13.1 illustrates the secondary market for Game 5 of the 2015 NBA Final Series between the Golden State Warriors and the Cleveland Cavaliers. Here the huge demand with high scarcity led to high prices listed by sellers on the secondary market rarely seen before.

BOX 13.1 GOLDEN STATE WARRIORS

The 2015 NBA Finals series between the Cleveland Cavaliers and the Golden State Warriors from the outset had many storylines that suggested there would be a high demand for tickets. The Cavaliers had the return of LeBron James after winning several NBA championships and MVPs at Miami Heat. The Cavaliers had never won a NBA championship, and James himself expressed extreme confidence in his own abilities to lead his team to championship rings. The Warriors had the best regular season record in the NBA and featured the 2014/15 MVP Stephen Curry. The Warriors had not won a NBA championship for 40 years,

Games 1 and 2 were in Oakland. It was reported that the market for Game 1 secondary market tickets was "stronger than any Finals game in at least the last five years."[7] Games 3 and 4 were in Cleveland. Cleveland-based ticket broker Amazing Tickets owner Mark Klang said that the demand for tickets for this year's Finals "was double the market" for the 2007 Spurs–Cavaliers Finals, the last time it came to Cleveland. After four games, the teams were two games each.

Seat Location	Primary Market	Secondary Market Seller List Prices		
	Average Price per Regular Season Home Game for Season Ticket Holders	June 14, 2015 NBA Finals Game 5 Price Range**		
		Example Section	Low	High
VIP AA	$2,000.00	VIP on Court (First Row)	$11,999.50	$49,053.49
Courtside Club	$540.00	Mid Section 1	$9,197.68	$20,970.00
Courtside Club	$525.00	Upper Section 15	$6,745.35	$11,941.25
Courtside Club	$360.00	Section 7	$4,905.82	$10,118.03
Mezzanine Club	$285.00	N/A	N/A	N/A
Sideline Club	$280.00	Lower Section 128	$2,799.50	$8,737.50
Sideline Club	$225.00	Mid Section 127	$2,912.50	$8,249.37
Sideline Club	$180.00	Upper Section 102	$2,504.75	$6,698.75
Lower Level	$135.00	Lower Section 124	$1,531.98	$6,132.56
Lower Level	$120.00	Lower Section 122	$1,349.07	$5,650.25
Lower Level	$100.00	Section 104	$1,963.03	$3,740.82
Lower Level	$85.00	Upper Section 121	$1,316.45	$3,679.07
Club 200	$60.00	Section 202	$778.22	$2,912.50
Club 200	$42.00	Section 216	$774.73	$2,277.58
Club 200	$36.00	Section 227	$778.22	$1,226.75
Club 200	$30.00	Section 223	$694.34	$982.10

EXHIBIT 13.8 Golden State Warriors Dynamic Pricing for June 2015 Playoff Games

** Note: High and Low price ranges for Seat Sections captured from TicketMaster website on 6/13/2015 from 12:03pm – 12:23pm.

* Source: Golden State Warriors Season Ticket Webpage and TicketMaster

Exhibit 13.8 shows the secondary market ticket price ranges for Game 5 in Oakland. These ranges are for listed prices rather than actual transactions. Some season ticket holders appear to have set very high prices they were prepared to sell at and bypass the opportunity to be inside the venue with its high-energy atmosphere. All tickets listed on the secondary market were sold by Ticketmaster and were guaranteed to be authentic. The average ticket prices quoted for Exhibit 13.8 for the primary market are for regular season games. During the NBA post-season, the primary market ticket price increased following each round at the playoffs.

One message of Exhibit 13.8 is that secondary markets now provide fans with the opportunity to access even the most highly demanded games. It is just a matter of willingness to pay what to many are very steep ticket prices.

Exhibit 13.9 presents how in 2015 StubHub has a partnership with the LA Galaxy (MLS) to operate its secondary market. Shown in this Exhibit are the average secondary market ticket prices for the last eight home games in Section 132 at StubHub Center in 2015 (formerly called Home Depot Center). Section 132 is premium seating, being on the bottom deck on the half-way line. On this market, individual season ticket holders can list their tickets for resale. These are list prices and potential buyers may choose not to buy at these prices.

The secondary market listings that underlie Exhibit 13.9 were done on Monday June 22, two days before the LA Galaxy versus Portland Timbers game on a Wednesday night. A general pattern observed for non-elite games in secondary markets is a decline in listed selling prices – see Box 13.2. The average

Date and opponent	Primary Market		Secondary Market Seller List Prices		
	Season ticket holder price	Individual game ticket price	Number of tickets listed	StubHub ticket price range	Average ticket price
Wed. June 24 v. Portland Timbers	$64	$75*	34	$54.65–95.60	$69.67
Sat. July 4 v. Toronto FC	$64	$75*	51	$89.95–221.96	$140.91
Fri. July 17 v. San Jose Earthquakes	$64	$75*	33	$101.45–195.05	$127.30
Sun. Aug. 9 v. Seattle Sounders	$64	$108*	23	$113.15–149	$133.66
Sun. Aug. 23 v. New York City FC	$64	$108**	27	$113.15–177.50	$137.25
Sat. Sept. 12 v. Montreal Impact	$64	$75*	47	$89.75–148.25	$109.72
Sat. Sept. 26 v. FC Dallas	$64	$75*	37	$78.05–148.25	$112.00
Sun. Oct. 18 v. Portland Timbers	$64	$75*	25	$122.98–148.25	$132.22

EXHIBIT 13.9 Primary Market and StubHub Secondary Market Ticket Prices in 2015 for Section 132 (Sideline) of LA Galaxy (MLS)

Note: *$87.25 with facility fee of $1.00 + service charge $11.25.
**$122.50 with facility fee 1.00 + service charge $13.50.
Source: StubHub Center (as of June 22, 2015)

secondary market ticket price in Exhibit 13.9 for the June 24 game ($69.67) is well below the average price for the October 18 visit by the Portland Timbers to StubHub Center ($132.22). Several of the individual listed prices for the June 24 game were below the lowest average cost to purchase full season tickets on the primary market. This willingness to price below primary market cost reflects the perishability of a ticket to a sporting event that is not used.

BOX 13.2 SECONDARY MARKET TICKET PURCHASE DECISION: WHEN TO BUY?

The secondary ticket market has opened up many opportunities for fans and entertainment seekers to access tickets to events of all profiles. Brokers, speculators, and ticket owners with scheduling issues have many ways to move their inventory of tickets. This has led to much discussion about when is best to buy tickets, supply and demand issues, and speculation about how to get those "sought-after" tickets.

But, and contrary to what many think, secondary ticket prices for many sporting events typically drop considerably in the final days or even hours before the start of the game or event. With a few exceptions (such as the Super Bowl), it is normally recommended to be patient on the secondary market if price is an issue for a potential buying decision as to whether to purchase a certain high-value ticket or not. A number of reports support this advice.

A 2012 report by *Business Wire* noted that on StubHub, ticket prices for a major event were dropping 30 percent in value from one month out to one day prior. The chief marketing officer of StubHub explained: "Because event tickets eventually expire, we find that sellers often lower their prices gradually as the event date approaches, and dramatically on the day of the event."[8]

A 2012 *Bleacher Nation* report[9] similarly discusses that buying baseball tickets late in the season in the secondary market often results in deeply discounted tickets (often below face value), particularly if the club is not performing well. In response, many clubs now have rules in place for the resale of tickets, such as not allowing resale on StubHub after six hours before game time.

A 2012 article by *Deal News* also supports the notion of patience in purchasing high-demand tickets in the secondary market, which the author describes as a "perishable good," that loses all of its value if it is not consumed by its "expiration date."[10] The article cites a study by SeatGeek that found that from 24 to 48 hours before a game, tickets lost the same 30 percent in value as quoted in the *Business Wire* article above. In one example in the article, a ticket to a particular NFL game was priced at $217 a few weeks out, dropping to $118 a day prior to the game.

Clearly, patience is a virtue that will be rewarded when buying on the secondary market, unless measures are put in place (e.g., time limits, extra fees to the re-seller, etc.) to prevent a sale.

Exhibit 13.10 illustrates how the San Francisco 49ers use the NFL Ticket Exchange, run by Ticketmaster for its secondary market.

As noted in Exhibit 13.10, Ticketmaster pays many NFL clubs for the right to be their official ticketing companies. A major plus with the secondary market underlying Exhibit 13.10 is that the tickets are authentic. There is also a high level of efficiency in the transaction process. In addition, insight can be gained into the type of buyers on the primary market who are reselling their tickets. Several

Date	Opponent	Game Classification	Primary Market		Secondary Market		
			Season ticket price	Single ticket price	Number of tickets listed	Ticket price range	Average ticket price
Sun August 23	Dallas Cowboys	Pre-season	$63	$63	75	$83–306	$135.00
Thurs Sept 3	San Diego Chargers	Pres-season	$63	$63	157	$63–306	$106.20
Mon Sept 14	Minnesota Vikings	Marquee	$156	$211	155	$156–428	$196.92
Sun Oct 4	Green Bay Packers	Marquee	$156	$211	150	$244–500	$359.84
Sun Oct 18	Baltimore Ravens	Prime	$125	$180	184	$140–428	$183.34
Thurs Oct 22	Seattle Seahawks	Marquee	$156	$211	172	$211–501	$283.06
Sun Nov 8	Atlanta Falcons	Prime	$125	$180	189	$138–428	$177.90
Sun Nov 29	Arizona Cardinals	Prime	$125	$180	188	$137–428	$203.03
Sun Dec 20	Cincinnati Bengals	Marquee	$156	$211	174	$165–428	$211.17
Sun Jan 3	St. Louis Rams	Prime	$125	$180	173	$125–428	$189.23

EXHIBIT 13.10 Primary Market and NFL Exchange Secondary Market Ticket Prices in 2015 for Section 126 (End Zone Lower Bowl) of San Francisco 49ers' (NFL) Levi's Stadium (as of June 22, 2015)

examples illustrate the increased transparency. There are eight regular season games at Levi's Stadium in the 2015 season – see Exhibit 13.7. Demand and supply across these eight games is far from uniform. The listed prices in Exhibit 13.10 are for Section 126, an end zone on the lower bowl. The average secondary market ticket price in this section ranges from $359.84 for the Green Bay Packers game to $177.90 for the Atlanta Falcons game. One can find fascinating insights into seller behavior by analyzing listed prices on the secondary market. For example:

- Two tickets in Row 5 of Section 126 (seats 1–20) are listed for resale in seven of the eight games. In six of these seven games it is the highest list price of any seats in the Section 126 secondary market. These seats are listed at $428 each game compared to season ticketprices of $156 for marquee games to $125 for prime games. The seller here is seeking arbitrage profits.
- Eighteen tickets are listed by one seller for each and every regular season game in Section 126 – Row 21 (seats 3 to 20). There is a high probability this is a broker reselling tickets on the secondary market.

When clubs go to the playoffs, secondary markets can offer very large arbitrage opportunities for those interested in making profits as opposed to sharing in the at-venue experience for playoff games – see Box 13.1 on the large potential arbitrage opportunities for Game 5 of the 2015 NBA Finals should the listed prices actually become transaction prices.

13.7 SUITE REVENUES

Exhibit 13.1 has separate pillars for regular seats in a venue and suites at a venue. Venues differ greatly in the investment made in suites and in the ability to yield high levels of revenues from this area. Often suite sales are made on a negotiated basis within some basic guidelines provided by a club's marketing group. Moreover, suites can differ in terms of size, location, and whether high-end food and beverage is included in the quoted price or is separately billed.

Exhibit 13.11 has summary information from the RSV database about the potential dramatic differences across NFL clubs in 2015 clubs in their suite revenue. The data here is indicative as the assumption is that all available suites are sold at the midpoint of the price range reported by RSV. It is also assumed that food and beverage is included in the quoted suite price ranges. The message in Exhibit 13.11 is that several NFL clubs at the top end can have suite revenues five or six times those of the NFL clubs at the bottom end. The top four NFL clubs by estimated suite revenues (Dallas Cowboys, New York Giants, New York Jets, and San Francisco 49ers) average $72.89 million. In stark contrast, the bottom four NFL clubs (Kansas City Chiefs, Seattle Seahawks, Arizona Cardinals and Buffalo Bills) average only $8.074 in estimated suite revenues using the assumptions underlying Exhibit 13.11.

13.8 INDUSTRY EXAMPLE: OAKLAND ATHLETICS EMBRACE VARIABLE PRICING AND DYNAMIC PRICING

The Oakland Athletics of Major League Baseball play in the O.co Coliseum in Oakland, California. They share the stadium with the Oakland Raiders of the NFL. For NFL games the capacity of the

Team	# of suites	Term	# Seats low	# Seats high	Price low	Price high	Price mid	Est. revenue
Dallas Cowboys	200	20 years max	12	20	$ 100,000	$ 1,000,000	$ 550,000	$ 110,000,000
New York Giants	200	—	16	24	$ 150,000	$ 500,000	$ 325,000	$ 65,000,000
New York Jets	200	—	16	24	$ 150,000	$ 500,000	$ 325,000	$ 65,000,000
San Francisco 49ers	165	10–20 years	16	20	$ 125,000	$ 500,000	$ 312,500	$ 51,562,500
Washington Redskins	244	5–10 years	10	16	$ 90,000	$ 250,000	$ 170,000	$ 41,480,000
Minnesota Vikings	131	4 years min	10	10	$ 110,000	$ 500,000	$ 305,000	$ 39,955,000
Cleveland Browns	147	4–10 years	10	20	$ 350,000	$ 125,000	$ 237,500	$ 34,912,500
Carolina Panthers	158	6–15 years	10	50	$ 87,000	$ 325,000	$ 206,000	$ 32,548,000
Philadelphia Eagles	172	5–10 years	14	30	$ 125,000	$ 250,000	$ 187,500	$ 32,250,000
Miami Dolphins	160	3–10 years	10	36	$ 50,000	$ 300,000	$ 175,000	$ 28,000,000
Houston Texans	185	6–10 years	14	24	$ 50,000	$ 250,000	$ 150,000	$ 27,750,000
Detroit Lions	125	—	10	30	$ 110,000	$ 225,000	$ 167,500	$ 20,937,500
Indianapolis Colts	142	3–10 years	8	21	$ 40,000	$ 235,000	$ 137,500	$ 19,525,000
Tampa Bay Buccaneers	195	5–10 years	8	46	$ 45,000	$ 150,000	$ 97,500	$ 19,012,500
Atlanta Falcons	164	3–7 years	16	24	$ 52,000	$ 175,000	$ 113,500	$ 18,614,000
Chicago Bears	133	5–9 years	12	32	$ 75,000	$ 200,000	$ 137,500	$ 18,287,500
Baltimore Ravens	108	5–7 years	20	24	$ 60,000	$ 250,000	$ 155,000	$ 16,740,000
New Orleans Saints	137	1–5 years	16	38	$ 90,000	$ 150,000	$ 120,000	$ 16,440,000
Green Bay Packers	166	4 years	16	21	$ 57,000	$ 133,000	$ 95,000	$ 15,770,000
New England Patriots	80	10 years	—	—	$ 85,000	$ 305,000	$ 195,000	$ 15,600,000
Tennessee Titans	175	5–10 years	16	22	$ 52,000	$ 125,000	$ 88,500	$ 15,487,500
Cincinnati Bengals	114	6–12 years	12	12	$ 76,000	$ 165,000	$ 120,500	$ 13,737,000
St. Louis Rams	124	4–15 years	10	36	$ 58,000	$ 135,000	$ 96,500	$ 11,966,000
Denver Broncos	106	—	14	18	$ 86,000	$ 130,000	$ 108,000	$ 11,448,000
Pittsburgh Steelers	129	6–10 years	6	12	$ 46,000	$ 125,000	$ 85,500	$ 11,029,500
Oakland Raiders	143	1–10 years	12	20	$ 50,000	$ 100,000	$ 75,000	$ 10,725,000
San Diego Chargers	112	3–10 years	12	36	$ 45,000	$ 135,000	$ 90,000	$ 10,080,000
Jacksonville Jaguars	90	5–10 years	12	20	$ 75,000	$ 135,000	$ 105,000	$ 9,450,000
Buffalo Bills	164	3–5 years	12	31	$ 21,000	$ 88,000	$ 54,500	$ 8,938,000
Arizona Cardinals	88	3–7 years	12	12	$ 65,000	$ 125,000	$ 95,000	$ 8,360,000
Seattle Seahawks	82	5–9 years	12	34	$ 50,000	$ 150,000	$ 100,000	$ 8,200,000
Kansas City Chiefs	80	4 years	18	54	$ 42,000	$ 128,000	$ 85,000	$ 6,800,000

EXHIBIT 13.11 Potential NFL Clubs Suite Revenues in 2015 Using RSV Database

Note: Estimated revenue assumes that all suites are fully sold at the midpoint price of low and high per suite.

Source: RSV Database

Coliseum is approximately 56,000. For MLB games, the Athletics play with a capacity of approximately 35,000 with much of the third deck blocked out under tarps. The context of the Athletics' ticket pricing at the start of the 2015 season was one with both positives and challenges. The Athletics had performed superbly on the field in the long era with Billy Beane as its general manager (since 1998) – see Chapter 6. The positive publicity associated with Michael Lewis' *Moneyball* book and the subsequent movie with the same title starring Brad Pitt strengthened the Oakland Athletics' brand. The challenges included playing in an oversized stadium that had been renovated to benefit the Raiders, the stadium itself being one of the least attractive in the MLB as a ballpark, and the ownership expressing multiple times a strong desire to move to San Jose and build a new state-of-the-art stadium. In addition, the Athletics shared the Bay Area market with the San Francisco Giants who had won the World Championship in 2010, 2012, and 2014 and played in one of the most attractive stadiums in all of baseball. It is in this context that the Athletics' ticketing executives have exhibited much creativity and a willingness to experiment and innovate. Like most MLB clubs, they also have used many game-day promotions and events to boost demand – such as bobblehead days, T-shirt days, and firework nights. Exhibit 14.7 outlines the top giveaways and promotions across all MLB games in 2014.

13.8.1 Oakland Athletics Use a Gold/Green/White Classification of Games to Guide Variable Pricing Decisions

The full season ticket package for the Athletics includes 81 regular home games. As with many MLB clubs, the Athletics also offer multiple "mini-ticket" packages. Their most popular mini-pack is a 24-game "Pick Plan." These full season and mini-plans are available for fans to buy before the season at set prices known at the time of the purchase. Outside of these multi-game plans are a large number of individual game tickets. Most Athletics home games are not sell-outs. Exhibit 13.2 shows that its average capacity utilization is less than 65 percent.

For the 2015 MLB season, the Athletics classified games into three categories when setting the ticket prices of individual games for their season ticket holder packages: gold (eight games), green (32 games), and white (41 games). Gold game tickets were priced highest and white game tickets were priced lowest. There were several factors underlying the gold/green/white classification:

1   Day of the week: Fridays, Saturdays, and Sundays typically have higher demand than those on Monday through Thursday. None of the 2015 white games are on a Saturday. A breakdown of the 81 home games by the gold/green/white classification is:

Game tier	Monday	Tuesday	Wednesday	Thursday	Friday	Saturday	Sunday	Total
Gold games	1	1	0	0	1	3	2	8
Green games	3	1	2	1	9	11	5	32
White games	3	10	11	9	3	0	5	41

Six out of the eight gold games were on a Friday, Saturday, or Sunday. The majority of the Tuesday, Wednesday, and Thursday games are classified as white games.

2   The eight gold games have multiple aspects that made management anticipate high demand for tickets. One aspect was a premier status opponent with high-profile star players – the New York

Yankees, the Los Angeles Angels, the Los Angeles Dodgers, and the cross-town team rival the San Francisco Giants. The average payroll of the visiting clubs for the eight gold games is $189 million versus $123 million for opponents in green games and $122 million for opponents in white games. Opening day on April 6 (versus Texas Rangers) was classified as a gold game, on the basis of many years of its being one of the highest demand games in the season. The Tuesday August 18 night game against the LA Dodgers, the club with the highest club payroll in 2015 was classified as a gold game.

3   Public holidays: all three public holidays were categorized as green games as opposed to white games – Memorial Day (Detroit), July 4 (Seattle), and Labor Day (Astros).

The Athletics have multiple promotion days – such as the Saturday July 5 game against the Seattle Mariners (Tote Bag Day), the Saturday July 18 game against the Minnesota Twins (Hello Kitty Bobblehead), and the Tuesday night August 18 game against the Los Angeles Dodgers (Mark McGwire Bobblehead). Jim Leahey, vice-president of sales and marketing stated:

> Mark McGwire is one of our most popular players and had not been back to be honored … We decided to do a bobblehead for the Tuesday August 18th game versus the Dodgers. McGwire's popularity combined with the fact that it is a high profile team (Dodgers) who doesn't visit us often and it's in summer, led us to believe it would be a high-demand game. One of the main points of emphasis in determining the color of a game was to spread demand. Over the past few seasons – when the team was especially hot – we had many weekend promotion days when we left money on the table because demand was too high. Season ticket holders who could choose games were taking up most of the inventory on those games. By creating a three tier system, we tried to spread demand.

13.8.2 Oakland Athletics Expand the Role of Dynamic Pricing

The path of many MLB clubs experimenting with dynamic pricing is to first adopt variable pricing (Era #3) for both season ticket packages and individual game ticket prices, with individual game tickets for a given game being priced higher than the season ticket package for the same game. The individual ticket prices for different games under variable pricing formed what is called the "base price" for individual tickets sold before the start of the season. Early adopters of dynamic pricing started with this base price and then later allowed dynamic pricing to subsequently shift prices due to changing demand and supply factors. Subsequently, some clubs have moved to dynamic pricing of individual game tickets from the outset without having a "base price" period.

Steve Fanelli, executive director of ticket sales and operations at the Oakland Athletics provided the following background to the team expanding its use of dynamic pricing for tickets not sold to season ticket holders:

> In 2011, after 2 years of careful pricing and data analysis, we decided to implement our first phase of dynamic pricing with the help of our partner QCue. QCue had been working with our team, to evaluate our historical sales and pricing data in order to create a customized algorithm to accurately establish a base value for A's tickets, while defining triggers that would move pricing in either direction. While dynamic pricing was not a new concept and consumers were

accustomed to price variability when purchasing airline tickets, hotel rooms, and more, it was a change from the traditional sports ticket pricing structure. Further, until QCue and others created a platform to overcome the technical barrier to making an actual price change in a timely manner, dynamic pricing was not feasible for sports teams to implement full scale. With technical barriers overcome, we selected our 9 premium games and dynamically priced all single game ticket inventory in order to introduce the concept to the market, as well as test the validity of the pricing strategy. Our goals were to drive revenue for our biggest games, encourage earlier buying within the sales cycle, and create additional value for our season package holders who purchased fixed-price tickets. After a successful roll out in 2011 which included us selling out 4 dates in advance of day-of-event, as compared to zero in 2010, and an overall increase from projected revenue for those events, we decided to implement full dynamic pricing for all single game ticket sales in 2012.

Since 2012, Oakland A's single game tickets have been dynamically priced for all games and in all single ticket seating categories. Prior to our annual single ticket on-sale, base prices were set for each of the seating categories and once demand was established by initial single ticket velocity, prices were adjusted accordingly. We made a tactical change in 2014, and eliminated the base pricing strategy in favor of a more true dynamic pricing plan. Price categories for each individual game were set based on multiple factors, well in advance of the single ticket on-sale date and adjusted accordingly. These pre-single ticket sales factors included group tickets, suites, and season packages sales. At the time of the individual ticket on-sale, fans were now buying tickets at the true market rate and not setting the rate with initial on-sale per-game velocity.

Dynamic pricing continues to be one of the top benefits for season package holder retention and the "Lock-in and Save" message has been prevalent in our renewal marketing strategy. Season packages through 2014 had fixed pricing, regardless of the package plan. Our philosophical change in how we evaluate base pricing allowed us to make a fundamental change in our season ticket pricing strategy as well. In 2015, we implemented a change in our season package pricing for our most popular plan, the 24-game Pick Plan. Prior to 2015, fans could pick 24-games of their choice at one fixed rate. Starting in 2015, we established a 3-tiered variable price structure for these pick-plans. The Gold, Green, and White tiers for pick plan packages were implemented to incentivize season package holders who purchased fixed-seat, fixed-game plans, to maintain their level of commitment as well as encourage pick-plan holders to consider additional savings per game by upgrading their account. This tiered structure has been successful in varying the type of events selected across the pick-plan accounts, therefore opening additional inventory for top-tier games for single sale while at the same time, increasing the base of season tickets for projected lower attendance games.

13.8.3 Dynamic Pricing in Action at Oakland Athletics for Six Series of Games

Exhibit 13.12 illustrates the dynamic prices set for six series of games in the late July to late September period in 2015. For each of the 19 games in Exhibit 13.12, we show prices for four sections – Section 121 (superb seats behind the Athletics' dugout), Section 221 (on the second deck, but sight lines over Athletics' dugout), Section 106R (on bottom deck in right field), and Section 242 (the bleachers, behind center outfield). For each section there are many different prices across games, as one would expect with dynamic pricing. Section 121 has 12 different prices for the 19 games, Section 221 has ten different prices, Section 106R has ten different prices, and Section 242 has 11 different prices.

EXHIBIT 13.12 Oakland Athletics Single-Ticket Primary Market Pricing Using Dynamic Pricing for Six Series in July to September 2015

Opponent	Date	Day of week	Time	Game tier color*	Promotion day with example**	Primary market			
						Section 121 (behind A's dugout)	Section 221 (second deck)	Section 106R (bottom deck right field)	Section 242 (bleachers)
Cleveland Indians	30 Jul	Thurs	7:05	White	Yes	$54	$30	$30	$10
	31 Jul	Fri	6:35	Green	Yes[a]	$72	$40	$46	$15
	1 Aug	Sat	6:05	Green	Yes	$63	$40	$40	$12
	2 Aug	Sun	1:05	Green	Yes[b]	$63	$40	$40	$5
Baltimore Orioles	3 Aug	Mon	7:05	White	—	$55	$34	$36	$9
	4 Aug	Tues	7:05	White	Yes[b]	$57	$34	$32	$12
	5 Aug	Weds	12:35	White	—	$54	$34	$32	$2
Houston Astros	6 Aug	Thur	7:05	White	Yes	$54	$32	$30	$12
	7 Aug	Fri	7:05	White	Yes	$57	$34	$32	$12
	8 Sep	Sat	1:05	Green	Yes[c]	$62	$41	$40	$12
	9 Aug	Sun	1:05	Green	—	$62	$40	$40	$12
Los Angeles Dodgers	18 Aug	Tues	7:05	Gold	Yes[d]	$76	$42	$38	$20
	19 Aug	Weds	12:35	Green	—	$65	$40	$34	$2
Tampa Bay Rays	21-Aug	Fri	7:05	Green	Yes	$62	$40	$40	$12
	22-Aug	Sat	6:05	Green	Yes[e]	$74	$46	$45	$21
	23-Aug	Sun	1:05	Green	—	$62	$40	$40	$12
San Francisco Giants	25 Sept	Fri	7:05	Gold	Yes	$116	$60	$55	$30
	26 Sept	Sat	1:05	Gold	—	$123	$66	$70	$36
	27 Sept	Sun	1:05	Gold	—	$122	$55	$55	$32

* **Game tier color** signifies expected strength of demand: Gold is Highest tier, Green is second tier, and White is lowest tier.

** Promotion day with examples: (a) Fireworks; (b) Mike Gallego Windmill Windup Toy; (c) Chevy Free Parking; (d) Mark McGuire Bobblehead; (e) Fireworks + Star Wars R2D2 Beanie.

There are 76 possible prices points in Exhibit 13.12 – 19 days × the four sections examined. Under ticket price Era #1, there would be one listed ticket price across all 76 combinations. Under Era #2 of tiered pricing there would be four potentially different listed ticket prices as each section is a tier and all games for a given tier are priced the same. Under Era #3 of variable pricing, using the Athletics gold/green/white categories of games there would be 12 potential different listed price points (three categories of games in each section × four sections). Under Era #4 of dynamic pricing there are 36 different listed ticket prices in Exhibit 13.5, as the same price points appear for multiple games. Eras #1 to #3 of listedticket pricing effectively suppresses important differences across games in demand and supply factors that can be recognized by dynamic pricing.

The gold/green/white classification of games in terms of expected strength of demand are supported by the actual market list prices observed in Exhibit 13.12. The average listed ticket prices in Exhibit 13.12 for each of the four sections of interest are:

Game tier	Section 121	Section 221	Section 106R	Section 242
	MVP Infield	Plaza Infield	Lower Box	Bleachers
Gold games (four games)	$109.25	$55.75	$54.50	$29.50
Green games (nine games)	$65.00	$40.78	$40.56	$11.44
White games (six games)	$55.17	$33.00	$32.00	$9.50

The average ticket price when purchased by a full season ticket holder was $44 for Section 121, $25 for Section 221, $32 for Section 106R, and $10 for Section 242. The Athletics use information about dynamic prices being well above the season ticket average prices for multiple games in their full season package as part of their "Lock-in and Save" marketing message promoting season ticket purchases.

13.9 SUMMARY

The ticket arena continues to evolve driven by a continual flow of new products on the primary and secondary markets. While the single biggest driver of ticket and suite revenue is the position of the sport in the general sports landscape and the attractiveness of the individual game or event, much room exists to increase venue revenues by creative pricing strategies. The expertise to develop and execute these strategies often requires a greater use of partnerships with third party companies than in the past.

APPENDIX 13A AVERAGE TICKET PRICE TRENDS FOR NFL, MLB, NBA, AND NHL

The Team Marketing Report tracks stadium-related costs for fans across the NFL, MLB, NBA, and NHL. Their standard report for each year includes the average primary market ticket price per game which is computed as "a weighted average of season ticket prices for general seating categories, determined by factoring the tickets in each price range as a percentage of the total number of seats in each venue."[11] Exhibits 13.13 and 13.14 highlight major trends in average ticket prices.

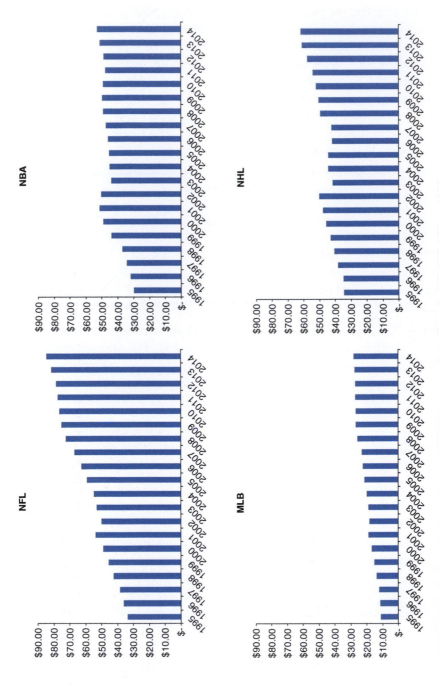

EXHIBIT 13.13 Team Marketing Report 1995/2014, Average Ticket Prices for NFL, MLB, NBA, and NHL
Source: Team Marketing Report Fan Cost Index

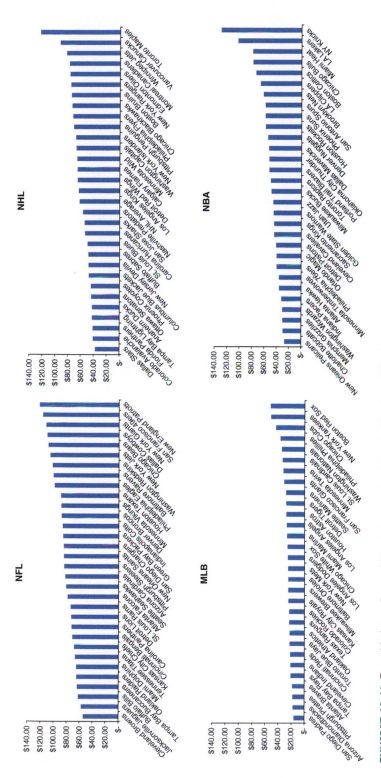

EXHIBIT 13.14 Team Marketing Report 2014, Average Ticket Prices for NFL, MLB, NBA, and NHL

Source: Team Marketing Report Fan Cost Index

Exhibit 13.13 shows the average ticket price per league over a 20-year period since 1995.The NFL benefits from very high demand and only eight regular season home games. In contrast, MLB has large inventories of tickets and 81 home games in the regular season to sell. The NBA historically was aggressive in raising ticket prices in the early 2000s. The NHL was impacted by a lost season in 2004/5. The ticket prices for that season were what was quoted at the start of a season that never occurred.

Exhibit 13.14 shows the variation across clubs in their average ticket prices in 2014. This is yet another area where leagues have great variations at any one time on financial, especially revenue related variables. Leagues that impose constraints on player payroll (especially the NFL, NBA, and NHL) effectively provide a windfall to clubs that have high venue revenues vis-à-vis other clubs in the same league that have relatively low venue revenues. As noted in Section 13.2.1, clubs such as the New England Patriots (NFL), New York Knicks (NBA), and Toronto Maple Leafs (NHL) have average ticket prices in their primary market more than twice those of the club with the lowest average ticket price in their same league.

NOTES

1 The Oakland Athletics play in the O.co Coliseum, which it shares with the Oakland Raiders of the NFL. The capacity of the Coliseum for NFL games is 56,000. For MLB games, part of the Coliseum is kept under "wraps." Several dedicated baseball stadiums have capacities of approximately 37,000 to 38,000 – such as Marlins Park of the Miami Marlins and PNC Park of the Pittsburgh Pirates.

2 Capacity estimates are often approximate as clubs experiment with temporary seating extensions and seeking new ways to add extra seating. Some clubs now sell "standing room only" tickets that mean that average attendance can exceed total capacity, which is typically based on total seating capacity.

3 www.teammarketing.com.

4 An example is for the Wimbledon tennis major. The property rights-holder is AELTC, the body that owns the Wimbledon tennis complex. Wimbledon sells a package of 65 tickets for five years of elite tickets. After the first sale of the 65 tickets, AELTC then offers to buy back one or more of these tickets at preannounced prices. These bought-back tickets are sold by AELTC a second time.

5 J. McCarthy, "Selling out with Russ Stanley," *Selling Out*, November 20, 2013.

6 http://m.tigers.mlb.com/news/article/42674478/mlbam-experience-partner-to-deliver-mobile-seat–experience-upgrades.

7 "NBA Finals ticket prices highest in five years; Gilbert profiting from flash seats transfers," *Sports Business Daily*, June 9, 2015.

8 "StubHub finds savvy fans save 30 percent making last minute plans," *Business Wire*, May 16, 2012, www.businesswire.com/news/home/20120516006359/en/StubHub-Finds-Savvy-Fans-Save-30-Percent#.VOZ_x0JDZVs.

9 B. Taylor, "Reselling tickets on StubHub this year: price floor, extra fees, sale ending six hours before event," *Bleacher Nation*, February 22, 2013, www.bleachernation.com/2013/02/22/reselling-tickets-on-stubhub-this-year-price-floor-extra-fees-sale-ending-six-hours-before-event.

10 L. Carlozo, "How to score cheap NFL tickets with the SeatGeek team," *Deal News*, September 17, 2012, http://dealnews.com/features/How-to-Score-Cheap-NFL-Tickets-with-the-Seat-Geek-Team/614500.html.

11 www.teammarketing.com.

14 BUILDING SPORTS ENGAGEMENT
LIVE SPORT EVENT TIME AND BEYOND LIVE SPORT EVENT TIME

Many stakeholders are themselves highly engaged in key aspects of the sporting world or are investing heavily to pursue their own interests by promoting higher levels of sports engagement by others. This chapter examines some select aspects of sports engagement to showcase the diverse areas that fall under this umbrella. We highlight how rapid advances in technology and the widespread embracing of digital tools are driving change in this area. Both the minefields and the opportunities of increased and more diverse sports engagement are examined.

14.1 MANY AREAS OF SPORTS ENGAGEMENT

Exhibit 14.1 (Panel A) outlines important distinctions when examining the sports engagement landscape. Different areas of engagement are:

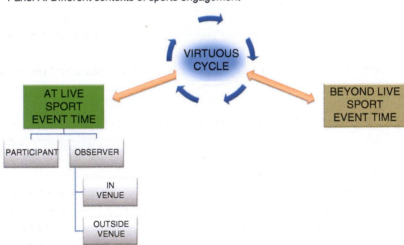

EXHIBIT 14.1 Rich Landscape of Sports Engagement

- Live event time(s) versus times when the event(s) of interest is (are) not occurring. Event time is when the action is on the field, on the court, at the raceway, etc. While what occurs at the event time is central to the whole sports ecosystem, the time taken is typically a small amount of the total time available to consume sports. Many live sports events last between two and three hours. Others are shorter and some, such as NASCAR events, can last three to five hours. These relatively short broadcast times leave many hours available for replays, discussion of on- and off-field stories, interviews, and more.
- Participant versus observer. Participants can be professionals or amateurs with the latter typically participating in organized events or in a less structured recreational mode. Participant obstacle races are an important growing category, where companies such as Tough Mudder, Spartan Run, and Warrior Dash have attracted thousands of participants to their individual events in multiple countries.
- Observer as a spectator at the venue where a sporting event occurs versus viewing the event from a location outside of the event location. Examples of the latter are at a home, at a sports bar, or at community center square for, say, a game that the national soccer team is playing in far away.

There is a mutually reinforcing relationship between the two boxes at the top of Exhibit 14.1, as shown by the virtuous circle positioned between them. High levels of engagement beyond the live sports event are fueled by great live events. Great pre-event build-up can drive a heightened level of excitement for the live event. The sports world is one where winning on the field can have a significant positive effect on many of the other areas of sports engagement.

The virtuous circle in Exhibit 14.1, however, can work in the opposite direction – what some call the "vicious circle." A sporting team that sizably underperforms on the field can negatively impact the experience of spectators at the live event venue or viewers outside the live event venue. This in turn can lead to less interest in engagement beyond the event time period. One of the challenges for sport business managers building engagement platforms at the club level or player level is their "limited control" over a key variable. A major driver of engagement – winning by a team or performing superbly for a player – is beyond their direct control. One goal of sport business managers in this context is to build strong engagement platforms that can sustain extended periods when a team or a player underperforms on the field. Companies working with athletes in team sports can face high levels of frustration when they sponsor an athlete who, although playing at the highest levels, is with a team that is not winning and consistently does not make the playoffs. One sports agent referred to their task in this context as "running uphill with lead weighted shoes."

14.2 MULTIPLE PLATFORMS AVAILABLE TO BUILD SPORTS ENGAGEMENT

The richness of the options available to the sports consumer continues to expand. Exhibit 14.1, Panel B, presents some key platforms. We first discuss some traditional platforms and then cover more recent additions for engagement. Traditional here means that the platform has existed for a long time period. These include (a) the game/sport on the field, (b) the club/event, (c) players/athletes and their coaches, (d) the sporting venue, (e) broadcast media, (f) print media, (g) sponsors and advertisers, and (h) sports gambling. More recent additions to the engagement platform arena draw heavily on the digital revolution that is transforming the business world in general and the sports business world in particular. These include (i) online sports content websites, (j) social media, (k) fantasy sports, and

(l) electronic games. Many of these platforms are discussed elsewhere in this book. Below we expand on those aspects less covered elsewhere.

Labeling a platform as "traditional" does not mean that advances for that platform have necessarily been slow relative to more recent additions. For example, one broadcaster (ESPN), which started in 1979, has very much been on the cutting edge for many years with regards to new ways to deepen the engagement of its community. This has included extensive partnering with several of the newer platforms of sports engagement. Decisions by key stakeholders seeking to build broader and deeper engagement almost without exception now are using combinations of the many platforms noted in Panel B of Exhibit 14.1.

14.2.1 Traditional Platforms of Sports Engagement

Traditional engagement platforms are now discussed in the following section:

Game/Sport on the Field

Leagues and federations in many sports have made multiple efforts to make their on-field product more engaging. These include competitive balance mechanisms (such as draft rules for rookies that aim to improve the playing talent of the lower performing clubs), rule changes to increase scoring, and rule changes to speed up the game or reduce the times when action on the field is on hold while the game clock is ticking.

An example is NASCAR restructuring their approach to deciding the Season Winning Driver. For many years, points per race were accumulated and the winning driver decided at the end of the season based on the number of total points accumulated during the entire race season (36 races currently). In several cases the drama of who would be the Season Winning Driver was over well before the last few race weekends. Drivers such as Jeff Gordon in an earlier era and more recently Jimmy Johnson are examples of having enough points to be unbeatable even if they drove none of the remaining few races. To create more excitement at the end of the season, NASCAR in 2004 moved to a "Chase for the Cup" format in its elite racing series. The 2015 format has 16 of the more than 40 NASCAR drivers qualify for the "Chase" based on their racing results over the first 26 races. For the last ten races of the season, this set of 16 drivers is progressively reduced based on a weighting from the first 26 races and on their performance in the final ten races. All NASCAR drivers run the last ten races, but it is only those qualifying for the "Cup" that can be the winner of the Season Championship. The final race of the season has the four remaining drivers in a "winner takes all" format. The effect of this "Chase for the Cup" innovation has been an increased interest in the back end of the season, especially in the final few races. NASCAR, in effect, moved to a playoff series format to decide their Series Champion.

Events in a playoff series invariably attract higher average viewer television ratings than do events during the regular season. Major League Baseball has, over time, added more teams and more games to its playoff season to better capture this higher level of fan engagement. MLB started with just two teams in a single World Series playoff until 1968, then moved to a four-team format from 1969 to 1993 when a Championship Series was added, then to eight teams from 1994 to 2011 when a Divisional Series was added, and then, most recently, to an updated format with ten teams since 2012 due to the addition of a Wild Card Round. With an increasing number of teams eligible for the playoffs, MLB has also found higher interest from fans in the month before the playoffs when there is greater hope and anticipation by more teams that they will indeed make the playoffs.

Club/Event

Many fans and viewers have a deep attachment to a specific sporting club or a specific sporting event or series. Family attachment to some sporting clubs can extend over multiple generations, even after some of the family have moved to other cities or even other countries. Liverpool FC of the EPL, for instance, has many fans on multiple continents, in part due to a large number of people who emigrated overseas from that city and then raised their own children to continue being fans of their heritage club. Multiple soccer clubs are now scheduling overseas "friendly games" in their pre-season warm-up. One factor in the choice of where these "friendlies" are played is the location of past generations of their hometown emigrants (their diaspora). Social media enables better identification of fan depth in different parts of the globe.

Some clubs have very active membership programs that increase the avidity of their fans around the world. For example, FC Barcelona is structured as an association (see Chapter 4 for further details on this structure), that has more than 150,000 members who are called "socis."

Major global events such as the Olympic Games and the FIFA World Cup in soccer are destination viewing for some individuals even if in other time periods they are not even casual viewers of Olympic sports or soccer. Social media now has identified such events as periods of high engagement. For example, consider Germany's 2014 World Cup victory over Argentina in Rio De Janeiro. The event:

> smashed global records on Twitter, and [became] the biggest sporting event in Facebook's history … Facebook said that 88 million global users made a record of 288 million interactions – posts, likes and comments – during the World Cup final. The social network site easily broke through the previous record held of 245 million interactions, set by the Super Bowl in 2013. The top five countries participating in the global "buzz" were, in order, US, Brazil, Argentina, Germany, and Indonesia.[1]

Players/Athletes and Coaches

Players/athletes and their coaches have long been important in fueling fan engagement in a sport. For many decades, the engagement was via their on-field performance and via interviews surrounding the game or outside of the game. These interviews were in what is now called a "one-to-many" format with no provision for the viewers to interact with the athletes and/or coaches being interviewed. Over time, players and coaches have been a central part of many of the other engagement platforms in Exhibit 14.1. Section 14.5 discusses rankings of the top ten athletes as regards both Facebook and Twitter followers.

Sporting Venue

Many sporting venues were constructed in a different technology era. Not surprisingly, technology played little role in building fan engagement in these older venues. Improvements in the fan experiences here first focused on areas such as better traffic flow in and out of the venue, ease of parking, higher quality/more diverse food options, and maintaining the venue in a clean condition. Section 14.4 outlines the major changes occurring now and going forward with regards to the in-stadium experience with major adoptions of technology at new and revamped venues.

Broadcast Media

This includes the traditional television and radio platforms. Broadcasters benefit greatly by attracting large viewership or audiences. For many years, this stakeholder in the sports ecosystem has been a major leader in seeking ways to improve the television experience, and more recently expanding to consider the mobile experience for fans.

Storytelling is a central part of sports broadcasting. Broadcasters now invest heavily in building background stories to promote to their audiences with the goal of having a deep emotional connection with key athletes scheduled to appear in the broadcasts. One example here is Olympic broadcasts where stories are told about how athletes built their sporting prowess over many years before they "competed for the gold" on Olympic event day. The broadcaster's goal is to have the viewer emotionally connect to the athlete. A second example is HBO's *Road to the Fight* storyline series that tracks the two competing boxers over several weeks before they step into the ring to fight for a world championship. The 2007 Oscar De La Hoya versus Floyd Mayweather fight set records for both in-arena revenues and pay-per-view subscriber revenues. It was promoted as "The World Awaits: De La Hoya vs. Mayweather." In the lead up to the fight, HBO produced a four-part series titled *De La Hoya–Mayweather 24/7* that aired in the four weeks before the May 5 fight day. The HBO series aired on the last three Sundays in April and on Thursday May 3. It very effectively 'played up' many emotional aspects that either increased fans' like or dislike for either of the fighters. In combat sports, the emotional connection for some fans can include cheering to see a fighter lose as much as cheering to see a fighter win! Here, boxing promoters play both the hate and the love ends of the emotional spectrum in building their audience. This HBO series is widely viewed as a landmark in the way boxing events (and also mixed martial arts events) are now produced and promoted in the weeks before the fight to build pay-per-view revenues on fight night.

Both the quality and quantity of cameras at major sporting events continues to increase. In-game technologies, such as graphics outlining the "first and ten" lines in football and the various instant replay formats, have greatly enhanced the viewer experience. For example, MLBAM incorporates technology from Sportvision in its broadcasts, including, for example, the Pitchf/x tracking system that "tracks the velocity, movement, release point, spin, and pitch location for every pitch."[2] Formula 1 and MotoGP now have multiple cameras in and on every car and motorcycle, allowing the producer to choose from dozens of different image feeds to make the storytelling of a race much more engaging. Formula 1 has experimented with the option of having fans choose the camera they want to see at any point in time that shows the area of interest for them, which could include the battle for leadership, the view of a particular turn, tire changes at pit row, the view of a spotter for a driver above the racetrack, and so on. These options allow the viewer to personalize their viewing experience by effectively being a self-producer of the content they watch, as well as a consumer of the event overall. Chapters 15 and 16 highlight these developments in detail.

The American national sport network ESPN has been a pioneer in continually improving the viewer experience. This pioneer status results from both investments in building engaging storylines, as well as staying at the forefront of broadcast technology. From the launch of ESPN in 1979, news show *SportsCenter* has been a signature program for its viewers. It now cycles more than eight times a day so that viewers know there is a regular "go-to" program that is always on and will provide updated results, highlight reels, top ten plays of the day, and featured hosts. Today, it is always live. *SportsCenter* is, for many fans, destination viewing and is now available on many devices as well as television.

Print Media

This includes hard-copy newspapers and magazines. For many decades, the single most accessed sports content was the daily sports pages and weekly magazines such as *Sports Illustrated*. This area has decreased sizably as a source of information and even more as a source of fan engagement. Millennials rarely access this platform for their sports engagement.

Sponsors and Advertisers

Chapter 10 discussed marketing *through* sports, where companies seek to leverage sports to better connect to their existing and potential partners and customers. Major sponsors of sporting leagues negotiate access to key inventories of tickets for elite events they use as competition prizes, such as trips to a Super Bowl, a UEFA Championship final, or a Rugby World Cup Final. These same sponsors also use these events to strengthen their partnerships with key business partners. For example, MasterCard is a major sponsor of World Rugby and activates this sponsorship through invites of senior executives of the many bank issuers of its cards to high-end hospitality at successive Rugby World Cups. The investment in these hospitality packages is motivated, in part, by these executives being excited to be a part of a major global sporting event.

Creative advertising using athletes can elevate and amplify the athlete's brand in a way that is not often possible on game day. The effective use of humor in advertising has often opened fans eyes to aspects of an athlete's personality that further deepens their avidity for anything involving that athlete.

Sports Gambling

Sports gambling gives an individual fan (or consumer) heightened (and in some cases very heightened) interest in the outcome of an event or aspect of an event (such as a point spread or finish order). In some countries, such as England and Australia, sports gambling has been legal for many years and is an important driver of fan interest in sports. In the United States, sports gambling is legal in a very limited way, such as in-person betting at casinos in the state of Nevada. In Canada, tight restrictions are placed on sports gambling, which require bettors to transact at physical locations run by provincial government bodies. While reports of large-scale illegal gambling in North America appear frequently, it is very much an underground industry and one that leagues and sponsors to date have not been able to directly embrace. Many believe that the continued growth in fantasy sports described below, especially daily fantasy sports, captures some of the same adrenaline that drives the high engagement levels of sports gamblers.

14.2.2 Addition of New Platforms with Greater Ability to Build More Personalized Engagement Programs

Two often-used expressions associated with the growing emergence of the internet since the early 1990s were: "the internet *has changed* everything" and "the internet *will change* everything." The sports engagement world is living testimony to both expressions holding true. The internet has been the foundation for multiple new platforms that have greatly increased the opportunities to build sports engagement.

Commentators distinguish between the Web 1.0 and Web 2.0 eras. In the Web 1.0 era, content was put on a website with no personalization to individual online readers. It was a one-to-many communication in the same way as traditional newspapers. The Web 1.0 world was a more efficient distribution platform than was hard-copy print media. Web 1.0 content also had the benefit of being able to be continuously updated as new information emerged. The Web 2.0 era is distinguished by user-generated content (UGC), where one-to-one communication between users of the internet occurs. Examples of Web 2.0-driven advances are illustrated later in this chapter and in many other chapters of this book.

Online Sports Content Websites

The first generation of sports websites were very much "one-to-many" sites, where content was developed that could be accessed by many people but with no interaction capability – the classic one-to-many communication. On such websites, users could find a set of websites that better fitted their interests, but the website learning about the interests of different users and tailoring content to them did not occur. The first editions of league and club websites were very much in the Web 1.0 tradition. Over time, Web 2.0 versions of league and club websites have emerged, as have updated versions of event, association, and athlete websites.

The Web 2.0 era saw multiple sports content websites emerge that allowed for many fans, as well as journalists, to post content and interact with readers who agree or disagree with them. Exhibit 14.2 outlines the 15 highest ranked online sports content websites in three selected months of 2014.

The leading sites attract more than 50 million unique US visitors each month, which is many times the readership base of newspapers and magazines in prior decades when they were the leading written providers of content. Over time, these online sites have increased in richness with the addition of video and interactive content as well as text. The continual updating of content attracts multiple daily visits by regular users of these sites. Several content sites have year-long high monthly usage, such as ESPN.com and Yahoo.com. Content sites related to specific leagues (such as MLB.com, NFL.com, and NHL.com) have higher usage patterns during their playing months. For example, MLB's lowest ranked months are in the November to March period when there are no MLB regular or post-season games.

Social Media

Key characteristics of social media include (a) UGC (sometimes called community based-input), (b) content-sharing, and (c) interaction among users. Exhibit 14.3 provides a timeline of some important social media companies starting with SixDegrees.com.

The activity levels in social media have engagement numbers previously not even imagined several decades earlier. Another feature of social media engagement is the frequency of multi-platform usage. At venues, spectators can be using Instagram and Periscope while also watching the live game on the field. At home, viewers can be using Facebook and Twitter while watching the live game on

Name	Feb 2014		June 2014		Dec 2014	
	Uniques	Rank	Uniques	Rank	Uniques	Rank
ESPN	56.488	2	80.689	1	88.384	1
Yahoo Sports – NBC Sports Network	63.637	1	58.201	2	66.547	2
Bleacher Report – Turner Sports/NBA	48.238	3	56.396	3	51.309	6
FoxSports.com on MSN/Sporting News*	46.275	4	44.298	4	56.650	4
USA Today Sports Media Group	40.508	5	39.552	5	40.513	7
NFL Internet Group	25.361	9	26.301	9	57.706	3
CBS Sports	26.197	8	25.432	10	51.806	5
SB Nation	28.949	7	28.196	8	36.185	8
Sports Illustrated	18.412	10	17.516	11	20.527	9
Deadspin	11.997	12	11.330	13	14.38	11
MLB	13.127	11	36.350	6	15.499	10
NHL	—	—	9.708	15	10.277	14
Sporting News Media**	32.302	6	28.882	7	—	—
Active.com	7.655	13	10.243	14	—	—
CineSport	7.219	15	—	—	10.579	13
FIFA	—	—	13.906	12	—	—
Stack Media	7.259	14	—	—	—	—
MSN Sports***	—	—	—	—	14.266	12
Huff Post Sports	—	—	—	—	8.900	15

EXHIBIT 14.2 US Sports Website Monthly Unique Visitors (Millions) and Ranks in Selected Months of 2014

* In February 2014 and June 2014, includes MSN; in December 2014 includes Sporting News.
** Sporting News Media included with FoxSports.com in December 2014.
*** MSN Sports included in FoxSports.com in February 2014 and June 2014.
Source: Sports Business Journal

a high-definition television. Subsequent sections of this chapter provide multiple examples of social media being used as an integral part of fan engagement initiatives. The high level of new company entrants in Exhibit 14.3 highlights the importance of major incumbents continuing to upgrade their offerings as new entrants.

Fantasy Sports

In the season-long versions of fantasy sports, participants build their own individual teams for the coming season to compete against the teams of other fantasy players. Each sporting game (football, soccer, cricket, etc.) for which a fantasy game has been developed has an algorithm that maps individual actions in actual games to an aggregate score for the fantasy team. While fantasy sports had its genesis in the 1960s, it was the growth of the internet that facilitated the efficient and fast updates of fantasy databases. After a lukewarm reaction by key sporting leagues to fantasy sports, most have come

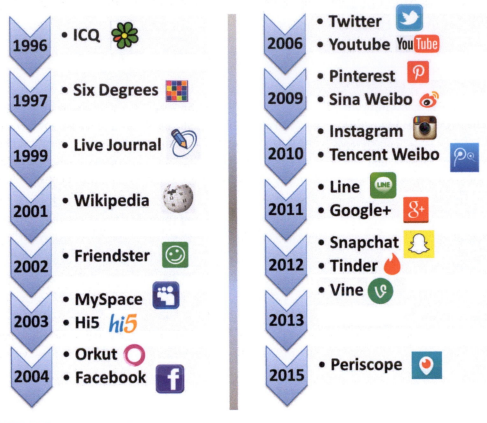

EXHIBIT 14.3 Selected Social Media Networks Timeline

to embrace it as an important pillar of building fan engagement for their sport. Companies with heavy involvement in fantasy include ESPN, Yahoo, CBS Sports, and Fox Sports, as well as NFL.com.

The Fantasy Sports Trade Association reports that the number of fantasy sports players in the United States and Canada in 1991/4 stood at no larger than three million.[3] Subsequent growth highlights the importance of fantasy sports to many millions of fans:

2003	2007	2009	2011	2014
15.2 million	19.4 million	28.4 million	35.9 million	41.5 million

One important dynamic here is that fantasy players focus less on actual clubs and more on the individual players on their own fantasy team. Fantasy sports are one of the factors that have heightened the role and stature of individual athletes in the sports engagement landscape.

Fantasy sports, for many years, focused on teams being chosen for a season. More recently, daily fantasy products have been developed, including those marketed by FanDuel and DraftKings. Daily fantasy appeals to fans who want a relatively fast payoff from the fantasy choices they make. In this sense, daily fantasy is closer to sports betting on individual games than are the season-long fantasy products. The MLB has chosen to prohibit their athletes playing daily fantasy games that involve a prize as part of the same rule (Rule 21) that prohibits their athletes from gambling on MLB games.[4]

Electronic Games

One of the earliest deep engagements in sports for many children is playing an electronic sports game. Over time, there have been advances on multiple fronts that have led to more realistic and engaging products available: (a) advances in the realism of players in the games; (b) advances in the number of playing formats (from one-to-one games to now also including multiplayer games that can be played versus players in other locations via the internet); (c) advances in the options (from consoles to now also having web-based games that can be played on mobile devices); and (d) more frequent real-time updates of player statistics.

Madden NFL is an example of a game series that has been an engagement pillar for a specific sport for many years. Electronic Arts released the first version of the game in 1988 and there have been annual editions ever since. More than 100 million copies of this game reportedly have been sold. Some young players often learn more about the rules of the game from *Madden* than from a coach they may have at a high school. There is frequent publicity each year about which player will be on the cover of the forthcoming edition of *Madden*. The *Madden* game is played by many users 12 months of the year, even in the many months there are no actual NFL games being played. Most leagues and clubs around the globe are seeking to stay engaged with their fan bases 12 months of the year and not just when the games are being played.

14.3 DECISIONS ABOUT SPORTS ENGAGEMENT

Exhibit 14.4 provides a broad overview of the various options an individual faces when making decisions about the consumption of sports. The focus of Exhibit 14.4 is on a live sports event. Three decisions embedded in Exhibit 14.4 highlight the importance of recognizing that decision making inevitably involves a choice between alternatives: the decision to be a participant or an observer; the decision to consume or not consume a sporting event; and the decision to observe a live game at the venue as a spectator or outside of the venue as a viewer.

The decision to be a participant or an observer is affected by ability levels and motivations. The number of professional athletes in most sports is a very small percentage of the total number of participants and an even smaller percentage of the number of amateur participants and observers. Most athletes with the ability to compete at the very highest professional levels will choose, at least for some time, to engage as an active professional. However, even here alternatives are often considered and different paths are occasionally chosen. For example, several male and female professional tennis players ranked 50th to 100th in the world after some time choose to exit the global ATP/WTA tours because they conclude that other options (such as going to business school) are a better use of their ongoing energies. Some athletes have retired early because they no longer want to risk injuries that would impact their subsequent life. Many individuals who participate as amateurs are likely to also choose to be an observer for multiple events. Being an active amateur can indeed increase the passion for observing professional games as these individuals likely have heightened appreciation of the skills being showcased by professionals.

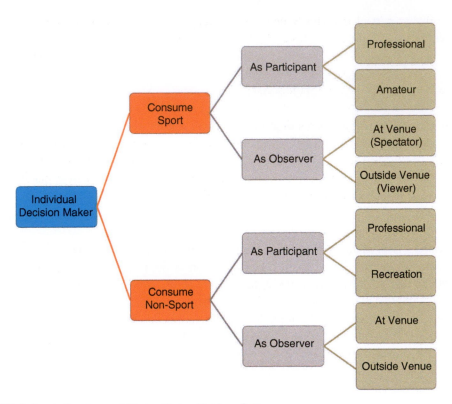

EXHIBIT 14.4 Sports Engagement Choice Made with Many Options

The decision to consume or not consume a sporting event is influenced by the attractiveness of available options. The attractiveness of a specific sporting event option can increase or decrease depending on the attractiveness of other options. Weekday sporting events are typically held at night because many people during the day are at their paid day-jobs or their children are at school. Sports that operate on a single event per week basis (such as football) typically schedule those events on a weeknight or on a weekend. Historically, weekend professional sporting events were scheduled in the afternoon or night slots, in part so as not to compete with many children's participatory sporting events on a Saturday morning and church events on a Sunday morning. With high-profile events, leagues and their broadcast partners have a strong incentive to not place games in time slots where they know there will be major competition for their target audience. For example, in June 2015, the NBA Finals and the NHL Finals were both held in the same time period. The NBA (with ESPN as the broadcaster) was the first league to publicly announce the dates for their seven-game final series. This NBA series had compelling storylines with MVPs on each of the opposing clubs (Cleveland Cavaliers with LeBron James versus Golden State Warriors with Stephen Curry). Curry and James received the #1 and #2 number of votes in the All-Star Ballot in 2015. The NHL, a league that attracts much lower ratings with some crossover audience for its final series, strategically chose with its broadcast partner NBC not to schedule a single game on a date when there was already a NBA Finals game set. The June 2015 Finals event dates for each league were as follows:

League	Game 1	Game 2	Game 3	Game 4	Game 5	Game 6	Game 7
NBA	4 (Thurs)	7 (Sun)	9 (Tues)	11 (Thurs)	14 (Sun)	16 (Tues)	19 (Fri)
NHL	3 (Weds)	6 (Sat)	8 (Mon)	10 (Weds)	13 (Sat)	15 (Mon)	17 (Weds)

The NFI's Super Bowl is typically held on a Sunday in early February starting at 6pm Eastern Standard Time in North America. Neither the NBA nor the NHL and their broadcaster partners schedule games in this time slot as they know in advance that the bulk of their potential audience has a more attractive alternative to observe.

The decision to observe a live game at the venue as a spectator or outside of the venue as a viewer (say, via television or a mobile device) is affected by the feasibility and attractiveness of each option. The fans of many sporting clubs or events often live long distances away from where an event of interest is being held. For example, Manchester United has many fans outside of England that may never have attended a single English Premier League game. The geography for most of Manchester United's fans in Asia, Africa, and the Americas makes observing the live game at an English stadium not feasible. Here, the decision to be a viewer outside of the stadium is almost a given.

BOX 14.1 MANCHESTER UNITED'S STRATEGY FOR BUILDING A MAJOR SOCIAL MEDIA PRESENCE AROUND THE GLOBE[5]

Manchester United (MU) of the EPL is one of the highest-profile soccer clubs in the world. Panel A of Exhibit 14.5 demonstrates its social media reach on the six channels of Twitter, Facebook, Google +, Instagram, as well as two Chinese channels Sina Weibo and Tencent Weibo.

Panel A: Social media reach by channel

Twitter	Facebook	Google+
Over **6.3m** followers	Over **64.8m** followers	Over **5.3m** followers
The fastest sports page to reach 1m followers Most retweeted club in football	Over 22m more 'likes' than any other Premier League club More popular than Disney, McDonald's, Family Guy, and Barack Obama	Fastest growing sports team on Google+ Fastest sports club to reach 1m followers

Instagram	Sina Weibo	Tencent Weibo
Over **3.4m** followers	Over **8.9m** followers	Over **5.2m** followers
40,000+"Likes" per photo 22 days to become the biggest Premier League club	The No. 1 football club on Sina Weibo Within a month of launch MU overtook Bayern Munich and Liverpool FC	50,000 followers in the first 24 hours after launch Within just 4 months, MU became the site's biggest football club

Panel B: Fan engagement versus other EPL clubs and Premier League

- Manchester United fans are the most engaged in the Premier League, the most popular league in Europe The club has over double the engagement of the next most popular team.

EXHIBIT 14.5　Manchester United Leverages Social Media
Source: Manchester United internal document

Panel B of Exhibit 14.5 highlights the success that has come from this high focus on building fan engagement. The comparison here is MU's engagement vis-à-vis other clubs in the EPL. MU's level on the average monthly "People Talking About This" metric[6] over the 24 months from June 2012 to May 2014 is indexed to 100. Then the same metric for other EPL clubs is expressed as a percentage of the MU level. The second ranked EPL club on engagement is Chelsea, a club with many trophies (championships) in recent years, including winning the EPL twice, the FA Cup twice, and the UEFA Champions League. However, with regards to this engagement metric, Chelsea is only 48 percent of MU's level, which means that MU's engagement level in Facebook is more than double that of Chelsea. Further, MU's level of 100 percent is more than three times that of the Barclay's Premier League itself on this metric.

For each of its six social media channels noted in Panel A, MU had explosive growth. Its social media strategy to increase fan engagement in all parts of the globe employs five techniques:

1　**Localization – speak the language of your fans.** MU's Facebook presence was launched in English in July 2010. It now has sites in 20 different languages. Its Twitter presence was launched in July 2011 and is now in six languages. MU has built its presence in social media sites that dominate individual countries or regions – such as Sina Weibo (July 2013), Tencent Weibo (January 2014), and WeChat (April 2015) in China, and KakaoStory (September 2014) in Korea.

2　**Wording.** Use of words in the social media posts that trigger engagement – such as asking questions or "demand feedback."

3　**Content that gives fans a reason to return.** Provide exclusive and high-quality content that is not available anywhere else. The content should be easy to share.

4　**Device optimization.** Content should be optimized to the users' device preferences. The general principle is "mobile first." The focus is on short form content that can be consumed "on the go" – such as short videos, and short text.

5　**Analysis-based understanding of consumers' behavior.** Use of all data points in this analysis to understand your fans. Steer content and frequency accordingly.

Even for fans who are geographically close, other factors can make it not a feasible option to be at a specific live event of interest. Events such as the Masters Golf Tournament, a Champions League Final, or a Super Bowl have very few tickets available for the general public relative to the demand. Many events now have dynamic pricing (see Chapter 13) with the result that some fans may be economically precluded from attending events. For example, tickets for the Men's Final at Wimbledon can start at £2,000. Tickets on the official website three days before the 2015 NBA Finals for games held at the Golden Star Warriors' home arena in Oakland ranged from $1,000 to more than $15,000. Many fans do not have the budget to buy tickets at these prices.

There are many fans who continue to evaluate the pros and cons of attending a live event in person at the venue versus viewing the event outside. The pros of attending the event include the communal excitement of seeing the event at the venue and the often high octane from the attendees when great happenings occur at the venue. However, going to a live event requires travel time, the purchase of often expensive tickets, and the potential exposure to bad fan behavior, sometimes of a kind that can be a very negative experience for a family. Improvements in the high-definition television experience at home or at a sports bar, as well as the greater ability to have a multi-screen experience outside the venue, means that venues are having to invest more to, at a minimum, retain their relative attractiveness to many potential attendees. New venues are now being built that place a greater emphasis on the use of technology to promote to attendees about having great experiences and feelings of greater safety and security at the venue.

14.4 EVALUATING THE IN-STADIUM EXPERIENCE

14.4.1 External Surveys of In-Stadium Experience

ESPN: The Magazine annually conducts an online survey of the fan experience covering all 122 clubs in the four largest North American sporting leagues – the MLB, NBA, NFL, and NHL. One question in the survey focuses specifically on the "stadium experience." Exhibit 14.6, Panel A, shows the average ranking of all the clubs in each of the four leagues. Over the eight-year period – from 2007 to 2014 – the MLB had the best average stadium experience at 48, followed by the NHL (59), the NBA (66), and the NFL (73). MLB clubs often have a strong family focus in their game-day planning. MLB also benefits by having many games in the summer, when the outdoor experience is more favorable than in the fall and winter months. Exhibit 14.7 outlines the top ten giveaways and the top ten promotions in 2014 across all the 30 MLB clubs.

Each MLB club has the largest number of games to sell per year (81 home games per year) compared to the other leagues, which has led to heightened emphasis on seeking diverse ways to attract attendees to their venues.

Panel B of Exhibit 14.6 reports the "stadium experience" rank of the Memphis Grizzlies of the NBA over the 2007/14 period. During the more recent years, the Grizzlies have been amongst the highest out of the 122 clubs ranked: second out of 122 in 2013, and first in 2014. Marketing executives at the Grizzlies gave the following explanations for the high stadium experience ranking by their fans at the FedEx Forum:[7]

- **Appealing overarching theme.** "Believe Memphis, greater Memphis or other thematic devices all are being used and supported with in-arena activities. Believe Memphis, in particular, was born

Panel A: Average ranks over time for NFL, MLB, NBA, and NHL (1 = best)

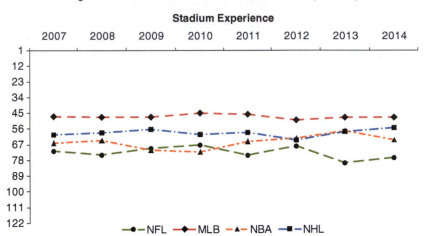

Panel B: Stadium experience rank for Memphis Grizzlies (1 = best)

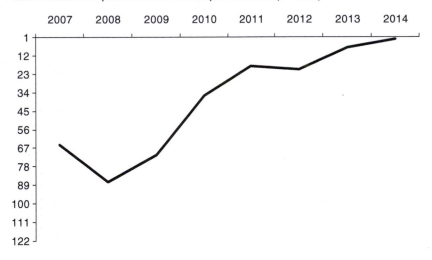

EXHIBIT 14.6 ESPN Fan Satisfaction Survey Ranking 2007/14 "Stadium Experience"
Source: ESPN

during the playoffs from the strong support the Grizzlies and its players gave to Memphis at the time of a serious flood. The club and players were major supporters of helping the city believe in itself."

- **Fans become insiders.** "Fans are encouraged to become insiders to the in-game experience. They are in on the narratives and jokes, know their cues, and ultimately play a direct role in the entertainment. They are participants, not mere observers."

- **Rhythm and consistency.** "There is a rhythm and consistency with most of our game-day promotions – between entertainment, promoting tickets, merchandise, food, reporting on the game, and sharing highlights."

- **Authenticity.** "Our players are not portrayed as hard-working and down-to-earth, but instead represent those traits inherently. And whether through the introductory video, subsequent

Panel A: Top MLB giveaways in 2014

Top giveaways

Rank (2013 rank)	Category	Number of participating teams	Number of dates (2013 dates)
1 (1)	Bobblehead	29	146 (108)
2 (2)	T-shirt	25	99 (100)
3 (4)	Headwear	26	86 (73)
4 (3)	Wall hanging	23	56 (92)
5 (5)	Backpack/bag	28	53 (63)
6 (7)	Magnet schedule	26	45 (46)
7 (10)	Jersey	19	42 (28)
8 (6)	Retail coupon	11	36 (48)
9 (8)	Toy	15	34 (33)
10 (9)	Beverage item (cup/mug/koozie)	19	27 (32)

Panel B: Top MLB promotions/events in 2014

Top Promotions/Events

Rank (2013 rank)	Category	Number of participating teams	Number of dates (2013 dates)
1 (2)	Fireworks	24	205 (205)
2 (3)	Concession discount	11	192 (152)
3 (1)	Ticket discount	10	180 (253)
4 (7)	Charitable causes	17	147 (115)
5 (4)	Autographs	9	145 (138)
6 (5)	Student day	12	129 (135)
7 (6)	Festival	19	103 (119)
8 (9)	Run the bases	15	97 (98)
9 (14)	Military day	17	87 (54)
10 (11)	Family day	9	79 (81)

EXHIBIT 14.7 Top Giveaways and Promotions/Events at MLB Games in 2014
Source: Sports Business Journal

highlights throughout the game, and other player features, we reinforce this authentic image of them and our brand."

■ **Innovative giveaways.** "Our chosen giveaways reinforce our unique fan engagement strategies and authentic connection with our players and city. For example, one giveaway for a playoff game was a mask. This linked with Mike Conley having to wear a mask whilst playing to protect his injured face. Another very popular giveaway was a Southern-style bow-tie with Zach Randolph's face on them."

■ **Uniquely Memphis experience.** "From the moment a fan walks in the arena to the moment they leave, they are engrossed with unique and authentic Memphis experiences from food offerings such a Rendezvous BBQ to wrestling promotions between quarters to live Memphis music during halftime."

14.4.2 Club Based Surveys of In-Stadium Experience

After each game, the San Francisco 49ers of the NFL conduct a poll of their attendees. Exhibit 14.8 presents extracts from this post-game online survey.

The survey covers multiple areas of the attendee experience, including the in-game experience, concessions, technology, retail, security, and cleanliness, as well as the ease of getting to and from the stadium. The regular use of digital feedback is increasing the reliability of the information that the 49ers collect. The information helps target areas of good experience that warrant reinforcing. It also highlights areas where resources need to be invested for improvement. Not included in each survey, but available given the date of the survey, is the outcome of each game. Not surprisingly, the average level of fan satisfaction is much higher when the team wins than on days when it has lost. This is one of many areas in sports where winning on the field brings a number of added benefits to many other areas.

14.4.3 Technology Drives a New Era for the In-Stadium Experience

Many new venues are being designed from the outset to leverage technology to promote enriched and memorable experiences for those attending. Panel A of Exhibit 14.9 highlights nine areas where the use of technology can be an integral part of the venue build (or renovation).

Panel B of Exhibit 14.9 illustrates several areas from Panel A where the app available to attendees at Levi's Stadium (home of the San Francisco 49ers) has enhanced the in-venue experience. The 49ers spent more than two years during the build phase of Levi's Stadium developing and extensively testing the ability of this app to be operable with 68,000 fans in the building. The app is a "continual work in process" as new developments occur in technology and as more is learned by the fans and the 49ers about ways to more effectively leverage this app platform. During its first year, more than 60 percent of season ticket holder accounts linked their tickets to the app. The "killer uses" of the app in its first year were "ticketing, wayfinding, and food and beverage."[8] The Barclay's Center app gives fans the option to order food from their seats, send messages to be displayed on the scoreboard, and interact with other fans in the stadium via social media. The app also offers replays from four different angles. Ticketing technology is enabling a better profiling of the fans attending the stadium – see Chapter 13.

Exhibit 14.10 summarizes key survey responses by stadium operators about the 2014 use of technology in more than 70 sporting venues.

As noted, older venues have significant limitations because they were designed before the information technology revolution happened. Some of these venues do not have enough mobile bandwidth for the full venue and, in turn, fans cannot reliably use smartphones or other mobile devices while in the venue. Less than 40 percent of those surveyed reported that their existing stadium infrastructure enabled high-quality Wi-Fi to all seating areas in the venue. The 2014 survey found that 27 percent of fans at the venue are now using social media to share their experiences with friends outside of the venue. Security and safety are key aspects of venue planning and management. Design parameters include metrics such as time to evacuate the premises (in case of a bomb threat, for example), as well as very strict fire and health regulations. Redundancy of the structure and ductility of joints and connections increase the safety of the venue in case of explosions. Technologies are now available to identify every single person in a venue. The Borussia-Park Stadium at Monchengladbach in Germany records detailed video of the stands. Police can now zoom into a section of the stadium as soon as an incident occurs. The new Stade de Hainaut in France uses innovative software to monitor the movements of people coming to the stadium to have the staff ready for the different waves of fans by size and club identity. Software is also used for crowd simulation in designing the safety of stadiums. Stadiums hosting teams that are known for their hostility often include separate access and segmented seating for those fans.

1. PUBLIC TRANSPORTATION EXPERIENCE IF USED

- Please rate your public transportation experience: friendliness/helpfulness of staff; travel time; value; appearance and cleanliness; overall experience

2. PARKING IF USED

- How would you rate your parking experience? – five-point scale.
- What factors contributed to any poor parking experience? Traffic flow getting into parking lot; ease of getting from car to stadium; cleanliness/availability of restrooms; helpfulness of uniformed police directing traffic flow; helpfulness of parking lot staff; affordability of parking; signage directing you to parking lot; availability of parking lot staff

3. IN-GAME EXPERIENCE

- Please rate your ticketing experience – five-point scale on each: staff; friendliness/helpfulness; wait time; overall experience
- Please rate our in-game entertainment – five-point scale on each: videoboard content; energy level; player introductions/anthems; halftime entertainment; volume of pa system; clarity of PA system; overall

4. CONCESSIONS

- Please rate our concessions – five-point scale on each: quality; variety; speed of service; staff helpfulness; overall

5. TECHNOLOGY

- Please rate our mobile app – five-point scale on each: wayfinding; tickets; replays; food and drink; parking passes; restroom wait; times; overall
- Please rate your Wi-Fi experience? – five-point scale: poor; below average; average; good; excellent)

6. RETAIL

- Please rate our retail stores on the following criteria – five-point scale on each: accessibility of locations; availability of staff; friendliness of staff; helpfulness of staff; variety/selection of merchandise; availability of merchandise; sizing options; speed of checkout; overall

7. SECURITY

- Please rate our security – five-point scale on each: security screening process upon entering the stadium; feeling of personal safety while inside the stadium; helpfulness of security staff; feeling of personal safety while outside the stadium; availability of security to assist you; helpfulness of uniformed police stationed inside the stadium; overall

8. CLEANLINESS

- Please rate the cleanliness of Levi's Stadium – five-point scale on each: concourse; seating area; restrooms; parking lots; retail store; concessions; overall

9. DEPARTURE

- How would you rate your departure experience? – five-point scale.
- What factors contributed to any poor departure experience? Traffic flow getting out of parking lot; traffic flow in the streets around the stadium; helpfulness of uniformed police directing traffic flow; ease of getting from the stadium to your car; signage directing you to exists, surface streets and expressways; availability of parking lot staff

10. OVERALL

- How satisfied were you with your event experience at Levi's Stadium? – five-point scale.
- How likely are you to attend another event at Levi's Stadium? – five-point scale.

EXHIBIT 14.8 Fan Satisfaction Areas to Target: Examples from Fan Experience Survey Emailed by San Francisco 49ers of NFL After Each Game

Panel A: Multiple areas of enhancing the fan experience

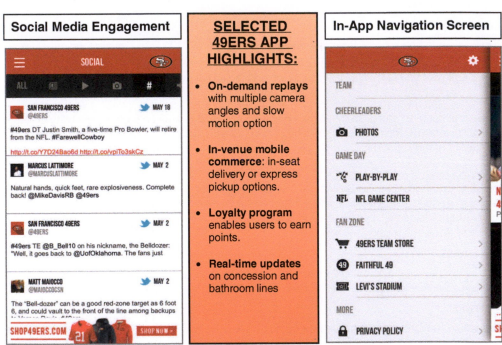

* PERSONALIZED OFFERS

* MOBILE DVR & INSTANT REPLAY CAPABILITY

* MATCH STATISTICS DATA VISUALIZATION

* SOCIAL & GAMIFICATION

* MOBILE TICKETING

* IN-SEAT ORDERING & SEAT UPGRADES

* LIVE TRAFFIC MANAGEMENT & PARKING INFORMATION

* PREMIUM VENUE/CODE/CLUB MEMBER SERVICES

* QUALITY CELLULAR & WI-FI NETWORK INFRASTRUCTURE

Source: Stuart Taggart At Relevant Innovation

Panel B: Example of 49ers mobile app

Social Media Engagement

SOCIAL

ALL

SAN FRANCISCO 49ERS
@49ERS   MAY 18

#49ers DT Justin Smith, a five-time Pro Bowler, will retire from the NFL. #FarewellCowboy

http://t.co/Y7D24Bao6d http://t.co/vpiTo3skCz

MARCUS LATTIMORE
@MARCUSLATTIMORE   MAY 2

Natural hands, quick feet, rare explosiveness. Complete back! @MikeDavisRB @49ers

SAN FRANCISCO 49ERS
@49ERS   MAY 2

#49ers TE @B_Bell10 on his nickname, the Belldozer: "Well, it goes back to @UofOklahoma. The fans just

MATT MAIOCCO
@MAIOCCOCSN   MAY 2

The "Bell-dozer" can be a good red-zone target at 6 foot 6, and could vault to the front of the line among backups

SHOP49ERS.COM   SHOP NOW

SELECTED 49ERS APP HIGHLIGHTS:

- **On-demand replays** with multiple camera angles and slow motion option

- **In-venue mobile commerce**: in-seat delivery or express pickup options.

- **Loyalty program** enables users to earn points.

- **Real-time updates** on concession and bathroom lines

In-App Navigation Screen

TEAM

CHEERLEADERS

📷 PHOTOS

GAME DAY

PLAY-BY-PLAY

NFL   NFL GAME CENTER

FAN ZONE

🛒 49ERS TEAM STORE

49   FAITHFUL 49

LEVI'S STADIUM

MORE

🔒 PRIVACY POLICY

EXHIBIT 14.9 Innovative Design and Use of Technology Enhances the Live At-Stadium Experience at Levi's Stadium of San Francisco 49ers

What is the current state of Wi-Fi networks at your arena?

- High Quality Wi-Fi to all seating areas — 35.7 %
- High Quality Wi-Fi to premium seating only — 9.5 %
- Other — 54.8 %

What do your fans use Wi-Fi services most for?

- General internet access/email — 16.2 %
- Social Media Updates — 27.0 %
- Fantasy Games — 0.0 %
- Replays — 0.0 %
- Ordering Food/Concessions — 0.0 %
- Not currently tracking user activity — 56.8 %

What is your most successful social media outlet?

- Facebook — 37.5 %
- Twitter — 37.5 %
- League/Team App — 6.2 %
- Email — 15.6 %
- Instagram — 3.1 %
- Vine — 0.0 %
- Google+ — 0.0 %

Do you solicit and use fan comments/tweets on team media outlets?

- Yes, in stadium only — 16.7 %
- Yes, online only — 20.0 %
- Yes, both live and online — 56.7 %
- No — 6.7 %

Do you have a stadium-wide digital signage system?

- Yes — 43.8 %
- No — 34.4 %
- In evaluation/planning — 21.9 %

What percentage of fans connect to the Wi-Fi service?

- 0–10 % — 22.2 %
- 10–20 % — 13.9 %
- 20–30 % — 13.9 %
- 30–40 % — 16.7 %
- 40–100 % — 2.8 %
- Not Applicable — 30.5 %

Does your Organization use a CRM Platform?

- Yes — 72.7 %
- No — 15.2 %
- In Planning/Evaluation — 12.1 %

What types of data do you most include in CRM?

- Ticketing — 96.4 %
- Social Media — 28.6 %
- Sponsor Activities — 39.3 %
- Concessions — 17.9 %

What do you primarily use social media for?

- Drive Ticket Sales — 15.6 %
- Increase Fan Loyalty — 43.8 %
- Build Team "Buzz" — 0.0 %
- Community Outreach — 0.0 %
- Marketing Messages — 18.8 %

Do you solicit and/or use fan-created video clips?

- Yes, in stadium only — 3.3 %
- Yes, online only — 13.3 %
- Yes, both live and online — 26.7 %
- No — 56.7 %

What is the primary focus of your digital signage strategy?

- Advertising — 89.3 %
- Video Replays — 50.0 %
- Concessions — 53.6 %
- Game Info/Stats — 53.6 %
- Safety/Messaging — 46.4 %

EXHIBIT 14.10 Stadium Technology Landscape: Survey by SEAT/Mobile Sports Report
Source: SEAT and MSR/Mobile Sports Report 2014, *State Of The Stadium Technology Survey*

BOX 14.2 VISA WINS SOCIAL MEDIA GOLD AT THE 2014 SOCHI WINTER OLYMPICS[9]

Visa is a premier payments technology company. Its global network connects thousands of financial institutions with millions of merchants and cardholders every day. It is only one of three companies, along with Coca-Cola and Panasonic, that have been a TOP (The Olympic Program) sponsor of the International Olympic Committee (IOC) for all eight four-year cycles of the TOP since Cycle I in 1985/8 (see Section 11.8 of Chapter 11 for more specifics). Cycle VIII included the 2014 Winter Olympics in Sochi, Russia. The challenge for Visa management for activating its investment for Sochi was how to use the Olympics to launch a new brand idea. Its branding heritage included the highly successful "Everywhere you want to be" campaign that highlighted the many physical locations where Visa cards were accepted. The following list highlights key elements of the Sochi campaign and its successful outcome. It draws on presentations done by Andrew Cohen, Visa's head of global Olympic sponsorship marketing.

- The new brand idea centered on the theme that "Everywhere is an aspiration" and not just a physical place. "Everyone has an everywhere, and only Visa helps you get there."
- The activation used a team of 36 Olympic and Paralympic athletes from ten countries. A digital-first campaign leveraged the pre-eminent social media channels in the relevant countries. "Newsrooms" in Sochi and New York created content based on live and broadcast schedules. Teams in Toronto, Moscow, Tokyo, and Seoul focused on placing and amplifying the content. Visa's social construct was predicated on *introducing* the world to the Team Visa athletes, *capitalizing* on their participation, performance, and achievements, and then *amplifying* the content that consumers were engaging with.
- The imperative "was to create content that was both (a) *timely* (both when consumers might check on live events as well as when events were broadcast), and (b) *relevant* (we were presenting content that consumers were interested in). Our *copy* and *creative* needed imagery and headlines that were visually arresting but also intellectually stimulating."
- Individual athlete stories were used to build high levels of engagement with viewers of the broadcasts. For example, "we introduced the world to David Wise, American free skier, whose event, ski pipe debuted in Sochi. When David won gold, we invited the world to congratulate him on Twitter and sent everyone a mosaic with his winning moment made up of all the Twitter avatars of people who sent congratulations. The mosaic was digi-graphed with David's signature, and one lucky fan received a Twitter shoutout with thanks from David."
- Posts capitalizing on winning moments were made: American Julia Mancuso's bronze, Korean Lee Sag Haw's gold; Russians Tatiana and Maxim Trankov's gold; and Kazakh Dennis Ten's bronze. Visa developed the capability to have the images ready within minutes of any of its athletes competing. See Exhibit 14.11.
- Visa's proprietary research reported unprecedented interactions with consumers. "Engagements surpassed our expectations … We broke every Visa social media record around the world – 28 million engagements such as retweets, likes and shares; 574 million earned impressions; and an 8.78% engagement rate on Twitter."[10]

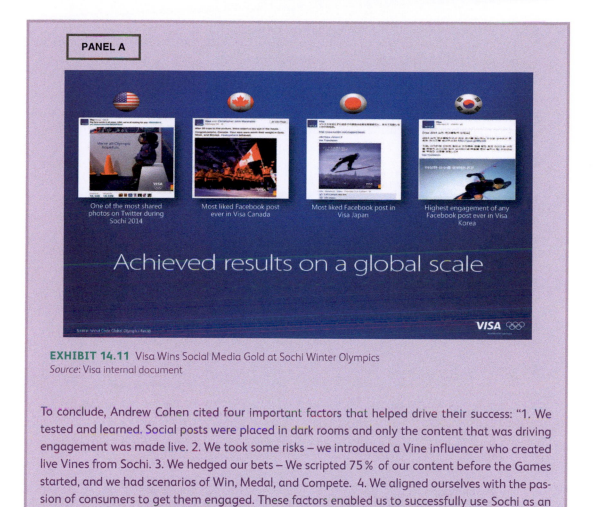

EXHIBIT 14.11 Visa Wins Social Media Gold at Sochi Winter Olympics
Source: Visa internal document

To conclude, Andrew Cohen cited four important factors that helped drive their success: "1. We tested and learned. Social posts were placed in dark rooms and only the content that was driving engagement was made live. 2. We took some risks – we introduced a Vine influencer who created live Vines from Sochi. 3. We hedged our bets – We scripted 75 % of our content before the Games started, and we had scenarios of Win, Medal, and Compete. 4. We aligned ourselves with the passion of consumers to get them engaged. These factors enabled us to successfully use Sochi as an amplifier for Visa's message."

14.5 ATHLETES DRIVING HIGH LEVELS OF ENGAGEMENT

Exhibit 14.12 presents, as of May 2015, the top ten athletes with the largest followings on Facebook and then separately across the sports/leagues of soccer, the NFL, MLB, NBA, and NHL. Exhibit 14.13 shares comparable rankings for athletes with the largest followers on Twitter. The numbers in Exhibits 14.12 and 14.13 are for worldwide Facebook and Twitter users. Several aspects are readily apparent:

1   First is the absolute large size of the followers. Each of the top ten athletes on Facebook have more than 20 million followers, while each of the top ten on Twitter have more than ten million followers. Soccer player Cristiano Ronaldo (Real Madrid) is #1 on both lists with more than 100 million followers on Facebook and more than 35 million followers on Twitter.

2   Second is the dominant number of soccer athletes in the top ten lists (eight out ten on Facebook and seven out of ten on Twitter). This reflects both soccer being the dominant sport globally and the growing use of social media in many regions of the world.

3   Third is the inclusion of Sachin Tendulkar, the recently retired cricketing star from India, as #9 on Facebook. Tendulkar, who played elite cricket from 1989 to 2013, has a huge following in a country with more than a billion people, as well as being recognized as a star in all of the countries playing cricket. Box 14.3 illustrates the use of social media in a Cricket World Cup context.

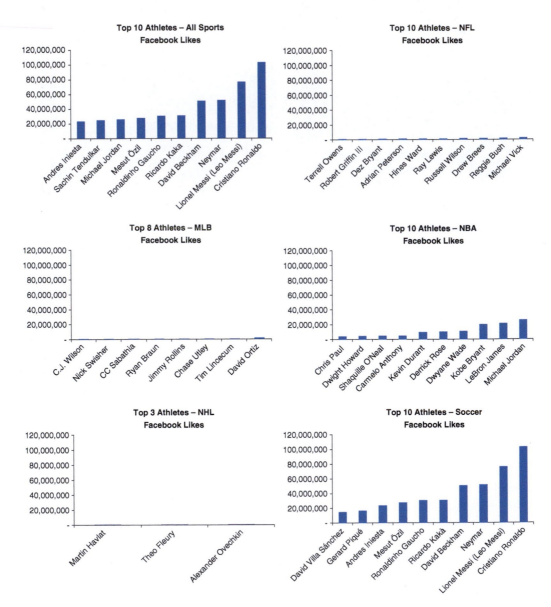

EXHIBIT 14.12 Facebook Likes – Top Ten Overall and by Selected Sports
Source: Facebook/Fanpagelist.com as of May 25, 2015

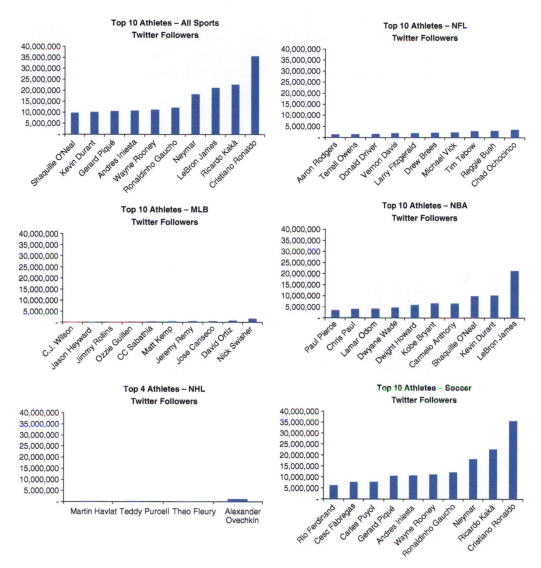

EXHIBIT 14.13 Twitter Followers – Top Ten Overall and by Selected Sports
Source: Twitter/Fanpagelist.com as of May 25, 2015

BOX 14.3 SPORTZ INTERACTIVE PARTNERS WITH STAR SPORTS TO AMPLIFY INDIAN FAN ENGAGEMENT FOR THE 2015 CRICKET WORLD CUP[11]

The Cricket World Cup was held in Australia from February to March 2015. Teams from 14 countries participated. Star Sports, the broadcaster in India, worked with Sportz Interactive to "revolutionize the fan experience on digital." The goal of Star Sports was to build as large and as engaged an audience for its broadcasts as possible. Social media played a central role in enabling Star Sports to have viewer numbers that were in the hundreds of millions. Indeed, *The Telegraph* on February 15 reported "India beat Pakistan by 76 runs as an estimated one billion viewers tune in to World Cup clash."[12] Cricket is the #1 sport in both India and Pakistan with a long history of rivalry between the two countries.

Exhibit 14.14 summarizes some of the results of high levels of engagement achieved.

EXHIBIT 14.14 Cricket World Cup Fans Use Twitter to Share Experiences
Source: CWC internal document

Arvind Iyengar, CEO of Sportz Interactive, outlined some key activities of the partnership:

1 **Own the jersey.** We kick-started Star Sports' World Cup campaign in early January this year with this campaign. This was a unique TV-plus-Twitter-based quiz activation with more than 1.6 lakh[13] tweets received during the activity. The hashtag trended at number one in India. It also trended worldwide.

2 **Real-time Facebook cover photo update.** A cricket game goes through multiple ups and downs, and using Facebook's cover photo to highlight match status was a truly unique innovation. This was achieved through some nifty technology innovations and the result was a highly engaging cover photo that was updated real-time to reflect match status. A first for cricket anywhere!

3 **Digital Tug of War.** A unique digital + outdoor activation, the Digital Tug of War got fans to support their team – India or Pakistan. Using Twitter as the primary medium, fans of India and Pakistan tweeted their support to their team with #IndWins or #PakWins and the number of tweets received were converted into a virtual tug of war that was visible at leading malls in Mumbai. We received over one lakh tweets through the activity.

4 **Stats cards.** One of the most engaging digital activities during the World Cup gave fans an opportunity to collect player stats "cards" of all quarter-final teams. All they had to do was tweet using a hashtag and an algorithm determined what card to generate for that fan. They then received the virtual card on Twitter through a personalized reply. To top this, five winners were given a cricket kit for their efforts! Totally, over two lakh tweets were received for this activity and it trended in India for more than 24 hours.

5 **Maukaticons!** A character called "Maukaman," in line with Star's overall marketing campaign, was used to react to events during games. Sportz Interactive brought him to life digitally through 'Maukaticons'. His passion, anguish, disappointment, and happiness were all captured and digitized for sharing across all platforms. Easy to download, the Maukaticons were a rage during India's and Pakistan's matches. It was as easy as sending a hashtag (#Maukaticons) to @StarSportsIndia to get all the emoticons in a ready-to-use format. Bestmediainfo.com reported that "@StarSportsIndia's #MaukaMauka campaign has consistently kicked build-up to India game days with a video for the upcoming game as well as a follow-up revealed almost immediately after the game. Star Sports asked users to tweet to them with the hashtag #MaukaMauka to reveal the ad on Twitter before it got revealed on TV, which was great for engagement since this really got viewers involved. They also continued to provide commentary on the games, which ensured that people kept engaging with them through the weeks."[14]

6 **Quizster.** While the players battled it on the field, fans were invited to a battle of wits on Twitter. #Quizster offered the user four categories to choose from and the entire quiz was run on Twitter. This was a first-ever interactive, personalized quiz on Twitter where fans would get questions sent to them individually and follow-up questions based on their answers. Users had to follow a simple mechanism to get started and continue playing. Winners got the chance to meet their cricketing heroes at the Star Sports studios for a once in a lifetime experience.

4   Fourth is the NBA being the dominant North American league with regards to their athletes on these two social media channels. Michael Jordan at #10 is the only North American athlete on the top ten overall list for Facebook. LeBron James (#3), Kevin Durant (#9), and Shaquille O'Neal (#10), all from the NBA, are the only North American athletes on the top ten Twitter follower list. Looking across the other three North American leagues in both exhibits, both the MLB and NHL have relatively low social media presence.

5   Fifth, multiple athletes with large followings on Facebook are not active on Twitter. These include Lionel Messi, David Beckham, and Mesut Özil in soccer and Michael Jordan in basketball.

Commentators stress that athletes that are authentic and have a regular pattern of posting new items are factors driving fan engagement as well as the athlete being a superstar on the field.

Rapid advances in the digital world are giving rise to much richer engagement options as well as presenting problems previously not encountered. The new digital world provides many more options for opinions to be expressed by athletes and other individuals in varying stages of thoughtfulness or responsibility. It also has "blown-up" traditional notions of privacy. In many contexts it is wise now to assume that athletes live their lives in a fishbowl with any number of people taking photos and instantaneously sharing them with many thousands or even millions. Leagues and clubs are increasingly taking proactive steps to advise players (and their own management) about the pitfalls of rapid social media responses that after the fact appear naïve at best and are at most cause for discipline and in some cases exits from a club.

14.6 INDUSTRY EXAMPLE: GOLDEN STATE WARRIORS

The Golden States Warriors of the NBA for many years invested little in embracing new technologies. In July 2010, the NBA announced that a syndicate led by Joe Lacob and Peter Guber were the new owners of the Golden State Warriors. Lacob had a very successful background as a partner for 20+ years of Kleiner Perkins Caufield & Byers (KPCB), a leading venture capital firm specializing in new technology ventures. Guber had a storied career in Hollywood as a movie producer as well as successful investments in Minor League Baseball clubs. Under the prior ownership, the Warriors had struggled on the court, even experiencing a 12-year period (1995 to 2006) without a single playoff appearance. The new ownership came with high ambition and a commitment to make across-the-board quantum improvements on and off the court.

Multiple NBA clubs before the new ownership at the Warriors arrived had been active in building their social media audience, notably the Los Angeles Lakers, Miami Heat, Chicago Bulls, and Boston Celtics. The new Warriors management made use of technology to greatly enhance the fan experience, making this a high priority. Social media was an important pillar of this embracing of technology. Important hires in this area included Kenny Lauer, Kevin Cote, and Laurence Scott. Panel A of Exhibit 14.15 shows the multiple social media channels used by the Warriors and their year-over-year growth from April 2014 to April 2015.

A central focus of the Warriors social media team was building deep engagement and not just audience size, which is often passive. Panel B of Exhibit 14.15 highlights the success made in this area by the Warriors. Engagement is measured by the aggregate total number of interactions across the multiple social media channels in Panel A, such as "likes" on Facebook, retweets on Twitter, and comments on Instagram photos and YouTube videos. Whereas the Warriors are #8 in total audiences as of April 2015, they are a clear #1 across the 30 NBA clubs in terms of interactions.

Some comments from the social media team at the Warriors provide insight into their impressive leadership in social media interactions:

Panel A: Golden State Warriors Engagement via multiple social media channels

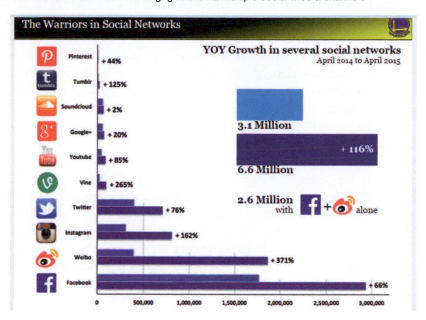

Panel B: Golden State Warriors Total social media audience versus interactions

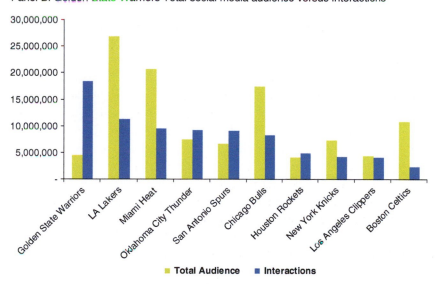

EXHIBIT 14.15 Social Media Engagement by the Golden State Warriors

Note: Total audience and YTD interactions from various social networks such as Facebook, Twitter, Instagram, and YouTube

Source: Golden State Warriors internal document

- Kenny Lauer noted the importance of strategic modeling of content: "One of the reasons our interactions (engagement) is so high is that we do behavior modeling first. We identify the behavior we would like to drive, and then design for that behavior. We will use whatever tools are the best fit to drive the behavior. So when we use our social footprint, we are confident that it will drive the behavior we want. We deliver on many different channels and work to optimize the content on each one. Just as you would say something different on the phone than you would on twitter, we look at each channel independently and ensure that we are optimizing our content to drive identified behavior on each channel. A lot of our success in social is also due to the fact that we believe in trying new things and are OK with failure (as long as there is a process for learning). We were the first to have a dedicated Instagram wall, the first to do a true app for Google Glass, and the first to really capitalize on proximity marketing driving revenue (through beacons)."
- Kevin Cote stressed the key points of: "Buy-in and encouragement from the highest levels and the Warrior fan base. The Warriors fans are the most engaging audience imaginable … It was imperative for us to embrace and invest in content creation, storytelling, digital fitness and the evolution of social media." He further noted that the strategy was to "think both locally and globally … Social media provides a worldwide audience to be engaged with 24 hours a day, 365 days a year. With the Warriors, we made a concerted effort to invest time and resources in enhancing brand awareness on a global level, and once again, focusing on engaging content and conversation via social media was the most effective way to do so."
- Laurence Scott, who came to the Warriors with a cable sports network background, works at the coalface for capturing key Warrior player moments that can be put out on different social media channels. He stated: "Covering the Warriors on the road is a key component to our efforts in sharing stories that bring our fans inside the organizations and and into the lives of our players. Thinking fan-first is the overriding goal of my productions as the Host and Commentator of Warriors TV. It's a role that essentially morphs into team evangelist and tour guide as we travel to the various cities around the NBA. From being with Stephen Curry at the White House as he met President Obama in support of the President's Malaria Initiative, to an unexpected team trip to a bowling alley in Minneapolis one morning before practice, the key is bringing timely and relevant access to the fans."

14.7 SUMMARY

Many stakeholders are investing heavily to build more and deeper engagement with fans and other key actors in the sports ecosystem. It is important to examine both engagement levels and their drivers (a) at the live sport event time, and also (b) beyond the live sport event time. Actual event time is only a small percentage of the total 24/7 time available for using the many different platforms of engagement. Both the digital revolution and rapid advances in technology are creating a very rich environment, but one in which informed choice is even more important to make effective use of resources devoted to building sustained engagement strategies and their execution.

NOTES

1 M. Sweney, "World Cup final breaks Facebook and Twitter records," *The Guardian*, July 14, 2014.
2 www.fangraphs.com/library/misc/pitch-fx.
3 www.fsta.org/?page=Demographics.

4 D. Rovell, "MLB, union prohibit players from daily fantasy games," ESPN, April 10, 2015.

5 This box is based on internal documents provided by Manchester United. The assistance of Jamie Reigle, board member and managing director for Asia Pacific of Manchester United is greatly appreciated.

6 Facebook developed the "People Talking about This" metric to measure engagement. It is "the number of unique users who have created a 'story' about a page in a seven-day period. On Facebook, stories are items that are displayed in News Feed. Users create stories when they: like a page, post on the page wall, like a post, comment on a post, share a post, answer a question, RSVP to a page's event, mention the page in a post, tag the page in a photo, check in at a place, share a check-in deal, like a check-in deal, write a recommendation, or claim an offer" www.adweek.com/socialtimes/people-talking-about-this-defined/273447.

7 This section was greatly aided by input from Matt Thiry and other executives at the Memphis Grizzlies.

8 A. Madkour, "49ers feel they are 'beginning to shift fan behavior' with new VenueNext app," *Sports Business Daily*, June 11, 2015.

9 This box is based on internal documents provided by Visa. The assistance of Andrew Cohen, head of global Olympics sponsorship marketing is greatly appreciated.

10 "2014 IAS: Visa, Sochi and Brazil: activation lessons learned and applied," On the Ground blog, *Sports Business Daily*, May 30, 2014.

11 This box is based on information provided by Sportz Interactive. The assistance of Arvind Iyengar, CEO of Sportz Interactive is greatly appreciated.

12 S. Berry, "India beat Pakistan by 76 runs as estimated one billion viewers tune in to World Cup clash," The Telegraph, February 15, 2015.

13 In India, one lakh is equivalent to 100,000.

14 www.bestmediainfo.com/2015/03/star-sports-continues-to-lead-twitter-brand-index-as-group-stage-wraps-up.

15

SPORTS BROADCASTING 1
CONTENT AND DISTRIBUTION DECISIONS

Sports content dominates the lists of the most watched television programs in many countries. These ratings showcase the power of elite sports as a viewer drawing card. For example, the NFL's Super Bowl heavily populates the list of the 20 most watched programs in US television history (out of all programming and based on total viewers). Super Bowl viewership from 2010 to 2014 exceeded 100 million viewers each and every year (ranked by viewership):

Game	Participants	Date	Total viewers
Super Bowl XLVIX	New England Patriots 28 Seattle Seahawks 24	Feb 1, 2015	112.5 million
Super Bowl XLVIII	Seattle Seahawks 43 Denver Broncos 8	Feb 2, 2014	108.4 million
Super Bowl XLVI	New York Giants 21 New England Patriots 17	Feb 5, 2012	111.0 million
Super Bowl XLVII	Baltimore Ravens 34 San Francisco 49ers 31	Feb 3, 2013	111.3 million
Super Bowl XLV	Green Bay Packers 31 Pittsburgh Steelers 25	Feb 6, 2011	106.5 million
Super Bowl XLIV	New Orleans Saints 31 Indianapolis Colts 17	Feb 7, 2010	106.5 million

In Canada, the most watched program in Canadian history is the men's ice hockey gold medal game from the 2010 Vancouver Winter Olympics, which saw Canada defeat the United States 3–2. A total of 16.6 million Canadian viewers watched the game. Similarly, in Australia, the two most watched programs are the 2005 Australian Open Men's Singles Final (Marat Safin of Russia defeated Lleyton Hewitt of Australia) with a reported 4.045 million viewers, followed by the 2003 Rugby World Cup Final (England defeated Australia) with 4.016 million viewers reported. In Germany, the 2014 FIFA World Cup Final (Germany beat Argentina 1–0) with 34.65 million viewers is the most watched broadcast followed by the 2014 FIFA World Cup Semi-Final (Germany beat Brazil 7–1) with 32.570 million viewers.

The broadcast of sports content plays a central role in the decisions of many stakeholders in the sports industry. This chapter and the next discuss the growth and importance of sports broadcasting – from building awareness and fan relationships, its content and distribution, and its increasingly pivotal role in the economics of sport enterprises. We highlight how broadcast decisions over time have become increasingly more complex, and involve a greater number of stakeholders. Driving many of these decisions are rapid changes in technology, and an increasingly sophisticated set of sports content producers, distributors, and consumers. Appendix 16A outlines some of the many key companies in the US Sports Television Broadcast world.

Throughout this chapter and the next, the multiple roles that these companies play in the sports broadcasting world will be discussed.

15.1 ALTERNATIVE MODELS OF DELIVERING LIVE SPORTS CONTENT TO THE CONSUMER

Historically, combinations of four key areas of the sports broadcast value-chain have been important:

1 **Sports rights-holder.** Examples are described in Section 15.1.1. They include leagues, clubs, events, and other competitions.

2   **Production of content.** Included here are decisions about the "on-air talent," the number of cameras at an event, the use of graphics to enhance the viewer experience, and access to on-field interviews with players, coaches, etc.

3   **Distribution of content.** This includes the way in which content is delivered to a consumer such as via the internet, over-the-air signals, or below-the-ground cables.

4   **Consumption of content.** The alternatives included here are viewing at home via television, on mobile devices, or in sports bars. There is increasing use of simultaneous use of multiple platforms to consume sports content – such as television and a mobile device to track and contribute to social media commentary on the event being watched.

We briefly overview alternative broadcasting models for this content based on varying combinations of the factors above and the roles played by different stakeholders in the sports ecosystem. Exhibit 15.1 overviews the broadcasting models discussed in this section.

15.1.1 Sports Rights-Holder Direct-to-Consumer Model

This is the simplest broadcasting model. However, it has only recently emerged as a real alternative to the delivery of live sports content to consumers. Here a sports rights-holder produces a

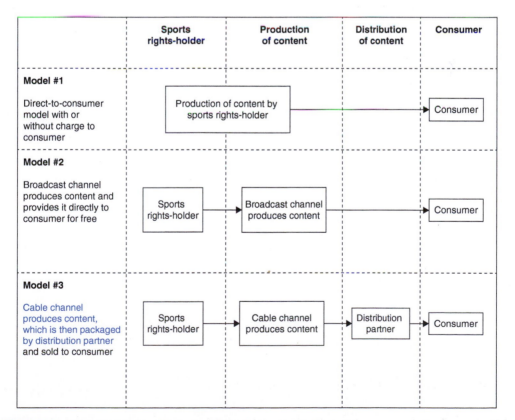

EXHIBIT 15.1 Alternative Models of Delivering Sports Content to the Consumer

live broadcast (often with subcontractors) and uses the internet (also often with subcontractors) to deliver the content to consumers. The revenue sources to the sports rights-holder in this model could include one or more of the following:

■ Payments from consumers
■ Payments from advertisers
■ Payments from sponsors

An example here is World Wrestling Entertainment's WWE Network. This network was launched in February 2014 as a streaming internet channel available 24/7 to consumers who pay the WWE a monthly subscriber fee. The WWE is the content rights-holder and also the content producer. Box 15.1 describes the first year experience of the WWE Network.

BOX 15.1 WWE NETWORK, WORLD WRESTLING ENTERTAINMENT'S OVER-THE-TOP (OTT) NETWORK, HAS A ROCKY START AFTER ITS FEBRUARY 2014 LAUNCH

In February 2014, the World Wrestling Entertainment (WWE) company launched on the internet its WWE Network. This OTT network was an example of Model #1 in Exhibit 15.1. Subscribers to the WWE Network would receive access to live content as well as to an extensive archive of past wrestling events and programs. The most attractive live content to be shown on the WWE Network would be the monthly pay-per-views (PPVs), including the banner WrestleMania. Prior to launching its own network, the WWE's three largest sources of revenues (taken from the Annual Report of the publicly traded WWE) were:

1   Television rights sold to broadcast and cable channels – $106.9 million in 2013.
2   Live events – $111.5 million in 2013.
3   Pay-per-view – $82.5 million in 2013.

Pay-per-views were produced by the WWE from its live events, but prior to February 2014 exclusively distributed by third parties. The average revenue yield per customer to the WWE from its PPVs ranged from $20 to $22 per event, despite the cost to the consumer often being above $50. With an OTT network, these middleman distributors would be eliminated. For the WWE Network, the WWE subcontracted with Major League Baseball Advanced Media (MLBAM) to assist in the delivery of its content over the internet. MLBAM had deep expertise in this area from its own online streaming of many thousands of live MLB games.

Launching its WWE Network, security analysts and media observers in 2014 expressed uncertainty about:

1   Television rights revenues. Would broadcast and cable television networks continue to pay high amounts to the WWE for the rights to show weekly television programs produced by the WWE (such as *Monday Night Raw* and *Smackdown*)? Subscribers to the WWE Network would be able to access some of the content provided on these weekly television shows. Would broadcast and cable stations penalize the WWE for providing content no longer exclusive to their traditional distribution partners?

> 2   Size of the new revenue stream from WWE Network subscriber fees and the expected associated decline in PPV revenues. When launched in February 2014, the WWE Network channel was available on the internet for a $9.99 per month subscription package, with a six-month minimum purchase period.
>
> In conference calls with financial security analysts in 2014, the WWE suggested that subscriber bases of more than two million were reasonable to expect for the WWE Network. The early take-up of the six-month packages at $9.99 per month was sizably less than expected. Mid-2014, the WWE dropped the six-month signup requirement in an attempt to promote more signups by subscribers. The third quarter of 2014 saw a subscriber base of only 731,000. Also challenging for the WWE was the relatively high "churn" rate in its early days. For the third quarter of 2014, the net gain in subscribers of 31,000 came from 286,000 new subscribers and 250,000 dropped subscribers.[1] By March 2015, the WWE Network had a subscriber count of more than 1,300,000. March 2015 included the WrestleMania 31 event. Concerns were raised as to how many March 2015 subscribers signed up for only one month for $9.99 as opposed to buying the WrestleMania PPV via a cable station for $59.99.
>   Wall Street took a cautious attitude to the first year of the launch of the WWE Network. The WWE reported a net loss of $30.1 million for the fiscal year to December 2014. On March 19, 2014, the WWE had a stock price of $31.39 and a market capitalization of approximately $2,300 million. On March 31, 2015, the WWE's stock price stood at $14.01 and a market capitalization of $1,025 million. Vince McMahon, Chairman of the WWE, however, remained more bullish after year one on the future performance of the WWE Network than did many on Wall Street.

In some cases, a sports rights-holder may seek to obtain revenue from all three sources. Some sports rights-holders attempting to build consumer interest may decide to provide content over the internet free to consumers, but obtain revenues from either advertisers or sponsors.

One possible form of the consumer pay revenue source in Exhibit 15.1 is a single event that a sports rights-holder produces and streams on the internet. An example would be a pay-per-view boxing event that the rights-holder produces and streams direct to consumers who pay the event-viewing fee.

15.1.2 Sports Rights-Holder Partners With a Broadcasting Channel Who Produces the Content and Provides the Content Free of Charge to Consumers

Model 2 is the broadcast television model that was for many decades the dominant way in which live sports content was delivered to consumers. The term "broadcast television" is used in the industry to describe a model where the consumer can access the channel without making a payment. Before the advent of paid cable television, almost all television channels operated with this model. Consumers had television receivers that picked up the content via over-the-air signals.

Broadcast television stations had one or both of two main revenue sources to pay for the production of the content:

1   **Advertising.** A football program could have, say, 15 minutes of advertising every hour of broadcasting. Examples include the four major broadcast network channels in the US (ABC, CBS, NBC, and Fox), CTV in Canada, ITV in the UK, and Channel 9 in Australia.

2   **Government financial allocations.** Here governments provide funds to a so-called "public" television station, such as PBS in the US, CBC in Canada, BBC in the UK, and ABC in Australia.

In most cases, the sports broadcaster will pay the sports rights-holder for the right to broadcast the content. Highly rated sports content will require higher payments to the rights-holder, as the broadcaster will be able to charge advertisers higher rates per each advertising time slot.

An alternative version of this model is where the sports rights-holder pays the broadcast channel to show its content. This is called a "buy time" approach and is often used by sports rights-holders seeking to build their profile. It is also called a "sports infomercial" approach due to its similarities to products that buy 30- or 60 -minute television time slots that are typically broadcast late at night or early in the morning.

15.1.3   Content is Delivered Via a Double Set of Partnerships – (A) Sports Rights-Holder Partners With a Cable Channel Who Produces the Content, and (B) the Cable Channel Partners With a Distributor Who Delivers Content to the Consumer

Model 3 is now the dominant way in which many consumers receive sports content. Here consumers typically pay for sports content in one or both of two ways:

1   Monthly payments to the cable distributor for packages of channels that provide 24/7 content.
2   Event-based payments – such as pay-per-events for boxing and mixed martial arts.

This double set of partnerships results in the end consumer paying for sports content through paying the cable distributor. The cable distributor then pays each cable company, typically on the basis of the number of cable subscribers receiving the cable channel. The cable channel in turn pays the sports rights-holder for the right to produce and have the content on their cable channel.

Examples of cable channels with sports content include:

- US: ESPN, Fox Sports 1, NBC Sports Network, YES Network, and CSN Chicago
- Canada: TSN and Rogers Sports Network
- UK: Sky Sports
- Australia: Fox Sports

Examples of cable distribution channels include:

- US: Comcast, Time Warner Cable, DirecTV, and DISH Network
- Canada: Rogers Cable and Bell Satellite
- UK: BSkyB
- Australia: FOXTEL

Exhibits 15.2 and 15.3 illustrate how the financial magnitude of the partnerships with the sport rights-holders are in the billions of dollars.

Years	NFC Sunday	AFC Sunday	Sunday Night	Monday Night	Sunday Package	Thursday Night	Total
1970–73	18 CBS	12 NBC		9 ABC			39
1974–77	22 CBS	19 NBC		18 ABC			59
1978–81	48 CBS	42 NBC		58 ABC			148
1982–86	133 CBS	118 NBC		130 ABC			381
1987–89	150 CBS	120 NBC	51 ESPN	120 ABC			441
1990–93	263 CBS	186 NBC	223 ESPN/TNT	222 ABC			894
1994–97	395 Fox	217 NBC	255 ESPN/TNT	230 ABC			1,097
1998–2004	563 Fox	511 CBS	610 ESPN	558 ABC	400 DIRECTV		2,642
2005–11	713 Fox	623 CBS	600 NBC	1,109 ESPN	700 DIRECTV		3,745
2012–13	1,100 Fox	1,000 CBS[b]	950 NBC[b]	1,900 ESPN[c]	1,000 DIRECTV[d]		5,950
2014	1,100 Fox[b]	1,000 CBS[b]	950 NBC[b]	1,900 ESPN[c]	1,000 DIRECTV[d,e]	275 CBS[f]	6,225

EXHIBIT 15.2 Summary of NFL broadcast/cable average annual contracts ($M) since 1970

a 1987 strike affected year
b to 2022
c to 2021
d to 2014
e $1,500 million annually from 2015 to 2022
f $275 million for 2014 and $300 million for 2015

Years	Average annual contract	Rights-holders (number of games)
2001–4	$559.3 million	Sky Sports (106)
2004–7	$519.6 million	Sky Sports (138)
2007–10	$866.7 million	Sky Sports (92) Setanta Sports (46)
2010–13	$904.8 million	Sky Sports (115) Setanta Sports (23)
2013–16	$1,530 million	Sky Sports (116) BT (38)
2016–19	$2,610 million	SKY Sports (126) BT (42)

EXHIBIT 15.3 EPL Average Annual Contracts (translated to US dollars) from UK Broadcasters
Source: "English Premier League is Big Winner from $7.7 Billion Television Rights Auction," *Sports Business Daily,* February 11, 2015

15.1.4 Consumer Options Can Include Several Broadcasting Models

Several of the three models in Exhibit 15.1 may be simultaneously available to a consumer. Consider several examples:

- Consumers may have the option to either receive free an over-the-air broadcast channel via Model #2 or pay for the channel via Model #3. In Model #3 the consumer receives the same broadcast channel as part of a package that a cable distributor charges the consumer on a monthly basis.
- Consumers may have the option to receive a pay-per-view event via Model #1 with a direct payment to the rights-holder or the same pay-per-view event via Model #3. In Model #3 the consumer receives the same pay-per-view but payment is made to the cable distributor. Box 15.1 outlines how the WWE allowed its fan base to receive WrestleMania on its own internet-based WWE Network for $9.99 a month (Model #1) or pay a cable company $59.99 (Model #3).

Over time, consumers have seen an expanding set of options to receiving the same content. Sports rights-holders have a vested interest in exploring whether Model #1,where they retain control over production and distribution, is financially more attractive for some of its content. Model #1 effectively cuts out one middleman in the case of Model #2, and two middlemen in the case of Model #3. However, Model #1 means the sports rights-holder faces the risk of demand uncertainty. In contrast, in Models #2 and #3, the sports rights-holder typically receives an agreed known revenue stream, often for many years in the future.

15.2 BROADCAST REVENUES AS A PIVOTAL REVENUE SOURCE FOR MANY SPORTS RIGHTS-HOLDERS

Broadcasting and media revenues are a central pillar of many sporting leagues and sporting bodies. Exhibit 15.2 presents a summary of NFL broadcast contracts since 1970. The 2014 year broadcast contracts are conservatively estimated to be $6.225 billion. This $6.225 billion figure for 2014 is a 66 percent increase from the prior contract period. Recent broadcast contracts across the major North American leagues have typically resulted in the already sizable broadcast revenue category increasing at a faster rate than other major revenue categories. Exhibit 15.3 reports the average annual broadcast contract payments that the English Premier League receives for its domestic United Kingdom rights. Note here the same general pattern of high rates of increase at each new round of broadcast contracts.

Deloitte provides a breakdown of the five major European soccer league revenues by category, including broadcast, game/match day, sponsorship, and other commercial. Exhibit 15.4 shows the percentage of league revenues by each of these categories for the five leagues.

The English and Spanish leagues present data only for the first three categories. Based on the average numbers reported for each league between the 2009 and 2013 seasons, the broadcast category is the highest revenue source in England, Spain, Italy, and France. In Germany, broadcast and sponsorship are tied as the highest revenue source. Of note is that in Exhibit 15.4 the traditional primary source of team revenues, game/match-day revenues, is below 30 percent of total league revenues in all five leagues.

Country – league Years	Broadcast	Game/ match-day	Sponsorship	Other commercial	Total	€(millions)
England – EPL						
2009	49 %	28 %	23 %	—	100 %	2,326
2011	52 %	24 %	24 %	—	100 %	2,515
2013	47 %	23 %	30 %	—	100 %	2,946
Average: 2009–2013	50 %	25 %	25 %	—	100 %	2,637
Germany – Bundesliga						
2009	31 %	23 %	31 %	15 %	100 %	1,575
2011	30 %	23 %	30 %	17 %	100 %	1,746
2013	31 %	23 %	29 %	17 %	100 %	2,018
Average: 2009–2013	30 %	23 %	30 %	17 %	100 %	1,775
Spain – La Liga						
2009	41 %	28 %	31 %	—	100 %	1,501
2011	45 %	25 %	30 %	—	100 %	1,718
2013	48 %	22 %	30 %	—	100 %	1,859
Average: 2009–2013	45 %	25 %	30 %	—	100 %	1,693
Italy – Serie A						
2009	55 %	14 %	18 %	13 %	100 %	1,494
2011	60 %	13 %	27 %	—	100 %	1,553
2013	59 %	11 %	30 %	—	100 %	1,682
Average: 2009–13	58 %	13 %	26 %	3 %	100 %	1,562
France: Ligue 1						
2009	55 %	14 %	18 %	13 %	100 %	1,048
2011	58 %	13 %	17 %	12 %	100 %	1,040
2013	49 %	11 %	15 %	25 %	100 %	1,297
Average: 2009–13	55 %	12 %	17 %	16 %	100 %	1,119

EXHIBIT 15.4 Breakdown of Total League Revenues for Five Major European Soccer Leagues: 2008/9 to 2012/13

15.3 SHORT HISTORY OF BROADCASTING IN SPORTS

15.3.1 Broadcast World Expands to a Broadcast and Cable World

Prior to the advent of radio and television, the only way to watch a sport contest was to go to the stadium. Today, the majority of fans watch games on television, and increasingly on mobile devices, either independently or complementing their television experience. The broadcast of sport began in the film industry in the late 1800s with the recording and distribution on kinetoscopes of athletic events such as boxing.[2] In 1910, a rights agreement to film and show highlights of a sporting event was signed between Major League Baseball and representatives of the movie industry for $500.[3]

The sport television era began in the 1930s. In 1936, cameras filmed events at the Olympic Games in Berlin that were later shown in public halls near the Olympic venues through closed-circuit television. In 1937, the British Broadcasting Corporation (BBC) televised a boxing match to the 20,000 British households that owned a television. The following year in June, the BBC telecast the Wimbledon

Tennis Championship.[4] The year 1939 marked the debut of North American sports broadcasting when a baseball game between Columbia and Princeton Universities was televised (using a single camera) to an estimated audience of 400 households. The 1964 Olympic Games in Tokyo showcased an early live sports broadcast to countries around the world. Previously, broadcasts mostly aired on television after the event as films needed to be physically transported to broadcast centers for transmission.[5]

During the 1950s and 1960s, network television dramatically increased its production and distribution of live sport content, driven by a few major broadcasting networks. This is Model #2 in Exhibit 15.1, where the major revenue source to a privately owned broadcaster is advertising. In the United States the three national networks (ABC, CBS, and NBC) jockeyed for the rights of popular events such as the Olympics, NFL, MLB, and NBA. CBS was the first network to broadcast the Winter Olympics at Squaw Valley in 1960, for a reported $50,000 rights fee. In 1961, congress passed the Sports Broadcasting Act, allowing sport leagues to collectively negotiate their television contracts.[6] Prior to this ruling, each team was required to negotiate their own television contracts. NFL commissioner Pete Rozelle was the first to take advantage of this new law and in 1962 the first league-wide television contract was signed by the NFL.[7]

Until the end of the 1970s, the number of television broadcast channels in countries around the world remained small, resulting in the slow growth of rights fees. Often public broadcasting networks played an important role in television broadcasting in general, and especially in sports broadcasting. The arrival of cable and satellite television in the 1980s and 1990s brought in a new era of greater competition for sports content. This is the world of Model #3 in Exhibit 15.1. Here cable stations received two revenue streams (subscription revenues and advertising revenues), which greatly increased their ability to bid large amounts for sports content.

15.3.2 Enhancing the Broadcasting Experience via Storytelling

The important role of storytelling in building compelling sports content is a key theme in broadcasting history. For example, the US broadcast network ABC in the 1960s enjoyed much broadcasting success by promoting a storytelling perspective on sports broadcasting. Its highly rated *Wide World of Sports* program opened with music behind dramatic sports clips with a resonant voice (Jim McKay) saying:

> Spanning the globe to bring you the constant variety of sport … the thrill of victory … and the agony of defeat … the human drama of athletic competition … This is ABC's *Wide World of Sports!*[8]

David Hill, a creative force in sports broadcasting across three continents for more than four decades (starting in Australia in the 1960s, followed by a stop in the UK, and then the US) stated:

> Sport is a microcosm of life. It always has been. And at any given sports event, you're going to have cowardice and heroism, you're going to have luck, and you're going to have bad luck, and you're going to have stupidity, and you're going to have great insight, and you're going to have incredible skills, and you're going to have people who forget what the basics are and fall on their butts as a result. Any sporting event has all those, the various conflicts of life, which has always made sport so compelling.[9]

Hill's approach to broadcasting promotes viewers having emotional connections to the events being presented. These connections could be to the event itself, the teams and athletes on the field, or to the broadcasters presenting the content. He also viewed the broadcast from the viewers' perspective. An example of Hill's viewer-based perspective is the "onscreen scorebox" that is now part and parcel of many sports broadcasts. Hill created this box when he was watching soccer and not hearing mention from the broadcasters of the score. His solution was the ever-present onscreen box score. Hill viewed the ongoing evolution of broadcasting technologies as important only if it enabled the viewer to have an enhanced viewing experience.

15.3.3 Onscreen Personalities Become Part of the Entertainment Experience

One pillar of sports broadcasting becoming a major entertainment experience is having engaging personalities in the broadcast. These personalities could be on the field or part of the onscreen broadcast team. They can also be part of the "shoulder programming." This refers to the programming before and after a live event where that event is either previewed or reviewed.

An example from the early years is Howard Cosell. In 1970, Roone Arledge of ABC hired Cosell to present *Monday Night Football* (MNF). He paired Cosell with two former football players – Frank Gifford and "Dandy" Don Meredith. Cosell stayed as a central part of the broadcast team from 1970 to 1983. Discussion of a MNF game after a broadcast often included comments about the broadcast team as well as the game itself. Viewers were far from unanimous in liking Cosell's outsized personality, but returned regularly to be entertained, amused, and sometimes revolted by his commentary.[10] Cosell also announced major boxing events, including many Muhammad Ali fights. The Cosell–Ali onscreen interactions became part of boxing and sports broadcasting lore. A 1995 *New York Times* obituary stated:

> Howard Cosell, who delighted and infuriated listeners during a 30-year career as the nation's best-known and most outspoken sports broadcaster, died yesterday. He was 77. From his first days on radio in the 1950s to the peak of his fame during his 14 years on Monday Night Football, Cosell – once simultaneously voted the most popular and the most disliked sportscaster in America – tended to be loved and loathed for his undisputed characteristics: his cocksure manner and his ebullient, unqualified immodesty. "Arrogant, pompous, obnoxious, vain, cruel, verbose, a showoff," Cosell once said. "I have been called all of these. Of course, I am." … Partly because he entered sports broadcasting in the mid-1950s, when the predominant style was unabashed adulation, Mr. Cosell offered a brassy counterpoint that was first ridiculed, then copied until it became a dominant note of sports broadcasting.[11]

Central to decision making by media executives is the choice of the broadcasting talent that appears on the screen before, during, or after the broadcast of a sports event.

15.4 THE CHANGING LANDSCAPE OF SPORTS BROADCASTING

Decision making regarding sports content now takes place in a rapidly changing landscape. Major trends include:

15.4.1. The Digital Revolution, Mobility and Proliferation of Devices

The demand for and supply of sports content being delivered on mobile devices continues to grow. The myopic focus on television that characterized the mindset of many broadcast executives now is being replaced by a "screens everywhere, new world" mindset. The CEO of CBS, Leslie Moonves, has stated: "I don't care where or when you watch our shows – just watch them. We just want it to get counted and we want to get paid accordingly."[12]

In 2014 the Bleacher Report, a leading online sports content site, saw its mobile page views exceed that of its monitor (web) page views. This shift requires recognition that content provision to smartphones and other mobile devices can be different than content provision to larger monitors and screens.

Global trends in sport media consumption highlight the growing influence of digital media. A 2013 survey covered 14 global markets. A common finding was that people are spending more time consuming sport than ever before. While television is still the #1 outlet for following sport, other methods – namely mobile, online, and social media – are making significant in-roads into consumers' viewing habits. For some, these in-roads are often occurring as complements to traditional television. This is what is now called the "second screen" phenomenon. The use of these second-screen technologies has displaced print as the second most used method to follow sport after television in many countries.[13]

15.4.2 The 24/7 News Cycle and Differing Strategies

For many decades, news content came at regular time periods – daily editions of newspapers, morning and evening broadcast news programs, and hourly news updates on radio. Today's world of continual flow of information (and misinformation) due to technology advances has implications on the information distribution strategies of content providers. These strategies include:

- to be the breaking source of new information;
- to be the first credible source of breaking stories (even if not the first source);
- to be the first source to have reflective and insightful commentary on the implications of breaking stories.

Many content providers do not have a consistent strategy on their positioning. Moreover, there are often apparent conflicts between media ownership and the content of potential news that make it difficult to always have a consistent strategy. For example, a league-owned cable broadcast channel may be reluctant to break negative stories that relate to their clubs until they have highly credible support from multiple sources. For sports stories that are more positive, they may well broadcast the story much earlier, with fewer credible sources.

15.4.3 Video and Pictorial Content Revolution

Television has long provided real-time content that subsequently could be provided on a tape, disc, etc., or on a program repeat basis by the channel itself. YouTube built its early status on being the largest repository of videos that includes both "professional" and user-generated content (UGC). Content platforms that can package multiple types (text, video, and pictorial) have an inherent advantage in providing a richer experience to viewers. Tweets that result in the largest numbers of retweets often now incorporate clips/photos as well as text.

15.4.4 Increase in Social Media Options

Social media to many was initially synonymous with companies such as Myspace and Facebook. Then Twitter from its beginnings in 2006 grew to be another important player in the media content landscape, allowing fans as well as on-air broadcasters to provide running commentary on a broadcast. Instagram, launched as a photo- and video-sharing service in 2010 and acquired by Facebook in April 2012, has also become an important online player. Vine, founded in mid-2012, was quickly acquired in late 2012 by Twitter. It distributes video clips of short duration. The lesson here is rapid evolution of the social media product both (a) within the larger social media companies, and (b) by startups that can have their financial exits as trade sales to those larger companies or continue to remain independent at the investor level (but not necessarily at the product level).

15.5 DECISION MAKING BY SPORTS RIGHTS-HOLDERS

Sports rights-holders are a central stakeholder in the sports broadcasting world. This section outlines some of the diversity among rights-holders and the complexity of their decision making.

15.5.1 Diversity in Sports Content Rights-Holders

Rights-holders range from bodies with sizable negotiating presence to those that have much less ability to attract interest by media companies to their content.

- **Global sporting bodies.** The major high-profile bodies such as the International Olympic Committee (IOC), FIFA (soccer), Formula 1 (open wheel motor racing), ICC (cricket), and World Rugby (rugby union) have high interest from multiple countries for their content. At the other end of the spectrum, there are many international sports federations who have smaller fan bases or less global demand for their content – such as the Badminton World Federation or the International Gymnastics Federation.
- **Regional sporting bodies.** The regional bodies (confederations) of FIFA vary greatly in their negotiation strength. The European Zone Federation (UEFA) has much negotiation strength whereas the Oceania Zone (OFC) has the weakest negotiation strength of the six FIFA confederations.
- **County/region-based sporting bodies.** The major professional sporting leagues in North America (NFL, MLB, NBA, and NHL) have high demand for their content. In contrast, a league, such as the National Lacrosse League (NLL), will have a smaller (albeit often very avid) fan base and lower media demand for their content. Minor leagues often have only small regional fan bases, with the result that demand for national distribution of their content is low.
- **NCAA and College Conferences in the US.** The so-called "Power Five College Conferences" in the US (ACC, Big Ten, Big 12, Pac-12, and the SEC – see Chapter 8) have strong demand for their content. In contrast, there is lower demand for the content of lower profile conferences such as the Mid-American (MAC), the Western Athletic (WAC), or Canadian Interuniversity Sport (CIS) in Canada.
- **Sporting facilities and events.** The All England Club holds the rights to the Wimbledon tennis tournament, one of the crown jewels of individual sport properties. A similar high demand event

is the Masters golf tournament, the rights to which are held by the Augusta National Golf Club. In contrast, there are numerous tennis and golf tournaments around the world where the demand for coverage is much lower.

15.5.2 Varying Objectives of Sports Rights-Holders

Decisions by sports rights-holders can include a diversity of objectives, including:

1   **Maximize the financial returns/revenue yield.** Some leagues adopt a very aggressive position to negotiate the most attractive financial package. In many negotiations, the financial focus by a rights-holder is on the total payments to be received from a broadcaster for the length of the contract. There is increasing recognition that sports rights-holders can build valuable assets by having equity in the broadcast or distribution stages. Model #1 in Exhibit 15.1 is one approach to a rights-holder seeking to capture returns from production and distribution. An alternative approach is a sports rights-holder taking equity in a cable network producing and broadcasting its games. Chapter 16 discusses decisions by leagues, teams and other sports rights-holders to build these broadcast or distribution assets.

2   **Broadest possible distribution of content.** For many years, leagues chose free-to-air broadcast partners, in part because they ensured the broadest distribution of their content. The advent of cable networks with their typically lower distribution, but often sizable subscriber fee revenues, now means that conflicts can exist between obtaining the best financial package and obtaining the broadest distribution of content. Concern by sporting bodies with having a broad distribution of content can also come from political pressure. Box 15.2 illustrates how politicians in the UK and Australia have "ring-fenced" multiple sporting events that must have "free-to-air" television as part of their live content distribution.

BOX 15.2 UK AND AUSTRALIAN POLITICIANS PASS LEGISLATION TO MAINTAIN "FREE-TO-AIR" DISTRIBUTION OF DESIGNATED SPORTING EVENTS

A major trend in sports content delivery is the declining percentage of sports content available on a "free-to-air" model basis – Model #2 in Exhibit 15.1. Concerns have been expressed about this trend by several stakeholders. One fear is that many financially challenged fans cannot afford to buy cable packages and hence will be precluded from seeing cable televised games and events in their own home. Sports rights-holders often express concern if there is limited distribution of their content as with some cable televised games.

In the United Kingdom, the early growth of cable television in the late 1980s and early 1990s was fueled by an increasing number of EPL soccer games being shown on cable (especially on the Sky Sports cable channel, which was distributed by BSkyB). Previously, elite soccer games in the UK were broadly available on a "free-to-air" basis, such as on the BBC. Politicians were lobbied to limit this growing trend. One outcome was what is now called the "Ofcom Code on Sports and Other Listed and Designated Events." The Broadcasting Act in the UK gives the Independent Television Commission (ITC) the right to exclude certain events from only being available on a cable or pay-per-view (PPV) basis. Examples of events that must have a "free-to-air" option available for consumers to watch live include:

- Soccer: FIFA World Cup; UEFA finals; FA Cup Final.
- Rugby: World Cup Final in rugby union; Challenge Cup Final in rugby league.
- Horse racing: Epsom Derby; Grand National.
- Tennis: Wimbledon Championships Men's and Women's Finals.
- Olympics: Summer and Winter Games; Paralympic Games.

Not surprisingly, much lobbying occurred as decisions were being made as to the events to be included or excluded from the "free-to-air" mandated list.

Australia has enacted similar legislation. The phrase "anti-siphoning" is used to describe legislation that gives free-to-air broadcasters first right of refusal to designated sporting events. The minister for sports in Australia has the ability to add or delete designated events from the list. Examples include events in the Olympic Games, Commonwealth Games, horse racing (Melbourne Cup), Cricket, Australian rules football, rugby league, rugby union, golf, tennis, and motor sports.

In the US, there is ongoing debate about the pros and cons of broad distribution of major events versus obtaining higher rights fees from cable companies wanting exclusive distribution rights. For example, although the NFL sanctioned its first regular season on cable in 1987 (shown on ESPN with the proviso that local channels could also show the game), it was not until 2015 that the NFL sanctioned a playoff game to be shown exclusively on cable television (being a "wild card" game in the first round of the playoffs).[14] For the five NFL media contracts starting in 2012, ESPN was the only cable broadcaster. However, it paid the NFL the largest rights fee ($1.9 billion per year) – see Exhibit 15.2. It also had the largest absolute and highest percentage increase in the rights fees paid (a 71 percent increase compared to 61 percent for CBS, 58 percent for NBC, 54 percent for Fox, and 43 percent for DirecTV).

3   **Control the presentation and showcasing of a sport.** Rights-holders can view broadcasting as an essential aspect of their brand building and protection. One extreme is they do the broadcasting themselves, having direct control of what is presented. This is one benefit of Model #1 in Exhibit 15.1. A less extreme position is when the rights-holders impose tight restrictions on the presentation of the broadcast as part of the contract. An example is CBS's contract with Augusta National Golf Club. Augusta limits the broadcaster to only four minutes of commercial time per hour (most events have 12 to 15 minutes) and places great emphasis on showcasing the sport of golf and the beauty of the course itself.[15]

4   **Build a fan base for a sport.** For new leagues, having a regular broadcast slot on a widely distributed channel can be an essential part of a fan growth strategy. Indeed, some new leagues adopt what is called a "buy time" approach where they pay a network to broadcast their content. Existing leagues seeking to build fan bases in new geographies often provide their content to broadcasters in those new regions at minimal amounts, and certainly well below the amounts in their "home country" contracts. Both the MLB and the NBA for many years were prepared to write "low revenue" contracts with Asian, European, and Latin American broadcasters as part of a long-term strategy to build larger, more avid, fan bases in those regions.

5   **Protect the game-day experience for fans attending an event.** Having a "full" venue is attractive to sports rights-holders for many reasons – including atmosphere, and revenue from food, beverage and tickets. For many years, key rights-holders (falsely in most cases) assumed that fans would not attend live games if live broadcasts were available in their home market. This led to so-called "blackout" requirements as regards live broadcasts of local games.

15.6 NEGOTIATION AND CONFLICT IN SPORTS BROADCAST VALUE-CHAINS

At key points, negotiations between key parties in the sports broadcasting value-chain can become very strained. Examples include:

■   Rights-holders often will be demanding higher rights fees than television stations view as economic to pay. Broadcasters in general now receive less loyalty from rights-holders, even those with which they may have multiple past broadcast contracts.

■   Cable stations will often demand higher subscriber fee rates than distributors view as economic to pay. High profile disputes regularly occur between cable stations and cable distributors. These include disputes between the YES Network and Cablevision in the early 2000s and more recently between the Pac-12 Network and DirecTV.

■   Consumers may view the rates that cable distributors charge as excessive. Phrases used to describe responses by consumers include "cord shavers" (those who reduce their cable package) and "cord cutters" (those who stop their cable package). The phrase "cord nevers" describes potential consumers who decide not to start subscribing to any cable package.

15.7 GLOBAL SPORTING BODY DECISION MAKING – INTERNATIONAL OLYMPIC COMMITTEE (IOC)

The signature events managed by the IOC are the Summer and Winter Olympic Games. There is much global interest in live Olympic sports content. The high number and diversity of events at each Olympic Games provides broadcasters with highly rated programming. Exhibit 15.5 highlights the continued growth in revenues the IOC receives from its many broadcast partners.

The Charter of the IOC puts great emphasis on selecting broadcast partners who can provide broad distribution of its content: "The IOC takes all necessary steps in order to ensure the fullest coverage by the different media and the widest possible audience in the world for the Olympic Games."

This stated objective of "broad distribution" led to challenging decisions over several decades regarding European television partners. In 1956, the IOC entered into the first of its many rights deals with the European Broadcast Union (EBU). This is a consortium of public service broadcasters that together provides free-to-air television coverage to all European homes. For nearly three decades, there was no real competition to the EBU until private commercial cable operators began to emerge in the 1980s. During this time the IOC stayed true to its mandate, turning down a $10 million bid for the Italian rights fees for the 1984 Los Angeles Games. This bid from Silvio Berlusconi's nascent commercial channel, Canale 5, was rejected because it did not have universal reach in Italy. A few years

Panel A: Summer and Winter Olympic Games broadcast revenue

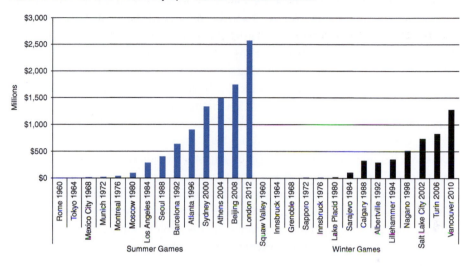

Panel B: Summer and Winter Olympic Games broadcast hours and broadcast revenue per hour

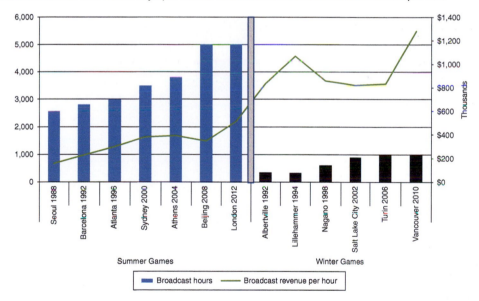

EXHIBIT 15.5 Broadcast Revenue History for Olympics
Source: IOC Marketing Report, 2014

later, the IOC rejected a $300 million bid for the European rights for the 1996 Atlanta Games from German commercial media group Bertelsmann for similar coverage reasons.[16] More recently, the IOC has encouraged multiple channels to form partnerships that combine "free-to-air" broadcasters with cable channels. In 2008, Sky Italia received IOC broadcasting rights when it outbid the state broadcaster Rai. However, Sky was obligated by both Italian law and the IOC to sub-license some coverage to a free-to-air broadcaster.

Timo Lumme, the IOC's director of television and marketing, said at the time: "The Sky deal is a reference point in that we were able to look at the European market in a new light and this flexibility will be carried forward into negotiations for 2014 and 2016." Lumme went on to say that the Italian deal did not represent a change of strategy for the IOC, noting that the objective was still to get the widest possible coverage with the best financial terms.[17] The Sky experience led the IOC to encourage the creation of consortium groups who mixed free-to-air and pay television coverage.

The US has long been the single largest source of broadcast revenue for the IOC. When live broadcasting of the Olympics to the US began in 1960, there were three major US national "free-to-air" broadcast networks – CBS, ABC, and NBC. Each of these three networks has broadcast either the Summer or Winter Olympics at some time. NBC has been the sole holder of Olympic broadcasting rights since 2000. Fox became the fourth major US broadcast television network in the 1990s, but has not been a successful bidder for Olympic rights. Having a broadcast network as the US distributor is consistent with the Olympic Charter promoting broad distribution. Over time, however, the US broadcasters have also added cable stations to their broadcast platforms to increase the live content available to viewers while also increasing their revenue streams. In 1992, NBC offered viewers a pay-per-view option of having live content of lesser profile events on three cable channels. Box 15.3 describes this so-called "triple-cast" experiment.

BOX 15.3 NBC'S HIGH-PROFILE BUT EXPENSIVE EXPERIMENT WITH TRIPLE-CAST PAY-PER-VIEW LIVE COVERAGE OF THE BARCELONA 1992 SUMMER OLYMPICS

Two major challenges that Olympic broadcasters have faced are: (a) more content produced than hours available to show on a single broadcast channel, and (b) time differences between when events are being held and the ideal broadcast times for ratings in different parts of the world. In 1992, NBC had the US broadcast rights to the Summer Olympics to be held in the July–August period in Barcelona, Spain. NBC's traditional approach for such a non-US-based Olympics would be to show high-interest events in US television prime-time on a taped delay basis and provide only limited coverage of many other events. NBC decided, in partnership with a New York-based cable operator, Cablevision, to complement this traditional approach with what they labeled a "triple-cast." The triple-cast consisted of three cable channels that could be purchased in different packages. The blue cable channel showed live swimming events and athletic events. The white cable channel showed live individual sports such as boxing, wrestling, equestrian, and gymnastics. The red cable channel showed live team sports such as baseball, basketball, and water polo.

Even before the Olympics began, skepticism was expressed about the likely commercial success of the triple cast experiment. An article in *The New York Times* stated:

The Olympics triple-cast has the potential of being the pay-per-view equivalent of a mega-flop movie with a greater chance of losing $100 million than of making a cent ... Cablevision would split profits 50–50 and cover half of all loses up to $100 million. NBC would have no cap on its losses. The price for the pay-per-view would be $95 for the "bronze "package, the first week or the weekends; $125 for the "silver" package, all 15 days: and $170 for the "gold" package, all 15 days plus extras (such as Olympic pins).

Tom Rogers, the president of NBC Cable said: "It's a whole new way to present sports on television." ... Rogers characterized the number of advance orders as "insubstantial." Many cable systems expect their subscribers to buy in numbers below NBC's and Cablevision's hopes, which range from 2 million to nearly 5 million.[18]

There was also a single-day option initially advertised at $29.95, but later reduced to $19.95 to stimulate demand.

While exact subscribers were not disclosed, estimates of the number of PPV subscribers for the triple-cast ranged between 200,000 and 250,000. This was well short of the numbers budgeted for a breakeven situation. Losses of at least $100 million were estimated to be shared by NBC and Cablevision. Explanations for the losses included: (a) limited tradition in 1992 of customers paying the premium prices charged for sports content, especially the Olympics; (b) limited promoting of the packages, with NBC reported to be concerned that advertising may reduce ratings for their prime-time broadcasts; and (c) poor execution/broadcasting at some events. A *New York Times* sports business journalist, Richard Sandomir, covering the situation commented: "I think people just weren't ready for it…It was just done in the wrong way at too high a price."[19]

NBC in subsequent Olympics shifted its strategy to using a platform of cable channels (and later also internet streaming) to supplement its free-to-air broadcasting of high-interest events (often with time delays). With this strategy viewers did not have additional out-of-pocket outlays to receive the Olympic content, although they had implicitly paid for that content via monthly cable subscriber fees.

NBC/Comcast holds US Olympic media rights to 2032. Their current approach has placed the highest rated Olympic content on its free-to-air broadcast channel and supplemented it with other content on cable channels that it also owns (such as USA Network, Bravo, and Spanish coverage on Telemundo). Box 15.4 describes the negotiation dynamics that led to the IOC renewing the NBC contract without a competitive auction occurring.

BOX 15.4 IOC AWARDS US OLYMPIC RIGHTS THROUGH 2032 TO NBC: THE POWER OF LONG-TERM RELATIONSHIPS!

Starting with the Sydney Summer Olympics in 2000, NBC has been the sole US broadcasting partner with the International Olympic Committee (IOC) for its Summer and Winter Olympics. Estimates of rights fees paid by NBC to the IOC are:

- 2000 Summer and 2002 Winter – $1.25 billion
- 2004 Summer, 2006 Winter, and 2008 Summer – $2.3 billion
- 2010 Winter and 2012 Summer – $2 billion

In June 2011, the IOC and NBC announced that NBC had won a bidding contest from ABC/ESPN and Fox Sports for four Olympic Games through 2020 (Winter Olympics in 2014 and 2018, and

Summer Olympics in 2016 and 2020). NBC's successful bid was approximately $4.4 billion. It was reported that "the three networks submitted sealed bids to the IOC in Lausanne, Switzerland. FOX went first, ESPN went second, and NBC went last in presentations. This was the first US media rights auction since NBC secured the rights to the 2010 and 2012 Olympics with a $2.3 billion deal in 2003." Fox issued a statement on Twitter congratulating NBC. ESPN said on a company website that paying more for the Olympics "would not have made good business sense for us."[20] The NBC bid was reported to have exceeded each of the Fox and ESPN bids by more than $1 billion.

In May 2014, the IOC and NBC announced that NBC had been awarded exclusive Olympic broadcast rights from 2022 to 2032. The contract was reported to be for approximately $7.75 billion. Competing bids from other US broadcasters were not sought. Reports relating to the negotiations behind this announcement provide insight into the decision processes at both the IOC and NBC. Included in the negotiations on the IOC side were Thomas Bach (president of the IOC – a German lawyer by background and Olympic gold medalist in fencing), Timo Lumme (director of TV and marketing services), and Christophe De Kepper (IOC director). On the NBC side were Brian Roberts (Comcast chairman and CEO), Mark Lazarus (NBC Sports chairman), Gary Zenkel (NBC Olympics chairman), and Steve Burke (NBC Universal CEO). An article in *Sports Business Journal*[21] provides much insight into the negotiation dynamics and decision making:

- "IOC executive Timo Lumme, who worked with Bach for years on European TV rights negotiations, said the German lawyer prioritizes long-term security over short-term rights. 'His philosophy always was that the best model is a long-term partnership.'"
- "Bach first let NBC know he was interested in a long-term extension two months after being elected president. He was in New York City for an event with the United Nations and scheduled a dinner with NBC Olympics President Gary Zenkel, IOC Director General Christophe De Kepper, and Lumme. Over dinner Bach floated the idea of extending NBC's deal early. Zenkel was interested and took the idea back to his boss, NBC Sports Chairman, Mark Lazarus."
- "The day after the opening ceremony of the 2014 Winter Sochi Games in Russia, Zenkel and Lazarus joined Comcast CEO Brian Roberts and NBC Universal CEO Steve Burke in the IOC presidential office at the Olympic Club. They told Bach, Lumme, and De Kepper that they wanted to make a deal. The question everyone had was: How long? … That was left open."
- "Zenkel traveled to the IOC's headquarters in Lausanne, Switzerland, in March 2014 with a green light to cut a deal. He met with Bach, Lumme and De Kepper. They quickly reached consensus on a $7.65 billion deal for six Olympics, from 2011 through 2033. They ended the negotiation with a handshake."

    "Handshake deals," however, do not always end up in signed contracts. All parties in the negotiation put high priority on maintaining secrecy until the contract was signed.

- "The IOC looped USOC Chairman Larry Probst and USOC CEO Scott Blackmun into the conversation in March, jump-starting contract negotiations. De Kepper, Lumme and Zenkel worked with NBC attorneys and the IOC's lawyers at O'Melveny & Myers to finalize the agreement. They worried at times that news of the negotiation might leak to the press and did their best to limit who knew about it. Between the IOC, NBC, and USOC, fewer than 15 people knew the deal was close. Blackmun said: 'We were all aware of how important keeping it quiet was to making the deal happen. Everybody was advised that this was on a need-to-know basis.'"

- "Lumme said the IOC debated whether it could get more revenue than an auction process in the future but ultimately decided it was more important to have a long-term agreement with a partner it trusted than make a few extra dollars. 'You can maybe in one deal make one or the other dollar more and maybe have your product destroyed,' Bach said last week. 'We are thinking long term in the IOC … We want to leave a good legacy there to our successors.'"
- Roberts outlined why NBC moved to keep the Games as follows: "We've been fortunate to be profitable since we got involved in the Olympics with London and Sochi. We have a lot more experience. This long-term partnership allows you to invest and innovate."

A Fox News article[22] included the following comment: "Almost as stunning as the deal itself was how the IOC and NBC managed to keep it under wraps. 'Sorry that we proceeded in keeping it secret, but it's also an expression of the excellent partnership that we've enjoyed [with NBC] and those we can rely on each other,' Bach said. The secrecy shut out NBC's rivals. There was no bid process open to all networks as there was in 2011. Bach said he saw no reason 'to take any risk' with anyone other than NBC."

In Canada, a consortium of cable channels (Bell Media and Rogers Communications) and the public broadcaster (CBC) won the Olympic rights for the 2014/20 period. In addition, the consortium also offers streaming to a variety of second screen devices.

15.8 NFL'S BROADCAST STRATEGY LEVERAGES ITS RATINGS POWER

Live coverage of NFL games has, for several decades, been the gold standard for television ratings and viewership in the US. Regular season ratings consistently outperform the regular season ratings of all other sports and even the playoff games of other sports. Exhibit 15.6 shows the drawing power of regular season NFL games and the Super Bowl vis-à-vis the MLB regular season games and the World Series.

The NFL has used this rating power to negotiate ever-increasing broadcast/cable contracts. The examples presented in the two following sub-sections are illustrative.

15.8.1 Fox wins the 1994/7 NFC regular season package with a 50 percent increase over the prior contract paid by CBS for the 1990/3 package

For many years ABC, CBS, and NBC were the only national broadcast networks in the United States. Each had more than 95 percent coverage of households. From 1970 to 1993, each network had the same NFL package of regular season games, as reported in Exhibit 15.2. CBS and NBC had the Sunday daily packages and ABC the *Monday Night Football* (MNF) package. In 1987, Rupert Murdoch's News Corp launched Fox as a fledging fourth national broadcast network. Murdoch saw NFL sports as a platform to build the growth of Fox as a national network and to convince some television stations to shift their affiliation to the Fox network. In a bold decision on both sides, the NFL awarded Fox the NFC Sunday package for 1994/7. The annual rights fee Fox would pay was a record $395 million per year. CBS, who held the package in the 1990/3 period, paid the NFL $263 million per year in that period.

Game night/event	2010	2011	2012	2013	2014
NFL REGULAR SEASON AND SUPERBOWL					
FOX/NFC SUNDAY	20.110	20.096	19.700	21.200	20.341
CBS/AFC SUNDAY	18.747	18.400	17.700	18.700	18.629
NBC/SUNDAY NIGHT	21.848	21.542	21.463	21.747	21.275
ESPN/MONDAY NIGHT	15.657	13.252	12.826	13.679	13.349
NFL SUPER BOWL	106.476	111.010	111.346	108.414	112.500
MLB REGULAR SEASON AND WORLD SERIES					
ESPN/ALL GAMES	2.177	2.294	1.784	1.850	1.808
MLB WORLD SERIES	14.268	16.645	12.660	14.900	13.800

EXHIBIT 15.6 NFL Averages Audience for Regular Season Games and Super Bowl versus MLB Average Audiences for Regular Season Games and the World Series Games (Millions Of Viewers)
Sources: "NFL game audience relatively flat in '14: Fox has its second-best season yet," *Sports Business Daily*, January 7, 2015; "MLB TV partners see mixed regular-season results during first year of new deal," *Sports Business Daily*, October 2, 2014; "Despite blowout, Super Bowl XLVIII ends up as most-watched program ever in the US," *Sports Business Daily*, February 4, 2014;. "World Series audience finishes down from '13, but well above record low in '12," *Sports Business Daily*, October 13, 2014.

The other two successful broadcast bidders for the 1994/7 period slots were NBC ($217 million per year) and ABC ($230 million).

This was a risky decision by the NFL on several grounds. Fox had lower household coverage than the other three networks. It also had a limited US track record in sports broadcasting. However, there were several powerful pluses to the NFL. First, it was the highest bid by many millions. Second, Fox was attracting a younger demographic than the other three established networks, which was also an area of weakness for the NFL. Most importantly, it enabled the NFL to add a fourth bidder for the three slots it had for national broadcasts. This created for the NFL the attractive bidding dynamic of more bidders than slots. The result has been large increases in the rights fees bid for subsequent NFL contracting rounds. A *New York Times* article in December 1993 accurately predicted that "Fox's acquisition of NFC games will not only affect the way viewers watch football but could also affect the balance of power among the major networks in terms of ratings and advertising."[23]

Fox benefited greatly by using the NFL content for its own "asset-build." It enabled Fox to build a highly valuable network with broad national coverage in a shorter time than would have been the case without the NFL content. In a narrower sense, advertising revenues from the NFL game timeslots were below the $395 million paid by Fox each year to the NFL. Fox also had setup costs and production costs for covering the NFL games. However, these costs were an investment in building the highly valuable larger asset that is the fourth US national broadcast network. The legitimacy and anchor content of the NFL was central to this asset-build. Fox also differentiated itself from the other traditional broadcasters by creating a more irreverent style that appealed to younger audiences, and promoting the onscreen personalities that resonated with many viewers.

15.8.2 DirecTV Successfully Bids for Exclusivity with NFL Sunday Ticket Package

The two main distribution platforms on which cable television is delivered to US viewers are cable video and satellite:

- Cable video is through cables placed under the ground. Major companies here include Comcast Corporation and Time Warner Cable, both of which have strong incumbent positions.
- Satellite distribution occurs by satellites that have been launched into space. The two leading companies are DirecTV and DISH Network.

Competition among these distributors was leveraged by the NFL in its negotiating strategy for a new package called "NFL Sunday Ticket." This package shows all NFL Sunday games by the NFL's broadcast partners except those available in a local market. The two main customers are avid NFL fans who want to watch as many NFL games as possible, and fans of a team that does not play in the local market in which they now live (such as a Dallas Cowboys fan who lives in Miami). When the NFL decided to make this package of games available, it faced the decision of whether to make it generally available to all potential distributors (say on a revenue-sharing basis) or to have possible distributors bid for the package on an exclusive basis. The NFL did the latter. It has awarded, on an exclusive basis, the NFL Sunday Ticket package multiple times to DirecTV. For DirecTV, having the NFL Sunday Ticket package on an exclusive basis reduces the likelihood of existing subscribers switching to other distributors. It also increases the likelihood of attracting new subscribers. DirecTV subscribers typically pay an extra fee for the NFL Sunday Ticket package, although it is often provided at minimal cost to new subscribers. The major benefit of a subscriber to DirecTV comes from monthly subscriber fees each and every month and not just the specific purchase cost of the NFL Sunday Ticket. The amount DirecTV was willing to bid for this package includes this broader "customer value" computation. By offering the package on an exclusive basis, the NFL was able to capture part of this broader customer value in the higher amount DirecTV was prepared to bid. The annual amounts the NFL receives from DirecTV have been sizable – $400 million per year in the 1998/2004 period, $700 million per year in the 2005/11 period, $1,000 million per year in the 2012/14 period, and $1,500 million per year in the 2015/22 period – enough in the view of the NFL to offset the benefits of a potential wider distribution reach.

15.9 SUMMARY

Revenues from broadcast partners are increasingly pivotal to the growth and economics of leagues, clubs, and events in many parts of the globe. This chapter highlighted the diversity and complexity of multiple decisions in this area. Multiple models exist by which sports rights-holders can have content delivered to consumers. Moreover, there can be conflicts, or at least compromises, among key objectives of a rights-holder – such as maximizing revenue yield versus maximizing widest possible distribution. Technology is also making the landscape for the key stakeholders in this arena ever-changing. Chapter 16 further discusses this broadcast landscape, emphasizing developments with respect to national and regional sports networks.

NOTES

1 V. Johnson, "WWE releases new subscriber numbers for WWE Network, change price point again, offer November free to new subscribers," *The Squared Circle*, October 30, 2014.
2 R. Gamache, "Genealogy of the sportscast highlight form: from peep show to projection to hot processor," *Journal of Sports Media*, 5(2), 2010: 77–106.
3 M.J. Haupert, "The economic history of major league baseball," *EH.net Encyclopedia*, December 2007, https://eh.net/encyclopedia/the-economic-history-of-major-league-baseball/.

4 J. Owens, *Television Sports Production* (Focal Press, 2007).

5 C. Jeanrenaud and S. Késenne (eds.), *The Economics of Sport and the Media* (Edward Elgar Publishing, 2006).

6 B. Schultz and W. Wei, "Sports broadcasting," *Routledge Handbook of Sport Communication*, 84, 2013.

7 Rozelle convinced the NFL owners to share the television revenues equally, which was an important building block in the NFL's efforts to promote competitive balance among the clubs.

8 "*Wide World of Sports* Intro 1978," YouTube.

9 A. Block "Fox sports chief talks Dodgers TV deal, NFL coverage (Q&A)," *The Hollywood Reporter*, September 14, 2011.

10 M. Ribowsky, *Howard Cosell: The Man, the Myth, and the Transformation of American Sports* (W.W. Norton, 2011).

11 R. McG. Thomas, "Howard Cosell, outspoken sportscaster on television and radio, is dead at 77," *The New York Times*, April 24, 1995.

12 A. Ha, "CEO Leslie Moonves explains CBS's streaming strategy: 'I don't care where you watch our shows,'" Techcrunch.com, January 7, 2015.

13 www.sportbusiness.com/knowledge-centre/sportbusiness-numbers-7-broadcast-digital-media-global-sports-media-consumption.

14 M. Yoder, "Arrival of NFL playoffs is the final frontier for ESPN and cable sports," *Awful Announcing*, January 2, 2015.

15 M. Thompson, "The Masters: a sports property unlike any other," TROJAN360.com, April 9, 2014.

16 F. Dunne, *Case Study: The IOC Media Rights Strategy*, www.sportbusiness.com/knowledgecentre/casestudyiocmediarightsstrategy.

17 Dunne (2009).

18 R. Sandomir, "Olympics; triple-cast: an Olympian blunder or innovation?" *The New York Times*, June 29, 1992.

19 Sandomir, "Olympics; triple-cast."

20 M. McCarthy, "NBC wins rights to Olympics through 2020; promises more live coverage," *USA Today*, June 7, 2011.

21 T. Mickle and J. Ourand, "NBC deal shows focus by Bach, IOC on loyal partners," *Sports Business Journal*, May 12, 2014.

22 "IOC and NBC: 5 things to know about the landmark Olympic rights deal," Fox News, May 8, 2014.

23 "NBC gets final NFL contract while CBS gets its Sundays off," *The New York Times*, December 21, 1993.

16

SPORTS BROADCASTING 2
NATIONAL AND REGIONAL SPORT NETWORKS

National networks and regional networks for many years have provided much of the live sports content that is delivered to consumers. Within each of these two categories, we often find both broadcast and cable options. The decisions made by these networks have played a major role in changing the landscape of the sports industry. This chapter examines key areas of decisions at these networks. Appendix 16A presents an overview of key players in the US sports television network landscape. Examples from other countries are provided in the text of this chapter. Appendix 16B provides an overview of five companies that are major sports broadcasters, but also play multiple other roles in the sports industry.

As consumption of sports expands to broader and more diverse outlets, the companies in Appendix 16A have also broadened their footprint to extend well beyond the delivery of content via television. As Jeff Krolik, executive vice-president of Fox Sports Regional Networks, has stated: "We are at a point where fans expect to watch their games wherever they want on whatever device they want. We're working hard with our teams and our distribution partners to meet that expectation."[1]

16.1 SPORTS CONTENT ON BROADCAST AND CABLE TELEVISION

Exhibits 16.1 and 16.2 present an overview and sample of four combinations of (a) national and regional networks, and (b) broadcast and cable networks. These combinations are discussed in this section.

16.1.1 Multiple National Broadcast and National Cable Networks Show Sports Content

A national network (NN) has content distributed across a large region, typically a country, where there is often zero or minimal localization of that content. The two main categories of national networks delivering sports content are national broadcast networks (NBNs) and national cable networks (NCNs).

Examples of NBNs include ABC, CBS, Fox, NBC, and PBS in the United States; CTV and CBC in Canada; ITV and BBC in the United Kingdom; and, the Nine Network, the Seven Network, and ABC in Australia. Each of the above examples relate to what Chapter 15 called "broadcast networks," as

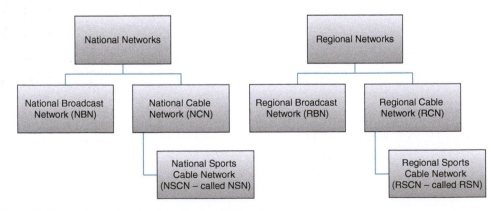

EXHIBIT 16.1 Categories of National and Regional Networks

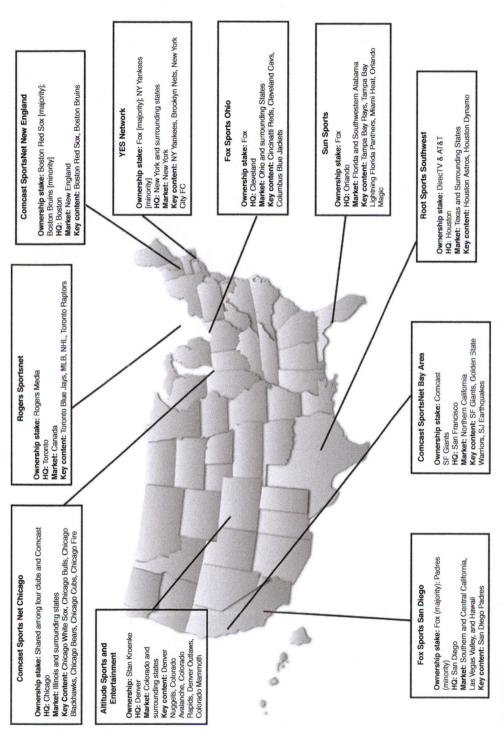

Comcast Sports Net Chicago

Ownership stake: Shared among four clubs and Comcast
HQ: Chicago
Market: Illinois and surrounding states
Key Content: Chicago White Sox, Chicago Bulls, Chicago Blackhawks, Chicago Bears, Chicago Cubs, Chicago Fire

Rogers Sportsnet

Ownership stake: Rogers Media
HQ: Toronto
Market: Canada
Key content: Toronto Blue Jays, MLB, NHL, Toronto Raptors

Comcast SportsNet New England

Ownership stake: Boston Red Sox [majority]; Boston Bruins [minority]
HQ: Boston
Market: New England
Key content: Boston Red Sox, Boston Bruins

YES Network

Ownership stake: Fox [majority]; NY Yankees [minority]
HQ: New York and surrounding states
Market: New York
Key content: NY Yankees, Brooklyn Nets, New York City FC

Fox Sports Ohio

Ownership stake: Fox
HQ: Cleveland
Market: Ohio and surrounding States
Key content: Cincinnati Reds, Cleveland Cavs, Columbus Blue Jackets

Sun Sports

Ownership stake: Fox
HQ: Orlando
Market: Florida and Southwestern Alabama
Key content: Tampa Bay Rays, Tampa Bay Lightning Florida Panthers, Miami Heat, Orlando Magic

Root Sports Southwest

Ownership stake: DirecTV & AT&T
HQ: Houston
Market: Texas and Surrounding States
Key content: Houston Astros, Houston Dynamo

Altitude Sports and Entertainment

Ownership: Stan Kroenke
HQ: Denver
Market: Colorado and surrounding states
Key content: Denver Nuggets, Colorado Avalanche, Colorado Rapids, Denver Outlaws, Colorado Mammoth

Comcast SportsNet Bay Area

Ownership stake: Comcast SF Giants
HQ: San Francisco
Market: Northern California
Key content: SF Giants, Golden State Warriors, SJ Earthquakes

Fox Sports San Diego

Ownership stake: Fox (majority): Padres (minority)
HQ: San Diego
Market: Southern and Central California, Las Vegas Valley, and Hawaii
Key content: San Diego Padres

EXHIBIT 16.2 Sample of North American Cable Sports Networks

for many years they have been broadcast on a free-to-air basis (i.e., no cable package was required to watch the network on a home television). Government broadcast networks (such as the BBC in the UK, CBC in Canada, and ABC in Australia) have often been funded largely from taxation revenues. Corporate-owned broadcast networks (such as NBC in the United States and CTV in Canada) for many years relied just on advertising revenues. In recent years, where cable operators have redistributed these broadcast channels, the networks have also received retransmission fees from these cable operators, which are expected to become more important in the future. These networks typically show a broad range of content such as news, dramas, and comedies as well as sports. For many years, most live sports content was shown on such broadcast networks and they still play a key but diminishing role.

NCN channels are available only on a "cable basis," where the cable distributor pays the channel for rights to distribute the channel. The distributor, in turn, charges the consumer, often in the form of a package ("bundle") of cable channels. Many cable channels have very little sports content. Examples are CNN, Fox News, the Food Network, the Disney Channel, and the Cartoon Network. Several national networks show live sports, but have a broader range of programming. Examples in the United States include TBS and TNT, which have sports rights to MLB and NBA games, as part of a larger set of content that includes a majority of non-sport programming. HBO and Showtime, both of which are widely distributed in the US, as well as in many other countries, regularly show boxing events along with many of their other non-sports programs.

16.1.2 National Cable Sports Networks Emerge To Be Major Content Providers

Prior to the 1980s, most channels showing live sports provided viewers with a broad range of non-sports and sports content over a weekly 24/7 cycle of programming. In 1979, ESPN (Entertainment and Sports Programming Network) launched as a national cable sports network (NCSN) – more commonly called a national sports network (NSN). An NSN has 100 percent (or dominant) sports content that is distributed across a large region. Typically there is zero or minimal localization of that content with a NSN. In its early years, ESPN showed a collection of low-profile sports to the US audience. ESPN's growth to be one of the most valuable assets in all of broadcasting and all of sports was a gradual progression rather than being an "instant" or "early" success. ESPN is now the flagship national sports network. The major revenue source for ESPN is subscriber fees. While most networks do not publicly disclose revenue numbers, third parties often make estimates. A Barclays Security Analyst Report[2] in January 2015 estimated that ESPN in 2013 received from its United States distributors $5.54 per month for each of 97.8 million subscribers giving an estimated $6,501 million in 2013 subscriber revenues. The closest US national cable network in revenue was TNT at an estimated $1,526 million in 2013 subscriber revenues ($1.29 per subscriber fee × 98.6 million subscribers × 12 months).[3] Kagan, an industry advisory firm, estimated that by 2015, ESPN was receiving $6.61 as a monthly subscriber fee while TNT was receiving $1.65 as a monthly subscriber fee.[4]

In many countries, NSNs are now a major source of live events across many sports. Examples of NSNs that cover a broad range of sports include ESPN, FS1, CBCSN, and NBCSN in the US; TSN and Rogers Sportsnet in Canada; Sky Sports in the UK; Fox Sports in Australia; and Star Sports in India. These cable networks have two main sources of revenues – subscriber fees from distributors and advertising revenues. Appendix 16C provides details of Rogers Sportsnet's portfolio of sports content on its NSN.

16.1.3 Regional Broadcast Networks and Regional Sports Networks

In the US, there are more than a thousand regional broadcast stations. Many national broadcast networks have regional stations that are either owned by or affiliated with the national network. For example, NBC is a national broadcast network that also has more than 200 "regional"/local stations that take some national content from NBC as well as having much local content (such as news, talk shows, and local sports). In many regional markets there are also independently owned broadcast stations. These regional broadcast channels have long been a rich source of live sports content to their viewers. For example, each of the 30 MLB clubs plays 162 games per season. Many of these local games appear only on a regional television basis rather than on a national basis. Initially, these local games appeared only on regional broadcast networks.

Starting in the late 1970s/early 1980s, some regional sporting games started appearing on cable networks (such as HBO) rather than regional broadcast channels. This shift of some live games to cable was the genesis of the major shift of live game content to regional sports networks (RSNs). A RSN has 100 percent (or dominant) sports content that focuses on sporting events and teams in a designated regional area. In North America, there are more than 50 RSNs that show packages of live sports that include one or more professional or college sports teams in that region. RSNs are available on a cable distribution basis. For example, Comcast Sports Net Chicago is a major RSN that is operated by Comcast (which has 20 percent equity). Its shows live games from four major Chicago-based sporting clubs, each of which owns 20 percent equity – Chicago Cubs and Chicago White Sox of the MLB, the Chicago Bulls of the NBA, and the Chicago Blackhawks of the NHL. Its main distribution areas are Illinois, Indiana, Iowa, and parts of Michigan and Wisconsin. Many professional sporting leagues restrict the transmission of live sporting games beyond the regional geography of each particular club so as to "protect" the local media rights of each club. These restrictions are effectively barriers to entry for other clubs in that league from competing for viewers against the local club in its home market.

Many of the current RSNs emerged from earlier ventures. For example, Fox Sports has two RSNs for the Los Angeles/Southern California, Las Vegas, and Hawaii markets: Fox Sports West and Prime Ticket. The current Fox Sports West started out as a Los Angeles-based Prime Ticket RSN in 1985. It was later purchased by Liberty Media who started building a portfolio of different RSNs. In 1996, Fox purchased a majority interest in these RSNs from Liberty Media. The RSN industry is one in which there has been many changes of ownership as well as multiple changes in the sporting rights held by individual RSNs. Sports content on Fox Sports West and Prime Ticket includes games of the Los Angeles Clippers (NBA), Los Angeles Angels of Anaheim (MLB), Los Angeles Kings (NHL), and the Anaheim Ducks (NHL), as well as college games from the Big West Conference. Recent losses of content to new RSNs are games of the Los Angeles Lakers (in 2013) and the Los Angeles Dodgers (2014).

16.2 SPORTS CONTENT CONTRACTS WITH BROADCASTERS AND DISTRIBUTORS

Chapter 15 and Exhibit 15.1 outlined three different models by which sports content is delivered to consumers:

Model #1: Sports rights-holder direct to consumer model.
Model #2: Broadcast channel produces content and provides it directly to the consumer for free.
Model #3: Cable channel produces the content, which is then packaged by a distribution partner and sold to the consumer.

Much of this chapter examines sports content contracting issues relevant to Models #2 and #3. The two major areas we now discuss are:

1. Contracts between a sports rights-holder and a broadcaster for content to show on either a broadcast channel (Model #2) or a cable channel (Model #3). Examples would be a regional broadcast station or a regional cable network negotiating to acquire rights from a MLB, NBA, or NHL club to show locally their live games. The contract amount will be a cost-line item in the income statement of the broadcast station/regional network and a revenue line item in the income statement of the sports rights-holder.

2. Contract between a national or regional cable network with a distributor (such as Comcast or DirecTV) that will include the cable channel to be sold to their subscribers. This is Model #3. The contract amount will be a revenue-line item in the income statement of the cable channel and a cost-line item in the income statement of the distributor.

We will first discuss sports contracts between the sports rights-holder and a broadcaster. It is these contracts that are an important revenue source for many sporting leagues, clubs, and other sporting event rights-holders.

16.3 CONTRACTS BETWEEN SPORTS RIGHTS-HOLDERS AND BROADCASTERS

Some key decision areas for negotiation are:

1. The broadness of media rights being negotiated. In the early pre-internet years, contracts were signed for televised rights for a given well-defined national or regional area. More recently, contracts are being signed in a world where content can also be delivered via online streaming to multiple devices as well as television. Contracts now are more explicit as to what content is being negotiated and over what delivery platforms.

2. Any upfront payment to the sports rights-holder. In some contracts, the broadcaster will be pay an upfront fee in addition to the annual rights fee.

3. The annual rights fee. Section 16.4 outlines some factors that affect the amounts broadcasters are willing to pay the rights-holder. In most cases, details of these contracts are intended to be confidential, although third parties frequently make informed (and sometimes uninformed) estimates.

4. The length of the contract. Contracts can frequently range from five to 20 years or longer. The Los Angeles Dodgers of the MLB have a 25-year contract with SportsNet LA.

5. The annual increases in rights fees over the contract length. Sometimes it is flat over time, while in many cases there is either a percentage or a fixed dollar amount of increase each year.

6. Reset provisions. Especially where contracts are lengthy, provisions can be included that allow both sides to seek a revised contract if either the rights-holder or the network believes that the contract is no longer "at current market rates." There can be guidelines included in the contract as to the procedures by which any revisions in the contract are determined. In most contracts for club sports rights, the league will also be a contracting party. Some leagues are now mandating reset provisions being included in contracts that have long periods – such as a 15- or 20-year period. Most resets have a narrow focus with no new broadcasters permitted to bid for the sports rights whose financial terms may be reset to a "new market rate."

7　The number of games to be covered. In many leagues, not 100 percent of the games are available to be included in a RSN contract. League contracts for a subset of games to be shown by a national broadcaster may result in games not available for a RSN contract. Some contracts will have two regional broadcasters sharing the games – such as a regional broadcast network and a regional sports cable network.

8　Equity in the broadcast network to be owned by the sporting rights-holder. This has occurred within several RSN negotiations. In the early years, RSNs were rarely willing to allow equity to be a negotiable term. In more recent years, especially in contexts where the bargaining power of rights-holders is strong, sports rights-holders have received significant equity interests. An example is the San Francisco Giants acquiring a 30 percent equity in Comcast Sportsnet Bay Area when signing, in 2007, a 25-year contract to provide 135 MLB games each season exclusively to the RSN.

9　Rights to tickets and access to different areas at live games. Some contracts will include a specified number of tickets to each live game. The broadcaster could use these tickets, for example, to host advertisers on their live broadcasts of games.

10　Access to coaches/players for content to use in pre- or post-game broadcasts. In recent years, several contracts have included access to coaches for short comments while a live game is in progress.

16.4 FACTORS AFFECTING AMOUNTS BID FOR BROADCAST RIGHTS

Three important categories of factors that impact decisions by broadcasters about sports content bidding and negotiations are:

1　the attractiveness of the sports content to key stakeholders such as consumers/viewers, distributors, and advertisers;
2　financial and strategic factors at the broadcaster level; and
3　the bidding/negotiation context.

16.4.1 Attractiveness of Sports Content to Stakeholders

Individual factors in this category include:

- **Size of audience attracted.** The larger the potential viewer audience, other things equal, the more attractive sports content is to a broadcaster. Sports differ greatly in their ability to attract viewers. National networks with large distribution are attracted to sports that have general broad attraction. Sports with highly regional interest or a narrow viewer clientele are less likely to be shown on the major national networks. Sports with minimal audiences are likely to attract low bidding from broadcasters. Some nascent sports even pay broadcasters to show their content in an effort to build a larger audience and their brand.

- **Quality/demographics of the audience.** Not all audiences of sports content are alike in demographics. Some audiences are highly attractive, such as those in the 16–34-year-old demographic as regards purchasing power. Sports such as skateboarding and beach volleyball attract viewers with young demographics, with the result that advertising rates are often higher when compared to sports with older demographics. Other sports attract audiences that are less attractive to broadcasters and their advertisers. Consider bowling (sometimes called ten-pin bowling). This sport has a focused audience that many advertisers view as "blue-collar," with its lower expected purchasing power. Professional wrestling content, which has strong national television ratings, also falls in this category. The advertising revenue per rating point of professional wrestling is relatively low, which translates to broadcast channels not bidding as high for broadcast rights vis-à-vis other sports.

- **Quantity/inventory of programming acquired.** Broadcasters operate on a year-round basis and benefit from accessing a large volume of live content. MLB sports rights are especially attractive as there are 162 regular season games each season. NBA and NHL seasons both have 81 regular season games per season. Several RSNs have rights to both a MLB club (regular season running from April to September) and a NBA or NHL club (regular seasons running from October to April), which means each month there are live games to be broadcast.

- **Stickiness.** Sports content that has an extended season of games regularly attracting a large targeted audience is highly prized by both advertisers and the network. Networks are often ranked on average ratings over a season. Sports content that, on a weekly or more frequent basis, draws high ratings can make an important contribution to boosting total station ratings.

- **"Live destination programming" reputation.** Many broadcast programs are increasingly being viewed on a "tape-delayed" basis, where viewers choose to access only part of the content and can aggressively skip advertisements – examples include soap operas, crime dramas, and situation comedies. In contrast, many sports events are what are called "live destination programming," in that viewers place a high premium on viewing the event live. There is also the attractive feature that pre-event and post-event programming often maintains high ratings. Commentators on the shifting habits of media consumers often call "live sports" the leading example of live destination programming, with the NFL often viewed as the gold standard.

- **Audience propensity to experiment with other programming.** Audiences that view an event on a network and then experiment to see other content on that same network are very attractive to a new network or a network seeking to reposition itself as a general sports network. Chapter 2 distinguished between general sports fans and singular-sport-specific fans. A viewer whose interest is in "tennis and tennis alone" may be attractive as a repeat viewer as long as tennis is being shown, but is unlikely to be attracted to viewing other sports on that same network. Consider Fox Sports launching in 2013 the FS1 and FS2 national sports cable channels offering a broad set of programming. Fox Sports' strategy is to show major live sports games/events on FS1 and FS2 as an investment in having general sports fans view these channels as their "home" to sports viewing. ESPN took many years to develop their brand, and Fox Sports will gain much by having a sizable number of ESPN regular viewers start viewing FS1 and FS2 as comparable or even better in terms of content and entertainment value.

16.4.2 Strategic and Financial Considerations of the Broadcaster

Broadcast and cable networks can differ in the strategic factors considered when bidding for the rights to include sports content on their channels. Factors considered in these decisions include:

- **Estimated revenues and costs from acquiring the sports rights.** When broadcast companies first started bidding for sports content, advertising revenues were the dominant revenue source. Financial analysts could look at the expected ratings for each sports property and make estimates of the likely advertising rates and the number of advertisements that could be shown during the event.

This information could offer a guide as to which sports properties to bid high or low and still have a positive surplus after covering production and administrative costs. When sports content increasingly shifted to cable television, with its dual revenue sources of cable subscription revenue and advertising, financial analysts at the cable company also had to consider the likely impact of acquiring specific sports rights to the fees that cable distributors were willing to pay the cable company.

- **Asset-build strategy of the broadcaster.** Section 15.8 gave several illustrations of companies with "asset-build strategies" bidding for sports rights amounts well above the "narrow" revenue benefits from acquiring that content. A RSN attempting to build greater presence in a region could be willing to bid "high" for sports rights fees in order to transform them to be the dominant RSN in a region.

- **Competitive strategy of the broadcaster.** Companies differ with the aggressiveness with which they attack existing competitors or seek to pre-empt potential competitors entering their market. *Forbes* argued that this factor was a key reason for Fox bidding aggressively in 2010 for its Fox Sports Southwest RSN to retain the rights to the Texas Rangers of the MLB: "Hell-bent on keeping its foothold in Texas and preventing Comcast or any other competitor from forming another RSN in the Dallas-Fort Worth Metro area, Fox Sports made a bold move."[5] *Forbes* also noted that the owner of the Dallas Mavericks of the NBA, Mark Cuban, had indicated interest in entering the Dallas–Fort Worth RSN market by setting up a team-based RSN that included the Rangers sports content with the Mavericks sports content. Further discussion of this contract is presented in Section 16.4.4 of this chapter.

16.4.3 Bidding Context of the Negotiations

In the early years of RSNs, there was typically only one RSN in each market. The result was that most competition for sports rights came from regional broadcast networks that relied only on advertising revenues to cover the amounts bid for sports rights. This limited competition usually meant the RSN had sizable negotiating power due to its combination of subscription revenue and advertising revenue. Over time, there has been an increase in the number of networks bidding for sports rights in a region with no increase in the number of sporting clubs in that region. Consider two of the largest markets in the United States: New York and Los Angeles.

New York

Up to 2002, Cablevision – with its MSG and MSG+ networks – was the dominant cable company in the largest US regional market and had rights to the content of all major sporting clubs in the region. The first new competitor in the market was the YES Network (starting in March 2002), which acquired rights to the New York Yankees of the MLB and the (then) New Jersey Nets of the NBA. The next major entrant was Sports Net New York (starting in March 2006) with rights to the New York Mets of the MLB.

Los Angeles

As noted in Section 16.1.3 of this chapter, up to 2012, Fox Sports, with its RSN duo of Fox Sports West and Prime Ticket, was the dominant cable company in the second largest US metropolitan market. In the 2012–14 period, three new RSNs entered the LA market by outbidding Fox Sports. In 2012, two new RSNs – Time Warner Cable SportsNet and Time Warner Cable Deportes – started broadcasting with the Los Angeles Lakers of the NBA as their lead sports content. The LA Lakers received the (then) largest sports rights contract for an NBA club, reported to be a 20-year cable contract averaging at $125 million a year.[6] Starting in 2014, a third new RSN entered the LA market with Time Warner Cable SportsNet LA. This new RSN acquired the rights to the Los Angeles Dodgers of MLB games for a 25-year period. An article on MLB.com noted that:

> SportsNet LA [was] controlled by American Media Productions, a club subsidiary. Terms of the deal were not announced, but media reports have speculated that it could be worth between $7 billion to $8 billion over 20 to 25 years. The team's current rights deal with FOX pays about $40 million annually. The new deal, which begins for the 2014 season, would be worth at least $280 million annually. The current cable contract, which runs through the 2013 season, gave FOX an exclusive 45-day window at the end of the 2012 season to negotiate an extension. The Dodgers and FOX reportedly agreed to a $6 billion deal, but it was not finalized as the club and MLB debated how much of it would be subject to revenue-sharing. Meanwhile, the exclusive window expired and Time Warner Cable escalated the bidding.[7]

Without taking the reported contract amounts at face value, the LA Dodgers example highlights how increases in competition among current and potential RSNs can increase what broadcasters have to pay to acquire or retain the rights to elite sports content that is attractive to consumers, distributors, and advertisers.

16.4.4 Reported Contract Amounts Can Diverge from Actual Contract Amounts

Although clauses of each broadcast contract are typically confidential, third parties often make informed and, in some cases, uninformed estimates. Consider the press commentary on the Texas Rangers renewing in 2010 its contract with Fox Sports Southwest. The prior contract was reported to pay the Rangers $20 million per year.

- *USA Today* reported on September 27, 2010 that the Rangers had signed a 20-year contract with Fox Sports Southwest "that will guarantee them $3 billion … That's about $150 million a year … In comparison, the Los Angeles Dodgers make about $45 million a year off their TV deal with FOX."[8]
- *The Dallas Morning News* on November 30, 2010, after noting the $150 million a year amount reported by *USA Today*, stated: "Turns out the report may have inflated the dollar figure by a wee bit. FOX Sports headquarters in New York called the figure 'wildly inflated' before reporting that was all it would say on the matter." The reporter then quoted a "TV executive in the know" who stated that "a more accurate figure … is 'somewhere between $1.5 billion and $1.6 billion' that translates in the neighborhood of $75 million to $80 million a year."[9]

Often the press will continue to report the highest amount other reporters or commentators have cited, even after there is considerable evidence the amounts being requoted are sizably wide of the mark.

16.5 CONTRACTS BETWEEN BROADCASTERS AND DISTRIBUTORS

In many countries, cable is now the dominant way in which sports and other content is provided to the consumer, see Model #3 in Exhibit 15.1. Cable here refers to either "under the ground" physical cables or via satellites. The distributor is effectively a middleman between cable stations and the consumer. Here there are two types of contracts:

1   Contract between an individual cable channel and each potential distributor: the revenues to the cable channel are typically a function of the fee per subscriber paid by a distributor to the channel, and the number of subscribers who receive the channel from the distributor.
2   Contract between a distributor and its consumers/customers: the revenues to the cable distributor are the total monthly cable bills consumers pay to receive the different packages of content.

We now discuss key elements of these two contracts. Decisions related to the second kind of contract listed above will be discussed first as they can dramatically affect the ability of cable channels and individual distributors to come to an agreement. Two major decisions made by a distributor as regards contracting with its customers are: (a) whether to sell cable channels as part of a bundle of stations or on an individual (à la carte) basis, and (b) how broadly or narrowly to distribute individual cable channels.

16.5.1 Alternative Distributor Packaging of Cable Channels to Consumers: Bundling versus à la Carte

The bundled approach is characterized by the distributor packaging multiple channels and offering the package to a consumer as a single product for a single price. An example would be a "basic" package that is $50 per month and includes, say, 80 channels comprising national broadcast channels, regional broadcast channels, national cable networks, national sports networks, and several regional sports networks. The consumer may be only interested in ten of these channels, but is forced to pay $50 per month and receive 70 channels of little interest. This approach has been compared to dining at a smorgasbord where you pay a single all-inclusive price for a menu that includes many items you do not or maybe even cannot eat.

An alternative approach is each channel having its own stand-alone purchase price, effectively an open market for each individual channel. Here the consumer could choose just that subset of available channels of interest given their set prices. This approach has been compared to dining at a restaurant where each item on the menu has its own price and you only pay for what you eat. It has been called "à la carte" pricing.

In many countries, distributors have adopted the bundled approach to the packaging of channels sold to consumers. While this is a constraint on consumer choice, the cable distribution industry to date in many countries has been able to maintain this approach. Over time, there will be increasing pressure that will likely see more channels available on an "à la carte" basis, or at least an increasing number of smaller bundles in which consumers are not being forced to purchase a large number of channels that they do not intend to watch.

16.5.2 Broad versus Narrow Distribution of Channels

There are two main factors that affect the distribution of a cable channel:

1   **National versus regional distribution.** National distribution has the largest potential market for a cable channel. In the US, the maximum national cable market is approximately 100 million households. Regional markets vary greatly in size. Nielsen regularly publishes rankings of

regions by market size. In 2015, Nielsen ranked regions from #1 (New York with 7.442 million households) to #210 (Glendive with 4,330 households). Even within the top 20 markets there are large differences: as can be seen when comparing #2 (Los Angeles with 5.523 million), #5 (Dallas–Fort Worth with 2.603 million), #10 (Houston with 2.301 million), and #20 (Sacramento with 1.345 million).[10]

2   **"Basic" versus specialty/tiered distribution.** Cable distributors typically have a "basic package" that has the broadest distribution in their market area. They also offer specialty packages that consumers can buy at extra amounts. For example, there could be a specialty sports package that includes sports channels not placed on the "basic" package, such as an out-of-market, college sports network or an overseas sports channel specializing in non-domestic sports with a narrow interest group. These specialty packages often have a much smaller number of subscribers.

Cable channel revenue is maximized by having both (a) the highest monthly rate by subscriber, and (b) the highest possible distribution. ESPN has high levels for both of these drivers of cable channel subscriber revenues.

16.5.3 RSN Subscriber Revenues from Distributors

Regional sports networks, by definition, have much lower distributions than do their national counterparts. This translates into much lower subscriber revenues. A Barclays Security Analyst Report[11] in January 2015 estimated that ESPN in 2013 received from its US distributors $5.54 per month for each of 97.8 million subscribers. The result for 2013 was an estimated $6,501 million in annual subscriber revenue.[12] The Barclays Report also provided estimates of the subscriber fees and number of subscribers for the top 40 most expensive cable networks in the US. Examples from this report are:

Network name	2013 monthly subscriber fee	2013 subscribers	Annual subscriber revenue
New England Sports Network	$3.91	4.1 million	$192 million
Comcast SportsNet Bay Area	$3.30	3.6 million	$143 million
YES Network	$3.20	12.0 million	$461 million
Fox Sports West	$2.15	6.9 million	$178 million
Altitude Sports	$1.66	3.0 million	$60 million

Each of these RSNs is distributed on a "basic" broad distribution package in their regional markets.

16.5.4 Most-Favored-Nation Clauses in Distributor Contracts With Cable Channels

Disputes between RSNs and their distributors occur on a regular basis at the time of contract renewals. The RSN will be asking for both (a) higher fees per subscriber, and (b) remaining on a "basic" broad distribution package. The distributor often pushes back in the negotiations and offers either a lower subscriber payment fee or a shift from inclusion in a "basic" package to inclusion in a specialty package that a much smaller number of consumers are willing to pay for.

Many distributors insert in their contracts with cable channels a "most-favored-nation" (MFN) clause. This clause effectively says that the same price is charged by a cable station to each and every distributor. Suppose RSN-LA (a hypothetical RSN) is a new cable sports station that has rights to a premier MLB club. RSN-LA proposes to each and every distributor in its region that they pay RSN-LA $4 for each "basic" subscriber of each distributor. The cable station wants the channel to be distributed on a "basic" package as that has the broadest distribution with an estimated total five million households. The maximum potential cable subscriber revenues for RSN-LA would be $240 million per year ($4 per month × five million subscribers × 12 months). Assume that only six of the 25 distributors in the region accept the $4 price and that these six have a combined distribution of 1.5 million. The result is that RSN-LA will have only 30 percent coverage of the Los Angeles region. Many fans of the baseball club will not be able to see live games in their own home. The remaining 19 distributors with 3.5 million subscribers refuse to include RSN-LA on their basic channel at the $4 demanded price. Suppose, however, that all 19 would accept a price of $3 per subscriber for distributing RSN-LA. Here the MFN clause in the contracts with the six distributors willing to pay $4 per subscriber would mean that RSN-LA would now only receive $3 per month per subscriber from those distributors.

The existence of a MFN clause by a distributor in its contracts with cable stations means that cable stations face a challenging decision in deciding on the price per subscriber they ask distributors to pay. Many disputes between cable channels and potential distributors arise when distributors view the price per subscriber the cable channels ask for to be excessive and not capable of being passed on to the customers of the distributor. Boxes 16.1 and 16.2 highlight two of the most high-profile and contentious disputes between RSNs and their distributors.

BOX 16.1 THE YES NETWORK'S ROLLER-COASTER EARLY JOURNEY TO GAINING BROAD DISTRIBUTION

The Yankees Entertainment and Sports (YES) Network is the leading RSN in the US based on revenues and number of viewers. However, its path to its current leading position was far from smooth.[13] Prior to 2002, Cablevision's two New York RSNs – MSG (Madison Square Garden) and MSG+ – effectively held dominant rights to sport content from the New York/New Jersey MLB, NBA/WNBA, NHL, and MLS teams. Distributing the New York Yankees of MLB was one of the "jewels in the crown" for MSG. Cablevision was also the largest cable distributor in the New York market as well as having ownership of the New York Knicks of the NBA and the New York Rangers of the NHL. Cablevision had distribution to more than 2.5 million homes, which comprised nearly half the area's cable households.

In 2000, Cablevision's 12-year $486 million cable contract with the New York Yankees was due to expire. This created an opportunity for a new RSN to be set up, subject to acquiring the rights to show Yankees games. The game plan was a RSN in which the Yankees themselves would take a major equity interest. Other investors in YES were Goldman Sachs, Providence Capital, and two individuals (Leo Hindery and Bill Bresnan). Hindery was the first CEO and a powerful driver of the formation and growth of YES in its early years. His background included investment banking, media, and president of Tele-Communications, Inc. (TCI), then the world's largest cable distribution company. The initial plan was to combine Yankees content with the rights to the NBA games of the New Jersey Nets and NHL games of the New Jersey Devils. Early challenges for YES included both acquisition of sports rights and distribution.

Acquisition of sports rights

Although the Yankees contract expired in 2000, Cablevision had first right of refusal for a new contract. YES ended up paying Cablevision $30 million to buy back the rights to show Yankees games starting with the 2002 season. YES agreed to pay $54 million per year to the New York Yankees for the rights to show live regular season games. Of the 162 regular season games, Fox and ESPN owned rights to up to 12 Yankees games over the entire season. YES signed a three-year contract at $12 million per year with a local broadcast channel, WCBS, to show 20 games per season. This left 130 live games available to show on YES. In August 2002, YES signed a 20-year agreement to acquire the rights to show around 75 New Jersey Nets games. In the first year, YES would pay the Nets $8 million a year for these rights. The original plan to include the New Jersey Devils did not eventuate.

Distribution

Cablevision quickly became a major obstacle to YES gaining 100 percent distribution on a "basic" cable package. In the 2001/2 period, YES signed three- to ten-year carriage agreements with more than 30 regional cable distributors. Every "under the ground" cable operator in the region, except Cablevision, agreed to pay YES approximately $1.85 per subscriber per month on a broad "basic" distribution basis. One of the two satellite distributors (DISH Network) refused to carry YES on the same terms that the other distributors except Cablevision had agreed to. DirecTV, the major satellite competitor to DISH, agreed to the distribution terms offered by YES.

Cablevision offered YES $0.50 per basic subscriber, which increased to $0.55 after litigation began. The alternative Cablevision offer was placement at a higher rate of YES on an à la carte premium package that had much lower distribution. YES rejected both options and filed legal briefs against Cablevision, citing anti-trust and anti-competitive behavior by Cablevision. During the 2002 MLB season, YES was not distributed by Cablevision, leaving a major gap in YES's budgeted revenue projections. The New York media continually ran stories that included many complaints from Yankees fans as well as reports from the ongoing litigation.

In March 2003, prior to the start of the 2003 MLB season, *The New York Times* reported that:

> the feud between the YES Network and Cablevision ended yesterday with a one-year deal that will make the network's Yankees and Nets games available to Cablevision's nearly three million subscribers. The deal was brokered by Mayor Michael R. Bloomberg. The long running dispute was played out in public hearings, federal court, the New Jersey Legislature, press releases presenting dueling versions of the tense squabble, advertisements and offers from DirecTV to lure Cablevision subscribers to watch YES by satellite. Cablevision's refusal to accede to YES's monetary demands made it "Exhibit A" in a national debate about the soaring costs of regional sports networks like YES that are ultimately absorbed by consumers.[14]

The YES clash with a major distributor was an early example of many subsequent such clashes between cable networks and cable distributors.

BOX 16.2 TIME WARNER CABLE AND THE LOS ANGELES DODGERS' STRUGGLE TO GAIN BROAD DISTRIBUTION IN SOUTHERN CALIFORNIAN MARKET

The Los Angeles Dodgers is one of the two leading baseball clubs in the Los Angeles basin. Moving east from Brooklyn, New York to Los Angeles in the 1950s the team has a very large fan base in Southern California. It has for many years been in the highest tier of revenue generating clubs, which has enabled it to continually invest in having a highly paid and high-profile set of players and coaches. A contentious dispute between the then owner of the Dodgers, Frank McCourt, and MLB (especially commissioner Bud Selig) over the 2010/12 period ended up with the Dodgers being placed into bankruptcy and then sold to a new owner for a record $2,150 million. The new owner was Guggenheim Baseball Partners. A central part of the valuation analysis for the $2,150 million bid was the expected future media revenues of the Dodgers.

Prior to 2014, the broadcast partners of the Los Angeles Dodgers were (a) Fox Sports West/ Prime Ticket as its RSN partner, and (b) KCAL-TV as its regional broadcast television partner. Estimates of the broadcast revenues from the contracts expiring in 2013 were in the $45–55 mil- lion range.[15] While Fox Sports had first right of refusal for a new contract starting in 2014, the own- ership dispute between the McCourt family and MLB created delays and obstacles in Fox Sports finalizing a deal. In January 2013, the Los Angeles Times reported that the Dodgers had signed a 25-year agreement with Time Warner Cable (TWC) at an average amount of $250 million to $280 million a year. TWC committed to start a new regional sports network (Time Warner Cable SportsNet LA) that would be focused heavily on the Dodgers. TWC had in 2013 launched a then new RSN (Time Warner Cable SportsNet) focused on its newly signed contract to show Los Angeles Lakers games. The Lakers contract was reported to pay the club an average of $125 million a year. TWC was a major cable distribution company in Southern California and could commit to carry the new Dodgers RSN for its own subscribers.

The Dodgers RSN channel was set to launch with the start of the 2014 season. As with many RSNs that have signed high priced contracts for sports rights, negotiations to gain broad distribution at an expected high carriage (subscriber) rate were expected to be both difficult and protracted. Both proved to be the case. TWC reportedly set a carriage rate of $4–5 for a monthly subscriber, The 2014 MLB season saw very few cable distributors besides TWC carry the Dodgers RSN. TWC required that distributors carry the new channel on a basic cable package rather than on a specialty sports package, which would have had a much lower number of subscribers. For the 2014 MLB sea- son, approximately only 30 percent of the target market had the Dodgers RSN available in their cable package. DirecTV, a major distributor in the Los Angeles basin and other parts of the Dodgers carriage area, was vocal in its refusal to pay the carriage rates demanded by the Dodgers RSN. Dan York, DirecTV's chief content officer commented that "Time Warner Cable has unilaterally decided to pay an unprecedented high price and now wants all of their own customers as well as those of their competitors, none of which had any say in the matter, to pick up that tab."[16]

Having only 30 percent carriage in the market meant that the television ratings of the Dodgers would reset new minimums for the club. The Sports Business Daily reported that the Dodgers aver- age ratings of 0.80 were the lowest in the clubs history:

Dodgers games on SportsNet LA were averaging 42,000 homes, paltry numbers for a division-winning team playing in the country's second-biggest market. By comparison, the cross-country rival Los Angeles Angels' audience was more than twice as large averaging 95,000 homes. Ratings for Angels' games on FOX Sports West jumped 49 percent this season, the biggest increase in baseball.[17]

At the end of the 2014 season, it appeared that the key parties in the dispute were very much entrenched in their own positions. Interview after interview, each group repeated the same talking points that they had at the start of the season. Industry observers were expressing the opinion that the impasse in the negotiations reflected some basic trends in the industry. The impasse showcased the major shift in the Los Angeles RSN market with multiple new entrants, each demanding high carriage rates, at the same time cable consumers were strengthening their resolve to not accept a continuation of the past record of cable distributors charging ever increasing costs.

16.6 SPORTING LEAGUE CABLE NETWORKS

The success of many regional sports networks highlighted to sporting leagues the opportunity to create their own RSN. One benefit here was from the subscriber and advertising revenue streams that other successful RSNs were receiving. Other benefits included (a) being able to have control over content shown on the league-owned RSN, and (b) the potential at some stage to add a live game option to the programming, which could lead existing and potentially new channels to bid higher amounts to retain rights to show league games live on their networks. Examples of league initiatives in this area are:

- **March 1999, NBA TV:** Started as a cable national network owned and operated by the NBA. Since 2007 it has been operated by Turner Broadcasting System, a subsidiary of Time Warner. Turner has long been a major broadcast partner for live NBA games. In October 2014, it was announced that "Turner Broadcasting System, Inc., and the National Basketball Association (NBA) have reached a new nine-year media rights agreement. Turner Sports will also continue to manage NBA Digital, the league's robust multimedia portfolio including NBA TV, NBA.com, NBA Mobile, NBA LEAGUE PASS, WNBA.com, and NBADLeague.com … The new agreement will increase TNT's regular season coverage to 64 live games annually."[18]
- **October 2001, NHL Network (Canada):** Started with equity interests held by the NHL and two Canadian companies (CTV Specialty Television and Insight Sports); the NHL has a minority equity position due to restrictions on non-Canadian companies owning Canadian broadcasting companies. The channel is operated by TSN, one of the two major Canadian cable sports network companies.
- **November 2003, NFL Network:** Started by the league with limited national cable distribution. In 2006, live games started being shown on the NFL Network with an eight-game Thursday/Saturday package. Over time, the NFL Network has expanded to have a full season of weekly games. It is owned and operated by the NFL. Kagan, an industry advisory company, placed the NFL Network as receiving the fourth highest 2015 monthly subscriber fee for all US cable networks: ESPN #1 at $6.61 a month per subscriber, TNT #2 at $1.65, Disney Channel #3 with $1.34, and the NFL Network #4 with $1.31.[19]
- **October 2007, NHL Network (US):** A joint venture between the NHL and NBC Universal (Comcast). It broadcasts a select number of live games and much commentary and highlight packages.

■ **January 2009, MLB Network:** Majority owned by the MLB, with minority equity positions held by Comcast, Time Warner, DirecTV, Time Warner Cable, and Cox Communications. Each of these minority owners are cable distributors, and helped the MLB Network start with a relatively broad distribution. The MLB is at the forefront of digital innovation in sports. In 2000 it started Major League Baseball Advanced Media (MLBAM) which is one of the most successful digital assets created in sports. It provides online access for subscribers to all out-of-market MLB games. MLBAM also operates MLB.com as well as the websites of each of the 30 MLB clubs (see Box 3.5 in Chapter 3).

The building of these league-based cable networks and multiple digital properties is part of the broader strategy of these leagues to become producers of content that is widely distributed across multiple platforms. This is a fundamentally different mindset than most leagues had in the past.

16.7 COLLEGE CONFERENCE CABLE NETWORKS

The growing interest in college sports content by broadcasters was first manifested in the increasing amounts that broadcasters were paying for college sports rights. Large increases in contracts made at the NCAA level and at the conference level showcased the potential high interest by many consumers – see Chapter 8. Much of the economic power in college sports is at the individual conference level. Examples of cable networks set up by several of the major conferences are:

■ **August 2007, the Big TEN Network (BTN):** Established as a joint venture between the Big TEN Conference and Fox Sports (now 21st Century Fox). While many high profile football games are shown by other broadcasters (under lucrative contracts with the Big TEN Conference), there is broad coverage of college football as well as multiple other college sports, such as basketball and baseball. It is a joint venture in which 21st Century Fox has a 51 percent interest and the Big TEN Conference a 49 percent stake.

■ **August 2010, the Pac-12 Network:** Owned and operated by the Pac-12 Conference. With a large inventory of live content, it has several regional channels that are tailored to different geographic regions of the 12 universities in the conference. Box 16.3 discusses the launch of this network and its struggles with DirecTV when seeking to get broadest possible distribution on a basic cable package.

■ **August 2014, the SEC Network:** Owned and operated by ESPN and provides a rich set of live and non-live content. This network benefited by having ESPN as its owner when negotiating with cable distributors.

BOX 16.3 THE PAC-12 NETWORK

The Pac-12 Network was launched in 2012 with several strong leverageable assets. These include:

■ **Colleges with rich and storied traditions in selected sports.** Relative to several other conferences, the Pac-12 has fewer high profile powerhouses in the men's football and men's basketball sports. USC and UCLA have a longer tradition than many of the other eight colleges in the then Pac-10 Conference (i.e., Stanford, Berkeley, Oregon, Oregon State, Washington, Washington State, Arizona, and Arizona State). The University of Colorado at Boulder and the University of Utah joined in 2011. The Pac-12 calls itself the "Conference of Champions," to reflect its #1 ranking in NCAA championships. One challenge here is that many of these championships are in sports with much lower popularity (and TV ratings) than the ratings program powerhouses of football and men's basketball.

- **Colleges with large alumni bases.** Many of the state colleges in the Pac-12 have large student bodies.
- **Conference covers large population's areas.** California is the most populous US state, providing the conference network with a major potential market opportunity. However, the other states (Washington, Arizona, Oregon) are much smaller. When the conference added two new colleges in 2011, one advantage was the expansion in its basic cable distribution area. Designated market area (DMA) rankings for the Pac-12 Network include Los Angeles (#2), San Francisco–Oakland–San Jose (#6), Phoenix (#12), Seattle–Tacoma (#13), Denver (#17), and Sacramento (#20). Overall, there is a potential base of more than 20 million cable households. The conference also includes several high-profile business and entertainment regions and cities with global brand companies (i.e., San Francisco, Silicon Valley, Los Angeles, Seattle, Denver, Salt Lake City, and Portland), which provide access to financial rewards and other benefits (e.g., Phil Knight's many contributions to Oregon and Stanford).
- **Leadership/management strength.** Larry Scott became commissioner of the then Pac-10 in 2009 and has since exhibited high levels of entrepreneurship for a conference that for many years had a relatively low profile and "sleepy" reputation. A $3 billion, 12-year contract with ESPN and Fox was signed for Pac-12 college football. It has been reported that ESPN and Fox paid the Pac-12 Conference $185 million in 2013, which increases by 5.1 percent annually through 2024.[20] The Pac-12 Network was launched as the first 100 percent college conference owned network.

Although most reports regarding broadcast and cable networks highlights the successes, not all ventures have been commercially successful. The college conference network area is no exception. In September 2006, the Mountain West Sports Network started broadcasting. It was 30 percent owned by the Mountain West Conference, 30 percent by Comcast, and 40 percent by CBS. From September 2006 to June 2012 it operated showing live college sports. However, the value of the sports content was sizably decreased over this period as several leading universities left the conference to join other higher-profile conferences – such as University of Utah joining the Pac-12 Conference, Brigham Young joining the West Coast Conference, and Texas Christian University joining the Big 12 Conference. In June 2012, the Mountain West Sports Network was shut down.

16.8 SUMMARY

This chapter outlines the decisions and roles of NSNs and RSNs in the sport industry, including how they interact with other stakeholders. It outlines some of the key networks, business realities and challenges facing league, collegiate, club and other content-based networks.

APPENDIX 16A KEY PLAYERS IN THE US SPORTS TELEVISION NETWORK LANDSCAPE

Parent company	National networks: broadcasting and cable	National cable sports networks	Regional broadcast networks	Regional sports cable networks
Disney	ABC	ESPN ESPN2 ESPNU ESPN Classic ESPN Deportes ESPN News	ABC regional stations	
CBS Corp.	CBS CW Network Showtime (cable)	CBS Sports Network	CBS and CW regional stations	
21st Century Fox	Fox	FS1 FS2 Fox Deportes	Fox regional stations	Fox Sports (FS) Arizona FS Detroit FS Florida FS Indiana FS Kansas City FS Midwest FS New Orleans FS North FS Ohio FS Oklahoma FS San Diego FS South FS Carolinas FS Tennessee FS Southwest FS West and Prime Ticket FS Wisconsin Sun Sports Sports South Sports Time Ohio YES Network Fox College Sports (FCS) Atlantic FCS Central FCS Pacific Big TEN Network
Comcast	NBC	NBC Sports Network Golf Channel Universal Sports	NBC regional stations	Comcast Sports (CS) Bay Area CS California CS Chicago CS Mid-Atlantic CS New England CS Northwest CS Philadelphia

Parent company	National networks: broadcasting and cable	National cable sports networks	Regional broadcast networks	Regional sports cable networks
Time Warner	HBO (cable) TBS (cable) TNT (cable)			Time Warner Cable SportsNet Time Warner Cable Deportes Time Warner Cable SportsNet LA
Univision		Univision Deportes Network		
"Independent" networks		beINSport	"Independent" regional stations	Altitude Sports & Entertainment MSG MSG 2 Mid-Atlantic Sports Network New England Sports Network Root Sports Southwest SportsNet New York
Sporting league networks		NFL Network MLB Network NBA TV NHL Network		
College conference networks				Big TEN Network Pac-12 Network SEC Network
Individual college networks				BYUtv Longhorn Network

APPENDIX 16B MAJOR COMPANIES WITH MULTIPLE ROLES IN THE US SPORTS BROADCASTING LANDSCAPE

This appendix describes the multiple roles that five of the companies referenced in Appendix 16A play in the broader US Sports broadcasting landscape: Comcast Corporation, 21st Century Fox/News Corp, the Walt Disney Company, CBS Corporation, and Time Warner Incorporated/Time Warner Cable.

Comcast Corporation

Comcast, headquartered in Philadelphia, has its roots in the 1960s, when Ralph Roberts led a group that purchased a small cable distributor. Comcast Corporation became the name of the company in

1969 and it publicly listed its stock in 1972. In 1990, Brian Roberts succeeded his father as president. Its portfolio of sports related assets includes:

- **Sports rights-holders.** Owns via acquisition in 1996 a major equity interest in the Philadelphia Flyers of the NHL. Previously also owned a major interest in the Philadelphia 76ers of the NBA.
- **Broadcast television.** Owns, via a 2011 acquisition, NBC Universal – whose major subsidiary is NBC, one of the four major US broadcast networks. NBC's rights to show sports include the NFL and the Olympics.
- **Cable television.** National sports cable networks of Comcast include the NBC Sports Network and the Golf Channel. Comcast's first RSN – Comcast SportsNet Philadelphia – was launched in 1997 to show games from each of the NBA (76ers) and NHL (Flyers) clubs it owned. Subsequently it has acquired or launched six other RSNs featuring clubs from Boston, Chicago, the San Francisco Bay Area, and Washington – see Appendix 16A.
- **Cable distribution.** Through continual acquisitions and internal growth, Comcast is now the largest "below the ground" cable distributor in the US with more than a 20 percent market share.
- **Sporting facilities.** Through holding major or controlling interests in Comcast Spectator and Global Spectrum, it manages and operates many sporting facilities in the US – e.g., Wells Fargo Center in Philadelphia (NBA and NHL anchor tenants) and University of Phoenix Stadium (with Arizona Cardinals of the NFL as the anchor tenant).

21st Century Fox/News Corp

Fox Sports has its heritage in Sir Keith Murdoch's News Limited acquiring control of an Australian newspaper (*The Adelaide News*) in 1949. Rupert Murdoch became head of News Limited in 1952 when his father died. After establishing a major position in the Australian media industry, News Corp made important acquisitions in the UK, and then in the US In 2012, News Corp was split into two companies with the Murdoch family having strong control over both companies – 21st Century Fox and News Corp. The most global of world media companies, its portfolio of sporting assets across the two companies includes:

- **Sports rights-holders.** In the US, News Corp owned the Los Angeles Dodgers from 1998 to 2004, in part to "guarantee" content to their Los Angeles based RSNs. In Australia, from 1998 to 2012, News Corp held a 50 percent interest in the National Rugby League (NRL), which came from the founding of a new league that competed for one season (1997) with the then established Australian Rugby League competition. The two leagues combined after one season as a joint venture. News Corp still owns a major equity interest in the Brisbane Broncos, a leading club in the NRL.
- **Broadcast television.** News Corp in the 1980s and 1990s made acquisitions in the US that provided the building blocks for Fox Broadcasting Corp to become one of the four major broadcast networks in the US. Sporting rights in the US held by Fox Sports for broadcast television include the NFL, MLB, and NASCAR.
- **Cable television.** Fox Sports' leading national sports networks are FS1 and FS2. These two networks were launched in 2013 with access to an impressive set of sports rights, including MLB, multiple leading soccer rights, UFC, NASCAR, and USGA championship golf events. News Corp in the 1990s put together the building blocks for the largest portfolio of RSNs in the US – see

Appendix 16A. Fox Sports also has a majority equity in the largest RSN (YES Network – showing games of the New York Yankees of the MLB and the Brooklyn Nets of the NBA) and one of the leading college sports networks (Big TEN Network). In the UK, 21st Century Fox operates and has 39.9 percent equity in Sky Sports, which has the leading set of cable sports channels. Major sports rights include EPL soccer, cricket, rugby league, and Formula 1. In Asia, ownership is held in Star TV, with major sports channels in India. In Australia, Fox Sports has the leading set of sports cable channels.

■ **Cable distribution.** 21st Century Fox's major distribution asset is in the UK with a 39.9 percent of the largest cable distributor (BSkyB). In Australia, News Corp has 50 percent equity in FOXTEL, the largest cable distributor.

The Walt Disney Company

The Walt Disney Company has continued to broaden its portfolio of assets over successive decades since its founding in the early 1920s as a cartoon network. Acquisitions have been an important contributor to this growth. Many of its acquisitions themselves had grown by their own prior acquisitions. As highlighted below, ABC acquired a 10 percent stake in ESPN in 1982 and then over time built up its equity to 80 percent (with Hearst Corporation owning the remaining 20 percent). Capital Cities in 1986 merged with ABC. In 1996 Walt Disney merged with ABC/Capital Cities. The result of these various mergers is that Disney now has a large portfolio of media assets, many of which have a strong presence in the sports industry.

■ **Sports rights-holder.** ESPN has built up impressive collections of sports events that it can showcase on Disney's broadcast and cable channels. These include the X Games and ownership or rights to many of the US college football sports bowls that are held each year in the December to January period. It previously owned the Anaheim Ducks (1992/2005) of the NHL, and the Californian Angels/Anaheim Angels (1997/2003) of MLB.

■ **Broadcast television.** ABC was one of the three early major broadcast networks in the US. ABC sports content has long been an important pillar of ABC's success over many decades. It held Olympic Games rights to many games prior to NBC starting its long sequence of Olympic broadcasting in 1992. Since ABC acquired majority control of ESPN in 1984, there began a gradual integration of the ABC Sports brand and the ESPN brand. That integration process continued after the Disney merger with ABC/Capital Cities. What was formerly known as ABC Sports is now called ESPN on ABC.

■ **Cable television.** Disney acquired control of ESPN as part of its 1996 acquisition of Capital Cities/ABC. ESPN is 80 percent owned by Disney and 20 percent owned by the Hearst Corporation. Appendix 16A illustrates the multiple ESPN channels in the US. Sports content shown on ESPN channels includes NFL, soccer, MLB, tennis, and NHRA. ESPN also has equity in multiple ESPN-branded channels in Latin America and equity in sports channels in other countries (such as CTV in Canada).

CBS Corporation

CBS, started in the 1920s as a radio network, and then expanded to become one of the three leading US broadcasting networks (with ABC and NBC). After several major changes in ownership (such as Westinghouse Electric and Viacom), in 2006 it was spun off by Viacom as a publicly traded company with CBS Broadcasting as a key asset. Viacom kept multiple cable channels in a separate company called Viacom Media Networks.

- **Broadcast television.** The CBS Broadcast Network is a major US broadcast network. Sports shown on CBS include the NFL, college football, NCAA men's basketball, PGA golf, and the Masters golf tournament.
- **Cable television.** CBS's leading national cable network is the Showtime portfolio of channels. Elite boxing events are shown on Showtime. CBS rebranded its national sports cable network as CBS Sports Network. It shares live sports with CBS Broadcast, as well as content from lower-tier leagues such as the Arena Football League and Major League Lacrosse.

Time Warner Incorporated and Time Warner Cable

Time Warner's roots go back to many media companies that have themselves been built by a combination of acquisitions and organic growth – such as Time Inc., Warner Communications, Turner Broadcasting, and AOL.

- **Sports rights-holder.** Turner Broadcasting previously owned multiple sports properties such as the Atlanta Braves of MLB, the Atlanta Hawks of NBA, the Atlanta Thrashers of the NHL, and World Championship Wrestling.
- **Broadcast television.** Time Warner owns a regional broadcast channel in Atlanta – WPCH-TV.
- **Cable television.** Time Warner's rights to major sports are with their national cable channels (TBS and TNT) that came with the Turner Broadcasting acquisition in 1996. TBS has rights to MLB and NCAA men's basketball championship games. TNT has rights to NBA games and PGA golf. Time Warner's HBO channel came from the Time-Life initial 20 percent equity in an early cable station that was formed by the founder of Cablevision. HBO holds rights to elite boxing events. Turner Broadcasting, with its Atlanta-based hub, launched Turner South in 1999 as a regional network carrying sports content from the Atlanta Braves, Atlanta Hawks, and the Atlanta Thrashers. In 2006, Fox Cable Networks purchased Turner South and later relaunched it as Fox Sports South, a Fox-run RSN.
- **Cable distribution.** Prior to 2009, Time Warner Cable was a majority-owned subsidiary of Time Warner. In 2009, it was spun out by Time Warner as an independent company. Time Warner Cable had by 2009 become the second largest "under the ground" cable distributor (after Comcast) in the US, and the third largest distributor (after DirecTV with its satellite distribution and Comcast). Comcast in 2013 made an acquisition bid for Time Warner Cable that would make it the largest cable distributor. In 2015 Comcast withdraw from the merger when the Justice Department failed to quickly approve the merger.

APPENDIX 16C ROGERS SPORTSNET "BULKING UP" IN CANADA USING A MULTI-PLATFORM STRATEGY

The Canadian broadcasting landscape includes both broadcast and cable networks. The CBC (Canadian Broadcasting Corporation) is a government-funded broadcast channel that had its genesis in radio broadcasting in the early 1900s. In 1952, CBC started a television station as a "free-to-air" broadcaster

(Model #2 in the language of Exhibit 15.1 in Chapter 15). By the late 1950s, CBC had greatly expanded the regions that received its signals. In 1961 the CTV Television Network, owned by Bell Canada, launched as the first privately owned broadcast network in Canada. Like the privately owned networks in the US (such as ABC, CBS, and NBC), advertising revenues were the dominant revenue source of the CTV Network. In 1968, the Canadian Radio-Television Commission (CRTC) was established as the regulatory body that would supervise both broadcast and cable systems. It was later renamed the Canadian Radio-Television and Telecommunications Commission in 1976.

For many years The Sports Network (TSN), based in Toronto, was the dominant cable sports network in Canada – Model #3 in the language of Exhibit 15.1. TSN was launched in 1984 with Bell Canada, a major Canadian telecommunications company, as the major shareholder. ESPN is a minority shareholder. The major competitor to TSN now is Sportsnet, which was launched in 1998. It is owned by Rogers Communications, which is a large Canadian media company also based in Toronto. Sportsnet has recently greatly increased its investment in sports content. Central to these investments is building a multi-platform to expand and deepen engagement with consumers of sports content – television, radio, online, print, and mobile. Examples of content on several of these platforms are now discussed (television, online, and mobile).

Television

The most recognized Sportsnet platform is their seven television channels. There are three national (Sportsnet ONE, Sportsnet World, and Sportsnet 360) and four regional channels (Sportsnet Pacific, West, Ontario, and East). Although the four regional channels primarily broadcast sporting events tailored to their own region, they also carry national programming. All four regional channels are available in both standard and high-definition formats and are carried through digital as well as satellite services. Sportsnet has strong rights positions across multiple high interest sports in Canada.

■ **Hockey:** Ice hockey is very much the Canadian national sport. For many decades, the majority of players in the NHL came from Canada. Even after the influx of hockey players from Europe and the growth of hockey in the US, Canada is the birthplace of approximately 50 percent of players in the NHL. Sportsnet currently has multi-year broadcasting contracts with four of the seven Canadian NHL clubs: the Vancouver Canucks, Edmonton Oilers, Calgary Flames, and Toronto Maple Leafs. Sportsnet has the exclusive rights to broadcast more than 250 Canadian NHL games a year on their regional networks. TSN has rights to the remaining three Canadian NHL clubs. In November 2013, Rogers and the NHL announced a "blockbuster" new broadcast and multimedia rights agreement that provided Rogers with national Canadian NHL broadcast rights. This 12-year, $5.232 billion deal was both the largest media rights deal in NHL history and Canada's largest sports media rights agreement. Commencing in the 2014/15 season, Rogers is the exclusive national rights-holder to all NHL games including Stanley Cup playoffs and NHL special events. In addition, the multimedia rights will allow Rogers to use digital technology to stream games on the internet, wireless and mobile devices, and satellite radio to Canadian consumers. To supplement the NHL national rights agreement, Sportsnet signed a 12-year extension with the Canadian Hockey League to make Sportsnet the exclusive broadcaster for junior hockey through the 2025/26 seasons. Examples include the Ontario Hockey League, Quebec Major Junior Hockey League, and the Western Hockey League.

- **NFL:** Sportsnet, in conjunction with City TV, broadcasts the NFL's *Thursday Night Football*. It also has NFL rights for Sunday afternoon games (normally offering a choice of two different games across the four regional networks) and all three American Thanksgiving games.
- **MLB:** Sportsnet is the home of the Toronto Blue Jays, Canada's only MLB team. It has the exclusive rights to broadcast all 162 Blue Jays games nationally across the four regional networks or Sportsnet ONE. Sportsnet covers the Blue Jays through six platforms: television, digital, magazine, radio, mobile, as well as the Blue Jays home stadium, Rogers Centre. Sportsnet also has Canadian rights to many regular season MLB games, the MLB All-Star Game and Home Run Derby, as well as the World Series Playoffs. In January of 2014, Rogers announced an eight-year extension with the MLB to maintain exclusive multi-platform broadcast rights until the conclusion of 2021.

The Sportsnet regional channels offer much additional live sports content, including: the NBA, soccer (EPL, UEFA Champions League, UEFA Europa League, and World Cup Qualifying), NCAA football and basketball, and tennis (Davis Cup and ATP Tour), and the exclusive rights to the Verizon IndyCar series.

Online

The Sportsnet webpage provides sports news, scores, highlights, and analysis. Sportsnet.ca has features and blogs from top journalists, as well as reader polls and comment sections. Sportsnet.ca also offers a section with various sports fantasy games.

Mobile

Sportsnet's mobile apps are available on multiple mobile operating systems including iOS, Android, and BlackBerry. The mobile app allows customers to stream live games on a tablet or smartphone.

Sportsnet and TSN Become Co-Investors as Well as Competitors

Sportsnet and TSN compete on multiple platforms as is evidenced by the following brief overview of TSN. TSN also uses a variety of platforms to provide fans with sports news, highlights, scores, and analysis. These platforms include television, radio, online, and mobile. TSN also has exclusive Canadian broadcasting rights to multiple sports properties including the CFL, MLS, NASCAR, the preliminary rounds of the PGA Tour, Formula 1, the Tour de France, and the Brier (Canadian curling championship). Prior to the Rogers Communications – NHL contract starting with the 2014/15 season, TSN was the previous holder of the NHL national broadcast rights. TSN has broadcast rights for three of the seven Canadian NHL clubs – the Montreal Canadians, Winnipeg Jets, and Ottawa Senators. Bell Canada, the major investor in TSN, owns a minority interest in the Montreal Canadians.

One interesting twist in the relationship between Sportsnet and TSN is the recent change in ownership of Maple Leaf Sports & Entertainment (MLSE). Based in Toronto, MLSE is the leading professional sports group in Canada. MLSE owns the Toronto Maple Leafs of the NHL, the Toronto Raptors of the NBA, and Toronto FC of MLS. It also owns or operates multiple sporting facilities, including the Air Canada Centre in Toronto where the Maple Leafs and the Raptors are anchor tenants. Both Rogers Communications (owner of Sportsnet) and Bell Canada (owner of TSN) each have 37.5 percent equity in MLSE.

NOTES

1 M. Reynolds, "RSNs To tip off live, in-market streaming of NBA games," *Multichannel News*, October 28, 2013.
2 Barclays Equity Research, *Twenty-First Century Fox – Fox: Understanding Sports Exposure*, January 6, 2015.
3 Third-party estimates of HBO revenues from distribution fees placed it above TNT, albeit with a much lower number of subscribers. HBO was not included in the Barclays Security Analysts Report. *Forbes* in July 2014 reported that "HBO US currently has 43 million subscribers and charges an estimated $6.77 monthly distribution fee, translating to over $# billion." "Sustained demand for HBO's original programming drives subscription fee growth to benefit TW," *Forbes*, July 1, 2014.
4 *USA Today*, April 23 2015, article cited in *Sports Business Daily*, April 23, 2015.
5 C. Settimi. "Baseball's biggest cable deals," *Forbes*, March 21, 2012.
6 J. Flint, "Time Warner Cable, Lakers strike 20 year TV deal," *Los Angeles Times*, February 14, 2011.
7 K. Gurnick, "Dodgers to launch network with Time Warner TV deal," MLB.com, no date. See also "Report: TWC wins Dodgers TV deal," Foxsports.com, May 28, 2014.
8 B. Nightengale, "Texas Rangers to receive $3 billion in new 20-year TV deal," *USA Today*, September 27, 2010.
9 "Rangers' new 20-year TV deal worth $80 million a year," *The Dallas Morning News*, November 30, 2010.
10 Nielsen, "Local Television Market Universe Estimates," (January 1, 2015).
11 Barclays Equity Research. "Twenty-First Century Fox – FOX: Understanding sports exposure," (January 6, 2015).
12 See footnote 3 above.
13 This box draws heavily on A. Wusterfeld, *Yankees Entertainment & Sports (YES) Network LLC: Team-Affiliated Television Networks* (Stanford GSB Case, 2003).
14 R. Sandomir, "Baseball: Cablevision agrees to carry the YES Network," *The New York Times*, March 13, 2003.
15 L. Stewart, "Dodgers headed to KCAL," *Los Angeles Times*, December 1, 2004; R. Sandomir, "Bankrupt Dodgers will benefit from robust TV market," *The New York Times*, December 3, 2011; "Dodgers further sever News Corp ties with new TV deal," *Sport Business Daily*, December 1, 2004.
16 J. Flint, "Dodger channel debuts Tuesday but much of the region will be shut out," *Los Angeles Times*, February 24, 2014.
17 J. Ourand and D. Broughton, "Ratings for Dodgers, Astros show the challenges of starting RSN," Sports Business Daily (September 29, 2014).
18 "Turner Broadcasting and the National Basketball Association reach nine-year media rights extension," pressroom.turner.com (October 6, 2014).
19 *USA Today*, April 23, 2015 article cited in *Sports Business Daily*, April 23, 2015.
20 J. Solomon, "Ed O'Bannon lawsuit reveals terms of Pac-12 contract with ESPN and FOX," AL.com, June 6, 2013.

17

BUILDING NEW VENUES AND VENUE MANAGEMENT

Stadiums, arenas, and other types of sports venues are the places where participants get to play and where spectators get to observe and experience live sports. Most cities have sporting venues of some kind. At the high-capacity end, there are several motor racing tracks that hold more than 150,000 spectators. Examples include the Shanghai International Circuit and the Indianapolis Motor Speedway. Multiple college football stadiums in the United States, such as Michigan Stadium and Ohio Stadium, have attendance capacities of more than 100,000, as does the Melbourne Cricket Ground in Australia. Many arenas have capacities in the 20,000 range, including the O2 in London, the Beijing National Indoor Stadium, the Air Canada Centre in Toronto, and the United Center in Chicago. At the low-capacity end are many community baseball and soccer fields where the capacity is in the hundreds and seating is often minimal or non-existent. This chapter discusses many decisions related to the building of sporting venues and their management subsequent to their being opened.

Many existing venues where sports are played were built in an era when the only events in that venue were sporting ones and where there was minimal investment in technology. In recent years, there have been dramatic advances on both the demand side and the supply side that are causing a major mind-shift in the way that executives think about, build, and manage new ventures:

- **Demand side:** Patrons have increasingly higher expectations of their in-venue experience. These higher expectations relate not only to being able to use multiple applications of new technologies (such as apps for replays and ordering food to their seat), but also to traditional areas such as the quality of concessions, bathroom cleanliness, and the ease of entry and exit to and from the venue. A motivating factor here is improvements in the at-home experience for consuming sports. Chapter 14 discussed this increase in the quality of options that influence the decision of a potential fan as to where and when to consume sports.

- **Supply side:** Recent new venues are showcasing a new frontier for venue architecture and in-venue experience. Levi's Stadium, which opened in 2014 in San Francisco, has raised the bar in multiple areas such as fan experience, use of technology, and the flexibility to have many different types of non-game-day events. After its first year, the venue won the Sports Business Award for "Sports Facility of the Year."[1] Many older stadiums are now accessing many new products to improve their in-stadium experience for attendees. These include hardware products such as larger and clearer scoreboards/large screens, as well as software products that relate to game replays, ticketing, concessions, and safety. Stadium partners and vendors, such as in ticketing and concessions, are themselves investing heavily in their own capabilities as they compete with new innovations or more fan-friendly deliverables against other vendors to retain and/or acquire contracts with their existing and new stadium clients.

We first cover the landscape of new venue building and venue management and the importance of decisions being guided by key business concepts. Both "good" and "bad" outcomes have been observed in many of the areas covered in this chapter. Financing new venues is then covered, with links to the multiple stakeholders who play roles in new venture building. We next examine new venue design and planning including a discussion of multiple choices that impact decision making after the venue is opened. Portfolio planning of the event calendar is then covered. The final section provides a case study of Avaya Stadium that opened in 2015. Avaya is the home of the San Jose Earthquakes of MLS. Chapter 14 is a related chapter and discusses how the ever-increasing advances in technology and management know-how are enhancing spectator engagement at many new and recently renovated venues.

"Venue" as discussed in this book is a generic term that includes facilities variously called stadiums, baseball parks, arenas, racetracks, race courses, and golf courses. There is a great spectrum in the size and investment in the venues in each of these categories. Sporting clubs that are contracted to play in a venue are often called "anchor tenants." The term "anchor" implies that the tenant commits to having a sizable number of playing days in the venue. For example, NBA and NHL clubs are committed to playing a minimum of 41 regular season games per year in their venue, while MLB clubs are committed to playing 81 games per year in their home venue.

17.1 KEY BUSINESS CONCEPTS

This section outlines some key business concepts and abilities that affect the likelihood of good or bad outcomes in venue building or venue management. Many high-profile "good" and "bad" outcomes highlight why these concepts are pivotal to guide decision making.

17.1.1 Stakeholder View with Required Coalition and Partnership-Building

Multiple stakeholders have or believe they should have substantive say in many decisions in this area. Exhibit 17.1 presents an overview of selected stakeholder roles to illustrate their sizable number and diversity.

As will be described later in this chapter, often one group will be performing several of these roles, such as a venue owner also being the venue operator. Building these different stakeholders into a workable well-functioning coalition requires much management and people-skills. Related here is the ability to manage via multiple formal and informal partnerships across the various stakeholders. Many business partnerships are abandoned quickly (often in acrimony) or fail to sizably deliver on their expected benefits. Venue building requires continued multiple efforts to keep the existing partners believing their roles are respected and that any emerging problems are caught before they reach the stage of severely damaging progress on the new venue.

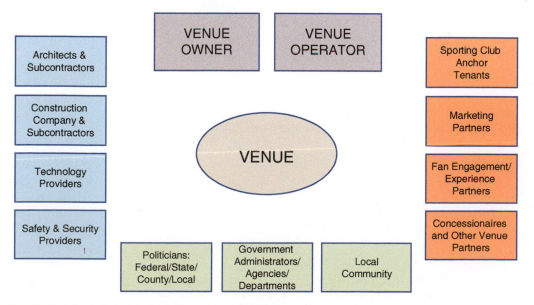

EXHIBIT 17.1 *Illustrative Stakeholder Roles in Venue Building and Management*

17.1.2 Building Community Support Amid Potential Opposition Groups

Very few proposals for venue construction, no matter of what kind and whether for sporting or non-sporting purposes, will have the unanimous support of all sections of the community. The San Diego Padres (MLB) opened Petco Park in downtown San Diego in 2004. However, initial explorations for moving from its aging Qualcomm Stadium that it shared with the San Diego Chargers (NFL) reportedly started as early as 1996. In November 1998, the Padres got the green light from voters in a ballot that gave them 60 percent approval. Over the next six years, the Padres juggled multiple constituencies and contractors and had delays on the project due to political infighting within the City of San Diego political world.[2]

In 2014, the Golden State Warriors (NBA) made a major change in venue planning when they decided to abandon an extensively developed new arena proposal on Piers 30–32 of the San Francisco waterfront and shift to a site close to but not on the waterfront. The Warriors ran into opposition for its first choice from multiple groups, including those opposed to new buildings on or near the waterfront, and those more directly affected by potential traffic problems associated with the proposed arena. One commentator noted: "The shift in location provides the Warriors with predictability and fewer regulatory hurdles … The Warriors have already spent about $20 million on design, engineering, consultants and other work for building on Piers 30–32. Some of that will transfer over."[3] Opposition to building new sporting venues has to be anticipated and strategies developed to manage the concerns of the different opposing groups. Multiple times voters have rejected specific proposals for public funding of sporting facilities, which had led to either delays in the building of a new venue or the total abandonment of the venue project itself.

17.1.3 Project Management Abilities

Most new venue plans have high levels of complexity and long timelines from the start day with initial plans to a venue opening. They also involve many different contractors and subcontractors. Understanding what are the critical stages that need to be done before other stages can be integrated into an evolving venue-build is essential to keeping the project on schedule as regards both time and budget. Venues that come in underbudget with regards to estimated cost and time are invariably managed by executives with superb project management skills.

17.1.4 Uncertainty, Risk, and Negotiation Astuteness

There are many areas of uncertainty and risk in the new venue area. Multiple new venue projects have had either sizable cost overruns or time overruns or both, often finishing way overbudget in cost or opening years later than planned. The causes of these overruns are both diverse and often unexpected. Astute negotiators write contracts that both motivate the various stakeholders to take actions that reduce these risks and help ensure that, if bad outcomes occur, they are not overly exposed to carrying the major part of those risks. For example, the lead contractor for the San Francisco 49ers Levi's Stadium, which opened on time, had financial penalties for not meeting the time schedule. One report was that the contractors faced a $6 million penalty for each 49er game missed in the 2014 NFL season.[4]

Astute negotiators also write contracts that enable them to capture much of the upside with regards to unexpected operating revenue increases and limit their downside as regards unexpected operating cost increases. Many sporting contracts have revenue-sharing or cost-sharing aspects. A manager who understands such aspects and negotiates to more frequently benefit under different scenarios can bring large value to the owner or operator of a venue.

17.1.5 Technology Opportunities Embraced and Exploited and Risks Managed

The continual evolution of new technologies affects all areas of venue building and management. Consider the area of stadium connectivity. Many operating partners in planning and managing events are developing technology to assist in areas such as ticketing, delivery of food to seats, guiding patrons to shorter lines in bathrooms, and in patron safety and security. The successful adoption of several of these technologies can bring both enhanced patron satisfaction and, in some cases, do so in cost-effective ways. However, there are numerous proposals in all these areas being continually made to the executives that are managing the stadiums. These managers need to have deep skills in evaluating these different proposals and be able to understand the likely benefits and costs of each proposal being seriously considered. Vendors here range from very large companies offering integrated solutions (such as Cisco with its "Connected Stadium" offering) to other, smaller companies offering individual components of technology.

17.1.6 Innovation Mindset Balanced With Rigorous Operational Management

Venue building and management benefit from managers who lead and develop a culture where (a) there is the opportunity and encouragement for innovation where appropriate, but also (b) a commitment to disciplined operational excellence in areas that need to be delivered with the highest levels of consistency to set standards. Examples of innovation can range broadly, from exploring and having the playing field use grass that is sturdier yet requires less water to identifying and successfully attracting new lucrative events to the venue. Ticketing and concessions are areas where, at the execution level, there is less scope for staff at the customer interface to continually seek ways to innovate on game day when the focus of game-day staff should be on fast and efficient service delivery.

17.2 MULTIPLE MOTIVATIONS FOR NEW VENUE BUILDING

There are multiple motivations for new venues being constructed. Several relate to the benefits offered by a new (or renovated) stadium. These include:

- Increasing revenues from both existing streams (tickets, suites, food and beverage) or new streams (personal seat licenses and expanded corporate entertainment rooms).
- Enhancing the spectator experience, such as better availability of Wi-Fi, increased number of bathrooms, and added security for patrons. Venues with retractable roofs ensure that events will not be cancelled due to weather. As will be discussed later in this chapter, an enhanced spectator

experience was a major motivation for multiple MLS clubs moving from sharing NFL stadiums with 60,000+ capacities to smaller venues with 20,000–30,000 capacities that better matched the typical MLS club spectator demand.

■ Expanding the ability to attract new and different events, such as concerts, truck events, corporate events, and conventions.

■ Expanding the focus of club management to include real estate opportunities associated with land adjacent to new venues. An example is the Atlanta Braves (MLB) moving approximately 20 miles out of downtown Atlanta to suburban Cobb County.[5]

■ Enhancing the community in an area that was run-down. The relocation of the San Diego Padres (MLB) to Petco Park was strongly supported by many officials and citizens on the basis of rejuvenating the Gaslight Area of downtown San Diego.

Several motivations related to the above have their genesis in problems with an existing venue. These include:

■ Existing venue being well below the standards of other venues in the same league in a relative sense, or below existing fan minimal expectations in an absolute sense.

■ Existing venue having safety concerns, such as tiles falling from a roof (as happened with the now demolished Kingdome in Seattle just before the start of a Mariners baseball game[6]) or the existing venue being below seismic/earthquake requirements.

■ Existing venue has real estate with high opportunity cost and the club or the city can gain by relocating venue to other locations and redeveloping the real estate occupied by the current venue.

In most cases, multiple of the above motivations will apply when a new venue is constructed or an existing venue is sizably renovated.

17.3 EXAMPLES OF NEW VENUE BUILDING IN SPORTS

Exhibit 17.2 provides examples of new stadiums and arenas constructed in the NFL, MLB, NBA, and NHL leagues in North America since 2000.

Some caveats about Exhibit 17.2 are appropriate. The numbers for the estimated stadium or arena construction cost are approximate. In some cases there are different numbers depending on the source used and the definitions used. The numbers given for the capacity are as of 2015 and in most cases they are relatively close to the capacity at the time the stadium or arena was opened. The names of each stadium or arena in Exhibit 17.2 are those as of 2015. Names of stadiums can change for multiple reasons:

■ Company with an existing naming rights contract chooses not to renew its contract when it expires and a new naming rights partner enters. The Oakland Athletics (MLB) and the Oakland Raiders (NFL) jointly play in what since 2011 has been called the O.co Coliseum after Overstock/O.co purchased the naming rights from the Oakland Alameda County Coliseum Authority in that year. It had been called McAfee Coliseum up to 2008, but McAfee chose not to renew the agreement. There was no naming rights partner from 2008 to 2011.

Panel A: National Football League (NFL)

Year stadium opened	Club	Stadium name	Estimated construction cost ($M)	Capacity (in 2015)
2000	Cincinnati Bengals	Paul Brown Stadium	455	65,600
2001	Denver Broncos	Sports Authority Field	365	72,000
2002	Houston Texans	NRG Stadium	352	69,500
2002	New England Patriots	Gillette Stadium	325	68,000
2002	Seattle Seahawks	Century Link Field	430	72,000
2003	Chicago Bears	Soldier Field	600	61,500
2006	Arizona Cardinals	University of Phoenix Stadium	455	63,000
2008	Indianapolis Colts	Lucas Oil Stadium	720	63,000
2009	Dallas Cowboys	AT&T Stadium	1,200	80,000
2010	NY Giants/NY Jets	MetLife Stadium	1,600	82,500
2014	San Francisco 49ers	Levi's Stadium	1,300	68,500
Average capacity				**68,600**

Panel B: Major League Baseball (MLB)

Year ballpark opened	Club	Ballpark name	Estimated construction cost ($M)	Capacity (in 2015)
2000	Detroit Tigers	Comerica Park	300	40,000
2000	San Francisco Giants	AT&T Park	357	40,800
2001	Milwaukee Brewers	Miller Park	400	42,500
2003	Cincinnati Reds	Great American Ballpark	290	45,000
2004	San Diego Padres	Petco Park	450	42,000
2006	St. Louis Cardinals	Busch Stadium	365	46,861
2008	Washington Nationals	Nationals Park	611	41,222
2009	NY Mets	Citi Field	860	42,500
2009	NY Yankees	Yankee Stadium	1,500	52,235
2012	Miami Marlins	Marlins Park	634	37,000
Average capacity				**43,012**

EXHIBIT 17.2 (cont.)

Panel C: National Basketball Association (NBA)

Year arena/center opened	Club	Arena/center name	Estimated construction cost ($M)	Capacity (in 2015)
2001	Dallas Mavericks	American Airlines Center	420	19,200
2002	San Antonio Spurs	AT&T Center	186	18,500
2003	Houston Rockets	Toyota Center	235	18,500
2004	Memphis Grizzlies	FedEx Forum	250	18,190
2005	Charlotte Bobcats	Time Warner Cable Arena	265	19,023
2010	Orlando Magic	Amway Center	480	18,600
2012	Brooklyn Nets	Barclays Center	1,000	18,000
Average capacity				**18,573**

Panel D: National Hockey League (NHL)

Year arena/center opened	Club	Arena/center name	Estimated construction cost ($M)	Capacity (in 2015)
2000	Columbus Blue Jackets	Nationwide Arena	175	18,137
2000	Minnesota Wild	Xcel Energy Center	170	18,064
2001	Dallas Stars	American Airlines Center	420	18,000
2003	Arizona Coyotes	Gila River Arena	220	17,500
2007	New Jersey Devils	Prudential Center	375	17,625
2010	Pittsburgh Penguins	Consol Energy Center	321	18,087
Average capacity				**17,902**

EXHIBIT 17.2 Examples of New Venue Construction Since 2000 in NFL, MLB, NBA, and NHL Leagues

■ Company owning the naming rights has financial problems and exits the agreement early. Gillette Stadium of the New England Patriots was initially CMGI Field, but CMGI exited associated with the financial problems many dot.com companies faced in the early 2000s.[7]

■ Company with naming rights is acquired by another company who then assumes the naming rights. The San Francisco Giants moved in 2000 to a new ballpark in downtown San Francisco called Pacific Bell Park. Since then it has had two more names under the same naming rights agreement. This arose from successive mergers in the telecommunications industry. It was called Pacific Bell Park from 2000 to 2003, SBC Park from 2003 to 2006, and AT&T Park since 2006. AT&T acquired SBC Communications in 2006, which had previously acquired Pacific Bell in 2003.

■ The venue owner/club may opt out of the agreement early and sell to another company. Scotiabank Place changed to Canadian Tire Centre under this scenario for the Ottawa Senators (NHL) in 2013.[8]

As a general rule, NFL stadiums have higher construction costs than MLB parks and MLB parks have higher construction costs than NBA or NHL arenas. A major factor here is the relative size of the buildings. The average capacities reported in Exhibit 17.2 are 68,600 for the 11 NFL stadiums, 43,012 for the ten MLB ballparks, 18,573 for the seven NBA arenas, and 17,902 for the six NHL arenas. The 14 soccer-specific stadiums in the MLS described later in this chapter (see Exhibit 17.9) have an average capacity of 20,806.

One illustration of how advances in building technology are blurring traditional distinctions occurs with respect to the category of stadiums/ballparks versus the category of arenas. For many years, there was an accepted distinction between a stadium (which was open to the elements) and an arena (which was closed to the elements with a roof). Event risk was said to exist at large stadiums (such as a baseball game being "rained-out") but was avoided in the smaller arenas. However, with multiple facilities now having retractable roofs, the distinction between stadiums and arenas is more blurred. Multiple new stadium venues have now been built with a retractable roof, such as the NRG Stadium in Houston with its 70,000+ capacity (home of the Houston Texans of the NFL and the Houston Livestock Show and Rodeo) and Etihad Stadium in Melbourne with its 50,000+ capacity (home of multiple Australian rules football clubs). Older existing venues have also now been retrofitted to have retractable roofs to avoid problems arising from key events being rained out, such as Wimbledon (technically the All England Lawn Tennis and Croquet Club) in 2009.

17.4 FINANCING NEW VENUES

Exhibit 17.2 shows the escalation over time of the construction costs of sporting venues across four North American leagues. We are now seeing billion-dollar-plus investments being made in venues where football, baseball, basketball, and hockey are played. North American soccer-specific stadiums are now starting at approximately at $100 million (see Exhibit 17.9).

Globally, there is also escalation in new venue costs. For example, the New Perth Stadium in Australia with a capacity of 60,000 is planned to be ready for use in 2018. The projected costs are more than $1,000 million (more than AU$1,200 million). This will be the home of the two Perth-based Australian rules football clubs (the Freemantle Dockers and the West Coast Eagles), as well as having international cricket matches. Typically much of these amounts are required upfront to pay architects, construction companies and their many contractors, technology providers, safety and security providers, and many others.

Exhibit 17.3 shows eight categories of potential financing sources linked to key stakeholders associated with building a new venue.

- Government financing

- Owner/equity financing

- Sporting league financing

- Debt financing

- Venue construction partner financing

- Venue marketing partner financing

- Venue operating partner financing

- Customer financing

EXHIBIT 17.3 Stakeholder Options for New Venue Financing

Two central aspects here are the magnitude of the construction cost and the timing of the associated cash flows (with large costs incurred early for a venue in which the revenue streams occur later in future years). Attempts to reduce the levels of financing required can work in three main areas:

- **Reducing the total venue construction cost:** Exhibit 17.2 shows dramatic differences in the construction cost of new venues in the same league built at approximately the same time. Causes include:
  - the size and complexity of the venue planned;
  - the location of the project (large city projects, such as in New York, are more costly);
  - how much work the venue owner or operator does internally;
  - whether changes in design or outfitting of the venue were made after the project commenced ("change orders" can add greatly to actual construction costs);
  - the skill with which the venue owner or operator conducted the bidding process (having multiple bids typically results in lower amounts being bid on a project).
  There are many decisions in this area. Project bidding and project management skills are a major determinant of the actual total construction cost of a new venue.
- **Back-ending of cash payments for construction costs:** Venue owners or operators can reduce their cash flow requirements in the early stages of venue construction by having various stakeholders (such as architects and contractors) accept cash payments at a later stage than would normally be their commercial practice. This effectively means a third party is being part of the financing plan.
- **Front-ending of cash payments from future revenue streams of the new venue:** Some stakeholders of a new venue may be willing to front-end cash to increase the likelihood of winning a bid as a venue marketing partner or a venue operating partner. Personal seat licenses are a means of having season ticket holders (customers) front-end cash to the benefit of financing the new venture.

There has been much innovation over time in the financing sources used by the owners and operators of new venues. We now consider the eight sources of new venue financing outlined in Exhibit 17.3.

17.4.1 Government Financing

The traditional source of funding for new sporting venues has been public money, where governments pay a significant amount of the total upfront investment. For many years, this was simply a line item allocation in a government budget. More recently, funds raised have been linked to specific taxes, such as hotel taxes, car rental taxes, parking taxes, taxes on alcohol and tobacco, etc. This source of funding is still common for Olympic venues and large stadiums for world cups such as for the FIFA World Cup.

To illustrate government financing, consider AT&T Stadium of the Dallas Cowboys (NFL). Convention Sports & Leisure estimated its public financing, at more than $444 million, was 37 percent of the total construction cost of $1,194 million.[9] The public funding sources for this sizable amount included:

- 0.5 percent city sales tax increase;
- 2 percent city hotel tax increase;
- 5 percent city car rental tax increase;
- 10 percent admissions tax;
- $3 parking tax;
- $25 million county contribution.

For the 20 new NFL stadiums that opened between 1997 and 2011, the average proportion from government financing was 58.8 percent. For the 12 stadiums opening from 2002 to 2011, the average was 48.8 percent compared to 73.7 percent for the eight new stadiums opening in the earlier 1997 to 2001 period. The range was from 100 percent government financing for the Raymond James Stadium that opened in 1997 for the Tampa Bay Buccaneers to 0 percent for MetLife Stadium of the New York Giants/New York Jets that opened in 2009. The general pattern over time has been a decline in the proportion of total construction cost coming from government financing.

The arguments presented for allocating government money or raising new taxes for new sporting venues include combinations of:

- sporting venues are public goods that benefit many citizens in the same way that public parks and other community venues do;
- sporting venues attract extra spending and branding for a local economy via extra spending by visitors and broadcasting of games; and
- the construction phase provides employment for many workers on the site.

For instance, the Formula 1 Grand Prix in Barcelona is argued to attract more than 100,000 visitors from outside the city, staying an average of four days in the local area and spending about €150 per day in activities other than the race (food, lodging, etc.).

In many areas, there is increasing opposition to government funding of elite sporting facilities. Arguments presented against public funding include:

- sporting venues are lower priority to investments in areas such as hospitals and education;
- governments have a track record of writing contracts that excessively benefit very wealthy sporting club-owners and highly paid athletes who can appear less than appreciative;

■ benefits alleged to occur with a new venue are greatly overstated. For example, opponents to the government support of the Barcelona Grand Prix argue that many visitors to a football match or an Olympics would nevertheless have gone to Barcelona.

17.4.2 Owner/Equity Financing

As described in Section 17.4.1, private ownership of stadiums has been increasing, although this is still in the minority relative to government funding. Where wealthy individuals or syndicates buy sporting clubs and then relocate the club to a new venue, the ownership group can be one important source of financing directly (or indirectly via covering large losses at the old stadium where the club is playing prior to the relocation). Owners typically will have advice on the most tax efficient ways to structure their investments in sporting venues.

The existing San Francisco Giants (MLB) syndicate purchased the club in 1992 and then moved to a new ballpark in 2000. Chapter 1 provides background on how this investment syndicate from 1992 to 1999 covered large ongoing losses of the club when playing in the aging Candlestick Park. If the Giants had borrowed to cover those losses, their ability to raise even extra debt associated with the new ballpark would have been much more constrained.

Wealthy individuals have long supported selected sporting clubs in many countries and have been one source of investments in either new venues or renovating existing venues. Examples include soccer and basketball venues in Europe (such as Olympiacos, the famous Greek basketball team).

17.4.3 Sporting League Financing

In new venue financing, some leagues play important roles in either being a direct source of financing or as providing guarantees using league contractual revenue streams. For example, the National Football League's G-3 program provided $150 million to each of the two anchor tenants – the New York Giants and the New York Jets – of MetLife Stadium, which opened in 2009 with a construction cost of $1,600 million. Under this program, money each of these two clubs would otherwise have shared with all the NFL clubs from the visiting teams share (VTS) of club seat ticket revenue could be used to repay both the principal and interest on the $150 million. This loan had a 7 percent interest rate with a 15-year loan period.[10] Under the G-4 program, the NFL provides up to $200 million to individual clubs for venue financing. The G-3 and G-4 new venue financial support programs are part of the NFL's philosophy that all clubs benefit when modern stadiums are built and clubs stay in large markets that often have higher construction costs for new venues. The G-3 and G-4 programs have all NFL clubs sharing equally in the repayment of principal and interest on the amounts borrowed by the individual club. Some clubs that may have had to sell minority equity in their ownership to fund a new venue have been able to keep their full ownership by accessing the NFL's G-3 or G-4 funding.[11]

17.4.4 Debt Financing

There is an active debt market available for some sporting clubs and venue owners to access. Examples of lenders include Bank of America, Goldman Sachs, and JP Morgan Chase. The San Francisco Giants ballpark (see Section 17.4.2 and Chapter 1) that opened in 2000 had an estimated construction cost of $360 million. The first bank loan was for $140 million in September 1996. It was structured as a construction project-financing loan with a provision allowing it to be financed before the end of the fifth year. The loan syndicate was led by Chase. In November 1997, Chase offered a new $170 million loan package with a 20-year, 8 percent fixed rate.

Bloomberg lists examples of Bank of America tombstones (formal announcements of financing deals) of multiple diverse types of debt financing. Examples include:[12]

- PILOT and Rental Revenue Bonds of $955 million for the New York Yankees and New Yankee Stadium in August 2006.
- Stadium Revenue Bonds of $475 million for the Dallas Cowboys in May 2007.
- Acquisition Financing Senior Credit Facilities of $277.5 million for SMG (motor sports tracks) in July 2007.

Debt financing in some leagues is constrained by limits on the level of debt that clubs can borrow. For example, the MLB has restrictions that the debt of a club cannot exceed 10× a multiple of EBITDA. Some commentators question whether this rule is a hard cap as opposed to a recommended cap.[13]

17.4.5 Venue Construction Partner Financing

Construction companies can benefit greatly by being associated with a major new venue, especially if that venue attracts both much positive media and is built on time/on budget. Ways that construction partners can assist in venue financing include:

- Agreeing to a lower price than they would normally commercially quote. This reduces the total amount of financing required.
- Agreeing to being paid at a much later stage than they would commercially quote. This effectively means that the construction company is carrying part of financing the new venue. It is sometimes called "cost payment back-ending of a project."

17.4.6 Venue Marketing Partner Financing

Marketing partners of a sporting club or venue are an important ongoing revenue source when the venue is in operation. Exhibit 17.4 shows the naming rights for 20 MLB stadiums.

The reported dollar amounts in Exhibit 17.4 on an annual basis range from $20 million per year for Citi Field/New York Mets to as low as $1 million for Tropicana Field/Tampa Bay Rays. In some cases, companies bidding for naming rights are willing to make a large initial upfront payment at the venue build stage and then pay the remaining amounts of the total naming rights deal on a yearly basis once the venue opens. The $20 million figure for Citi Field is very much an outlier and highlights that care is always needed when basing comparisons on the basis of only public sources. Citibank was also a financing partner for the New York Mets' new ballpark and it is not made public whether the very high naming rights deal for Citi Field is part of a larger "financing/marketing partnership" between the Mets and Citibank. Box 17.1 provides an example of a $700 million naming rights deal that was a central part of a proposal (eventually abandoned) to build a new NFL stadium in downtown Los Angeles.

Team	Venue	Location	Buyer	Expiration date	Term	Avg. annual
New York Mets	Citi Field	Flushing, NY	Citigroup	2026	20	$20,000,000
Houston Astros	Minute Maid Park	Houston, TX	Minute Maid Co.	2030	28	$6,071,429
Minnesota Twins	Target Field	Minneapolis, MN	Target Stores/Dayton Hudson	2032	25	$5,000,000
Cleveland Indians	Progressive Field	Cleveland, OH	Progressive Insurance	2023	16	$3,600,000
Chicago White Sox	US Cellular Field	Chicago, IL	US Cellular	2023	20	$3,000,000
San Diego Padres	Petco Park	San Diego, CA	Petco	2025	22	$2,727,273
Cincinnati Reds	Great American Ballpark	Cincinnati, OH	Great American Insurance	2031	30	$2,500,000
Los Angeles Angels	Edison International Field	Anaheim, CA	Edison International	2017	20	$2,500,000
Philadelphia Phillies	Citizens Bank Park	Philadelphia, PA	Citizens Bank	2028	25	$2,300,000
Detroit Tigers	Comerica Park	Detroit, MI	Comerica Bank	2029	30	$2,200,000
San Francisco Giants	Pacific Bell Park	San Francisco, CA	Pacific Bell/AT&T	2024	24	$2,083,333
Milwaukee Brewers	Miller Park	Milwaukee, WI	Miller Brewing Co.	2021	20	$2,050,000
Seattle Mariners	Safeco Field	Seattle, WA	Safeco	2019	20	$2,000,000
Pittsburgh Pirates	PNC Park	Pittsburgh, PA	PNC Bank	2020	20	$1,500,000
Oakland Athletics	O.co Coliseum	Oakland, CA	Overstock.com	2017	6	$1,333,333
Arizona Diamondbacks	Bank One Ballpark	Phoenix, AZ	Bank One Corp.	2038	30	$1,103,333
Tampa Bay Rays	Tropicana Field	St. Petersburg, FL	Tropicana	2028	30	$1,000,000
Texas Rangers	Global Life Park	Arlington, TX	Globe Life	2024	10	ND
St. Louis Cardinals	Busch Stadium	St. Louis, MO	Anheuser-Busch	2025	ND	ND
Colorado Rockies	Coors Field	Denver, CO	Coors Brewing Co.	ND	ND	ND

EXHIBIT 17.4 Ballpark/Stadium Naming Rights Agreements in Major League Baseball (MLB) in 2015

Source: RSV database

BOX 17.1 FARMERS FIELD GETS SCRATCHED IN THE NFL STADIUM STAKES FOR LOS ANGELES

The 1995 NFL season started in a way many in Los Angeles had thought unlikely several years earlier. There would be no LA-based home NFL clubs in 1995 and for the immediate future! The two NFL clubs that played in the Los Angeles basin in 1994 had relocated – the Los Angeles Raiders to Oakland and the Los Angeles Rams to St. Louis. The Los Angeles Raiders had played in the LA Coliseum that had a full football capacity of more than 90,000. However, the Raiders averaged approximately 55,000 per game in the ten years up to and including 1994. The Los Angeles Rams had shared Anaheim Stadium with the Anaheim Angels of MLB. The Rams averaged approximately 53,000 per game in the ten years up to and including 1994 in a stadium with a football capacity of 69,000. The cities of both Oakland and St. Louis put together stadium deals that were sufficient to attract each club to leave what is the second largest DMA market in the US. Since 1995, the NFL and many groups have looked at the best way to have one (possibly two) NFL clubs be based again in this highly important market.

Bringing a NFL club back to Los Angeles required three key pieces of the puzzle to be put together:

1 Having a club to be in the new market. The two options were a new expansion club or a relocated club. Multiple clubs have been mentioned as relocation candidates since 1995 – including Minnesota Vikings, Jacksonville Jaguars, San Diego Chargers, and the two clubs that exited the market after 1994 – the Oakland Raiders and the St. Louis Rams.
2 Building a new stadium or sizably renovating an existing one. Given that the existing stadium options in LA (such as the LA Coliseum or the Rose Bowl) required quantum upgrades, the NFL's strong preference was for a new stadium to be built. This raised the question of where to locate the new stadium. Sites at Carson, City of Industry, Hollywood Park, Dodger Stadium, and downtown LA have been discussed.
3 An investment group capable of raising or having several billion dollars. If the NFL voted to have a new club, an investment group willing to invest both in the new club and in a new stadium had to be found. If an existing club relocated to LA, the NFL would ask a very sizable relocation fee, which could well be beyond the financial capacity of several clubs that could potentially relocate. With many wealthy individuals based in LA, a long list of names from the entertainment, sporting, and other business areas were frequently mentioned every time discussions about a new NFL club in LA arose.

In the 1997/9 period, the NFL pushed hard to have a viable Los Angeles-based candidate when making the decision on the expansion 32nd NFL club. However, no viable LA group with the stadium/NFL club/investor combination in place existed in 1999, when the NFL awarded the 32nd club to the Houston Texans who started playing in 2002. Subsequent to 1999, multiple entrants would enter the LA market stakes. Two major ones in 2008/10 focused on the new stadium aspect without locking down an NFL club as its anchor tenant. Two new entrants in the 2014/15 periods came with NFL clubs closely linked to their new stadium proposals.

From 2008 to 2011, two well-developed plans to build a NFL stadium emerged. In 2008, Majestic Royalty (owned by Ed Roski) announced plans to build the "Los Angeles Football Stadium" at the City of Industry, which is 20 miles from downtown Los Angeles. It would be a open aired stadium with a capacity of 75,000. The estimated cost was $800 million. Majestic Royalty received support from the City of Industry and had its environmental plans approved. In 2010, AEG announced a more stunning proposal. Their proposed stadium was to be in downtown Los Angeles with a $1,300 million cost, a retractable roof, and a capacity of 72,000 to be built next to the LA Convention Center and Staples Center. One of the most stunning aspects of the AEG proposal was a 30-year, $700 million naming rights agreement between AEG and Farmers Insurance for the venue to be called Farmers Field. It was reported that the $700 million would increase to $1,000 million if two NFL clubs became anchor tenants in Farmers Field. The city of Los Angeles strongly supported the AEG proposal, seeing it as part of a further development around the Convention Center. A key lead proponent within AEG of the Farmers Field project was its CEO Tim Leiweke, widely viewed as one of the most successful and creative sports executives. In March 2013, it was announced that Leiweke was leaving AEG with multiple speculations as to the reasons for his sudden AEG exit.[14] After Leiweke's exit, AEG's very public commitment to the Farmers Field project greatly slowed. In 2015, AEG Vice-Chairman Ted Fikre was quoted in an AEG press release stating: "After years of work on the stadium project, including execution of a term sheet with the NFL and over a year of negotiations in earnest with the league, it has become evident that a transaction that would be satisfactory to AEG, the City and the NFL is not achievable in any foreseeable time frame."[15] Various reports estimated that AEG had already invested $50 million on the abandoned Farmers Field project.[16]

Subsequent to AEG's exit, two new entrants entered the NFL new stadium stakes race in LA. In 2015, Stan Kroenke (owner of the St. Louis Rams) announced a partnership with Stockbridge Capital (owner of sizable land in Hollywood Park) to build a new $1,800 million NFL stadium.[17] Also in 2015, the Oakland Raiders and the San Diego Chargers jointly announced a new LA- based stadium $1,700 million proposal.[18] Both these new proposals appeared to make the Majestic / Royalty /City of Industry stadium proposal more of a long-shot in the race. One winning group has already emerged in the LA Stadium stakes –the architects for at least four new stadium proposals. A second winner likely is Farmers Insurance which received high profile publicity without having to pay any of the $700 million in its proposed naming rights agreement with AEG.

17.4.7 Venue Operating Partner Financing

Two major operating partners of a venue are (a) concessionaires for food and beverage (F&B), and (b) ticketing companies such as Ticketmaster and Tickets.com. There is much competition within each of the major categories of venue operating partners and here there is the opportunity for a venue owner or operator to negotiate upfront cash payments to be the designated category partner. Consider concession companies: Exhibit 17.5 illustrates how four companies dominate the sporting landscape in major North American team sports: Levy Restaurants, Aramark, Sportservice, and Centerplate.

These four companies are very competitive with each other and with a new entrant such as Legends. To gain a contract at a new venue for, say, an MLB club, one of these companies could offer to front-end some cash and (possibly) reduce the percentage of venue revenue they share with the club once the venue opens (say, from 10 percent to 9 percent sharing of venue concession revenues with the club). The MLB club here is gaining added cash flow in its ballpark build stage while receiving lower cash flow from its concessionaire once the ballpark is in operation.

Concessionaire	NFL	MLB	NBA	NHL	MLS	Total
Levy Restaurants	2	5	20	10	3	40
Aramark	9	12	3	6	2	32
Sportservice	6	9	2	5	2	24
Centerplate	9	2	1	3	2	17
Legends	1	1	—	—	3	5
Ovation	2	1	—	—	2	5
MSG	—	—	1	1	—	2
Sodexo	—	—	—	—	2	2
Other	1	—	1	2	—	4
Owner/Club	1	—	2	3	2	8
N/A	1	—	—	—	2	3
Grand Total	**32**	**30**	**30**	**30**	**20**	**142**

EXHIBIT 17.5 Concessionaire Companies in North American Sporting Leagues
Source: RSV database

17.4.8 Customer Financing

Customer financing of venue building is becoming an increasingly major part of new venue building in sports. Several categories are observed with some frequency:

Personal Seat Licenses (PSLs)

This is a right to buy individual season tickets and in many cases that right can be resold to third parties. Consider Levi's Stadium of the San Francisco 49ers of the NFL as an example. The customer, who will be a season ticket holder at Levi's, has two purchase points:

1   the purchase of the seat license; and then
2   the purchase of a season set of tickets (two pre-season and eight regular season games) on a season-by-season basis.

The stadium, which opened for the 2014 NFL season, is owned by the Santa Clara Stadium Authority. Legends Sales & Marketing was contracted to sell the PSLs.[19] Ground-breaking for the new venue was in April 2012. During 2012, Legends started selling PSLs at prices ranging from $80,000 in the high-end premium section to a low of $2,000 in the upper deck. They stated that a PSL "is a one-time cost that gives buyers control of their seats for 49ers home games. They are good for the life of the building and have additional benefits, including priority to purchase tickets for most other events that will be held at the stadium."[20] The Santa Clara Stadium Authority generated more than $530 million with its PSL program, the largest single source of funding for Levi's Stadium, which was estimated to cost approximately $1,300 million.

PSL-based financing is now a central part of financing for many new venues. For example, MetLife Stadium (jointly shared, as previously noted, by two NFL clubs – the New York Giants and the New York Jets) opened in 2009. PSLs sold by the two clubs raised $800 million and covered 50 percent of the $1,600 million construction cost. Customers buying PSLs typically have the right to resell those rights. Some clubs manage the selling and buying of the PSLs of their venue. There are also companies that offer to match sellers and buyers for the PSLs of multiple clubs – such as PSL Source.[21]

Suite Revenues

Suites in many venues are sold on a multi-year contract basis, often with some discount for a front-end payment that covers the multi-years of the contract. Consider the following example for a ten-year contract for suites at a new venue being built. Potential customers could choose between two options: (a) immediate payment of $4 million or (b) an annual payment plan that costs $500,000 per year for each of 10 years. Customers who choose option (a) are effectively helping with the financing of the new venue, as they are front-ending cash that does not need to be raised from other sources.

17.5 NEW VENUE DESIGN AND PLANNING DECISIONS

This section illustrates some key decisions that are made in the design and construction stages that later affect event planning and management at the venue. Examples from Major League Baseball will be mostly used to illustrate concepts introduced and distinctions being made in this section. Box 17.2 outlines the different stages in the building of the new downtown arena for the Sacramento Kings as well as discussing the challenges of a club playing in an increasingly substandard arena.

BOX 17.2 SACRAMENTO KINGS USE SOCIAL MEDIA AS PART OF A FAN EXCITEMENT RAMP FOR NEW ARENA IN DOWNTOWN SACRAMENTO

The Sacramento Kings of the NBA are the sole major league sporting franchise playing in the capital of California. Nielsen in 2015 ranked Sacramento as the #20 DMA size market in the US.[22] From 1998 to 2013, the Maloof family owned the Kings and its venue – variously called ARCO Arena, then Power Balance Pavilion, and more recently Sleep Train Arena. The arena opened in 1988 and was long viewed as the most basic and, over time, the least "NBA attractive" venue. A 2013 *ESPN: The Magazine* survey of fans of all 122 clubs in the NBA, MLB, NFL, and NHL ranked the Kings last at #122 in Overall Fan Satisfaction – subcategories included Fan Relations (#122), Ownership (#121), and Stadium Experience (#122).

In May 2013, the NBA voted a change of ownership in the Kings to an investor group led by Vivek Ranadivé, founder and a former CEO of TIBCO. The May 2013 transaction that valued the Kings at $535 million was a then-record transaction value for the NBA. A prior deal to sell the Kings to an investor group led by Chris Hansen and including Steve Ballmer (who was later to buy the Los Angeles Clippers in 2014 for $2,000 million) was not approved by the NBA. The NBA's policy is to ensure that every effort is made to keep each club in their existing markets.

Many efforts had been made over the years to build an alternative arena to Sleep Train Arena. For example, in November 2006, the county of Sacramento voted on a set of measures to fund a new arena in downtown Sacramento, to be financed by an increase in the county sales tax by a quarter-cent for 15 years. The voters rejected each measure by more than a 70/30 percent margin.[23]

The Ranadivé investor group committed from the earliest stage in its negotiations to working with the city of Sacramento and its mayor Kevin Johnson to build a new downtown arena that would make the club a viable economic club while remaining in Sacramento. Prior to being elected as mayor, Johnson had an outstanding basketball playing career at the University of California at Berkeley and then in the NBA with the Cleveland Cavaliers and the Phoenix Suns. In May 2014 it was announced after a city council vote (seven yes to two no) that a new arena at Downtown Plaza at a cost of $477 million would be constructed. Summary details were:[24]

- City of Sacramento ownership of the arena with the Kings on a 35-year lease.
- City to contribute $254 million with the Kings investor group contributing the rest and being responsible for cost overruns. The city would raise much of the money via a parking bond.
- The city would transfer $32 million of land that enables the Kings to construct "the arena and develop surrounding land with a hotel, office tower, and shopping."

In June 2014, the Kings released the following timeline for the project which included demolition of the Downtown Plaza Mall before work could start on the new arena:[25]

- **Summer 2014** – truck deliveries and barrier/fence set up. Street re-striping. On-site abatement work and utilities shut off. Demolition and removal of existing buildings, including use of excavators, hoe rams, and forklifts.
- **Summer–fall 2014** – mass excavation of site.
- ***Fall 2014–winter 2014/15** – drilled displacement piles and foundation construction.
- ***Winter–summer 2015** – concrete slab pours. Steel structure erection, welding and installation (includes installing vertical steel, but not roof steel).
- ***Summer–fall 2015** – building facade of precast concrete, metal, and glass built. Roof constructed.
- **Fall 2015–fall 2016** – interior assembly.
- **Fall 2016** – complete and open to the public.

A key focus of the Sacramento Kings' new ownership was active interaction with fans and the broader community. New syndicate owner Ranadivé had a deep background in technology and information-sharing networks, and led from the front with this focus. He stated: "When I look at the business of basketball it's more than basketball. It's really a social network. You can use technology to capture that network, expand it, engage it, and then, obviously to monetize it."[26] The Sacramento Kings app gives points to users that can accumulate and then be redeemed for tickets and Kings merchandise. The app is available to a fan watching a game beyond the arena (such as in Mumbai) on a device as well as those at Sleep Train Arena. The Kings benefit from many of its investors being deeply immersed in the business technology sector. For example, in addition to Ranadivé is Paul Jacobs, executive chairman of Qualcomm. The Kings are already using the Gimbal mobile engagement platform from Qualcomm at Sleep Train, "to engage fans through a combination of physical location, activity, time, and personal interest as a major enhancement of its loyalty program."[27]

One high-profile area of fan engagement is giving regular updates on the construction progress for the new arena. Exhibit 17.6 shows examples of using Twitter (Panel A) and Instagram (Panel B) to continue building fan excitement leading up to when in 2016 the Kings move into their new technology showcase arena in downtown Sacramento.

Panel A: Twitter fan engagement

Panel B: Instagram fan engagement

EXHIBIT 17.6 Sacramento Kings Use of Social Media to Engage with Fans on Developments in Building of New Downtown Arena

17.5.1 Decision #1: Who Will Own the Venue?

Exhibit 17.7 outlines the two major options for sporting venue ownership. Panel A has examples from the 24 (80 percent) MLB venues that are publicly owned – typically by a city, county, or state. Panel B has examples from the six (20 percent) MLB venues that are privately owned.

Many sporting venues were built in an era when few in the private sector relished spending many millions on a venue when the government sector appeared willing to do so. Public ownership of sporting facilities was traditionally viewed as delivering a community benefit, similar to a city-owned opera house or museum. Often such facilities made operating losses as well as required capital investments out of public funds. It is only in recent decades that sporting facilities have been viewed as investment assets capable of generating profits even after the capital investments in them have been taken into account.

The pros of private ownership of a venue include: (a) more control of the revenue-generating options of the stadium, including ticket-pricing, naming rights, or other uses of the stadium (concerts, political rallies, corporate events, conferences, and more), (b) better access to the stadium, parking and other amenities, and (c) less accountability to politicians who often try to insert themselves into decision making for sporting venues in their elected areas. Private owners of sporting venues almost always are the owners of one or more of the anchor tenants playing in that venue. Two examples of privately owned stadiums and their anchor tenants are:

Panel A: Public ownership (23 clubs)

Examples of public ownership

Club	Venue	Ownership
Kansas City Royals	Kauffman Stadium	Owned by Jackson county; operator is Jackson County Sports Authority
Colorado Rockies	Coors Field	Owned by state of Colorado; operator is club
Oakland Athletics	O.co Coliseum	Owned by city of Oakland and Alameda county; operator is AEG Facilities

Panel B: Private ownership (seven clubs)

Examples of private ownership

Club	Venue	Ownership
Boston Red Sox	Fenway Park	Owned by Fenway Sports Group; operator is owner
Los Angeles Dodgers	Dodgers Stadium	Owned by Guggenheim Baseball Management; operator is owner
Toronto Blue Jays	Rogers Centre	Owned by Rogers Communications; operator is owner

EXHIBIT 17.7 Alternative Ownership Models for Sporting/Entertainment Venues – Examples from 30 Major League Baseball (MLB) Clubs

■ Gillette Stadium, which is owned by the same investor group (Kraft Sports Group) as is its two anchor tenants, the New England Patriots (NFL) and the New England Revolution (MLS).

■ Pepsi Center, which is owned by the same investor group (Kroenke Sports Enterprises) as is its three anchor tenants: Colorado Avalanche (NHL), Denver Nuggets (NBA), and Colorado Mammoth (NLL).

17.5.2 Decision #2: Who Will Operate the Venue?

The venue operator is in charge of booking and managing events and for keeping the venue as a well-functioning facility. Exhibit 17.7 illustrates several different models of owner/operator relationships. The larger and more diverse the number of different parties in owner, operator, and anchor tenant relationships, the more complex the financial and operating arrangements that must be arranged. In most cases there will be structured legal agreements. It is central to have explicit guidelines about the revenue-sharing, cost-sharing, and decision making rights to guide decisions by executives in the various units of these bi-party or tri-party contexts.

Panel A in Exhibit 17.7 provides three examples of public ownership of a venue with differing operator arrangements:

1 **Public-sector owner of venue with public-sector operator.** For example, in Exhibit 17.7 the Kansas City Royals (MLB) play at Kauffman Stadium, which is owned by Jackson county and operated by the Jackson City Sports Authority. The Atlanta Falcons (NFL) play in the Georgia Dome, which is owned by the state of Georgia. The operator is the Georgia World Congress Center Authority (GWCCW). GWCCW, which books events at the Georgia Dome for days that the Atlanta Falcons are not playing, is also the operator of the Georgia World Congress Center and the Centennial Olympic Park.[28] Management at the Atlanta Falcons within this context is not tasked with managing the full calendar of events.

2 **Public-sector owner of venue with private-sector anchor tenant as operator.** The Colorado Rockies is the operator for Coors Field, which is owned by the state of Colorado. The San Jose Sharks (NHL) play at the SAP Center which is owned by the city of San Jose. The Sharks' parent company (Sharks Sports and Entertainment, SSE) is the operator for this arena. As noted later in this chapter, SSE books and manages more than 80 other non-Sharks NHL events at the SAP Center each year. In 2015, the city of San Jose extended the operating lease agreement with SSE as the operator. The contracts commit the Sharks to play in the SAP Center from 2016 to 2025 (called a fixed-term lease) and thereafter the operating lease is on a yearly renewal basis.[29] Management at the San Jose Sharks here has the responsibility to manage the full set of events at the venue with the opportunity to profit from booking all events (see Section 17.6 of this chapter).

3 **Public-sector owner of venue with private-sector corporate operator.** For example, the Oakland Alameda County Coliseum is an agency established by the city of Oakland and the county of Alameda. The Coliseum Authority contracted with a private operator – AEG Facilities – to operate the Coliseum Complex.[30] Management of the two anchor tenants at the venue (the Oakland Athletics and the Oakland Raiders) here is not tasked with managing the full calendar of events at the venue.

Panel B in Exhibit 17.7 outlines three examples of owner/operator relationships in venues with private ownership. In most cases here, the owner of the venue is also the operator. Examples from Exhibit 17.7

are found with Dodger Stadium (with the LA Dodgers as the anchor tenant) and the Rogers Centre (with the Toronto Blue Jays as the anchor tenant). In some cases, the private owner subcontracts to a private-sector corporate operator such as AEG, Global Spectrum, or SMG Facilities. For example, Barclays Center in Brooklyn, New York (with the Brooklyn Nets/NBA and the New York Islander/NHL as its anchor tenants) is privately owned and operated by AEG Facilities.

Anschutz Entertainment Group (AEG) is one of the largest operators of sporting and entertainment venues in the world. AEG has contracts in many countries including Australia (Suncorp Stadium in Brisbane), Brazil (Maracanã Stadium in Rio de Janeiro), China (MasterCard Arena in Beijing), Germany (Mercedes-Benz Arena in Berlin), Russia (Galactica Park Arena in Moscow), Sweden (Tele2Arena in Stockholm), and the United Kingdom (O2 Arena in London).

17.5.3 Decision # 3: How Many Different Sports Anchor Tenants in the Venue?

For many years in multiple North American cities, baseball and football clubs shared venues with large capacities. Examples were:

- **Candlestick Park in San Francisco.** Opened in 1960 with two major anchor tenants for many years: the San Francisco Giants (MLB) from 1960 to 1999, and the San Francisco 49ers (NFL) from 1971 to 2013.
- **Metrodome in Minneapolis.** Opened in 1982 with two major anchor tenants for many years: the Minnesota Twins (MLB) from 1982 to 2009 and Minnesota Vikings (NFL) from 1982 to 2013.
- **Qualcomm Stadium in San Diego.** Opened in 1967 with two major tenants for many years: the San Diego Padres (MLB) from 1969 to 2003 and San Diego Chargers (NFL) from 1967 to present.

The main motivation for these shared multi-sport venues was to increase the utilization of a fixed resource that had infrastructure in place. Increased utilization by several anchor tenants was viewed as attractive as alternative non-sport uses of these open low-technology venues were not many. However, there were many downsides for fans in these stadiums. Each sport had different playing field dimensions and layouts. Fans in multi-sport venues can have poor sight-lines in certain areas or have long distances from front row seats to the actual playing area for certain sports. Over time, the strong trend has been to build purpose-built stadiums that are dedicated to a single sport where the venue can be built to enhance fan experience.

Multi-sport venues are more commonly found in arenas. Arenas often have multiple tenants such as NBA and NHL clubs. These two sports are relatively more compatible in the same venue.[31] Venues with multiple anchor tenants can have challenging decisions to make relating to the sharing of common revenues. For instance, assume luxury boxes which are sold for the entire year provides the buyer the right to use the box for any "public event" happening at the arena.[32] Therefore, if two (or more) clubs share the arena, there needs to be an agreement as regards how revenues from naming rights and year-long suite contracts will be shared. The Staples Center in Los Angeles is privately owned (by Philip Anschutz and Edward Roski) and has four main anchor tenants – the Los Angeles Clippers and Los Angeles Lakers of the NBA, the Los Angeles Kings of the NHL, and the Los Angeles Sparks of the WNBA. It is operated by AEG. For central revenues the sharing rule is 50 percent to the owners, 25 percent to the Los Angeles Lakers and 25 percent to the Los Angeles Kings.

Some venues have multiple anchor tenants from one sport. In Milan, two leading Italian soccer clubs – Inter Milan and AC Milan – have shared the famous San Siro stadium since 1926. The San Siro stadium is owned by the City of Milan, but jointly operated by the two Milan-based professional teams. As noted, the New York Giants and the New York Jets, are joint operators of MetLife Stadium, which is owned by the New Meadowland Stadium Co. that opened in 2010. Both clubs gave up much relative autonomy compared to having their own stadium, but each greatly benefited from only having to be responsible for half the $1,600 million venue construction costs and the annual operating costs.

17.6 VENUE MANAGEMENT – BUILDING THE PORTFOLIO OF EVENTS

Venues provide a fixed capacity that goes unused every day that it remains empty or if certain parts are not used. A large portion of the costs are fixed and are associated with the initial investment or the maintenance of the infrastructure. Another set of costs is associated with each event, such as setting up the stage for a concert or the ice rink for a hockey game. The additional cost of having an extra fan at an event is usually very small. In such a case, the variable cost is no different from hotels, airplanes, or movie theaters. These assets offer a set number of rooms or seats. The more frequently these rooms and seats are filled and the higher the revenue every time they are used, the more profitable the venue is:

> Venue economics = average capacity use per event × number of events × average revenue per seat – cost of delivering events and maintaining the venue.

Exhibit 17.8 shows the event portfolio of the SAP Center from 2002 to 2014.

The main anchor tenant is the San Jose Sharks of the NHL. There are 41 regular season events from the October to April period each NHL season. There is a maximum extra 16 possible home play-off games if the Sharks play all four rounds of the playoff series. In the 2002/14 period there were two lockouts, which explain the lower number of games played in several calendar years. The San Jose SaberCats of the Arena Football League (AFL) play approximately nine to ten home games per year. No games were played in 2009 and 2010 due to the AFL playing no games before it was restructured and started again in 2011.The SaberCats joined the AFL in 1995 and has been one of its most success-ful clubs. The result is that the SAP Center has approximately 300 days when there is not a Sharks or SaberCats game on the schedule. Exhibit 17.8 shows the diversity of extra events run at the SAP Center with an average of 111 extra events per year.

Venue managers planning the portfolio of events have to consider multiple factors:

■   The number of "committed events" and hence the number of potential open slots available to book. Here, there can be sizable differences across venues. At one end of the spectrum are sport-ing venues where there are many events locked into the schedule. The Staples Center has, at a minimum, 123 NBA and NHL regular season games each year and potentially many extra playoff games. MLB baseball parks have 81 regular season games. In contrast, some motor racing tracks have at most four or five major events (typically a week or two weeks long in occupancy) where the track is booked, with a high-revenue yield.

Number of events at SAP Center per calendar year

Year	02	03	04	05	06	07	08	09	10	11	12	13	14
Sports													
San Jose Sharks (NHL)	52	47	33	21	52	47	54	46	51	52	47	30	46
San Jose SaberCats (Arena Football)	11	10	10	8	10	10	10	—	—	9	9	10	9
San Jose Stealth (NLL – Lacrosse)	—	1	9	8	8	8	9	—	—	—	—	—	—
Fight Night at the Tank	4	5	5	5	5	4	4	—	—	—	—	—	—
Dew Action Sports	—	—	—	4	4	0	0	—	—	—	—	—	—
Motorsports events	3	3	3	—	3	0	0	0	0	0	0	0	3
SAP Open (tennis)	13	13	13	13	13	13	13	—	—	—	—	—	—
MMA/Other boxing	—	2	—	2	4	2	4	8	4	3	4	2	1
College Basketball	2	5	5	5	6	8	5	3	8	3	3	5	0
Other Sports	1	—	1	—	—	7	1	25	16	15	24	19	2
Subtotal	86	86	79	66	105	99	100	82	79	82	87	66	61
Entertainment													
Disney on Ice	18	18	18	18	19	18	19	16	10	11	20	21	21
Other family events	20	3	11	8	8	19	19	29	9	16	9	24	17
Concerts	30	30	46	36	32	37	35	19	37	29	30	35	32
Wrestling/WWE	1	3	1	3	1	2	1	2	1	1	2	2	2
Cirque Du Soleil	—	—	—	—	4	0	0	—	—	—	—	—	—

EXHIBIT 17.8 (cont.)

Year	02	03	04	05	06	07	08	09	10	11	12	13	14
Ringling Bros. Circus	10	9	9	9	10	9	8	0	0	9	9	8	9
Subtotal	**79**	**63**	**85**	**74**	**74**	**85**	**82**	**66**	**57**	**66**	**70**	**90**	**81**
Other													
City	2	1	5	3	4	1	2	—	—	—	—	—	—
Motivational/religious	6	3	6	4	4	9	10	—	—	—	—	—	—
Other	5	4	5	2	1	1	2	—	—	—	—	—	—
Subtotal	**13**	**8**	**16**	**9**	**9**	**11**	**14**	**0**	**0**	**0**	**0**	**0**	**0**
Grand Total	**178**	**157**	**180**	**149**	**188**	**195**	**196**	**148**	**136**	**148**	**157**	**156**	**142**

EXHIBIT 17.8 Portfolio of Events at Venue: SAP Center in San Jose, California – Home of San Jose Sharks of NHL
Source: Sharks Sports and Entertainment

■ The net revenue yields from different potential events that could be booked. Events differ greatly in their expected revenues and in their expected set-up and operating costs. Consider an arena where events could include concerts, family events, and the circus. Contracts can vary substantially per event. For example, some elite artists offer very little net revenue yield to a venue as they demand a contract where they pay only minimal rent and do not share ticket revenues with the venue. The argument by the artist is that their event adds to the prestige and brand of the venue. Other artists or events can be booked on more favorable terms to a venue.

■ Any positive or negative effects of different events to the brands of the venue or its owner. Artists attracting a high percentage of fans that will enter with "concealed illegal drugs" are likely to have a negative brand impact and most likely will not be booked. In contrast, family events such as *Disney on Ice* add to the venue brand.

■ Community-building events. The city of San Jose views having high-school and college graduations and "San Jose Sports Hall of Fame" award dinners as important events for the San Jose community to celebrate.

FC Barcelona plays its home games at Camp Nou, a stadium that was built in 1957. This venue area is constantly used for hosting company events and tours, most of which do not use the soccer pitch. The FC Barcelona museum (now relabeled the FC Barcelona Experience) includes a tour of the stadium, with a visit to the changing rooms as a central part of the tour. This museum is the most visited in the city, ahead of the Picasso and the Miró museums, with more than 1.5 million visitors per year (more than the total number of fans going to games). The price to enter the FC Barcelona Museum is twice the price of getting into Louvre in Paris or the Museum of Modern Art in New York. Not surprisingly, the exit of the museum leads directly into the FC Barcelona shop, where fans are encouraged to transform their passion of experiencing the history of the club into merchandise purchases.

Managers of venues with only a small number of very high-revenue events (called "tent-pole" events) face high risks if one of those tent-pole events is not renewed. Formula 1 and NASCAR racetracks are illustrative. The Formula 1 Grand Prix or NASCAR event itself might use the track 15–20 days a year. If the track is lucky, it might also host a MotoGP Grand Prix for another 15–20 days. But there are still 11 months for it to be used, more than 300 days! While the Formula 1 Grand Prix can easily represent 90 percent of the revenues of the track, it is still important to use it the rest of the time. This additional revenue flows to the profits of the venue because a large part of the costs are fixed and can mean the difference between making a profit or a loss. Tracks often fill up the rest of the time with events such as lower level car and motorcycle competitions, racing team training sessions, new car presentations, driving courses, and corporate events.

17.7 INDUSTRY EXAMPLE: SAN JOSE EARTHQUAKES' ROLLER-COASTER RIDE TO THE OPENING OF AVAYA STADIUM[33]

Since its start in 1996, Major League Soccer has sought to have their clubs play in soccer-specific stadiums. In the early years of MLS, many clubs played in NFL stadiums with their capacities averaging above 60,000. With MLS attendance averaging below 20,000 per game, televised games were often showing stadiums with 70 percent empty seating. The in-stadium experience for many MLS games in these NFL stadiums was substandard. Exhibit 17.9 shows the systematic building of soccer-specific stadiums in North America since 1999.

Panel A: Clubs playing in soccer-specific stadiums in 2015 (14 clubs)

Year stadium opened	Club	Year entered MLS	Stadium name	Estimated construction cost ($M)	Capacity (in 2015)
1999	Columbus Crew	1996	Mafre Stadium	28	22,485
2003	LA Galaxy	1996	StubHub stadium	150	27,000
2005	FC Dallas	1996	Toyota Stadium	80	20,300
2006	Chicago Fire	1998	Toyota Stadium	98	21,000
2007	Toronto FC	2007	BMO Field	63*	20,000
2007	Colorado Rapids	1996	Dick's Sporting Goods Park	131	18,000
2008	Real Salt Lake	2005	Rio Tinto Stadium	110	20,000
2010	New York Red Bulls	1996	Red Bull Arena	200	25,189
2010	Philadelphia Union	2010	Union Field at Chester	120	18,500
2011	Sporting Kansas City	1996	Sporting Park	200	18,467
2011	Portland Timbers	2011	Providence Park	83*	20,000
2012	Houston Dynamo	2006	BBVA Compass Stadium	95	22,000
2012	Montreal Impact	2012	Saputo Stadium	40*	20,341
2015	San Jose Earthquakes	2008	Avaya Stadium	100	18,000
Average capacity					**20,806**

* Renovation cost shown is for renovation construction.

Panel B: Clubs playing in larger (typically football) stadiums in 2015 (six clubs)

Year stadium opened	Club	Year entered MLS	Stadium name	Estimated construction cost ($M)	Game capacity (in 2015)	Full capacity (in 2015)
1936	Orlando City FC	2015	Citrus Bowl	—	41,000	61,000
1961	DC United	2006	RFK Stadium	24	19,647	68,800
1983	Vancouver Whitecaps	2011	BC Place	126	20,000	54,000
2002	NE Revolution	1996	Gillette Stadium	325	20,000	68,800
2002	Seattle Sounders	2009	Century Link Field	430	39,000	67,000
2009	New York FC	2015	Yankee Stadium	1,500	27,500	52,325
Average Capacity					**27,858**	**61,988**

EXHIBIT 17.9 Major League Soccer's Transition to Soccer – Specific Stadiums
Source: Multiple sources including Nihar Naik, RSV Database

By 2012, ten new stadiums had been built, with an average capacity of 21,294. In 2015, the San Jose Earthquakes moved into its Avaya Stadium with an 18,000 capacity to rave reviews from its fans, sponsors, and the media. However, the path to the opening of Avaya was far from smooth with multiple delays and challenges on the journey. The following section tells this story.

The San Jose Earthquakes were a charter member of MLS in 1996. They played at Spartan Stadium, which was owned by San Jose State University. Opened in 1933 and last renovated in 1985, Spartan Stadium was built for football and had capacity of approximately 31,000. The Earthquakes played at Spartan Stadium from 1996 to 2005, averaging approximately 13,000 spectators per game. Despite much success on the field, the continuing financial losses led to the Earthquakes relocating to Houston as the Houston Dynamos starting with the 2006 MLS season.

In July 2007, MLS, along with new owners John Fisher and Lew Wolff, announced the San Jose Earthquakes as a new MLS club. After an early failed effort to rebuild Spartan Stadium in conjunction with San Jose State University, a location for a new venue was identified by the city of San Jose next to San Jose International Airport. The location was more than 70 acres, with 14.5 acres for the soccer stadium and the remaining land available for a mixed-use commercial development. It was a former industrial site and home to the FMC Corporation, which built the M2 Bradley Fighting Vehicle for the US Army at the location. Early on, there were serious challenges in the permitting and the construction process, which delayed the stadium approval and created significant challenges for management and ownership. The stadium was initially set to open in 2009 after playing just one year at a temporary home – Buck Shaw Stadium with 10,500 capacity – on the campus of Santa Clara University. It soon became apparent that this timeline would not occur. The financing for the stadium was contingent upon the adjacent real estate deal and in 2008 the global financial crisis was in full swing. Credit was tight and commercial real estate deals were in limbo. The result was that the stadium plans were put on hold. Fans and season ticket holders were upset. The 5,000 season ticket holders from the inaugural 2008 year had assumed they were buying into a new venue as well as a winning team. The club's inability to compete as an expansion team, as well as the uncertainly over the stadium and poor conditions at Buck Shaw Stadium, led to losing more than half of the season ticket holders by the end of 2009.

In 2009, Dave Kaval, a co-founder of Golden Baseball League, was hired as President of the Earthquakes. His key charge was developing and delivering a soccer-specific stadium with a $60 million budget. Exhibit 17.10 presents selected key stakeholders in the stadium build process that ended with the opening of Avaya Stadium in March 2015.

From its inception, the stadium featured a European inspired design. This was unique to MLS, which had soccer-specific stadiums that were mostly just smaller versions of American football stadiums. In 2006, Earthquakes co-owner John Fisher had attended the World Cup in Germany and seen the intimate designs with steeply raked stands, roofs, and dedicated supporters sections. Brad Schrock (the principal designer) and 360 Architecture (the architectural firm) carried forward this design ethos in developing the stadium. Over the course of its development, the Earthquakes' management team visited all MLS stadiums as well as made several trips to Europe to see the best venues from a fan experience. There was also a focus on how to reduce unneeded space and how to optimize the stadium for the California climate with outdoor patios and not indoor club space. Keith Wolff and Kaval led the efforts of design from 2010 to 2012 to internally manage costs while delivering on the European design. The stadium was built with one concourse, vastly reducing the cost. The design phase also developed the concept of premium seating at the field level, which was unprecedented at that time. This created an experience similar to NBA court-level seats while reducing the cost of possibly elevating the suites and clubs.

Category	Stakeholder	Description/role
City	San Jose	Granted permits and entitled land; helped navigate other third-party claims.
Owners representative	Keith Wolff and Dave Kaval	Sourced internally. No dedicated project manager.
Architect	360 Architecture	Designed stadium; developed working drawings; heavily involved in construction administration.
General contractor	Devcon	Handled construction; bid out project to subcontractors; delivered building on schedule.
Structural engineer	Mangusson Klemencic (MKA)	Handled unique structural system with cantilevered roof; maintained seismic standards.
Steel erector	Schuff Steel	Installed steel and SPS terrace system.
Demolition	Campenella	Handled complicated underground bunker demolition.
Field designer	Verde Design	Designed Bermuda grass field.
Field construction	Bothman & Associates	Built world class natural grass pitch.
Concessionaire	Ovations	Managed design and build out of $2.5 million concessions equipment.
Video	Daktronics	Installed both world class video boards on scoreboard and fascia ribbon board.
Integrator	Assured Technologies	Local IT integrator oversaw converged network roll out and Wi-Fi integration.
Ticketing	Ticketmaster	Deployed ticketing system and associated access points.
Wi-Fi	Avaya	Design and deployed robust Wi-Fi network with over 200 wireless access points.
App Developer	ArcTouch	Design and built Avaya Stadium app.
Seating	Camatic	Avaya Stadium features both Forte and Quantum seats.
Neighborhood group	Newhall Neighborhood Association	Opposed project due to sound impacts. Led to delay of concert permitting.

EXHIBIT 17.10 Selected Key Stakeholders in Construction of Avaya Stadium: Home of San Jose Earthquakes of MLS
Source: San Jose Earthquakes/Dave Kaval.

Although premium seating was initially not planned, field-level suites and clubs were later added to the design. In order to convince ownership to make the additional investment in these amenities, Kaval and his team packaged and sold all 12 field suites and more than 1,000 club seats over a six-month period in 2012. This gave ownership more confidence in the success of the endeavor and enhanced the construction budget to accommodate these upgrades. The owners raised the stadium budget voluntarily to $100 million to fund these revenue-generating features that also included enhanced LED boards.

In parallel to the design work, the Earthquakes sought a planned development permit with the city of San Jose. However, a local neighbor group – the Newhall Neighborhood Group – opposed the project due to concerns regarding noise at the location. The irony here was that the stadium site sits next to a freeway, train tracks, and an international airport. The Newhall group was successful in appealing the planning permit to the city council. In a San Jose city council meeting in February 2012, over 500 Earthquakes fans packed city council chambers to advocate for the stadium to be built on the site. Hundreds of fans and community members had large "Build it now" signs. The city council unanimously rejected the Newhall group's appeal and the stadium project could now move forward. The success that night was tempered by the almost nine-month delay that the appeal had caused in terms of timing. The earliest the stadium could open would now be 2014.

In October of 2012, the Earthquakes had a ceremonial ground-breaking. Instead of a couple of dignitaries and some gold shovels, the club decided to attempt to break the existing Guinness record for the largest participatory ground-breaking. More than 7,000 blue shovels were ordered and 6,526 people showed up and dug for two minutes to set the record. It was a joyous day for the community and the stadium was set to open in March 2014.

However, just as the stadium was getting on track, a new challenge emerged. In the demolition phase of the project, the construction team from Devcon encountered underground basements, sub-basements, and bunkers associated with the old military complex. Many of the underground chambers had old tank parts and even old munitions that were fortunately not explosive. This created another difficult delay and the stadium was initially pushed back to mid-2014 and then all the way to March 2015.

In November 2014, a ten-year deal with Avaya was announced for the naming rights of the facility. Avaya is a telecommunications company headquartered in Silicon Valley. The partnership was $20 million over ten years and was one of the largest in MLS. In addition to the rights fees, Avaya would be investing in a world-class Wi-Fi system that would enhance the technology benefits of the venue, which was viewed to be critical in Silicon Valley.

On March 22, 2015, Avaya Stadium opened to great fanfare in front of a sellout crowd of 18,000 fans. Its unique design and atmosphere was immediately positively received. Fans and community members alike raved about the open concourses, the field level seats, the steep rake of the seating bowl, and the signature scoreboard bar – the largest exterior bar in North America. The *San Jose Mercury News* asked whether Avaya Stadium could be the "best in North America." The venue was shortlisted for the 2015 Venue of the Year at the Sports Building Awards in Barcelona, along with such iconic stadiums as Camp Nou, Wembley Stadium, Levis Stadium, the Maracanã in Brazil, and the Sydney Cricket Ground.

17.8 SUMMARY

Venue building and management is a central aspect of sports management. Venues bring together players and fans and provide a platform for the creation of content that is broadcast to a wider community. Multiple demand and supply factors are driving the building of more technologically advanced venues that enhance the in-venue experience for attendees. New venue-building projects have many complex facets. Communities rarely support each aspect of a project proposal. Often groups will form that oppose the total venue proposal. Venue financing also is requiring more ingenuity as the costs of venues continues to increase. Astute management recognizes uncertainty and risk in contracting and aligns the interests of multiple stakeholders, which can substantially increase the likelihood of new venues being built on time and at or below budget.

NOTES

1　B. Fischer, "Sports Business Awards: Levi's Stadium wins sports facility of the year," *Sports Business Daily*, May 21, 2015.

2　See *San Diego Padres: Petco Park as a Catalyst for Urban Redevelopment* (Graduate School of Business, Stanford University, 2008).

3　J. Coté, "Warriors shift arena plans to Mission Bay," *SF Gate*, April 22, 2014.

4　R. Leuty, "49ers stadium's surprising score on construction, seat licenses," *San Francisco Business Times*, March 25, 2015.

5　R. Phillips, "Braves release rendering of new stadium and community," *Birmingham Business Journal*, July 30, 2014.

6　E. Nalder and T. Guillen, "Years of fixes turned leaky Kingdome roof into sodden disaster – flawed from the start, structure fell prey to birds, bad weather, bad maintenance," *The Seattle Times*, August 28, 1994.

7　Further examples are in B. Watson, "The 9 worst corporate stadium names in America," DailyFinance.com, February 25, 2013; G. Lubin and S. Foxman, "The Enron Field curse: why you should avoid companies that put their name on a stadium," *Business Insider*, January 18, 2012.

8　S. Krashinsky, "Canadian Tire puts its name on Ottawa Senators' arena," *The Globe and Mail*, January 18, 2013.

9　www.vikings.com/assets/docs/stadium/DES-recent-nfl-stadiums.pdf.

10　Under NFL revenue-sharing, 34 percent of the ticket revenues at a home game are classified as the "visiting team share" (VTS). The VTS revenues for all NFL games in a season are pooled into one central single pool which is then shared equally by all clubs. Effectively, under the G-3 and G-4 programs all the other NFL clubs are subsidizing the club that accesses the G-3 or G-4 "loan." The G-4 loan program is even more beneficial to the borrowing club and can result in all 32 NFL clubs paying equal shares of the interest and principal repayments on a $200 million loan.

11　M. Layer, "The limits of the NFI's G-4 stadium loan program," Newballpark.org, October 17, 2013.

12　www.bloomberg.com/ss/08/10/1002_power100/64.htm.

13　"Report: debt issues cast wider MLB net," ESPN, June 4, 2011.

14　"The AEG shocker: what happened," *Sports Business Daily*, March 18, 2013.

15　S. Farmer, "AEG reiterates that it's moving on from Farmers Field in downtown LA," *Los Angeles Times*, March 10, 2015.

16　"NFL stadium plan in downtown Los Angeles scrapped amid competition from neighboring cities," Fox News, March 10, 2015.

17　R.L. Cash, "Wake up: boring NFL stadium, LA talks finally get interesting," *Sporting News*, June 3, 2015.

18　http://www.foxsports.com/nfl/story/oakland-raiders-san-diego-chargers-los-angeles-area-stadium-042415

19　The PSLs were called stadium builders licenses (SBLs) for Levi's Stadium.

20　www.levisstadium.com/2012/06/pricing-announced-reserved-seating-new-stadium.

21　See www.pslsource.com.

22　www.tvb.org/media/file/Nielsen_2014-2015_DMA_Ranks.pdf.

23　K. Johnson, "Railyard arena backers will keep trying," *Sacramento Business Journal*, November 7, 2006.

24　www.elmets.com/news/new-sacramento-kings-arena-closer-to-reality-after-historic-7-2-city-council-votes.

25　www.sactownroyalty.com/2014/6/26/5844518/downtown-kings-arena-timeline.

26　S. Riches, "This man wants to makes the NBA a social network – and take it global," *Wired*, December 26, 2013.

27　K. Cracchiolo, "Sacramento Kings implementing cutting-edge technology to enhance the fan experience," NBA.com, April 17, 2014.

28　www.gwcc.com/about/Default.aspx.

29　J. Wadsworth, "San Jose Sharks, city extend lease agreement at SAP Center," *San Jose Inside*, May 12, 2015.

30　www.oraclearena.com/oacca/about-the-authority.

31　Some venue owners and operators prefer to operate with a NHL dedicated or a NBA dedicated facility as there are some differences in arena layout for the playing area for NHL versus NBA games that can impact some sight-lines in an arena.

32　Many venues have "private events" that are not automatically open to suite holders and other "full year" ticket holders. Examples are an "All-Star NBA Weekend" where the NBA assumes control of the venue and a political convention for a presidential candidate of a major party.

33　Much information for this section was provided by Dave Kaval and the San Jose Earthquakes.

18

VALUATION OF CLUBS, COMPANIES, AND OTHER SPORTING-RELATED ASSETS

Many stakeholders in the sports industry have high interest in the valuation of clubs, companies and key assets. This chapter outlines key principles of valuation and discusses how the principles apply or may be adjusted when examining applications in the sporting industry. To illustrate, we first discuss the valuation of clubs and companies and then move to the valuation of related sporting assets. This chapter should be viewed as a complement to Chapter 4, which highlighted the importance of leverageable assets and inherited liabilities to club management. These two concepts are also important to club valuation.

18.1 VALUATION OF SPORTING CLUBS

Sporting club valuations are frequently mentioned in the media. There are multiple prompts to public comment on valuations.

18.1.1 Sporting Club Ownership Changes

One major prompt to valuation disclosures is when a sporting club changes ownership, especially where there are "interesting" aspects of the ownership change. These include:

- Ownership changes that set "record" prices for franchises traded in a league. Given the upward trend in franchise transactions over the past two decades, this is a seemingly regular event. Examples include the NFL (Miami Dolphins in 2008 and Buffalo Bills in 2014); NBA (Golden State Warriors in 2011, Sacramento Kings in 2013); NHL (Colorado Avalanche in 2000, Toronto Maple Leafs in 2012); and MLB (Boston Red Sox in 2002, Chicago Cubs in 2009).
- Ownership change due to league-related sanctions or actions. One example is the Los Angeles Clippers. In August 2014, Steve Ballmer acquired ownership for a record $2 billion after the prior owner was given a lifetime ban by the NBA associated with accusations of racist behavior (See Chapter 4, Box 4.1). A second example is the sale of the Los Angeles Dodgers in 2012 to the Guggenheim Baseball Partners. Box 18.1 discusses the 2012 Dodgers transaction as well as the prior 1998 and 2004 Dodgers transactions.

BOX 18.1 LOS ANGELES DODGERS OF MLB: FOUR OWNERSHIP GROUPS OVER TWO DECADES AND A SIX-FOLD INCREASE IN VALUATION

Ownership changes in sports clubs can occur for a diverse set of reasons. The following three transactions for the Los Angeles Dodgers in 1998, 2004, and 2012 highlight the valuation uplifts for the club as well as some of the diverse motives and contexts in which ownership changed hands.

Fox Group of News Corp in 1998 acquires the Los Angeles Dodgers from the O'Malley family who had owned the Dodgers since 1950

Included in the transaction was "Dodger Stadium and its surrounding 300 acres, the club's spring training complex in Vero Beach, Florida, and a baseball academy in the Dominican Republic." MLB owners approved the sale for $311 million, which was considered to be the most money ever paid for a pro sports franchise at the time. Peter O'Malley commented that "Professional sports today is as high risk as the oil business … You need a broader base than an individual family to carry you through the storm." One motivation for the Fox acquisition was to prevent ESPN setting up a regional sports network in Los Angeles with the Dodgers 162 games as lead programming. Fox subsequently experienced sizable operating losses with the Dodgers. *Forbes* estimated the operating losses of the Dodgers under the Fox ownership to be more than $100 million. In January 2003 "Fox retained the New York investment banker Allen & Co to shop for a buyer for the Dodgers." Multiple buyers were reported to be interested. For example, Dave Checketts was reported to offer "$650 million, but only if it includes control of Fox Sports Net West 2, which broadcasts Dodgers games."[1]

McCourt family in 2004 acquires the Los Angeles Dodgers from News Corp for a reported $420–30 million in a transaction with a large amount of debt[2]

A key part of the transaction was Fox's LA regional sports network obtaining an extended contract to broadcast Dodgers games to 2013. Some observers viewed this contract as below the market rate.

The McCourt family ownership initially gained positive praise from the media. Major investments were made in upgrading Dodger Stadium. However, personal problems associated with the divorce of Frank and Jamie McCourt led to a flow of negative press and accusations and counter-accusations.[3] In April 2011 baseball commissioner Bud Selig announced that MLB would "seize control of Dodgers." In June 2011, Selig rejected a proposed TV deal with Fox that would have provided the cash flow to enable Frank McCourt to retain control of the Dodgers and make a divorce settlement. In June 2011, the Dodgers filed for bankruptcy protection. In November 2011, Frank McCourt "agreed to sell the Dodgers, abruptly surrendering the team after fighting to retain it over two years and in two courts. The sale is expected to sell for two to three times as much … as the $421 million McCourt paid in 2004."

At least six groups were reported to be interested in buying the Dodgers. On March 23, 2012 the *Los Angeles Times* reported that "the field of Dodgers bidders was cut to three." The three finalists were reported to be:

1   Guggenheim Baseball Partners, a group that included former Atlanta Braves executive Stan Kasten, former LA Laker Magic Johnson, and Peter Guber.
2   Group led by hedge-fund billionaire Steven Cohen and Los Angeles billionaire and philanthropist Patrick Soon-Shiong.
3   Stan Kroenke, whose family owned or held major stakes in the St. Louis Rams (NFL), Denver Nuggets (NBA), Colorado Avalanche (NHL), and Arsenal (EPL).[4]

Guggenheim Baseball Partners announce in late March 2012 the purchase of the Los Angeles Dodgers for $2,000 million

In addition, it was announced that McCourt "and 'certain affiliates' of the new ownership will be 'forming a joint venture,' which will acquire the Chavez Ravine property for an additional $150 million."[5] Reports were that to remain in the bidding, each of the three finalists had to commit to a minimum bid of $1,400 million for the Dodgers. Guggenheim then made a pre-emptive bid that very quickly and effectively ended the auction.

A major part of the financial analysis done by the Guggenheim Baseball Partners was based on the expectation of a major increase in local media rights. The existing Fox contract was reported to pay the Dodgers less than $40 million per year. In January 2013 it was announced that the Dodgers had signed a contract with Time Warner Cable for a "team-owned 'Sports Net LA' channel starting in 2014. It covers 25 years and is believed to be worth between $7 billion and $8 billion to the team."[6] At an average payment of $280 million per year, the new media contract with Time Warner Cable illustrates the increasingly central role that media contracts play in the valuation of sporting clubs.

■ Ownership change with international investors buying a club. One aspect of the globalization of sports is the purchase of sporting clubs by owners outside the domestic base of the competition. Such changes often come with high publicity. The examples here are many including: (a) English Premier League (EPL) – Arsenal and Manchester United with US-based major investors, Chelsea with a Russian major investor, Liverpool with American major investors in both of two ownership changes, Manchester City with a UAE major investor, and Queens Park Rangers with a Malaysian major investor; (b) French Ligue 1 – Paris Saint-Germain FC with a Qatar-based major investor; (c) MLB – Seattle Mariners with a Japanese major investor; and (d) NBA – Brooklyn Nets with a Russian major investor.

18.1.2 Public Market Signals About Sporting Club Valuations

Where sporting clubs are publicly listed, there are ongoing signals about valuation. A high-profile example is Manchester United. This club has undergone several changes in its corporate status, more recently being listed in August 2012 on the New York Stock Exchange.

A variant of a public market setting occurred with the Indian Premier League. Starting as a new league in 2008, bids were requested for franchises to enter a new Twenty20 cricket competition. Box 18.2 examines the different valuations for the initial eight franchises and three additional expansion franchises.

BOX 18.2 INDIAN PREMIER LEAGUE (IPL) LAUNCHES WITH AUCTION FOR EIGHT FRANCHISES: VALUATIONS RANGE FROM $111.9 MILLION FOR MUMBAI INDIANS TO $67 MILLION FOR RAJASTHAN ROYALS[7]

Cricket in India is the dominant professional and participant sport. Traditionally, the major cricket games had been played in a five-day or a one-day format. In 2003, a short form of the game was introduced called Twenty20. These games last approximately three hours and involve each side having 20 overs of six balls each over to score runs. The format encouraged high scoring and aggressive play and attracted much attention from fans and the media. Launched in March 2008, the Twenty20 Indian Premier League represents one of the most successful ever new leagues that started strong and has maintained much of its early momentum.

The Board of Control for Cricket in India (BCCI) is the powerful central body controlling cricket in India. In 2007, a new Twenty20 league – the Indian Cricket League (ICL) – was started by ZeeTV, a media company that had been unable to win the rights to show cricket in India. This league met with strong opposition from the BCCI, including the threatened blacklisting of cricketers who played in the ICL. In late 2007, the BCCI announced that, with IMG as a partner, it was launching its own Twenty20 league – the Indian Premier League (IPL). Each club would play in a six- to seven-week season (April–May) that had been negotiated with the International Cricket Council (ICC). The basic structure was a single-entity league (see Chapter 3) with eight individual franchises. Rather than set a price to be paid for each franchise, the BCCI conducted an auction where bids were solicited for each franchise. Each franchise would receive an equal percentage of the IPL's central revenues (largely from media rights and sponsorship). Franchises would be based in one of 12 cities the BCCI had qualified – two criteria were access to a stadium seating at least 25,000, and the capability of lighting the stadium for night games.

The BCCI awarded franchises to eight clubs. Exhibit 18.1 lists the eight teams and their bids. A mixture of corporations, individuals, and syndicates were the bidders. The top bid of $111.9 million came from the Reliance Group for the Mumbai franchise. The lowest accepted bid was $67 million for the Rajasthan Royals. The bid amounts were to be paid over ten years in equal amounts. Several franchise bids included Bollywood stars (such as Shah Rukh Khan and Preity Zinta). One of the major success factors for the IPL was its emphasis on dramatically increasing the entertainment aspect of the game, in part fueled by a heavy association with Bollywood. The IPL attracted the very best cricket players in the world, largely by offering very high salaries for the short six- to seven-week season.

Team	Auction bid ($M)	City of team	Years in IPL
2008 AUCTION			
Mumbai Indians	111.9	Mumbai	2008 →
Bangalore Royal Challengers	111.6	Bangalore	2008 →
Deccan Charges	107	Hyderabad	2008–12
Chennai Super Kings	91	Chennai	2008 →
Delhi Daredevils	84	Delhi	2008 →
Kings XI Punjab	76	Mohali	2008 →
Kolkata Knight Riders	75.1	Kolkata	2008 →
Rajasthan Royals	67	Jaipur	2008 →
2011 AUCTION			
Sahara Pune Warriors	370	Pune	2011–13
Kochi Tuskers	333	Kochi	2011
2013 AUCTION			
Sunrisers Hyderabad	80	Hyderabad	2013 →

EXHIBIT 18.1 Indian Premier League Teams and Auction Bid Valuations

After two very successful seasons, the BCCI in March 2010 held an auction for an additional two IPL clubs. Out of 12 bidders, the BCCI selected a $370 million bid from the Sahara Group and a $333 million bid from Rendezvous Sports World. Both these franchises had a short life in the IPL. The Rendezvous franchise (Kochi Tuskers) lasted just one year and had both syndicate disagreements and financial difficulties. When it defaulted on its financial commitments, its franchise was terminated by the BCCI. The Sahara Group franchise (Sahara Pune Warriors) lasted three years. It withdrew its franchise amid allegations and counter-allegations between the BCCI and the franchise.

The Deccan Chargers franchise played in the IPL for the first five years. When its parent company ran into financial difficulties, it chose to have its franchise terminated rather than sell at a "fire-sale" price. Starting in 2013, a new Hyderabad franchise entered the IPL via the auction process, winning with a bid of $80 million. The lower franchise fee paid reflected a general viewpoint that the two 2011 new franchise groups had sizably overpaid in the auction format.

The success of the IPL has had multiple impacts on the global world of cricket. Many young cricketers have both improved their skills by playing with elite cricketers from other countries and have had a high-profile platform to showcase their talents. Other cricket bodies have set up Twenty20 leagues that draw heavily on the IPL format – such as Cricket Australia and its successful launch of the Big Bash League. The enthusiastic acceptance by players, media, and fans of the Twenty20 game format has raised the profile of the ICC's Twenty20 country team-based World Cup. It is now on a four-year cycle akin to other major global tournaments such as the FIFA World Cup and the Rugby World Cup.

18.1.3 Magazine Estimates of Sporting Club Valuations

Starting with *Financial World* in the early 1990s and followed by *Forbes*, business magazines in the United States have been regularly publishing valuation estimates for an expanding set of sporting clubs. Exhibit 18.2 shows average club valuation estimates by *Forbes* since 1999 for the four major North American leagues.

Mean, highest, and lowest estimated 2014 valuations by *Forbes* across the four leagues in Exhibit 18.2 are (in $ millions):

	Mean	Highest (Name)	Lowest (Name)
NFL	1,428	3,200 (Dallas Cowboys)	930 (St. Louis Rams)
MLB	1,199	3,200 (NY Yankees)	625 (Tampa Bay)
NBA	1,106	2,600 (LA Lakers)	600 (Milwaukee Bucks)
NHL	490	1,300 (Toronto Maple Leafs)	190 (Florida Panthers)

These estimates are often given high publicity and reported in multiple news outlets. Included in Exhibit 18.2 are the annual compound growth rates for the average valuations.[8] These annual compound growth rates range from a high of 12.99 percent for NBA clubs over the 2000/14 period to 8.67 percent for NFL clubs over the same time period.

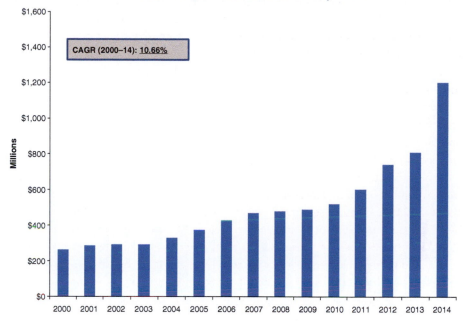

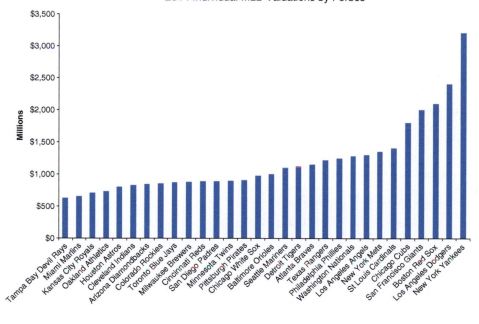

EXHIBIT 18.2 (*cont.*)

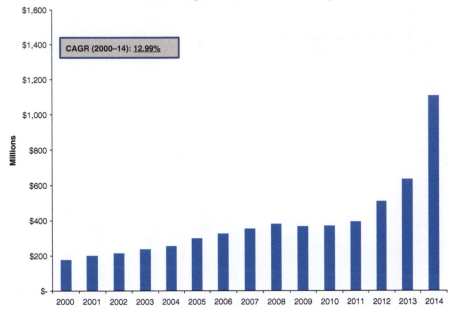

Forbes Average Annual NBA Valuations by Forbes

CAGR (2000–14): 12.99%

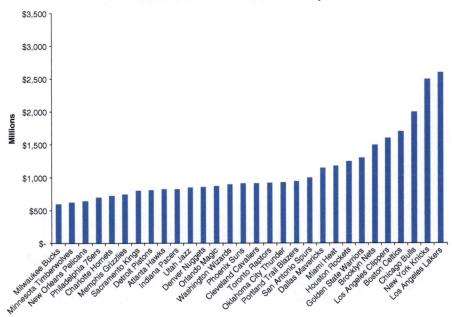

2014 Individual NBA Club Valuations by Forbes

EXHIBIT 18.2 (cont.)

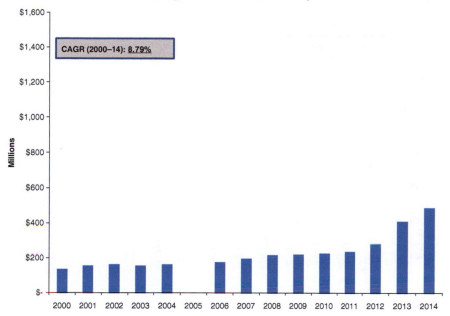

Average Annual NHL Valuations by Forbes

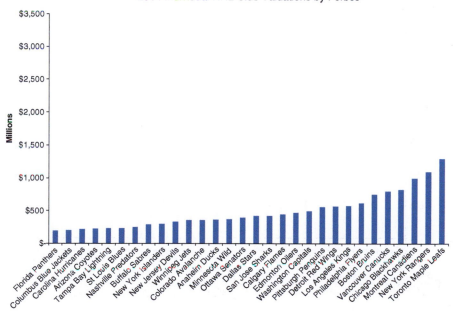

2014 Individual NHL Club Valuations by Forbes

EXHIBIT 18.2 (cont.)

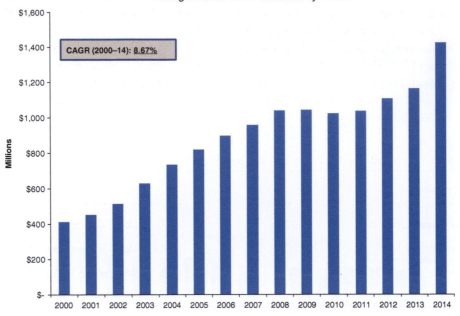

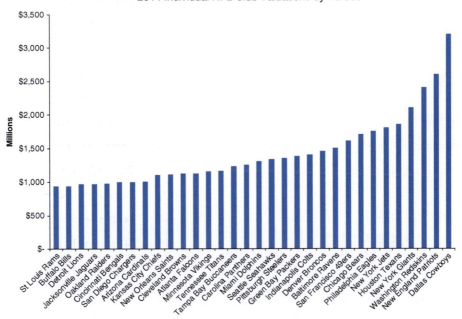

EXHIBIT 18.2 *Forbes'* Valuations of Clubs in North America – NFL, MLB, NBA, and NHL

The increasing interest around the globe in the business of sports has led *Forbes* to expand its valuation estimates to include sporting clubs beyond North America. Exhibit 18.3 shows the *Forbes* 2014 list of the 50 most highly valued sporting clubs in the world.

NFL clubs comprise 30 of the 50 clubs, followed by MLB with six clubs, then both the NBA and the EPL with four clubs. *Forbes* estimated the two leading Spanish soccer clubs – Real Madrid at $3,440 million and Barcelona at $3,200 million – to have the highest valuations in 2014. Both these Spanish clubs have an association model (see Chapter 4) that effectively precludes them being bought or sold in a 100 percent acquisition context.

(Rank in list; name; estimated valuation in 2014 in $millions)

SOCCER				*NFL*		
1.	Real Madrid (La Liga)	3,440		5.	Dallas Cowboys	2,300
2.	Barcelona (La Liga)	3,200		8.	New England Patriots	1,800
3.	Manchester United (EPL)	2,810		9.	Washington Redskins	1,700
7.	Bayern Munich (Bundesliga)	1,850		10.	New York Giants	1,550
16.	Arsenal (EPL)	1,331		12.	Houston Texans	1,450
48.	Chelsea (EPL)	867		14.	New York Jets	1,380
49.	Manchester City (EPL)	863		17.	Philadelphia Eagles	1,314
50.	AC Milan (Serie A)	856		18.	Chicago Bears	1,252
				19.	Baltimore Ravens	1,227
	MLB			20.	San Francisco 49ers	1,224
4.	New York Yankees	2,500		21.	Indianapolis Colts	1,200
6.	Los Angeles Dodgers	2,000		24.	Green Bay Packers	1,183
11.	Boston Red Sox	1,500		25.	Denver Broncos	1,161
21.	Chicago Cubs	1,200		27.	Pittsburgh Steelers	1,118
37.	San Francisco Giants	1,000		28.	Seattle Seahawks	1,081
39.	Philadelphia Phillies	975		29.	Miami Dolphins	1,074
				30.	Tampa Bay Bucc.	1,067
	NBA			31.	Carolina Panthers	1,057
13.	New York Knicks	1,400		32.	Tennessee Titans	1,055
15.	Los Angeles Lakers	1,350		33.	Kansas City	1,009
37.	Chicago Bulls	1,000		34.	Minnesota Vikings	1,007
45.	Boston Celtics	875		35.	Cleveland Browns	1,005
				36.	New Orleans Saints	1,004

EXHIBIT 18.3 *(cont.)*

	FORMULA 1	
21.	Ferrari	1,200

	NHL	
26.	Toronto Maple Leafs	1,150

40.	Arizona Cardinals	961
41.	San Diego Chargers	949
42.	Atlanta Falcons	933
43.	Cincinnati Bengals	924
44.	Detroit Lions	900
45.	St. Louis Rams	875
47.	Buffalo Bills	870

EXHIBIT 18.3 *Forbes'* Most Highly Valued Sporting Clubs in 2014

18.2 SPORTING CLUB VALUATION DRIVERS

This section looks at the drivers of club valuations through several different lenses. We first link valuation drivers to the discussions in Chapters 3 and 4 regarding league and sports club management. Then industry perspectives on club valuation drivers are discussed.

18.2.1 Valuation Drivers and Club Management

Exhibit 18.4 outlines categories of valuation drivers for a sporting club. These categories help guide estimating the inputs used in alternative valuation methodologies. Other things being equal, the stronger a sporting club on each of the categories in Exhibit 18.4, the higher the estimated valuation. Each category is explained below.

1 Country/sport strength	• Economy size and strength • Sport stature in country
2 League strength	• Revenue-generating capacity • Economic/business model • League revenue-sharing with clubs
3 Ownership strength	• Capacity and willingness to invest • Power base/relationship networks
4 Management strength	• Leadership abilities • Domain experience
5 City/region strength	• Market size and economy strength • Competitive landscape
6 Arena/stadium strength	• Revenue-generating capacity • "State-of-the-art" status • Sharing rules with city/county

EXHIBIT 18.4 *(cont.)*

7 Team on-field performance strength	• Current/recent success stature • Heritage success stature
8 Strength of players/coaches	• Current squad stature and contract context • Heritage player/coach status
9 Branding/sponsorship strength	• Revenue-generating capacity • Brand resilience to shocks • Global aspects of the brand
10 Fan strength	• Size and loyalty of fan base • National/regional mix of fans • Global reach of the fan base
11 Media contract/asset strength	• Revenue-generating capacity • Potential for renegotiation • Media ownership assets
12 Real estate asset strength	• Revenue-generating capacity • Ability to "capture" new real estate assets
13 Other factors	

EXHIBIT 18.4 Sporting Club Financial Valuation Drivers

Country/Sport Strength

Both the size and strength of an economy and where a sport stands in the sporting hierarchy in that country affect valuation. The combination of the large United States economy and the high status of the NFL across North American sporting leagues, helps explain why the NFL has 30 of the 50 most highly valued clubs by *Forbes*, as reported in Exhibit 18.3.

In large European economies, soccer is the dominant professional sport. This combination helps explain the relatively high valuations for top tier clubs in the larger economies of England, Spain, Germany and Italy vis-à-vis clubs in smaller economies such as Belgium, Greece, and Sweden.

League Strength

Chapter 3 outlined key aspects of leagues that can lead to higher or lower valuations. Leagues with high central revenues that are equally distributed (such as the NFL) lead to both higher average club valuations, a lower ratio of the highest valuation to the lowest valuation, and a lower percentage of total club aggregate valuation that is concentrated in the most highly valued clubs.

Chapter 4 introduced the concept of relegation that occurs in many soccer leagues. In relegation, each year several low on-the-field performing clubs exit the Premier League and play the next season (and often for many subsequent seasons) in leagues with lower revenue yields. Clubs that have a higher likelihood of relegation will have a "relegation discount penalty" in their valuation. Box 18.3 highlights how the EPL has a much more tiered valuation structure within its clubs than do the four North American leagues in Exhibit 18.2.

BOX 18.3 RESEARCH ON SPORTING CLUB VALUATIONS HIGHLIGHTS THE LARGE DIFFERENCES IN ENGLISH PREMIER LEAGUE (EPL) CLUB VALUATIONS

Research in many areas has the opportunity to create new knowledge that is valuable to many of the stakeholders in the sporting ecosystem. An example is Tom Markham's research on the valuation of clubs in the EPL. The EPL setting is enhanced by each club having audited financial statements publicly available. Markham sought to develop a single quantitative model that estimates club valuation based on multiple variables. Four variables were used after multiple efforts at refinement:

1   Revenue + net assets – "A club's revenue figure is added to its net assets as these underpin a club's ability to generate future revenue and make up the backbone of the valuation model. The net assets figure is made up of a club's fixed assets added to current assets less current and long term liabilities."
2   (Net profit + revenue) / Revenue – "This figure examines a club's profitability in comparison to its overall revenue. Profitable clubs will have a figure greater than 1."
3   Stadium capacity percentage – "The stadium utilization percentage illustrates how effectively the club is using its core differentiating asset … The higher the utilization, the higher the valuation."
4   Wage ratio percentage of revenues – "Illustrates a club's ability to control its major expenditure … the lower the percentage the higher the club's valuation."

An important part of Markham's research was validating the model by comparing the predictions of the model with actual reported values for 15 transactions involving the sale of English soccer clubs between 2003 and 2011. On average, the Markham model was within 20 percent of the reported actual transaction valuations.

Exhibit 18.5 shows Markham's estimated valuations for the 20 clubs in the EPL at the start of the 2012/13 season. These valuations highlight the extreme tiering of EPL clubs in their valuations.

Manchester United's valuation is more than 24 times that of Wigan Athletic. The six highest valued EPL clubs comprise 72.28 percent of the total aggregate of all the 20 EPL clubs in Exhibit 18.5. Appendix 18A discusses relegation risk in the EPL. Clubs that have consistently stayed well above the relegation risk zone in recent years prior to 2012 have the highest valuations. The four highest valued clubs in Exhibit 18.5 have never been relegated in the EPL era (starting in 1992/3). In the four years up to and including the 2011/12 season, the end-of-season ranking of these four clubs was never lower than tenth. In contrast, the bottom six valued clubs in Exhibit 18.5 have predominantly been in the second-tier Championship League over this four-year period. Only Wigan Athletic remained in the EPL all four years from 2008/9 to 2011/12. At the end of the 2012/13 season, Wigan placed 18th in the EPL and was one of the three EPL clubs relegated to the Championship League for the 2013/14 season. This relegation sizably reduced the expected revenue-generating ability of the club.

Rank	Club	Valuation estimate in 2012 (£m)	End of season rank in EPL competition			
			2008–9	2009–10	2010–11	2011–12
1	Manchester United	1,060.4	1	2	1	2
2	Arsenal	942.9	4	3	4	3
3	Chelsea	510.5	3	1	2	6
4	Tottenham Hotspur	436.3	8	4	5	4
5	Manchester City	401.1	10	5	3	1
6	Liverpool	352.2	2	7	6	8
7	Newcastle United	275.8	18	CL	12	5
8	West Bromwich Albion	126.9	20	CL	11	10
9	Sunderland	121.8	16	13	10	13
10	Everton	112.3	5	8	7	7
11	Fulham	108.7	7	12	8	9
12	West Ham United	104.3	9	17	20	CL
13	Aston Villa	102.5	6	6	9	16
14	Stoke City	94.9	12	11	13	14
15	Norwich City	90.1	CL	CL	CL	12
16	Swansea City	64.8	CL	CL	CL	11
17	Queens Park Rangers	59.9	CL	CL	CL	17
18	Reading	58.0	CL	CL	CL	CL
19	Southampton	57.5	CL	CL	CL	CL
20	Wigan Athletic	42.8	11	16	16	15

EXHIBIT 18.5 English Premier League 2012 Valuations Using Markham Model

Note: CL = Championship League.

Those low on-the-field performing EPL clubs with resulting high relegation risk have relatively lower valuations than do comparable low on-the-field performing clubs in the North American leagues without relegation in Exhibit 18.5.

Ownership Strength

Owners who are willing to make ongoing astute investments in their playing squad and in their other assets (such as stadiums, media companies, and real estate) will likely have higher valuations than owners who either do not have the capacity or the willingness to make such investments.

Management Strength

Across most industries, astute and experienced management is likely to make more value-adding deci-sions than management with less quality judgment and experience. The sporting industry is no dif-ferent in this respect. Note that here "strength" refers to managers whose focus is on value-adding. As noted in Chapter 4, some owners or managers have a dominant focus on winning-on-the-field, which in some cases can lead to them "tolerating" very high operating losses. From a valuation perspective, a new owner should focus on what is the likely financial situation with a potentially different strategy that has a more financial discipline focus.

City/Region Strength

Cities and regions in any country can differ sizably in their economic strength. Consider a league such as the MLB, where local revenues are central to a club's financial strength. Clubs in cities with depressed economies and high unemployment will likely have fewer fans able to purchase high-priced tickets, as well as fewer corporations able to purchase suites or engage in large sponsorship deals with a local MLB club. Such cities and regions will likely have lower valued sporting clubs than clubs in regions with thriving local economies.

Arena/Stadium Strength

There can be large differences across clubs as regards the revenue-generating ability of their stadiums or arenas. Factors here include the size of the stadium, its relative capacity utilization, and the amount of recent investment in its digital capabilities. Clubs that have recently built or upgraded to state-of-the-art stadiums can have local game-day revenues double that of other clubs with aging stadiums. An import-ant additional factor here is the revenue-sharing agreements a club has with a city or county. Some clubs own or have long-term operating rights to manage all events in an arena or stadium. In contrast, some other clubs may be "game-day-only tenants" in a building that can greatly reduce their revenue streams.

Team On-Field Performance Strength

Clubs with sustained on-field success typically have enhanced financial valuations in part due to the virtuous circle aspect noted below for brand, sponsorship, and fan base. A past heritage of on-field suc-cess can enable a brand to have more resilience to a period of lower on-field success or some negative events (such as a salary cap violation).

Strength of Players/Coaches

Players and coaches can be either value-enhancing or value-diminishing. Clubs with elite athletes with exemplary behavior off-the-field (either current or heritage) benefit from the positive attributes these players bring to the club. One potential asset or liability here is the contracts written for current players. Clubs with very large contractual obligations for underperforming or retired players have effectively liabilities on their "club balance sheet" such that the net club value is lower. Leagues with guaranteed player contracts (such as the MLB or the EPL) are more likely to be in this situation than leagues without guaranteed player contracts (such as the NFL). A potentially important asset for clubs playing in elite soccer leagues is the ability to sell player contracts.

Branding and Sponsorship Strength

These two factors often reinforce each other such that there can be either a "virtuous circle" or a "vicious circle" – clubs with strong brands can attract ongoing high levels of sponsorship, while clubs with weak brands attract minimal sponsorships. Clubs with very strong brands can better withstand periods of on-the-field underperformance, as well as the inevitable crises that any club will face over an extended time period.

Fan Strength

The size and avidity of the fan base is an important determinant of club revenues. For example, many fans outside the geographical footprint of the venue may never or rarely attend games but will still purchase fan club memberships and club merchandise. Also of interest here is the global nature of these aspects. In recent years, major clubs in several leagues have invested heavily in expanding their global footprints.

Media Contracts/Asset Strength

In leagues where local media contracts are important, large differences across clubs in the annual revenues from these media contracts are the norm. The two dominant Spanish soccer clubs – Real Madrid and Barcelona – had for many years media contracts that were multiples of the contracts of most other clubs in the Spanish La Liga. Similarly, the highest RSN contracts in the MLB, NBA, and NHL can each be more than five times those for the clubs with the lowest contracts. Such differences contribute to large differences in the valuations of clubs in the same league. In some cases, clubs have equity in the media company broadcasting their games. This equity can be an important factor in increasing the valuation of the sporting club as a broader entity.

Real Estate Asset Strength

Some individual clubs either for many years have owned real estate associated with their sporting facilities (such as the Los Angeles Dodgers) or have in recent years aggressively acquired real estate to further enhance their revenue streams or club valuation (such as the Green Bay Packers). These assets add to the value of the sporting club as a broader entity.

18.2.2 Value to an Owner versus Value in Exchange

The categories in Exhibit 18.4 cover a broad set of areas where sporting club value is either created or destroyed by different stakeholders. Valuation exercises often distinguish between value to an owner of an asset versus value in an open market exchange where there are potentially multiple buyers and multiple sellers for an asset with agreed attributes. One attribute of sporting clubs in elite leagues is their exclusivity or "trophy asset" status. In Chapter 4 and Exhibit 4.4, this was described as the "Profile P" of ownership intent. It also related to the "Power P," where club ownership is sought for the advantages it provides. For example, there are only 30 NBA clubs, only 32 NFL clubs, and so on. Having ownership of an asset that attracts the attention of potentially millions of fans and viewers on a week-by-week basis brings to some individuals its own attractive features (in most cases). This celebrity aspect of ownership is sufficiently attractive to some owners that they are willing to not demand a potential sporting club investment pass the same stringent financial hurdles as they would for other financial investments. Industry observers emphasize the importance of this celebrity element when tracking and explaining sporting club transactions.

18.2.3 Industry Perspectives on Club Valuation Drivers

Financial institutions and advisory firms play a key role in many transactions in the sporting industry and have an incentive to build strong capabilities and a deep understanding of the industry. An illustration is the industry categorization of "drivers of sports franchise valuation" from John Waldron, co-head of the Investment Banking Division of Goldman Sachs:

1   **Strategic position** – for example, (a) historic team performance, and (b) brand equity and fan loyalty.
2   **Economics** – for example, (a) team operating performance, (b) league economies, and (c) upside opportunities.
3   **Comparable entity valuations** – for example, (a) recent transactions, and (b) expansion franchises.
4   **Ownership issues** – for example, (a) potential buyer universe, (b) league rules and restrictions, (c) tax consideration, and (d) rights of first refusal.
5   **Trophy statues** – for example, (a) limited opportunity to acquire a professional sports franchise, and (b) community standing.

Sporting clubs with publicly traded securities will typically have security analysts publicly issuing reports on a regular basis. These analyst reports can provide insight into many issues about the club and its league that impact the ongoing valuation of publicly traded clubs as well as other clubs in that league.

18.3 ALTERNATIVE VALUATION APPROACHES AND TRIANGULATION

Valuation is inherently a forward-looking exercise as the focus is on the likely distributions a holder of the asset being valued will receive over the life the asset is held. Valuation analysis rarely yields a precise number over which there is little difference of opinion among informed experts or via different methodologies. The recommended approach is one known as "triangulation," where a series of approaches are employed to estimate the value of the target property. Each methodology can play the role of a check and balance against the other methods used.

This section gives a brief overview of alternative valuation approaches. Only the basic structure of each approach will be noted. It is important to distinguish between "internal" valuations where access to private information (such as audited financials and player contracts) exists and "third-party" valuations (such as by *Forbes*) where no such access to private information occurs. There often are direct financial consequences associated with internal valuations such that there may be extensive due diligence underlying the valuation – such as a new minority investor agreeing to invest money at the figure that is yielded by the internal valuation.

Four valuation approaches are briefly presented in this section. There can be some overlap in the inputs used in these different approaches:

1   Adjustment to traded acquisition valuation approach;
2   Market multiple approach;
3   Sum of parts asset valuation approach; and
4   Discounted cash flow approach.

18.3.1 Adjustment to Traded Acquisition Valuation Approach

Transactions for equity in sporting clubs occur with some frequency in many leagues where trading of clubs is permitted.[9] These transactions result in market prices for clubs that become inputs into the valuations assessed for other clubs in the league or for the same club in subsequent transactions. Consider the NBA where transactions occurred over the 2000/15 period for a change in majority control for many of the clubs. Exhibit 18.6 is a summary document from public sources on the values of the NBA clubs sold in many of these transactions.

These transactions include both elite clubs as well as many clubs with less heritage and stature. Examples include the Boston Celtics, the Brooklyn Nets (formerly New Jersey Nets), the Golden State Warriors, the Dallas Mavericks, the Oklahoma City Thunder (formerly Seattle Sonics), Los Angeles Clippers, Atlanta Hawks, and the New Orleans Pelicans/Hornets. Each transaction will have a transaction figure.[10] For example, the elite Boston Celtics in 2002 traded for $360 million while the lower-tier Milwaukee Bucks in 2014 traded for approximately $550 million.

In addition to transactions for all the equity of a club, there also can be multiple transactions for individual blocks of shares held by minority investors. These transactions also result in implied club valuations (albeit without a control premium). Examples include when (a) a minority investor in one NBA club has to sell his equity due to acquiring another NBA club, or (b) a minority investor in a syndicate exiting for "personal reasons." The result of these multiple past transactions is a sequence of valuations over time that provide likely bands (especially at the lower valuation amounts) in which negotiations over valuation of a club commence. In this setting, an analysis is often then made of the leverageable assets and inherited liabilities of the club (and its league) being valued vis-à-vis other clubs that have valuations from past transactions. There is also typically an adjustment for likely future factors that may affect club valuation. An example that would affect NBA valuations is any major increase in NBA distributions to clubs from new media contracts.

Year of purchase	Club	Reported purchase price ($M)
2014	Los Angeles Clippers	2,000
2014	Milwaukee Bucks	550
2013	Sacramento Kings	534
2012	Memphis Grizzlies	377
2012	New Orleans Pelicans	338
2011	Detroit Pistons	325
2011	Philadelphia 76ers	297
2010	Washington Wizards	550
2010	Golden State Warriors	450
2010	New Orleans Hornets	300
2010	New Jersey Nets	260
2010	Charlotte Bobcats	175
2006	Seattle Sonics	350
2005	Cleveland Cavaliers	375
2004	Phoenix Suns	401
2004	New Jersey Nets	300
2004	Atlanta Hawks	189
2003	Boston Celtics	360
2001	Seattle Sonics	200
2000	Denver Nuggets	450
2000	Dallas Mavericks	200
2000	Vancouver Grizzlies	160
1998	Toronto Raptors	350

EXHIBIT 18.6 Estimated Transaction Valuations for NBA Clubs from Public Sources
Source: Various public sources; often multiple reported values were found

Exhibit 18.6 highlights both the upward lift in NBA club transaction valuations since 2000 as well as the diversity across clubs in their transaction valuations. Exhibit 18.6 also highlights how the reported $2,000 million transaction in 2014 by Steve Ballmer to purchase the Los Angeles Clippers (NBA) reset the bar from the previous record NBA amount of $550 million reportedly paid in the same year for the Milwaukee Bucks. We caution that the patterns in Exhibit 18.6 are based on publicly available information and no representations are made as to the accuracy or completeness of the information presented.

When sporting leagues expand their number of clubs, valuations by those leagues are placed on these expansion clubs. Major League Soccer in the United States has been aggressive at expanding the clubs in its league – such as seven new clubs from 2007 to 2012 (Toronto, San Jose, Seattle, Philadelphia, Portland, Vancouver, and Montreal). In 2015, the MLS admitted clubs in both New York and Orlando. The sequence of valuations in these expansion decisions by the MLS likely sets valuation bands in which negotiation over transactions for new or existing MLS clubs occur. For example, New York City FC entered the league at a MLS valuation of $100 million. This transaction for a large market club likely heavily guided the MLS setting a reported $100 to $110 million price for the Los Angeles FC club that enters in 2017.

18.3.2 Market Multiples Approach

This approach is widely used in security analyst valuations of publicly traded companies and is frequently found as part of the analysis of sporting club valuations. There are two key inputs – the financial amount of the variable, and the multiplier:

valuation = variable × multiplier

Variables often used in a multiples approach include revenues, earnings before interest and taxes (EBIT), income before taxes, and net income. The multiplier used is often taken from public equity markets or the acquisition market.

Consider a multiple approach to valuing: Liverpool FC in the EPL, June 2013. Assume that the variable used is the most recent years revenue (£206 million in year ending May 2013) and the multiplier is the revenue multiple of Manchester United (4.7 in June 2013). Manchester United is publicly traded on the New York Stock Exchange. The valuation for Liverpool FC with these inputs would be £906 million:

Liverpool FC 2013 valuation = £206 million × 4.7 = £906 million

Within this valuation approach there are many considerations. As further discussed in Appendix 18A, these (a) include whether the 2013 year's revenue is representative of the likely future stream of revenues, and (b) whether the Manchester United multiple needs to be adjusted downwards for Liverpool, which possesses fewer of the leverageable assets that Manchester United can exploit. A fundamental question is also the choice of the variable that is being multiplied. In many non-sporting contexts, profitability-based variables are used – such as EBIT or net income. However, in many sporting club valuations, profitability variables are precluded, as they are often negative.

18.3.3 Sum-of-Parts Asset Valuation Approach

Companies in which many of their individual assets are "tradeable" on a stand-alone basis will often use a "bottom-up" summing of the estimated valuations of those individual assets as one approach in a broader valuation analysis. An example would be a mutual fund examining their aggregate value based on summing the valuations of their individual equity investments. Some real estate companies use this approach in valuation by looking at the valuations of their individual real estate holdings.

One application of this approach in sporting club valuations is where trades are made for clubs with different combinations of assets. Possible assets of a sporting club that potentially can be traded independent of each other are:

1　Ownership of a sporting team with arena, sponsorship, and media revenue streams.
2　Ownership of player contracts that in some leagues can be individually sold – such as by clubs in European soccer leagues where some individual player contracts can have $50 million+ potential for a cash inflow.
3　Ownership or long-term operating rights to a stadium or arena – the Boston Bruins (NHL) ownership also owns the TD Gardens arena where the Boston Celtics is a tenant.
4　Ownership of media companies – the New England Sports Network (NESN) broadcasts Boston Red Sox (MLB) and the Boston Bruins (NHL) games. The Red Sox ownership has 80 percent equity of NESN while the Bruins ownership has 20 percent equity of NESN.
5　Ownership of real estate associated with a club – the Los Angeles Dodgers have partial ownership of 250 acres surrounding Dodger Stadium.

Clubs that have a combination of these assets can do a "bottom-up" approach when assessing the attractiveness of potential offers for those assets. Note that for these more complex packaging of assets there is, in effect, multiple valuations of individual assets being undertaken to estimate the value of the package of those assets. When clubs traded with different combinations of the assets listed above, it is important to make adjustments so that an "apples to apples" comparison is being made about the current market price of, say, just the sporting team that is a tenant in an arena and does not have either media company (#4 above) or real estate (#5 above) assets.

18.3.4 Discounted Cash Flow (DCF) Approach

This approach requires for each period over the life of the asset being valued:

- the expected cash inflows per period, and
- the expected cash outflows per period.

It also requires the discount rate to take account of the time value of money and the riskiness of the cash flows. This approach is widely used for individual capital budgeting projects and for individual publicly traded assets such as stocks and bonds. Historically, it has not been used widely in sports club valuations. One obstacle here is that historically many sporting clubs have negative net cash flows over extended periods, whereas most contexts that use the DCF approach typically have positive net cash flows over extended periods.

18.4 VALUATION OF RELATED SPORTING ASSETS

Valuations of sporting companies and properties, in addition to sporting clubs, are also of high interest to many stakeholders in the sporting industry. Three examples are regional sports networks, startup ventures, and sponsorship properties.

18.4.1 Regional Sports Network Valuation

Chapter 16 discussed regional sports networks (RSNs) and their growing importance in the sporting industry. The valuation approaches outlined in Section 18.3 are applicable to this sector of the sporting industry. The comparables for an RSN should include a broad base of cable companies and not just narrowly defined RSNs. The economics of the cable industry in general are an important backdrop to RSN valuation and there are many cable companies that can provide insights into this area. For example, one issue affecting RSN valuation is whether cable distributors will continue to be able to "force" cable subscribers to buy bundles/packages of cable channels or whether there will be an à la carte world where consumers can buy individual cable channels. This issue will affect the valuation of all channels and is an important concern for the entire industry.

18.4.2 New Startups Focused on Sports

The sports ecosystem is continually being broadened by a pipeline of new startups. In recent years, the venture capital industry has been a major investor in these ventures. Areas where new ventures have emerged include ticketing (such as StubHub and SeatGeek) and fantasy sports (such as FanDuel and DraftKings). There is a large literature on the valuation of venture-backed startup ventures that can be accessed when valuing these startups. One characteristic of many of these ventures in their early years is that they are cash flow negative. As with many sporting club valuations, traditional metrics (such as profitability multiple approaches) will likely have little adoption.

18.4.3 Sponsorship Valuation

Companies considering sponsoring leagues, events, players, and other properties use a variety of approaches to estimate the value of the sponsorship. One approach here is using a benchmark analysis. This involves seeking a series of similar properties where the cost is known and metrics are available as to the effectiveness of the sponsorship. Comparable here could be the same property in prior years, or similar properties in the current or prior years. An example would be sponsorship of a NASCAR race where the sponsor of previous years has changed its strategy of sponsorship and the track seeks new sponsors. A potential sponsor could examine what the NASCAR race in question attracts as regards attendance, television ratings, etc. At a broader level, metrics would be available as regards impressions on media for various sponsors of the same event last year and similar events in the current or past years. In some cases, points could be developed for various attributes that a potential sponsor views as important (such as recall factors, propensity to make purchases after exposure, etc.). Then alternative sponsorships could be evaluated as to their point scores and the expected cost per point.

18.5 SUMMARY

Valuation of sporting assets is an area with high interest. The valuation approaches discussed in this chapter have been illustrated with respect to sporting clubs in sporting leagues around the globe. A major overall trend has been the increase in average valuations since 2000 across each of the leagues examined. While increases in valuations give only part of the picture of the financial returns from club ownership (they ignore operating profits or losses), they do highlight the high demand for sporting properties with multiple leverageable assets. Valuation analysis can be much enriched by undertaking a systematic analysis of the leverageable assets and inherited liabilities of the asset being valued vis-à-vis other sporting assets for which transaction evidence or third-party estimates are available.

APPENDIX 18A SOME CHALLENGES IN USING MARKET MULTIPLES IN SPORTING CLUB SETTINGS

Section 18.3.2 illustrated the market multiple approach to estimating the valuation of Liverpool FC. Exhibit 18.7 expands the set of EPL clubs to highlight some of the complexity in this approach. This appendix raises issues that a detailed valuation analysis would address without an attempt to resolve them as this would have to be done on a case-by-case basis.

1   Choice of benchmark clubs for valuation multiples based on public stock exchanges. There are very few publicly traded soccer clubs for which market capitalizations can be computed. Exhibit 18.7 shows two public companies. Manchester United trades on the NYSE while Arsenal trades on a specialist exchange in the UK.[11] Each has published estimates of market capitalization based on the number of their shares outstanding times their current market price per share. In June 2013, the market to revenue multiple of Manchester United was 4.7 while Arsenal's market to revenue multiple was 4.1:

Club	Market capitalization	Revenue	Multiple
Manchester United	£1,706 million	£363 million	4.7
Arsenal	£996 million	£243 million	4.1

While there is an active market in Manchester United shares, there is very limited trading in Arsenal shares. Hence, questions arise about whether Arsenal's thinly traded stock provides reliable estimates of its market capitalization and its changes over time.

2   What revenue number to use in the valuation if a revenue multiple approach is used? The text example in Section 18.3.2 used the 2013 revenue numbers for Manchester United and Liverpool when taking Manchester United's revenue multiple to value Liverpool. The year by year revenues of the seven clubs over the 2009 to 2013 period in Exhibit 18.7 highlight some very different growth paths. Compound annual growth rates in revenues over this five year period were:
   ● Benchmark clubs: Manchester United (5.46 percent) and Arsenal (1.69 percent).
   ● Clubs being valued: Manchester City (25.58 percent), Chelsea (4.49 percent), Wigan (4.49 percent), Liverpool (2.22 percent), and Everton (1.63 percent).
Manchester United's compound growth rate of 5.46 percent is higher than that of five of the seven clubs in Exhibit 18.7. However, it is well below that of Manchester City (25.58 percent). Should this higher growth rate for Manchester City justify using a higher revenue multiple than

Manchester United's 4.7 or Arsenal's 4.1 multiples? Box 2.2 provides the background to an Abu Dhabi investment group in 2008 purchasing Manchester City for a reported £210 million.[12] Subsequent to this purchase Manchester City was transformed into a major force in the EPL. Parts of this transformation were a major increase in player payroll (from £82.633 million in 2009 to £233.106 million in 2013) and a major increase in the revenue (from £87.033 million in 2009 to £271.775 million in 2013).

3   How should profitability be taken into account when valuing the soccer clubs in Exhibit 18.7? Most valuations of companies using the multiples approach use a profitability variable rather than a revenue multiple. However, the multiple approach requires a positive profit figure to yield a positive valuation. Exhibit 18.7 reports the pre-tax profit series for the seven clubs. Only Arsenal has a consistent series of pre-tax profits in each and every year. Chelsea, Liverpool, and Manchester City each have pre-tax losses each and every year. Moreover, the magnitude of the cumulative losses over this five-year period is stunning – Chelsea with £264.393 million in cumulative pre-tax losses, Liverpool with £248.356 million in cumulative pre-tax losses, and Manchester City with £561.679 million in cumulative pre-tax losses.

4   When using revenue or profit variables, should revenues from the Champions League competition be adjusted to recognize their uncertainty? Each of the clubs in Exhibit 18.7 played in the EPL in the 2008/9 to 2012/13 seasons. At the end of each season, the top four clubs in the EPL competition table qualify to play in the Champions League competition for the following year. This competition is effectively a European "Super League" in which elite clubs from many countries compete. Panel B of Exhibit 18.7 shows the revenues each of the seven clubs earned each year from this elite competition. The more games a club plays in the competition, the higher the revenues earned, with the winner of the Champions League Final earning the richest prize in global club soccer competitions. Only Arsenal, Chelsea, and Manchester United appeared in the Champions League competition each year of the five-year period. There is uncertainty each year in the EPL over whether a club will qualify for the Champions League and then how many games it plays in that competition. Chelsea's distribution has ranged from a high of £62.9 million in 2011/12, when it beat Bayern Munich in the final, to a low of £30.9 million in 2008/9 when it lost in the semi-final to Barcelona. No club in the EPL is guaranteed a place in this competition, For example, Manchester United placed seventh in the 2013/14 EPL season and thus failed to qualify for the Champions League Competition in 2014/15.

5   How should the risk of relegation be taken into account when valuing clubs that have this "open league" format? From 1992/3 to 2013/14, only seven clubs have remained in the EPL each and every year – Manchester United, Arsenal, Liverpool, Chelsea, Tottenham, Everton, and Aston Villa. Over this 22-year period, 38 other clubs have played in the EPL for one or more but not all 22 seasons. When a club is relegated, there is a sizable reduction in its revenue-generating capacity, which can decrease its valuation. For many clubs in the EPL, relegation risk is an important negative on valuation. As an illustration, Wigan placed 18th in the EPL in the 2012/13 season and hence was relegated to the lower-tier competition (the Championship League) starting with the 2013/14 season. In that season, Wigan was not able to qualify for promotion to the EPL and remained in the lower-tiered competition for the 2014/15 season. The valuation of Wigan is negatively impacted by remaining in this lower-tier league as opposed to being in the EPL. Box 18.3 illustrates how a multi-factor valuation model ranked Wigan in 2012 as having the lowest valuation of all the clubs playing in the EPL in the 2011/12 season.

Panel A: Revenues	2009	2010	2011	2012	2013
Manchester United	278.476	286.416	331.441	320.320	363.189
Arsenal	224.018	224.352	226.825	234.893	243.627
Chelsea	208.779	212.510	228.574	261.046	260.056
Everton	79.669	79.076	82.021	80.531	86.397
Liverpool	184.782	184.839	183.690	169.038	206.205
Manchester City	87.033	125.050	153.186	231.140	271.775
Wigan Athletic	46.927	43.581	50.507	52.597	58.458
Panel B: Champions League revenues	2009	2010	2011	2012	2013
Manchester United	38.3	46.4	55.5	36.9	36.5
Arsenal	26.8	33.8	31.3	29.6	32.3
Chelsea	30.9	32.6	46.4	62.9	31.6
Everton	—	—	—	—	—
Liverpool	23.2	29.4	—	—	—
Manchester City	—	—	—	27.9	29.6
Wigan Athletic	—	—	—	—	—
Panel C: Pre-tax profit	2009	2010	2011	2012	2013
Manchester United	(108.930)	(44.273)	12.004	(4.664)	(8.793)
Arsenal	45.512	55.968	14.776	36.588	6.654
Chelsea	(47.356)	(77.286)	(78.262)	(4.324)	(57.165)
Everton	(6.920)	(3.093)	(5.413)	(9.106)	1.597
Liverpool	(54.862)	(19.880)	(49.317)	(54.679)	(69.618)
Manchester City	(92.562)	(121.300)	(197.491)	(98.705)	(51.621)
Wigan Athletic	(5.838)	(3.995)	(7.155)	(4.254)	(2.823)
Panel D: Player wage cost	2009	2010	2011	2012	2013
Manchester United	123.120	131.689	152.915	161.688	182.924
Arsenal	103.978	110.733	124.401	143.448	154.490
Chelsea	167.179	174.111	191.214	172.871	178.542
Everton	49.069	54.311	58.026	63.389	63.049
Liverpool	107.206	121.085	134.768	118.671	132.371
Manchester City	82.633	133.306	173.977	201.789	233.106
Wigan Athletic	42.198	39.421	39.948	37.679	45.290

EXHIBIT 18.7 Financials (£millions) for Seven English Premier League Clubs

NOTES

1   "News Corp–Los Angeles Dodgers timeline," *Sports Business Daily*, October 20, 2003.
2   "Owners approve $430M sale of team," ESPN, January 30, 2004.
3   Details taken from multiple sources including "The McCourts and the Dodgers," *Los Angeles Times*, June 27, 2011.
4   B. Shaikin, "Dodgers bidders cut to Cohen, Magic, and Kroenke," *Los Angeles Times*, March 23, 2012.
5   B. Shaikin and D. Wharton, "Magic Johnson-led group is picked as Dodgers' next owner," *Los Angeles Times*, March 27, 2012.
6   B. Shaikin, "Dodgers officially announce deal with Time Warner Cable," *Los Angeles Times*, January 28, 2013.
7   This box draws from D. Hoyt and G Foster, "Sports entrepreneurship: the case of the Indian Premier League," in D. Ciletti and S. Chadwick (eds.), *Sports Entrepreneurship: Theory and Practice* (Fitness Information Technology, 2012) and R. Sharma and G. Foster, *The Indian Premier League: Managing Beyond the Startup Years of the Most Successful New Cricket League* (Stanford GSB, 2015).
8   The compound growth rates should *not* be interpreted as the rates of return from owning a club over the designated period. For example, not included in the computation are the annual profits (or cash surpluses) or losses (or cash deficits) of clubs. Although most clubs do not report their financials, there are multiple reports that many clubs have sustained heavy total net operating cash deficits over extended periods. These cash deficits would reduce the compound annual rates of return based on *Forbes* estimates of valuations at different dates.
9   Leagues and clubs vary in the restrictions placed on the trading of all or part of the equity in individual clubs. In the German Bundesliga, restrictions are placed on the sale of all the equity in a club. Clubs that have an "association model" effectively cannot engage in a trade for all "equity" in the club.
10 It is important to understand the totality of the transaction. The actual transaction amount can be but part of the exchange agreement. For example, there can be differences in the assumption of debt, in the timing in which payments are to be made, and in the amount of the transaction amount that is held "in escrow" as security to the buyer in case representations by the seller do not eventuate. There can sometimes be subsequent litigation in which differences of opinion between a buyer and a seller are passed to a "third party" (such as an arbitrator or a court) for analysis and adjudication.
11 Tottenham Hotspur was publicly traded up to January 2012 when it went into private ownership and was delisted from the AIM exchange in the UK. B. Wilson, "Tottenham Hotspur delists shares from stock exchange," BBC News, March 7, 2012.
12 D. Conn, "Thaksin doubled his money in City sale, claim sources," *The Guardian*, October 7, 2008.

Names index

Topic index